BEYOND FABERGÉ

Imperial Russian Jewelry

Marie Betteley
David Schimmelpenninck van der Oye

BEYOND FABERGÉ

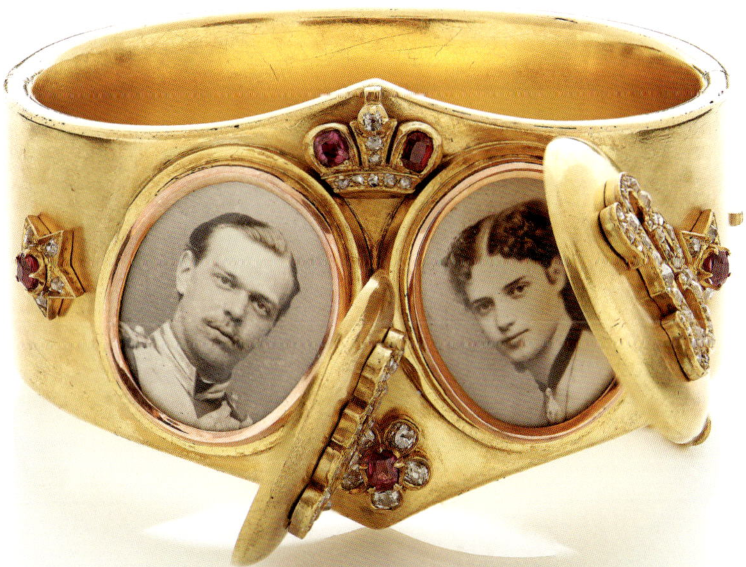

Imperial Russian Jewelry

SCHIFFER PUBLISHING
4880 Lower Valley Road • Atglen, PA 19310

Library of Congress Control Number: 2020930873

Designed by Danielle D. Farmer
Cover design by Danielle D. Farmer
Type set in Desire/Adobe Garamond Pro/Times New Roman

Front cover image: Diamond and cabochon ruby diadem (detail) by C. E. Bolin, St. Petersburg, ca. 1890. *Courtesy of Getty Images.*
Back cover image: Enamel punch bowl and ladle by Fedor Rückert. *Courtesy of Sotheby's.*
Title page image: Gold bracelet depicting Grand Duke Alexander Aleksandrovich and Grand Duchess Maria Fedorovna by Arnd. *Courtesy of the Royal Danish Collection, Amalienborg.*

ISBN: 978-0-7643-6043-5
Printed in China

Published by Schiffer Publishing, Ltd.
4880 Lower Valley Road
Atglen, PA 19310
Phone: (610) 593-1777; Fax: (610) 593-2002
E-mail: Info@schifferbooks.com
Web: www.schifferbooks.com

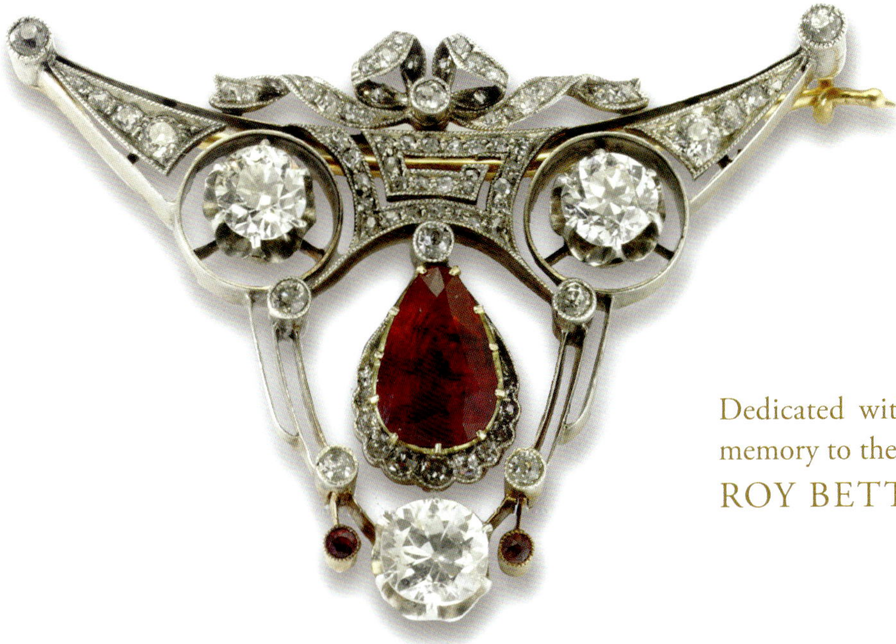

Dedicated with loving
memory to the late
ROY BETTELEY

CONTENTS

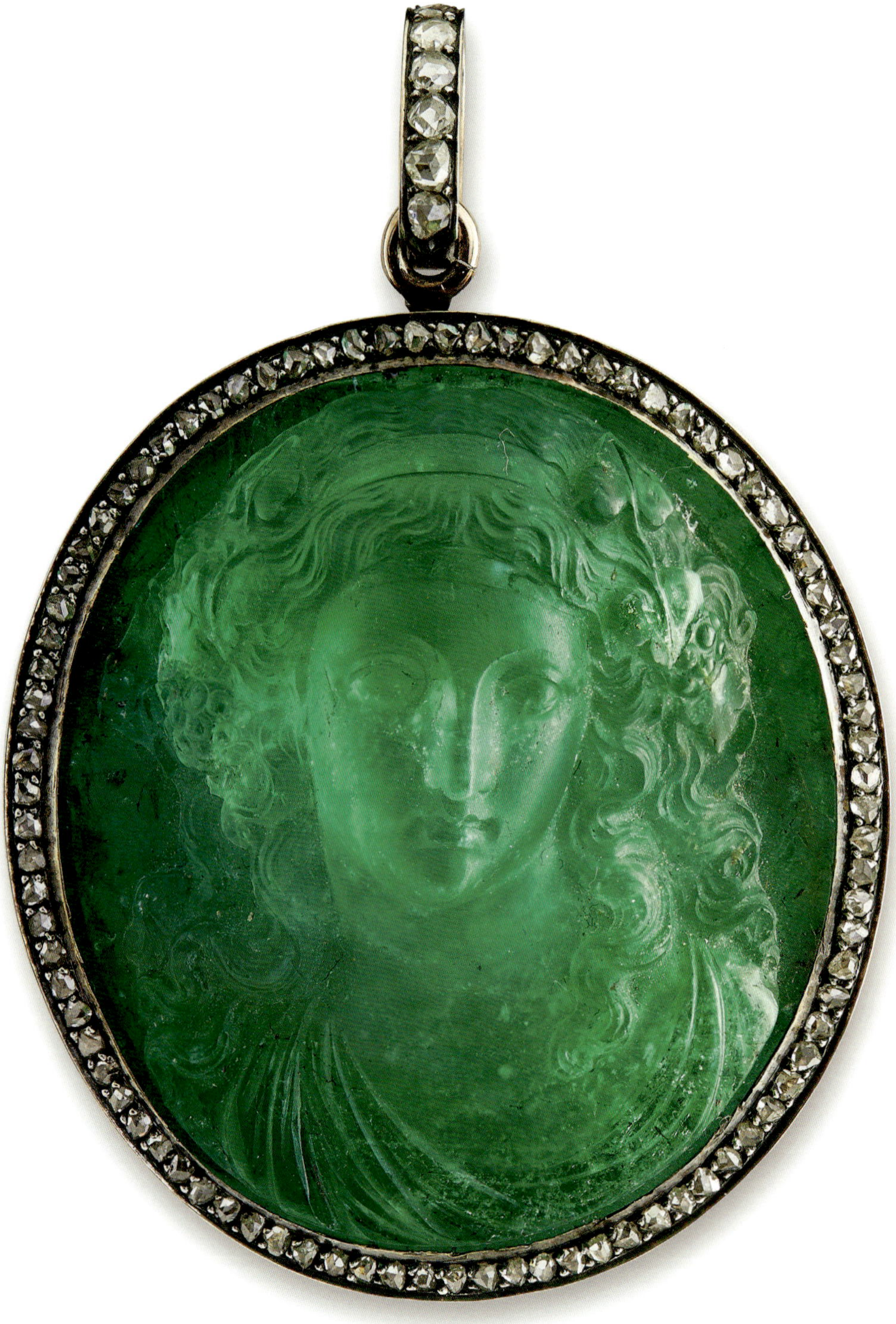

ACKNOWLEDGMENTS

Many have generously helped us along the lengthy path of writing this book. First and foremost, we thank the indefatigable and indispensable Mari Stock, who assisted us in so many ways through her tireless work in St. Petersburg's archives and library, among others. We are also grateful to Flora Allen, Mary Ann Allin, Noel Allum, John Atzbach, Lyudmilla Bakayutova, Lara Lvov Basirov, Wladimir Berelowitch, Roger Bester, Susan Bishop, Dominique and Armelle de Blanchard, Darin Bloomquist, Victoria Svederberg Bojsen, Christian Bolin, Morgane Brispierre, Mikkel Brogger, Cornelia Castan, Marie-Cécile Cisamolo, Judy Colbert, François Curiel, Andrew Currie, Alex Dove, Cindy and the late Joe Fanelli, Kate Flitcroft, Josh Gaddy, Princess Christine and the late Prince Alexandre Galitzine, Susana Garcia, Léa de Gramont, Jack Glover Gunn, Sue Heaser, Debra Healy, Gerard Hill, Steve Hirsch, James Hurtt, Rainier Kämmerer, Edward Kasinec, Iben Kaufmann, Margaret Kelly Trombly, Karen Kettering, Daria Khristova née Chernenko, Sandra Korinchak, Galina Korneva, Mette Korsholm, Olga Kostiuk, Peter Kristiansen, Dmitry Krivoshey, the late Liliia Kuznetsova, Gail Brett Levine, Marina Lopato, Adrienne Lynch, H.M. Queen Margrethe II of Denmark, Viacheslav Mukhin, Lyubov Nikolaevna, Stefano Papi, Howell Perkins, Irina Polynina, Michina Pope, Anita Purcell, Nikolai Rakhmanov, Annamarie Sandecki, Marie Sapozhnikova, Tanja Schaupp, Ji May Seo, Ti Sheffield, Valentin Skurlov, Aleksandr Solin, Nonna Tarkova, Ulla Tillander-Godenhielm, Yulia Tikhonova, Rose Tozer, Christina Vignoni, Sabrina Villani, Elisabeth von Buchwald, Pehr Wallin, Rob Wayman, Annemiek Wintraecken and Igor Zimin, as well as the staffs of the State Hermitage Museum, St. Petersburg; Russian State Historical Archive (RGIA), St. Petersburg; the Central State Archive of Cinema and Photo Documents, St. Petersburg; the Moscow Historical Museum; the Victoria & Albert Museum, London; the National Library of Russia; the Municipal and University Library of Geneva; and the New York Public Library, as well as the libraries of the Musée des Arts Décoratifs, the Frick Collection and Hillwood Estate Museum & Gardens.

NOTES

Transliterations from the Russian are generally according to the US Library of Congress system (without diacritics), except for names commonly known in the West. In the case of Russians with foreign names, we use the original version. Thus, Fabergé rather than Faberzhe.

Unless otherwise indicated, dates in the narrative are according to the Julian calendar in use in Russia before 1918. Auction catalogues and non-Russian publications in the bibliography and notes adhere to the Gregorian Calendar.

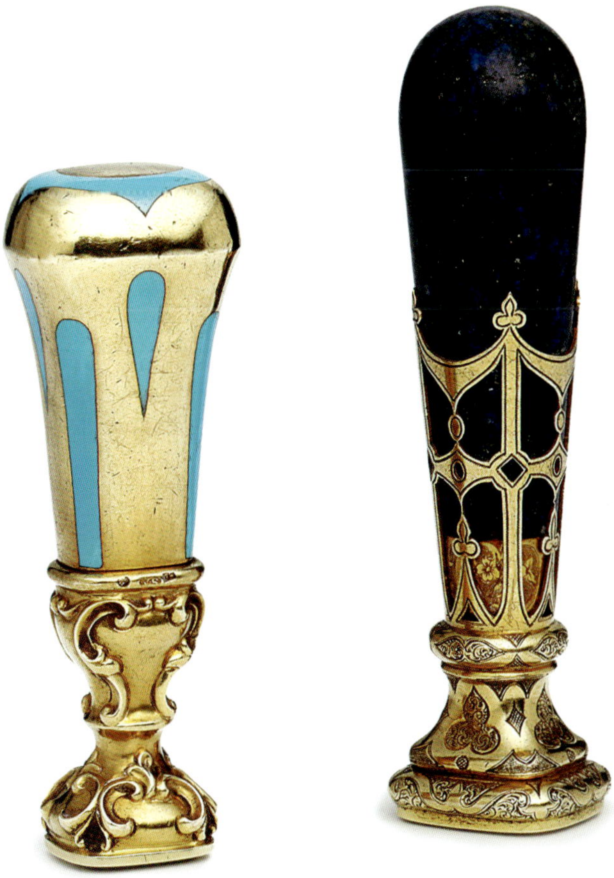

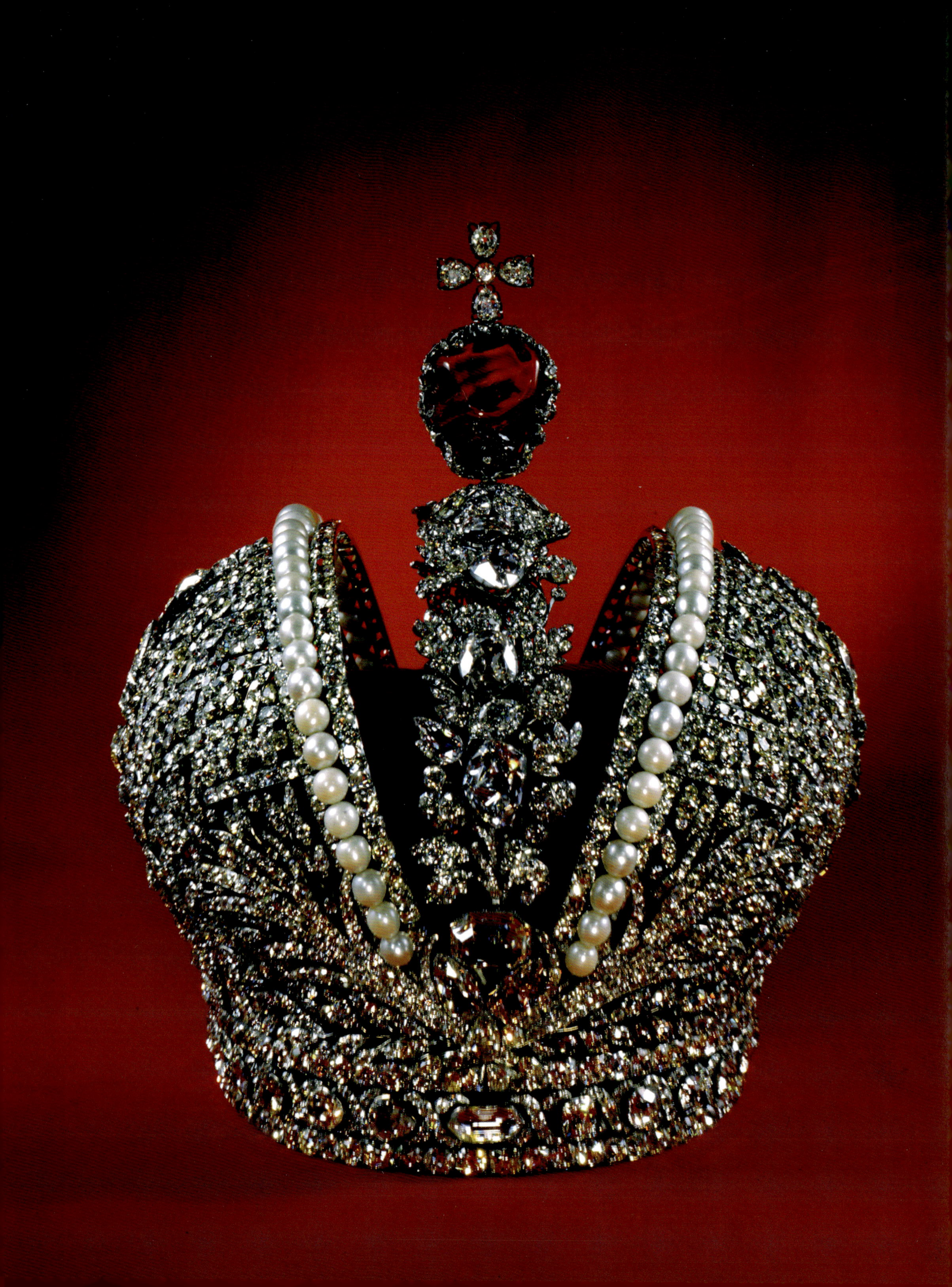

INTRODUCTION

Imperial Russia evokes images of a vanished court's unparalleled splendor: fancy dress balls, magnificent tiaras, gem-encrusted necklaces, snuff boxes and other diamond studded baubles from the tsars and tsarinas. During that time, jewelry symbolized power and wealth, and no one knew this better than the Romanovs.

Indeed, the Imperial era marked the high point of the Russian jewelers' art. For nearly two hundred years, Russian goldsmiths perfected their craft, and soon the quality of the imperial capital's jewelry equaled, if not surpassed, the best that Paris, London, Rome and Vienna could offer.

Until now, almost everything we know about Imperial Russian jewelry is tied to one name, Carl Fabergé. Long proclaimed Jeweler to the Tsars, Fabergé formed *only part* of an intricate network of the empire's finest jewelers, but today the names of the others are virtually unknown.

Beyond Fabergé: Imperial Russian Jewelry introduces the world to these masters and their creations, putting Fabergé in perspective by casting the firm as a shining star, rather than the sun in a constellation of master jewelers.

This book is divided into two parts: History and Market. The first two chapters provide an insight into the rich yet little-known history of Russian jewelry arts through the ages, as well as the intimate relationship between jewelers and the Imperial Court. The following chapters are organized by jeweler or silversmith, rather than style or period. Many of these masters were largely forgotten in the wake of the Bolshevik Revolution and are unknown in the West. The most prominent are featured in separate chapters. And yes, despite this book's title, there is one on Fabergé, as no work on Russian jewelry is complete without it. We also shed light on the lesser-known jewelers, mostly in St. Petersburg, and their place in history.

Throughout the Romanov dynasty, styles from Moscow differed from those of St. Petersburg, as the former reached back to its ancient Slavic roots while the other looked to Europe for inspiration. This is highly visible in silver and enamelware that emerged from the two centers of trade. We are lucky that many fine examples of Russian silver survived the melting pot of wars and revolution and made it to the western market. Kiev and Odessa produced two great masters of jewelry making: Marshak and Rokhumovskii, both of whom merit separate chapters.

The second section, "Market," gives an overview of the Russian art trade in Europe and North America, a source of continuing fascination to us and, we hope, to you. We begin with the 19th-century Russian fairs in St. Petersburg and Moscow, followed by the famous world fairs such as the Crystal Palace Exhibition of 1851 in London, which first brought the Russian jeweler's art to the attention of the West. We then go on to examine public sales of Imperial-era jewelry and silver in the West after 1917. In addition to the many treasures that those fleeing the Revolution took abroad, from 1927 to 1936, the Soviet government systematically sold a large number of the former dynasty's jewels. This is covered in chapter 26, "The Fate of the Russian Crown Jewels."

The book is filled with auction house records. Because all major houses publish hammer prices, they are the best barometers of the market. This is not to say that Christie's and Sotheby's always have the finest selection; but rather that over time, they tend to feature the most representative examples of a jeweler's oeuvre.

We would also not advise prospective buyers to buy *only* at auction. On the contrary, as the main houses continue to raise their buyer's premiums (as much as 30% of hammer price), and with high visibility of items online enabling global bidding, auction values now often equal retail. This may be good news for sellers, but there is also a danger of overexposure, death by auction we call it, as is the case in several pieces of Fabergé that continue to surface at various venues, accompanied by lower and lower prices. It may be advantageous to buy from the trade today. A handful of dealers offer fabulous Russian treasures. Direct, personal contact with trusted dealers is important, as opposed to buying online from unknown sources, since the market is filled with fakes.

If we do not include today's dealers of Russian art, it is because their selling prices are often difficult to assess. The posted price on websites is not always the final one, and many dealers choose to keep this information private.

History

1

History

RUSSIAN JEWELRY OVER THE AGES

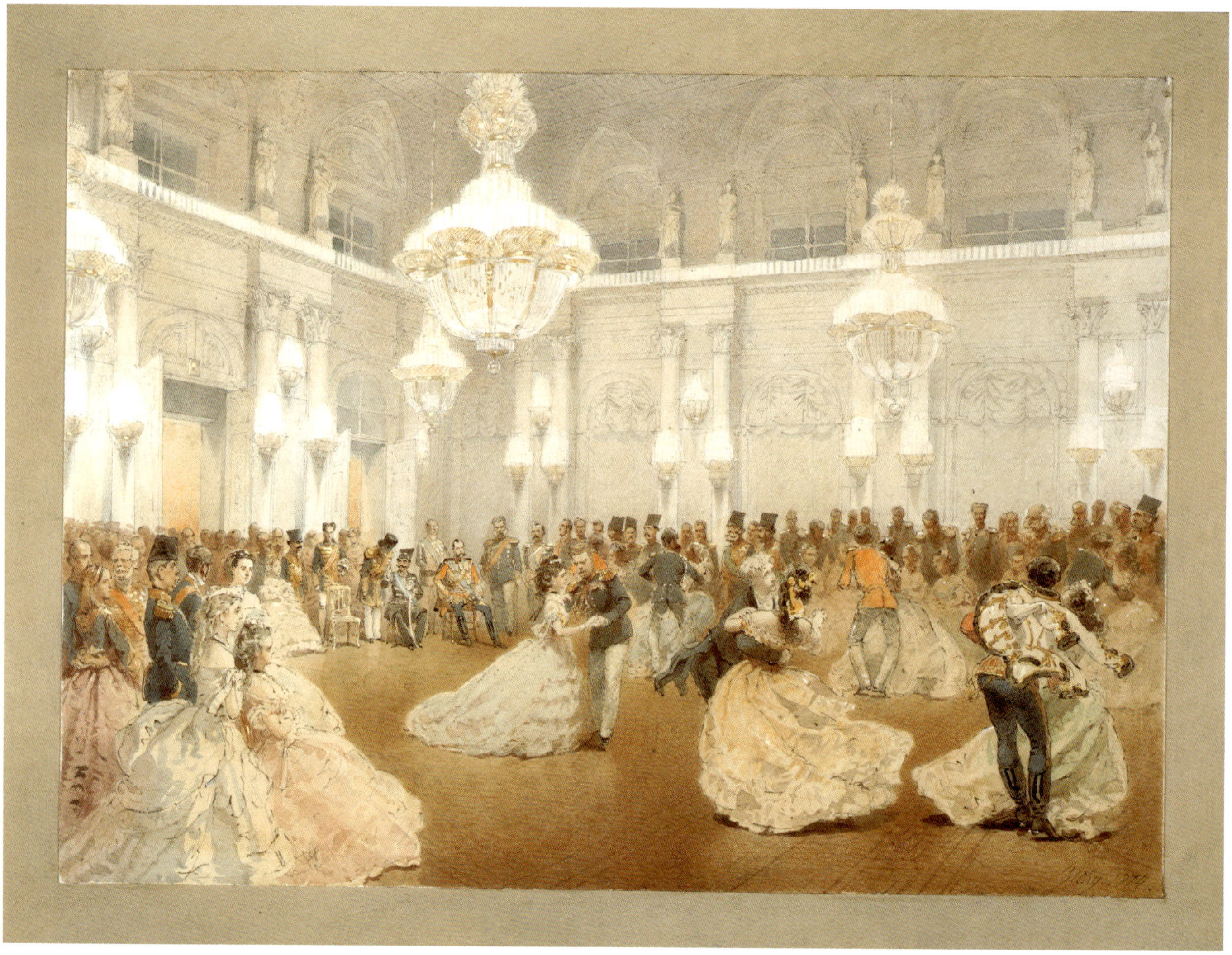

A strong sensual streak has always pervaded Russian culture. This is already evident in the semilegendary Primary Chronicle, the nation's first written history. It states that in 986, Grand Prince Vladimir of Kiev began to consider whether his pagan subjects should adopt a monotheistic faith from one of their more advanced neighbors. The chronicler tells us that Vladimir first considered Islam but was put off by its prohibition on alcohol. "Drinking is the joy of the Russes. We cannot exist without that pleasure," he proclaimed.[1] For various reasons the prince also rejected the arguments of the Catholic and Jewish emissaries. But when Orthodox clerics from Byzantium visited his court, he was intrigued and sent a delegation to Constantinople.

The Ball in the Concert Hall of the Winter Palace by Mihály Zichy. *Source: State Hermitage Museum © State Hermitage Museum photo by Vladimir Terebenin*

Upon their return from the great Byzantine metropolis, Vladimir's envoys reported about its magnificent churches. "We knew not whether we were in heaven or on earth," they gushed. "For on earth there is no such splendor or such beauty, and we are at a loss how to describe it. We only know that God dwells there among men, and their service is fairer than the ceremonies of other nations."[2] Within two years, Vladimir ordered his subjects baptized into Orthodox Christianity.

The Russian Church remains a feast for the senses. The soft glitter of the golden icon frameworks, the heady fragrance of the incense, and the mysterious harmonies of the sung liturgy are all meant to bring the faithful closer to God. For the Orthodox believe that the path to salvation lies not through the cold, reserved rationality of the intellect, as Protestants in the West assert. Rather, it is through the splendor of the Liturgy.

There was nothing subtle or restrained about this insatiable appetite for beauty in secular life as well—visitors to the court, whether in Moscow or St. Petersburg, were invariably struck by its opulence. And there was nothing discreet about this ardor. A French visitor once observed,

> One hardly encounters what the English call *comfort* and we describe as ease in Russia. You will never find anything that is sufficiently perfect entirely to satisfy the fancy of Russian magnates. . . . They love the splendor of their wealth rather than the pleasures it can provide.[3]

And what better way to flaunt one's fortune than with jewelry? Magnificence well describes the earliest precious objects archeologists found in what are now Russia and Ukraine.

The Scythians

These are the remarkable gold pieces left by the Scythians, the nomadic people who roamed the Pontic Steppe north of the Black Sea some 2,500 years ago. As hunters and warriors, they initially fashioned jewelry that featured deer, birds of prey, and large cats typically in combat or flight. Graceful flowing lines and fine detail characterize the artifacts Scythians left in their *kurgans*, the burial mounds of their chiefs. One celebrated example is the 600 BC gold plaque of a stag with curling horns and other flowing lines that strikingly anticipate Art Nouveau, which is now preserved in the Hermitage.

Over time, the Scythians began to interact with the Greek colonies that dotted the Black Sea's northern shore, which led to sophisticated hybrids. Men and gods now joined the fauna, often still in violent struggle. However, reflecting their increasingly sedentary existence, more pacific scenes of domestic life also began to appear. The most famous example is the remarkable 4th-century BC gold comb also at the Hermitage. Three men, possibly inspired by a Scythian myth, are in battle. The central figure, wearing a Corinthian helmet and nomadic trousers, neatly embodies this Greco-Scythian artistic symbiosis.

The Scythians eventually succumbed to the more vigorous nomadic Sarmatians, who by the 2nd century BC had cast them into the dustbin of history. However, when Catherine the Great conquered the region during the late 18th century, Russian archeologists began to unearth Scythian treasures to great acclaim. Many of them naturally found their way to the Romanov dynasty's most prestigious art collection, at the

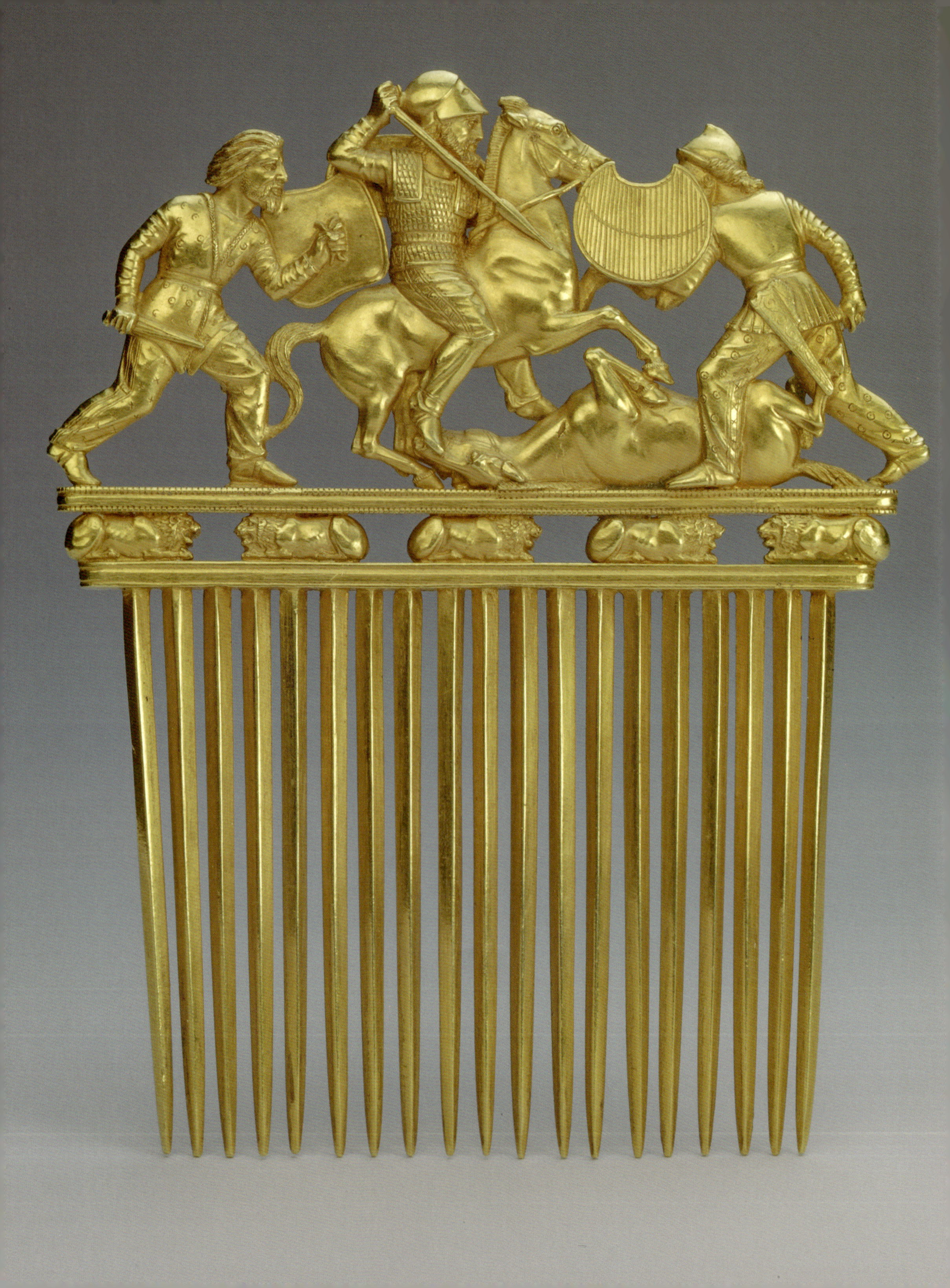

Left:
Gold Scythian comb, late 5th–early 4th century BC. As in Russia, the jewelry of the Scythians on the Black Sea steppe fused native with Western motifs. *Source: State Hermitage Museum © State Hermitage Museum photo by Vladimir Terebenin*

Right:
Kievan silver *kolts* (temple pendants) and buttons, 11th–12th century. Found in treasure troves in southern Ukraine and Russia, these precious objects may well have been hidden underground to escape the notice of the Mongol invaders in the early 13th century. *Source: Solntsev*

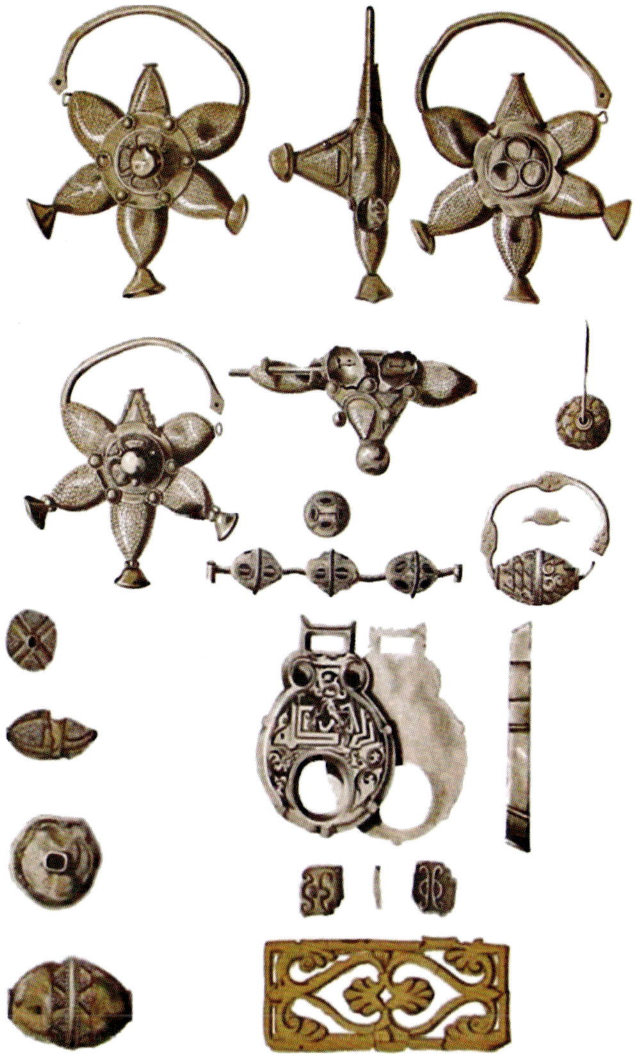

Hermitage in St. Petersburg. In 1867 Count Sergei Stroganov donated a particularly spectacular collection of Scythian gold that had recently been unearthed near the Black Sea to the museum. To catalogue and restore the objects, its curator turned to a young jeweler's son who had just returned from a study tour in Europe, Peter Carl Fabergé.[4]

Kievan Rus

While the Pontic Steppe remained in flux as wave after wave of nomadic nations swept over its grasslands, more sedentary Slavs slowly settled the forests to the north. It was only in the 9th century, when a group of Norsemen in search of trade routes from Scandinavia to Byzantium established their control over these lands, that these Eastern Slavs began to evolve into a semblance of political unity as Kievan Rus, which the Russians consider to be their ancestor. With its capital in Kiev, Rus developed over the 10th and 11th centuries into one of medieval Europe's most prosperous and culturally sophisticated states. Its waterways were the principal commercial conduits between northern Europe and Constantinople and markets farther east at the time. Kiev grew rich on this riverine trade "from the Varangians to the Greeks," as the route became known.

Situated at a crossroads between Christendom, Dar al-Islam and the great Eurasian Steppe, Rus was inevitably influenced by a variety of artistic traditions. After Prince Vladimir converted

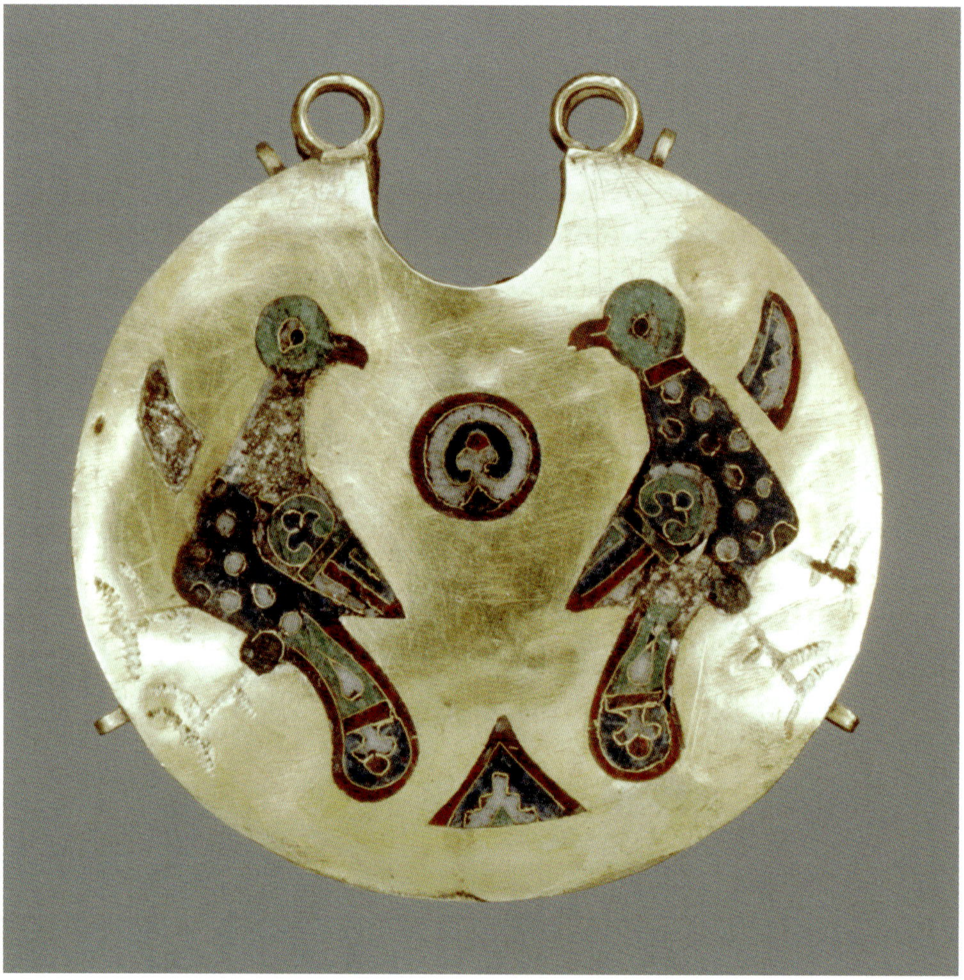

his realm to Eastern Orthodoxy, Byzantium's Christian culture became a dominant element. But Kiev did not blindly ape the Greeks. Instead, its artists and craftsmen created a distinctive style that tempered and humanized the severe asceticism of Constantinople's Eastern Orthodox tradition.[5]

The modest jewelry of the pre-Christian Eastern Slavs tended to find inspiration in the natural world of their surrounding forests. Birds, flowers, and other vegetation, often fashioned from bronze and iron instead of more precious metals, proliferate. Temple pendants were particularly popular among women. So named because they were worn near the temples, these adornments were fashioned from silver or other metals and were either suspended from a headdress or woven into braids of hair.

One popular variant was the *kolt*, a pendant made from two circular or semicircular disks that were soldered together to create a hollow interior. Women would fill the interior with fragrant herbs or scented oils as a perfume.[6] Those with smooth exteriors could be decorated with niello or enamel. The former is a technique that involves filling etchings in metal with a black compound to create intricate designs. Kievan craftsmen were highly skilled in the art, and their work attracted eager buyers in Constantinople. Niello still finds much favor among Russians today.

Contacts with Byzantium also introduced jewelers in Rus to a host of new skills, including filigree, granulation and cloisonné enamel. Cloisonné, the practice of applying different shades of enamel on metal in separate sections separated by gold wire partitions (*cloisons*), yields intricate designs when carried out by highly skilled hands. These were especially effective for portraits of saints and other Christian motifs on gold, which began to proliferate after Kiev adopted Orthodoxy in 988. Its baptism into the Greek faith also inspired craftsmen to turn their attention to devotional objects, such as pectoral crosses, communion beakers, icon covers (*oklady*) and Bible mountings.

Like enamel, gemstones added color. Since jewelers had not yet learned how to cut stones, they were *cabochon* (rounded, polished gems) and set into silver or gold. As in many cultures,

Gold and enamel Kievan kolt. 12th century. Kievan Rus craftsmen adopted enameling from Byzantium, the source of much of their early culture. *Source: Walters Art Gallery*

gems were believed to embody supernatural qualities. Thus emeralds were the stone of wisdom and bestowed hope and foresight, rubies imparted strength and valor, while sapphires promoted contentment.[7] Since the art of cutting diamonds to bring out their brilliance had not yet been developed, that stone's dull, gray luster made it less desirable.

None of these gems were native to Rus. Greek and Bukharan merchants imported precious stones from the mines of India, Ceylon and Burma via Constantinople. By contrast, the rivers abounded with freshwater pearls, which made them popular among all classes of society. Because of their association with purity, brides often wore the gem, sometimes in great profusion. Even in the reign of Nicholas II, pearl necklaces were the obligatory imperial wedding gifts to young ladies at their nuptials.[8] Meanwhile, pearls also found a place in Church, where they were used to decorate oklady.

Kievan Rus reached its apogee in the early 11th century and thereafter began a slow decline as its unity gradually disintegrated and trade patterns changed. The deathblow came in 1237, when the Mongol Batu Khan unleashed his hordes on the weakened realm. For the next two centuries, Russian culture languished, to be eventually reborn in a very different guise under Moscow's tsars.

In her history of Russian art, Tamara Talbot Rice suggests that "the high standards set in pre-Christian times by Scythian and Sarmatian metalworkers and jewelers were maintained in Kiev during the Early Christian period."[9] Over a millennium separates the Scythians from the Rus, but the precious artifacts that have survived suggest that she is right on the mark.

Muscovy

Toward the end of the 15th century, Tsar Ivan III ("the Great") definitively cast off the Mongol Yoke and restored unity to the Eastern Slavs. Centered in Moscow, deep in the forests on Europe's distant northeastern edge, his Russia was a more isolated and inward-looking realm. Kiev's fall had largely cut its commercial and cultural links with the West, and over the past centuries the differences between the Eastern and Western Churches had hardened them into two mutually hostile solitudes. At the same time, Byzantium's fall to the Turks in 1453 left Russia as the only major Orthodox nation, which only heightened its defensive insularity. Thus, as the Renaissance's warm rays of light began to reawaken the rest of Europe from the slumber of its dark ages, Muscovy continued largely to languish in somnambular solitude.

Ivan the Great's realm was also more rigidly centralized. Whereas its Kievan ancestor had been a loose confederation of principalities whose people enjoyed varying degrees of political self-determination, the Russian tsar considered the land to be personal property and its inhabitants his servants. All subjects, regardless of rank, addressed the sovereign with the standard formula "your slave obeys you."

Foreign visitors from the West described Ivan's Russia as "a rude and barbarous kingdom," a godless, alien nation no less Oriental than Cathay, Persia or Turkey. Nothing characterized Muscovy's exotic culture more dramatically than the strict segregation of well-born women from the world. When the Habsburg envoy Baron Sigismund von Herberstein returned from a mission to the Kremlin in the early 16th century, he reported, "No woman who walks in the street is deemed chaste or respectable. Thus, wealthy or important people keep their women so shut up that no one can see or speak to them."[10] Not only were wives of the tsar and his nobles entirely subordinate to their husbands, but they were also isolated in the *terem*, a separate quarter, together with their daughters. On those rare occasions when they were allowed on brief excursions beyond the terem's confining walls, blue-blooded women wore many layers of formless dress that concealed virtually all curves and skin, lest they arouse impure thoughts. Many also veiled their faces, and married women always covered their hair with a *kokoshnik* or other headdress.

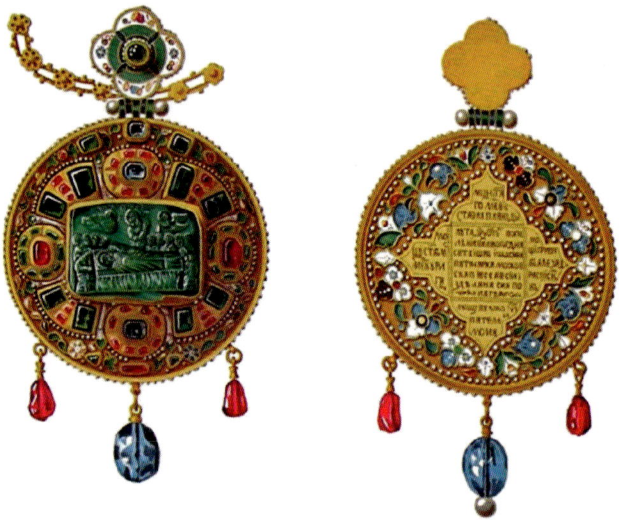

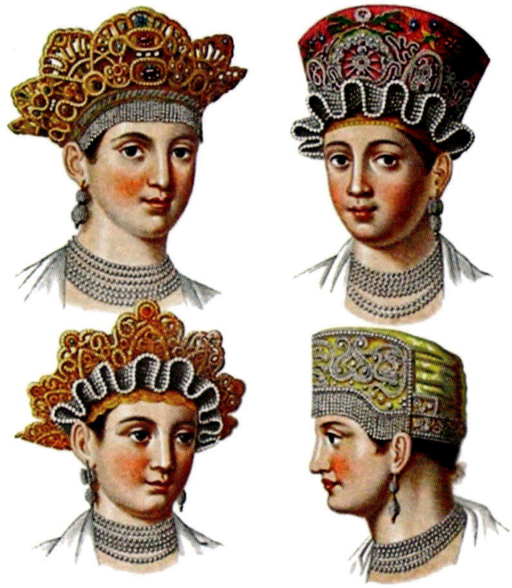

Left:
Gold *panagia* bearing a chrysoprase carving of the repose of the Mother of God and set with gemstones belonging to Patriarch Ioasaf II (ca. 1770). As in the medieval West, before the modern age Russian jewelers devoted much of their craft to serve their Orthodox faith. *Source: Solntsev*

Right:
Married women (*right*) and maidens' (*left*) headdress. 17th century. With great regional variations in style, a married woman's *kokoshnik* enclosed the crown, while a maiden's *poviazka* was open in the back. *Source: Solntsev*

Muscovite jewelers therefore tended to distract the viewer's eye away from a woman's femininity rather than draw attention toward it. Adornments such as gems were often sewn directly into formal garments along with gold or silver ornaments. The kokoshnik, a tall, curved headdress worn mostly by married women, could also be lavishly decorated with gold or pearls. As they began to be influenced by Western fashions, toward the end of the 17th century, some ladies also took to attaching *kruzhevo,* or precious metal imitation lacework, to the collars, hems and cuffs of their robes.

Earrings were popular in Muscovy both among women and men, although the latter only wore one. As in the rest of Europe, gentlemen also sported rings, sometimes in great profusion. The Danish diplomat Jacob Ulfeldt recalled his audience with Ivan the Terrible in 1578:

> His yellow velvet robe was decorated with precious gems. . . . While written treaties were being read to him . . . [Ivan] cheerfully summoned Bogdan Ivanovich Belskii and very affectionately showed him his rings (they were costly, and he had one on every finger of both his right and left hands).[11]

Cast in gold or silver, they were often decorated with enamel and set with precious or semiprecious stones.

Buttons were another way for both sexes to display their wealth. Like studs on a gentleman's evening shirt today, they were made of silver, gold, pearl or gems, and transferred from one garment to the other, as needed. However, rather than being flat, Muscovite buttons tended to be spherical or pear shaped, and could be elaborately enameled or carved. They also varied in size, with some being as large as a hen's egg. Like other precious objects, these jewels were carefully passed on to the next generation.

As in Kievan times, Russians were inordinately fond of colored gems and pearls. Both decorated religious objects, such as oklady, as well as beakers and other household objects, in addition to being worn as jewelry. Since Muscovite artisans

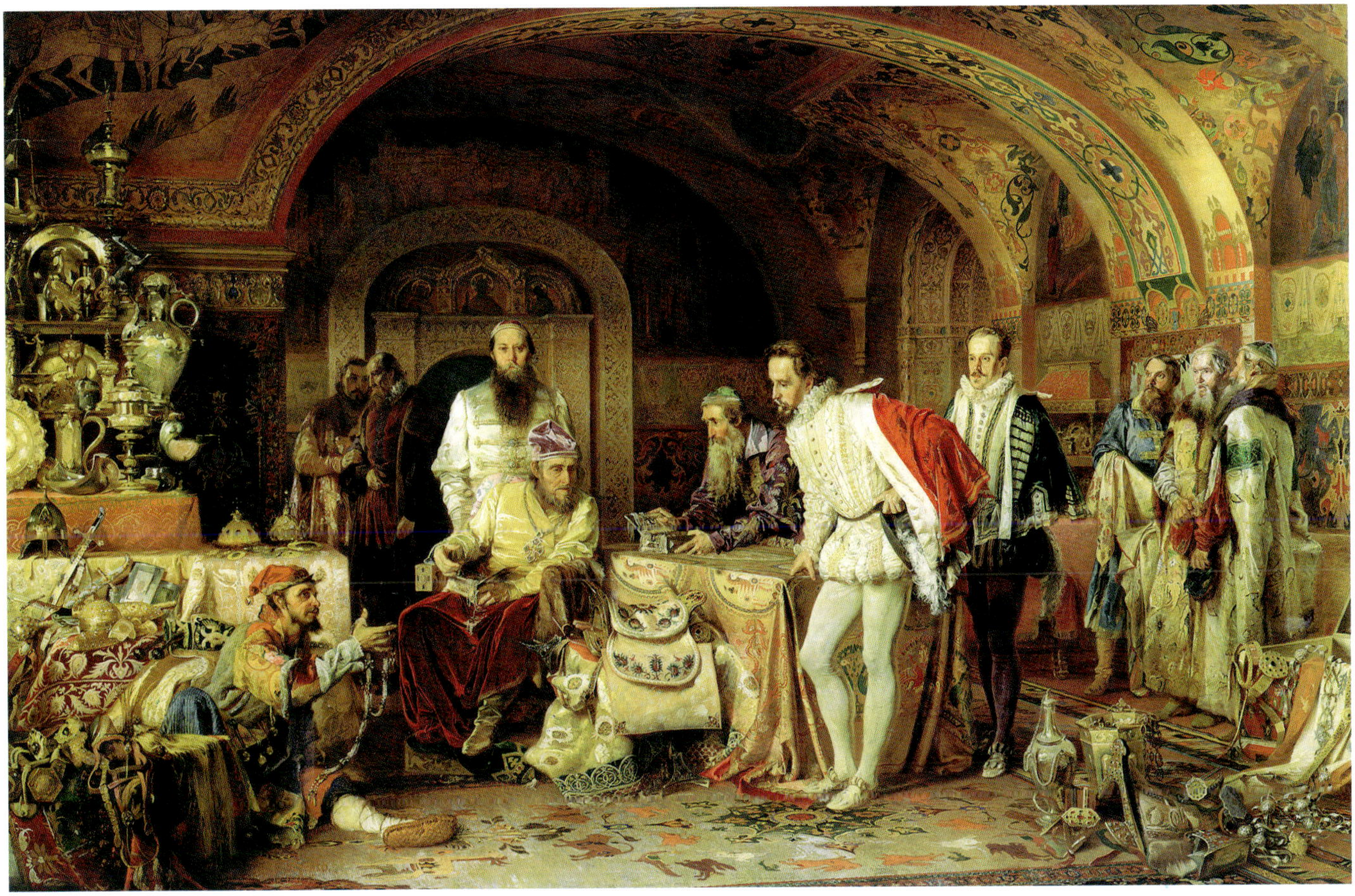

Aleksandr Litvichenko, "Ivan Shows His Treasure to English Ambassador Horsey." Medieval Russians believed in the healing powers of gemstones. *Source: Wikimedia Commons*

began to carve faceted stones only in the 17th century, most gems were still irregularly shaped cabochons in deep settings. Chosen for color rather than clarity or quality, sapphires, rubies and emeralds were especially prized.

Russians continued to believe that gems held magical qualities. One day the Englishman Sir Jerome Horsey, another diplomat to Ivan the Terrible's court, had the privilege of being invited into the Kremlin's treasury by the tsar. The ailing sovereign commanded attendants to array his precious stones before him and began to describe their properties. Pointing to a ruby, Ivan explained, "This is most comfortable to the harte, braine, vigar and memorie of man, clarifies congelled and corrupt bloud." Meanwhile, the emerald was "an enemye to uncleanness." As for the sapphire, "yt preserves and increaseth courage, joies the heart . . . clears the sight, takes awaye bloud shott, and streingthens the mussells and strings therof." More ominously, when the tsar had coral and turquoise placed on his arm, he woefully confessed to Sir Jerome, "I am poisned with disease; you see they shewe their virtue by the chainge of their pure cullor into pall; declares my death."[12]

Despite Muscovy's conservatism, jewelry styles did evolve. Through the 15th century, vegetation—plants, leaves and flowers—was the principal motif, albeit in a highly stylized form. During the next centuries, these patterns began to imitate nature more precisely as other European influences slowly began to filter through Russia's isolation. For now, these changes were incremental, and it would take until Peter's dramatic cultural opening to the West at the turn of the 18th century radically to transform tastes in jewelry, as well as in so much else.

The 18th Century

It would be going too far to suggest that the Russia of Peter the Great's forefathers was hermetically sealed from the rest of Europe. Already toward the end of the 15th century, Tsar Ivan the Great commissioned the Italian Aristotle Fioravanti to build a cathedral in the Kremlin. His grandson, Ivan the Terrible, actively promoted foreign trade, and there were strong Baroque influences on the architecture of 17th-century Moscow. Nevertheless, the

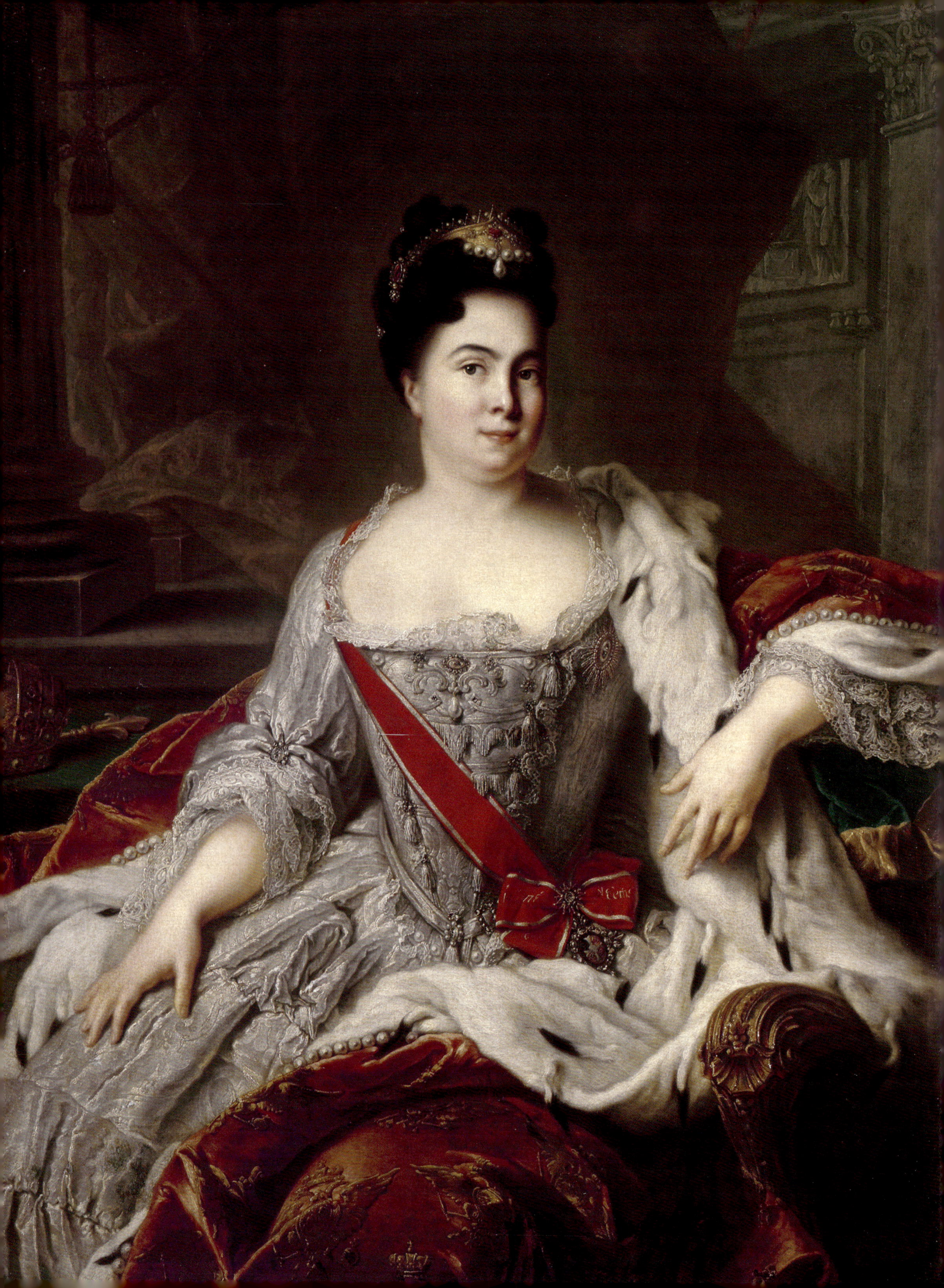

Empress Catherine I of Russia, Jean-Marc Nattier, 1717. Unlike her more austere husband, Catherine I did not disdain jewelry. *Source: Wikimedia Commons*

protean tsar is rightly credited for force-marching his often reluctant subjects into Western modernity. If his motives were largely to build a modern armed force that could take on more advanced powers such as Sweden, their effects on Russian culture proved no less thorough.

At the same time, Peter's reforms initially affected only a small stratum of Russia's population. His eponymous new capital of St. Petersburg, "that most abstract and intentional city in the world," imitated Dutch canals, northern German fortresses and Italian palaces. But beyond the banks of the Neva, the peasant millions carried on their lives much as they had for centuries. For now, the emperor's trickle-down Westernization mostly affected the artificial, hothouse world of his courtiers.

If Peter preferred to sup from wooden bowls himself, he encouraged his nobles to use gold plates. Like his Romanov heirs, he understood that splendor and magnificence broadcast imperial greatness. Extravagance was a spectacle that announced Russia's might to the world. According to Tatiana Zabozlaeva, "accumulating wealth, aside from its decorative and material merits, acquired a new purpose: Luxury became an instrument of state politics."[13] When Peter officially wed his new consort, Catherine, in 1712, the 30-kilo weight of her bejeweled crown and gold-embroidered robe caused her to stoop during much of the ceremony.[14]

The Western dress that Peter and his heirs imposed on their noblewomen exposed much more flesh than had been the case in Muscovy. The necks, arms, and decolletés of St. Petersburg's well-born ladies now called for increasingly lavish jewelry to accentuate their charms.[15] The result was a boom in the import and production of necklaces, rings, hairpieces, brooches, bracelets and other precious adornments in the new capital. By the second half of the 18th century, the quality of the city's jewelry began to rival that of Paris. Alas, little of it survives since gemstones were often remounted and their fittings recast to follow the latest trends.

Among the many other changes in fashion in Peter's time was the introduction of brilliant-cut diamonds, or "brilliants" (*brillianty*—not to be confused with the brilliant cut introduced in the early 20th century). In the West, the art of cutting many facets in diamonds to enhance their sparkle had been developed in the 17th century, and brilliants were already slowly making their way to Russia. In 1697, during his Grand Embassy to Europe's capitals, Peter visited the Dresden workshop of Augustus the Strong's celebrated goldsmith, Johann Melchior Dinglinger, where the jeweler personally taught him how to cut diamonds.[16] The lengthy war with Sweden that broke out not long after the tsar's return would occupy most of his attention during the next two decades of his reign. However, in 1721, the same year a grateful senate implored him to accept the title of emperor, Peter invited the Dutchman Pieter van Heesel to set up his own "state diamond mill" at his summer residence of Peterhof, just outside the capital.

Peter had little personal interest in jewelry. Such was not the case for his feminine successors during the rest of the 18th century. From the reigns of Catherine I (who ruled from 1725 to 1727) to Catherine the Great (r. 1762–96), mostly women wore the imperial mantle. Some were more effective rulers than others, but they all shared a passion for gems. One historian called this period "the Diamond Age" (*vek brilliantovy*).[17] Their lust for diamonds was truly aroused after Grand Duchess Anna Leopoldovna wore a magnificent bejeweled wedding crown at her nuptials in 1739.[18] Peter the Great's notoriously

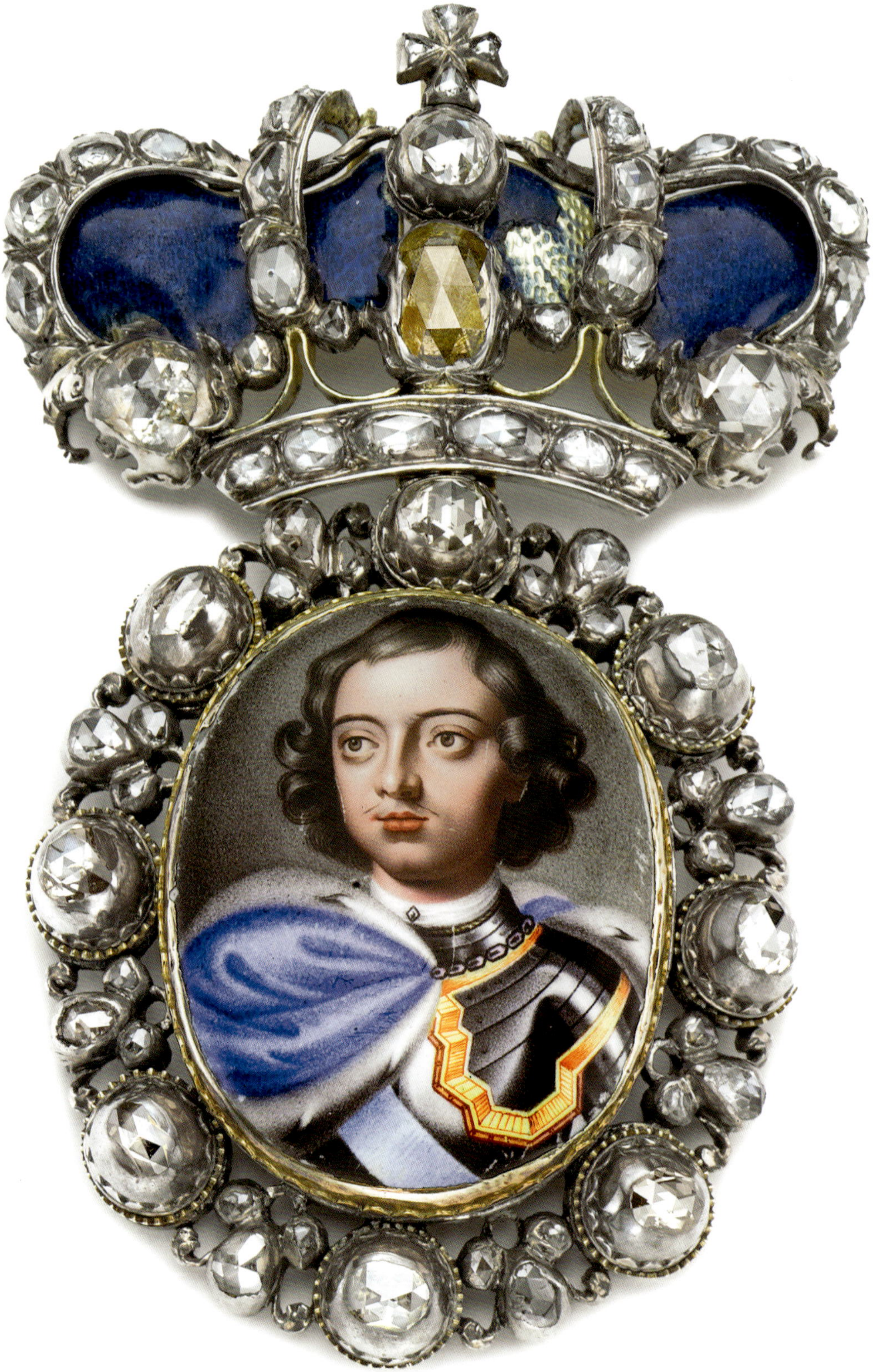

Diamond, silver and enamel Peter the Great portrait medallion. As with so much of Russian culture, jewelry began to be strongly influenced by Western styles and techniques beginning in Peter's reign at the turn of the 18th century. *Courtesy of Sotheby's*

self-indulgent daughter Elizabeth (r. 1741–62) aspired—and largely succeeded—to make her court the most dazzling in Europe. Ladies and gentlemen who were invited to her lavish balls and other amusements aggressively rivaled each other with the blinding glitter of their gems (imperial decree strictly forbade paste).[19]

Colored stones, especially emeralds and sapphires, remained popular during Elizabeth's reign, and were often arranged according to the asymmetrical and irregular rococo style of the day into such patterns as floral sprays. Unlike much of the age's jewelry, a few examples of these delicate creations by Jérémie Pauzié survive in the Hermitage (see chapter 3, "Jérémie Pauzié: A Jewel in the Crown"). To add variety, their diamonds could be backed by colored foil, endowing the stones with muted pastels. Adopting the French *en tremblant* fashion, some brooches, hair ornaments and aigrettes had gems mounted on stiff wires that shook whenever their wearer moved.

Never did Russia's brilliant century sparkle more brightly than during the decades after Catherine the Great seized power in 1762. Driving out other precious stones, diamonds now not only came to dominate such traditional jewelry as necklaces, pendants and brooches, but also became de rigueur for a host of other objects, from shoe buckles, sword hilts and snuffboxes to portrait frames and decorations. The English clergyman William Coxe, who traveled to Russia in 1778, recalled.

> The richness and the splendor of the Russian court surpasses all the ideas which the most elaborate description can suggest. It retains many traces of its ancient Asiatic pomp, blended with European refinement. . . . Amid the several articles of sumptuousness which distinguish the Russian nobility, there is none perhaps more calculated to strike a foreigner than the profusion of diamonds and other precious stones, which sparkle in every part of their dress. In most other European countries these costly ornaments are . . . almost entirely appropriated to the ladies; but in this the men vie with the fair sex in the use of them. Many of the nobility were almost covered in diamonds.[20]

Naturally, the empress had by far the most impressive collection of the gem. To keep them close at hand, she ordered a special Diamond Room set up near her bedchamber in the Winter Palace, to which she habitually invited guests to play cards—with the stones as the stakes. One of its highlights was the famous Orlov Diamond, whose massive 190-carat weight far surpassed the largest in any other European royal house; Catherine boasted to Voltaire that it was as large as an egg.[21] (See "The Fate of the Russian Crown Jewels," page 238).

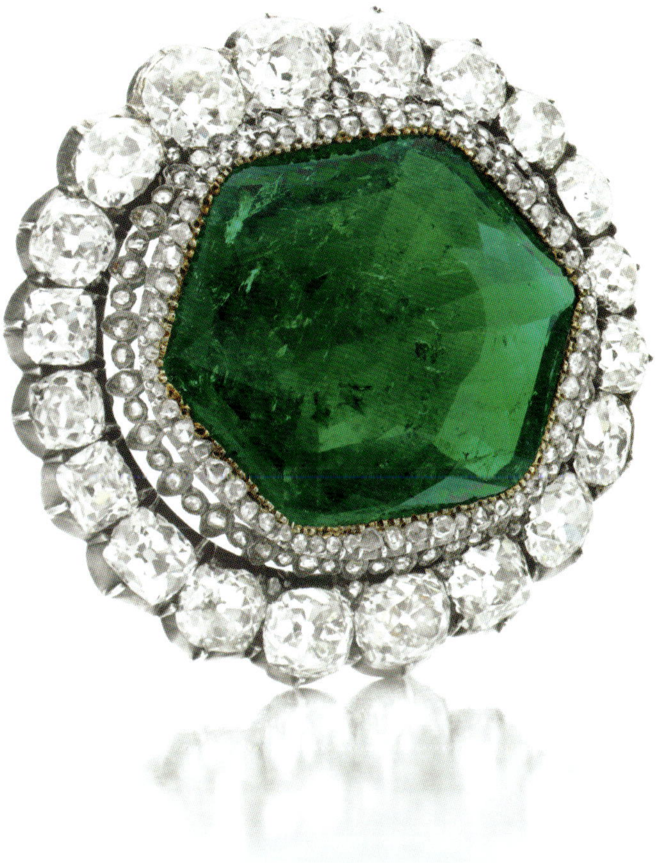

Emerald and diamond brooch, late 18th century. Catherine took great pride in her precious gemstone collection. © 2010 *Christies Images, Ltd.*

The jewel's origins are shrouded in legend. Some said that it had been stolen from a Hindu statue in southern India, while others claimed that it had come from the Persian shah's treasure. Whatever its provenance, the stone was eventually acquired by an Armenian merchant in Amsterdam. Reasoning that it was best suited for the woman who ruled the world's most extensive empire, he sold it to Catherine's former lover, Count Grigori Orlov, for some 400,000 rubles. The count, who hoped to rekindle her erstwhile ardor, presented it to the empress on her name day in 1773. The gift did not win the sovereign back from her new favorite, Grigorii Potemkin. However, she did present him with the Marble Palace and allowed him to take the title of prince of the Holy Roman Empire. As for the diamond, Catherine eventually had it set in a scepter that now forms part of the Russian crown jewels in the Kremlin Armory.[22]

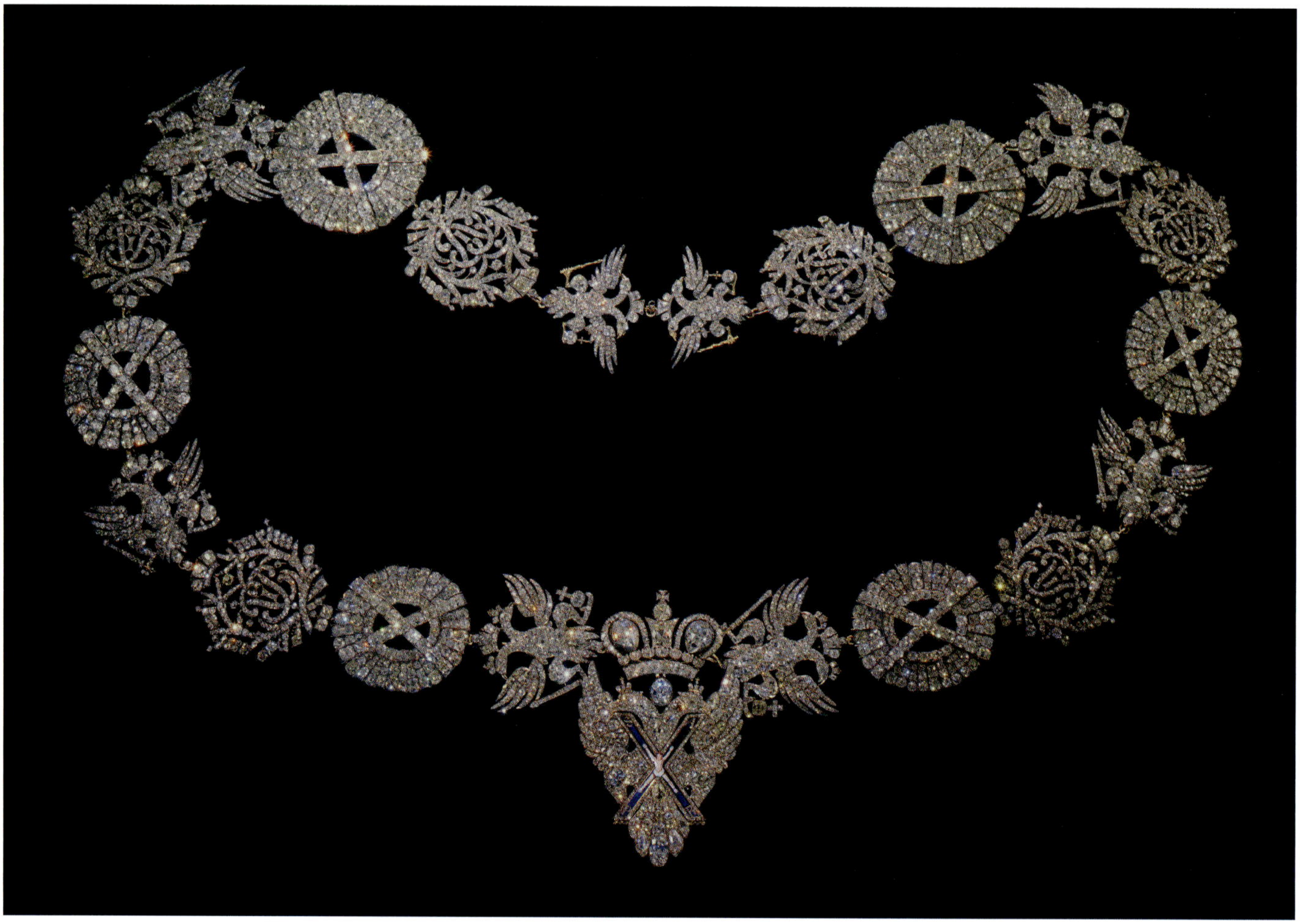

Foreign lands still remained the source for most gems in the 18th century. Jérémie Pauzié, the Swiss-born jeweler to the Romanovs, tells us in his memoirs that Empress Anna (r. 1730–40) sent a caravan to China every year to acquire precious stones along with porcelain. The immense ruby-red spinel that topped the magnificent crown Pauzié fashioned for Catherine the Great's coronation in 1764 had been acquired some 90 years earlier by Nicholas Spafary during his embassy to the Middle Kingdom. Many gemstones, including sapphires and rubies, reached Russia from the Indian subcontinent, which had also long yielded diamonds. However, by the 17th century vast deposits from Brazil began to flood the European market. While emeralds had traditionally come from Egypt and the Arabian Peninsula, new mines in South America supplanted those in the Near East as well.[23]

Peter the Great's efforts to develop his own empire's vast natural riches now began to provide sources for gemstones closer to home. The most important discoveries were in Siberia, which had only been absorbed into Peter's realm during the century before his reign. The emperor's attention focused on the Ural Mountains, which geographically separate European Russia from its Asian domains. By the late 1700s, Cossack settlers had already begun sporadically to mine its slopes, which were rich in amethyst, topaz, jasper, aquamarine and other stones. Peter began to send expeditions to Siberia to conduct more systematic searches, and in 1721 established a state monopoly to exploit minerals in the Urals.

Catherine the Great, whose craving for gems knew no bounds, was even more active. Already in 1765, only three years into her reign, she commanded General Iakov Dannenberg to lead a 30-man party to look for "diverse colored stones" in the area around Ekaterinburg. The group included two Florentine lapidaries, in whose honor a new amethyst mine was named "Talian." Upon returning from their 25-year mission, the expedition's men presented the empress with a map of more than 30 varieties of gemstones in the Urals, which she ordered mounted on taffeta and kept in her chambers to remind her of Russia's mineral wealth. Other searches over the next century would discover deposits of diamonds and many other gems throughout Siberia.[24]

Right:
Gold and enameled snuffbox with the portrait of Grand Duke Paul Petrovich, 1774, by Jean Paul Ador. Portrait snuffboxes were the most-prestigious gifts a Russian sovereign bestowed on deserving subjects, right up to the dynasty's fall. The empress herself was an avid afficionada of snuffboxes. *Source: State Hermitage Museum © State Hermitage Museum photo by Vladimir Terebenin*

Previous page:
This grand collar of the Imperial Order of St. Andrew set with diamonds, ca. 1795, was first worn by the Russian emperor Paul I during his imperial coronation. Diamond Fund of the Moscow Kremlin. *Photo by Nikolai Rakhmanov*

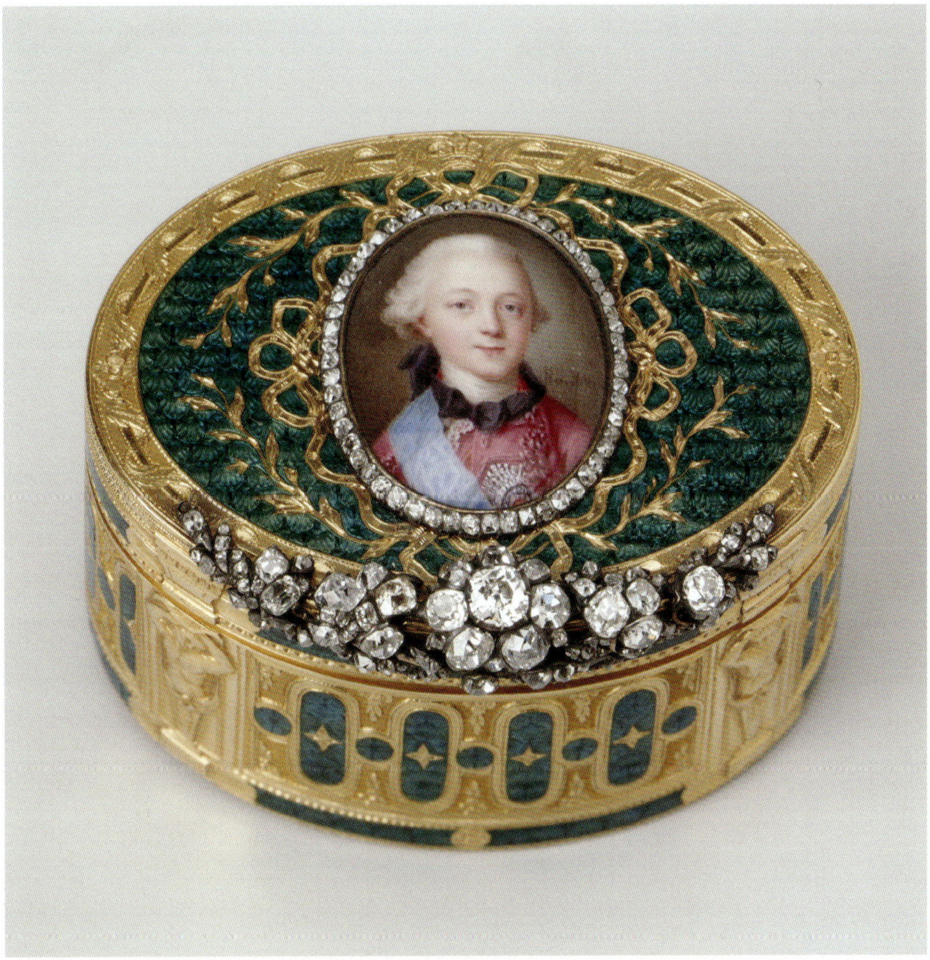

The vast lands east of the Urals were also found to contain precious metals. Until Peter's reign, the only source for jewelry in Russia was coins and ingots from abroad. However, in 1704 the first domestic silver mine opened near Lake Baikal in eastern Siberia, and some 40 years later, gold began to be mined in the environs of Ekaterinburg. By the 19th century, other Siberian mines also provided the metals, as well as platinum.[25]

Catherine decorated her palaces on a large scale with malachite from the Urals and eastern Siberian lapis lazuli. Together with other gemstones, they were also extensively used in jewelry and *objets de vertu*, such as snuffboxes, seals, *bonbonnières* and the other accoutrements indispensable for the nobles at the imperial court. The popularity of snuff made the former particularly prominent, and they became an important way to display the jeweler's art.

First introduced to the French court in 1561 by the diplomat Jean Nicot—ironically for medicinal purposes—the practice of inhaling powdered tobacco was already popular in Muscovy a century later. As in the rest of Europe, taking snuff reached its height among St. Petersburg's well born in the 18th century. Among the many objects Peter brought back from his foreign travels were some Dutch snuffboxes, and soon St. Petersburg's goldsmiths began making them as well. Their first efforts consisted of heavy gold objects parsimoniously covered with a few gems, but by the time of Catherine the Great they began to rival their most skilled Parisian competitors.

The empress herself was an avid afficionada of snuffboxes. Rather than carrying them, she kept a large variety within easy reach on tables and other convenient flat surfaces. Meanwhile, like some of her subjects, Catherine also passionately collected these objets de vertu. As for the snuff itself, she patriotically took only tobacco that had been grown in Russia, at Tsarskoe Selo. Apparently, the empress "always sniffed it from the left hand, because she extended the right one for her subjects to kiss."[26]

While snuffboxes were also fashioned from porcelain, mother-of-pearl, ivory, tortoise shell, or even wood, gold remained the preferred raw material. Often lavishly encrusted with diamonds, many of the boxes featured portraits of loved ones or pastoral scenes in exquisitely fine *en plein* enamel, the process of laying colored enamel on a plain gold surface. Goldsmiths also adopted

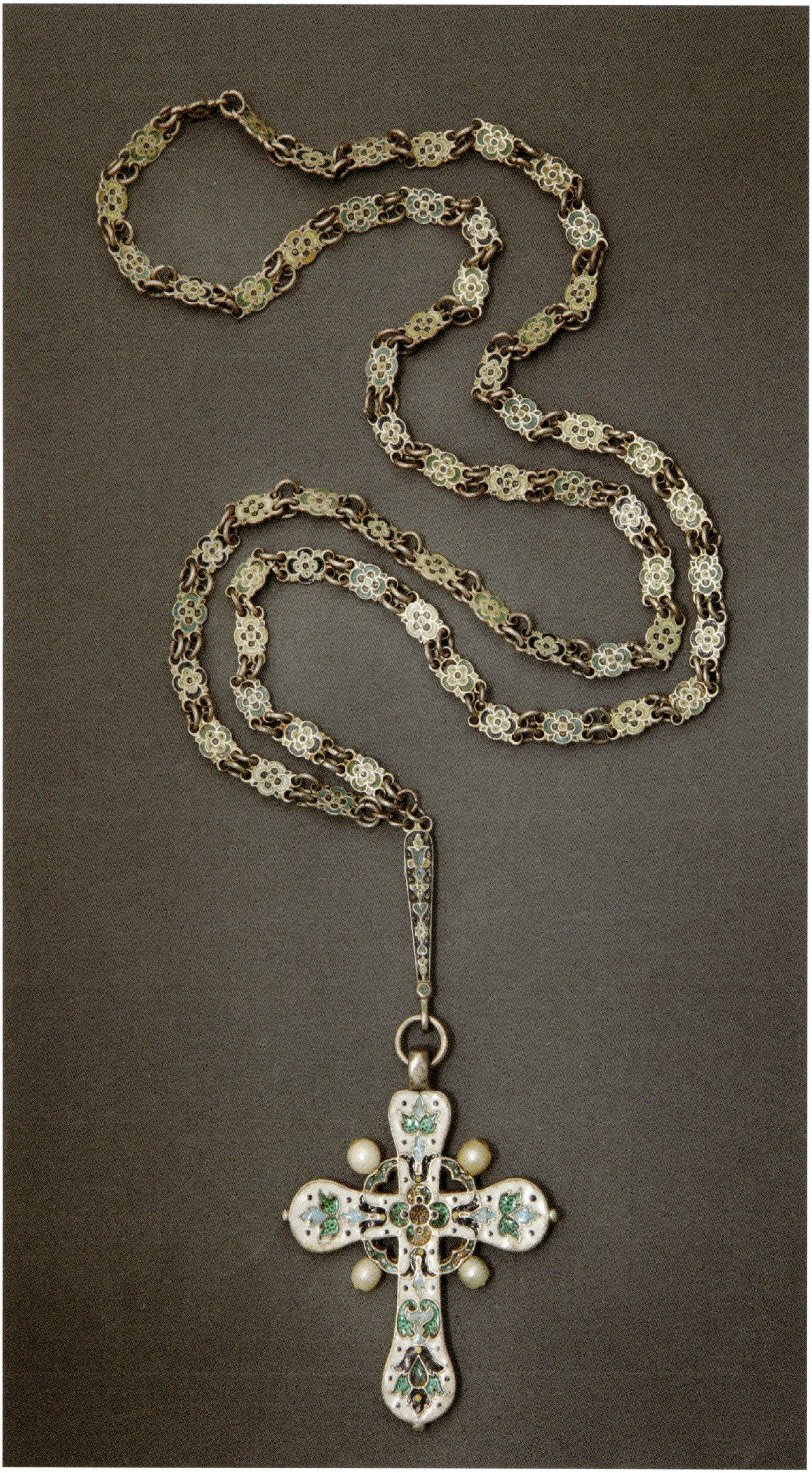

Enameled cross and chain, Velikii Ustiug, late 17th–early 18th century. Despite growing interest in more secular motifs, the church remained a major source of inspiration for the Russian jeweler's art. *Marie Betteley, photo by Noel Allum*

the French technique of decorating snuffboxes and other objects with *guilloché* enamel, which involved firing several coats of translucent colored enamel on incised metal.[27]

Of course, enamel was hardly new to Russia. Craftsmen had already been proficient in the medium since the Kievan age a thousand years earlier. During the 16th and 17th centuries, the skill was highly developed in such northern towns as Velikii Ustiug and Solvychegodsk, as well as the Kremlin's workshops. The motifs were often religious, embellishing the oklady of icons, *panagias* (clerical pectoral medallions), crosses and other liturgical items. At the same time, reflecting Muscovy's bicontinental influences, both more naturalistic Western motifs and the abstract ornamentation of the East were used for secular objects.[28]

Peter's journeys to Europe had also interested him in portrait enamels. When he moved his capital to the banks of the Neva River in 1713, among the Kremlin Armory craftsmen he brought over were the enamelers Grigorii Musinskii and Andrei Ovsov. Soon, Russia's emperors and empresses were presenting snuffboxes with their portraits to foreign ambassadors when they took their leave from the court, and as expressions of gratitude to their own subjects for important services to the Crown. The latter regarded them more highly than decorations, since they were a personal mark of imperial favor, while medals recognized merit. Those lucky to receive a presentation snuffbox often rushed to have them appraised by their jeweler to measure the degree of the sovereign's gratitude.[29]

Unlike their more soberly attired 19th-century sons and grandsons, the noblemen of St. Petersburg's diamond age were just as eager to display their jewelry as the ladies. The remark of Madame de Staël, who had spent some time in the imperial court during the Napoleonic era, was equally applicable to both sexes: "I heard that a Russian man had suggested making an alphabet with precious stones. . . . He understood that this was the best way to encourage Russians to learn to read."[30] In addition to the snuffbox they ostentatiously took out of their pocket at the right moment, gentlemen were often seemingly carapaced in glittering cuirasses of gems and gold. Decorations—the higher the order's grade, the more spectacular the bling—were practically de rigueur at court. Jeweled buckles decorated their shoes and the backs of their jackets, while the fronts were also festooned with several dozen buttons of enameled precious metals and gems. And as timepieces now began to shrink in size, gold pocket watches were another way to show off one's riches.

The Hermitage curator Marina Lopato points out that in the 18th century, St. Petersburg came of age as a center of the jeweler's art. While the styles were largely imported from Europe, they eventually blended with Russian tastes to create a unique vernacular that was "neither entirely Occidental, but no longer Muscovite."[31] She rightly concludes,

> It may be said without a doubt that the 18th century's second half marked the bright dawn of jewelry in St. Petersburg. During those centuries the capital housed a glorious *pléiade* of master craftsmen, who not only matched but, in some ways, surpassed their Western brethren.[32]

The 19th Century

Already in the latter years of Catherine's reign, Russian tastes began to react against the Rococo's extravagant excesses. In the 1782, the empress issued an edict to temper the lavish glitter at court, "[to] introduc[e] simplicity and moderation to retain and augment one's own prosperity, so that it brings greater profit,

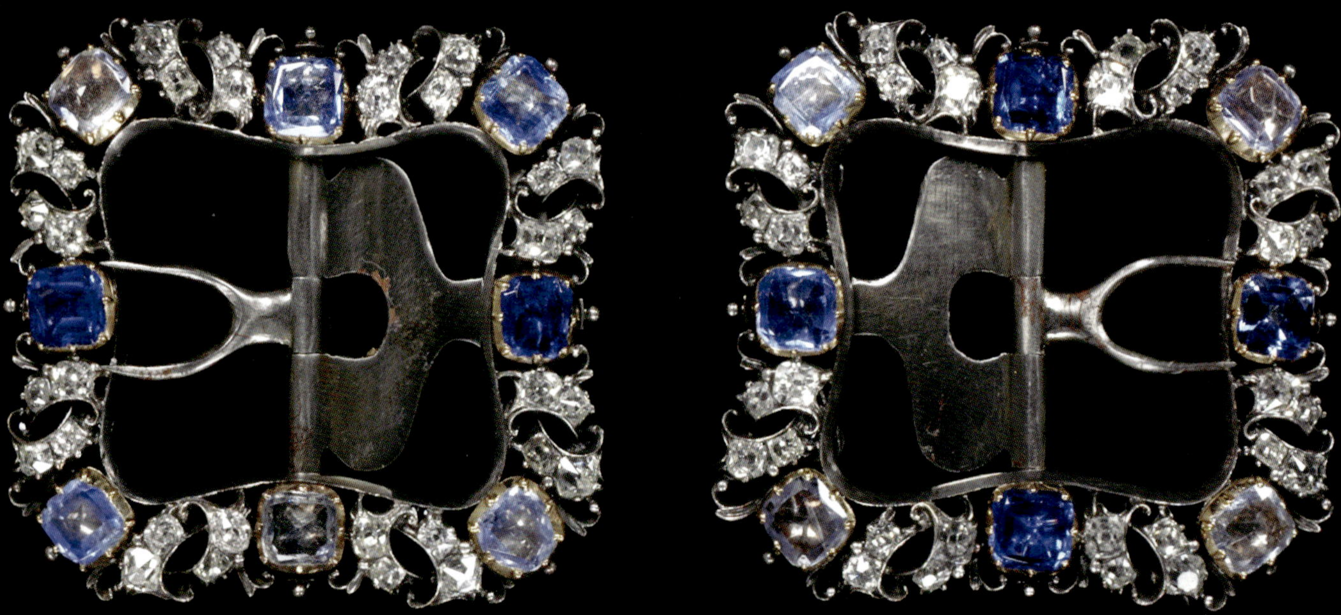

Shoe buckles, ca. 1750. © *Victoria and Albert Museum, London*

and because of an aversion to ruinous luxury."[33] Despite the decree's seemingly sensible goal, she was following the dictates of French fashion, which was replacing the exuberance of the Louis XV style with the more restrained neoclassicism of Louis XVI. Simple high-waisted dresses of delicate fabrics and less elaborate coiffures sought to echo the glories of ancient Greece. At the same time, ladies ornamented themselves more sparingly, now preferring a few pieces of excellent quality rather than displaying entire treasuries of gold and gems.

There were also direct allusions to Antiquity in the jeweler's art of the imperial capital as the 18th century drew to a close, with cameos of semiprecious stones such as carnelian fastening the shawls its frigid climes called for. Likewise recalling ancient Greece and Rome, tiaras became a popular way to wear brilliants. By far the age's preferred gem, faceted diamonds now began to be put into open settings to enhance their sparkle. Meanwhile, the plain, monochromatic surfaces of snuffboxes were sparingly chased with such Classical motifs as garlands, cornucopias, cupids, sphinxes and gryphons.

The reign of Alexander I (1801–25) was dominated by the more martial Empire style.[34] Close to neoclassicism with its restrained aesthetic, geometrical shapes and use of elements drawn from Antiquity, ironically the Alexandrine Empire was a Slavic variant of the fashion current at the court of the tsar's archfoe, the self-styled Emperor Napoleon of France. But unlike the latter, which celebrated the person of the monarch, in Russia the new style lauded the nation and its warriors.[35] Along with the fantastic creatures of Greek mythology, Roman military elements, including drums, standards, swords and armor, entered the jeweler's vernacular. The Romanov double-headed eagle also featured prominently, albeit now often with its wings turned down to create a raptor with more elegant, horizontal lines. Forged in the titanic conflicts that engulfed the continent at the turn of the 19th century, Alexandrine Empire was distinctly more nationalist, even patriotic, than the cosmopolitanism that had shaped tastes in St. Petersburg in the era of the empresses.

Inspired by the republican virtues of Alexander's Swiss tutor, Frédéric de La Harpe, and dictated by the exigencies of war, his court was also more austere than under his feminine 18th-century predecessors. Upon acceding to the throne, the tsar trimmed his court's spending by four million rubles, and one foreign diplomat was surprised that the monarch "wears no jewelry, not even a ring or a watch."[36] Empress Elisabeth Alekseevna likewise eschewed extravagance and adopted a relatively modest toilette, although she did have a particular fondness for aquamarines.[37]

Perhaps the Alexandrine Empire's most famous jewel was the magnificent diadem created for the empress, which blended the ancient Greek head ornament with the peak of the traditional kokoshnik. Featuring a 13-carat pink diamond from the era of Paul I at the center, set below three trains of briolettes, old mine cut, and pear-shaped diamonds, respectively, the "Russian tiara" inspired a number of similar jewels by Bolin, Fabergé, Boucheron and Cartier, among others.[38] (see page 227)

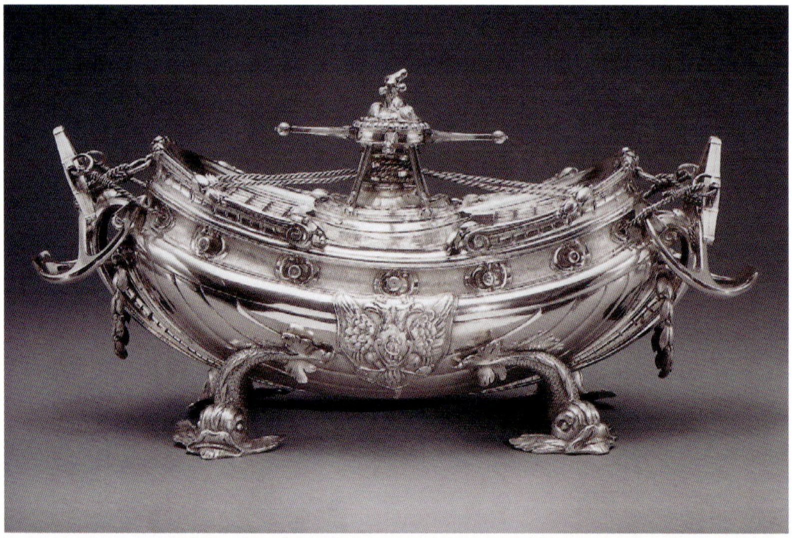

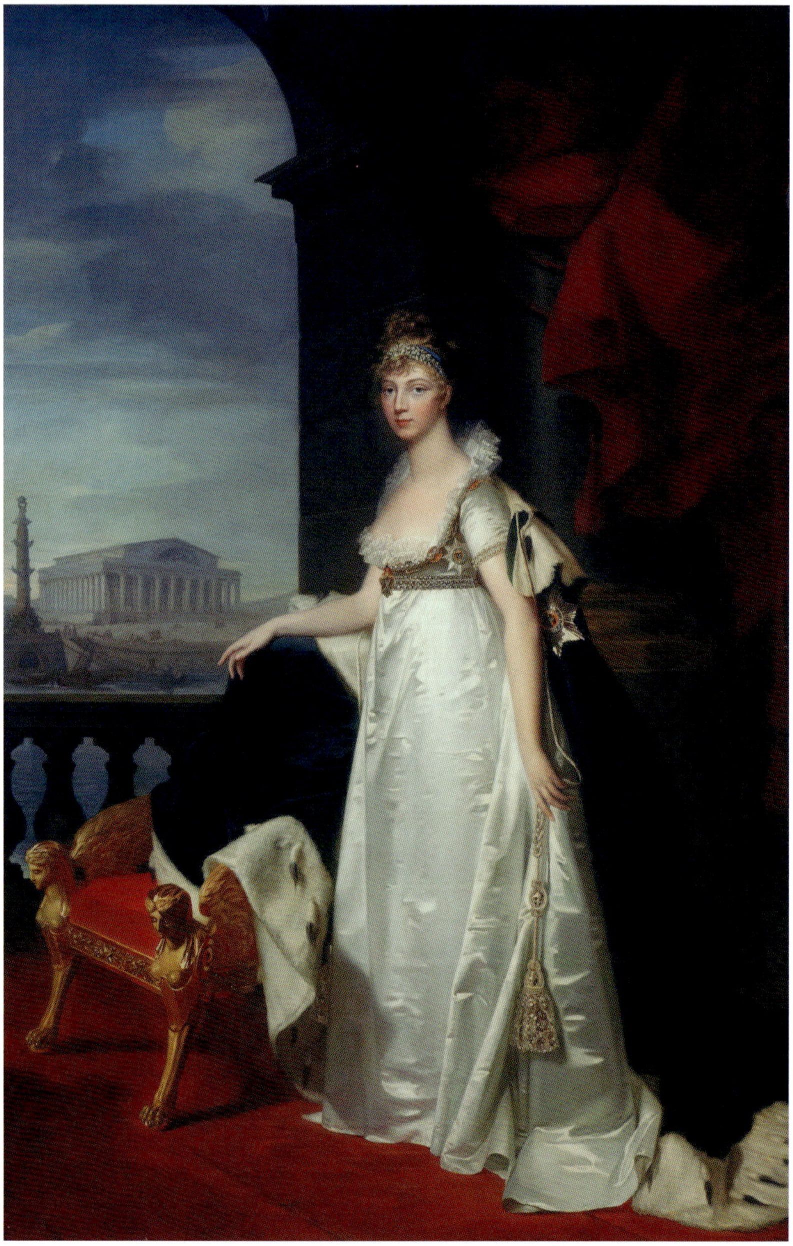

Silver tureen, Zacharias Deichmann, late 18th century. Shaped as a vessel, this silver tureen was an imperial presentation piece. *Courtesy of Sotheby's*

Empress Elizabeth Alekseevna, Jean-Laurent Mosnier, 1805. Even though Alexander I ultimately became his enemy, Russians enthusiastically adopted Napoleon's Empire style during the tsar's reign. *Source: Wikimedia Commons*

Baron Armin von Fölkersam, the Hermitage jewelry collection's curator at the turn of the 20th century, wistfully recalled the graceful style of Alexander's court a hundred years earlier:

> The Empire was the last age of work by hand, and therefore even one creation of the time always keeps its value. Subsequent factory-made jewelry, mass produced by comparison, seems to us plebeian, unattractive, and awakens the same, almost physical, revulsion as when we look at chromolithographs, stamped and cast metalwork, and counterfeits.[39]

No single fashion ruled over Russian jewelry after the Empire style expired along with Alexander in 1825. As in the West, much of the rest of the 19th century was dominated by historicism, a term used to describe a variety of influences from the past, real or imagined. Craftsmen did not necessarily strive for clinical verisimilitude. What was important was to capture the spirit of the age. The attitude was much like that taken by architectural restorers at the time. An article about the latter in 1840 explained,

> By the power of the poetic attuning of his soul and of his hypotheses, [the restorer] strives to convey the character of the original, not only with archaeological accuracy but also with that sublime feeling which moves the architect himself in moments of creation and lays upon his works the seal of true beauty and creativity.[40]

By the same token, St. Petersburg no longer looked solely to Paris for inspiration, as English and Prussian jewelers also began leave their mark. During the reign of Nicholas I (1825–55), the city's most famous store was the Magasin Anglais on the corner of Bolshaia Morskaia Street and Nevskii Prospect, whose British-born owners, Charles Nicholls and William Plincke, imported silver, jewelry and other luxuries from their homeland as well as making copies in the English taste (See "Nicholls & Plincke: Silver Purveyors to the Tsars").

Geographical proximity, the recent wartime alliance and dynastic ties (Nicholas had taken the Prussian king's daughter as his consort) also made German fashions popular in the imperial capital. These included jewels made of iron. Cast in delicate floral and other intricate patterns, and covered with shiny black lacquer, such adornments had been adopted by patriotic Prussian women who had received them for trading in their gold to help finance the struggle against Napoleon.

The popularity of designs that more accurately and luxuriantly imitated nature characterized the rise of Romanticism in the new century's early decades. Emotion and nostalgia for the nation's own past now replaced the cosmopolitan rationalism of neoclassicism. The new age also marked the return of more lavish ornamentation and a greater variety of materials. Ladies might sport acrostic rings with hidden messages, such as those set with a ruby, emerald, garnet, amethyst, another ruby and a diamond to spell the French noun "regard." Meanwhile lovers wore lockets that secreted a lock of their intimate's hair, and some even went so far as to weave hair into bracelets and necklaces.

Diamonds continued to reign supreme. However, other colored stones returned to the Russian jeweler's palette, now joined by coral, turquoise and agate, as well as exotic natural materials such as ivory and tortoise shell. At the same time, more discoveries in the Urals made a greater variety of their stones available, such as pale green demantoid garnets and alexandrite. The latter has the unusual quality that it changes color according to how it is illuminated. In natural daylight it is greenish, somewhat like an emerald, but it turns red under incandescent light. A type of chrysoberyl, alexandrite earned its name because it was found on the name day of Tsarevich Alexander Nikolaevich, April 17.[41]

The turn of the 20th century saw a revival of neoclassicism as well as the rise of *style modern*, as Russians call Art Nouveau. The latter was in part a protest against mechanization and the Victorian excess of the previous decades. Nature remained a leitmotif, but now in more vivid and stylized forms and iridescent enamels. Sinuous lines represented exotic flowers, insects and peacocks.

At the same time, jewelry now even invoked the female form, highlighting the sensuousness of the naked body. The style also mixed various precious and semiprecious stones, with demantoid garnets being particularly popular. However, the gems tended to be small, as discrete points of light that blended harmoniously rather than clashing with the jewel's flowing form.[42]

The proliferation of styles that recalled ages past, ranging from Etruscan and Byzantine to Gothic, Renaissance and Rococo, not to mention pre-Petrine Muscovy, reflected the imperial capital's increasingly diverse clientele.[43] As the city's population of officials, professionals, businessmen and others in the middle class grew, so did their requirements for adornment. An article of 1847 about St. Petersburg merchants out for a Sunday stroll in Elagin Island's parks reported, "everyone wears diamonds, from eight-year-old girls to men not accustomed to tidiness, who astonish us by wearing an enormous solitaire on their grimy shirtfronts."[44] Meanwhile, mechanization and other technological developments, such as the electrolyte process for plating base metals with silver and gold the Birmingham manufacturer George Elkington commercialized in the 1840s, made jewelry more affordable.

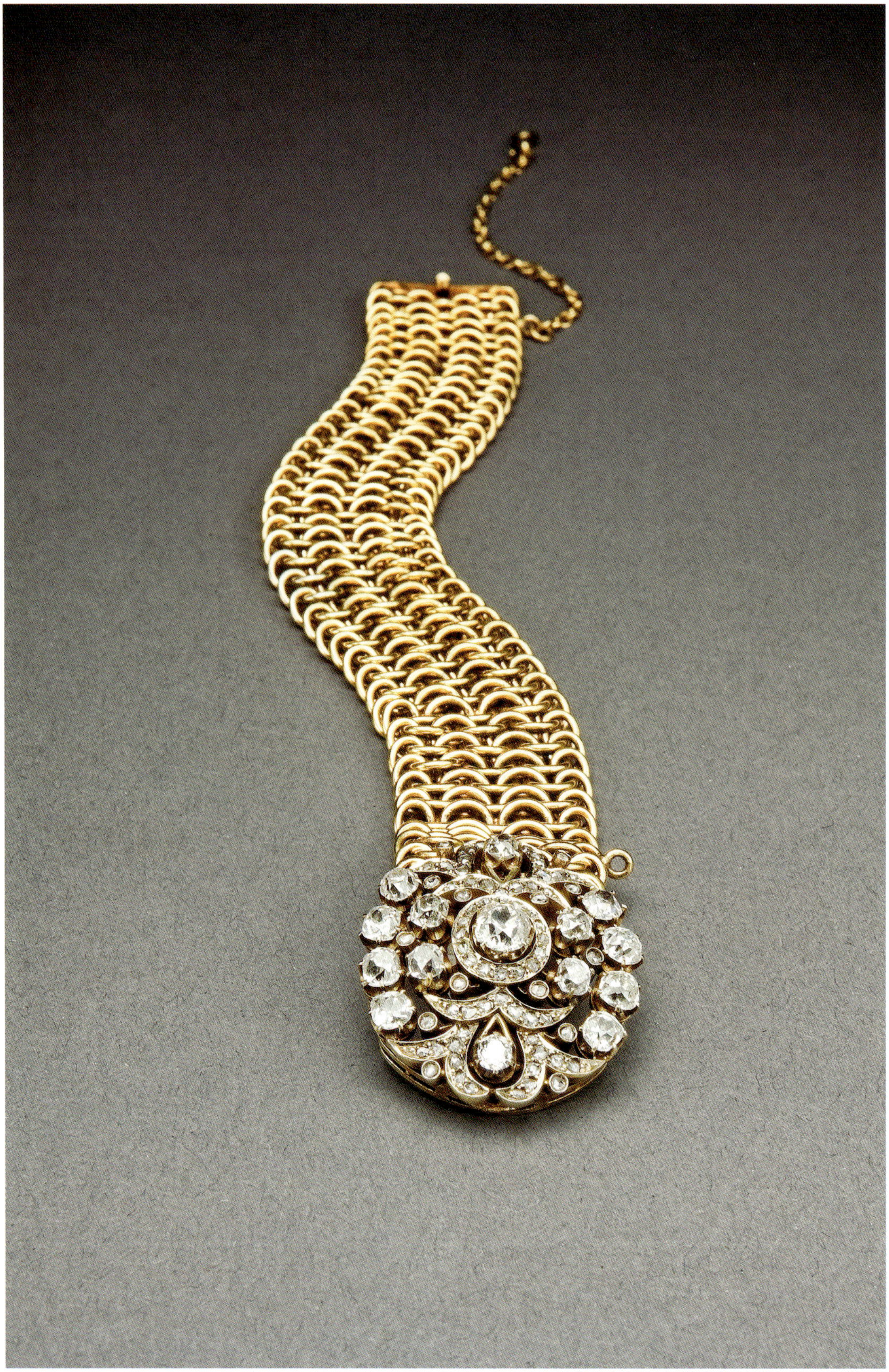

Gold-and-diamond bracelet, St. Petersburg, ca. 1840. Bracelets were popular throughout the 19th century and could adorn both wrists. *Marie Betteley, photo by Roger Allum*

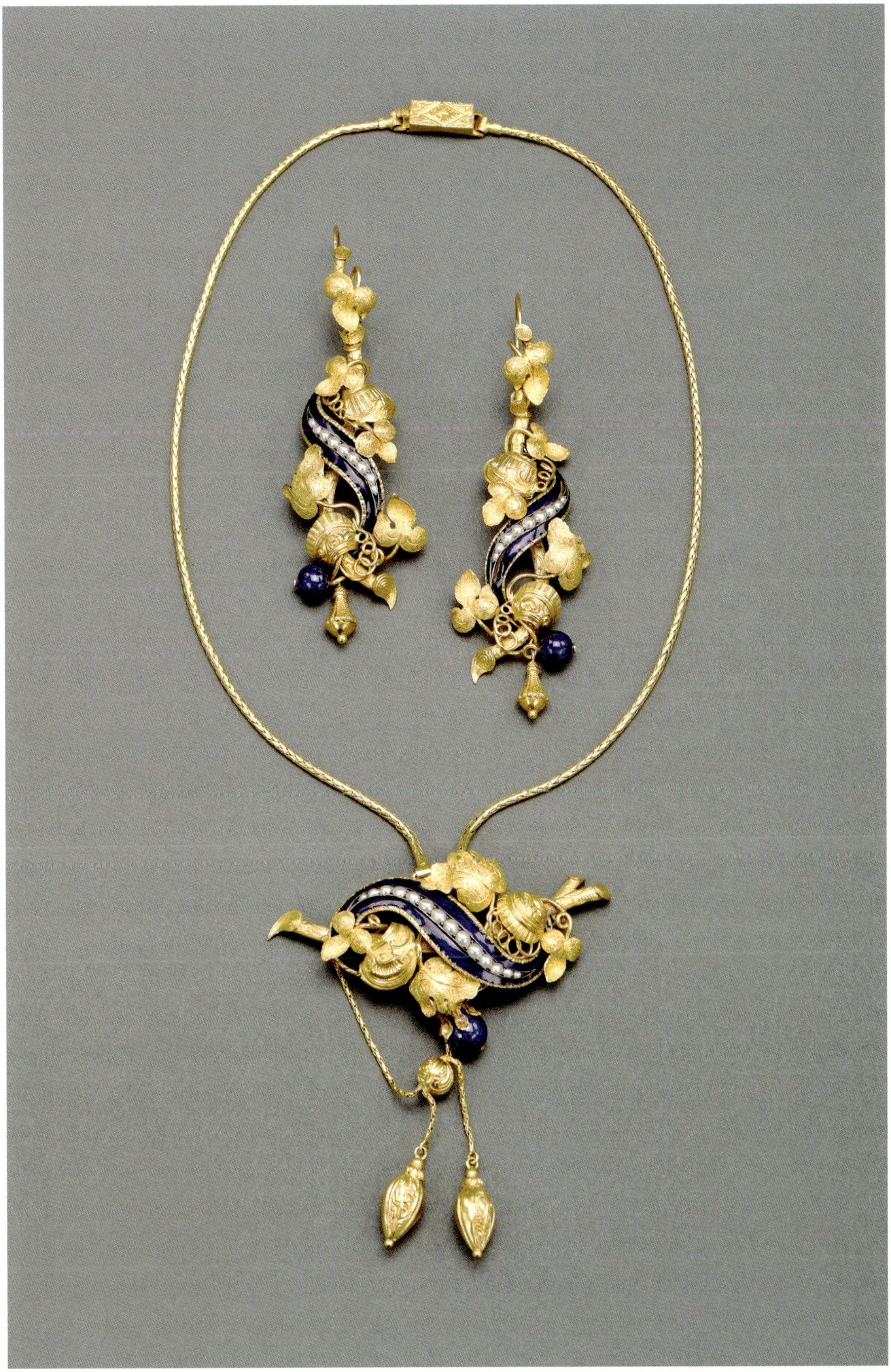

Gold, pearl and enamel parure from the era of Nicholas I, with Moscow maker's mark. To appeal to the town's wealthy merchants, Moscow jewelry tended to be more robust than in the imperial capital. *Marie Betteley, photo by Noel Allum*

If earlier jewelers such as Jérémie Pauzié personally attended to their rarefied clients at home, by the 19th century they sold from shops, with the more fashionable firms located on the capital's main commercial artery, Nevskii Prospect, and Bolshaia Morskaia Street, which intersects it not far from Palace Square. The Maison Anglais right on the corner of these two streets was the most prominent among them. Even Tsar Nicholas I patronized it, and the poet Alexander Pushkin also had an account there. Other prestigious establishments included Bolin, Breitfus, Jahn and Keibel, while St. Petersburgers of more modest means frequented the Gostinnyi Dvor, a labyrinthine mall further down Nevskii.[45]

During the Crimean War at midcentury, the Maison Anglais expediently changed its name to Nicholls & Plincke, and the firm survived until 1880. Bolin flourished right up to the Russian Revolution, and during the reign of the last tsar its principal rivals included Tillander, Fabergé, Hahn and Köchli. According to one survey, in 1889 there were some 52 jewelry firms in Russia, employing about 2,500 workers. Some foreigners, such as the Cartier brothers, Frédéric Boucheron and René Lalique, attempted to break into the market. Their efforts did not meet with great success (the murder of Boucheron's manager and his son during a robbery on the train from Baku to Moscow in 1914 was one of the hazards they faced[46]). But in stark contrast to the previous century, even if their owners had distinctly Germanic and Scandinavian names, Russian firms increasingly dominated the market. Imports accounted for a little over a tenth of the total value of jewelry sold in the empire during the 1890s.[47]

Much like the sale of their creations, the education of jewelers also became increasingly institutionalized during the 19th century. When they first established themselves in Peter's young city, workmasters solely passed on their skills by training apprentices—an arduous and often difficult process for those on the receiving end, as Jérémie Pauzié's memoirs suggest. In 1845, the silversmith Ignatii Sazikov added a new department in his St. Petersburg factory to train 80 young men in various aspects of jeweler production.[48] Some three decades later, a colleague in Moscow, Pavel Ovchinnikov, also opened a school attached to his large plant. The program took five to six years and taught its students the relevant skills as well as religion, singing, Russian, arithmetic, geometry and geography.[49] By the turn of the 20th century, private institutions such as Baron Stieglitz's Central College of Technical Design in St. Petersburg and the Moscow-based Imperial Stroganov School of Industrial Art also educated jewelers.

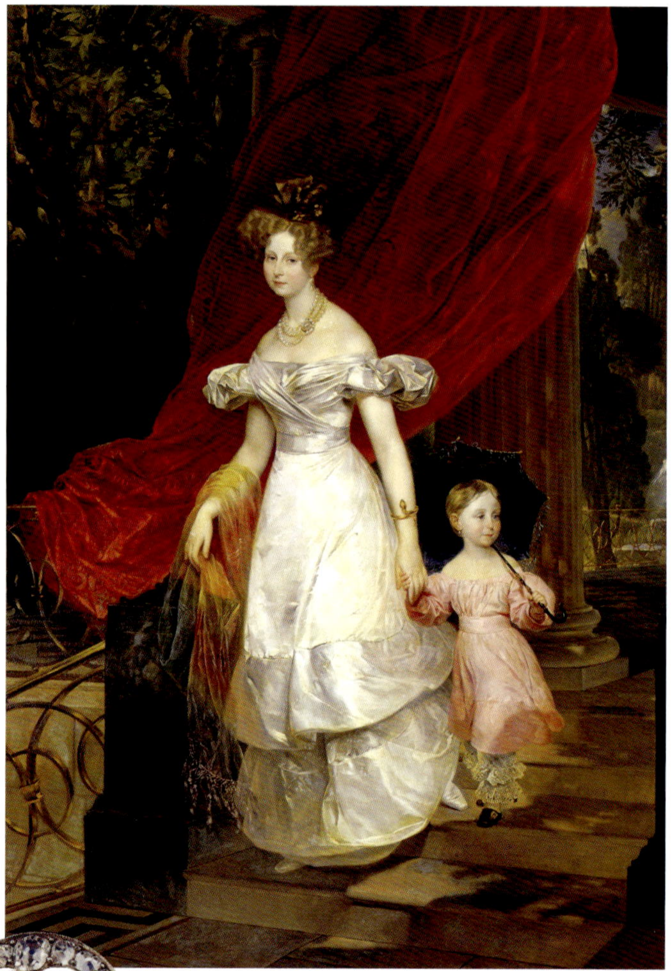

Grand Duchess Elena Pavlovna of Russia with daughter Maria, Karl Brüllow, 1830. Née Princess Charlotte of Württemberg, the grand duchess is fashionably adorned in pearls and a gold snake bracelet. *Source: Wikimedia Commons*

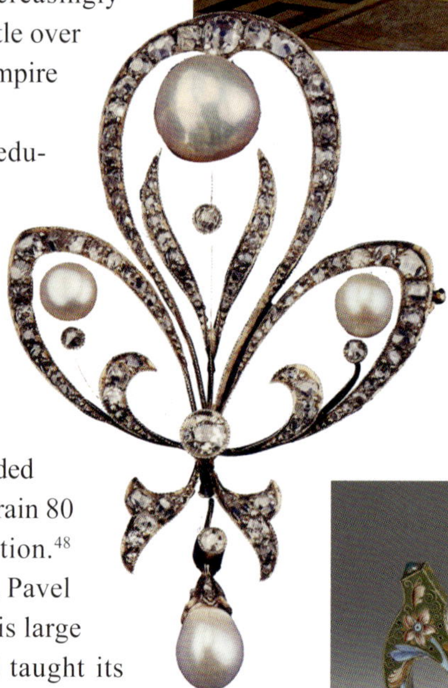

Pearl-and-diamond brooch, ca. 1880. Naturalism remained prevalent in Russian jewelry until the turn of the 20th century. *Marie Betteley, photo by Roger Bester*

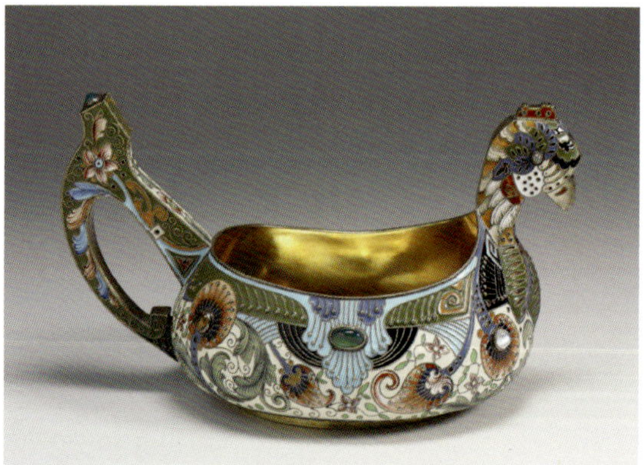

The imperial age marked the apogee of Russian jewelry. And from the beginning of the reigns of the 18th-century empresses until the end of Nicholas II's in 1917, St. Petersburg was the center. While its workmasters adopted many of their styles and skills from the West, they were no mere imitators. Within just a few decades under Elizabeth and Catherine the Great, the quality of their creations rivaled that of Europe's finest. Yet, Russian jewelry adopted its own distinctive style. Led by the dictates and desires of successive sovereigns and aristocracy who yearned for pageantry, color and displays of wealth best expressed through jewels and treasures, the imperial capital's craftsmen succeeded both in embracing Russia's Slavic and Byzantine roots while fusing them with the refinements of the West to produce outlandish yet exquisite adornments worthy of the Romanovs.

The dynasty's fall in 1917 and its replacement by a regime that claimed to represent the proletariat came as a death blow to St. Petersburg's jewelers. Despite proclaiming themselves to be socialist, Russian women of course did not lose their desire for adornments in precious metals and gems. However, Soviet craftsmen could never even aspire to match the elegance and splendor of the treasures their tsarist predecessors crafted. And sadly, wars and revolution have destroyed much of what the latter created. Those that did survive the cruel 20th century are therefore all the more precious.

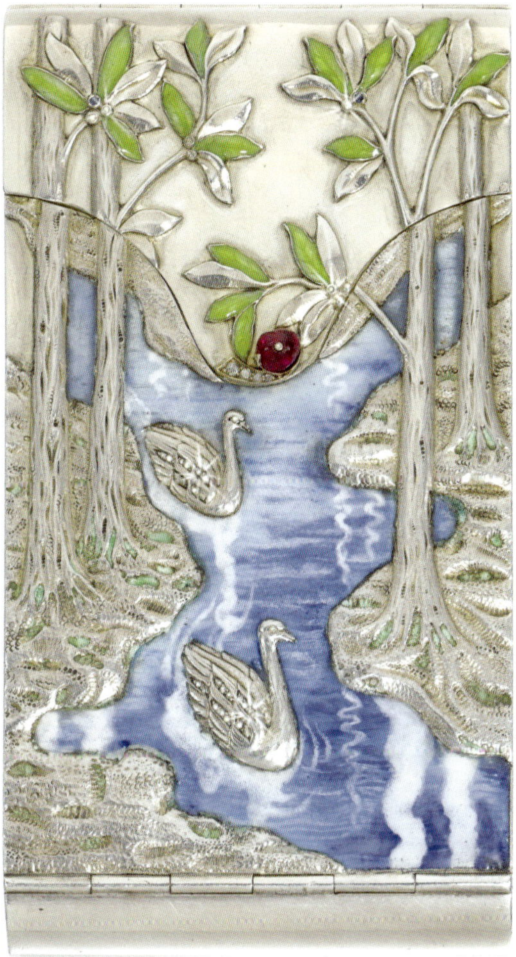

Previous page, bottom:
Silver and plique-à-jour enamel kovsh by Ovchinnikov, late 19th century. Moscow's Style Russe appealed to the "second capital's" more traditionalist clientele. *Courtesy of Walters Art Gallery*

Above right:
House of Bolin. Silver enamel cigarette case, ca. 1900. Long the court's leading jeweler, Bolin produced a wide variety of style moderne accessories. *Courtesy of Sotheby's*

HILLWOOD AS A TEENAGER

Hillwood was the home of the late Marjorie Merriweather Post (1887–1973), whose third husband, Joseph E. Davies (1876–1958), was ambassador to Russia in the late 1930s. As heiress of the Post Cereal and later General Foods fortune, Marjorie, already an established collector while stationed in Moscow, was intrigued by the huge quantities of Romanov treasures that Joseph Stalin was selling off to raise cash for his Five-Year Plans. She started buying small amounts and exporting them via diplomatic channels back to the US. Today, she is considered the Grand Dame of Russian art collectors, with Hillwood housing one of the most comprehensive collections of tsarist decorative arts outside Russia. It became a museum in 1973.

When I was 18 years old, my father, Roy, became the director of Hillwood and my family moved onto the 25-acre estate. Although it took a while and some growing up—at first I preferred the gardens—I eventually began to appreciate the splendor of the Romanov dynasty that surrounded me every day.

Soon, Russian treasures and their stories beckoned. Slowly the trappings of the tsars and their tragic demise took hold of me.

Mrs. Post bought two Fabergé Imperial Eggs, the blue 12 monogram Egg of 1895 and the Catherine the Great Egg of 1914, from the trade, both of which are still displayed in the house. But it was the other Romanov treasures that began to intrigue me—especially the imperial gold and silver, as well as the gems and jewelry, although even here there were not many distinct Russian examples.

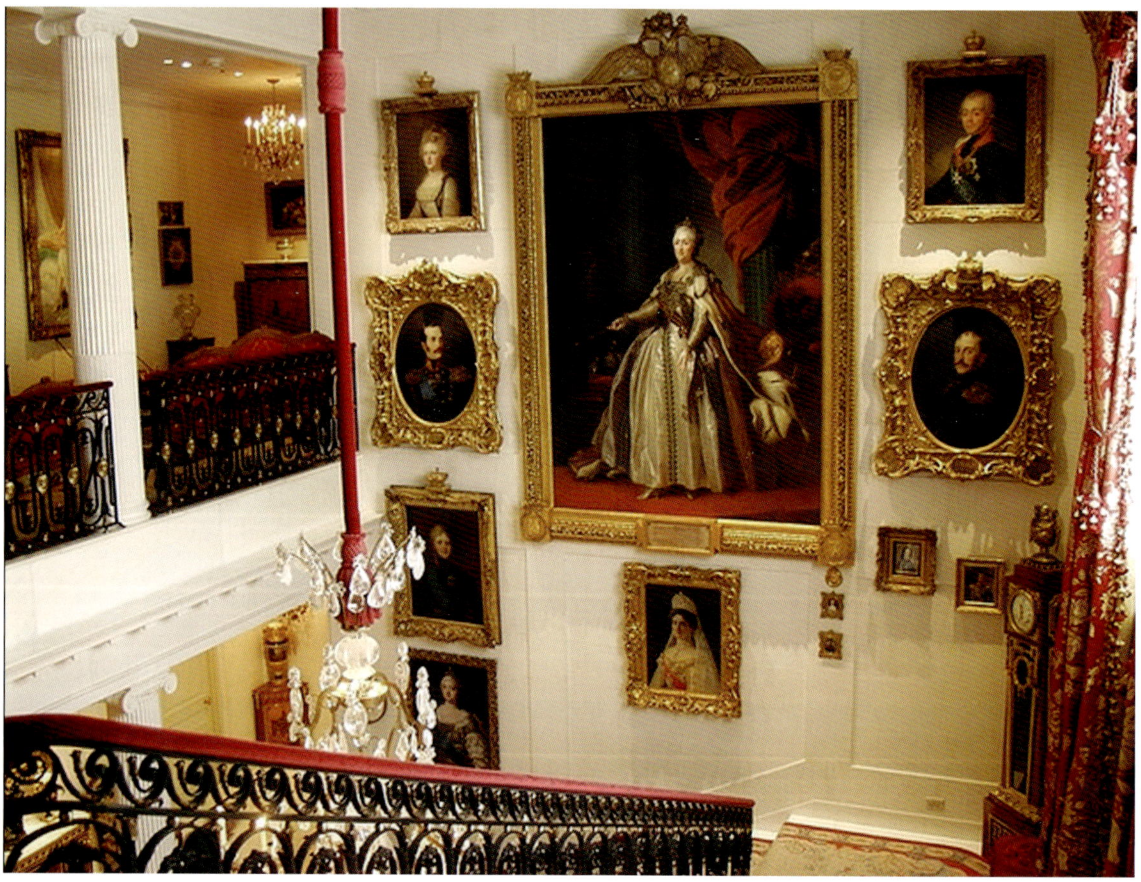

NOTES

1. Samuel Hazzard Cross and Olgerd P. Sherbowitz-Wetzor, eds. and trans., *The Russian Primary Chronicle: Laurentian Text* (Cambridge, MA: Mediaeval Academy of America, 1973), 97.

2. Ibid., 111.

3. Germaine de Staël-Holstein, *Mémoires de Madame de Staël (Dix années d'éxil)* (Paris: Charpentier Librarie-éditeur, 1861), 411.

4. Tatiana Fabergé, Eric-Alain Kohler, and Valentin Skurlov, eds. *Fabergé: A Comprehensive Reference Book* (Geneva, Switzerland: Slatkine, 2012), 33.

5. M. M. Postnikova-Loseva, *Russkoe iuverlirnoe iskusstvo: Ego tsentry i mastera* (Moscow: Nauka, 1974), 14.

6. Katherine Reynolds Brown, "Russo-Byzantine Jewelry in the Metropolitan Museum of Art," *Apollo* 111, no. 215 (January 1980): 6–9.

7. V. L. Zhuravleva, "Iuvelirnoe iskusstvo Drevnei Rusi," in V. L. Zhuravleva, I. D. Kostina, and T. N. Mutian, *Iskusstvo russkikh iuvelirov: Deviat vekov istorii* (Moscow: Khudozhnik i kniga, 2004), 27; and V. I. Martynova, *Precious Stone in Russian Jewelry Art in XIIth–XVIIIth Centuries* (Moscow: Iskusstvo, 1973), 7.

8. T. B. Zabozlaeva, *Dragotsennosti v russkoi kul'ture XVIII–XX vekov* (St. Petersburg: Iskusstvo-SPB, 2003), 130–38.

9. Tamara Talbot-Rice, *A Concise History of Russian Art* (London: Thames & Hudson, 1963), 95

10. Sigismund von Herberstein, *Description of Moscow and Muscovy, 1557* (New York: Barnes and Noble, 1969), 40–41.

11. M. M. Postnikova-Loseva, "16-17 veka," in *Russkie iuvelirnye ukrasheniia 16–20 vekov iz sobraniia Gosudarstvennogo ordena Lenina Istoricheskogo muzea*, ed. Galina Medvedeva et al. (Moscow: Sovetskii khudozhnik, 1987), 17.

12. Sir Jerome Horsey, "A Relacion or Memoriall," in *Russia at the Close of the Sixteenth Century*, ed. Edward A. Bond (London: Hakluyt Society, 1856), 200–201.

13. Zabozlaeva, *Dragotsennosti v russkoi kul'ture*, 314.

14. Olga Kolpakova, *Karl Fabergé i russkie iuveliry* (Moscow: Belyi gorod, 2008), 6.

15. Liliia Kuznetsova, *Peterburgskie iuveliry: Vek vosemnadtsatyi, brilliantovyi* (Moscow: Tsentrpoligraf, 2009), 35.

16. Ibid., 5

17. Ibid.

18. Zabozlaeva, *Dragotsennosti v russkoi kul'ture*, 64.

19. Ibid., 321.

20. William Coxe, *Travels into Poland, Russia, Sweden, and Denmark, vol. 2* (London: J. Nicholls, 1784), 154.

21. Susan Jaques, *The Empress of Art: Catherine the Great and the Transformation of Russia* (New York: Pegasus, 2016), 133.

22. Olga W. Gorewa, Irina F. Polynina, Nikolai Rachmanov, and Alfons

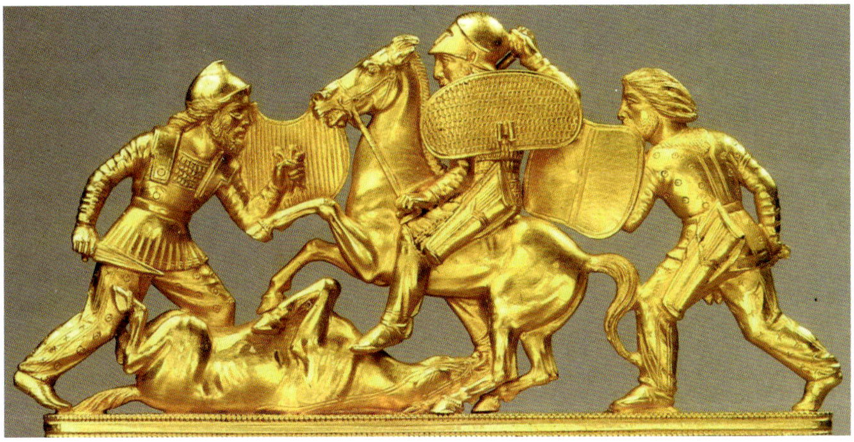

Left:
View of the grand staircase, Hillwood Museum. *Photo by Roy Betteley*

Right:
Detail of Gold Scythian comb, late 5th–early 4th century BC. *Source: State Hermitage Museum © State Hermitage Museum photo by Vladimir Terebenin*

Raimann, *Joyaux du trésor de Russie* (Paris: La Bibliothèque des Arts, 1991), 117–19.

23. Martynova, *Precious Stone*, 11.

24. *Russkii biograficheskii slovar*, s.v. "Dannenberg, Iakov Ivanovich"; Joel A. Bartsch, "Precious Stones and Noble Metals: Historic Sources for Russian Gems and Jewels," in *Kremlin Gold: 1,000 Years of Russian Gems and Jewels*, ed. T. D. Avdusina and N. S. Vladimirskaia (New York: Harry A. Abrams, 2000), 181.

25. Olga Kostiuk, "Introduction: The Guild of Foreign Masters," in *Gold of the Tsars: 100 Masterpieces of the Goldsmith's Art of the Hermitage, St. Petersburg. Guild of Foreign Masters*, ed. Fritz Falk (Stuttgart: Arnoldsche, 1995), 10, 15.

26. Ibid., 19.

27. Anne Odom, *Russian Enamels: Kievan Rus to Fabergé* (Baltimore: Walters Art Gallery, 1996), 82–83; and Alexander von Solodkoff, *Russian Gold and Silverwork, 17th–19th Century* (New York: Rizzoli, 1981), 138–40.

28. Odom, *Russian Enamels*, 28–63; and Postnikova-Loseva, *Russkie iuvelirnye ukrasheniia*, 170–78.

29. Kuznetsova, *Peterburskie iuveliry: Vek vosemnadtsatii*, 40–42

30. Staël-Holstein, *Mémoires*, 420.

31. Marina Lopato, *Iuveliry starogo Peterburga* (St. Petersburg: State Hermitage Publishers, 2006), 31.

32. Ibid., 85.

33. Kostiuk, "Introduction," 21.

34. Baron Armin von Fölkersam, "Iuvelirnye izdeliia vremen Aleksandra I," Starye gody, July–September 1908, 529–46.

35. Lopato, Iuveliry, 122.

36. Liliia Kuznetsova, *Peterburgskie iuveliry: Dnei Aleksandrovykh prekrasnoe nachalo* (Moscow and St. Petersburg: Tsentrpoligraf, 2012), 22.

37. Zabozlaeva, *Dragotsennosti v russkoi kul'ture*, 15.

38. Geoffrey C. Munn, *Tiaras: A History of Splendour* (Woodbridge, UK: Antique Collector's Club, 2001), 268–323.

39. Baron Armin von Fölkersam, "Relikvii Aleksandrovskogo vremeni v Imperatorskom Ermitage," *Starye gody*, July–September 1912: 67.

40. Evgenia Kirichenko, *Russian Design and the Fine Arts, 1750–1917*, comp. Mikhail Anikst (New York: Harry N. Abrams, 1991), 80.

41. M. I. Pyliaev, *Dragotsennye kamni: Ikh svoistva, mestonakhozhdeniia i upotrebleniia* (St. Petersburg: Suvorin, 1896), 76–77.

42. Tatiana F. Fabergé, A. S. Gorynia, and Valentin V. Skurlov, *Fabezhe i Peterburgskie iuveliry* (St. Petersburg: Neva, 1997), 179.

43. Lopato, *Iuveliry*, 125–27.

44. "Peterburgskoe kupechestvo," *Sovremennik* 1847, 3:177, in *Zabozlaeva, Dragotsennosti v russkoi kul'ture*, 313.

45. I. I. Pushkarev, *Opisanie Sankt-Peterburga i uezdnykh gorodov S.-Peterburskoi gubernii*, vol. 3 (St. Petersburg: Tip. S. Peterburgskogo gubernskago pravlenia, 1841), 4–5, 38, 96–97.

46. Magdalena Ribbing et al., *Jewellery & Silver for Tsars, Queens and Others* (Stockholm: W. A. Bolin, 1996), 128–30.

47. Geza von Habsburg, Alexandre de Solodkoff, and Robert Bianchi, *Fabergé: Imperial Craftsman and His World* (London: Booth-Clibborn Editions, 2000), 229.

48. Lopato, *Iuveliry*, 131–32.

49. S. M. Gontar, "Tendentsii razvitiia iuvelirnogo dela v Rossii poslednei tretii XIX-nachala XX veka," *Arkhiv Valentin Skurlova*, 10 October 2001. http://skurlov.blogspot.com/2011/10/xix.html.

2

History

THE TSAR'S JEWELERS

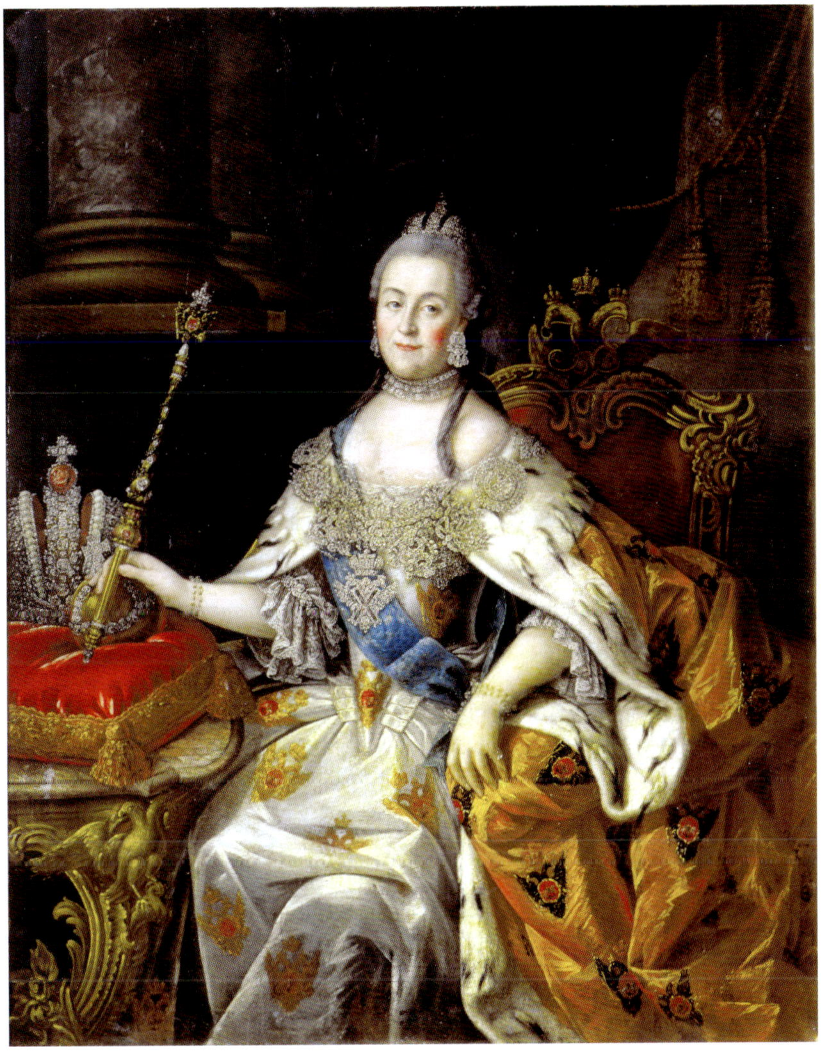

Empress Catherine II, Aleksandr Antropov, 1767. Wearing the diamond-studded Imperial Order of St. Andrew the First Called, Catherine holds the imperial scepter, with the orb and the crown fashioned by Jérémie Pauzié and Friedrikh Eckhardt resting on a pillow. *Source: Wikimedia Commons*

Monarchs use splendor to broadcast their power.[1] Together with grand palaces as well as immense parades of soldiers in magnificent uniforms, lavish displays of precious metals and gems are highly effective in this regard. Russia's rulers knew it well. According to Marina Lopato, they were meant "to demonstrate not only the tsar's own riches, but also his might."[2] Foreign visitors could not fail to be awed by the tsar's seemingly inexhaustible wealth. Already in the 16th century, an English guest at Ivan the Terrible's court marveled, "All the furniture of dishes and drinking vessels, which were then for the use of a hundred guests, was all of pure gold, and the tables were so laden with vessels of gold that there was no room for some to stand upon them."[3]

Jewelers therefore occupied a privileged position in the autocracy of the Romanovs. Some, such as Jérémie Pauzié, even enjoyed direct access to the sovereign. And they prospered as they worked hard to gratify the seemingly insatiable appetite of tsars, tsarinas and their grand ducal relatives for gold and diamonds. These august personages did not order such baubles solely for their own use; they also bestowed them in great profusion onto their subjects and foreign dignitaries. On average, Emperor Nicholas II distributed 2,000 gifts of jewelry worth 500,000 rubles every year, from a gem-encrusted portrait miniature costing 16,000 rubles to thank a senior minister upon his retirement, to a 20-ruble silver pocket watch bearing the double-headed eagle he might present to a deserving coachman or peasant who had performed some minor service.[4]

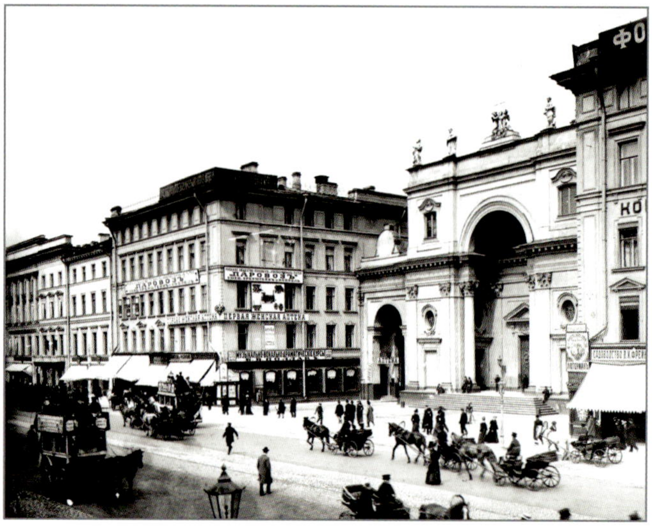

The St. Catherine Church and storefronts on Nevskii Prospect, 1901. Many jewelers set up their shops on St. Petersburg's most fashionable avenue. *Courtesy of the Central State Archive of Cinema and Photo Documents of St. Petersburg*

St. Petersburg's Jewelers

As with much else, it was Peter the Great who organized the jeweler's profession in Russia. The Kremlin Armory's workshop in Moscow had long employed its own goldsmiths and silversmiths. But in his zeal to modernize his empire, together with the shipwrights, engineers and physicians he brought over, Peter recruited craftsmen of luxury goods from the West for his new capital. Some had little choice in the matter. Among the first to settle on the Neva River were Swedish gold- and silversmiths who had been captured as prisoners of war during the long struggle with the Scandinavian kingdom. They were soon joined by Russian jewelers transferred (no doubt equally unwillingly) from Moscow's Kremlin Armory.

As the young capital grew, others freely made the move. Most were Germans. According to Baron von Fölkersam, among the 550 men registered in the foreign precious metalworkers' guild during the 18th century, no fewer than 400 were ethnically German, while another 100 were Swedes. Frenchmen, including Huguenot refugees and Francophone Swiss, also joined them during the reigns of the more Gallophile empresses Elizabeth and Catherine II in the century's latter half.[5] While less numerous, they included such prominent jewelers as Jean-Pierre Ador and the Duval brothers. This development so alarmed the French consul-general in St. Petersburg that in 1768 he urged his foreign minister to forbid any more craftsmen to leave France for Russia.[6]

Already by 1714, the immigrants formed their own guild, which would subsequently be known as the Amt der löblichen Gold- und Silberarbeiter in Sanct Petersburg (Office of the laudable gold- and silver workers in St. Petersburg). Six years later, Peter organized other trades into guilds as well. However, he had not been the first to establish regulations for the craft in his realm. As in most European jurisdictions, the production and sale of precious metals had long been regulated in Russia. Merchants in Moscow and other cities could conduct business only on the marketplace's silver row (*serebriannyi riad*). To gain admission, prospective members presented a sample of their work and signed a contract that bound them to follow the tsar's relevant edicts. Meanwhile, two aldermen assayed the purity and weight of their metals, stamping those pieces that passed muster. Craftsmen who tried to pass off work with too many impurities could expect the knout, while exile awaited anyone who dared to sell outside the silver row.[7]

Peter established separate guilds for foreign and Russian craftsmen. Based on the German model and refined by Catherine the Great and Paul I toward the end of the 18th century, their statutes strictly defined members' obligations. Only workmasters with at least seven years of training (eventually reduced to three years) as well as two years' experience as a journeyman could operate a workshop and join a guild. As on the silver row, aldermen strictly controlled the quality of their output, and they could destroy those objects that failed to meet their standards.

According to the regulations, masters had to house and feed their apprentices and limit their workdays to 12 hours, with Sundays and Church holidays off. At the same time, they had leave to whip their charges for theft, wastefulness, laziness, drunkenness and insolence, among other offenses. Discipline could be harsh. Franz Birnbaum, Fabergé's chief designer, recalled that when a member of the imperial family visited

Fabergé's workshop, he asked an old craftsman which tools were essential to practice his trade. The man's list included mallets and chisels as well as "a flat [leather] strap of sufficient thickness." Curious about the last item, the guest asked about its purpose. "Your highness, it is the first and most indispensable instrument" was the reply. "No apprentice has ever been taught the jewellery art without it."[8]

Until the 19th century, most jewelers in St. Petersburg were European immigrants. Whereas in 1793 the Russian guild comprised 44 masters, there were 59 goldsmiths, 51 silversmiths and 29 masters in related crafts in the one for foreigners.[9] The latter tended to form a closed caste as they congregated near the Winter Palace on Millionaia and Bolshaia Morskaia Streets, where few troubled to learn Russian, and their offspring often intermarried. The Europeans prospered. According to a Swedish guidebook to the capital published at the turn of the 19th century, "nowhere do [foreign craftsmen] live . . . as well as they do here, since nowhere can they earn as much and as easily."[10]

In an age when Russian society was highly stratified, the jewelry business was a private affair. Makers usually dealt with their well-born clients by commission directly from their workshops. While most of their trade was by word of mouth, some also advertised in the press. In 1753, a notice in the newspaper *Sankt-Peterburskie Vedomosti* announced, "The diamond cutter Johan Anton Franz Seidel recently arrived from Vienna. He can polish, engrave and set all diamonds, gems and pearls, and resides with the jeweler Pauzié."[11]

With the rise of a middle class in the 19th century, merchants such as Nicholls and Plincke began to open stores offering ready-made jewels to the general public. Meanwhile, industrialized production began to erode the authority of the guilds. Already in 1757, Vasili Kunkin operated a factory in Moscow with some 70 craftsmen to produce liturgical objects in precious metals. In the next century, individual workshops became increasingly rare, with some of them eventually banding together as *artels*, or cooperatives, to survive.[12]

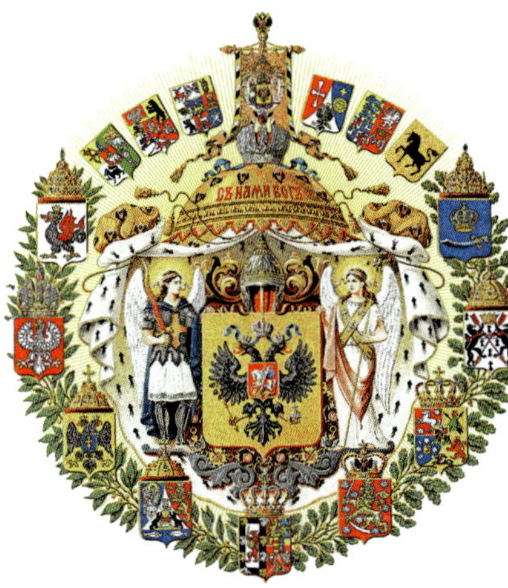

The Greater Arms of the Russian Empire. *Courtesy of Igor Barbe*. Adopted in 1882, the final version of the imperial arms displays the double-headed eagle with St. George, representing Moscow, on its breast, surrounded by the arms of the other lands subject to the tsar.

Purveyors to the Court

Like other monarchs to this day, the Romanovs favored faithful tradesmen with special designations that allowed them to advertise that they supplied the court with their goods or services. These distinctions were initially bestowed at the sovereign's whim. Peter III appointed Jérémie Pauzié court jeweler (*pridvornyi iuvelir*), with the civil service rank equivalent to a brigadier in the army.[13] By the 1840s, a few businesses began to be allowed to use and display the title of "Purveyor to the Imperial Court" (*postavchik Imperatorskogo dvora*) along with the double-headed eagle on their storefronts. Until 1855, 22 merchants, including the St. Petersburg jeweler Bolin and the Moscow silversmith Sazikov, enjoyed this privilege.[14]

Early in Alexander II's reign, the Ministry of the Imperial Court established standard procedures for the designation.[15] According to the regulations he authorized in 1856, firms now had to formally apply to the court ministry's chancellery to receive the title of purveyor. To be eligible, they had to have conducted business regularly and reliably with the court for eight to ten years at favorable prices. The appointment was made to an individual person, not his firm; it was valid only during the reign of the emperor who had given it and could not be passed on to any heirs. If a son inherited a firm from a father with the title, he had to make a new request. Meanwhile, the chancellery inquired with the police about the applicant's "commercial and moral aspects."

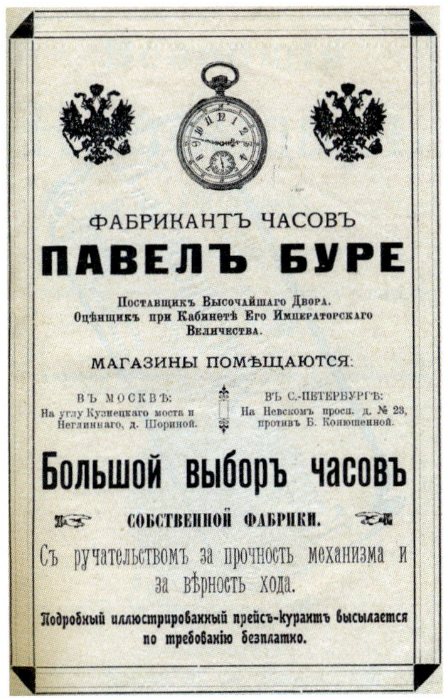

Newspaper advertisement for Pavel Buhré watchmakers, "Purveyor to the Imperial Court, Appraiser to the Cabinet of His Imperial Highness." As purveyors to the tsar, the firm was permitted prominently to display the Russian double-headed eagle in its publicity and on its storefront.

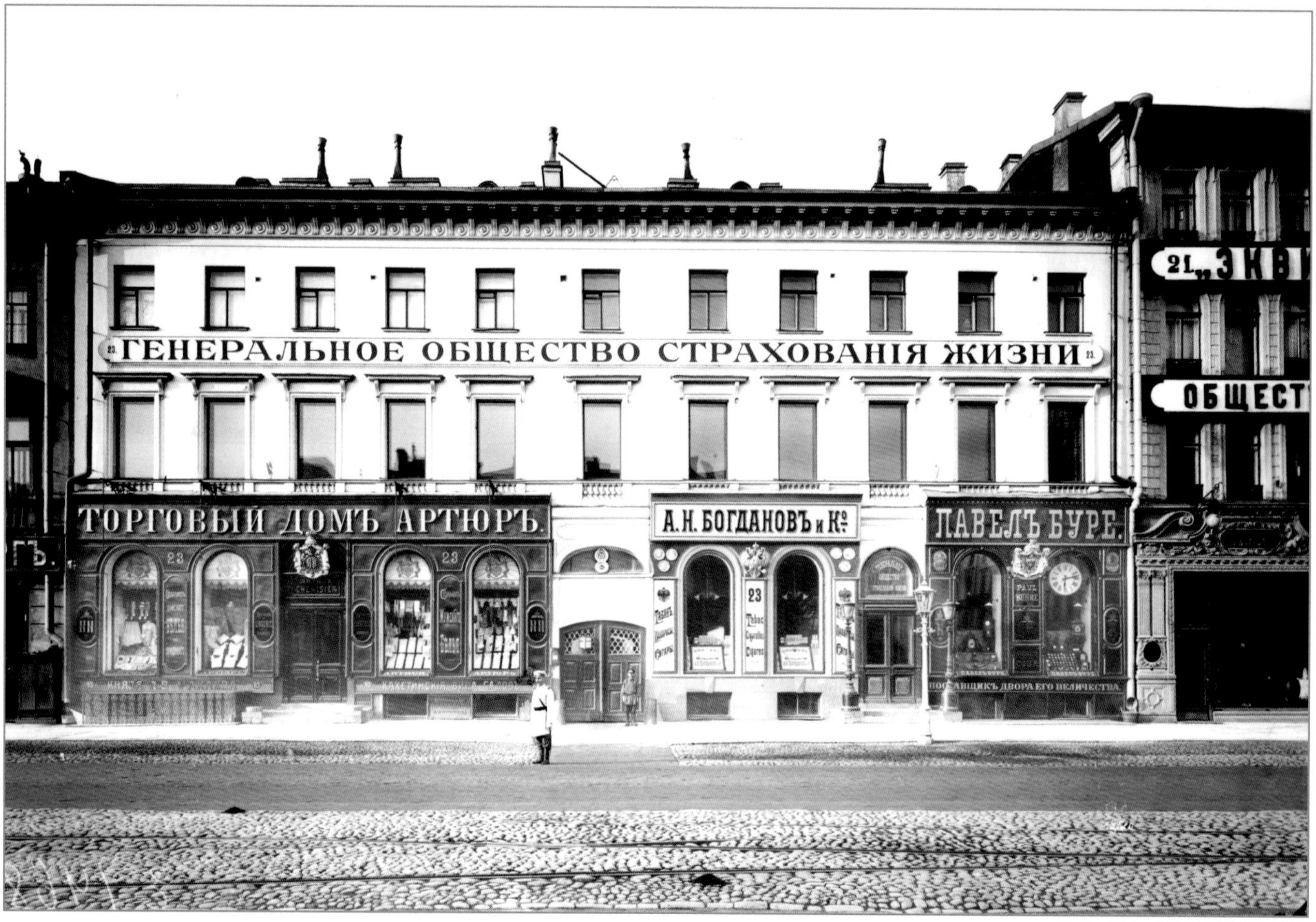

Two shops on 23 Nevskii Prospect proudly display the coveted Romanov arms on their storefronts: *To the left*, the shirt-maker Arthur, purveyor to Grand Duke Nicholas Nikolaevich; *on the right*, Pavel Buhré, watchmaker to the court of His Imperial Highness. The eagles on the facade of the tobacconist A. N. Bogdanov, in the center, were awarded at industrial exhibitions. *Courtesy of the Central State Archive of Cinema and Photo Documents of St. Petersburg*

Traditionally announced at Christmas and Easter, the prestigious title was highly coveted and sparingly given. Only about half of all applications were approved. Even Carl Fabergé was turned down on his first attempt in 1884.[16] Grand dukes and duchesses granted the distinction of purveyor to their own courts, although they did so less frequently. But, whereas those who supplied the emperor or empress displayed the imperial eagle on their storefronts and stationery, the latter showed only the relevant initials. To further complicate matters, the Finance Ministry also permitted firms that had won prizes at trade fairs to include the bicephalous Romanov raptor on their promotional material, albeit without the designation of purveyor. Some tsars granted the title more sparingly than others. In 1883, when Emperor Alexander III (r. 1881–94) occupied the throne, there were nine jewelers on the list of purveyors compiled by the Ministry of the Imperial Court. By 1915, toward the end of Nicholas II's reign, the number had grown to 31.[17]

The most prestigious distinction to which a jeweler could aspire in Imperial Russia was that of "Appraiser to the Cabinet of His Imperial Highness" (*otsenshchik Kabineta Ego Imperatorskogo Velichestva*). Until the early 19th century, the court employed two of them. Nicholas I began to appoint three, who now advised him without pay—the honor was sufficient compensation. Beginning in 1823 with its founder, Andreas Römpler, a member of the House of Bolin held the title right up to the Revolution of 1917. Carl Fabergé and the head of the Hahn firm were the other two who served the last tsar. While appraisers enjoyed preferential treatment for some commissions from the court, they were expected to assist the imperial cabinet with repairs and other tasks.[18]

HANDLE WITH CARE

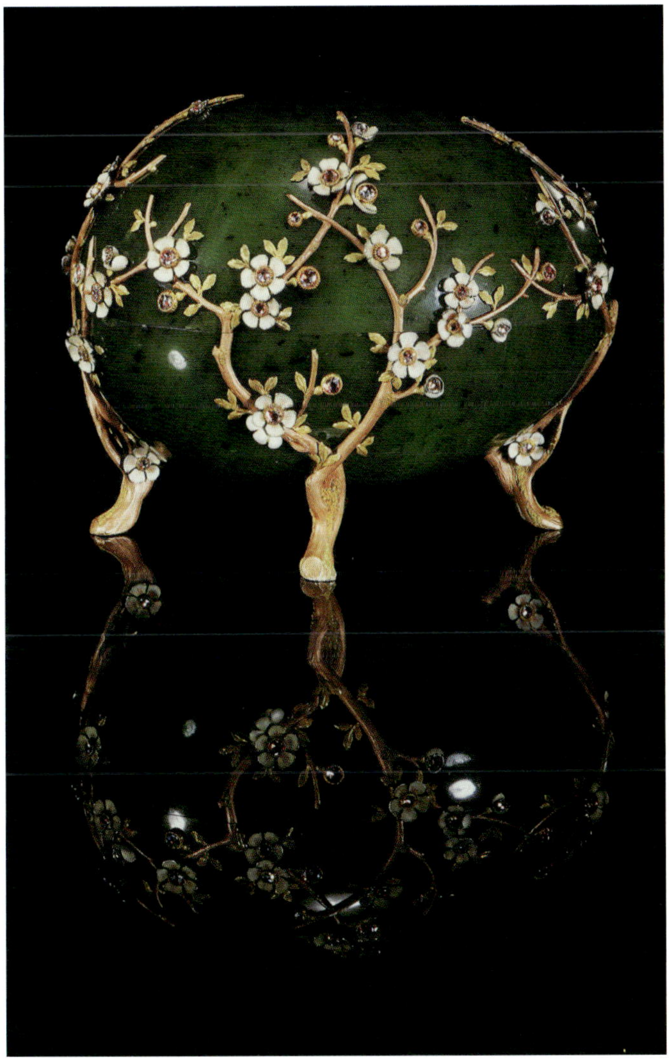

Apple Blossom Egg of 1901. © *1994 Christie's Images, Ltd.*

There's nothing like holding a real Fabergé egg in your hand—because, well, it's perfect. Then there's the surprise, often missing, but what a treat if it's still there! I've handled four as an auction expert, and several more as an appraiser. As an auction specialist you get the amazing privilege of inspecting it inside and out and even taking it apart if possible. So out would come the inner compartments holding surprises, in a quest to uncover hidden hallmarks and verify the way it was made. But one of my biggest thrills was having the blue Twelve Monogram Egg of 1895—I didn't take that one apart (along with the Fabergé Yusupov box and the Tsarina's *carnet de bal*) in my own Lexington Avenue apartment in New York. My father was hand carrying these treasures not yet sealed by customs from Hillwood Museum in Washington, DC, to the Munich exhibition of Fabergé.

Another highlight was transporting the Fabergé Bonbonnière Egg of 1903 from New York to London on the Concorde. My frequent flights toting Fabergé eggs to international exhibition and sales venues qualified me for this treat. My intern forecast disaster. "Don't you know the enamel will break with the speed of sound?" she warned. I scoffed upon hearing this but admit to feeling a tad nervous seated in front of the counter as it read first MACH 1 then MACH 2 followed by *BOOM!* each time, holding the bag, sealed by customs, up to my ear to check for a pinging sound of shattering enamel. Luckily the egg landed intact.

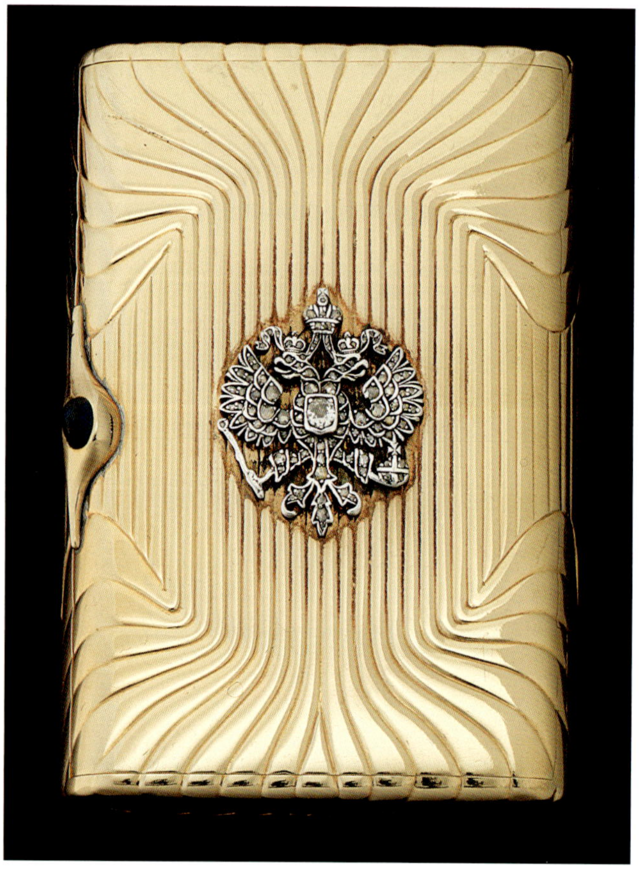

Gold Fabergé imperial presentation cigarette case with diamond double-headed eagle. Nicholas II began to give cigarette cases set with the Romanov eagle or his cipher to deserving gentlemen during his reign. *© 2010 Christie's Images, Ltd.*

Some businesses continued to advertise their status as purveyor to the court in Bolshevik Russia when the new government temporarily lifted its restrictions on private enterprise during the New Economic Policy it launched in 1921. The following year, Lenin's regime did get around to abolishing the title.[19] Nevertheless, a few firms abroad still proudly display their former distinction, such as some of Cartier's shops.

Imperial Gifts

While they did not enjoy a monopoly on its orders, purveyors to the court prospered from the many gifts the tsar liberally distributed throughout the year. Ulla Tillander-Godenhielm points out that these were not a frivolous extravagance, but a meticulously apportioned instrument of imperial rule. In her book about the Romanov dynasty's award system, she explains:

> These rewards were presented . . . to create bonds of loyalty between the ruler and those who served in his name, as well as to promote efficiency and zeal in the carrying out of one's official duties. They were compensation for services, both political and administrative, rendered to the state.[20]

At the same time, gifts were also an important aspect of diplomacy. While by the 19th century trains of envoys ceremonially bearing lavish and exotic treasures (*pomniki*) to the Kremlin were a thing of the past, a departing ambassador could still expect to receive a jeweled snuff box during his farewell audience with the emperor.

Before the 18th century, Muscovite rulers rewarded victorious commanders with gold, fur and estates. To receive the "fur coat from the Tsar's shoulder" (*shuba s tsarskogo plecha*) was a signal honor. When the prominent boyar Boris Godunov checked a Tatar raid on Moscow in 1591, Tsar Fedor

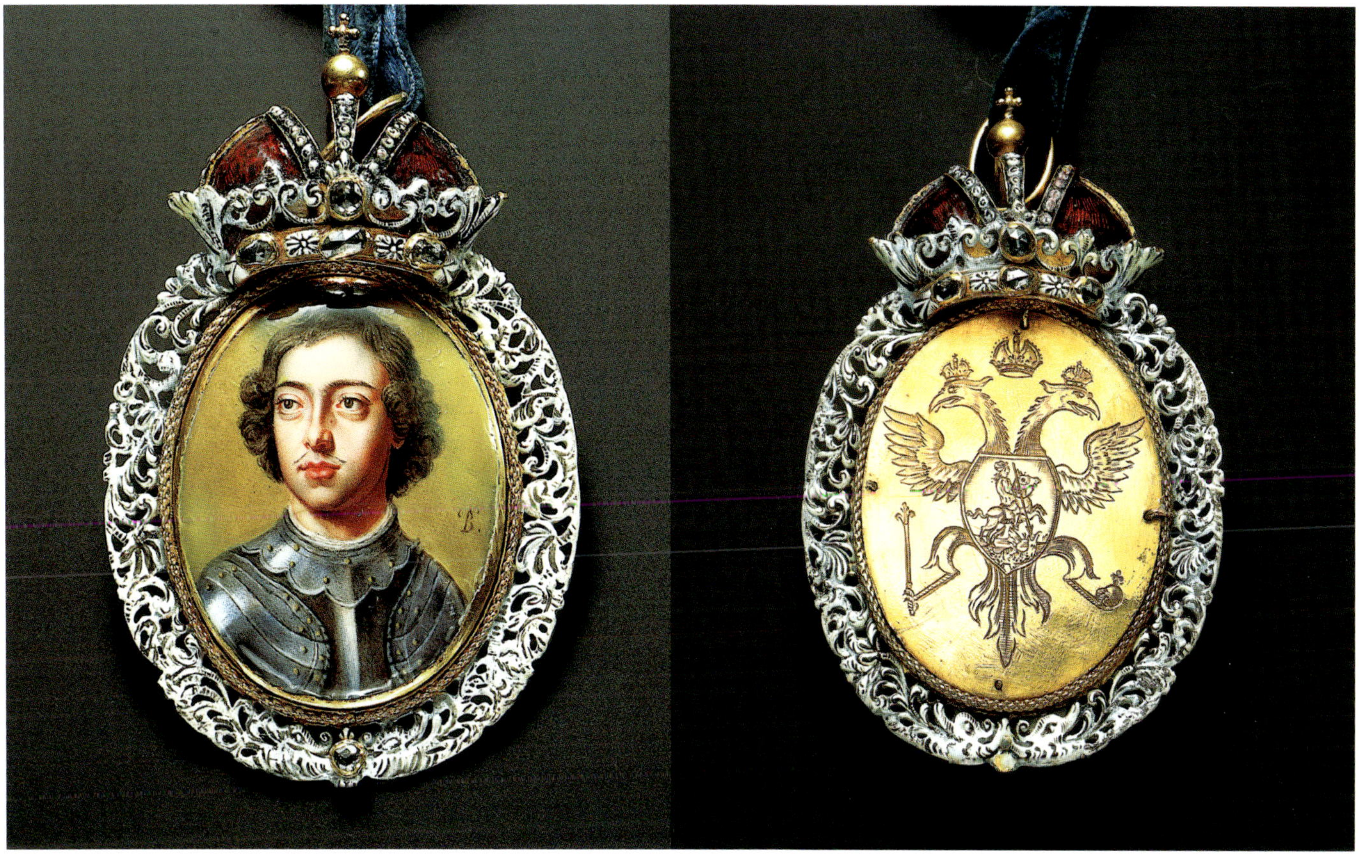

Peter the Great portrait medallion, front and back. The emperor presented jeweled likenesses of himself to particularly favored subjects. © *2011 Christie's Images, Ltd.*

Ivanovich presented him with a 1,000-ruble fur coat, a gold chain and plate, and three northern towns and promoted him to *sluga* ("Servant to the Tsar").[21]

Peter the Great reformed the system for imperial gifts to bring them more in line with Western practices. A man of spartan tastes, he liked to present wooden snuffboxes that he had made himself in his workshop. But the tsar was well aware that most of his subjects preferred something more substantial. As a result, he adopted the custom of European royalty to award a medallion with a miniature of his portrait, often set with diamonds, to particularly worthy individuals.[22] Until the fall of the Romanov dynasty, jeweled portrait badges were the highest distinction a subject of the tsar could receive, and they were worn with more pride than the most prestigious decoration.

Another one of Peter's most important innovations was his Table of Ranks. For centuries, nobles had been required to serve the tsar, usually by military means. As a child of the Age of Reason, in 1722 Peter established a precise hierarchy of 14 grades, which determined a gentleman's status either as an officer or official. Rather than birth, the principle was that a noble now had to earn his rank (*chin*) through merit. Russian subjects who were classed in the lower five ranks became lifetime nobles, while those of the eighth chin, for a captain or major in the army, or higher, were granted hereditary nobility (the threshold was subsequently raised to the fourth rank). With certain modifications, the Table of Ranks remained in force right up to 1917.

A little over a century later, Nicholas I began to link the categories for his gifts to Peter's Table of Ranks. Eventually, the Ministry of the Imperial Court followed a strict order based on the recipient's chin when recommending what the tsar should present to whom.[23] Medallions, rings, and snuffboxes with his portrait were meant only for those who had attained at the least the third chin (lieutenant-general or privy councilor in the bureaucracy). Even here the value could vary widely. In 1881, Alexander III gave a portrait medallion that cost over 16,000 rubles to General-Adjutant Count Alexander Adlerberg, who had been his father's court minister. Meanwhile, Finland's Governor-General, Count Fedor Heiden, received one worth a little under 6,000 rubles.[24] While fewer were presented, gifts with the emperor's cipher were designated for those holding the fifth (Brigadier or State Councilor) to third ranks.

Subjects below the fifth chin in status could expect to receive a gift decorated with an emblem of the Russian state, such as the double-headed eagle or the Romanov crown.[25] Termed "an ordinary gift" (*obychnyi podarok*), these included gold rings, cuff links, tie pins, earrings, and brooches, among other jewels. As smoking became more fashionable at the turn of the 20th century, cigarette cases also began to be awarded.

Watches were particularly popular. According to Valentin Skurlov, during the reign of Alexander III the court bought 3,477 watches from its principal supplier, Paul Buhré.[26] The custom had begun after the Napoleonic Wars, when officers noticed that the first item soldiers took from French captives was their watch, then a great rarity in Russia.[27] Officers typically received a gold pocket watch in a hunter's case with the eagle engraved in the lid, which cost the tsar's treasury between 75 to nearly 400 rubles. Silver equivalents worth between 20 and 50 rubles were meant for deserving other ranks. Even recipients of the latter valued them, since the average factory worker earned a monthly wage of 15 rubles at the turn of the century.[28]

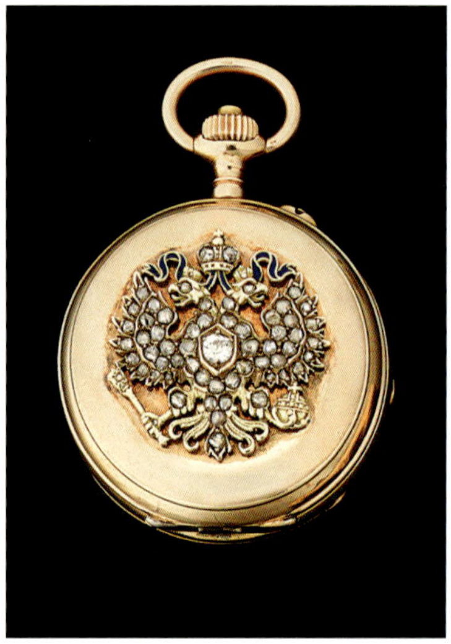

Pavel Buhré gold imperial presentation watch. Engraved with the double-headed eagle or the tsar's cipher, these "ordinary gifts" were commonly given to officers, while other ranks usually received silver timepieces. *Courtesy of Sotheby's*

The emperor presented such "ordinary gifts" for a wide variety of reasons, ranging from meritorious service to participating in charitable ballet and musical performances. For example, in 1826, Nicholas I gave a set of diamond and amethyst earrings worth 780 rubles to Avdotia Kartsova, the peasant woman who had served as his heir's wet nurse.[29] The tsar was particularly generous when traveling, both in Russia and abroad. Captain 2nd Rank N. Sablin recalls how Nicholas II thanked the crew of the imperial yacht *The Standard* in early autumn 1906 at the conclusion of his family's vacation in Finnish waters,

> On the morning we left the roadstead, the tsar gave [gifts to] everyone, including the sailors, who were leaving active duty for the reserves. Non-commissioned officers received watches with the state eagle and medals for zeal—gold for the senior, silver for the junior, while sailors each got five gold rubles as well as medals. To all officers, without exception, the empress and her children presented gold cigarette cases with eagles or cuff-links; the cigarette cases were all engraved with their signatures. I was given cuff links with the eagle on this sail.[30]

The procedure for awarding gifts was highly bureaucratized. When an individual's superior thought a gift was merited, he wrote a recommendation to the Cabinet of His Imperial Highness. Housed in Anichkov Palace and under the aegis of the Ministry of the Imperial Court, the cabinet functioned as the tsar's private office. Its responsibilities included, among others, all matters related to the imperial family's jewelry. Thus, it looked after the crown jewels, appointed purveyors to the court, handled the tsar and tsarina's purchases and administered their gifts.[31]

Once the court minister had approved the recommendation, his staff would select an appropriate award from the Cabinet of His Imperial Highness's large stock of presentation jewelry. Although his cabinet did most of the work, Nicholas II took a keen interest in such matters and often involved himself in deciding what would be appropriate.

Recipients typically rushed to a jeweler for an appraisal, by way of getting an objective measure of the emperor's esteem. At the same time, despite the honor such an award conveyed, many were returned for cash. This was an accepted practice, and it was not considered undignified to sell a gift back for its full price, less a 10 percent donation to charity. Ulla Tillander-Godenhielm describes the multiple reincarnation of one such award. Between

1904 and 1907, a diamond order of St. Alexander Nevskii made by Hahn for 2,000 rubles was recycled six times.[32]

The imperial cabinet did not object, since it provided a source of diamond orders for other worthy august recipients. In this way, a widow might supplement her meager pension. For example, more than two-thirds of the snuffboxes the tsar presented to his subjects were eventually redeemed.[33] Back in the Cabinet's storerooms, the jewel would be cleaned and kept for the next occasion.

The Cabinet of His Imperial Highness ordered gifts from a variety of jewelers. At the turn of the 20th century, among the major workshops in St. Petersburg that furnished it were Blank, Bolin, Butz, Fabergé, the Grachev Brothers, Hahn, Ivanov and Köchli, while in Moscow the silversmiths Khlebnikov and Ovchinnikov were also suppliers. Although it helped, having the status of purveyor to the imperial court was not obligatory, and the cabinet also turned to smaller firms such as Tillander.

The house of Paul Buhré, which had been founded by Swiss immigrants from Neuchâtel, furnished 95 percent of all presentation watches.[34] Aside from Buhré's virtual monopoly on timepieces, the cabinet tended not to limit itself to a single jeweler for any particular item. Thus, of the 174 snuffboxes Nicholas II presented with his cipher that could be identified, 68 were made by Fabergé, 59 by Hahn, 21 by Bolin and 10 by Köchli, while Ivanov, Butz and Blank each received a smaller number of orders.[35]

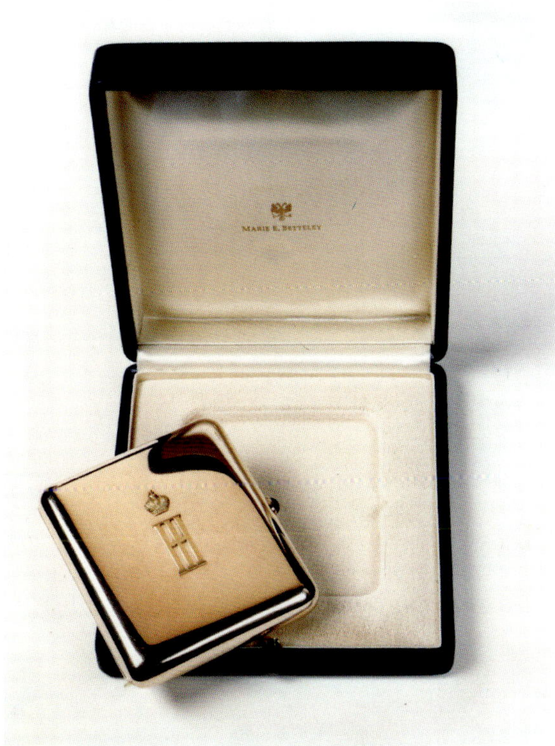

Grand Duke Nicholas Nikolaevich (the Younger) gold Fabergé presentation cigarette case. Other Romanovs also gave personalized jewelry to friends and for services rendered. *Marie Betteley, photo by Noel Allum*

Decorations

In an age when nearly every subject of the tsar affiliated with the state, from generals to university students, wore uniforms, decorations were an important distinction. Peter had also imported this monarchical prerogative from the West. During his visit to England on his Grand Embassy (1697–98), he was particularly impressed by that kingdom's Order of the Garter and, upon his return, instituted an equivalent for his empire, which he named after Russia's patron saint. Known to Orthodox Christians as St. Andrew the First Called (*Sviatoi Andrei Pervozvannyi*), the apostle was also one of Jesus's closest disciples. This made the saint's name appropriate for an honor bestowed on the tsar's most worthy subjects. The Order of St. Andrew was Russia's most prestigious knighthood.[36]

Initially limited to 24 men, Peter awarded the first order in 1699 to his intimate, Field Marshall Count Fedor Golovin, and the second to the Cossack Hetman Ivan Mazeppa the following year. However, when Mazeppa switched sides to his Swedish foe eight years later, the tsar stripped him of the honor. As for the Emperor, he insisted on joining the order only on the basis of merit and made himself the sixth knight in 1703 after he took two Swedish navy ships at the mouth of the Neva River. By 1916, the blue saltire (X-shaped cross) had been awarded about 900 times.[37] Like the Order of the Garter, it was worn with a light-blue ribbon. Some 15 years later, Peter established an equivalent honor for women, the Order of St. Catherine, to thank his eponymous wife for negotiating his release from Turkish captivity during an unsuccessful campaign in 1711.

Peter had also planned to create a third order, to reward military bravery. However, his death in 1725 intervened, and his successor, Empress Catherine I, first bestowed it that year. Contrary to her late husband's wishes, she also presented it to civilians. Third in seniority after the Orders of St. Andrew and St. Catherine, the new knighthood was named after the 13th-century prince Alexander Nevskii, who had routed the Swedes on the very site of the new capital and been subsequently canonized.

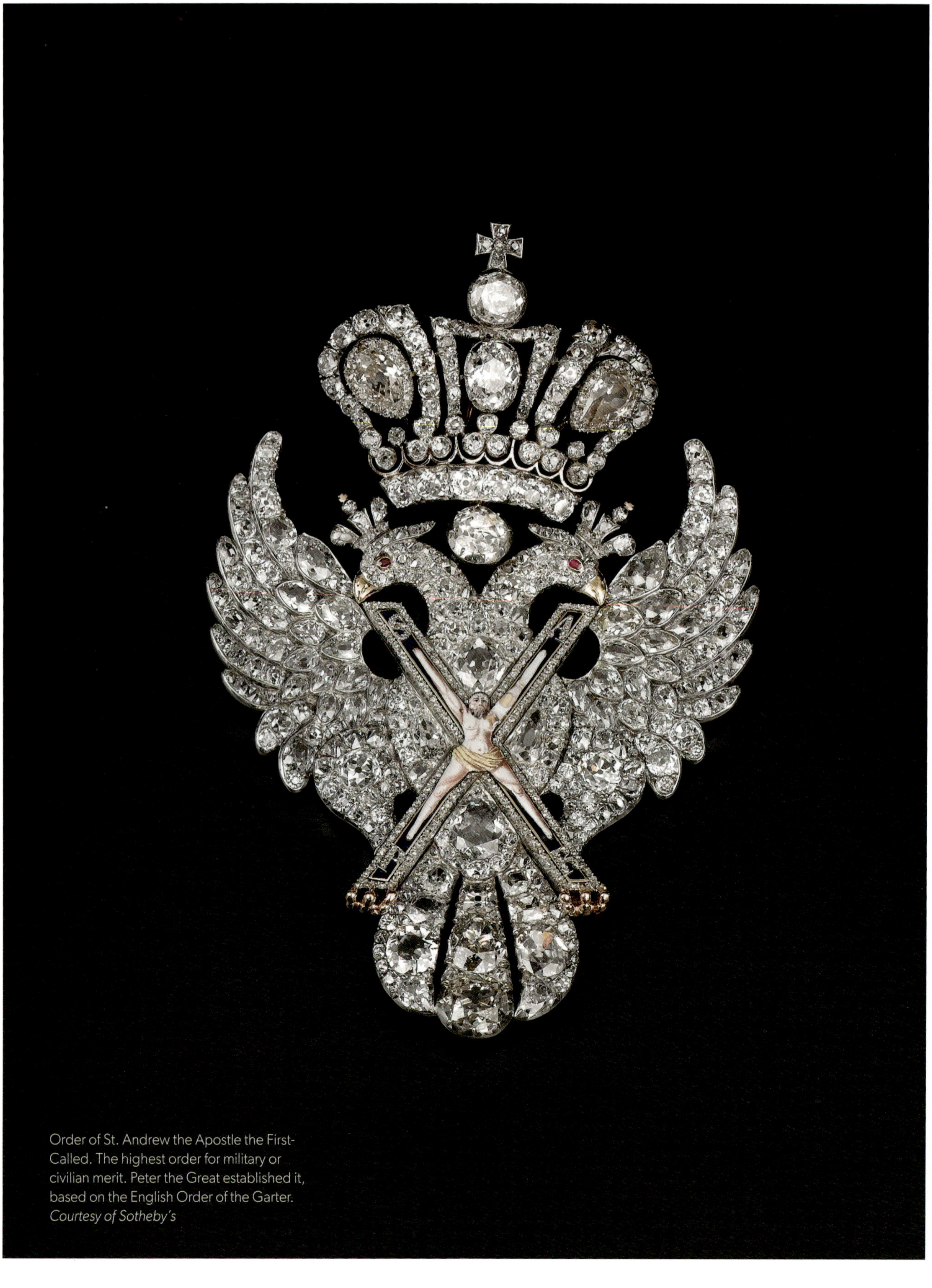

Order of St. Andrew the Apostle the First-Called. The highest order for military or civilian merit. Peter the Great established it, based on the English Order of the Garter.
Courtesy of Sotheby's

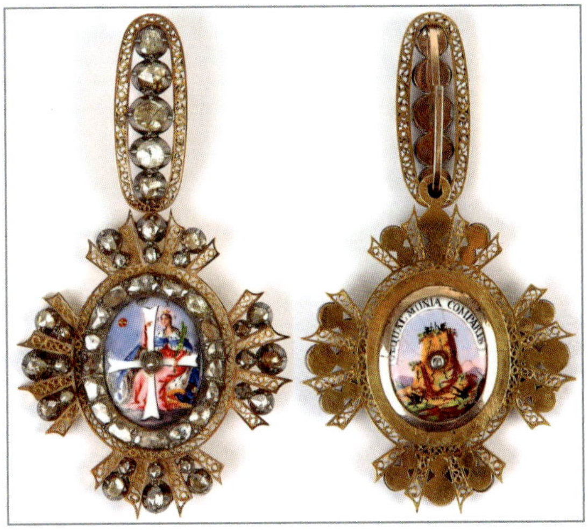

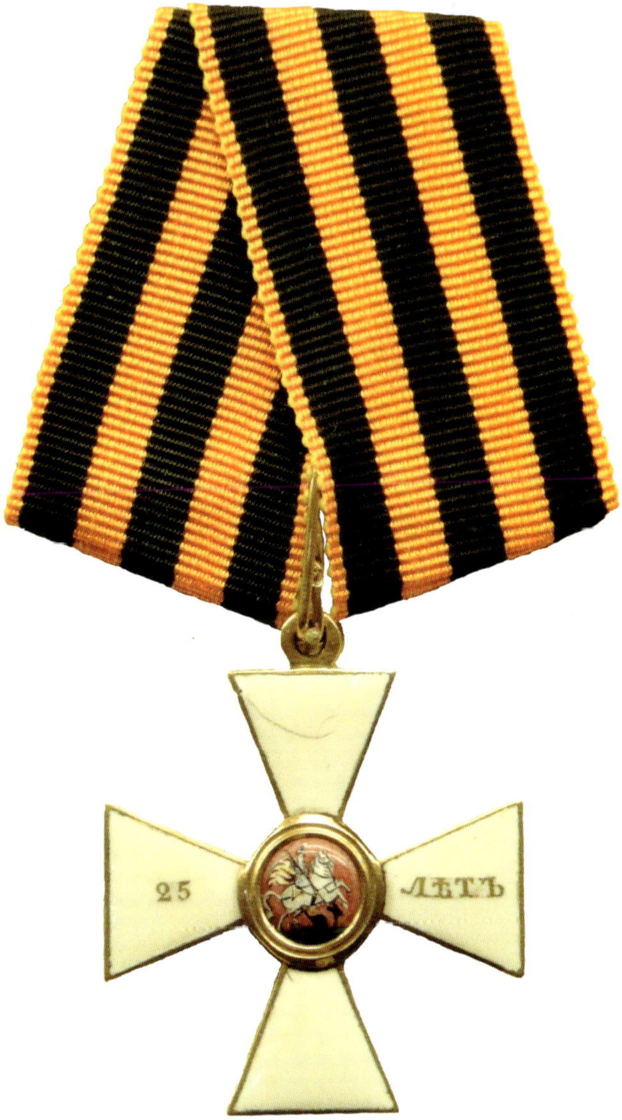

It would be up to Catherine II "the Great" to establish an award exclusively for military merit, with the Order of St. George in 1769. According to the knighthood's statute,

> Neither noble birth, nor the past merits, not yet the wounds received in battle, shall be of consequence. . . . A person may be granted that honour only in the event of distinguishing himself by gallantry of outstanding nature to the glory of the Russian arms, besides doing what his oath, honor and duty may demand.[38]

With its motto of "For service and bravery" (*Za sluzhbu i khrabrost*), the new decoration primarily rewarded feats of heroism in battle, although admission to the order's fourth class could also be earned through 25 years of military service and action in at least one battle.

Unlike Britain's Victoria Cross, the medal was exclusively meant for officers. Therefore, in 1807, Alexander I created an equivalent decoration for other ranks, the "Decoration of the Military Order of St. George." Whereas the Order of St. George came in the form of a gold cross pattée enameled in white, the "Soldier's George," as the latter came to be known, was a simpler, plain silver cross of similar shape. Both variants were suspended on a distinctive black-and-orange-striped ribbon, which in recent years has been adopted as a symbol of Russian patriotism.

In 1782, to mark the 20th anniversary of her accession to the throne, Catherine also founded the Order of St. Vladimir, which rewarded merit both in military and civil service. Named after another hallowed figure in Russia's past, the order commemorated the Kievan prince who had brought Christianity to his people eight centuries earlier. This was also a reference

Left:
Order of St. Catherine, front and back, Johann Keibel, 1870s. Also established by Peter the Great, the Order of St. Catherine was the highest imperial order for women. Ladies wore such decorations as brooches.
Source: Wikimedia Commons

Right:
The Order of St. George, Fourth Class. Established by Catherine the Great, the decoration was the highest award for military merit. Only officers were eligible. However, Alexander I decreed a plain gold or silver variant, the George's Cross, for other ranks. This variant, inscribed "25 years," was awarded for a quarter century of service and action in at least one battle.
Source: Wikimedia Commons

to contemporaneous events, since Catherine would finalize her hold on the empire's Ukrainian frontier by annexing Crimea the following year.

Possibly out of dislike of his mother, Catherine the Great, Paul I bestowed neither the Order of St. George nor St. Vladimir during his short reign at the turn of the 19th century. Filial spite also played a role in the Order of St. Anne, which the tsar recognized as a Russian knighthood immediately after acceding to the throne. The order had initially been founded in 1728 by the ruler of a minor German state, Duke Karl-Friedrich of Hostein-Gottorp, to honor his marriage three years earlier to Peter the Great's daughter Anna Petrovna. Their grandson, the future Emperor Paul, became grand master of the order via his father (Anna Petrovna's son), Peter III. However, he could award the foreign order only with the permission of his mother, Catherine the Great, which only embittered the tsarevich all the more. Paul gleefully recognized it as a Russian order immediately upon his coronation in 1797. In the hierarchy of Russian orders of knighthood, St. Anne was last in seniority; by 1831, over 170,000 had been awarded.[39] In the 19th century, after Poland was under their rule, Russian emperors also began bestowing two orders from that kingdom, the White Eagle and St. Stanislas.

For a brief time, a tsar also awarded the Order of St. John of Jerusalem. More popularly known as the Order of Malta, after the Mediterranean island where it was then based, this Catholic knighthood dated back to the Crusades. But when Napoleon seized Malta in 1797, its grand master sought protection from Emperor Paul, who was only too happy to be associated with the venerable brotherhood. With two new priories, one for Catholic Poles and the other for Orthodox Christians, noble subjects who could prove that their status had been granted to an ancestor for military valor at least 150 years earlier could be admitted for a 1,200-ruble fee. The order's Russian sojourn was short lived, and in 1817 Alexander I fully abolished its status as one of the empire's knighthoods.[40]

By the late 19th century, Imperial orders were generally ranked according to chin, ranging from St. Andrew with diamonds to St. Stanislas, third class for those at the lowest rung.[41] Aside from the highest grade, which was worn as a badge and a silk sash with its color diagonally across the tunic, the decorations were medals of enameled gold crosses. As a special honor, the orders could be inlaid with diamonds (those who received the regular version were forbidden by law to decorate it with gems). Hahn usually furnished the latter. These could be expensive, and in the case of Russians the cost was borne by the recipients. They weren't always keen to pay. In 1881, a physician to Alexander III's court sold his diamond-studded Order of St. Alexander Nevskii back to the cabinet for 4,000 rubles.[42]

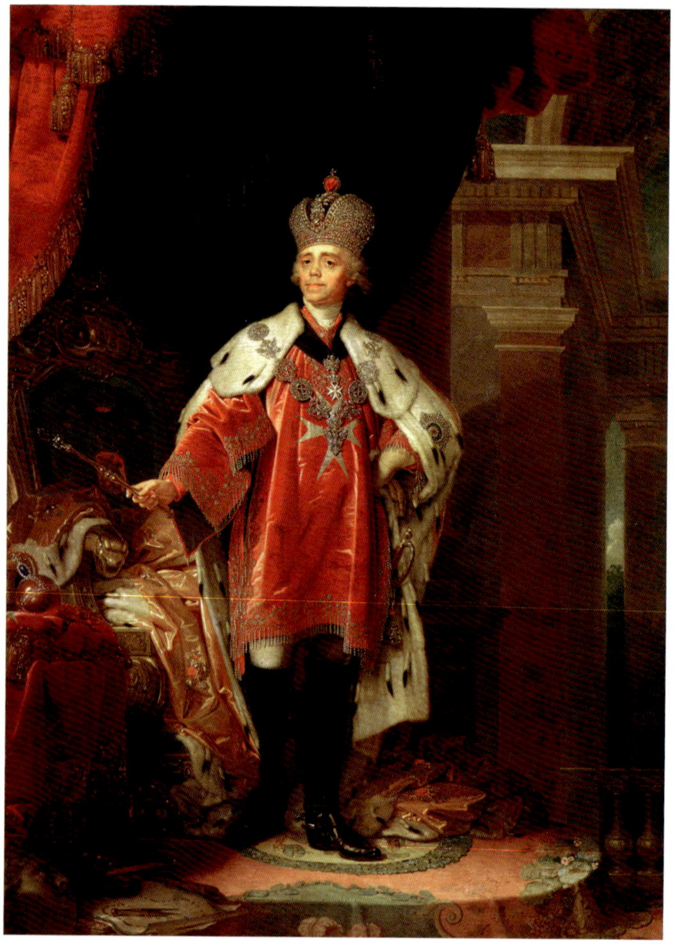

Vladimir Borovikovskii. "Emperor Paul I in Coronation Robes," 1800. In addition to the traditional Order of St. Andrew, Paul also wears the Order of Malta. During his brief reign, he awarded the Catholic order to Orthodox subjects, a practice his son, Alexander I, discontinued. *Source: Wikimedia Commons*

The Cabinet of His Imperial Highness also commissioned regular medals, and for much of the 19th century, the St. Petersburg firm of Keibel held the contract. Keibel lost the tender in 1906, when a smaller firm, Eduard, outbid it. But within a few years, recipients of gold stars began to complain that their edges were very sharp. Upon investigation, it emerged that the metal's content was below the stipulated weight. Shortly thereafter, the firm's owner took his own life, although his widow was allowed to carry on.[43]

While such jeweled insignia were not technically decorations, Russian sovereigns also gave them to their attendants at the court. Bearing grandiloquent titles such as Grand Master of the Stables, Grand Cup Bearer, and Grand Mistress of the Court, these officials were chosen from the most distinguished noble

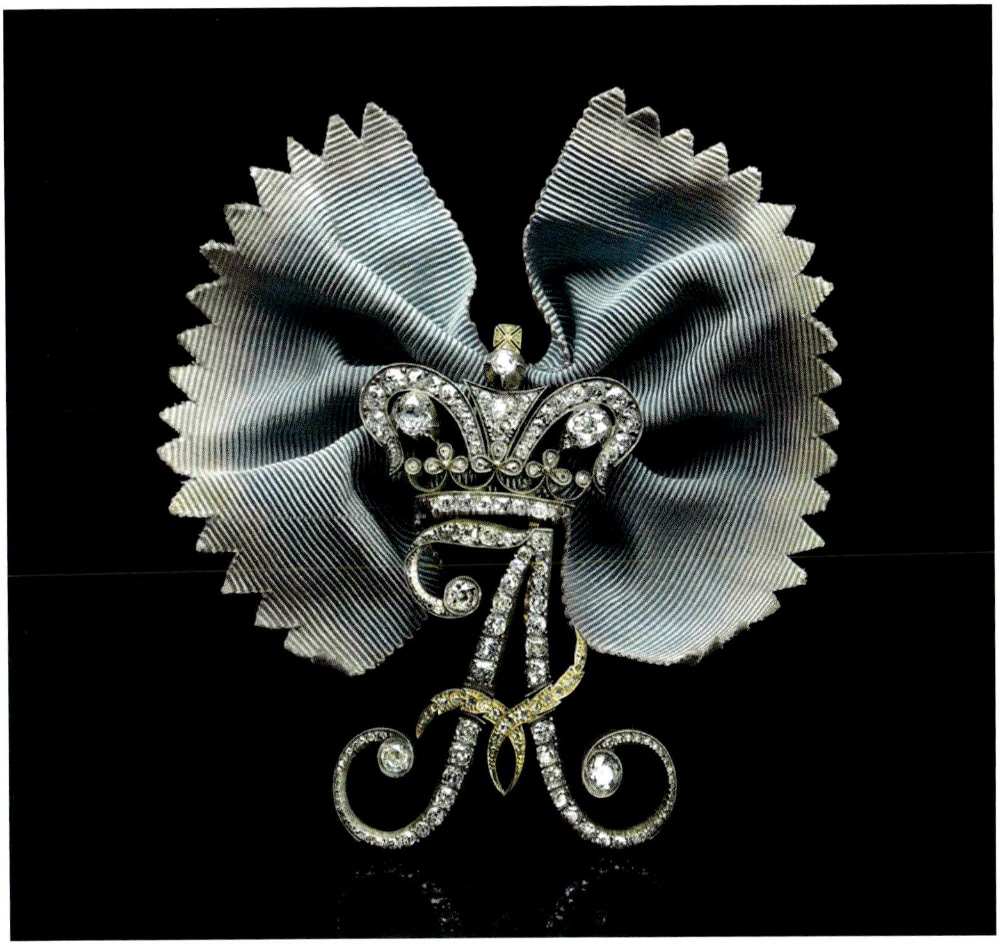

Diamond maid-of-honor chiffre with initial "A" for Empress Alexandra Fedorovna. *Courtesy of Sotheby's*

houses to act as glorified servants of the tsar and tsarina, much as in other European monarchies. Most of the gentlemen held the post of *kamerger* (lord-in-waiting), or, if younger, *kameriunker* (page). At the start of his reign, Emperor Nicholas II had 176 kamergery and 252 kameriunkery at his service, although most were not expected to perform many, if any, duties. The traditional insignia of the lord-in-waiting was a gold key, which those at the Russian court wore on a blue silk *moiré* ribbon fastened to the flap of their uniform's left pocket.

Meanwhile, Empress Alexandra had 17 *stats-damy* (ladies of honor) and 190 *freiliny* (maids of honor) to assist her. Also of impeccable breeding, the ladies were awarded a miniature of the empress framed in diamonds, which was worn on the left shoulder with a blue silk ribbon backing as well. As a result, these distinguished women were nicknamed *dames à portrait*. Meanwhile, the maids, who had to be unmarried blue bloods, wore a diamond-set cipher with their empress' initials surmounted by a diamond crown. Among the major suppliers of these jewels were the houses of Bolin and Hahn.[44]

The imperial court was swept into the dustbin of history in 1917. However, along with the double-headed eagle, some of its traditions have been reborn. Russia's president Vladimir Putin has been known to present gold and diamond rings to athletic champions.[45] At the same time, the Russian Federation once again awards its military heroes the Order of St. George, and its most prestigious decoration is the Order of St. Andrew.

Map

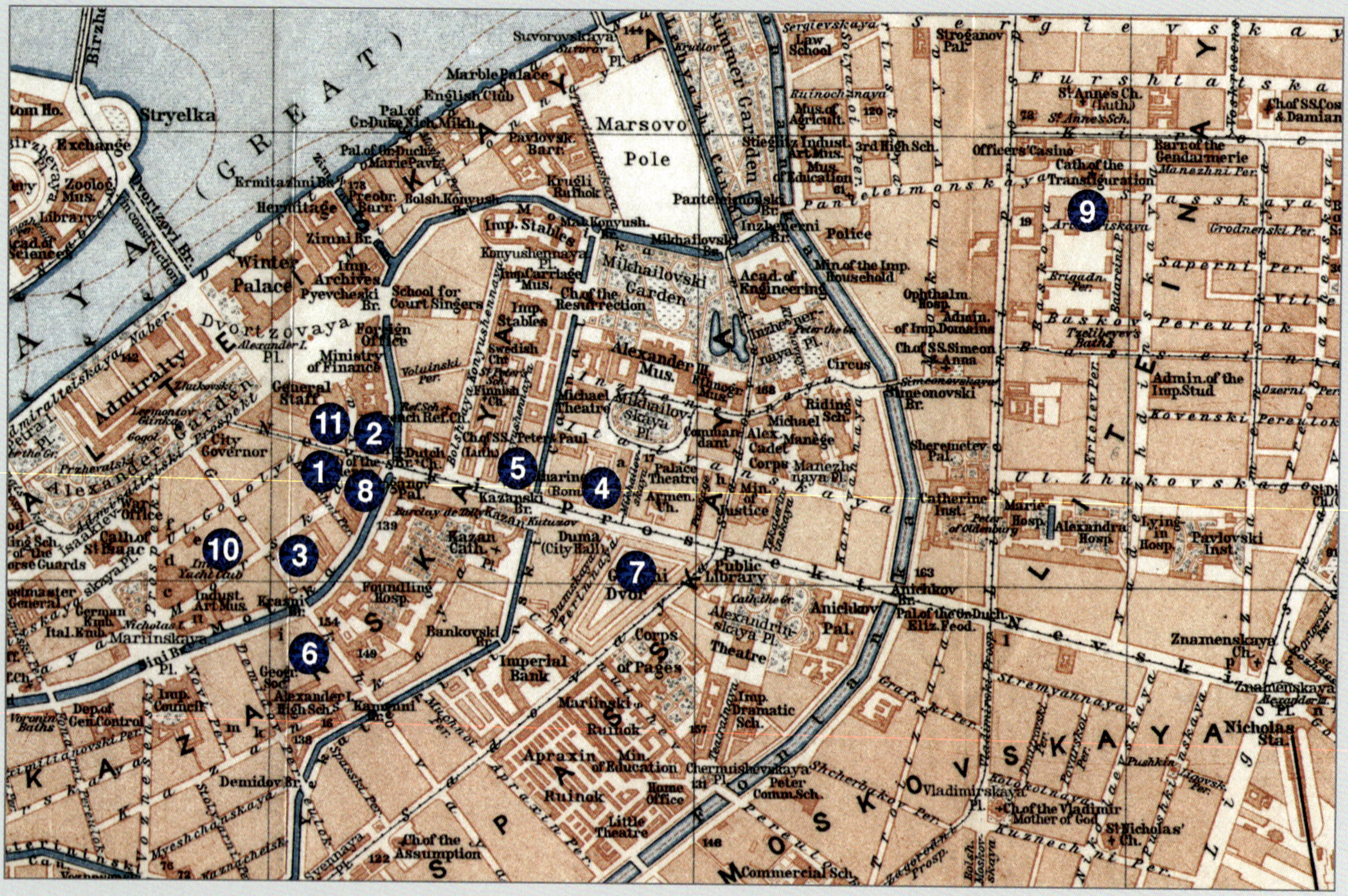

THE REIGNING JEWELERS OF ST. PETERSBURG

Beginning with Empress Elizabeth Petrovna (r. 1741–61) until the last tsar's tragic demise in 1917, the imperial capital grew to include hundreds of jewelers and silversmiths. Already by the late 18th century, numerous goldsmiths had opened their own workshops, plying their trade in the heart of the imperial capital, steps away from the Winter Palace along the famous Nevskii Prospect, the illustrious Bolshaia Morskaia Street, or, as in the case of Jérémie Pauzié, in the ancient artillery district of St. Petersburg. Of these many would earn the imperial warrant from the sovereign.

By the 19th century, Russia's most prominent jewelers were Bolin, Köchli, Hahn and Fabergé. The House of Fabergé, its most famous, rose to fame only at the end of the century, and it too relied on a network of jewelers and goldsmiths that was in place during and long before its tenure. These and other firms stood out because of the brilliance of their craftsmanship and their august clientele. The following chapters tell their stories.

The Jewelers

1. Bock
2. Bolin
3. Fabergé
4. Grachev
5. Hahn
6. Köchli
7. Morozov
8. Nicholls & Plincke
9. Pauzié
10. Sazikov
11. Seftigen

NOTES

1. For imperial Russia, the classic study is Richard Wortmann, *Scenarios of Power: Myth and Ceremony in Russian Monarchy*. 2 vols. (Princeton, NJ: Princeton University Press, 1995–2000).

2. Lopato, *Iuveliry*, 12.

3. Richard Hakluyt, ed., *The Principal Navigations, Voyages, Traffiques and Discoveries of the English Nation* vol. 3 (New York: Kelley, 1969), 66.

4. Fabergé, *Faberzhe i Peterburgskie iuveliry*, 237.

5. Baron Armin von Fölkersam, "Inostrannye mastera zolotogo i serebrianago dela," *Starye gody*, June–September 1911: 98.

6. Kuznetsova, *Peterburgskie iuveliry: Vek vosemnadtsatyi*, 57.

7. Solodkoff, *Russian Gold and Silverwork*, 19–20; and Kuznetsova, *Peterburgskie Iuveliry: Vek vosemnadtsatyi*, 59–60.

8. Franz Birnbaum, *The History of the House of Fabergé*, ed. Tatiana Fabergé and Valentin Skurlov (St. Petersburg: Russkie samostsvety, 1992), 35.

9. Solodkoff, *Russian Gold and Silverwork*, 21.

10. Kuznetsova, *Peterburgskie iuveliry: Vek vosemnadtsatyi*, 69.

11. A. E. Fersman, *Ocherki po istorii kamnia*, Vol. 1 (Moscow: Izd-vo Akademii nauk SSSR, 1954), 79.

12. Solodkoff, *Russian Gold and Silverwork*, 33.

13. Kuznetsova, *Peterburgskie iuveliry: Vek vosemnadtsatyi*, 118.

14. I. V. Zimin & A. Sokolov, *Iuvelirnye sokrovishcha Rossiiskogo imperatorskogo dvora* (Moscow: Izd-vo Tsentrpoligraf, 2013), 16.

15. Valentin Skurlov, *Postavchiki imperatorskogo Dvora* (St. Petersburg: Antikvarnoe obozrenie, 2008), 3–4; and Zimin and Sokolov, *Iuvelirnye sokrovishcha*, 11–39.

16. Marina Lopato, "New Insights into Fabergé from Russian Documents," in *Fabergé: Imperial Jeweler*, ed. Geza von Habsburg and Marina Lopato (Washington, DC: Fabergé Arts Foundation, 1993), 54–56.

17. Zimin and Sokolov, *Iuvelirnye sokrovishcha*, 45–53.

18. Kuznetsova, *Peterburskie iuveliry: Dnei Aleksandrovikh prekrasnoe nachalo*, 247–56.

19. Zimin and Sokolov, *Iuvelirnye sokrovishcha*, 39.

20. Ulla Tillander-Godenhielm, "The Russian Imperial Award System," *Journal of the Finnish Antiquarian Society* 113 (2005): 397.

21. S. M. Solovev, *Istoriia Rossii s drevneishikh vremen*, vol. 4 (Moscow: Mysl', 1989), 255; and Valentin Skurlov, "Podarok ot Imperatora," http://skurlov.blogspot.com/2009/.

22. Lopato, *Iuveliry*, 12.

23. Ulla Tillander-Godenhielm describes the system in exhaustive detail in her doctoral thesis, "Russian Imperial Award System," 145–255. See also Zimin and Sokolov, *Iuvelirnye sokrovisha*, 388–415.

24. Zimin and Sokolov, *Iuvelirnye sokrovisha*, 396.

25. Non-Russian subjects of the tsar in this category, such as Poles and Finns, typically received similar gifts without a state emblem. Tillander-Godenhielm, "Russian Imperial Award System," 221.

26. Tillander-Godenhielm, "Russian Imperial Award System," 387.

27. Ibid., 212.

28. Henri Troyat, *La vie quotidienne en Russie au temps du dernier tsar* (Paris: Hachette, 1969), 127.

29. Zimin and Sokolov, *Iuvelirnye sokrovisha*, 404.

30. Ibid., 427.

31. *Entsiklopedicheskii slovar' Brockhaus i Efron*, s.v. "Kabinet Imperatorskogo Velichestva."

32. Tillander-Godenhielm, "Russian Imperial Award System," 309.

33. Ibid., 180.

34. Ibid., 387.

35. Ibid., 179.

36. Gorewa et al., *Joyaux du trésor de la Russie*, 69.

37. S. S. Shishkov, "Orden Sviatogo Apostola Andreia Pervozvannogo," in *Nagrady Rossii*, http://web.archive.org/web/20090215014919/http://www.rusawards.ru:80/russia/001%20standrew/standrew.htm.

38. V. A. Durov, *The Orders of Russia* (Moscow: Voskresene, 1993), 36–37.

39. Shishkov, "Orden Sviatogo Apostola Andreia Pervozvannogo."

40. Frà Cyrille Toumanoff, *L'Ordre de Malte et l'Empire de Russie* (Rome: Palazzo Malta, 1979).

41. For a table correlating orders with civil ranks, see Tillander-Godenhielm, "Imperial Award System," 60.

42. Zimin and Sokolov, *Iuvelirnye ukrashenia*, 416.

43. Tillander-Godenhielm, "Russian Imperial Award System," 382–83.

44. *Entsiklopedicheskii slovar' Brockhaus i Efron* s.v. "Pridvornye chinyi i pridvornye vedomstvo"; Tillander-Godenhielm, "Russian Imperial Award System," 31–45; and L. E. Shepelev, "Imperatorskii dvor: pridvornye tituly i mundiry," Tituly, mundiry i ordena Rossiiskoi imperii, www.bibliotekar.ru/CentrTitul/29.htm.

45. Valentin Skurlov, "Podarok ot Imperatora," http://skurlov.blogspot.com/2009/

3

History

JÉRÉMIE PAUZIÉ: A JEWEL IN THE CROWN

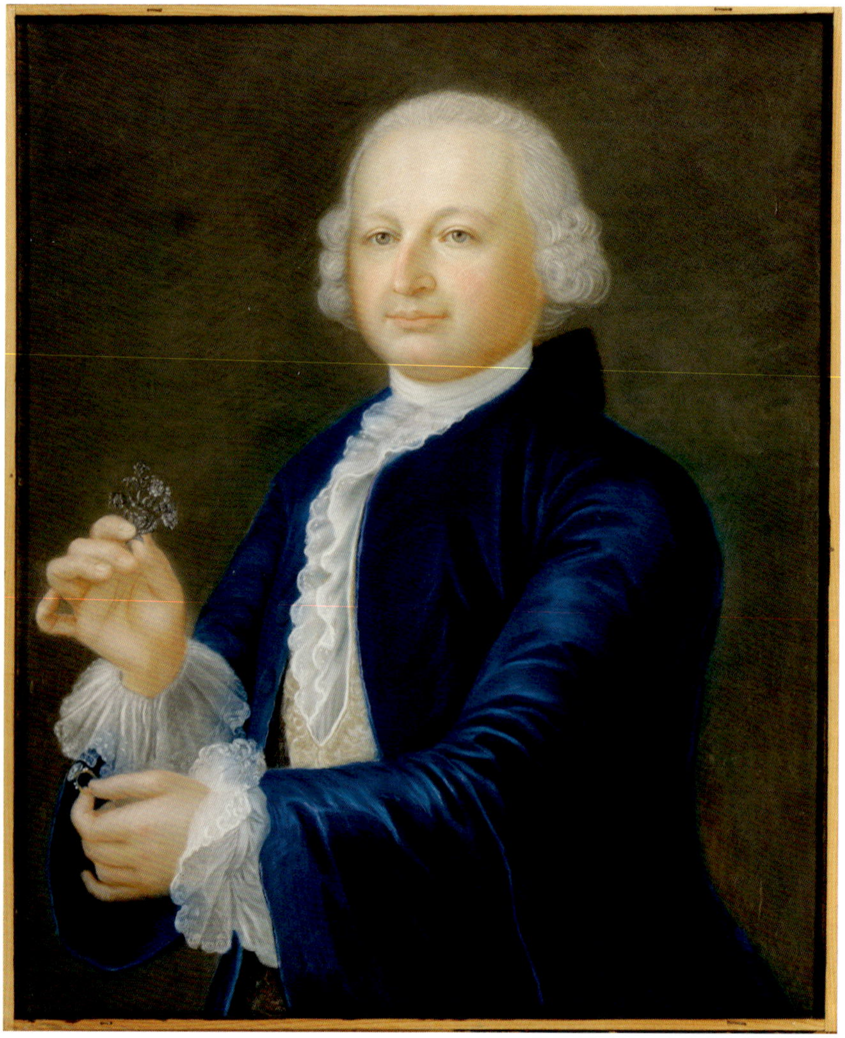

Although nearly forgotten today, Jérémie Pauzié (1716–79) created sumptuous jewels that bedazzled Russian empresses and grandees alike. The transplanted Swiss introduced new techniques of stone setting, and by combining both European and traditional Russian styles his lavish gem-encrusted masterpieces caught the world's attention. Indeed, during his tenure, the Russian imperial court became known as one of the richest in Europe. Pauzié's creations were personal, most by special commission for the empresses or noblewomen in St. Petersburg, according to their exacting wishes and using only the finest gemstones. Pauzié's career culminated in one of the most magnificent jewels ever created in Europe: Catherine the Great's Coronation Crown.

Portrait of Jérémie Pauzié.
Source: Cabinet d'arts graphiques des Musées d'art et d'histoire, Genève, Legs. Gustave Revilliod, Geneva, © Musées d'art et d'histoire, Ville de Genève, photo courtesy of Yves Siza.

Après Trente ans de Larmes, de peine et de Travaux
Je vais chercher un Lieue ou je puisse en Repos
Prier L'Etre Suprême d'y adoucir mes Meaux!

After thirty years of tears, pain and work
I will seek a place where I can rest
Pray to the Supreme Being to lessen my sorrows!

Jérémie Pauzié etched these words using a diamond on a window pane upon his return journey to his homeland in 1764.

Because the empresses were so besotted by his jewels, Pauzié enjoyed extraordinary court privileges, unheard of for jewelers before or after. Even Carl Fabergé had to arrange for an audience with the tsar. Not so for Pauzié. His word was gold, his position all powerful. Defying all protocol, he could enter the imperial Palace to meet the empress at will. Other than the Chamberlain, her favorites and a few members of the highest nobility, no one else had free access to the court. When the ailing Austrian ambassador Count Nicholas Esterhazy failed to secure an audience with Empress Elizabeth, the diplomat turned to Pauzié to transmit an urgent message to her.[1] A central player in court and political intrigues, Pauzié also witnessed five palace coups, including the most momentous one, orchestrated by Catherine the Great. Yet, with each successor, Pauzié managed to keep his position as court jeweler.

Fortunately, Pauzié left memoirs. Written after his return to Switzerland, they give us an invaluable insider's account of 18th-century court life in St. Petersburg—an age when women ruled Russia. In his era, memoirs were in vogue for well-born gentlemen and ladies with a literary bent. But it was unusual for jewelers to put pen to paper, particularly since they were so busy at work. We are lucky that Pauzié found the time to do so in retirement.[2]

Pauzié had arrived in Russia at an auspicious time, for during the reigns of the women who succeeded Peter the Great, production of gold work and jewelry for the court had skyrocketed. According to Pauzié,

> The gowns of the ladies are magnificent just like their jewels. They wore a surprising number of diamonds, the lesser quality worth at least 10 to 12,000 rubles. . . . I think that of all the sovereigns of Europe, none equals in richness the jewels of the Empress of Russia.[3]

By the mid 18th century, diamonds were all the rage. Empress Elizabeth would change gowns up to 10 times a day, and each new one required a different parure. The exorbitant cost of festooning herself with jewels for appearances at the court ruined many a noblewoman's family.[4] To satisfy the Romanovs' craze for lavish ornamentation, goldsmiths and jewelers from all over Europe flocked to the imperial capital. Pauzié's career flourished thanks to the insatiable appetites for finery of these female monarchs.

From Geneva to St. Petersburg

Jérémie was born on December 6, 1716, in the town of Clérac, near Geneva. Like Carl Fabergé, he was of Huguenot origin. His Protestant parents, Etienne, an impoverished dyer, and Suzanne Bouverot, had six children. When Jérémie was barely a teenager, his father decided to take him and his older brother, Philibert, to Russia to seek a better future there. A generation earlier, Tsar Peter had issued an *ukaz* (decree) inviting foreign artisans to help build his new capital, St. Petersburg, in exchange for religious freedom and other privileges.[5] This resulted in a huge influx of Protestant Europeans to the empire in the first half of the 18th century. Etienne had no doubt heard about the young empire's seemingly limitless opportunities from his brother Pierre, who had become a surgeon to the tsar.

Jérémie was only thirteen in 1729 when the trio crossed the Alps on foot and made their way across Alsace, Westphalia, the Dutch Republic and northern Germany. Philibert stayed behind in Hamburg to apprentice with a cutler. After seven grueling months of overland travel, father and son arrived in St. Petersburg, only to learn that Pierre had relocated to Moscow. When they rejoined him there, Pierre's house had been burned to the ground in one of the frequent fires that razed the wooden city. The pair then went to Archangel on the Arctic Sea for military service, where Jérémie described being stranded in a forest filled with bears.[6] Etienne could not survive his new homeland's hardships and died in 1731, to his son's inconsolable sorrow—but not before learning of Jérémie's impending apprenticeship to his brother Pierre's friend, the French court jeweler Benoît Gravereaux.[7] After a two-week vigil, the grief-stricken teenager returned to St. Petersburg by sleigh to begin his seven-year contract.

The Apprentice

The Parisian lapidarist Gravereaux had settled in the new imperial capital a quarter century earlier to become a jeweler to Peter the Great. By now, the master jeweler had built up an impressive clientele. Unrivaled in his knowledge of the field, he was an accomplished gem connoisseur. Charming and good looking, he suffered at the same time from a violent temper and an excessive fondness for drink, as well as the pleasures of the flesh. Pauzié nevertheless benefited from Gravereaux's expertise. He quickly learned how to cut, polish and set stones—and how to appraise them. Within two years, the youth was helping Gravereaux fill orders. After a full day's work at the bench, Pauzié had leave to create his own jewels, working late at night. It was not an easy apprenticeship, for his master often returned from his carouses in a drunken rage. One evening Gravereaux attacked Pauzié and continued beating him until some Catholic priests living nearby came to his rescue. Fearing for his life, Pauzié decided to flee to England but was dissuaded from doing so by Benoît's long-suffering wife, Elizabeth, née Vassoux.

Pauzié excelled as a gem cutter and began to establish his own network of clients. Often tasked with delivering Gravereaux's commissions, the apprentice frequented the most influential members of the Russian nobility, such as the grand chamberlain and guards officer Count Mikhail Vorontsov, who would later help Elizabeth overthrow Empress Anna Leopoldovna, as well as the powerful Shuvalov family.[8]

Gravereaux's most illustrious client was the empress herself, Anna Ioannovna (r. 1730–40). Like all Romanov tsarinas, Peter the Great's niece craved luxury. Particularly fond of gold and jewels, Anna patronized both city merchants and foreign suppliers via diplomatic channels. Intrigued by exotic precious stones, including unpolished rubies from the Orient, she sent caravans along the Silk Road to India and China to source them in vast quantities.[9] Impatient to have the sumptuous gems mounted as wearable parures, she ordered Gravereaux to transfer his workshop to her palace.

Having the stonecutting machines installed close to her private chambers, the formidable empress inspected the jeweler's progress several times a day. To try to appease the sovereign, Gravereaux often brought along his personable apprentice, Pauzié. Making matters worse for the carousing craftsman, Anna was an early riser. When Gravereaux failed to appear in the *laboratoire* one early morning, Pauzié told the empress that his master was ill. Unfortunately, when her Italian court jester, Petro Mira-Pedrillo, happened to mention that he had spent the night merrymaking in the countryside with Gravereaux, the Empress flew into a rage and struck his name from the register.[10] Banished from the court, Gravereaux lost all prospects of imperial patronage.

This left young Pauzié alone in the palace. With Gravereaux out of the way, Anna soon realized that his apprentice was endowed with extraordinary talent. Within a few days, she invited Pauzié to join the caravan to China to choose precious stones for her collection. While overwhelmed by this honor, the Swiss youth was a practical businessman, and he negotiated a payment of 2,000 rubles for the three-year journey in addition to a stipend of 10,000 rubles. Sadly, the offer never materialized since the empress died three weeks later. The infant Ivan VI was named tsar, with Anna's German lover, Ernst Johann von Bühren, as regent. Bühren was thoroughly loathed by Russians, and little Ivan's own mother, Anna Leopoldovna, had the foreigner arrested and exiled and replaced him as regent. This reign too was short lived, but it was with her that Pauzié scored his first coup as a goldsmith.

Like her aunt, Anna Leopoldovna had a passion for jewels. Early in her reign, she summoned Pauzié to the court to dismantle existing parures from the imperial treasury and reset their gems into more fashionable designs. When Pauzié respectfully reminded Anna that he was a stonecutter, not a stone setter, she shrugged and insisted that he do it anyway. The job took two days. Having gathered the broken gold into his hat to return the precious metal, Anna told him to keep it all. To Pauzié's delight, the mountings held many small diamonds that had been too difficult to remove on site. The value was 1,500 rubles for the diamonds, and 500 for the gold, which he then sold to buy fine colored gemstones.[11] His passion grew.

Master Jeweler

Pauzié's apprenticeship finally ended in 1740. But a lack of funds and a debt of 150 rubles forced him to stay with Gravereaux. Increasingly jealous and possessive of his charge, the disgraced jeweler continued to hold him in servitude. The latter's prospects did not look brilliant. Poverty among the capital's foreign craftsmen workers was common. With no steady work, most lived precariously in considerable hardship, often enduring the hostility of native Russian tradesmen.[12] But Pauzié had connections. One of them, Isaak Liebmann, a merchant banker who was also chief commissioner to the imperial court, lent him the money to repay Gravereaux.[13] Anticipating his master's violent objections, Pauzié carefully staged his exit. He first announced that he was leaving and then quickly put the money on the table. Enraged, Gravereaux was helpless to retain him. Pauzié was free at last.

Now a master jeweler himself, before the year was out Pauzié managed to open a workshop not far from the imperial palace.[14] Sponsored by Liebmann, he installed two stonecutting machines and other implements of the trade. With little capital, but great potential, Pauzié found favor with the well-heeled aristocrats he had earlier met as Gravereaux's go-between. They included various members of the Shuvalov family. Count Peter Shuvalov, who would become grand chamberlain under Elizabeth, was grateful

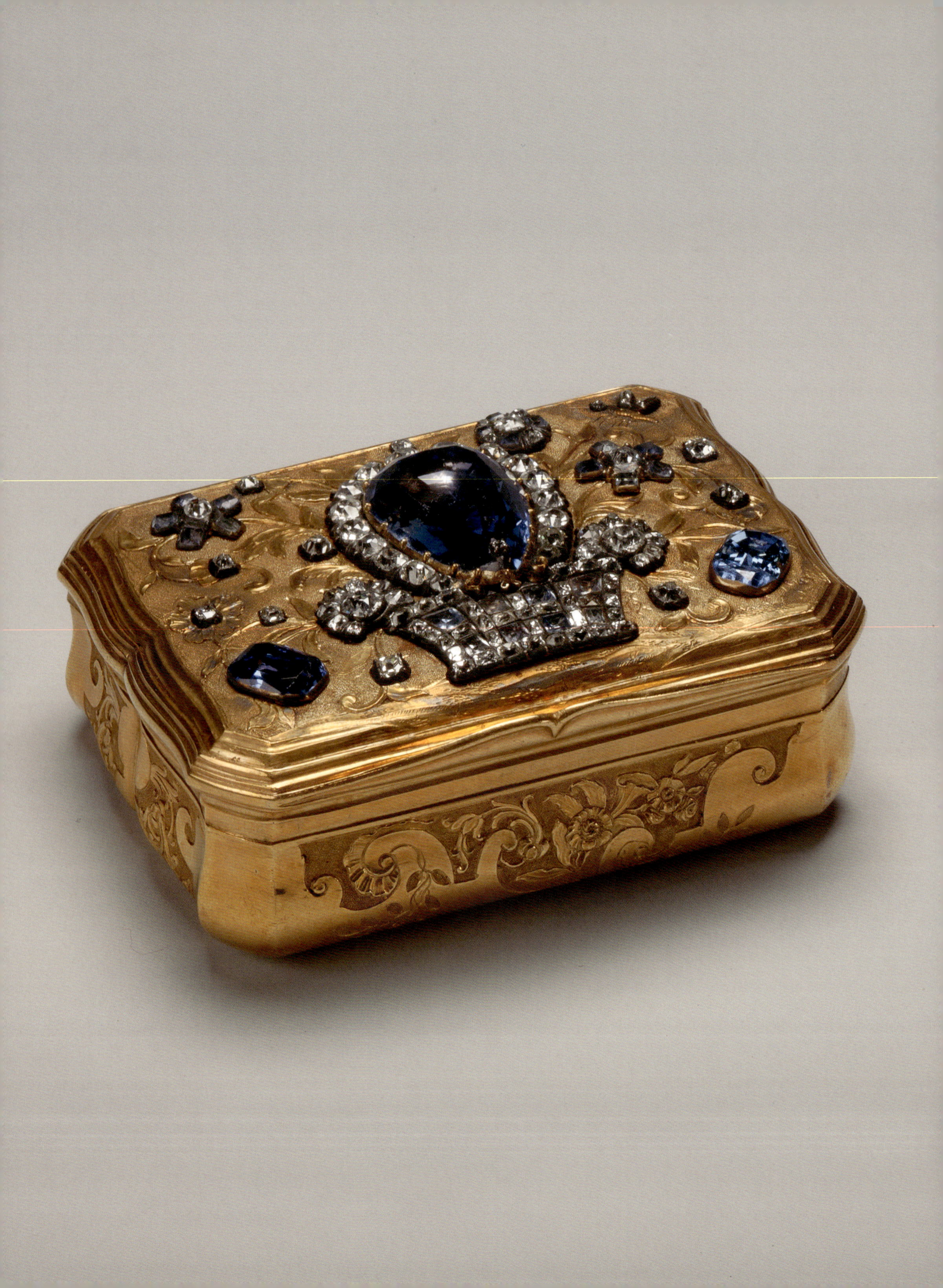

Gold and sapphire snuffbox by Pauzié, ca. 1750. *Source: State Hermitage Museum © State Hermitage Museum photo by Vladimir Terebenin*

to Pauzié for extending credit to him when he was in need. To show his appreciation, he pronounced the jeweler honest and trustworthy in front of a distinguished party of grandees and repaid his debt on the spot.[15]

The jeweler also forged ties within the trade. Unable to join the caravan to China, Pauzié nevertheless managed to come to an arrangement with the merchants who took part. This was strictly without the court's permission, since all the goods were meant for the imperial palace. Nevertheless, he bought exotic rough gems from the Far East, which he himself then cut, polished and resold at a great profit.[16]

Pauzié excelled in every facet of the business. First he had to source precious stones. This was no easy task since native mines were not yet exploited in the early 18th century. Once he had purchased the gems, he had to cut and polish them. If they were sold unmounted, he then sought a buyer, usually a merchant.[17] With imperial commissions, the process was more complicated. As an independent jeweler, it was up to Pauzié to design jewels, then to purchase the precious metals and gems to realize them. On his résumé, had he needed one, Pauzié would have listed buyer and seller, negotiator, dealer, goldsmith, stone polisher, stone setter, jeweler, designer, gemstone appraiser and connoisseur. And jeweler to the Empresses.

Most foreign jewelers joined guilds. Pauzié and his compatriot, the court jeweler Jean-Pierre Ador, did not need to do so, since both had already built strong ties with the imperial court. But this came at a price. Guild members received both materials and designs from the *pridvornaia kontora*, or imperial cabinet.[18] The master's payment would then be negotiated separately.[19] As an independent jeweler, Pauzié had to bear all costs up front. Adding to this financial burden was his clients' notorious tendency to buy only on credit. To pay his own suppliers, Pauzié was forever chasing down these aristocratic deadbeats. These included Grand Duke Peter and his wife, Catherine, the future empress. Pauzié claimed that for 15 years, he supplied jewels to the imperial couple without receiving more than a few kopeks from them. Empress Elizabeth herself had strictly forbidden Pauzié to extend credit to the Grand Duke during her reign, fearing perhaps that he would seize power from her, as she had done with Anna Leopoldovna. Having no allowance in no way restricted Peter from ordering personal jewels.

As Pauzié perfected his skills, he began developing new stone-setting techniques. One of his specialties was chasing, in which metal was formed usually from below. In the Rococo style prevalent in Russia in the 1730s, such settings would accentuate diamonds.[20] But by the mid-18th century, precious colored gemstones came to the fore. And Pauzié pounced. As both goldsmith and stonecutter, he created jewels uniquely his own. Bouquets of gems, each colorful stone cut into different shapes within conforming mounts, were set into vases to glittering effect. For whimsy, Pauzié would add small jeweled dragonflies, butterflies or beetles. Some could be worn as brooches on court occasions. The bouquets became his trademark. Pauzié proudly holds one in his right hand in his portrait. The Hermitage Museum in St. Petersburg has three such bouquets by Pauzié, bound with gold (see illustration, page 64).

While Van Cleef and Arpels popularized the invisible setting technique in Paris in the 1930s, Pauzié had already laid its foundation two centuries earlier. Under his deft hand, mountings virtually disappeared below faceted gemstones. This was meant to accentuate the beauty and cut of each gem. Pauzié also pioneered making a wax model to showcase his designs to the empress, as well as to work the material beforehand so as to create this feat of minimal setting.

Pauzié's creations for the imperial court included tobacco boxes and objects de vertu. According to the Hermitage curator of Russian jewelry, Liliia Kuznetsova,

> [his] smoky quartz tobacco box is remarkable for its beauty. Only a poet of stones such as Jérémie Pauzié could rework such a clean "Oriental stone" without the slightest inclusion and transform it into a beautiful object. . . . Its shades of golden smoke and color are enlivened by specks of enamel and flashes of diamond sparkles.[21]

By all accounts, Pauzié was a devout Calvinist. Unlike the Swedes, Germans and the Dutch, the French and Swiss did not live in distinct quarters of the capital but kept contact with

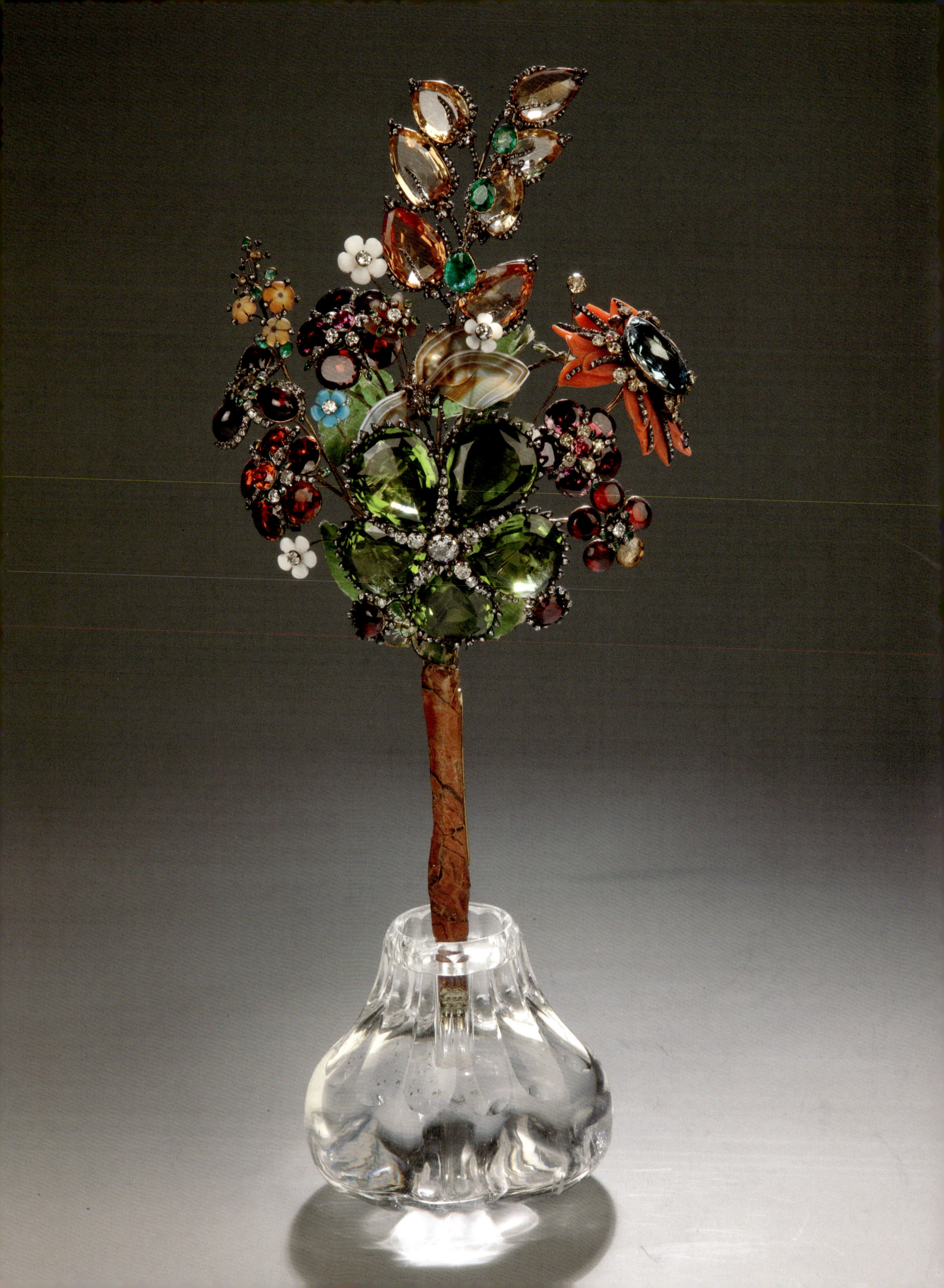

Bouquet of gem-set flowers by Pauzié. These unique creations held great appeal to the Empress Elizabeth, who wore them on her gown. *Source: State Hermitage Museum, St. Petersburg, photograph © State Hermitage Museum photo by Vladimir Terebenin*

each other though their churches.[22] Shortly after his arrival in St. Petersburg, the apprentice had received instruction for his first communion from Robert Dunant, the Swiss pastor at the French Reformed Church.[23] Pauzié later became its deacon and eventually lived in the church's courtyard.[24] Later on, Pauzié sent a donation in memory of his life in the imperial capital to build a new Calvinist church in St. Petersburg to replace the one destroyed by fire in the 1750s.[25]

Empress Elizabeth Petrovna

In 1741, Peter the Great's daughter orchestrated a military coup that deposed Anna Leopoldovna. On November 25, to the cheers of crowds gathered around the Winter Palace, Elizabeth Petrovna became Empress of All the Russias. Pauzié was there. Having already met Elizabeth through Shuvalov, the Swiss was well placed to be appointed her court jeweler. To gain her trust, he had to tread carefully. Greek, Armenian, Italian and German goldsmiths all vied for imperial court patronage. But their prices were exorbitant. Pauzié's were more modest, yet his workmanship superior. With this winning combination he quickly gained the confidence of the new court.

Early in her reign Elizabeth summoned Pauzié to produce his most important jewel to date: the Imperial Order of St. Andrew the Apostle the First Called, with Diamonds. The highest order of chivalry in Russia, it had been established by Peter the Great in 1698. That the court entrusted Pauzié rather than a guild jeweler with this order attests to the high regard in which it held him. Given a budget of 15,000 rubles by the empress's favorite, Ivan Shuvalov, he took great care with this commission. Pauzié began by making a wax model—an innovation at the time—on which he set the diamonds. The day he submitted it to Elizabeth for her approval was particularly tense. According to Pauzié,

> I waited a few moments surrounded by ladies in waiting who looked at me with suspicious eyes asking me what I wanted. They were not pleased, as I hadn't gone through them. The Empress left her chamber with Chamberlain Shuvalov, who motioned me to approach, which I did. She proffered her hand, which I kissed, and asked me to show her what I had brought. I withdrew from my pocket a box. She seemed very surprised . . . at the way I had arranged this, which she had not seen before.

The empress was most pleased with such magnificence, but she did grumble about its high cost. With a flourish the jeweler showed his august client a list with the cost of his diamonds. His own markup proved modest, thereby appeasing Elizabeth. She placed the order but insisted it must be carried out in great haste.

Pauzié lost no time in hiring six stone setters from Saxony and Vienna, and within four weeks the order, which included a Star and Badge encrusted with diamonds, was ready. Once again, the jeweler had an anxious moment when he presented the final version to Elizabeth at Peterhof. Marveling at Pauzié's *chef d'oeuvre*, the empress showed it to her ladies-in-waiting, one of whom maliciously claimed that the diamonds had appeared larger on the wax model than on the finished piece.

The jeweler flew into a rage, seized his pliers from his pocket, and set upon breaking up the precious Order, at which point the empress reentered. When he explained it would be better to destroy his creations than be accused of switching stones, Elizabeth chastised the agitated goldsmith for taking jealous ladies-in-waiting seriously. She herself was very happy with the result and was convinced of his good faith.[26] The empress never questioned his prices again.

Pauzié's most important contact was Count Mikhail Vorontsov's family. The count had helped Elizabeth in her coup to seize the throne, and remained a close confidant of the empress throughout her reign, ultimately rising to chancellor, the highest rank in tsarist officialdom. His wife, Anna, a lady-in-waiting with full access to Elizabeth's apartments, also liked Pauzié, as did Vorontsov's niece, Elizaveta, the mistress of the empress's nephew, the future Peter III.[27]

As the empress's chief diplomat, Vorontsov was in charge of ordering gifts for departing foreign dignitaries and court officials. The count turned exclusively to Pauzié for these imperial commissions, which also included diamond-set rings for the nobility. This meant continuous business at the most prestigious level. And, since the orders were issued through the Foreign Ministry, he was sure to be paid—not always a certainty in Russia at the time.

Pauzié now had more work than he could handle. At first, he was forced to toil late at night by candlelight, since most of his days were spent visiting his vast network of clients. Suppliers would arrive at 5 a.m., and the rounds would begin again. Eventually, he simply designed the jewels while Russian apprentices, as stipulated in his contract as court jeweler,[28] would complete them. However, he did find the time to marry Marie-Madeleine Scalogne in 1747 and father five children.

To meet the rising demand, Pauzié also employed foreign stone setters, enamelers and chasers. Yet, even once he was able to employ craftsmen to carry out his orders, Pauzié did not always enjoy a full night's sleep. An insomniac utterly besotted by jewels, Elizabeth habitually summoned him to the palace at all hours to dictate her exact desires, only to forget about them and keep him waiting for hours. Once, having spent the whole night without seeing the empress, he returned home, only to be recalled to the court. Elizabeth had an ardent desire to live in luxury. Most of her fortune was dedicated to buying jewels, dresses and accessories. Under her reign the Romanov court became one of the most sumptuous in Europe.[29]

A Sojourn in Europe

In 1750, yearning for change, Pauzié received permission to revisit his homeland. This was not without effort, since the Empress was reluctant to lose sight of him. "Bring me back some pretty things" were her parting words. Chancellor Vorontsov arranged for Pauzié's passport and provided letters of introduction to governors across the empire and into Prussia. In exchange, Pauzié was to bring back a suitable European governess for his daughter. He had not seen his family in Geneva in 20 years, and in Russia he left behind his wife, Marie-Madeleine, three children, and another on the way. It was a tearful departure, but one suspects that Mme Pauzié, by now accustomed to her husband's frequent absences, remained stoic.

This proved an important trip for Pauzié. As a dealer, he found suppliers for gems in Europe, thereby eliminating middlemen in Russia. In Berlin, he met a court jeweler to Frederick the Great, and in Geneva, Jean Jacques Pallard, jeweler to the Habsburgs in Vienna, who consigned gems to Pauzié.[30] Pauzié also visited the renowned engraver Jean Dassier, from whom he bought several medallions for Elizabeth. Thanks to Pauzié, his son, Jean-Antoine Dassier, would come to Russia to work for the Empress. In Dresden, the Saxon foreign minister, Count Heinrich von Brühl, arranged for him to tour the crown jewels and the magnificent collection of treasures amassed by August the Strong in the 1720s at Grünes Gewölbe. This exposure to precious European objects would later influence his designs.

Accompanied by a Mlle. Counent, the demoiselle he had found for the Vorontsovs in Berlin, Pauzié returned to St. Petersburg exhausted, with swollen legs and unable to walk. This did not deter the empress from immediately summoning Pauzié to her side at Peterhof. With great difficulty, Pauzié made his way to the palace to present to the Empress his cache of treasures. This included medallions, bonbonnières, a diamond necklace *en esclavage* and a rose-cut diamond ring set with a miniature pocket watch, which she placed on her finger. Perhaps the most astonishing item was a small *boîte à mouche* in the form of a diamond egg, with her Russian name, Elizaveta Petrovna, set in rose diamonds below the Romanov double-headed eagle. This was more than 130 years before Fabergé would introduce his famous series of eggs. The empress beamed with delight and complimented Pauzié profusely on his fine choice. It was one of the highlights of his career. According to Liliia Kuznetsova, Pauzié's other court creations under Elizabeth included a diamond-encrusted snuffbox for a Swedish general in 1759, and, the following year, a diamond ring for a prominent Habsburg courtier and another for a "Colonel de Bott."[31]

In 1753, Pauzié formed a short-lived partnership with Swiss jeweler Louis David Duval. Duval had started his career with his brothers as crown jewelers in London. In 1745, he established himself in St. Petersburg as a gem merchant. He would later open a workshop with his sons on the Nevskii Prospect as a court jeweler to Catherine the Great. By now, Pauzié's workshop had also become a fashionable jewelry shop, renowned for the high quality of its merchandise. After the merger with Duval, Pauzié increased his stock to include watches, étui, pinchbeck and other unusual items from England. But he wasn't entirely happy. His established clients were not receptive to foreign objets de vertu, since they preferred Pauzié's own work. Furthermore, Duval's taciturn character (he suffered from suicidal depression and was delusional) made him utterly unfit to meet clients. The partnership dissolved, but his brothers back in London remained on good terms with Pauzié. Duval's sons would go on to create the coronation crown of Elizabeth Alekseevna, the wife of Tsar Alexander I.

Toward the end of her reign, the empress listened to only two people: Shuvalov and Pauzié.[32] During one lengthy illness, she refused all audiences for half a year. Even Chancellor Vorontsov could not approach his sovereign, and he had to send Pauzié to the empress with important documents to sign. The jeweler disliked this role, but he could hardly refuse it.[33] On another occasion, on the pretext of delivering a ring to Elizabeth, Pauzié interceded on behalf of the Austrian ambassador, who was himself gravely ill, to take leave of her court without a formal ceremony. As the customary farewell gift, the empress commissioned a diamond ring and furs for the diplomat upon his departure. Yet, despite her caprices, the Swiss jeweler was quite fond of his august client, and he was crushed when she died on Christmas Day 1761.

Upon Elizabeth's death, her successor, Peter III, ordered Pauzié to create a funerary crown to be placed on her head on her gold parade bed when, according to Orthodox custom, her former subjects could pay their last respects. Pauzié described the wake in eerie detail. The new tsar's consort, Catherine—soon to be Russia's ruler herself—was having difficulty placing the crown on Elizabeth's head, so she turned to Pauzié for help. Court protocol dictated that up to six weeks after death, all must still kiss the sovereign's hand, so he did so. Aware that after one's death, the head tends to swell, he had designed the crown to expand. Pincers in hand, he adjusted it by altering miniature screws along its circumference. Then, lit by 6,000 candles, surrounded by weeping ladies-in-waiting, maids of honor, the highest court officials, archbishops and priests, Pauzié gingerly placed the enlarged crown on her head. It was all he could do not to break down.

Peter III

As tsarevich, Peter was in the habit of ordering jewels from Pauzié without paying for them.[34] In 1761, when Pauzié suffered from pleurisy, the heir sent a request for a diamond-set snuffbox. Fed up, Pauzié's wife, Marie-Madeleine, sent the officer away, insisting that her husband was too sick even to stand.[35] This did not, however, prevent Pauzié from soliciting his patronage when Peter became tsar. No doubt because of his affability and skill, the Swiss jeweler was high on Peter III's list of favorite goldsmiths. He also appreciated Pauzié's creativity. For his coronation in 1762, Tsar Peter commissioned several parures of imitation stones to be worn by his German relatives for court occasions. No one could tell them apart from the real thing, and the secret remained between the ladies and Pauzié. To show his gratitude, Peter elevated him to the rank of brigadier and allowed him to keep the title of court jeweler. Inept and thoroughly disliked, Peter III reigned as tsar for barely half a year before being swept from power by his wife, Catherine.

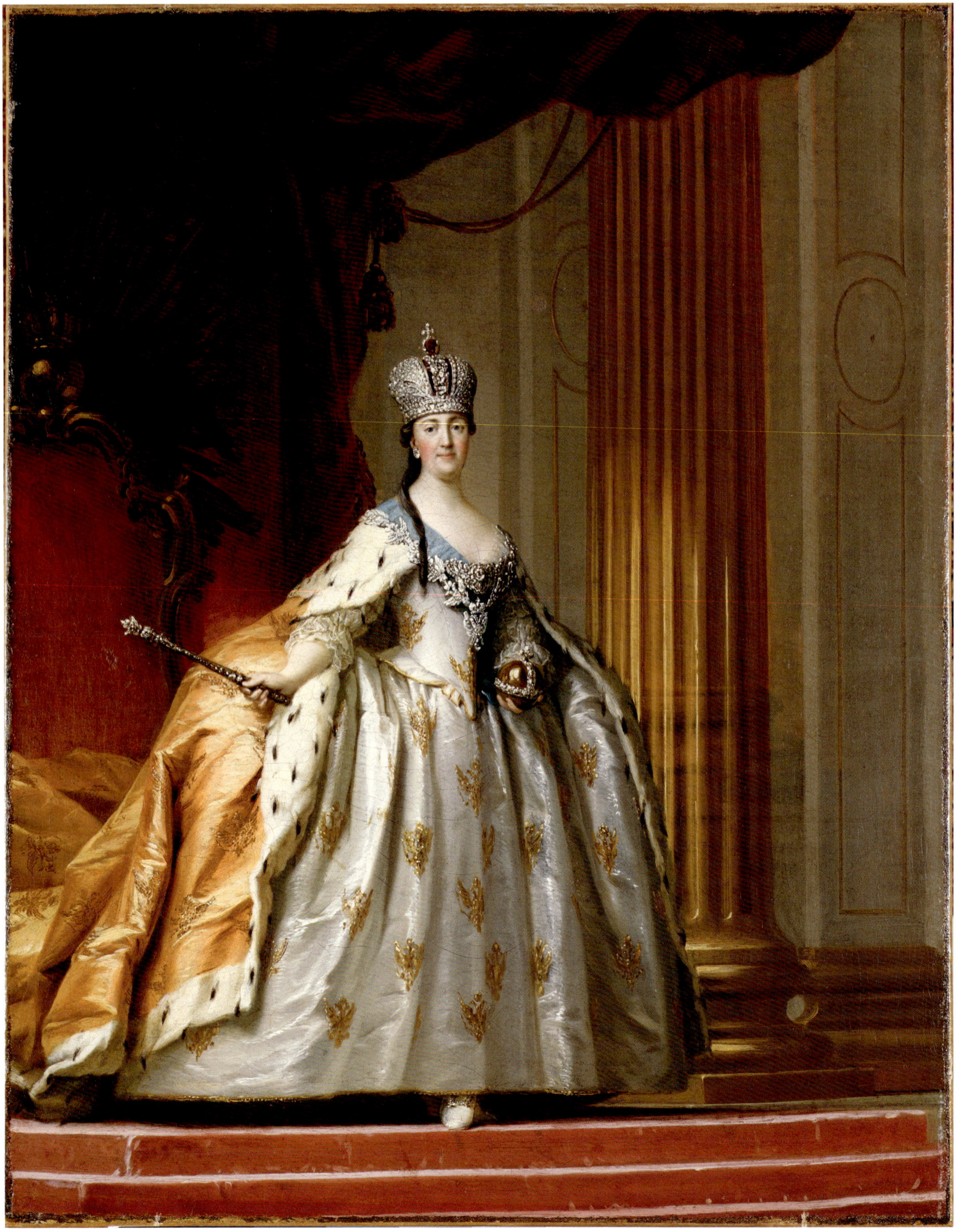

Catherine the Great

Not long into her reign, Elizabeth had chosen Sophie Augusta, the teenaged daughter of a minor German prince, to be wed to her nephew and heir, Grand Duke Peter. Taking the name "Catherine" upon converting to the Orthodox faith, the grand duchess proved much more popular among her adopted countrymen than had her husband. Accordingly, on June 28, 1762, officers of the imperial guard supported her in a coup that deposed the despised Peter III and hailed their new empress, Catherine II. On that very day, Pauzié was en route to Oranienbaum to deliver 200,000 rubles' worth of jewelry to the emperor when a military guard galloped up to his coach and advised him to return to the capital at once or risk his life. Pauzié arrived in St. Petersburg to scenes of wild jubilation. Soldiers everywhere were celebrating as huge crowds thronged the Palace Square. As Pauzié wondered how he might pay his respects to his new ruler, a carriage with four guardsmen arrived at his doorstep. "The Empress would like to know," one of them asked, "do you have the diamond-set chamberlain's key commissioned by Peter III for Count Sheremetev?"[36] This was the very object that Pauzié had been about to give to Peter. The soldier then suggested, "Would you change the donor's name from Peter III to Empress Catherine II, as she would like to personally present the key to Sheremetev?" The jeweler obliged and asked for a guard to be stationed at his home to protect his precious inventory from the day's disorderly mobs while he brought the key to the empress.

Pauzié arrived at the Winter Palace, where he found the leading nobles crowding around the throne to kiss their new sovereign's hand in submission. After waiting for an hour, he finally managed to hand her the chamberlain's diamond key in its fitted velvet case. Pauzié recalled,

> She found it magnificent. Its value was 10,000 rubles. She presented it to Grand Chamberlain Sheremetev, who was standing nearby and threw himself on his knees before her to kiss her hand. She turned toward me and said, "I am much obliged, Pauzié, by your exactitude." I seized the moment to tell her of the large amount of Crown Jewels in my house. And to whom should I deliver them? She said not to be concerned and ordered a guard to escort me back there.[37]

Catherine II in her coronation robe by Vigilius Eriksen, 1778–79. The David Collection, Copenhagen, inventory number 14/1967. *Photo courtesy of Pernille Klemp*

Pauzié was on good terms with Catherine, and she favored him with several commissions for imperial orders, including an Order of St. Catherine, a lavishly decorated star for the Order of St. Alexander Nevskii and a St. Andrew's badge. One, priced at 18,800 rubles, was destined for the newly elected king to the Polish throne, Stanisław Poniatowski.[38] Like her predecessors the Empress craved luxury and, thanks to her long reign, augmented the coffers like no other monarch; 40 percent of the Diamond Fund dates from her reign. Catherine transformed the imperial bedchamber in the southeast corner of the Winter Palace to the Brilliant Room, where, according to one visitor, she had the jewels laid out on a table under a great crystal globe, all the better to admire them.[39]

During Catherine's long rule, neoclassicism supplanted the curved lines and rich Rococo ornamentation popular in earlier decades with streamlined, symmetrical and monochromatic designs. This can be seen in snuffboxes given as diplomatic gifts. While still encrusted with precious stones, these took on a sparer look. Pearls and diamonds reemerged as gems of choice, although rubies, emeralds and sapphires were by no means neglected.

The jeweler's career reached its apogee with the magnificent Russian diamond crown for Catherine's coronation. Today it remains the highlight of the Diamond Fund in the Moscow Kremlin. Designed by Pauzié and another jeweler, it took several craftsmen a full two months to complete.[40] The crown weighed 5 pounds and was set with just under 5,000 diamonds, 75 natural pearls and a 398-carat spinel. Pauzié mistakenly identified the latter as a ruby, and so it is likely he did not have a hand in choosing or setting this stone. The largest diamond, at 56 carats, had been offered to Empress Elizabeth by the merchant guild in gratitude for exemption from taxes and duties.[41]

Although confident of Catherine's patronage, Pauzié was uneasy about his future. Noble clients who owed vast sums of money avoided him. The imperial court was no different. Bills remained unpaid. Yet, suppliers, whether abroad or in Russia, did not wait. Pauzié was caught in the middle. As the coronation approached and Catherine invited Pauzié to travel with the regalia to Moscow, he accepted but delicately asked whether the empress would be kind enough to acquaint herself with Peter III's outstanding debt of 15,000 rubles. Pleading scant resources in the treasury, Catherine advised Pauzié to settle some items with her secretary of state. The rest would be a loss. The official proved just as inattentive as the others. Catherine also commissioned from Pauzié a diamond St. Andrew Star and Badge, by now one of his specialties. He produced it in just two weeks, but the empress did not pay him. When pressed, she feigned indifference, and in desperation,

Pauzié bribed her treasurer by making a charitable donation to his children's hospital. The official then suggested he attend a masked ball to await his response. To Pauzié's considerable annoyance, the payment came in a vast quantity of copper coins from the imperial foundry.[42]

There were more blows. First, Pauzié fell ill. For six weeks he lay in his bed, unable to move. His mood was not improved when his accountant revealed that three-quarters of his fortune were tied up in the debt of his aristocratic clients. Then, in 1763, a young man in a blue cloak appeared on his doorstep, masquerading as a courier for Field Marshall Razumovskii to request diamond jewels for his master. Pauzié obliged, handing over 12,000 rubles' worth of inventory. It quickly emerged that Razumovskii had nothing to do with the matter. Although later recovered, the items were broken up, much like Pauzié's spirits as he descended deeper into debt.

The richest court in Europe had defied the jeweler. Neither the empress nor her nobles paid him, or they took far too long to do so. It was time to go back home. Using his illness as an excuse, he petitioned Catherine for leave to take a cure. She consented and, as a farewell gift, granted him the title of personal jeweler to the empress. The empress then asked him to deliver two portrait medallions to Voltaire and d'Alembert. Ever alert despite his infirmities, Pauzié seized the chance to ask for payment for this trip, since he was short of funds. Perhaps suspecting he would not return, Catherine immediately signed documents for the release of funds as Pauzié tearfully left the palace.

To maintain the fiction that he was taking a short trip, Pauzié arranged for two employees to stay in his workshop along with much of his inventory. Then, on September 4, 1764, having already sent his family ahead of him, he bade farewell to his closest friends and took his leave. Pauzié settled in Geneva with his wife and six children. An honest and pious man, he was heartbroken but undoubtedly reassured that he had done the right thing for his family and himself. After 30 years in Russia, the jeweler had accumulated about 28,000 rubles, enough to live in comfortable retirement.[43] And to write his memoirs. Pauzié died at the age of 63 on November 30, 1779.

A Magician

With sheer ingenuity and a profound knowledge of precious stones, Pauzié created masterpieces. According to Liliia Kuznetsova, he was "something of a magician, able to rework stones with natural defects to perfection."[44] His virtuosity with gems was remarkable. Few could equal it then or today. Although some are preserved in the State Hermitage's Diamond Fund, sadly, most of Pauzié's creations are lost. He did not sign his pieces, and it is difficult to identify them without marks. Add to that the habit of redesigning jewels to suit changing tastes, and the chance of finding any surviving Pauzié masterpieces is remote.

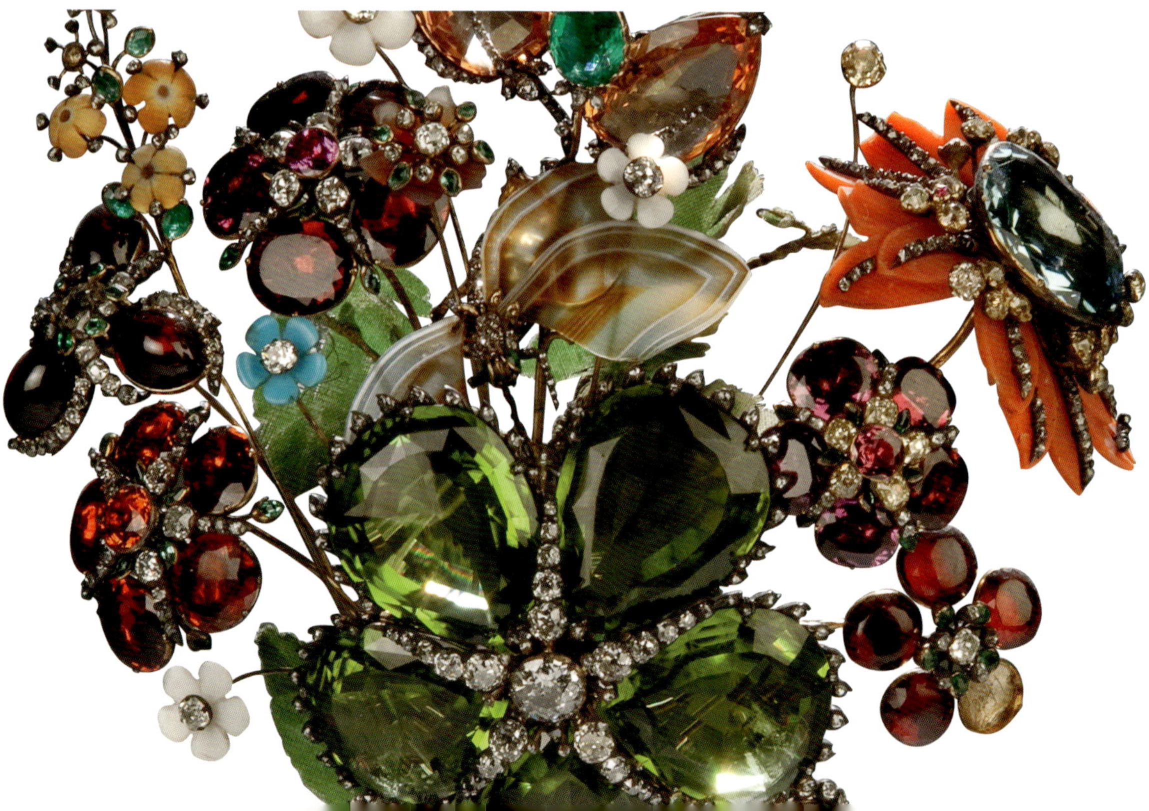

Detail of Pauzié gemstone bouquet on page 64.
Source: State Hermitage Museum, St. Petersburg, photograph © State Hermitage Museum photo by Vladimir Terebenin

NOTES

1. Prince Nikolaus Joseph Esterházy (1714–90), field marshal during the war of Austrian Succession and Seven Years' War.

2. Jérémie Pauzié, "Mémoire abrégé de la vie de Jérémie Pauzié né à Genève l'année 1716 en Septembre," Ms suppl. 1399, Public and University Library of Geneva. The 31-page manuscript, written in French, covers the years 1729–63. The manuscript was translated into Russian and published in part in 1870 in *Russkaia Starina*. The memoirs also appeared in excerpts in the periodical *Russkii iuvelir*.

3. Pauzié, "Mémoire abrégé," 24. Authors' translation.

4. Mélanie Draveny, "Edition critique introduite et commentée du mémoire de Jérémie Pauzié, joaillier à la Cour de Russie de 1730 à 1763" (master's thesis, University of Geneva, 2004), 44.

5. Peter the Great pronounced the ukaz on April 16, 1702. Draveny, "Edition critique," 12.

6. Pauzié, "Mémoire abrégé," 7.

7. Benoît Gravereaux (1695 or 1700–1766), Parisian master lapidarist, stone setter, and court jeweler to Empress Anna Ioannovna.

8. Draveny, "Edition critique," 40. Vorontsoff became grand chamberlain and lieutenant of the Imperial Guard after helping Elizabeth Petrovna overthrow Empress Anna Leopoldovna.

9. According to Liliia Kuznetsova, the empress was the first to inspect and take the items she desired. The rest would be sold publicly in her palace's "Italian Rooms." Kuznetsova, *Peterburgskie iuveliry: Vek vosemnadtsatyi*, 110.

10. This and much of the biographical information on individuals mentioned in Pauzié's memoirs is provided by Draveny, "Edition critique."

11. Pauzié, "Mémoire abrégé," 10.

12. Draveny, "Edition critique," 14–15, 16. A Russian carpenter's annual salary was 24 rubles, a government worker about 200–220 rubles, while more-exalted foreign artists such as Jean Jacques Lagrenée (1739–1821) received a tax-free salary of 7,347 rubles in his first year at the court.

13. Solodkoff, *Russian Gold and Silverwork*, 22.

14. Draveny, "Edition critique," 66. He rented a room from a fellow countryman, Philippe de Caro (1693–1750), a colonel with connections to the chancellery, whose son would later play a role in Pauzié 's return to Geneva.

15. Pauzié, "Mémoire abrégé," 11.

16. Kuznetsova, *Peterburgskie iuveliry: Vek vosemnadtsatyi*, 113.

17. Draveny, "Edition critique," 65.

18. Mélanie Draveny, "Jérémie Pauzié, joallier genèvois à la cour des tsars," in *Svejcarija-Russie-Lausanne*, ed. Laurent Golay ([Wabern-Bern, Switzerland]: Benteli, 2006), 54.

19. Solodkoff, *Russian Gold and Silverwork*, 21.

20. Draveny, "Edition critique," 31.

21. Kuznetsova, *Peterburgskie iuveliry: Vek vosemnadtsatyi*, 123.

22. Draveny, "Edition critique," 51.

23. Ibid., 61.

24. Kuznetsova, *Peterburgskie iuveliry: Vek vosemnadtsatyi*, 116

25. Ibid., 122.

26. Pauzié, "Mémoire abrégé," 12.

27. Draveny, "Edition Critique," 41.

28. Ibid., 33–34.

29. Ibid., 45.

30. Ibid., 35.

31. Kuznetsova, *Peterburgskie iuveliry: Vek vosemnadtsatyi*, 121.

32. Draveny, "Edition critique," 45.

33. Pauzié, "Mémoire abrégé," 21.

34. Karl Peter von Holstein, Anna Petrovna's only son, who married Sophie of Anhalt-Zerbst, future Empress Catherine II, on August 21, 1745.

35. Pauzié, "Mémoire abrégé," 21.

36. Count Petr Borisovich Sheremetev (1713–88), grand chamberlain under Catherine the Great.

37. Pauzié, "Mémoire abrégé," 30.

38. Kuznetsova, *Peterburgskie iuveliry: Vek vosemnadtsatyi*, 121.

39. Sotheby's, Geneva, *Russian Imperial Jewel*, November 17, 2005, single-lot catalogue.

40. The court jeweler and silversmith Friedrich Ekhardt, who was in charge of imperial regalia for the coronation in Moscow, completed the design. Kuznetsova, *Peterburgskie iuveliry: Vek vosemnadtsatyi*, 127. The Belgian diamond setter Jean Henroté (1727–1800) also worked on the crown.

41. Mélanie Draveny. "Genevois et Vaudois, joailliers de la Couronne et de la Cour, in *Suisses en Russie de Pierre le Grand à Alexandre Ier*, ed. Jean-René Bory (Pregny, Switzerland: Institut national de recherches de la Suisse avec l'étranger, 1996), 136.

42. Pauzié, "Mémoire abrégé," 35.

43. Draveny, "Edition critique," 22, n. 42.

44. Kuznetsova, *Peterburgskie iuveliry: Vek vosemnadtsatyi*, 123.

4

History

BOLIN: THE BRIGHTEST STAR

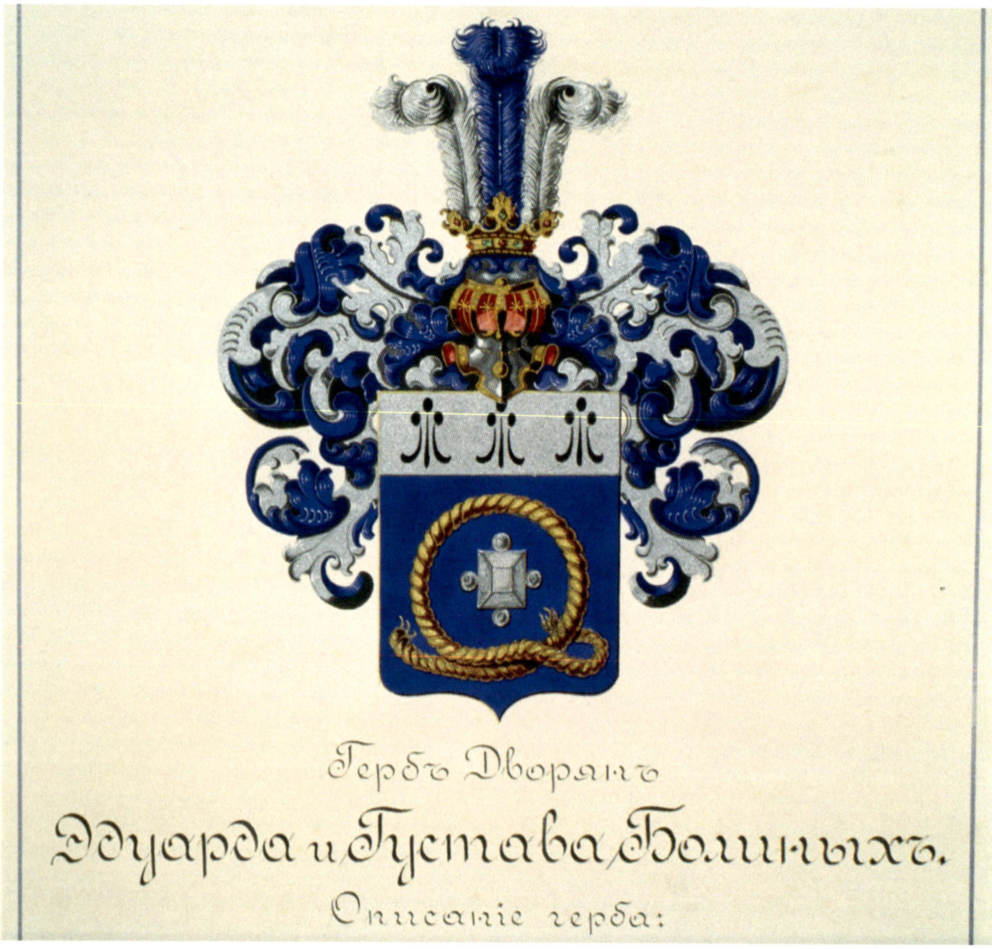

The Bolin coat of arms complete with heraldic diamond and bow line symbolizing the name's origin and the family's successful profession. The Russian imperial court rarely granted coats of arms to tradesmen. *Courtesy of Court Jewellers, W. A. Bolin*

Many believe that Carl Fabergé was Russia's best jeweler. But the distinction could just as easily be applied to any number of other, lesser-known firms, of which at least 40 also held the Romanov warrant at the turn of the 20th century in Russia. One particular powerhouse stood above all others: the House of Bolin. Unlike Fabergé, who served only the last two tsars of Russia, the storied Bolin enterprise produced jewels and silver for not just two, but *five* consecutive Russian sovereigns, starting with Tsar Alexander I in the early 19th century. But the story begins even earlier, under his grandmother, Catherine the Great. Most surprising is that today, over 100 years after the Bolshevik Revolution, the firm still continues in Stockholm. Originally from Sweden, Bolin is one of the oldest, still-active family-owned jewelry firms in history.

For much of the 1800s Bolin dominated the jewelry trade in Russia and was the jeweler of choice for the Russian imperial family and aristocracy. It was also the most expensive. Always held in high regard, the Bolins held the titles of appraiser to the imperial court as well as court jeweler decades longer than anyone else. As official court appraiser, familiar with the imperial treasury and in charge of repairs and alterations of crown jewels and objects, Bolin enjoyed priority over others.[1] The tsar even entrusted Bolin with transporting the crown jewels for coronations from St. Petersburg to Moscow.[2] In the 1920s, A. E. Fersman, a Russian gem expert in charge of cataloguing the Romanov crown jewels, called Bolin's magnificent pearl-and-diamond tiara the finest in the entire collection.[3]

Why is so little known about Bolin outside Sweden and Russia? For one, sadly, most of the sumptuous jewels from the imperial era are gone, melted down, disassembled, or destroyed. They were the first things to go during the revolution. Fabergé literature is also to blame. For decades and still today, Bolin and other Russian goldsmiths are dismissively labeled "competitors" or, worse, "contemporaries" of Fabergé. Both are misleading. Given Bolin's venerable history, if anyone was a contemporary of another, it was Fabergé of Bolin, and not the reverse. And while they were competitors in the strict sense, many jewelers, including Carl Fabergé and Edvard Bolin, were more inclined to collaborate with one another, especially on major commissions from the imperial court. In 1900, for example, on short notice both jewelers together created an emerald and diamond parure for Empress Alexandra Fedorovna, wife of Tsar Nicholas II, and her sister Elizabeth. They also bid together on jewelry from the imperial treasury at a secret auction in 1906 and at one point even considered merging as a single firm.[4]

Christophe Andreas Römpler

The story of Bolin begins with an immigrant from Saxony, Andreas Römpler. Römpler arrived in St. Petersburg around 1790 and promptly registered as a diamond master in the German guild. He had little choice, since unregistered craftsmen were punished and fined. Yet, this would work in his favor. Having been established by Peter the Great in 1714, the German guild was the oldest foreign one in the capital. Römpler's stars aligned, and he soon rose to become a court jeweler of the most demanding diamond patron of them all, Empress Catherine II.

At the time, Swiss, Germans and Swedes dominated the jewelry trade in St. Petersburg. Compared to native Russians, foreigners were seen as more creative and sophisticated. Many, such as Geneva-born court jeweler Jérémie Pauzié, were first generation,and therefore still influenced by prevailing European tastes. Born abroad herself, Catherine the Great preferred craftsmen and goldsmiths from the West to the more traditional Russian jewelers.

Little more is known about Römpler until 1802, when he married Anna Schell, the daughter of a German-born master tailor who owned a building on Bolshaia Morskaia Street in St. Petersburg. This was not just any building, but one that happened to house the Russian imperial court's diamond workshops.[5] How convenient for the young jeweler! Here, surrounded by imperial Russia's most glittering gems, Römpler became an expert in precious stones. By 1809, he had established his own company and taken Russian nationality, Russifying his name and including the patronymic Andrei Grigorievich, as well as buying the entire building.

Over the next two decades, Römpler perfected his trade. So high was the quality of his workmanship that in 1823, the empress's grandson, Tsar Alexander I, appointed him appraiser to the imperial court, an honor bestowed on only the most highly skilled jewelers. Along with purveyors to the imperial court, appraisers had the right to display the Romanov double-headed eagle emblem on their storefronts. Their role was to inspect and approve the jewels commissioned by the imperial family before allowing them to reach their recipients.

Römpler played an important role in the coronation of the next tsar, Nicholas I. According to the late Hermitage curator Liliia Kuznetsova, the burial of Tsar Alexander I in 1825 cost the treasury just under 830,000 rubles, and silver had to be melted down to replenish the reserves. In preparation for the coronation of the heir, Nicholas Pavlovich, the court summoned the best jewelers in the capital, including Philip Duval and Wilhelm Keibel. Andreas Römpler was entrusted with restoring the Crown of Kazan, which had lost a large emerald, two other gems, and parts of the mounting. In 1827, together with court appraiser Johan Friedrich Jannasch, Römpler appraised the diamonds of the late Empress Elizabeth Alekseevna, Alexander I's consort.[6]

The Swedish Connection

Eager to continue his legacy, Römpler wed his eldest daughter, Sofia, to Gottlieb Ernest Jahn, another court jeweler and also of German origin. Jahn himself was both appraiser and jeweler to the imperial court of Tsar Alexander I. When Römpler died in 1829, Jahn took ownership. That same year, he hired a Swede named Carl Edvard Bolin as bookkeeper.[7] Five years later, Bolin married Römpler's younger daughter Ernestine Catherine and became full partner in the firm. After Jahn's death in 1836, the

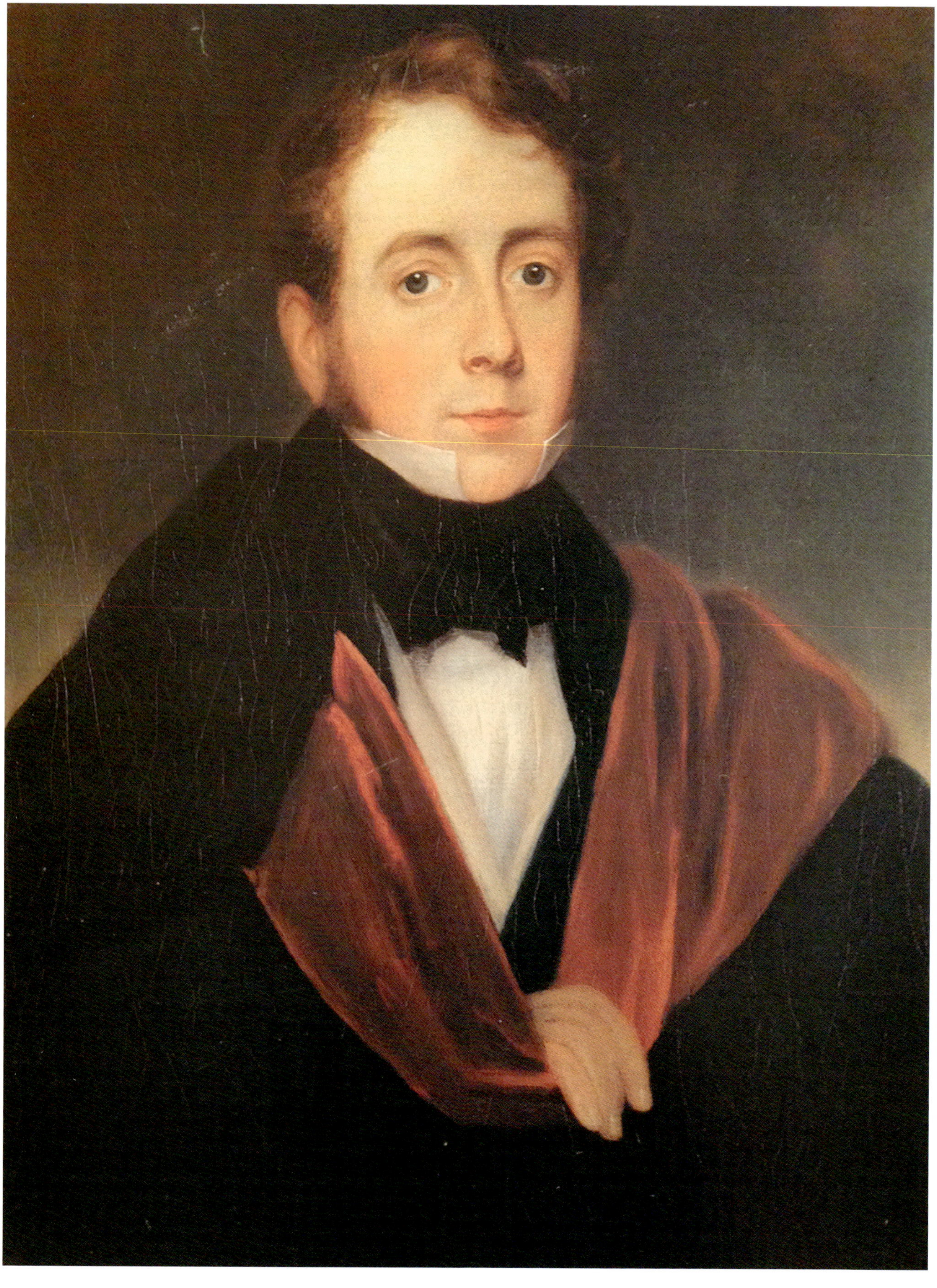

Portrait of Carl Edvard Bolin painted in St. Petersburg by an unknown artist. *Courtesy of Court Jewellers W. A. Bolin*

firm was renamed Bolin and Jahn. Sofia, Jahn's widow, continued to work there, apparently for another 20 years. In 1839 both Carl Edvard Bolin and Sofia Jahn were granted title of Court Jeweler by Appointment to the Tsar.[8]

C. E. Bolin, Court Jeweler

Thanks to his enterprising father-in-law, the future looked bright for Carl Edvard Bolin as a newly minted jeweler. Already in the 1840s, under the reign of Tsar Nicholas I, he enjoyed close ties with the Romanovs. Like Catherine the Great's jewelers—Pauzié, Ador and the Duval brothers—the goldsmith's main occupation was to disassemble older pieces to create new parures, particularly for imperial weddings. In addition, according to Ulla Tillander-Godenhielm, up to the 1880s the workshop produced hundreds of imperial presentation boxes as gifts from the tsars both to Russians and foreigners, and it was the leading manufacturer of diamond portrait badges.[9] At the time, Gustav Fabergé (Carl's father) had just established his business and was still unknown.

In 1845 the emperor's son, Grand Duke Constantine Nikolaevich (1827–92), commissioned Carl Edvard to reset one of Catherine the Great's magnificent cabochon sapphires, said to be the size of a pigeon's egg, into a diamond brooch.[10] A year later, the jeweler received a gold medal on a ribbon of St. Anna and another for the Order of St. Vladimir in 1857.[11]

One early imperial commission was a magnificent pearl and diamond diadem in the form of a Kokoshnik or traditional Russian headdress. Of uncertain date,[12] Bolin's jeweled masterpiece undoubtedly created a sensation when worn at court, as, suspended from diamond arches, its pearl drops swayed with the wearer's every movement. Symbolic both of Russia's Kievan past and of ancient Greece, the jeweled diadem epitomized the Bolin style, combining exquisite design with a line of sumptuous natural pearls.

Meanwhile, Carl Edvard's younger brother, Henrik Conrad the elder, had moved from Stockholm to Helsinki on July 12, 1834, where he apprenticed to a merchant for three and a half years. He arrived in St. Petersburg to join the family business on December 13, 1837.[13] In 1849 the Bolin shop relocated to 71–73 Nevksii Prospect and employed and housed 50 workers of native Russian background, most of whom were illiterate and trained by foreign masters.[14]

International Exhibitions

In 1851 Bolin & Jahn participated in the Great Exhibition of Industry of All Nations in London, which was to catapult them to international fame. More popularly known as the Crystal Palace Exhibition, this grand affair, the first of its kind, featured jewelers of great stature among thousands of exhibitors. Britain and France sent close to 60 goldsmiths, including their best and most revered: the British crown jewelers Garrard and Hunt & Roskell, as well as Froment-Maurice, Lemonnier, and Morel from Paris.

Despite its vast size, the Russian Empire was represented by only two important jewelers: Bolin & Jahn and Kämmerer & Seftingen. Both won medals.[15] The former's display of jeweled bracelets, brooches, demiparures, a *sévigné* (bow brooch with pendant) and a tiara dazzled both the press and the public. One critic deemed Bolin's jewels the finest in the exhibition. Another declared them of even greater interest that the Spanish queen's tiara by Gabriel Lemonnier of Paris.[16]

Bolin's diadem was unlike anything seen in Europe. Set with masses of diamonds of foliate design, it appeared light and feathery. The public marveled at the richness of its gems and the settings themselves. The jewels followed the naturalistic trends of the period—bracelets and brooches fashioned as flowers, knots, grapevines or branches, serpents—combined with remarkable technical excellence. One pin alone was set with over 700 turquoises of various sizes and shapes, and another featured a large natural pearl surrounded by a profusion of diamonds. Considered newcomers in the field of jewelry, the Russians were seen as innovative and masterful, a breath of fresh air compared to long-established French jewelers. The Great Exhibition secured Bolin's reputation as one of the world's finest jewelers.

Back on Russian soil, Bolin's fame continued to spread within the empire's borders. Business increased by collaborating with another St. Petersburg master jeweler, Alexander Butz, whose workshop was nearby—a partnership that lasted until Butz's death in 1856.[17]

The Bolin Imperial Style

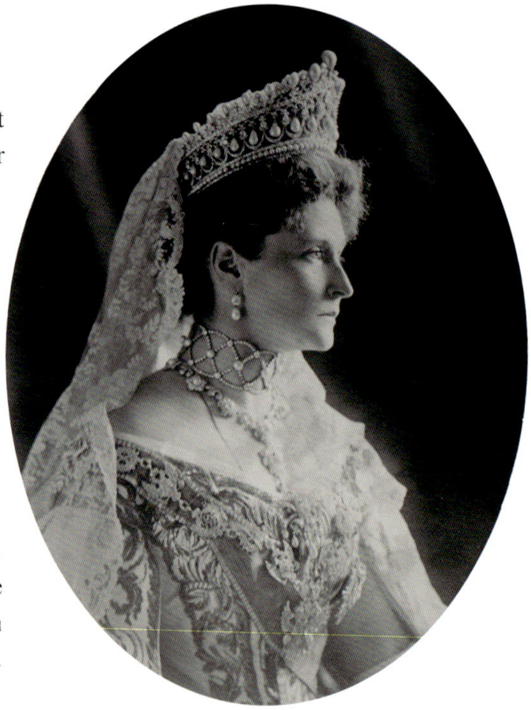

For its imperial patrons, the firm excelled in the classical style inspired by ancient Greece. Bolin's trademark tiara epitomized this, with masses of gems in tiered or garland designs arranged in time-honored fashion. These were enhanced with natural pearl drops, or enormous emeralds, the deepest sapphires, Burmese rubies, all in profusion and graceful settings. How better to evoke the sumptuous splendor of Europe's wealthiest and most lavish imperial court?

Like most 19th-century European jewelers, Carl Edvard Bolin experimented with various historical styles for his stock in trade, such as snuffboxes, tiepins, cuff links, brooches, pendants, rings and bracelets.[18] Naturalistic designs continued to attract interest. In the All-Russian Industrial Artistic Exhibition in St. Petersburg in 1870, Bolin displayed a large diadem designed as trailing ivy profusely set with diamonds, almost invisibly set. This technique would become a hallmark of Bolin, one that workmaster Sophia Schwan would later perfect. Twelve years later, for the 1882 Fine Arts Exhibition in Moscow, the jeweler designed a diamond bird brooch in the 16th-century Florentine style, an amethyst-and-diamond pectoral cross and a luxurious tiara worth 120,000 rubles. The House of Bolin won top prize.

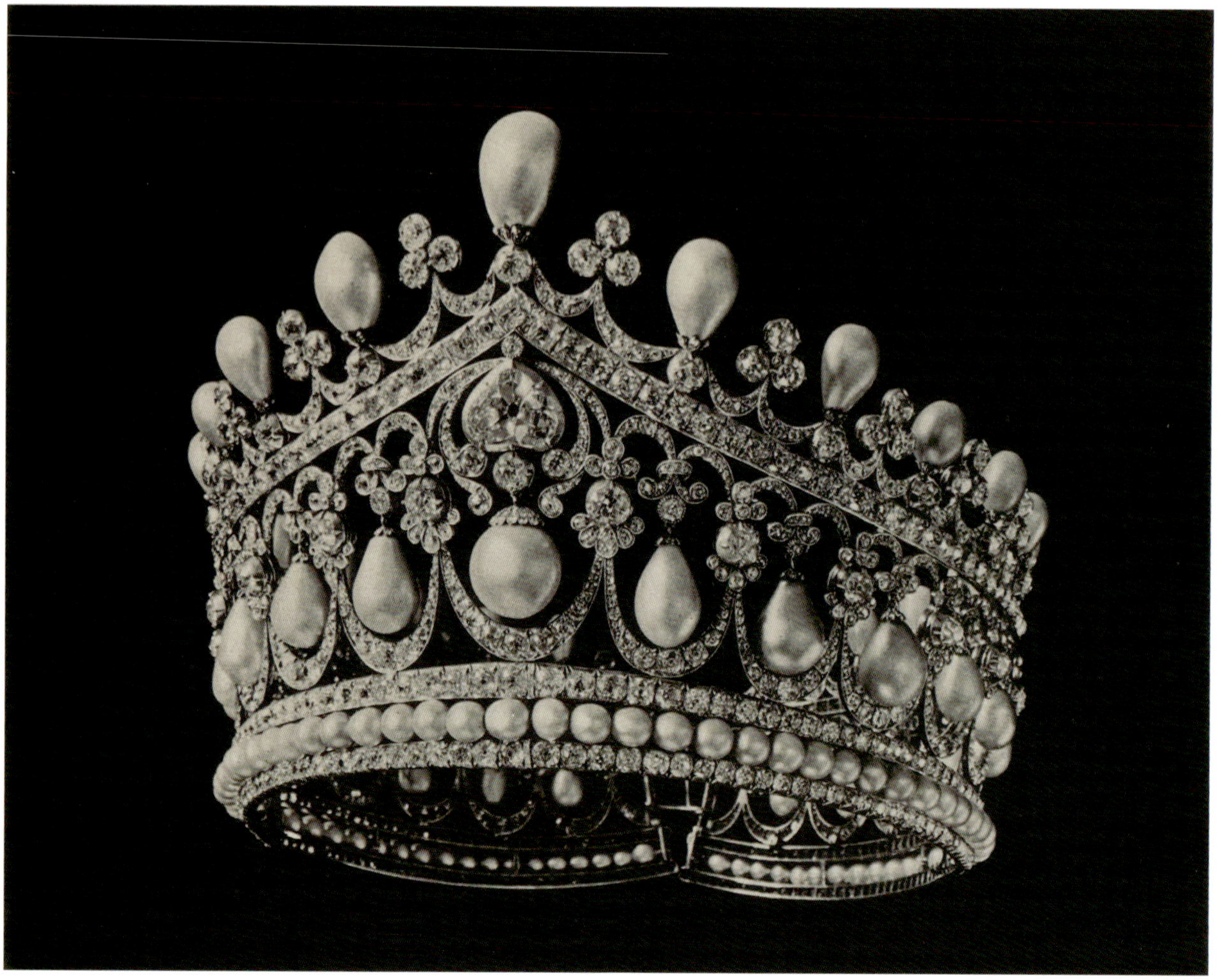

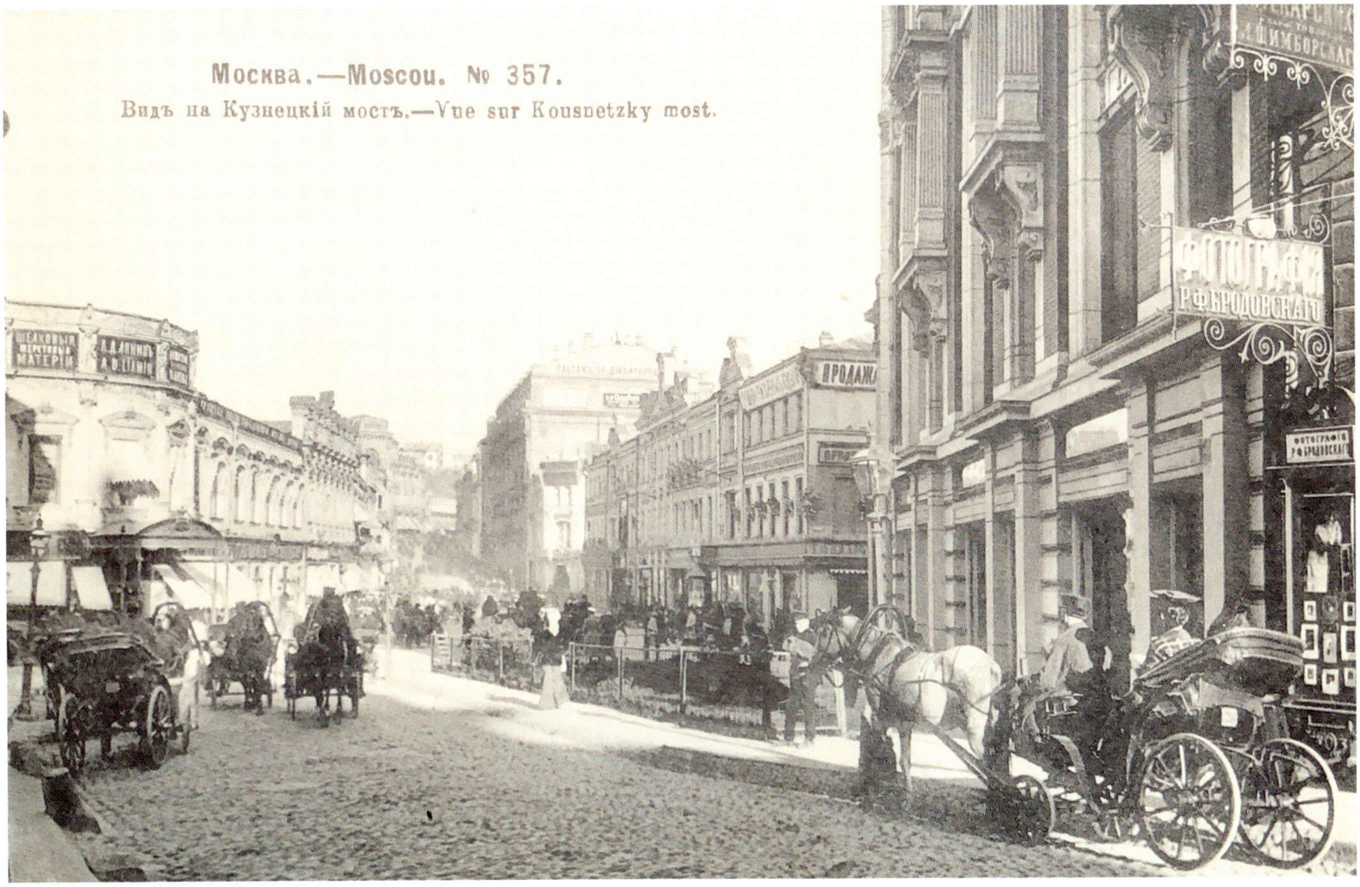

Moscow Branch

Above:
A view of the bustling Kuznetskii Most ca. 1906 in Moscow, the street on which both Bolin and Fabergé had their shops.

Previous page:
Empress Alexandra Fedorovna is seen in full court dress for the opening of the Duma in 1906. She wears a pearl and diamond tiered crown by Bolin, shown below. *Sources: Library of Congress and A. E. Fersman,* Russia's Treasury of Diamonds and Precious Stones *(Moscow: People's Commissariat of Finances, 1925), plate 12*

In 1852, Henrik Conrad Bolin moved to Moscow to open a store there with an English partner, James Stuart Shanks. The firm was named Shanks & Bolin Magasin Anglais (English store). Even in Moscow, jewelers had their names on storefronts and letterheads in French, the language of the court.[19] Established at 4 Lubianka Street, and later (in 1893 or 1894) at 12 Kuznetskii Most, both at the time among Moscow's most prestigious shopping streets, the enterprise was an immediate success.[20] Meanwhile, Henrik Conrad became court jeweler.[21]

The ancient capital had become an important center of trade, and home to a growing middle class with discretionary income. Traditional Old Russian styles prevailed there over the more modern European ones of St. Petersburg. At the same time, the best silversmiths lived in Moscow. Although a jeweler by profession, Henrik Conrad turned his talents to the silver trade. Bolin's Moscow branch became known for its focus on women's accessories and, later, silver-enameled art nouveau items, although it also stocked jewels from St. Petersburg. By appealing to newly wealthy merchants, the shop had a broad client base.

The Crimean War of 1853–56 caused much hardship in Russia. Pitting the empire against four countries, including France and England, and ending in the siege of Sevastopol, it was an uncertain time for most citizens, including the wealthy owners of Crimean estates. Carl Edvard Bolin cleverly adapted to changing conditions. One way of reassuring concerned clients over potential losses of their Crimean estates was to offer to repurchase their jewels at full price, which had the desired effect of enticing these grateful clients to buy more rather than sell their Bolin jewels.[22]

1860s–70s Renewed Growth

The reign of Tsar Alexander II (1855–81) witnessed a new interest in domestic gold and jewelry, and Bolin was there to ride that wave. By then, St. Petersburg had over 300 goldsmiths employing thousands of workers.[23] New advances in mining technology saw an increase in diamond production, which enabled St. Petersburg–based jewelers to make their wares more accessible. In addition to gems, Siberia and the Urals yielded enormous deposits of gold. Native rose gold (*chenvonnoe zoloto*), which had more copper, and cabochon-cut (domed) rather than faceted gemstones became popular, both in Moscow and St. Petersburg. The cabochon cut deepened gem color, and small rose diamonds served as accents, a style that Carl Fabergé would favor decades later.

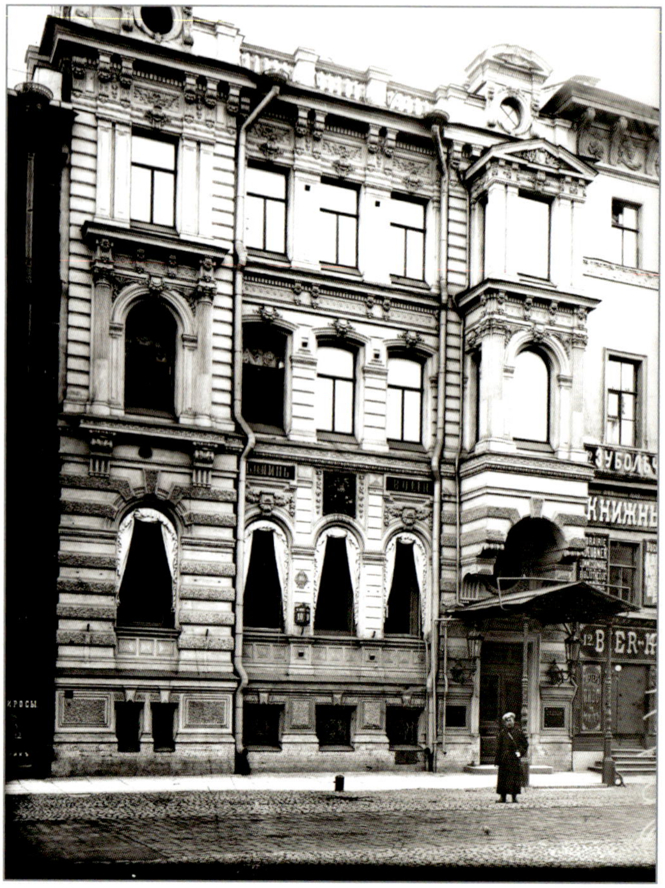

Bolin's St. Petersburg store ca. 1900. Its discreet facade shows the company name in Cyrillic and Latin, flanking a Romanov eagle. The salon was on the second floor. *Courtesy of Central State Archive of Film and Photographs in St. Petersburg*

The Bolin brothers purchased a house at 10 Bolshaia Morskaia Street in 1869, which became their St. Petersburg store. At the head of the imperial capital's famous diamond row and only steps from the Palace Square, it soon attracted the Russian aristocracy. Clients were invited to take tea in a private salon on the second floor, where they could calmly inspect designs or commission new jewels from earlier ones. Adding to its exclusivity, the shop rarely displayed its wares.[24] One can still see the name "Bolin" in Latin letters etched in the original facade today.

King of the Parure

The mid-19th century also saw the rise of the parure. Comprising a necklace, a tiara and a pair of earrings, parures might also include brooches, bracelets, rings, stomachers, pendants and more. As backs of mountings were now opened to let light shine through gemstones, jewels became lighter, and more could be worn in ever-greater combinations. The House of Bolin catered to the growing demand for ostentatious luxury and was the imperial capital's leading jeweler until the late 19th century.[25]

When Carl Edvard died in 1864, his sons Edvard (1842–1926) and Gustav (1844–1916) became principals and the business continued to grow. Following in the tradition of their grandfather, Andreas Römpler, both served as official appraisers to the Cabinet of His Imperial Majesty as well court jewelers, titles they would retain until the Revolution of 1917. As demand rose, Bolin began to sell jewels from other sources, including the Finnish-born jeweler Tillander.[26]

After 1865, court jewelers became subject to increasingly higher standards. The title was bestowed only on the owner, not the firm, and was not transferable. The jeweler had to have completed court commissions for a continuous period of eight to ten years, have displayed superior workmanship, and have charged reasonable prices (see "The Tsar's Jewelers").[27] In March of that year, the imperial family commissioned a tiara and additional jewels for the wedding of Tsarevich Alexander Aleksandrovich to Princess Dagmar of Denmark.[28] In 1870 Bolin participated in the exhibition of manufactures in St. Petersburg, further expanding its renown.

But it was the year 1874 that proved pivotal for crown jewelers C. E. Bolin. First, Tsar Alexander II ordered the now-famous lavish Burmese ruby and diamond parure for the wedding of his daughter, Grand Duchess Maria Aleksandrovna, to Alfred Duke of Edinburgh. The set consisted of a coronet, several brooches, a ring, a pair of earrings, a necklace and a bracelet (see the following four pages).[29] Bolin then created a magnificent pearl-and-diamond kokoshnik for the wedding of

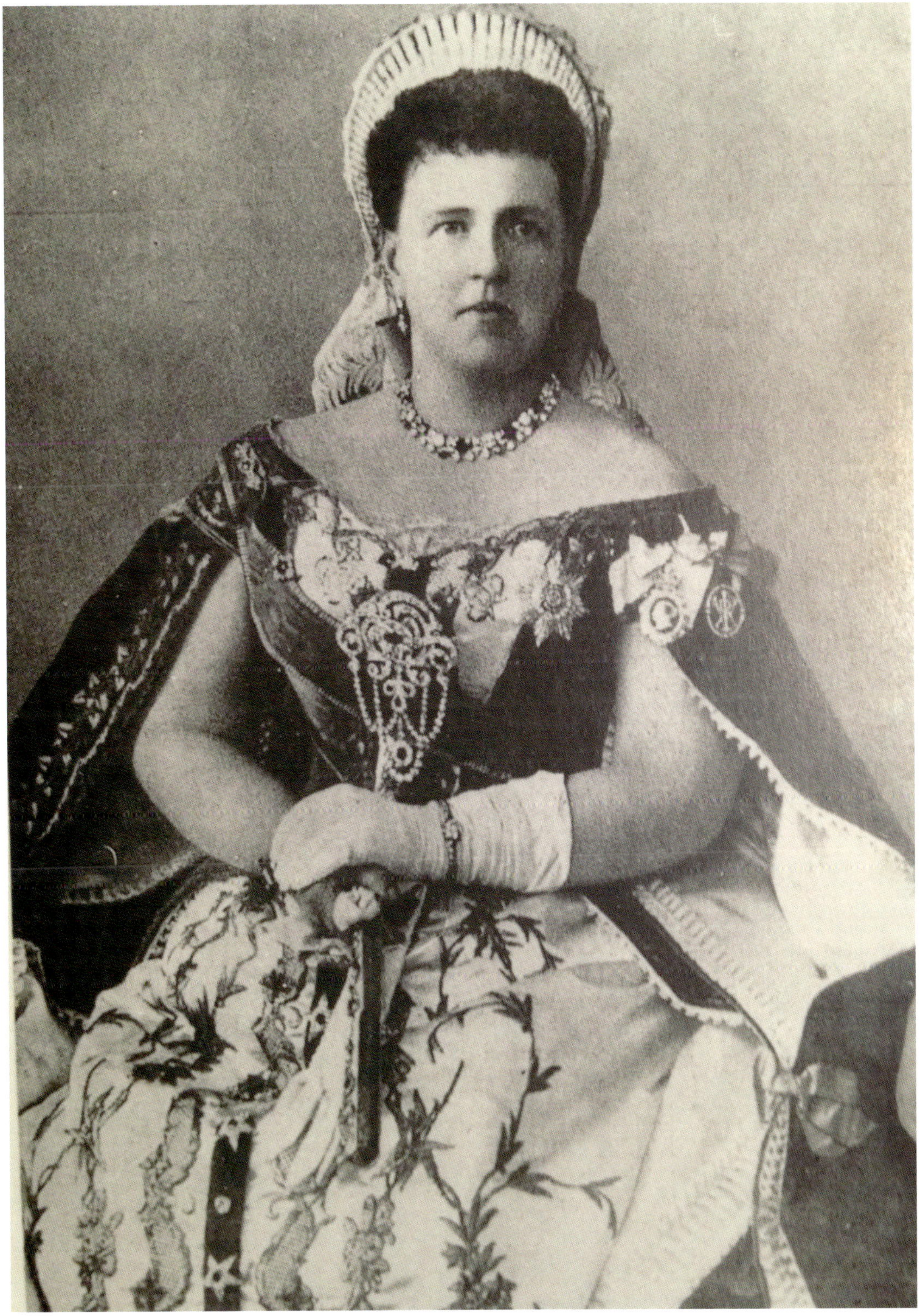

Above and following three pages:
This Bolin diamond and ruby parure, which was made for the wedding of Grand Duchess Maria Aleksandrovna to Alfred the Duke of Edinburgh in 1874, reappeared at auction in Geneva in the 1970s almost in its entirety. The sale included a tiara, a necklace, three brooches, a bracelet, a pendant, a pair of earrings and a ring. The grand duchess is seen wearing the necklace. *© 1978 Christie's Images Ltd.*

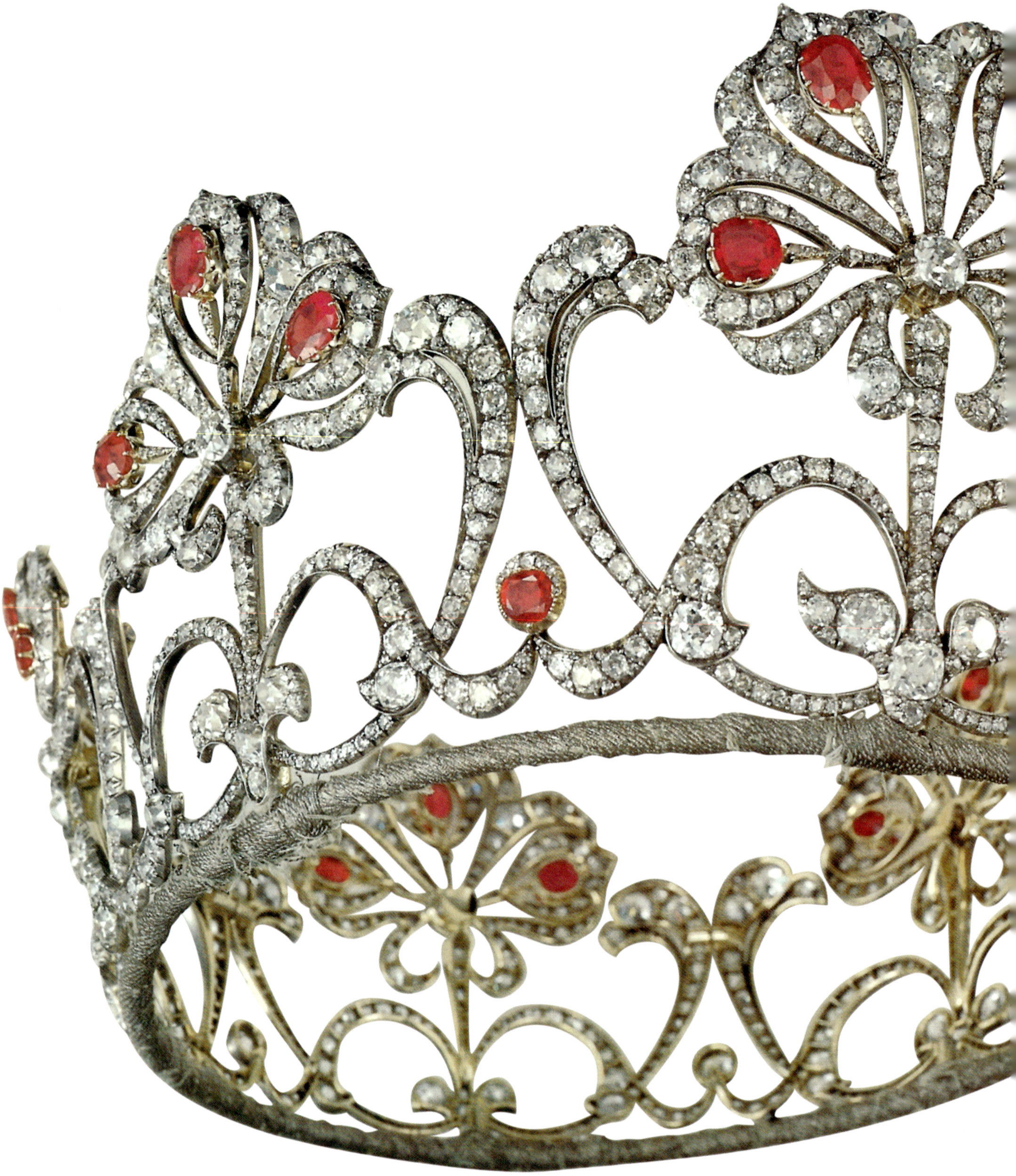

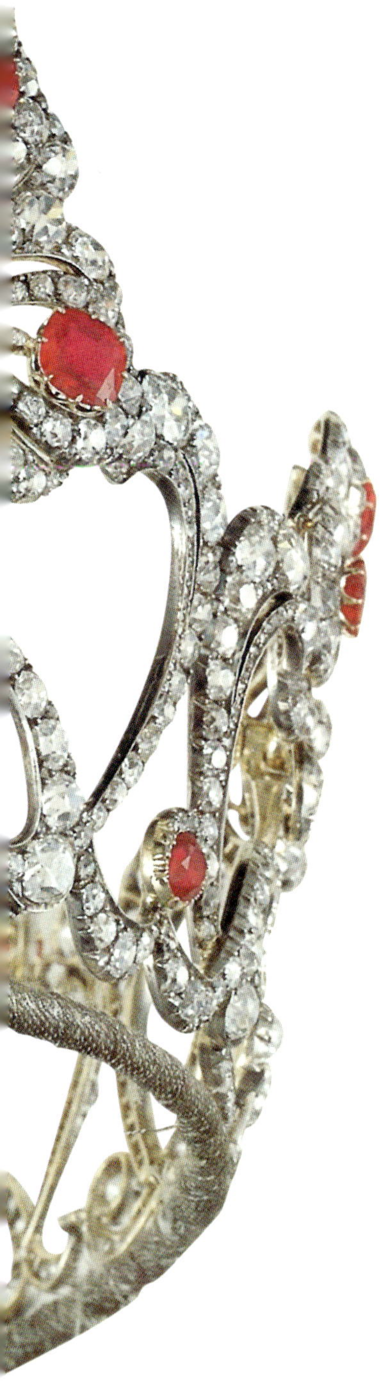

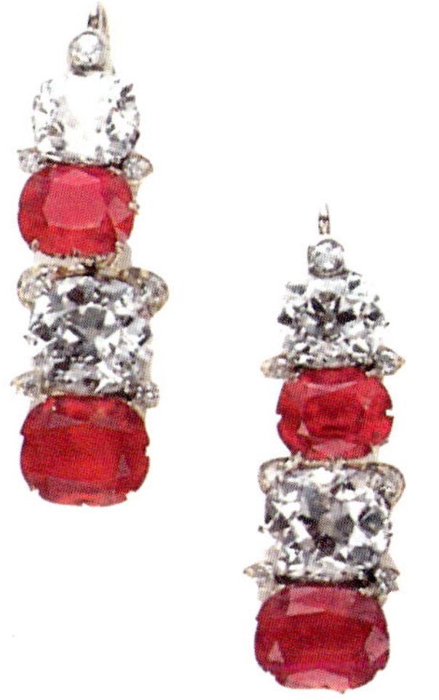

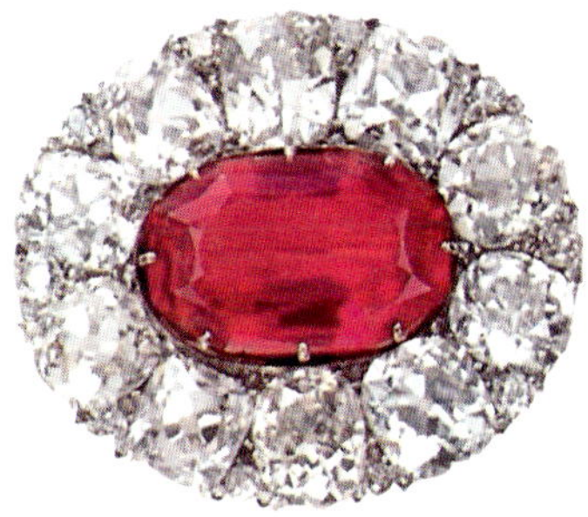

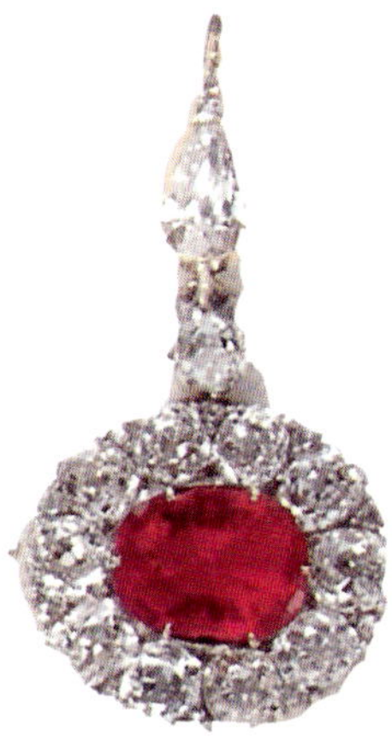

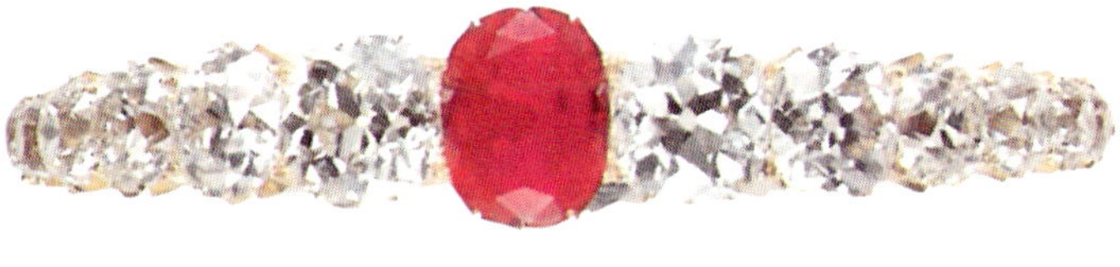

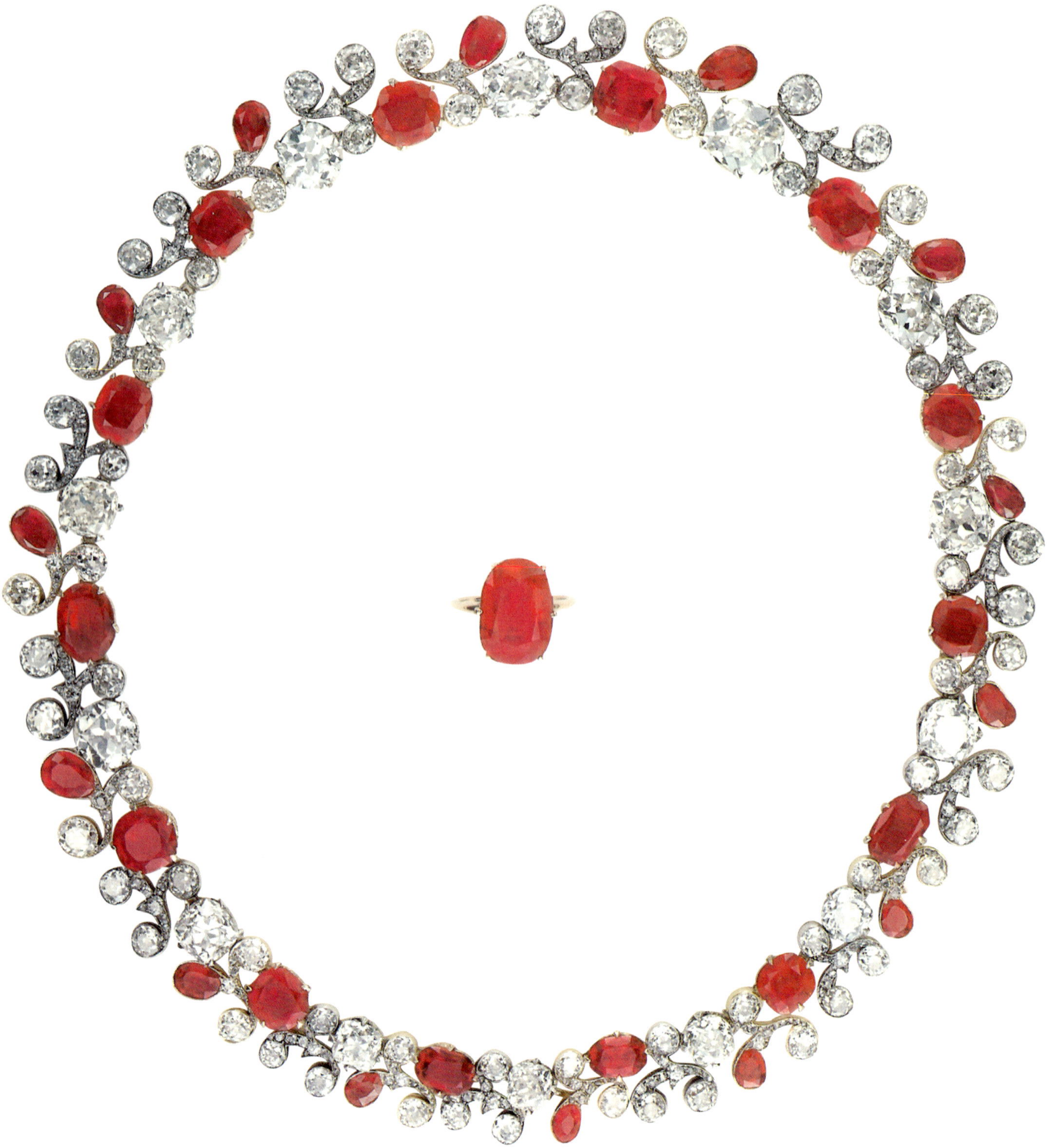

Grand Duchess Maria Pavlovna of Russia, née Duchess of Mecklenburg, to Grand Duke Vladimir Aleksandrovich, son of Tsar Alexander II. So successful was this design that, it is said, when the grand duchess visited Cartier, she left the tiara with the Parisian jewelers, who made three copies of it.[30] Among other presentation jewels, it would awaken an ardent passion in the grand duchess that continued all her life. According to David Chavchavadze, "Jewelery (sic) was a particular concern of Marie Pavlovna, and she assembled a collection of diamonds, emeralds, pearls and rubies that could be matched only by the Crown Jewels themselves."[31]

The grand duke himself also became one of Bolin's long-standing clients. At the Moscow Pan Russian Exhibition of 1892, he bought yet another tiara of pearls and diamonds. Rediscovered in the Swedish Foreign Office in Stockholm in 2008 and auctioned in London in 2009, Vladimir Aleksandrovich's personal collection contained several pairs of Bolin cuff links, along with an amusing silver cigarette case, its cover inscribed *assez d'enfants* (no more children) by Finikov, Bolin's chief St. Petersburg designer.

In 1894, Tsar Alexander III's daughter, Grand Duchess Xenia Aleksandrovna, married Alexander Mikhailovich of Russia. In his memoirs, *Once a Grand Duke*, Alexander describes his wife's wedding gifts as being by "Bolin, the best craftsman of St. Petersburg."[32] Since the bride was the daughter of a reigning emperor with access to the imperial treasury, the groom and dowager empress, Maria Fedorovna chose Bolin, Nicholls & Ewing and Fabergé to refashion select crown jewels into wedding jewels. Bolin supplied the most important: a briolette-cut diamond tiara mounted en tremblant, two large diamond *rivière* necklaces and a lavish ruby-and-diamond suite comprising a tiara, necklace and brooch, among others. Grand Duke Alexander gave Xenia a magnificent diamond-set tiara à la russe (or kokoshnik style), which could be converted into necklace.[33] A similar necklace of fringe design apparently dating from the period of Paul I formed part of the treasures sold by the Soviet government in the 1920s and may have served as inspiration.[34] This lavish *corbeille de marriage* symbolizing the wealth of the Romanov Court cost Tsar Alexander III just under 230,000 rubles.[35] In 1897 the cabinet purchased a brooch from Bolin for Alexander's sister Princess Olga Aleksandrovna for 19,200 rubles.[36]

The Silver Age

At the turn of the 20th century, Bolin continued to create diamond imperial orders, decorations, badges with the tsar's portrait, and crosses, as well as numerous presentation jewels and table items for Nicholas II.[37] Demand was so high that, together, Bolin, Fabergé, Hahn and Köchli produced 158 imperial presentation boxes for the tsar with his diamond cipher.[38]

Despite Carl Fabergé's rising fame, Bolin was still the tsar's jeweler, and it continued to supply personal jewels for the Russian imperial couple, including three diamond ornaments and a black-pearl-and-diamond brooch. When yet another grand duchess, Maria Pavlovna, daughter of Grand Duke Paul Aleksandrovich and Alexandra Georgievna of Greece, married Prince Wilhelm of Sweden in 1908, Bolin supplied a wedding parure, set with emeralds from the treasury of Tsar Alexander II.[39] The following year, the court commissioned a Bolin brooch for Duke Johann Albrecht of Mecklenburg.[40]

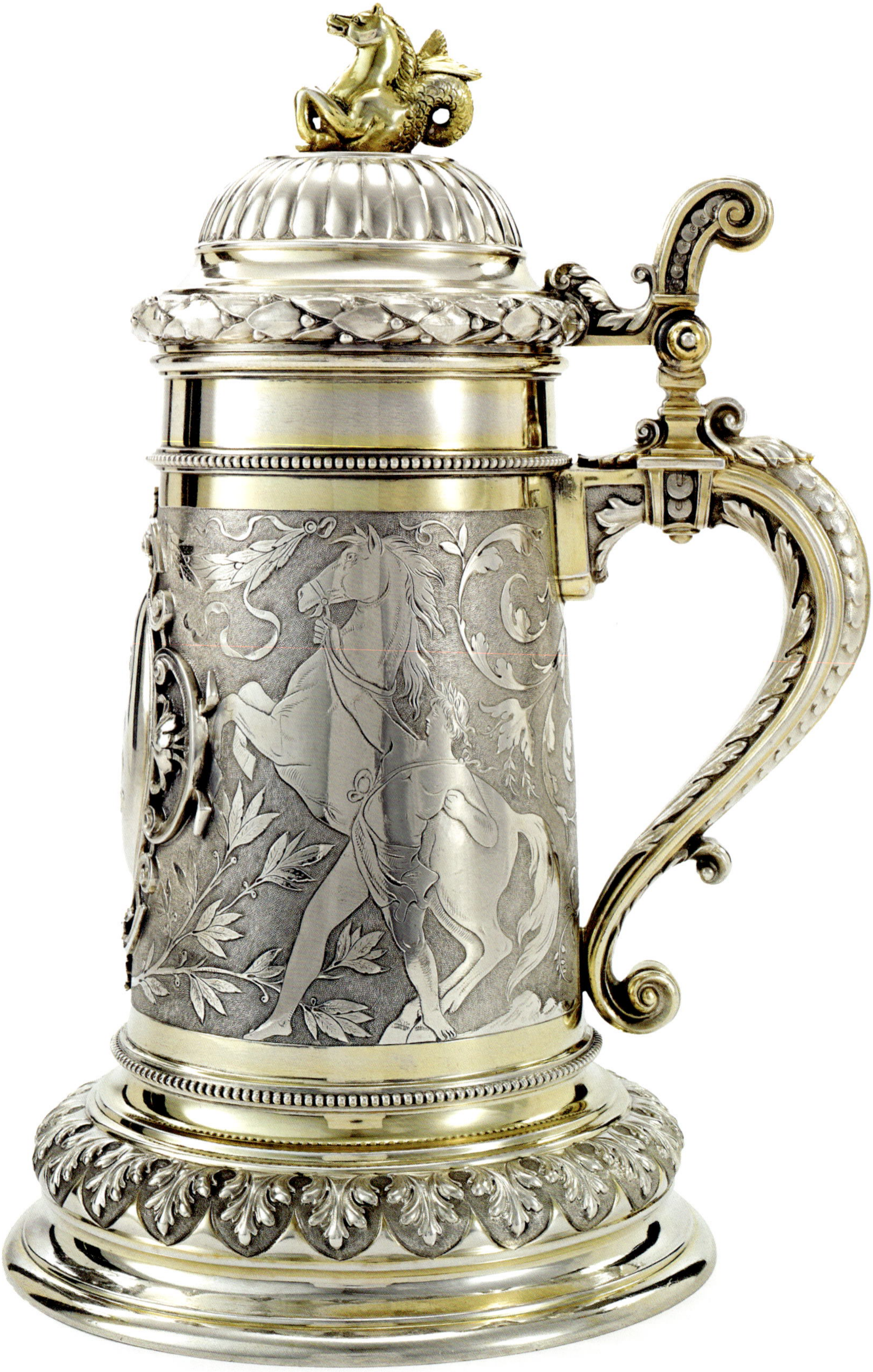

This large silver tankard, which was made by Konstantin Linke in 1893, probably as a special commission, depicts the horse tamers on St. Petersburg's Anichkov Bridge. Linke was in charge of all silver production in Bolin's Moscow branch. *Courtesy of Sotheby's*

Workmasters

The House of Bolin employed its own workmasters, both in Moscow and St. Petersburg. Each used their own hallmark, comprising their initials, either in Cyrillic or Latin, to identify their work.

Robert Schwan was one of Bolin's most talented craftsmen. In 1883, he created a pearl and diamond brooch shaped as a Romanov crown for Tsar Alexander III's coronation, with miniatures of the emperor and his consort, Maria Fedorovna, the daughter of the Danish king Christian IX.[41] Thirty years later, he made a jeweled brooch in the form of the ancient Monomakh crown for the Romanov Tercentenary in 1913.[42] Another beautiful Schwan brooch of scroll design set with a blister pearl surrounded by diamonds was displayed at the 2001 Bolin exhibition in the Moscow Kremlin.[43]

Perhaps Schwan's most memorable creation was a sumptuous cabochon emerald-and-diamond necklace for Empress Alexandra Fedorovna and her sister Elisabeth Fedorovna, circa 1900. As a part of a parure jointly created by Bolin and Fabergé, the tiara (unsigned but also by Bolin) was set with 11 Colombian emeralds weighing just under 100 carats and 225 carats of diamonds. Fabergé's Moscow workmaster, Oskar Pihl, produced the *devant de corsage* (bodice ornament). The three pieces formed part of the crown jewels that E. Fersman catalogued in 1925.[44]

Some of Bolin's most accomplished workmasters were women. Husbands and wives probably worked in tandem, although only men were allowed to become master jewelers. After the masters' death, widows carried on, establishing their own hallmark and excelling in their own right. One such person was Sophia Schwan. Schwan worked exclusively for C. E. Bolin and produced exquisite jewels, such as the star sapphire and diamond brooch circa 1910 (illustrated, page 266). The cushion-cut diamonds in the curved petal-shaped mounting appear to be invisibly set, foreshadowing Van Cleef and Arpel's celebrated *sertie mystérieux* technique introduced in Paris in the 1930s.

Nicholas Chernokov was entrusted with imperial presentation and Romanov jubilee items. Other Bolin workmasters included A. Karpenko and Ivan Flinck, although not much is known about them. Perhaps the most prolific was Vladimir Iakovlevich Finikov, Bolin's chief designer, who had his own workshop at 55 Moika until about 1916. In Moscow, Maria Linke was a Bolin workmaster along with her relative, Konstantin Linke. Maria owned a silver workshop from 1866 to 1894 with 36 employees, where she specialized in silver and enamel and silver-mounted glass table items. St. Petersburg jeweler Lorié also sold items by Linke.

When Henrik Conrad died in 1888, his son, Wilhelm Andreevich, took ownership. It was then that the Moscow branch was renamed C. E. Bolin.[45] The Moscow enterprise flourished; Wilhelm hired both French and German designers and opened offices in London, Paris and Berlin (around 1913, he even ran a summer shop at Bad Homburg, a German resort near Wiesbaden). Soon its Moscow sales almost matched those of the St. Petersburg branch. And while the tsar raised his cousins in the imperial capital to the nobility, Wilhelm declined to become naturalized. He was still a Swedish citizen, which would play a key role in the company's survival beyond the Russian Revolution.

A Triumphant Return

At the onset of the Great War, as borders between the combatants were closed, members of the Bolin branch in St. Petersburg were forced to remain in place. Based in Moscow as a Swedish citizen, however, Wilhelm could move freely between Germany and Sweden. He therefore transferred his inventory first from Moscow to Bad Homburg, and thence to a bank in Stockholm. It wasn't long before the enterprising shopkeeper, with the help of K. A. Wallenberg, a leading Swedish financier and the Swedish foreign minister, opened a shop in Stockholm and immediately became court jeweler to Swedish King Gustav V. In the tradition of the Russian branches, the firm employed various goldsmiths, silversmiths and stone setters and took private orders from its clientele.[46]

The fame of the House of Bolin, Russia's premier 19th-century court jeweler, continues in Sweden. Today, to its illustrious and unparalleled roster of Russian imperial patrons, crown jewelers W. A. Bolin can add three Swedish kings. Still family owned and now under the direction of Christian Bolin, the enterprise continues to thrive in Stockholm's fashionable residential Östermalm district.

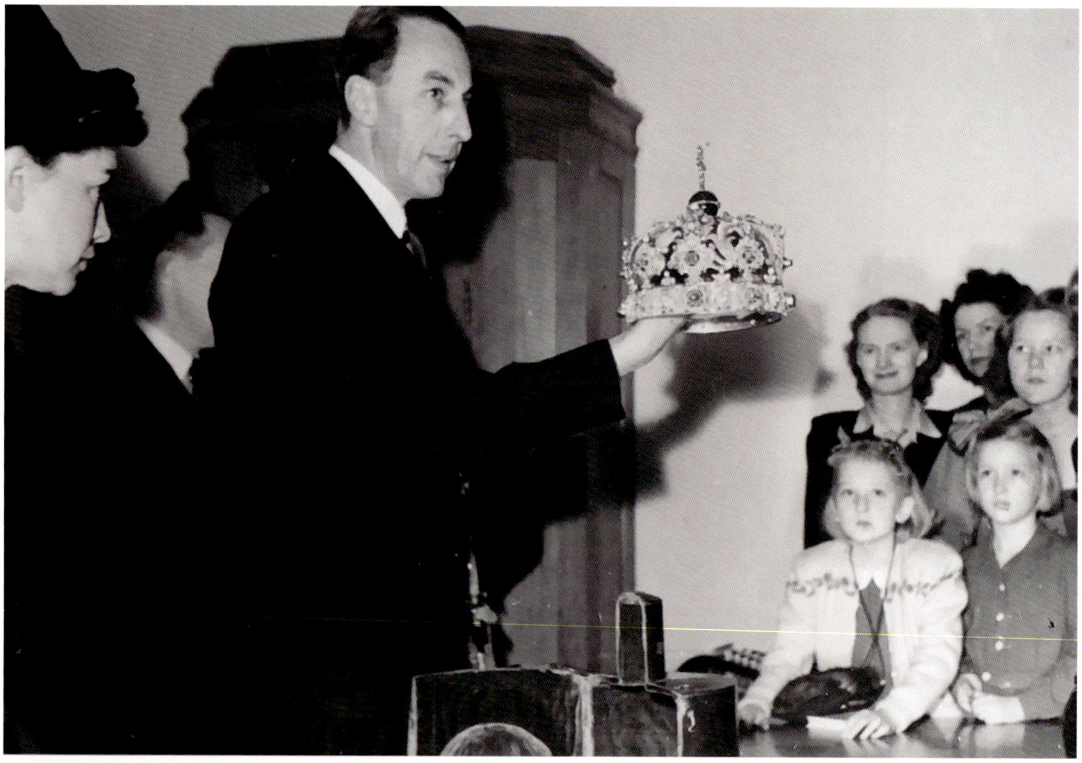

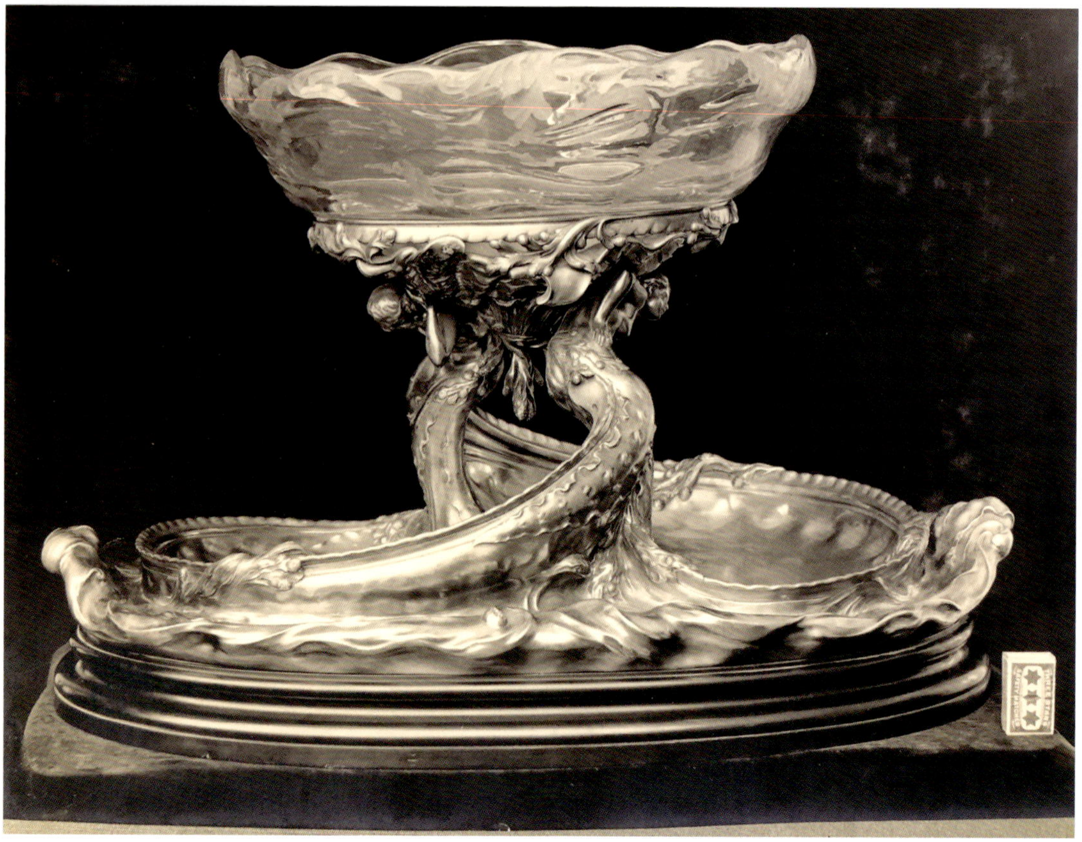

This centerpiece by Konstantin Linke from Bolin's Moscow shop catalogue was displayed at the opening of the Swedish store. Because parts of it were made in Moscow in 1916, then reassembled in Sweden in 1919, the silver bears Swedish hallmarks. Swedish court jeweler Henrik Conrad Bolin Jr. (1892–1986) shows the crown of Queen Maria Eleonora from 1650 to a rapt audience in 1947, on a special occasion when the public was allowed into the Royal Treasury in Stockholm. *From the Bolin family archives, courtesy of Christian Bolin*

NOTES

1. Tillander-Godenhielm, "Russian Imperial Award System," 382.

2. Graham Hughes, *Modern Silver throughout the World, 1880–1967* (London: Studio Vista, 1967), 23.

3. Fersman, *Russia's Treasures*, 28.

4. Geza von Habsburg, *Fabergé Revealed at the Virginia Museum of Fine Arts* (New York: Skira-Rizzoli, 2011), 46. In 1906, the imperial treasury offered over a million rubles worth of unmounted gems for sale. Both Fabergé and Bolin tried to buy these goods, but a French gem merchant, Georges Sachs, outbid them. See Marie E. Betteley, "A Bid for the Best Backfires," Russian Life, March–April 2017: 46–49.

5. Ribbing, *Jewellery & Silver for Tsars*, 22–24. The building was later occupied by Gustav Fabergé and many other famous jewelers.

6. Kuznetsova, *Peterburgskie iuveliry: Dnei Aleksandrovykh*, 253–56.

7. To maintain the title of court jeweler, and eventually to pass it down to her sons-in-law, Römpler's widow, Anna Geralselina, remained the firm's official representative until her death. Ribbing, *Jewellery & Silver for Tsars*, 26.

8. Ribbing, *Jewellery & Silver for Tsars*, 28.

9. Tillander-Godenhielm, "Russian Imperial Award System," 54.

10. Ribbing, *Jewellery & Silver for Tsars*, 38–40. The sapphire went to his daughter, Queen Olga of Greece (1851–1936), who bequeathed it to her granddaughter, Helen of Greece and Denmark (1896–1982). It was sold at Sotheby's London in 1966, but its current whereabouts are unknown.

11. Ribbing, *Jewellery & Silver for Tsars*, 52

12. A. E. Fersman dates it to 1815, during the reign of Alexander I, presumably made for his consort Elizaveta Alekseevna. In more-recent books the tiara is dated ca. 1841. It was lot 117 in Christie's 1927 Russian crown jewels sale, described as a "pearl and brilliant tiara, set with twenty-five large drop pearls in brilliant borders," where it fetched £310. In 1978 it was resold at Sotheby's for over £67,000 to the wife of the president of the Philippines, Imelda Marcos and has since been dismantled.

13. This information is from the archives of the Swedish parish of St. Catherine's in St. Petersburg and was kindly provided by Christian Bolin.

14. Ribbing, *Jewellery & Silver for Tsars*, 36.

15. *Official Catalogue of the Great Exhibition of the Works of Industry of All Nations, 1851* (London: Spicer, 1851), 301; Judy Rudoe, "Jewellery at the Great Exhibition," *American Society of Jewelry Historians Newsletter* 20 (May 2003): 17–18.

16. Ribbing, *Jewellery & Silver for Tsars*, 40–42. Bolin's prices were high, but not enough to discourage early sales. The firm sold a bracelet to a client described as a leading connoisseur and owner of the Hope Collection of precious stones. This probably describes the crown jewelers Hunt & Roskell of New Bond Street, who had secured the Hope Collection, including the 177-carat Hope Diamond, for the exhibition. The famous dealer's own contribution to the Great Exhibition of 1851 included a magnificent diamond set floral bouquet.

17. Ribbing, *Jewellery & Silver for Tsars*, 50–52.

18. The Bolin family owns a gold rococo-style box by Jahn & Bolin from around 1840. The Russian Museum in Moscow has a flexible gold serpent bracelet by Bolin from ca. 1850.

19. Ribbing, *Jewellery & Silver for Tsars*, 46.

20. According to Henrik Conrad Jr.'s personal notes in his family's archives, he worked for his brother from 1837 to the early 1850s. I am grateful to Christian Bolin for this information as well.

21. Solodkoff, *Russian Gold and Silverwork*, 191.

22. Ribbing, *Jewellery & Silver for Tsars*, 44.

23. Ulla Tillander-Godenhielm and Michael Wynne Ellis, "Tillander," in *The Master Jewellers*, ed. Kenneth A. Snowman (New York: Abrams, 1990), 110.

24. Ribbing, *Jewellery & Silver for Tsars*, 52.

25. Habsburg, *Fabergé Revealed*, 44.

26. Ribbing, *Jewellery & Silver for Tsars*, 54.

27. Skurlov, *Postavchiki imperatorskogo dvora*, 4–7.

28. Ribbing, *Jewellery & Silver for Tsars*, 54.

29. The parure reappeared almost in its entirety at Christie's in Geneva in 1978. The necklace resurfaced in 1998, while the other items remain at large, and the tiara apparently sold again in the 1980s and was taken apart (see "Bolin Market").

30. It is unclear whether the grand duchess placed the order or Cartier took the initiative. The Bolin tiara now forms part of the British crown jewels. Grand Duchess Elena, Maria Pavlovna's daughter, sold it to Queen Mary, consort of King George V. The tiara is sometimes illustrated with emerald drops rather than pearls and is one of Queen Elizabeth II's favorites.

31. David Chavchavadze, *The Grand Dukes* (New York: Atlantic International, 1990), 108.

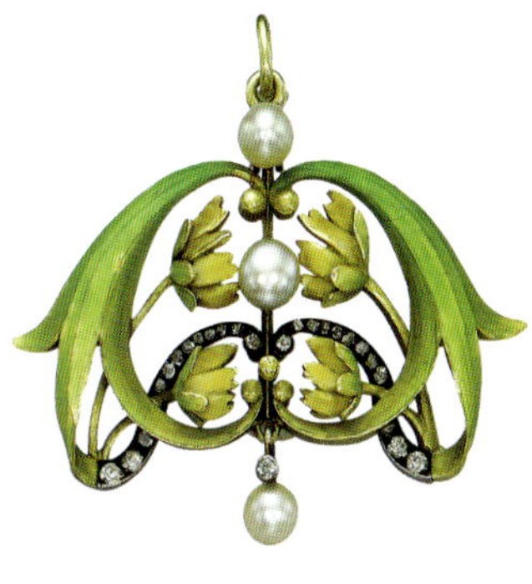

This Bolin Art Nouveau enameled pendant was possibly designed by European artisans working for the firm. @ *2007 Christie's Images Ltd.*

The fame of the House of Bolin, Russia's premier 19th-century court jeweler, continues in Sweden. Today, to its illustrious and unparalleled roster of Russian imperial patrons, crown jewelers W. A. Bolin can add three Swedish kings.

32. Grand Duke Alexander Mikhailovich Romanov, *Once a Grand Duke* (New York: Farrar & Rhinehart, 1932), 132.

33. The jewelry that Grand Duchess Xenia owned from 1880 to 1912 was inventoried in two albums, all hand-drawn and inscribed. The album set was sold at Bonham's London in 2011.

34. Fersman, *Russia's Treasures*, plate 21.

35. Hapsburg, *Fabergé Revealed*, 45.

36. Rossiiskii gosudarstvennyi istoricheskii arkhiv (hereafter RGIA), fond (f, *fund*) 468, opis (o, *register*) 8 delo (d, *file*) 274, list (l, *sheet*) 9.

37. Tillander-Godenhielm, "Russian Imperial Award System," 384.

38. Ibid., 179.

39. Munn, *Tiaras*, 272, plate 246. The suite later formed part of a parure worn by Princess Maria of Romania, consort of King Alexander II of Yugoslavia. The necklace was remodeled by Cartier and the tiara was acquired by its current owners, Van Cleef and Arpels of Paris, in 1949. The firm replaced the emeralds with paste imitations.

40. RGIA, f 468, o 8, d 1036.

41. Ribbing, *Jewellery & Silver for Tsars*, 68–69. At least two of these were made for this occasion, perhaps more. One was presented to Queen Louise of Denmark (1843–1912), wife of King Frederick VIII, which is now in the Danish Royal Collection, Rosenborg Castle. Queen Louise also owned another Schwan pearl-and-diamond jewel. This was shown in a Fabergé exhibition in 1986 in Munich. Geza von Habsburg, *Hofjuwelier der Zaren* (Tübingen, Germany: Wasmuth, 1986), 287, no. 564.

42. Geza von Habsburg, Fabergé (Geneva, Switzerland: Habsburg, Feldman Editions, 1987), 287, n. 563.

43. Christian Bolin and Pavel Bulatov, eds., *W. A. Bolin in Russia: Court Jeweller late XIX-early XX centuries*. (Moscow: Novyi Ermitazh-odin, 2001), 159.

44. Fersman, *Russia's Treasures*, table LXXI.

45. Ulla Tillander-Godenhielm, *Jewels from Imperial St. Petersburg* (London: Unicorn, 2012), 121.

46. Ribbing, *Jewellery & Silver for Tsars*, 104, 106, 108.

History

5

CARL AUGUST HAHN: THE DIAMOND KING

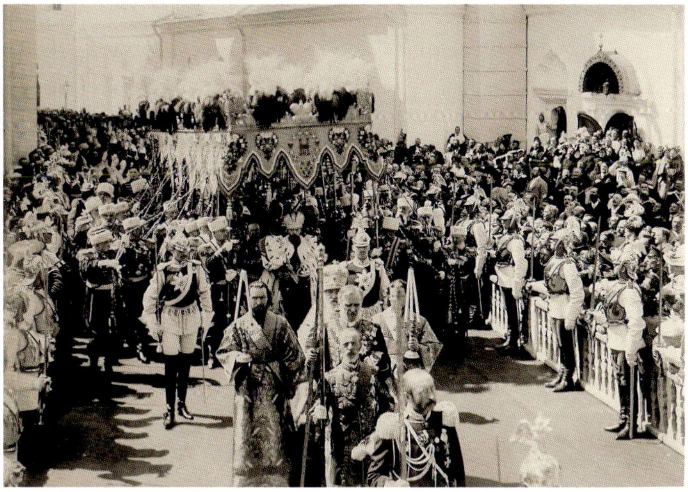

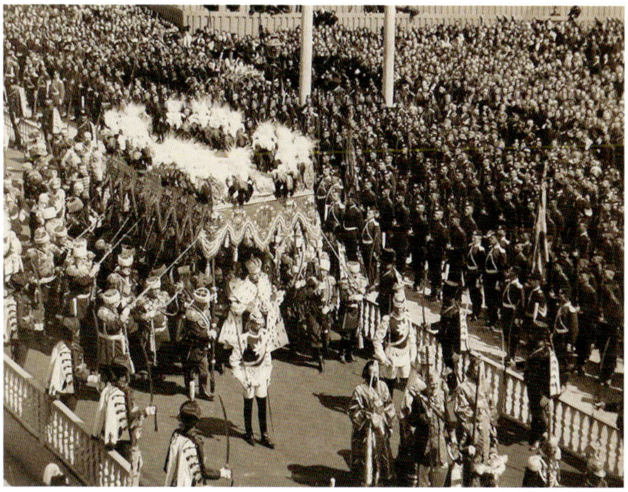

Nicholas II coronation procession.
Source: Wikimedia Commons

The coronation of Nicholas Aleksandrovich on May 14, 1896, in the Assumption Cathedral of the Moscow Kremlin dazzled the world. Costing millions of rubles, the ceremony was to be the final and most extravagant of Romanov coronations: kings, crown princes, presidents and other heads of state from around the world traveled to the old capital to participate in the 20-day festivity.

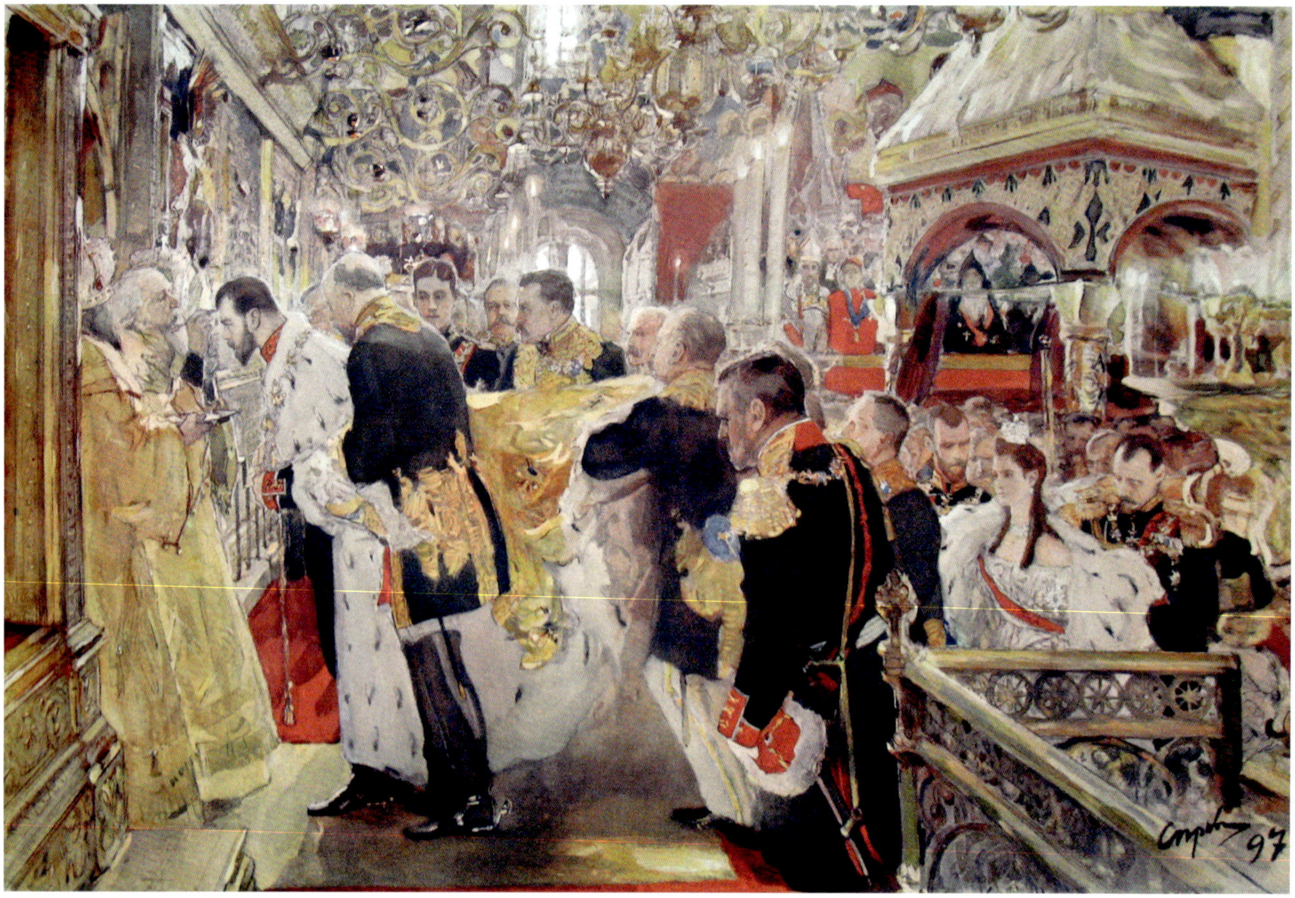

Valentin Serov, The Coronation of Nicholas II.
Source: Wikimedia Commons

As tradition dictated, for the grand ceremony, senior military and government ministers surrounded by Grenadier Palace Guards transported the imperial regalia from the Armory Chamber to the Grand Kremlin Palace. These included the magnificent 18th-century gold and sapphire orb and the Orlov diamond-capped scepter, foremost symbols of the tsars' power. The sovereign wore an ermine-trimmed robe, his shoulders encircled by a resplendent diamond-set collar of the Imperial Order of St. Andrew, and on his head, weighing over 5 pounds, rested Catherine the Great's famous coronation crown by court jeweler Jérémie Pauzié, set with just under 5,000 diamonds and a pigeon-blood 400-carat red spinel (see page 226).

Having donned a similar ermine robe on which rested a smaller diamond St. Andrew chain, Nicholas's consort, Alexandra Fedorovna, would kneel before the new sovereign to receive her own crown. The latter led to some complications. According to the Pauline Laws, the regulations of the House of Romanov that Emperor Paul I had decreed in 1797, the tsar's mother enjoyed precedence over her daughter-in-law, a privilege she insisted on invoking. Still good looking at the age of 47, Marie Fedorovna was passionately fond of fine

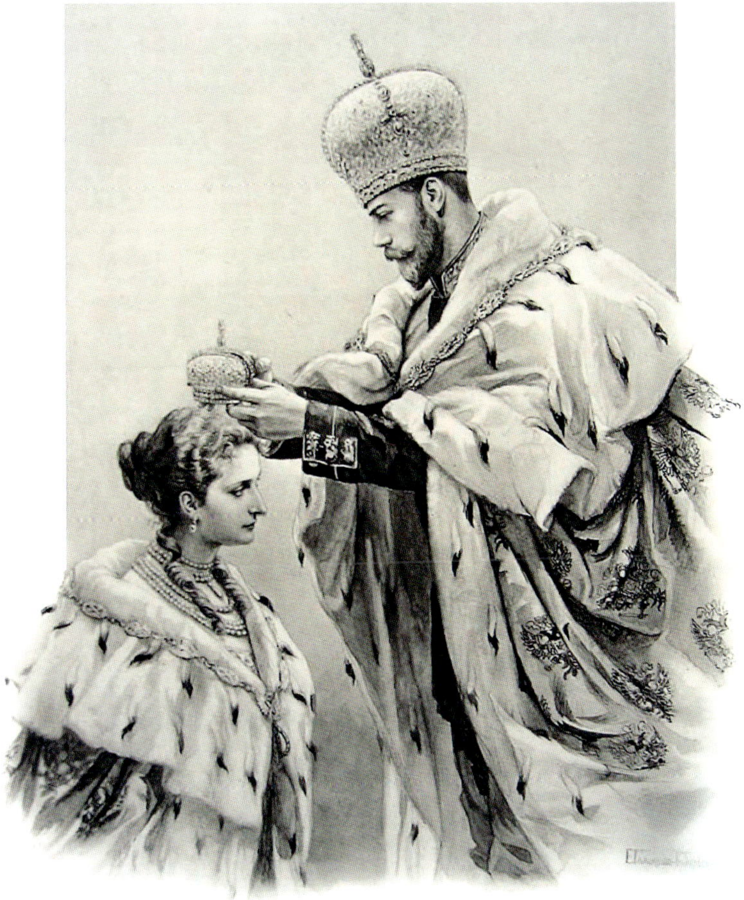

E. P. Samokish-Sudkovskaia, Emperor Nicholas II crowning Empress Alexander Fedorovna, May 14, 1896. The crown is by Carl Hahn. *Source: V. S. Krivchenko,* Koronatsionnyi sbornik *(St. Petersburg: Ekspeditsii zagotovlenniia gosudarstvennykh bumag, 1899), 1:230*

jewelry, and she was not about to attend the ceremony without the same magnificent diamond crown she had worn for her own coronation in 1881.[1]

There was no other suitable jewel in the imperial treasury's reserves. So what would the Empress-to-be Alexandra Fedorovna wear for this momentous occasion, probably the most important of her life? Thus, for the first time in decades, a new diamond crown was created. For this prestigious commission, the imperial cabinet chose neither Fabergé nor Bolin, the leading court jeweler, but an Austrian-born master goldsmith, Carl August Ferdinand Hahn (1836–99).[2] It was to be the highlight of his illustrious career as jeweler to the tsars. Unlike the two coronation crowns, which were set with diamonds from the imperial treasury, Hahn himself provided the diamonds.[3]

Today, despite an astounding tenure as court jeweler both for Tsars Alexander III and Nicholas II, the name Carl Hahn means little to us. Yet, the master goldsmith created some of the finest Russian jewels, diamond portrait badges and imperial presentation boxes ever made. It was to Hahn and his head workmaster, Carl Blank, that Tsar Nicholas II turned for the largest number of lavish diamond insignias or decorations for the court, including the highest orders, for elaborate diamond crosses destined for metropolitans, and for presentation rings adorned with his diamond cipher. Records indicate Nicholas purchased more diamond jewelry from Hahn than from any other goldsmith, including Fabergé.[4]

While the date of Hahn's arrival from Austria to St. Petersburg is unclear, by 1873 he had founded the C. Hahn firm at 26 Nevskii Prospect and lived in the nearby rectory of the Swedish Church. Eventually he would add two large workshops on that fashionable thoroughfare to his name—at numbers 26 and 42.[5] While few items and virtually no jewelry survive from the Hahn firm in the early period, by the 1890s, thanks to a surge of patronage by the court, the workshops were buzzing with activity.

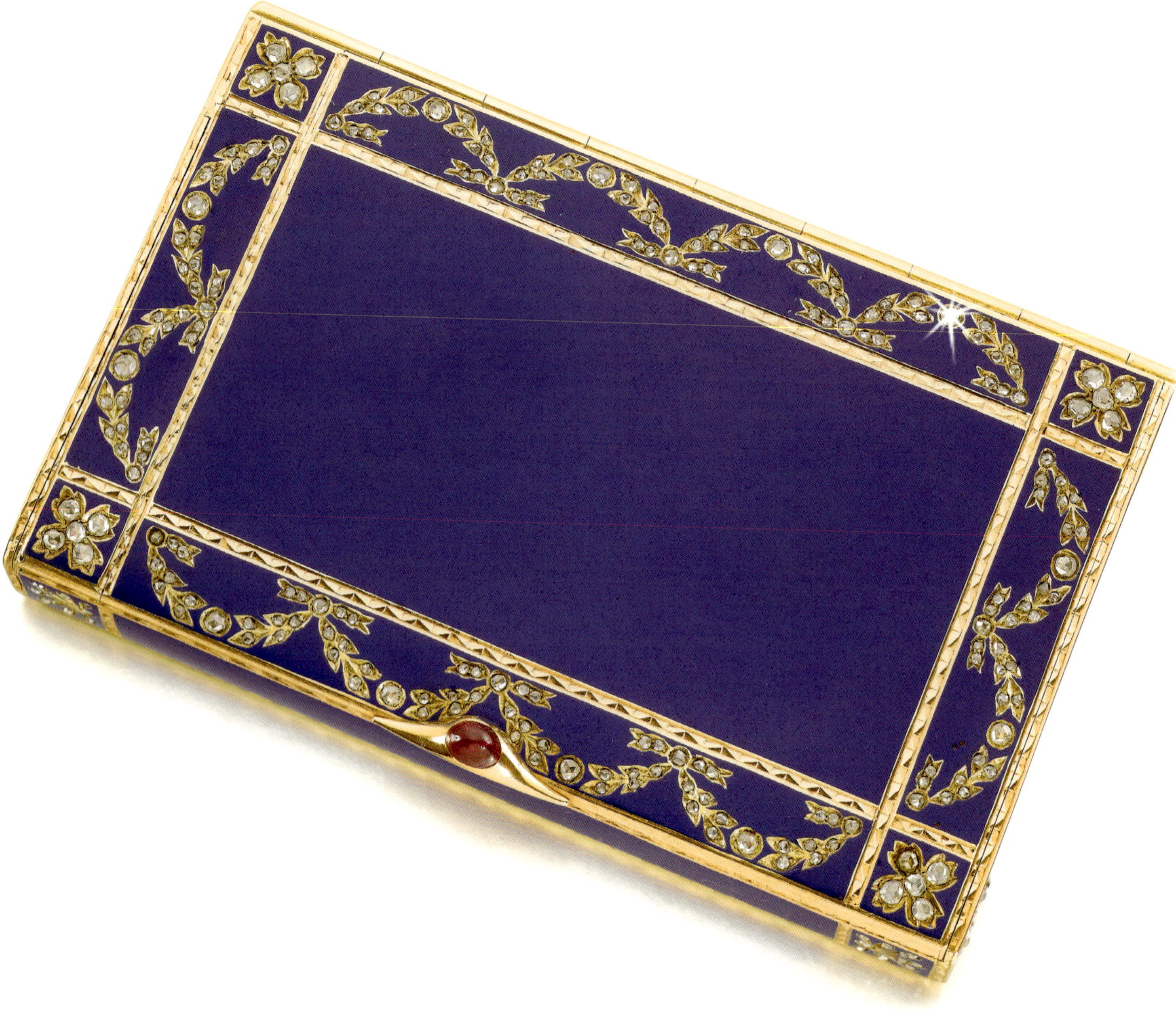

Empress Alexandra gave this Hahn enamel cigarette case to her new husband Nicholas II on the first day of 1895.
Courtesy Sotheby's

Hahn's Rise to Fame

The year 1895 proved busy, starting with the very first day. For New Year's Day, Empress Alexandra purchased from Hahn a beautiful, deep-blue enamel cigarette case for her new husband. Adorned on the border with diamond-set swags in the neoclassical taste, it was inscribed *For darling Nicky from Alix* and dated *January 1, 1895* (the couple almost always corresponded in English).[6] That same month, the workshop produced an Imperial Order and Star of St. Alexander Nevskii, a diamond monogram for a snuffbox, 11 rings and five tobacco boxes.[7] Hahn also made a jeweled cross on the occasion of the christening of Grand Duchess Olga Nikolaevna, the imperial couple's first born.[8]

The tsar had already entrusted Hahn with creating an imperial presentation box for her birth, to be presented to Alexandra's *accoucheur*, Dr. Dmitrii Ott. In May the Austrian jeweler completed two bracelets, one with rubies and diamonds, 19 boxes, three brooches, one fan and 11 pairs of buttons, all commissioned as gifts for Countess Elizaveta Andreevna Vorontsova Dashkova (1845–1924).[9] For this single order in 1895, Hahn received 22,759 rubles, a handsome sum, considering it was three times the cost of two Fabergé imperial eggs delivered by Carl Fabergé that same year.[10]

The jeweler was never busier than in the final decade of his life. As business grew, so did his stature. Or vice versa. In 1896, after becoming a Russian citizen and a Knight of the Order of St. Stanislaus, 3rd Class—no doubt as a result of producing Empress Alexandra's magnificent coronation crown—Carl Hahn received the three highest honors bestowed on goldsmiths: purveyor to the court, appraiser to the imperial cabinet and hereditary honorary citizen. When Hahn died in 1899, his widow, Adele Marie (or Adelaide), continued the business for two years, before passing the firm on to her son, Dmitrii.

As master jeweler in his own right, Dmitrii took little time to retrieve the title of court purveyor, which had lapsed with his father's death, and to reclaim that of appraiser to the court. During his tenure an additional designation, merchant of the first guild, would give the Hahn firm the right to export.[11] Compared to other prominent jewelers such as Bolin and Fabergé, and despite its prolific output, the enterprise employed only 30 workmen by 1893.[12] After Dmitrii's death in 1911, the St. Petersburg jeweler Alexander Tillander bought the lease to the shop for 12,000 rubles.[13]

Head Workmasters Carl Blank and Alexander Treiden

Hahn owed much of his firm's success toward the end of its tenure to master jeweler Carl Karlovich Blank. The son of a Finnish blacksmith, Blank was born in St. Petersburg and joined Hahn in 1882, where he worked for almost 30 years, although on separate premises. Records show that in 1885, Blank registered as a gold and silversmith and had a workshop at 36 Gorokhovaia Street with eight workers and three apprentices.[14] In 1896, he received an award for excellence at the Nizhnii Novgorod Exhibition.[15]

Blank was known for his honesty and fair prices, which kept him busy until the revolution. Like his employer, the goldsmith produced diamond-encrusted decorations, portrait badges, crosses, ceremonial swords and imperial presentation boxes. In 1909 Hahn invited Blank to become a partner of the firm, although its name remained unchanged. Blank went on to set up his own business after Dmitrii Hahn's death in 1911 and kept up the same caliber of work. In 1914 he created a field marshal's baton for 12,500 rubles.[16] In 1917, on the eve of the February Revolution, Blank produced one of the most expensive snuffboxes ever made in Russia. This last imperial commission, which cost 4,100 rubles, was meant for the emperor's lead banker, Lord Revelstoke, of Baring Brothers. Ironically, the lord received only it after Nicholas' abdication.[17]

Alexander Aldolfovich Treiden (b. 1858) was Hahn's other head workmaster. Little is known about this jeweler, although a few of his creations survive. The imperial presentation cases

Hahn design and invoice for a diamond rivière for Grand Duchess Irina, which was completed in time for her wedding to Prince Felix Yusupov. Below, her wedding trousseau, showing lavish family jewels—many of which had been refashioned by Chaumet, the Parisian jeweler—including jewels from her husband's family. The diamond necklace on the lower left (7) appears to be Russian and may have been made by Hahn. Princess Irina, age 17, by Boasson and Eggler, photographers located next door to Hahn at 24 Nevskii Prospect in St. Petersburg. *Sources: RGIA, Stolitsa i usadba, Wikimedia Commons*

he made for the Romanovs during the reign of Nicholas II are almost identical to those by Blank. Where Treiden made his mark was in smaller gold and enameled *objets* including triptychs and kovshs.

Jewels for the Ladies of the Court

In addition to the empress's coronation crown, Hahn specialized in grand personal jewels long associated with the imperial family. Diamond rivières were particularly in demand by the Romanovs and members of the highest aristocracy. Designed as a line of graduated cushion-cut diamonds within collet (closed) mounts, a diamond rivière necklace bespoke wealth and privilege. Hahn produced numerous diamond necklaces for grand duchesses and princesses alike.

One example is striking. In 1902 Hahn began to create an important diamond rivière for the only daughter of Grand Duke Alexander Mikhailovich (b. 1866) and niece of Tsar Nicholas II, Princess Irina Aleksandrovna (1895–1970). Irina's mother was Grand Duchess Xenia, Tsar Alexander III's daughter. The imperial cabinet placed its order in July. Although Princess Irina was only seven, no expense was spared. Judging from the size of the diamonds, the grand duke may have foreseen his daughter's future marriage to Prince Felix Yusupov, one of the empire's wealthiest aristocrats.

While the necklace's fate is uncertain, its original design, invoice and supporting documents survive. The drawing is a simple pencil sketch, perhaps a draft. Along the edges of the circles representing diamonds are dates. Within each circle is a precise weight, in ancient carats, written in pen. It is unclear whether Hahn was paid in full, or just for the two diamonds he furnished at the time. One wonders also how the jeweler knew the exact carat weight of each diamond unless he already had them in reserve. As a Romanov, Irina may have been entitled to diamonds from the imperial treasury, yet Hahn's invoice suggests otherwise.

According to the plan set forth by the imperial cabinet, beginning in 1902, two diamonds would start the necklace, one, probably for the clasp, weighing 6 $^{13}/_{32}$ carats (6.9 new carats) and another of 2 $^{22}/_{32}$ (2.8). Then, for the next 10 years, solitaire by solitaire in ever-increasing size, the necklace would grow. From July 1902 to 1906, Hahn would add a pair of diamonds, both on Irina's name day, May 5, and on her birthday, July 3. From 1907 onward, one solitaire would be added on each of these days.[18] The entire necklace would total 132 $^{23}/_{32}$ (136.7) carats of diamonds and cost 33,479 rubles. An invoice signed by Dmitrii Hahn for the gold mounting also survives.

The necklace would be completed by 1912, for Irina's 17th birthday. Ample time for her nuptials! Held on February 22, 1914, the wedding of Prince Felix Yusupov and Princess Irina Aleksandrovna was the grandest social event of the season. Her highness's jewelry would match the occasion. The November 1914 issue of the glossy St. Petersburg equivalent of *Town & Country*, *Stolitsa i usad'ba* (capital city and country estate), lists Princess Irina's lavish wedding jewels. Displayed on velvet stands as arranged by the Parisian jeweler Chaumet, who was responsible for redesigning much of the Yusupov family jewels, no. 7 features an original Russian creation: a diamond rivière necklace most likely by Hahn.

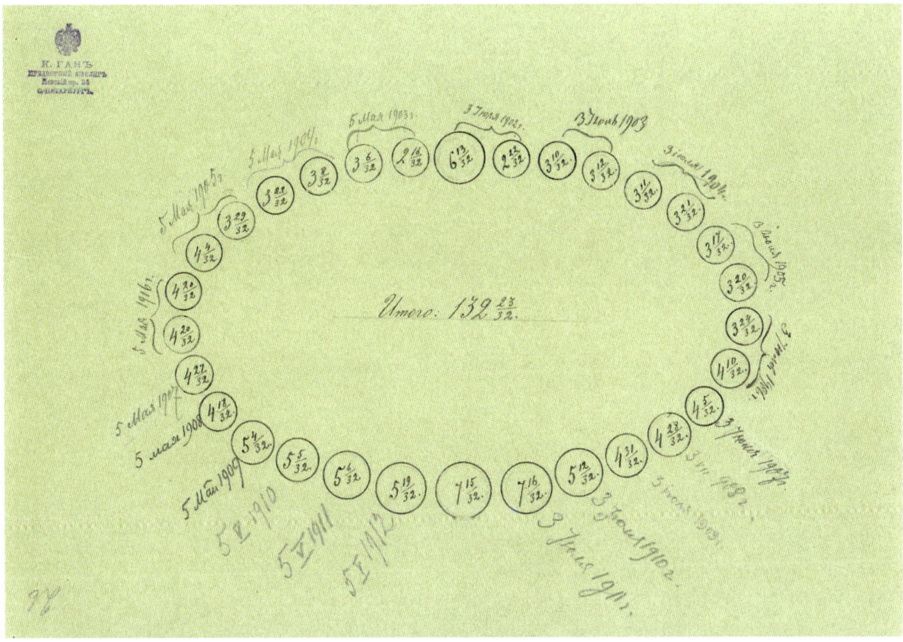
К. ГАНЪ
Итого: 132 23/32.

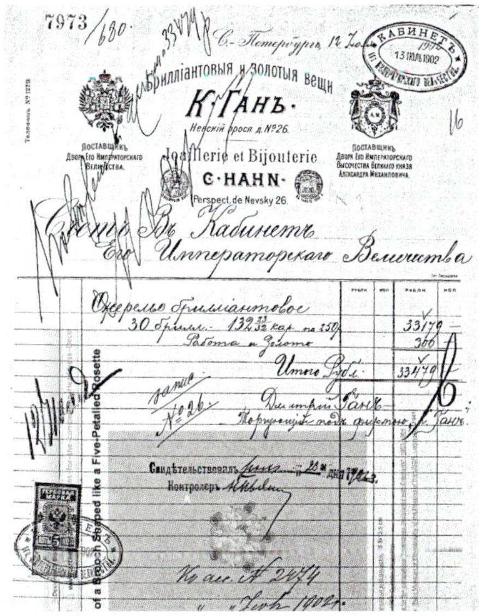
7973
С.-Петербургъ
КАБИНЕТЪ
Брилліантовыя и золотыя вещи
К. ГАНЪ
Невскій просп. д. №26.
Joaillerie et Bijouterie
C. HAHN
Perspect de Nevsky 26.
ПОСТАВЩИКЪ Двора Его Императорскаго Величества
ПОСТАВЩИКЪ Двора Его Императорскаго Высочества Великаго Князя Александра Михайловича
Въ Кабинетъ Его Императорскаго Величества
Свидѣтельствовалъ
Контролеръ

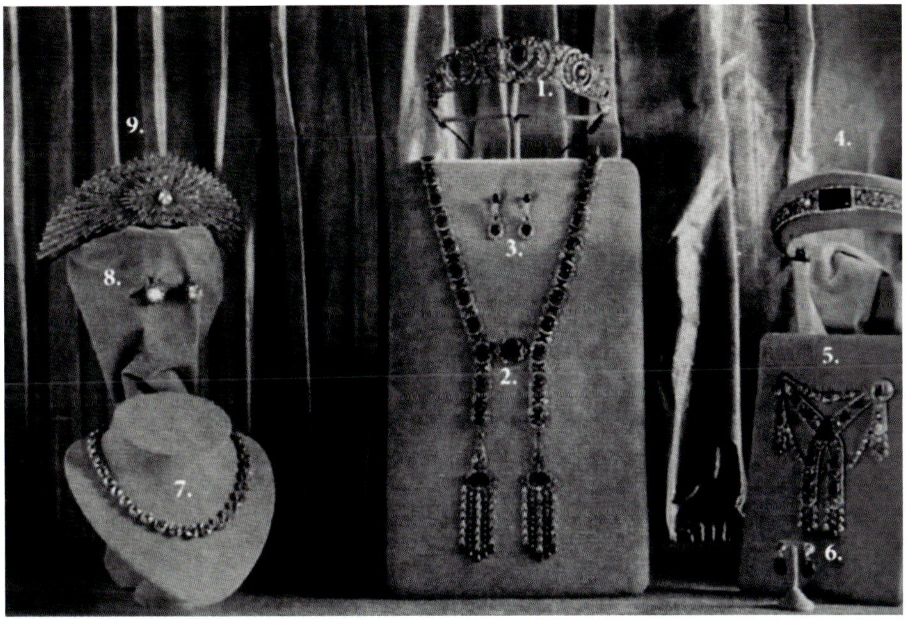
1.
2.
3.
4.
5.
6.
7.
8.
9.

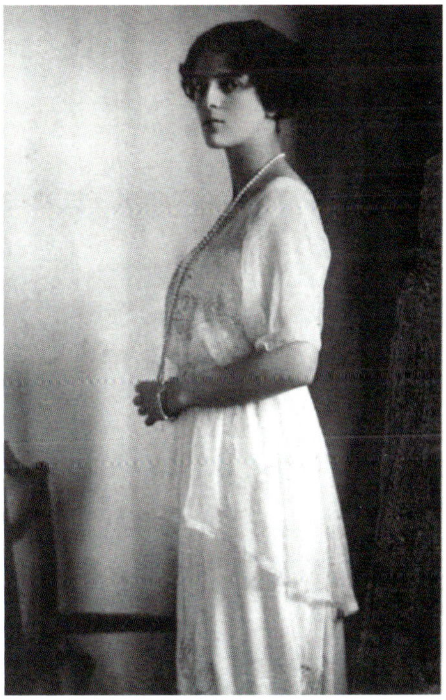

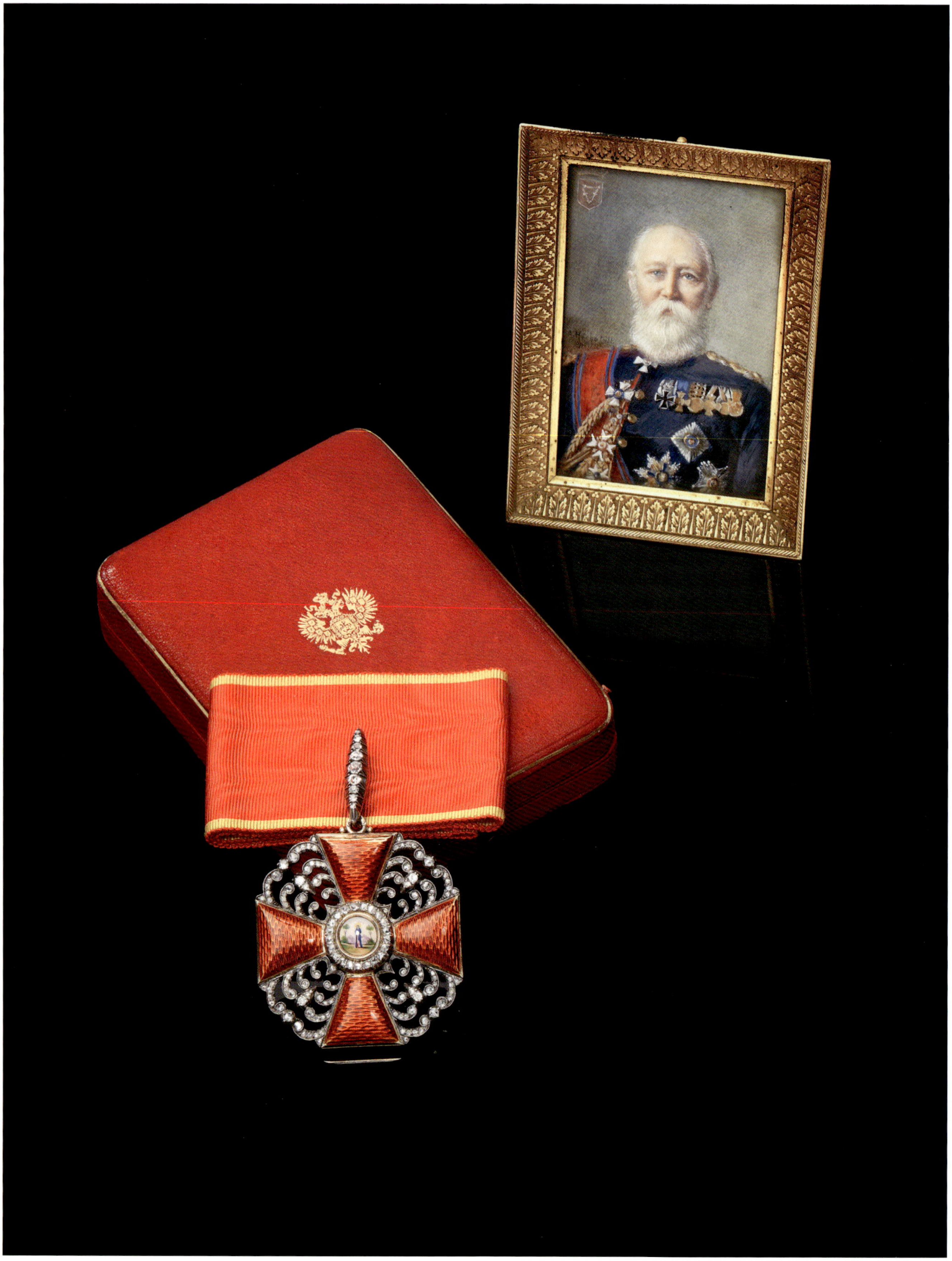

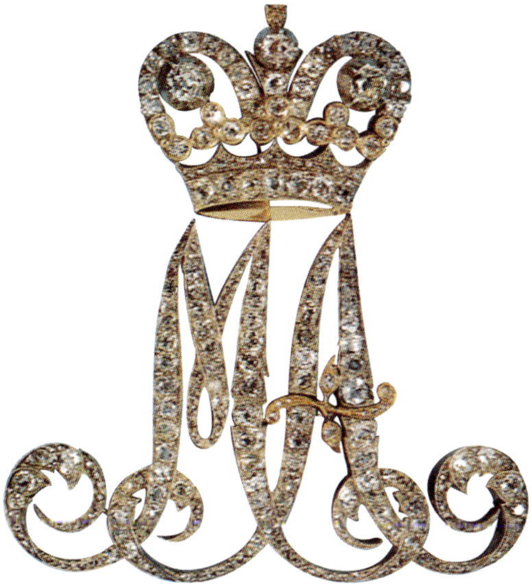

Imperial Presentation Orders

Carl Hahn also excelled in the diamond decorations for the imperial court. During the Romanov dynasty's final two decades, Hahn *père et fis* and later their protégé Carl Blank perfected these lavish jewels, which were commissioned by the tsar for the knights of the empire's highest orders and for important dignitaries. Like Bolin before him, Hahn made two of the most prestigious diamond awards: the imperial presentation Order of the St. Alexander Nevskii and the Order of the White Eagle. The cost for these ranged from 2,000 rubles for the first to 5,134 for the second, owing to the presence of more than 500 diamonds. The latter design was based on a 13th-century Polish decoration, reinstituted as a Russian enamel badge in the 19th century, and first set with diamonds in 1882. It was awarded to foreign dignitaries such as the princes of Persia, Siam and Prussia. Research reveals that either Hahn and Blank produced at least 12 out of only 24 diamond-set white eagle decorations ever made, and only two of these still exist.[19]

After Hahn closed shop, Carl Blank continued making diamond decorations under his own name. In 1913, for example, the jeweler produced two insignias of the Imperial Order of St. Alexander Nevskii, possibly for the Romanov tercentenary celebrations.[20]

The Dowager Empress and Empress Alexandra Fedorovna also patronized Hahn for diamond decorations for the ladies of the court. They wore the badge only on specific ceremonial occasions with a court dress in the traditional Old Russian style—white silk weighted by a gold and red velvet train.

The distinctly Russian design remained the same with each succeeding reign: a Romanov crown set with diamonds above the diamond-set initials of the empress. In 1902 the firm delivered to the imperial cabinet four diamond maid-of-honor badges averaging 600 rubles each. The price was low for the simple reason that jewelers were forbidden from charging the court more than the cost of diamonds and a minimum labor fee for its commissions.

Inventory numbers can now be traced to particular recipients. One badge, identified by a scratched number, was presented to Baroness Anna Vladimirovna Osten-Sacken Cobourg in May 1896. It sold at auction in 2013. By coincidence, the same award in paste rather than diamonds appeared a few lots later in the same sale.[21] Paste reproductions of some decorations were made by Russian jewelers presumably to allow the original recipients who had returned their diamond award for monetary value to wear its facsimile in the presence of the sovereign during important court celebrations.

Previous page:
A jeweled Order of St. Anne, 2nd Class, with original presentation box, by Carl Blank, ca. 1910. © *2012 Christie's Images Ltd.*

Above:
Diamond lady-in-waiting cipher, ca. 1860. The initials M A refer to Empress Maria Aleksandrovna, the wife of Alexander II, and the Dowager Empress Alexandra Fedorovna, respectively. © *1981 Christie's Images Ltd.*

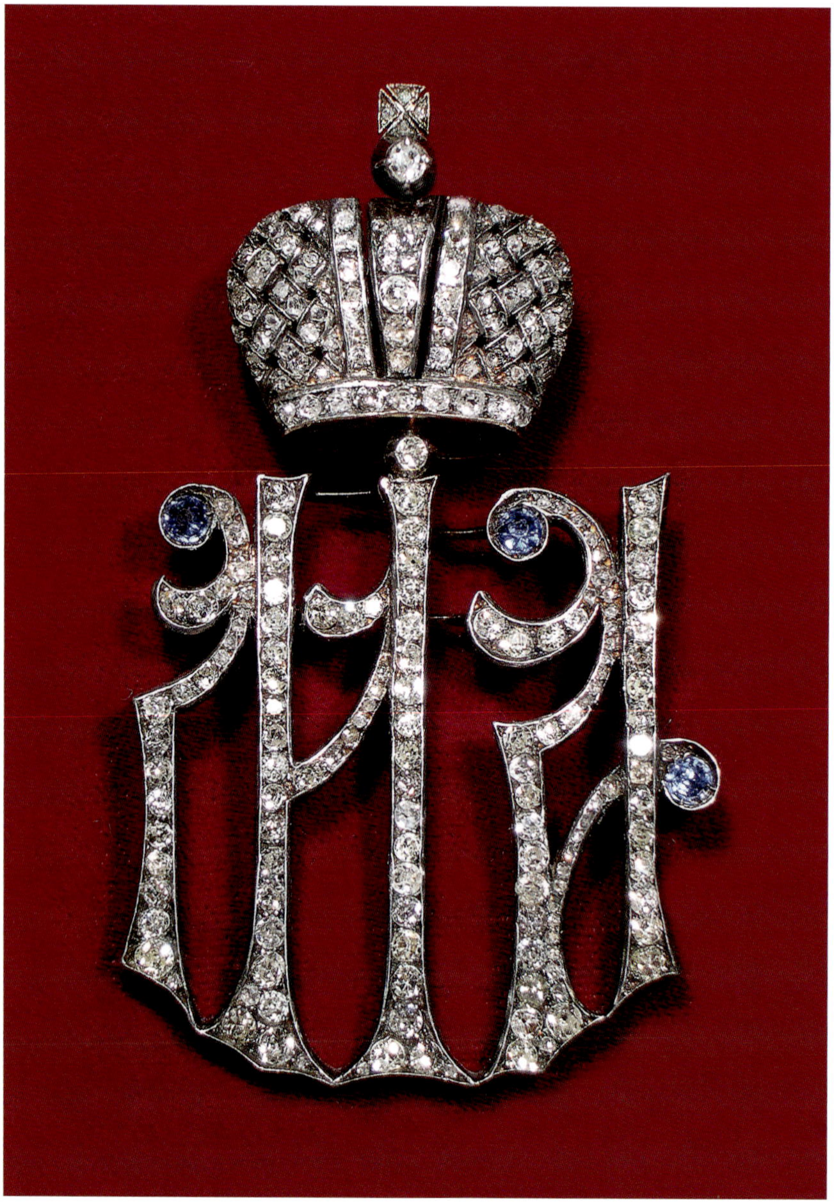

Russian imperial diamond maid-of-honor insignia by Carl Hahn. This cipher had the conjoined initials *M A* for both Dowager Empress Maria Fedorovna and Empress Alexandra. Although it is unsigned, designs from the archives indicate that Hahn made it between 1896 and 1911.
Marie Betteley, photo by Roger Bester

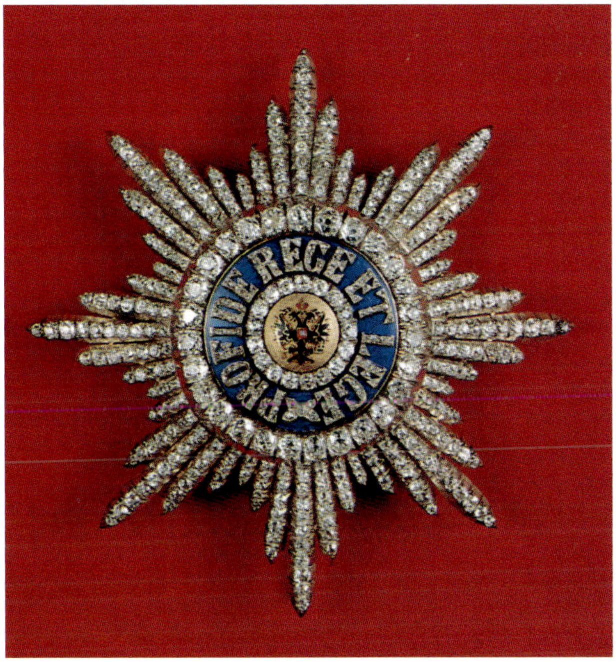

Ladies-in-waiting to Empress Maria Fedorovna received an insignia or chiffre of a single crowned initial *M* set with diamonds.[22]

Diamond presentation crosses for the clergy proved another source of steady income for Hahn. From 1907 to 1916, Hahn and Blank produced most of these orders from the imperial cabinet: 17 panagias (pendant icons) (500–1200 rubles each), 25 diamond crosses for miters (averaging 800 rubles) and 54 gold crosses.[23] Crosses bestowed on metropolitans were costly—the eight made by Hahn between 1896 and 1912 averaged 1,100 rubles. For the Chief Procurator of the Holy Synod, the value rose even higher, to 3,120 rubles.[24] Blank took over this role after 1911 and produced crosses for, among others, George, the patriarch of the Armenian Church, and for Gregory IV, the patriarch of Antioch.[25] In 1912, Blank redesigned a diamond presentation award that had belonged to the Chief Procurator of the Holy Synod, that was bestowed by the tsar upon a recipient outside the Orthodox faith, the emperor of Japan.[26]

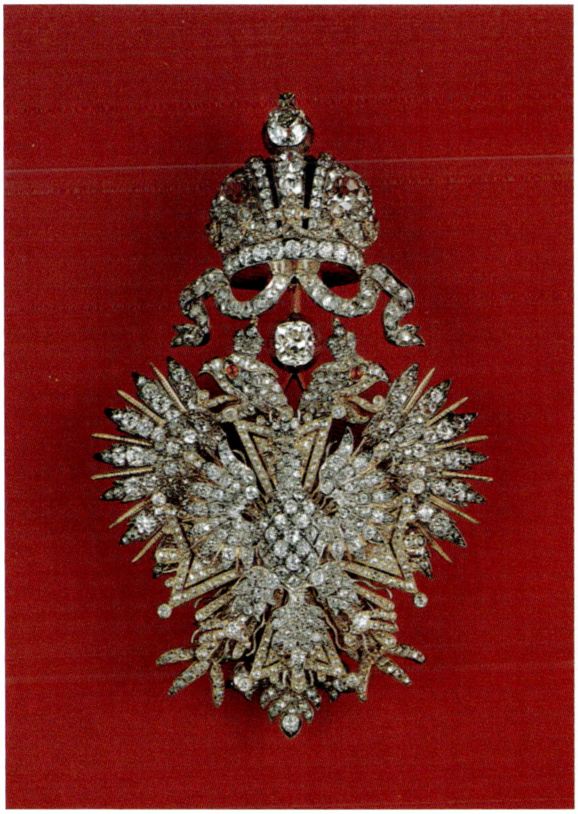

Above:
Diamond-set star of the Order of the White Eagle. Probably by Hahn. © *1981 Christie's Images Ltd.*

Right:
Order of the White Eagle badge. Probably by Hahn. © *1981 Christie's Images Ltd.*

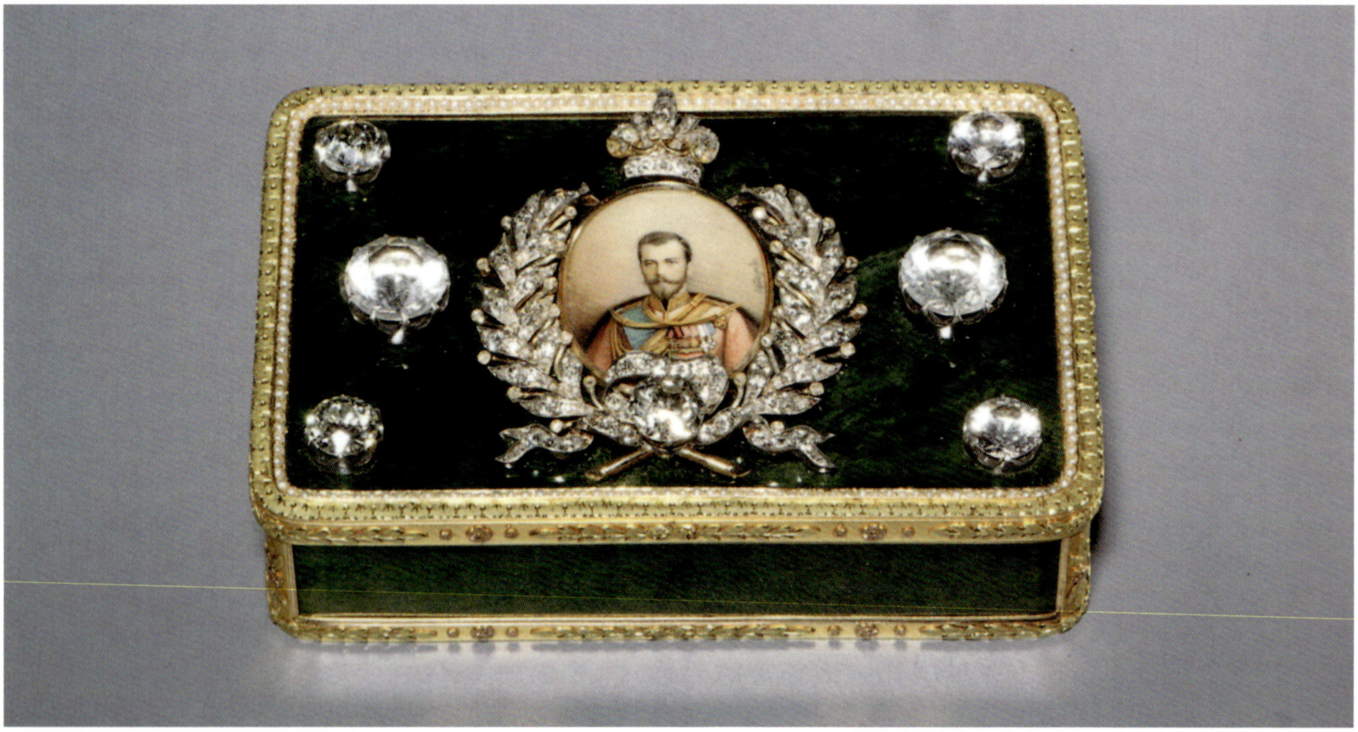

The Russian emperor gave this nephrite box to the French minister of foreign affairs, Théophile Delcassé (1852–1923), in 1901 for his role in the Franco-Russian accord. Since it cost 4,754 rubles, an enormous sum at the time, it is likely that four of the larger stones on the cover, which are now pastes, were originally diamonds. *Courtesy of Sotheby's*

Master Imperial Box Maker

Like Fabergé, Hahn created the finest and most expensive imperial snuffboxes for the court of Nicholas II. Gold snuffboxes bestowed by the emperor were either set with a diamond Romanov eagle, the sovereign's crowned cipher in diamonds, or his miniature portrait bordered by diamonds. Recipients were Russian subjects of high merit or rank or foreign dignitaries, including heads of state. Out of 14 boxes decorated with the sovereign's portrait made during this period, six were by Hahn, five by Fabergé. These two goldsmiths also created the highest number of boxes with the tsar's cipher, with a total of 68 by Fabergé and 64 by Hahn or Blank.[27] Competition between the two jewelers for these commissions was fierce. Between 1896 and 1899, Hahn had the upper hand, outproducing Fabergé's annual total by creating 17 such snuffboxes in 1896, while Fabergé prevailed by 1902. However, between 1896 and 1907, it was Hahn rather than his famous counterpart who sold the costliest of these boxes to the court, for 2,700 rubles.[28]

Fortunately, several Hahn boxes with imperial ciphers survive. Usually rectangular, but also with an oval and scalloped outline, many are decorated with translucent enamel over a guilloché pattern. The telltale color for Hahn boxes is bright pink, a shade never seen in Fabergé's palette of enamels. A box of shaped outline in Hahn pink—undoubtedly a gift to a lady—sold at Christie's in 2000.[29] Another presented by the tsar to the American financier J. P. Morgan is in the Metropolitan Museum.[30] At least two oval ones, both in deep-blue enamel, one bordered with red enamel applied with a diamond-and-gold garland, surfaced in the West over the past two decades (see page 276).[31]

One frequent recipient of jeweled snuffboxes was Dr. Dmitrii Ott, who delivered all five imperial children, beginning in 1895 with the birth of Grand Duchess Olga Nikolaevna. For his service to the imperial family, the accoucheur received a total of 12 presentation boxes, each set with the cipher either of Nicholas II or his consort in diamonds.[32] The first was in Hahn's trademark bright-pink enamel. Its cover featured the diamond cipher in Cyrillic *AF* of the empress below a Romanov Crown within a ribbon-tied gold laurel wreath. This *boite à chiffre* and another by Hahn in yellow enamel also bestowed on Dr. Ott sold at Parke-Bernet in the Lansdell K. Christie's Sale in 1967 for $9,000 each.[33] The latter was reoffered at auction in 2010.[34]

In the realm of presentation boxes, Blank workmanship can rival that of Fabergé, making it difficult to tell one from the

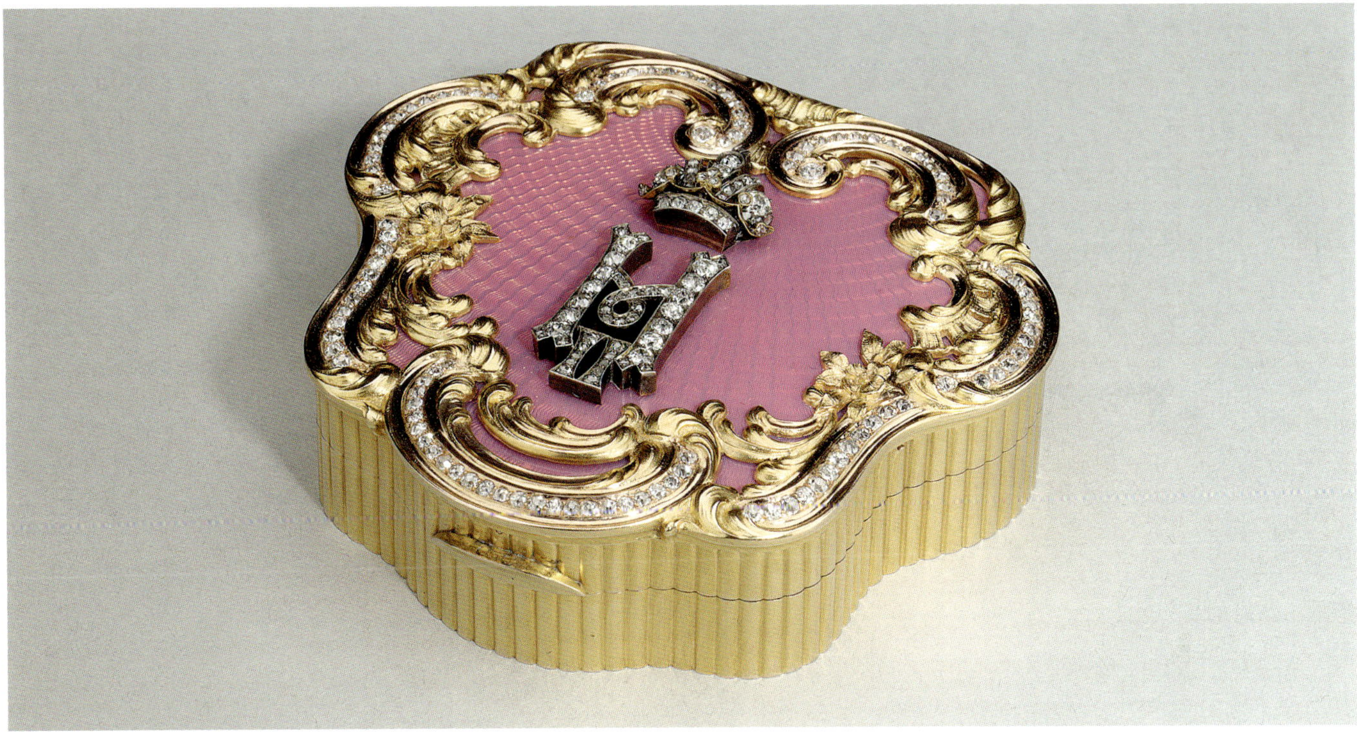

This snuffbox was made by Carl Blank of St. Petersburg as a gift from Tsar Nicholas II. © *2000 Christie's Images Ltd.*

other without looking at hallmarks. In one striking example, two sky-blue enamel boxes, one by each, have an almost identical diamond trellis pattern. Only the centers differ. The first by Blank, a gift from the emperor to an unknown recipient, bears the crowned diamond cipher of Tsar Nicholas II, while the second is by Fabergé and was commissioned by Grand Duke Alexis Aleksandrovich (1850–1908) for a mistress, Madame Elizaveta Balletta of the Imperial Mikhailovskii Theater.[35]

Rings from the Sovereign

Hahn and Blank also made most of Tsar Nicholas's presentation rings.[36] Adorned with either the sovereign's portrait trimmed in diamonds, a Romanov eagle, or his diamond cipher, few from the reign of Nicholas II survive, especially as the fashion of gentlemen wearing rings fell out of favor in the 20th century. However, as gifts awarded both to Russian and foreign subjects, rings remained popular. For the most part they were relatively inexpensive. Because of their small size, along with cuff links and tiepins, rings proved an ideal gift for gentlemen. Those adorned with state emblems and small rose diamonds cost as little as 30 rubles, while 400 rubles was the average price for a more elaborate imperial presentation ring. Their recipients included priests of various congregations, prelates, teachers and artists, as well as state councilors, other civil servants and stenographers.[37] One such ring survives in the Moscow Kremlin. Made by Blank, it features the imperial double-headed eagle set with diamonds.

Diamond Setter to the Tsar

The jeweler's work did not always demand creativity. As a diamond merchant, Hahn performed two main tasks for the Romanov court. The first was to set diamonds on the lids of imperial boxes, while the second was to upgrade presentation gifts, usually boxes, by embellishing them with larger and more-valuable diamonds. The tradition of producing gold boxes with an oval blank reserve by one jeweler to be subsequently embellished by another began under the reign of Alexander I. For over a century this proved an efficient and cost-effective way to meet the high demand for these important gifts. Boxes could easily be recycled, and many were. Only about 26 percent of the portrait boxes made during Nicholas II's reign were new creations.[38]

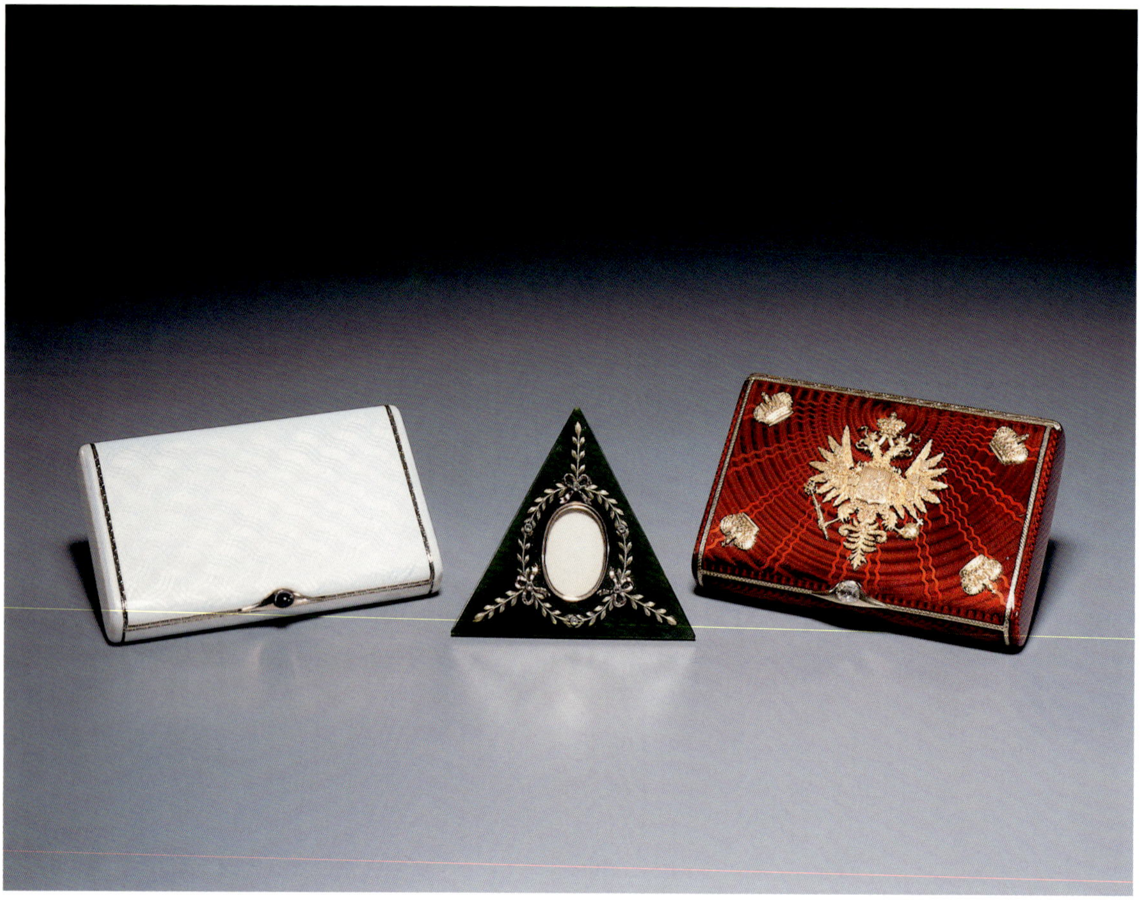

Hahn presentation cigarette case (right). While less varied than Fabergé's, Hahn's enamel palette was more vivid. While the provenance was not documented when sold, this cigarette case was clearly commissioned by the court, since it bears two emblems of the Romanov dynasty in gold. *© 1998 Christie's Images Ltd.*

Several boxes made by other St. Petersburg jewelers would land on Hahn's workbench for the final phase of diamond setting or upgrading. At least one example by Köchli that was later enhanced by Hahn survives.[39] In 1906, Dmitrii Hahn upgraded a lavish box for the Emir of Bukhara, made by the jeweler Ivanov.[40] On another occasion, Hahn doubled the value of a Fabergé Nicholas II *boite à portrait* by adding a large cushion-shaped diamond on each corner for presentation by the emperor to the papal secretary of state, Cardinal Mariano Rampolla.[41]

As with diamond insignias, recipients of boxes from the imperial cabinet would often return them for cash. Of the 424 boxes delivered from the cabinet's stock during the reign of Nicholas II, over half were recycled. At 70 percent, the return of boxes with the imperial cipher was even higher.[42] The imperial cabinet maintained the practice, since precious objects or jewels could be recycled faster and at a lower cost.

Like all Russian imperial goldsmiths, Hahn made many cigarette cases. One with Tsar Nicholas's cipher in diamonds was presented to an actual state counsellor in 1910.[43] Another one, of pink guilloché enamel and bordered by tiny diamonds formed part of the late John Traina's collection. The firm made at least two gold cigarette cases depicting battleships. One in blue and oyster guilloché enamel featured the famous battleship *Pamiat Azova*, and another was in gold chased with the warship *Rinda*. Set with a sapphire thumbpiece, this elegant *porte cigarette* was given to Grand Duke Alexander Mikhailovich in 1891 after he had completed a three-year voyage around the world on the vessel.[44] The firm also produced cuff links, fobs, bracelets, patch boxes, stickpins and brooches as well as perfume bottles and gold-mounted hardstone cups by either Blank or Hahn, or both, as well as fine gold and enamel triptychs by Hahn and his workmaster Alexander Treiden.

NOTES

1. The design was based on one that Louis David Duval made in 1797 for Empress Maria Fedorovna. Leopold Seftigen originally created this crown for the coronation of Maria Aleksandrovna, Emperor Alexander II's consort, in 1855.

2. Like that of the dowager empress, this crown was also patterned after Duval's. It cost 76,200 rubles ($2,228,483 today) and has not survived. Tillander-Godenhielm, "Russian Imperial Award System," 384 and 523, n. 26.

3. This was the only crown that the Bolsheviks dismantled, a testament to the high quality of diamonds used.

4. "A Rare Plique-à-Jour Enamel Kovsh by Alexander Treiden," http://atzbach.com/product arare-jeweled-gold-and-plique-a-jour-enamel-kovsh-byalexander-treiden-for-hahn/.

5. These were headed by master goldsmiths Carl Blank and Alexander Treiden, respectively.

6. Sotheby's, *Russian Art, Works of Art, Fabergé & Icons*, November 27, 2012, lot 586.

7. RGIA, f 468, o 8, d 186, ll 3, 14, 20, 23, 24.

8. Tillander-Godenhielm, "Russian Imperial Award System," 374 and 523, n. 11.

9. RGIA, f 468, o 13, d 1542, l.

10. The Blue Serpent Clock Egg cost 4,500 rubles; the Rosebud Egg, 3,250 rubles.

11. Tillander-Godenhielm, *Jewels from Imperial St. Petersburg*, 290.

12. Vyacheslav Mukhin, ed., *The Fabulous Epoch of Fabergé* (Moscow: Nord, 1992), 230.

13. Tillander-Godenhielm, *Jewels from Imperial St. Petersburg*, 260–61.

14. Fabergé et al., *Faberzhe i Peterburgskie iuveliry*, 114.

15. Christie's, New York, April 20, 2001, lot 136H.

16. Tillander-Godenhielm, "Russian Imperial Award System," 386.

17. Like the tsar, Blank fared badly that year. Besieged by the Bolsheviks, the Finnish jeweler fled back to his homeland with his family but never resumed his trade there. He became penniless, fell into a depression, and was haunted by tragic family events. Ulla Tillander-Godenhielm, "The House of Fabergé—Workmasters and Subcontractors," in *The Era of Fabergé*, ed. Marjo-Riitta Saloniemi (Tampere, Finland: Tampere Museum Publications, 2006), 126. On Lord Revelstoke, see Jennifer Siegel, *For Peace and Money: French and British Finance in the Service of Tsars and Commissars* (Oxford: Oxford University Press, 2014), 116–20.

18. The largest diamond, in the middle, is undated.

19. Valentin V. Skurlov, *Antikvarnoe obozrenie* 3 (2001); and Ulla Tillander-Godenhielm and Valentin V. Skurlov, "An Imperial Russian Presentation Order: The Diamond-Set White Eagle," in Habsburg et al., *Fabergé: Imperial Craftsman*, 326–28.

20. Tillander-Godenhielm, "Russian Imperial Award System," 393.

21. The diamond insignia sold for $100,091, while the paste one, with its ambitious estimate of $76,000–110,000, did not sell. Christie's, London, November 25, 2013, lots 275 and 277. It went on to sell in 2014 for £25,000.

22. One, probably misattributed as Fabergé, sold for $17,000: Sotheby's, Geneva, May 11, 1989, lot 298. Another St. Petersburg jeweler, N. S. Johansson, also made the same decoration for Maria Fedorovna. Tillander-Godenhielm, Jewels from Imperial St. Petersburg, 170.

23. Tillander-Godenhielm, "Russian Imperial Award System," 243.

24. Ibid., 511, n. 29.

25. Tillander-Godenhielm, "Russian Imperial Award System," 511, n. 42.

26. Ibid., 310 and 517, n. 9.

27. Ibid., 179. Sotheby's Geneva sold one by Hahn in 1998.

28. Tillander-Godenhielm, "Russian Imperial Award System," 181.

29. Christie's, New York, October 23, 2000, lot 112, $116,000.

30. Habsburg, *Fabergé*, 1987, 297, no. 613.

31. Sotheby's, New York, December 8, 1992, lot 184 (also featured on the catalogue's cover), sold to the trade for $56,100. This was resold at Sotheby's for $641,623 in December 2015, lot 420. Christie's sold a Hahn deep-blue enamel oval box in London on November 24, 2008, lot 229A, for $127,023.

32. Tillander-Godenhielm, "Russian Imperial Award System," 357. These boxes cost between 1,000 and 1,350 rubles. Of those that survive, usually only the covers are enameled, while the sides and base are in patterned gold.

33. Even back then, the Fabergé box that is illustrated with the Hahn boxes sold for more than three times that price, although it was not an imperial commission. A strong market for Fabergé had already been established by the 1960s.

34. When it sold for $115,000. Carl Fabergé made two boxes for Professor Ott: one for the birth in 1899 of Grand Duchess Maria Nikolaevna, and another for the long-awaited arrival of Tsarevich Alexis in 1904. Tillander-Godenhielm, "Imperial Award System," 358. The former also sold in the 1960s at Parke-Bernet for $12,500.

35. Compare Sotheby's, New York, October 22, 2002, lot 318, with Habsburg, *Fabergé: Imperial Jeweler*, 302, fig. 174.

36. Morozov also made many imperial presentation rings.

37. Tillander-Godenhielm, "Imperial Award System," 187 and 196–197. At 1,800 rubles, the most expensive ring was made by Fabergé for a Russian colonel.

38. Tillander-Godenhielm, "Imperial Award System," 167.

39. In July 1894, Tsarevich Nicholas Aleksandrovich ordered an elegant Köchli gold box before his trip to inaugurate a portion of the Trans-Siberian railway. The lid, first set with the diamond initials NA, was enhanced by Hahn just six months later with higher-quality diamonds and a diamond-set numeral "II" to designate Nicholas's new position as tsar.

40. Tillander-Godenhielm, "Imperial Award System," 218.

41. Sotheby's, Geneva, November 16 and 17, 1998, lot 420; and Tillander-Godenhielm, "Russian Imperial Award System," 167.

42. Tillander-Godenhielm, "Russian Imperial Award System," 180.

43. Ibid., 184.

44. Christie's, London, November 29, 2010, lot 252

6

History

FRIEDRICH KÖCHLI: THE GRAND DUKES' FAVORITE

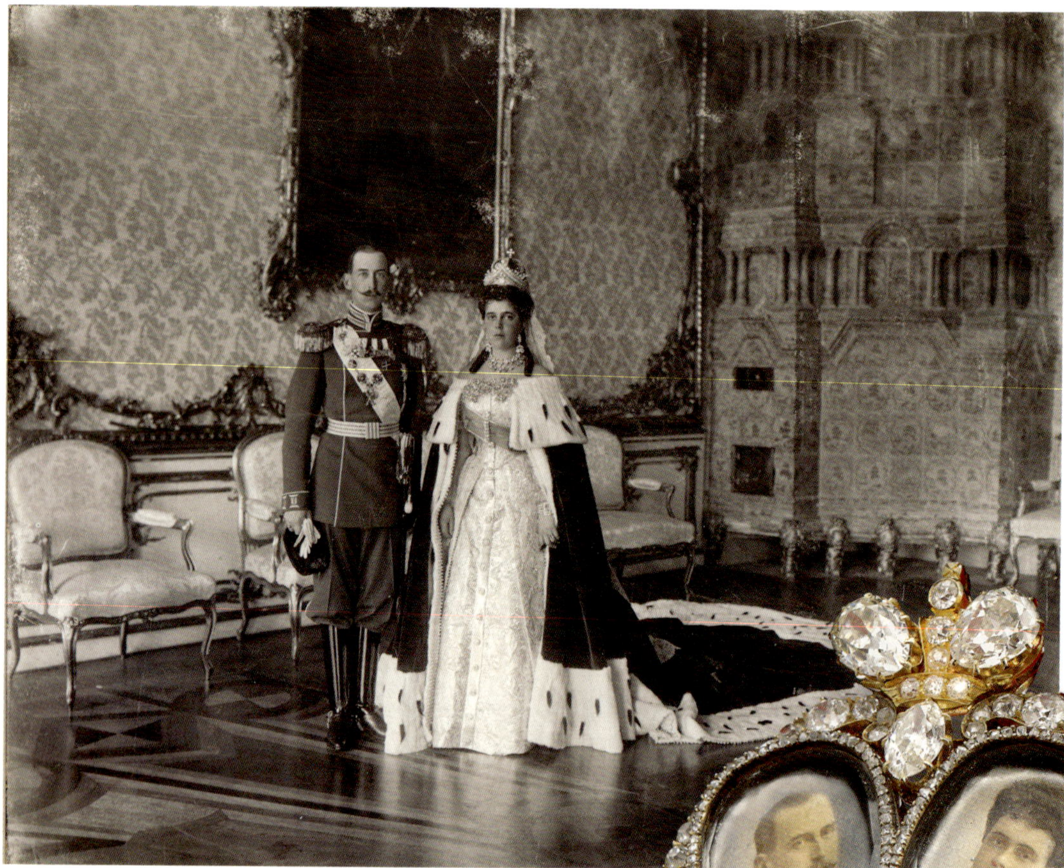

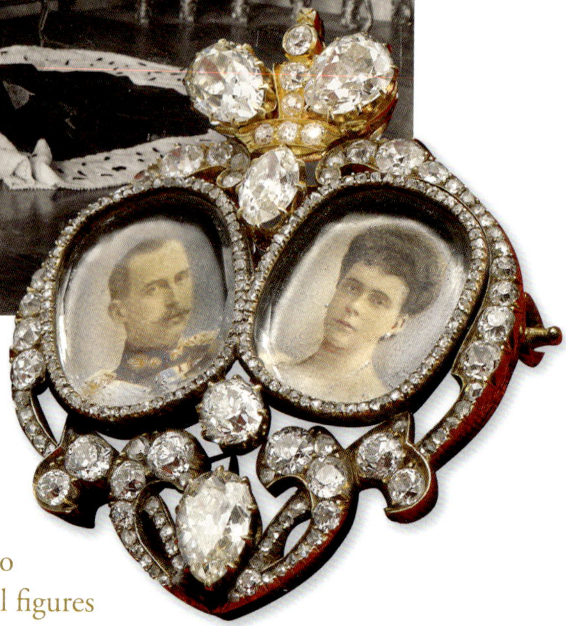

If the emperor was the most important client of Russia's more prominent jewelers, the grand dukes were not far behind. As sons and grandsons of the tsar, grand dukes played an important role in St. Petersburg society. Close to the court, but not of it, these men were rich and powerful figures in their own right. Their intimacy with the autocrat endowed them with an influence unmatched by even the most powerful minister in his cabinet. Some rose to the occasion, such as Grand Duke Nicholas Nikolaevich (1856–1921), whom Nicholas II would appoint as the army's commander in chief at the start of the Great War. Another grand duke, Alexander Mikhailovich (1866–1933), headed the new air force, while others had presided over the senate, commanded the navy, or served as viceroy in sensitive assignments on the frontier, such as Poland and the Caucasus. And then there were those who preferred to benefit from their august status by leading a more sybaritic existence.

Top left & right: This royal double-portrait diamond brooch of Prince Nicholas of Greece and Grand Duchess Elena Vladimirovna was made by Friedrich Köchli for their wedding in 1902. From the collection of Princess Elizabeth of Yugoslavia, © *2007 Christie's Images Ltd.*

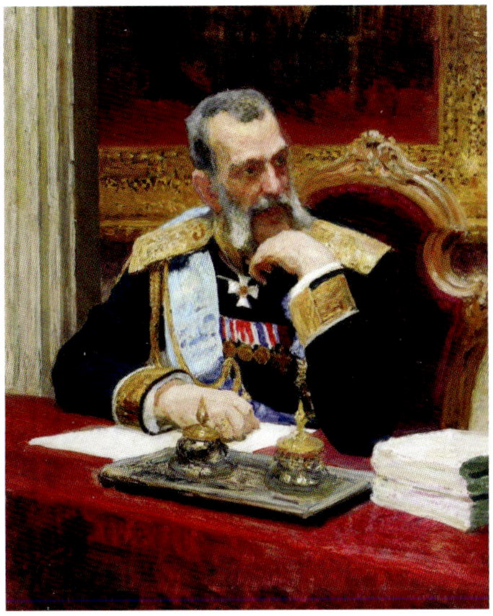

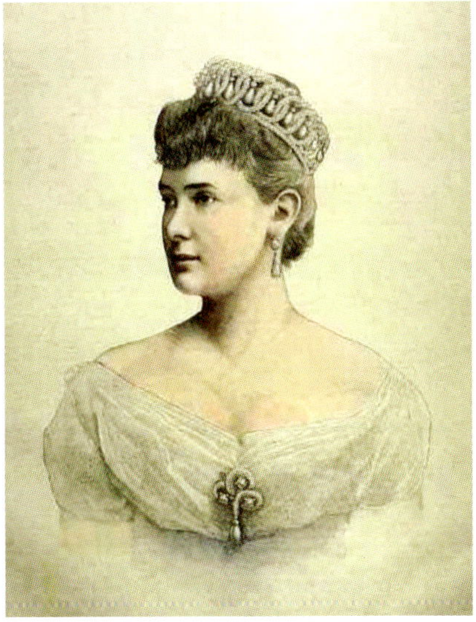

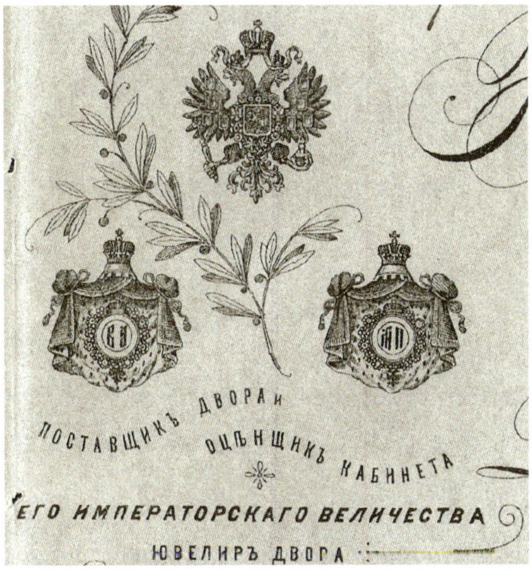

As jeweler to the courts of Grand Duke Vladimir Aleksandrovich and Maria Pavlovna, Köchli proudly displayed their grand ducal warrants on his letterhead. *Sources: Wikimedia Commons and RGIA*

Tsar Alexander II's son, Vladimir Aleksandrovich (1847–1909), was the senior grand duke of the House of Romanov. A particularly colorful figure in the imperial capital, Vladimir headed the Imperial Academy of Fine Arts and generously sponsored the imperial ballet. His frequent journeys to savor the pleasures of Paris had already earned him the nickname of "le grand duc bon vivant" there as a youth. Marriage did little to slow him down. After he wed the fun-loving Duchess Marie of Mecklenburg-Schwerin (subsequently Grand Duchess Marie Pavlovna), the grand ducal couple's magnificent residence at 28 Palace Embankment was the hub of the imperial capital's social life—all the more so when Nicholas II's dour consort, Alexandra Fedorovna, became chatelaine of the Winter Palace nearby upon her husband's accession to the throne.

The grand duchess's passion was fine jewelry, while her husband collected cuff links and cigarette cases. Both were particularly fond of jewels by Köchli. Indeed, when part of Vladimir Aleksandrovich's personal accessories surfaced at auction in 2009, it contained five pairs of cuff links by Köchli, one of which had been created for the wedding of his brother, Grand Duke Serge Aleksandrovich (1857–1905) (see illustration on page 107). Some were no doubt unique, created by special order. One pair was fashioned as gold ship's wheels, another as knots, polished gold lockets, or pearl trefoils with diamond stems. The most distinctive featured a "Man in the Moon" of carved moonstones against a deep-blue enameled background.[1] In 1907 Vladimir chose Köchli to embellish with diamonds a gold medal of Tsar Alexander II as a gift to Adjutant-General Count Ilia Tatishchev, for his role in completing the construction of the Christ Resurrection Cathedral in St. Petersburg.[2]

Along with Bolin, Hahn and Fabergé, Köchli was a leading court jeweler during the reigns of Alexander III and Nicholas II. By 1903 the firm had surpassed even Fabergé by accumulating no less than four grand ducal warrants. This is significant because grand ducal seals were more difficult to obtain than imperial warrants from the tsar and symbolized excellence of design and workmanship. First introduced during the reign of Alexander II, like the imperial warrant, the title of "supplier to the court of the grand duke" was awarded twice a year. To receive it, merchants had to apply, qualify and be selected. Only those who had supplied the imperial court for eight consecutive years were eligible for the distinction.

Grand Duke Vladimir Aleksandrovich owned this pair of man-in-the-moon enamel and moonstone cuff links by Köchli. Carl Fabergé and others repeated this popular motif in their jewelry. *Courtesy of Sotheby's*

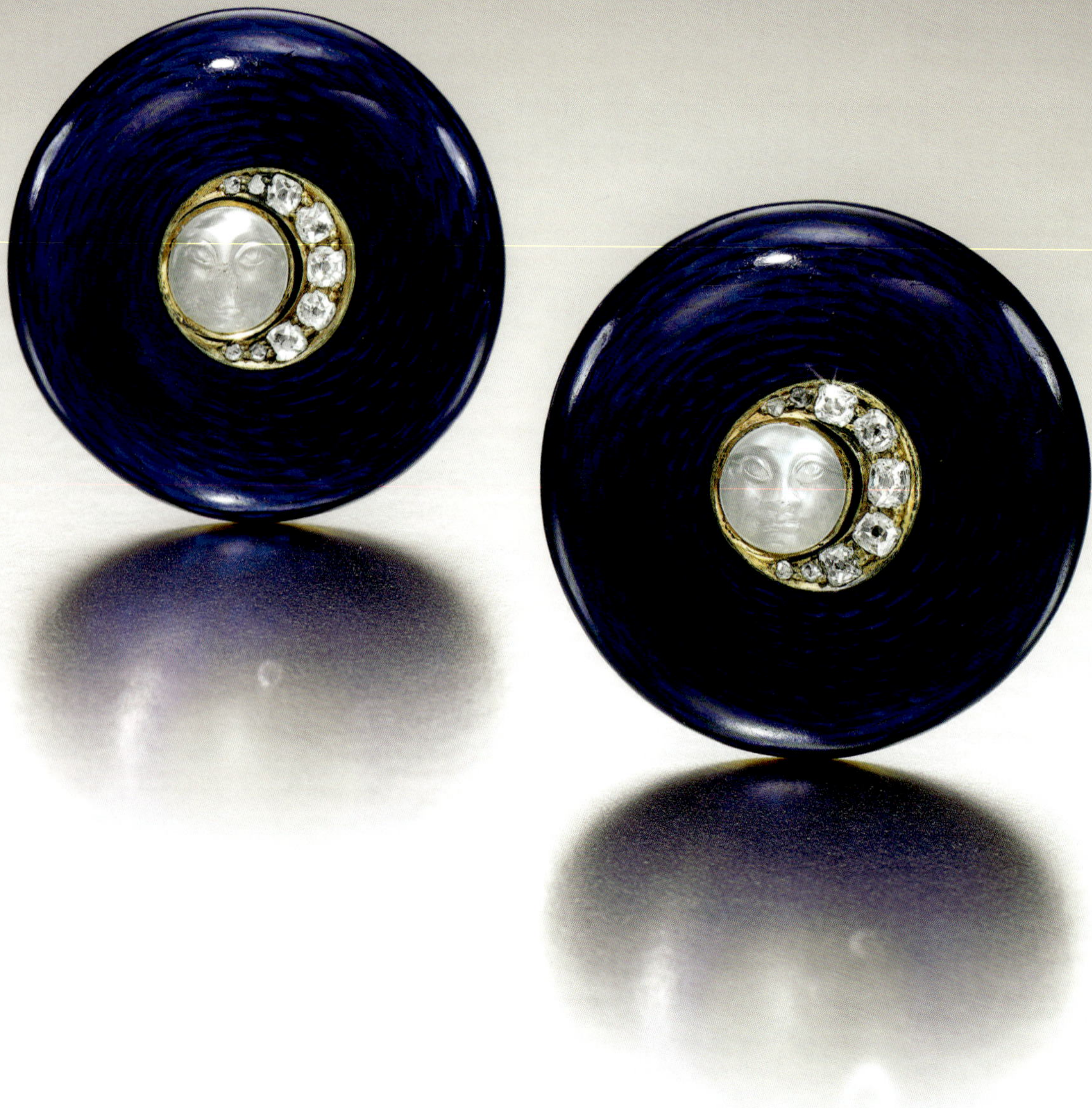

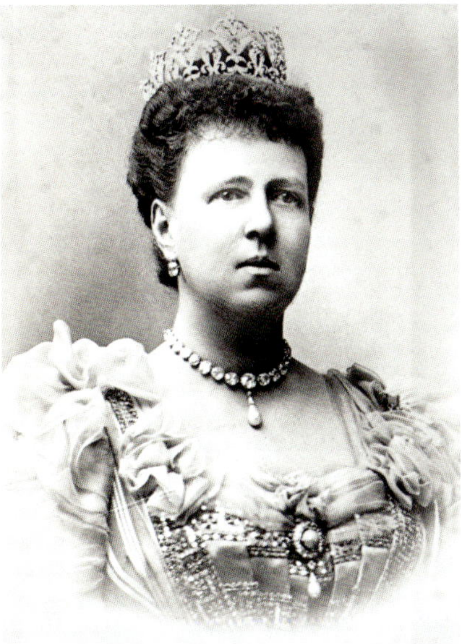

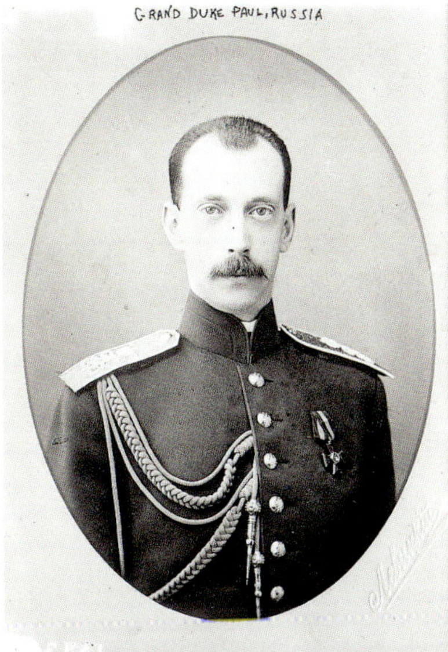

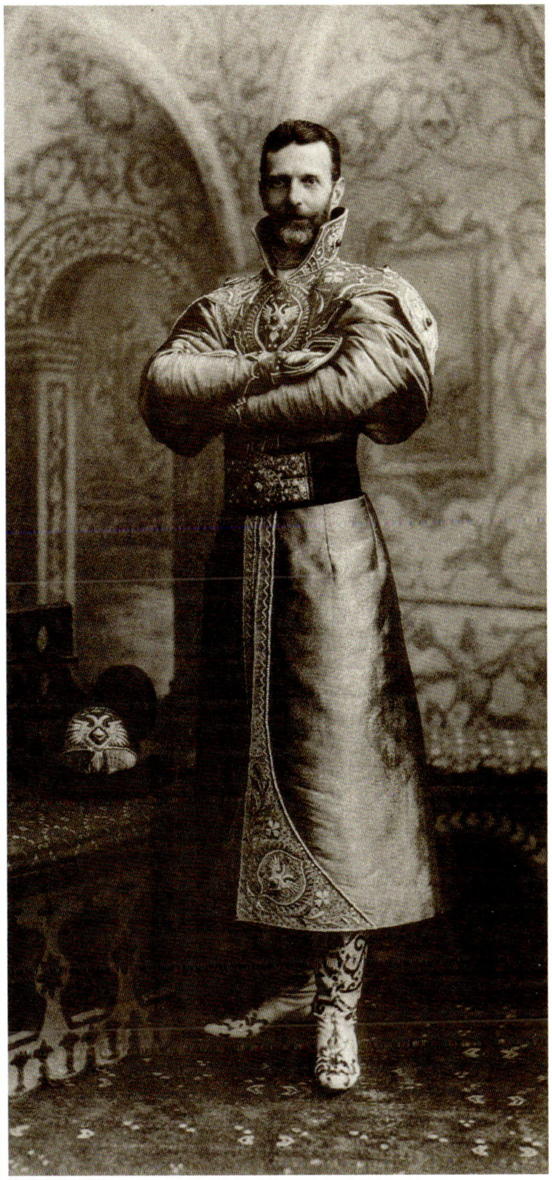

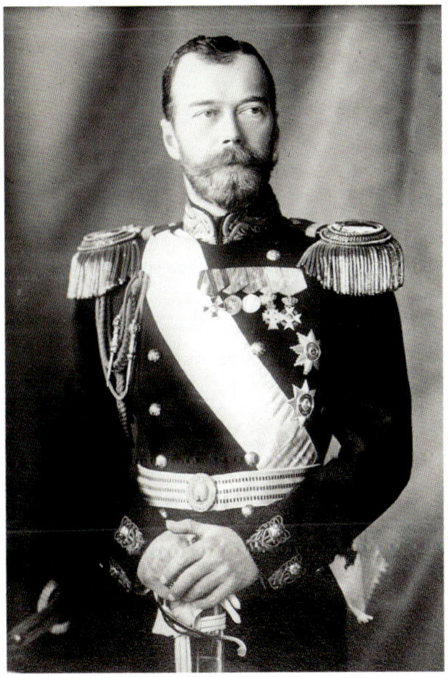

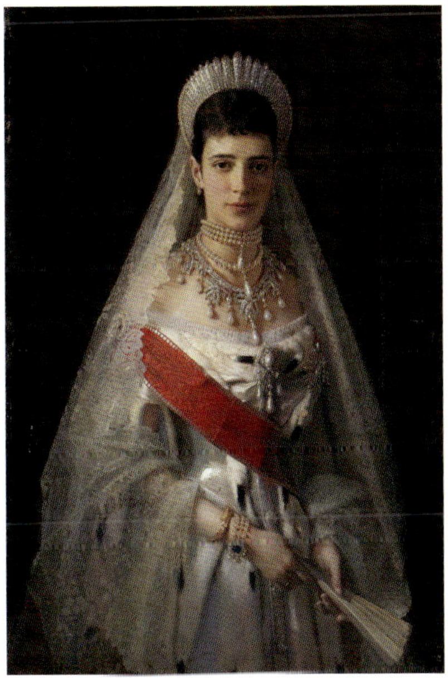

Friedrich Köchli's Romanov clients, *from top left*: Grand Duchess Maria Aleksandrovna (*née* Duchess Marie of Saxe-Coburg-Gotha), Grand Duke Paul Aleksandrovich, Grand Duke Serge Aleksandrovich and Tsar Nicholas II and his mother, Dowager Empress Maria Fedorovna, by Ivan Kramskoi. *Source: Wikimedia Commons*

Details of Köchli's life are sketchy. Like Jérémie Pauzié, Friedrich-Christian Köchli was born in Switzerland, in 1838. Records show that at age five, he was already in Russia and lived at Panteleimonskaia Street in the rectory of St. Simeon Church.[3] He worked as a goldsmith in 1864 and by 1874 opened a workshop at 7–10 Gorokhovaia Street, close to Palace Square. Other jewelers plying their trade on that street were Eduard Burchard (a member of St. Petersburg Jewelers' Association), Julius Butz (a close friend and competitor of Carl Fabergé), Victor Lindroos (a Finnish goldsmith) and Vladimir Finikov (Bolin's master jeweler). To get ahead, Köchli participated in shows and worked as the St. Petersburg administrator of foreign trade.[4] In 1870 Köchli received a bronze medal for "excellent and clean work" at the Pan Russian Exhibition in St. Petersburg.[5] By 1882 he was registered as a merchant of the Second Guild and had moved to 17 Gorokhovaia Street.[6]

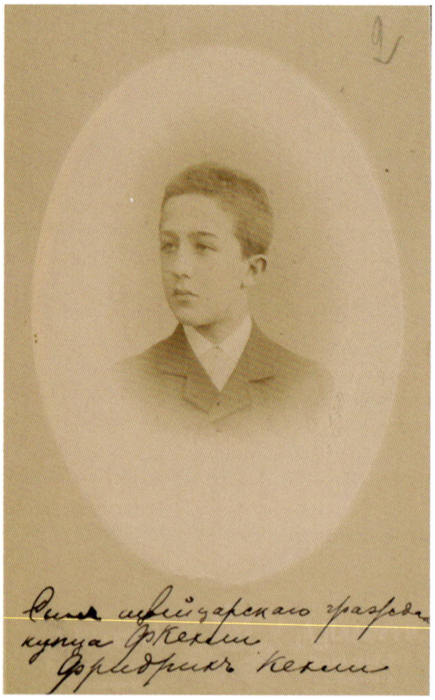

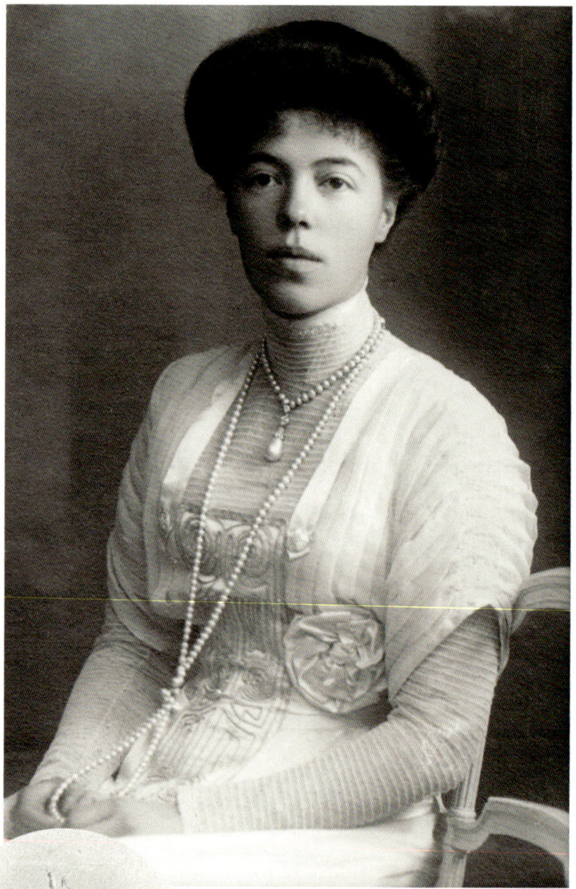

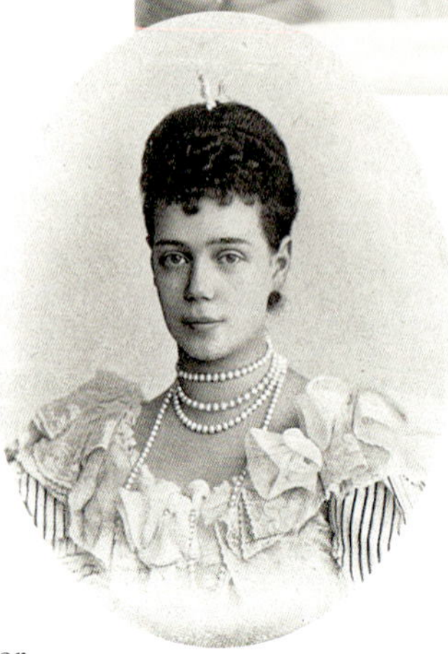

Counterclockwise from left: Friedrich Köchli's son Theodor, Grand Duchess Xenia Aleksandrovna and Grand Duchess Olga Aleksandrovna. As daughters of Tsar Alexander III, both received magnificent dowries of jewels and precious objects by Köchli. *Sources: RGIA, Romanovempire.com*

Business grew, but slowly. The first imperial commission was modest enough: a silver object (probably a cigarette case) with a gold rim and sapphire push-piece, which the jeweler made in 1888 for 133 rubles, for an artist of the Russian drama troupe.[7]

Two years later, however, the floodgates opened right on New Year's Day 1890,[8] when Alexander III's imperial cabinet placed a large order for a group of jewels including a pearl necklace and a diamond brooch for 2,877 rubles. This was followed four months later by a necklace with a diamond weighing 57 carats, for 8,000 rubles.[9] Friedrich now held the attention of the imperial court.

At this point Köchli, like Hahn, was not only making jewelry but also supplying gemstones to enhance premade pieces. It was common practice for jewelers from separate houses to join forces according to their expertise, with one making a box, and the other embellishing it with diamonds. Alexander III often turned to Köchli to enhance presentation boxes, cigarette cases, or signet rings with diamonds and rubies, although Köchli created several lavish imperial presentation boxes on his own as well.

Records show that on June 25, 1890, the cabinet commissioned 50 diamonds at 78 rubles per carat, for a total of 3,900 rubles from Köchli for this purpose.[10] In July the jeweler supplied 30 carats of rubies at 72 rubles each for 2,160 rubles, all for signet rings.[11] Orders continued throughout the year and the next. The archives reveal that Köchli adorned seven snuffboxes with diamonds and created one bracelet with Tsarevich's portrait between September and December 1890.[12] The latter was destined for Natalia Dmitrovna Logimova, the spouse of a grenadier guard major general.[13] Dowager Empress Maria Fedorovna also favored Köchli bracelets. Her imperial highness presented one each to two ladies of the chancellery of his majesty in April 1891.[14]

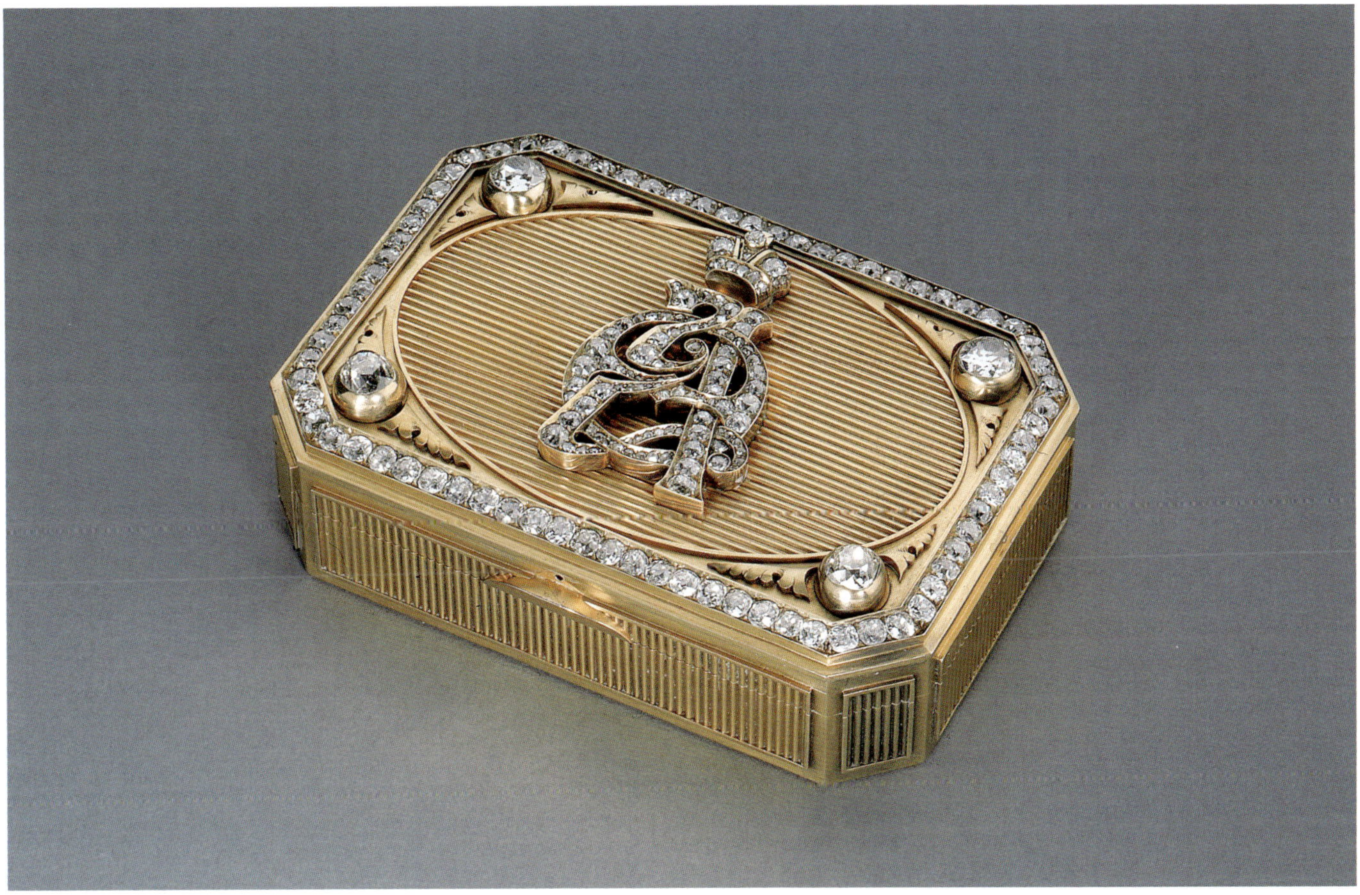

A diamond presentation box by Friedrich Köchli set with the crowned initials of Alexandra Fedorovna, ca. 1895. © *1999 Christie's Images Ltd.*

In 1892 the tsar commissioned two gold wedding bands for 70 rubles for the nuptials of Grand Duchess Xenia Aleksandrovna, his eldest daughter, a grand event that would take place two years later on July 25.[15] Köchli delivered the rings himself four days before in Peterhof.[16] This led to a spectacular commission for her *corbeille de marriage*: a sapphire-and-diamond diadem, necklace, brooch and earrings, for an astonishing 83,974 rubles.[17] The grand duchess also received lavish jewels by Bolin and Nicholls & Ewing, as well as icons covered with gold oklady and precious stones from the reserves of the cabinet, an enameled and silver presentation bread platter and salt cellar by the renowned Moscow silversmith Pavel Ovchinnikov, and a Fabergé Empire-style silver and nielloed serving set.[18]

For the wedding of Xenia's youngest sister, Grand Duchess Olga Aleksandrovna, to Peter of Oldenburg in 1901, Köchli produced a lavish set of large natural pearls with diamonds, 10 of which were 5¼ carats for 55,000 rubles.[19] Commissions for diamond presentation boxes, grand ducal *bibelots* and gem-encrusted dowries for imperial weddings kept the family busy for over two decades.

The years 1894 and 1895 proved particularly stellar for the Swiss artisan. To inaugurate a portion of the Trans-Siberian Railway (whose government committee he chaired), the future tsar, Grand Duke Nicholas Aleksandrovich, commissioned four out of the eleven presentation boxes from Friedrich Köchli. This was a coup for the small firm (compared to Fabergé's much-larger workshop). Bearing the future sovereign's miniature portrait, they were among the most-prestigious gifts the court ordered.[20] In August the jeweler made an emerald-and-diamond bracelet for the imperial cabinet, which was presented to the Mrs. Medep-Finger, an artist of the Russian opera troupe.[21]

But the firm's greatest honor to date that year was winning a competition to create the wedding parure for the future Empress Alexandra Fedorovna. A drawing of this sapphire and diamond ensemble, which included a tiara, a necklace, two pairs of earrings, a brooch and a *devant de corsage* or bodice ornament, is at the Hermitage in St. Petersburg. The Fersman inventory reveals, in original photos, the necklace, tiara, and brooch, now lost. The

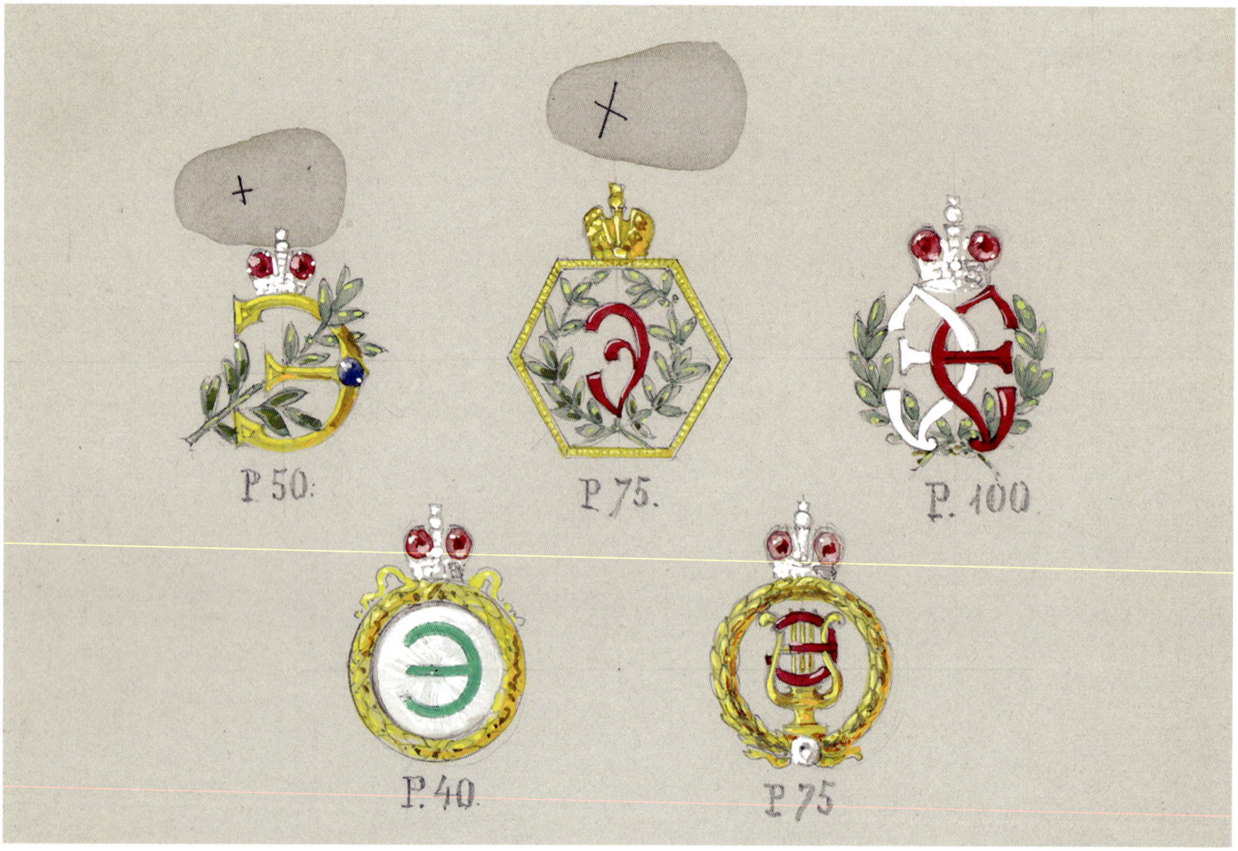
P. 50.
P. 75.
P. 100
P. 40.
P. 75

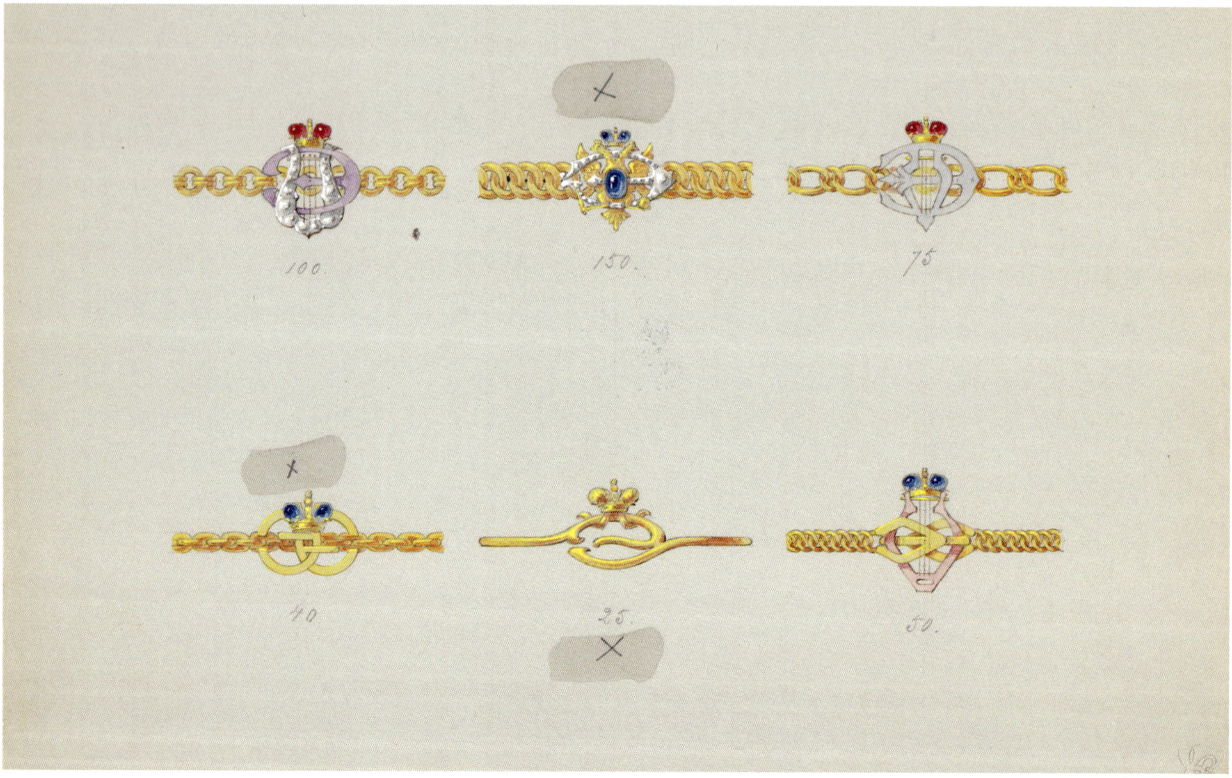
100.
150.
75
40.
25.
50.

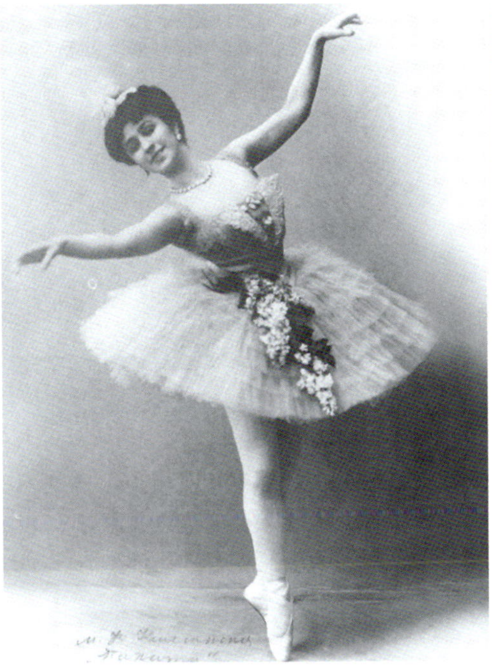

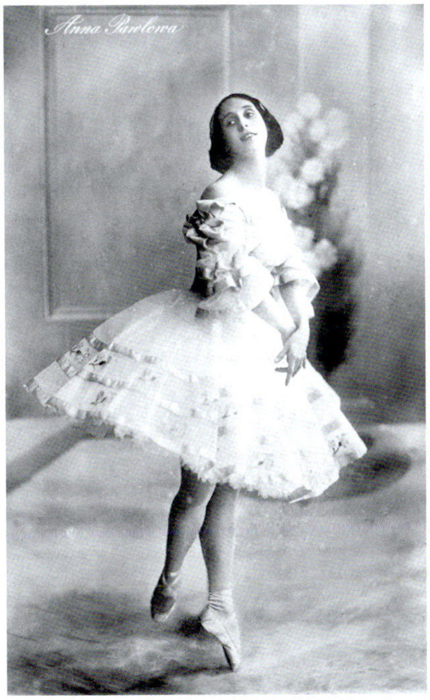

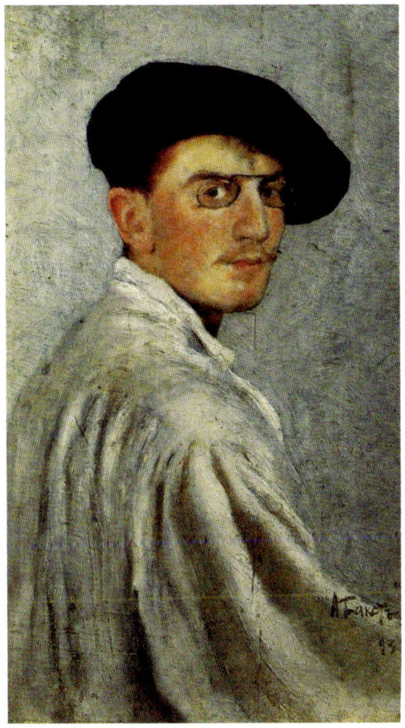

Original designs for imperial bracelets and other jewels from the workshops of both Fabergé (top) and Köchli (below). Marked with an X are those the tsar chose for gifts to the artists of the Imperial Theater in St. Petersburg, which included the famous dancers Mathilda Ksheshinskaia and Anna Pavlovna (above). Set designer Leon Bakst (above right) received a pair of diamond cuff links by Köchli. *Courtesy of RGIA and Wikimedia Commons*

tiara is set with faceted rather than cabochon-cut sapphires and appears in another photograph of the empress in profile.

In 1897 Köchli produced a brooch for the imperial cabinet set with three diamonds; the largest weighing just under 40 carats, which cost 51,000 rubles.[22]

As a transplanted Swiss, his French was fluent, and he attained international renown for his keen eye. In 1900, at age 62, Köchli served as juror *hors concours* in the Paris International Exposition. He also finally received the official title of imperial court jeweler, although the precise date is unclear.[23] Meanwhile, an invoice from 1902 indicates his position as cabinet appraiser and jeweler to the court of Dowager Empress Maria Fedorovna.[24]

Rich in ornamentation and detail, Köchli invoices attest to a distinguished aristocratic European and Russian clientele. St. Petersburg suppliers often used both French and Russian on their stationery. Köchli did so with abandon and filled every available space with decorative motifs, script, coats of arms and titles. An invoice from February 1903 shows, from top center, his position as member of the jury of the Paris Universal Exposition of 1900, followed by *Frederic Köchli, Joaillier de la Cour* and, below that, even a translation into French of the Russian street name: *Rue aux Pois*. The Russian name and address follow in bold Cyrillic lettering. The imperial double-headed eagle appears both on the right and left, each flanked by two grand ducal warrants—on the right, of Paul Aleksandrovich and Serge Aleksandrovich, and on the left, Vladimir Aleksandrovich and Maria Pavlovna. Then there is a reference to the firm's role as supplier to the court, as well as imperial jeweler to Empress Maria Fedorovna. Finally, in the center are the coats of arms and inscription *Supplier to the Imperial and Royal Courts of Duchess Marie of Saxe-Cobourg-Gotha*.

Köchli 's impressive array of titles of purveyor to the grand dukes, grand duchesses and the imperial Russian court led to brisk sales at the workshop at 17 Gorokhovaia Street. Jewels from the House of Köchli had the right look at the right price, which proved to be a winning combination for imperial gift giving on a massive scale. Perusing the designs must have pleased the emperor as well. Like his younger sister, Grand Duchess Xenia, Nicholas appreciated jewelry designs and kept an inventory of his own private collection, with drawings by his own hand.[25]

In 1902, the tsar turned both to Carl Fabergé and Friedrich Köchli for special jewelry designs. The renderings he chose would be presented as finished jewels to artists and performers of the Imperial Hermitage Theater. These colorful drawings of stickpins, bracelets and cuff links the two jewelers produced for this occasion are housed in St. Petersburg archives. Those chosen bear an "X" in pencil above coated with wax, standard practice for any notation the emperor made on official documents. By linking the Xs with Köchli's invoices, we see which jewels were selected and how many were ordered.

The emperor made his choice in the fall, and on November 2, 1902, the imperial cabinet ordered 170 jewels from Köchli: 85 pairs of cuff links priced at 25 to 150 rubles each, and 85 bracelets from 25 to 100 rubbles each. As with many Russian prerevolutionary bracelets, a gold motif adorns the center, sometimes set with diamonds or other gemstones on a gold link chain of varying width.[26]

The most expensive Köchli bracelet, which featured the crowned Russian imperial eagle enhanced with cabochon sapphires and diamonds, was presented to the famous dancers Mathilda Ksheshinskaia and Anna Pavlova. The set designer, Leon Bakst, received a pair of Köchli cuff links of similar inspiration with diamonds, as did the artists Baron Nikolai Klodt and Nikolai Figner. The late Tatiana Fabergé provides a fascinating look at the distribution of these gifts according to stature of the recipients and in some cases their peccadillos. Fedor Chaliapin turned down a pair of Fabergé cuff links for a diamond-encrusted watch, probably by Buhré, costing three times more. The artist Alexander Golovin also exchanged his pair of Köchli cuff links for a watch, but of the same price. The more stellar the performance or impression made, the more expensive the gift.[27]

The following year, again, by the order of the tsar for the artists of the Imperial Theatre, Köchli produced four bracelets and three pairs of cuff links with crowns and eagles together with two gold chains, for which he received 3,207 rubles.[28]

Friedrich's son, Theodor, graduated as a sculptor from the St. Petersburg Academy of Arts in 1890, where he won a silver medal for his skill before joining the firm. He was also an appraiser of the imperial court and a member of the Russian Applied Arts Society, together with many artists from the Fabergé firm.[29] In 1903, the two rechristened the shop FI and FF Köchli (for Fedor Ivanovich and Fedor Fedorovich, their Russian names). Sadly, it was not a long-lasting enterprise. Köchli père died six years later and his son closed the shop. The firm was purchased by a neighboring jeweler, Alexander Noskov who worked exclusively for Grand Duchess Maria Fedorovna.[30]

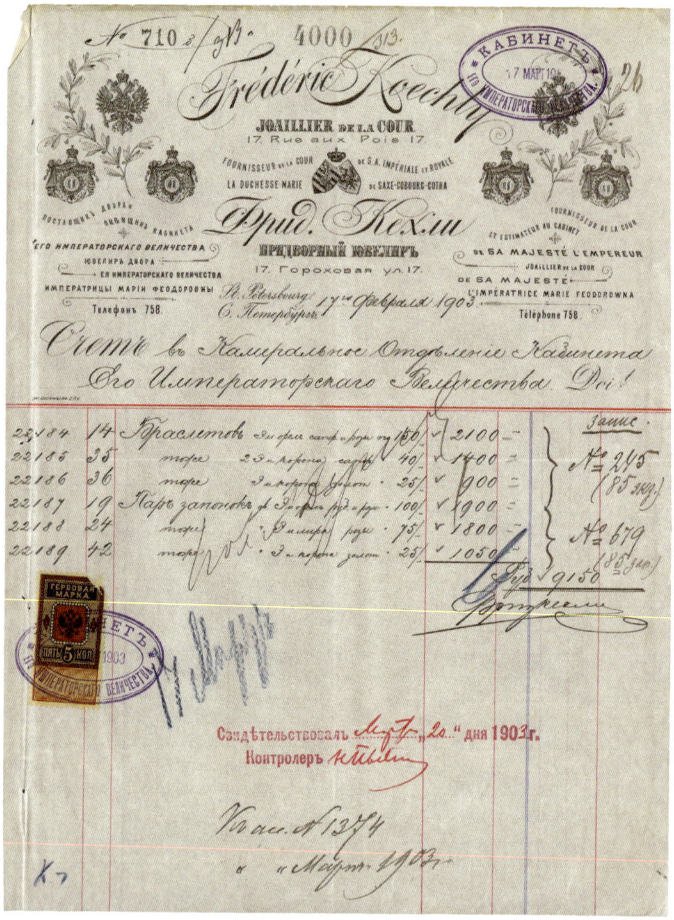
Frédéric Koechli
JOAILLIER DE LA COUR
17 Rue aux Pois 17
Фрид. Кехли
ПРИДВОРНЫЙ ЮВЕЛИРЪ
17. Гороховая ул. 17.
Телефонъ 758
Téléphone 758
КАБИНЕТЪ
Контролеръ

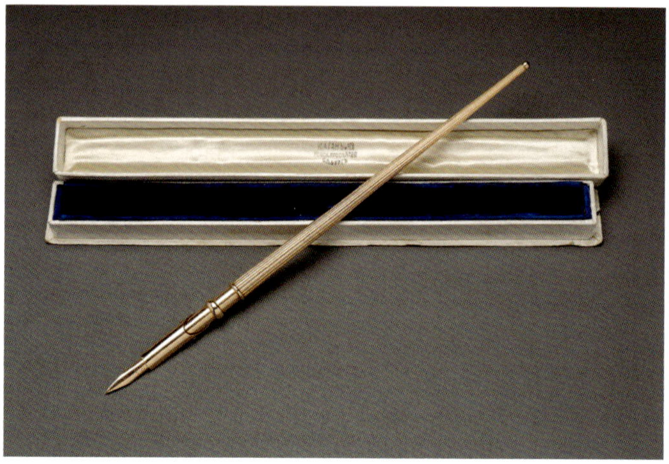

Top:
Köchli's bilingual invoice from the State Archives, dated 1903, shows the number of bracelets and cuff links ordered by Tsar Nicholas II for the performers of the Imperial Theater. *Courtesy of RGIA*

Bottom:
A reeded gold dip pen by Köchli is contained in an original box by Carl Hahn, whose store was well within walking distance of Köchli's. Another gold item, a travelling inkwell in the form of a cube by Köchli and also retailed by Hahn, sold in 1963 in London, confirming a collaboration between the two jewelers. *Marie Betteley, photo by Noel Allum*

NOTES

1. Sotheby's, London, *Romanov Heirlooms: The Lost Inheritance of Grand Duchess Maria Pavlovna*, November 30, 2009, lot 57. At over $80,000, the cuff links sold for more than 10 times the high estimate. However, in 2015, along with two other lots from the Romanov sale, they all failed to sell despite a much-lower estimate, a testament to their having been on the market too recently. Fabergé workmasters Wigström and Hollming also favored the man-in-the moon motif.

2. RGIA, f 468, o 14, d 2714, l 2.

3. RGIA, f 20, o 3, d 1985, l 32.

4. Tillander-Godenhielm, *Jewels from Imperial St. Petersburg*, 291.

5. He was among 12 jewelers from Russia participating in the fair, including Bolin, who won the top prize. *Vserossiiskaia manufakturnaia vystavka 1870 g.* (St. Petersburg: Obshchestvennyi listok, 1870), 117.

6. RGIA f 20, o 3, d 1985, l 32.

7. RGIA f 468, o 43, d 995, l 289.

8. According to the Julian calendar then used in Russia, which at the time followed the Gregorian calendar by 12 days.

9. RGIA f 468, o 43, d 995, l 10, nos. 24 and 25.

10. While earlier that month Köchli sold the imperial cabinet 75 diamonds at 60 rubles per carat for signet rings and brooches, in July, Köchli procured for the imperial cabinet 110 carats of diamonds totaling over 4,400 rubles. RGIA f 468, o 43, d 993, ll 2 and 3; f 468, o 43, d 992, l 58.

11. RGIA f 468, o 43, d 992, l 34.

12. RGIA f 468, o 43, d 993, l 3.

13. RGIA f 468, o 43, d 995, l 41.

14. RGIA f 468, o 43, d 995, ll 41–42 obverse.

15. RGIA f 468, o 43, d 995, l 366.

16. RGIA f 468, o 43, d 995, l 3667.

17. RGIA f 468, o 43, d 995, l 5 obverse. This was delivered to Empress Alexandra Fedorovna in 1895; RGIA f 468, o 43, d 995, l 6.

18. RGIA f 468, o 8, d 648, ll 1–2.

19. RGIA f 468, o 8, d 468, l 3 and f 468, o 43, d 995, l 13.

20. Three boxes were listed as enhanced with diamonds by Köchli in 1894. RGIA f 468, o 43, d 994, l 176 (obverse) 178.

21. RGIA, f 468, o 43, d 995, l 49.

22. RGIA, f 468, o 13, d 1843, l 3.

23. Köchli's name appears below the imperial warrant in his 1894 designs for Alexandra Fedorovna's wedding parure, which suggests that he already held the appointment of court supplier.

24. RGIA f 20, o 3, d 1985, l 32.

25. Alexander von Solodkoff, *The Jewel Album of Tsar Nicholas and a Collection of Private Photographs of the Russian Imperial Family* (London: Ermitage, 1997).

26. RGIA f. 468, o. 8, d. 697, ll. 26.

27. Fabergé et al., *Fabergé: A Comprehensive Reference Book*, 458.

28. RGIA F 468, o 8, d 694, l 15.

29. Tatiana Muntian, comp., *The World of Fabergé* (Moscow: Red Square, 2000), 219.

30. Fabergé et al., *Fabergé: A Comprehensive Reference* Book, 111.

7

History

FABERGÉ IN PERSPECTIVE

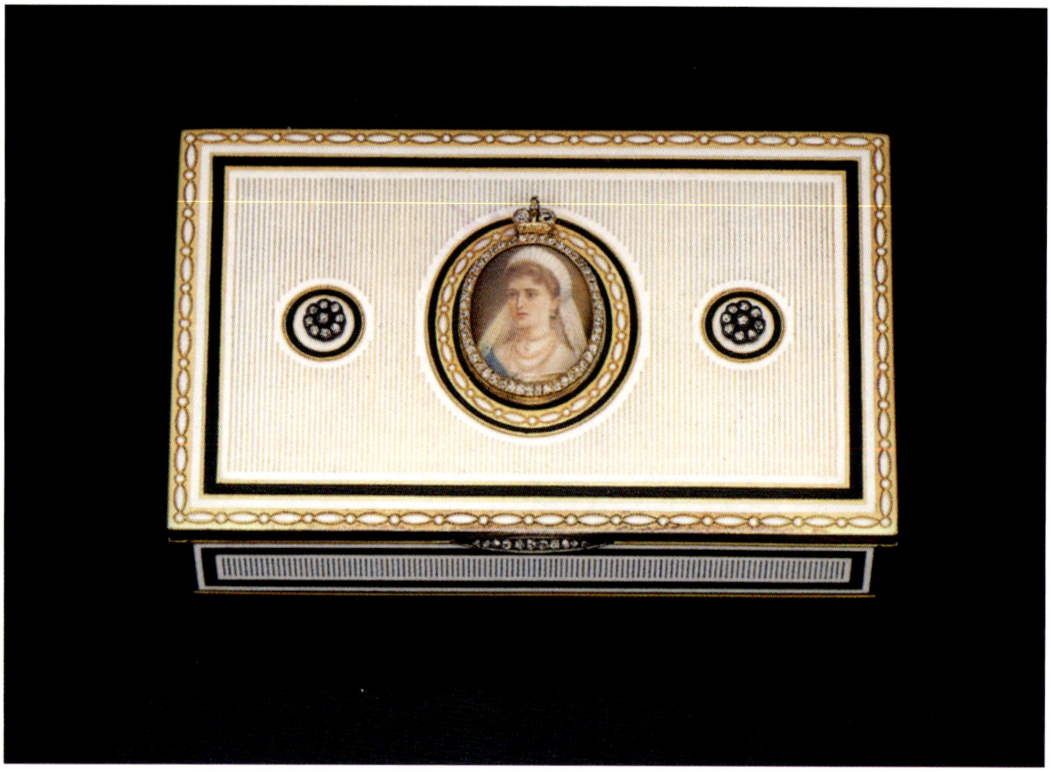

Carl Fabergé. The name evokes grand images of the glittering Russian Empire, the lavish riches of its court, of European royalty and, of course, the eggs. The 50 spectacular eggs the tsars commissioned every Easter are among the most celebrated artifacts of the Romanov dynasty's splendor before its tragic demise. As a European-trained goldsmith, Carl Fabergé led a multitude of artisan workshops with legions of enamelers, goldsmiths, designers, engravers, polishers, gem cutters and more to produce these exquisite objects. His story is well known. But was he himself a creative genius?

A Fabergé imperial presentation compact graced with the portrait of Alexandra Fedorovna from the estate of the Honorable Clare Booth Luce, American editor and ambassador. A superb example of Henrik Wigström's champlevé enameling technique. *Courtesy of Sotheby's*

Above all, Carl Gustavovich Fabergé (1846–1920) was a brilliant visionary. Energetic and decisive, he hired only the finest, whether as in-house workmasters or independent contractors, and even in his own day succeeded in elevating his company to cult status. That the eggs and his legacy still fascinate us today, over 100 years after the Bolshevik Revolution, is also testament to a creative marketing strategy, a trait he may well have inherited from his father.

When Estonian-born Gustav Faberg (1814–94) opened his shop on Bolshaia Morskaia Street in 1842, his first move was to add the accented *é* to his surname, knowing a French-sounding name would attract business.[1] Russia had admired France for its taste in luxury since the reign of Empress Elizabeth, and French was still the language of the court.

While Gustav lacked originality, he had excellent credentials, having trained under two of St. Petersburg's best master jewelers, Andreas-Ferdinand Spiegel (1797–1862) and Johann Wilhelm Keibel (1788–1862).[2] Court jeweler since 1841, Keibel had restored the coronation crown of Tsar Nicholas I in 1826. His father, Otto Samuel (1768–1808), was a leading court jeweler and among the best in St. Petersburg.

Gustav in turn hired help with great promise, mostly of European origin, including a number of Finns.[3] One, the jeweler Hiskias Pendin (1823–81), would manage the firm when his boss retired to Dresden in 1860, and mentor Fabergé *fils*, Carl.[4] The other, August Holmström (1829–1903), a future head workmaster under Carl, would become one of the finest jewelers/designers in Russia.[5] At first, the Fabergé shop sold traditional jewels to the public rather than the court. By comparison, in the 1860s master jewelers Bolin and Seftigen enjoyed close connection to the Romanovs and regularly received imperial commissions.

Gustav's sons, Carl and Agathon, were educated in Europe. Carl apprenticed in Germany and visited its various royal and princely collections in the mid-1860s, traveling with soon-to-be fellow jeweler Julius Butz. Sixteen years younger, his brother Agathon would join the family firm as a brilliant designer in 1882. When Carl took over the St. Petersburg workshop in 1870 (or 1872), he initially seemed content to keep the status quo.

A sensational discovery of ancient gold jewels in 1867 in the Kerch Peninsula east of Crimea would change the firm's direction. Still in his 20s, Carl had offered his services as restorer pro bono at the Hermitage for years. Therefore, when Count Sergei Stroganov, president of the Imperial Archaeological Commission, offered the treasures to the Hermitage Museum, its director approached Fabergé for an appraisal and restoration. Once exhibited, the hoard met with overwhelming interest from the public as it confirmed a rich cultural heritage similar to that of other great civilizations.[6]

Eager to capitalize on this trend, and sensing a potential windfall, Fabergé decided to make copies of the ancient gold objects.[7] Stroganov and German emperor Wilhelm II placed their orders. To fulfill them, Carl hired former Holmström apprentice Erik Kollin, a newly minted Finnish goldsmith. Kollin quickly mastered the long-forgotten techniques of ancient gold granulation and filigree, and it became his signature style. Fringe necklaces, bangles with ram's-head terminals, pins and chandelier earrings flew out of the shop on Bolshaia Morskaia Street. The collection caused a sensation.

While the House of Fabergé first thrived on copies, it was a departure from his father's tried-and-true stock in trade. With Kollin's jewels—technically perfect, but still replicas the master's early jewels reflected a nascent tendency to emulate historical styles.[8] It was younger brother Agathon rather than Carl who would provide the impetus for the creative direction the firm would follow. In 1884, the first Fabergé objects emerged, probably all based on Agathon's designs. Sadly, the designer died of pneumonia at age 33 before witnessing the firm's rise.

Like his fellow jewelers, Fabergé exhibited at trade fairs, both in Russia and abroad. The first was the Pan Russian Exhibition of Arts and Industry in Moscow in 1882, followed by Nuremberg in 1885 and Copenhagen in 1888. In Moscow, the illustrious House of Bolin won the top prize and exhibited several magnificent creations, including a luxurious tiara priced at 120,000 rubles, while Fabergé won the third gold medal for its Scythian-style copies. However, it was there that he met Tsar Alexander III, who made his first purchase from him: a pair of gold cicada cuff links. Even then, at shows it was not about sales, or even prizes, but contacts.

An Egg with a Surprise

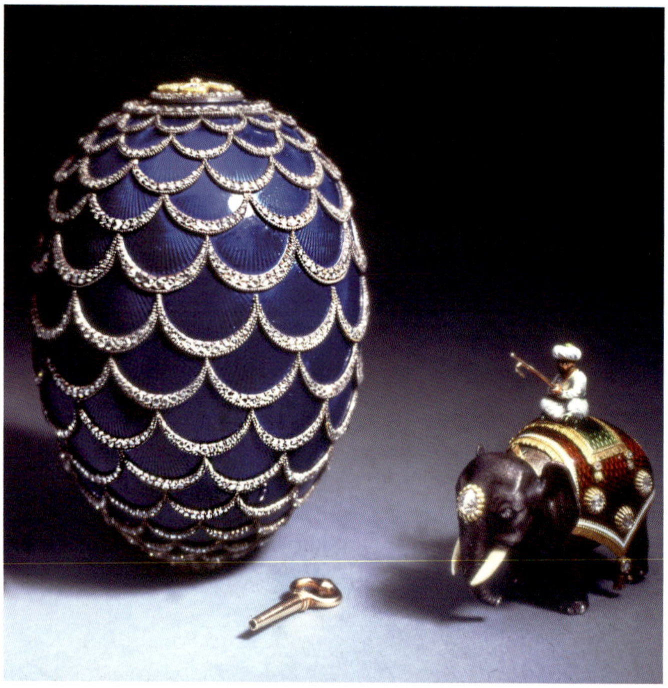

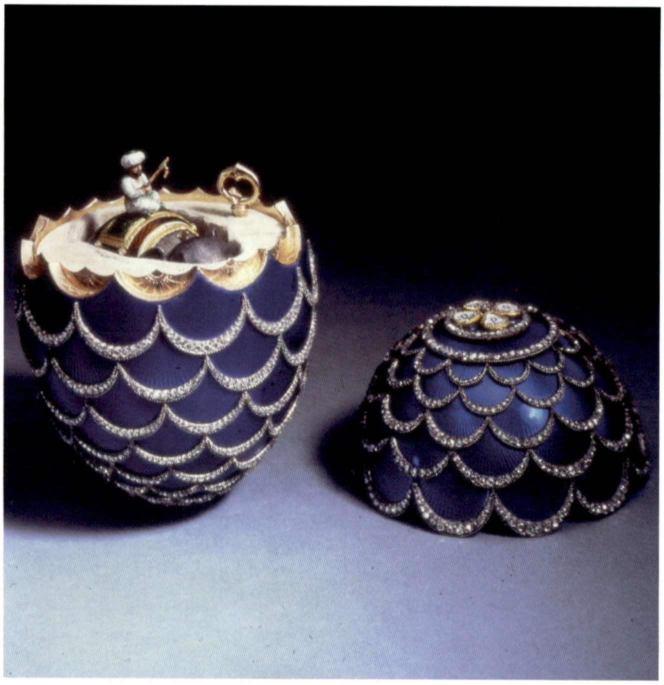

In 1885, after 43 years in business, the House of Fabergé received the coveted title of purveyor to the Russian court, allowing it to display the Romanov eagle emblem on its storefront and letterhead. With this honor, the firm joined Hahn, Bolin, Seftigen and others. Thereafter, its star would soar.

That same year, Tsar Alexander III commissioned Fabergé to create the first Easter egg as a present to his wife, Maria Fedorovna, née Princess Dagmar of Denmark. Ever attentive to his clients' demands and the empresses' background, Fabergé chose an 18th-century French prototype in the Danish royal collection as the basis of his design. The first egg contained not one but five surprises, the smallest of which are now lost (two ruby pendants and a Romanov crown). Of plain white enamel, it opened to reveal a two-color gold hen. The tsar's brother, Grand Duke Vladimir Aleksandrovich, was instrumental in its purchase and gave detailed instructions on how to open each section.[9] The idea of opening the egg to reveal a surprise proved irresistible to the imperial couple.

The emperor ordered another egg the following year and every year thereafter until his death in 1894. His son, Nicholas II, continued the custom and ordered two eggs each year, one for his widowed mother and the other for his consort, Alexandra. Except for the years 1904 and 1905 during the Russo-Japanese War, the practice continued until the empire's fall in 1917.[10]

Surprises enclosed in each imperial Easter egg proved the final manifestation of Fabergé marketing genius. Miniatures representing a theme, an occasion, a family celebration—all intimate and personal reflections of life at court—would become the firm's hallmark. Fabergé knew how to cater to his clients, and had an uncanny ability to create whatever *objet de fantaisie* would appeal to them most at a given time.

Based on existing 18th-century eggs already in museums, most of those Alexander III presented to Maria Fedorovna were not unique. Later the eggs became more intricate, distinctive and, except for the war years, larger (increasing in size from 2½ to 14⅜ inches). The Colonnade Egg was second largest and was hewn of bowenite, a light-green signature stone of the workshop. In 1913 Fabergé created perhaps the grandest of all, the Winter Egg. The most expensive, it symbolized spring.[11]

Surprises varied, although some, such as the elephant and clock mechanisms, were repeated. The most spectacular were those that had miniature replicas of imperial vessels, trains, palaces, or churches, such as the Coronation Egg enclosing the imperial coach in gold, platinum and rock crystal; the Trans-Siberian Railway Egg; the Gatchina Palace Egg; and the Memory of Azov Egg, which reproduced in exact detail the cruiser on a sea of aquamarine. The Moscow Kremlin Egg re-created the Cathedral of the Assumption, complete with miniature icons, gold cupolas and a chiming clock. Although not the first object to be made of platinum, the Alexander III Equestrian Egg of 1910 was Russia's greatest showpiece of the noble metal, of which the empire boasted the world's largest deposits.[12] In 1916, at the height of the Great War, Fabergé brought the St. George Cross Egg to Dowager Empress Maria Fedorovna, who had moved to Kiev and would keep the egg until her death in 1928 in Denmark.[13]

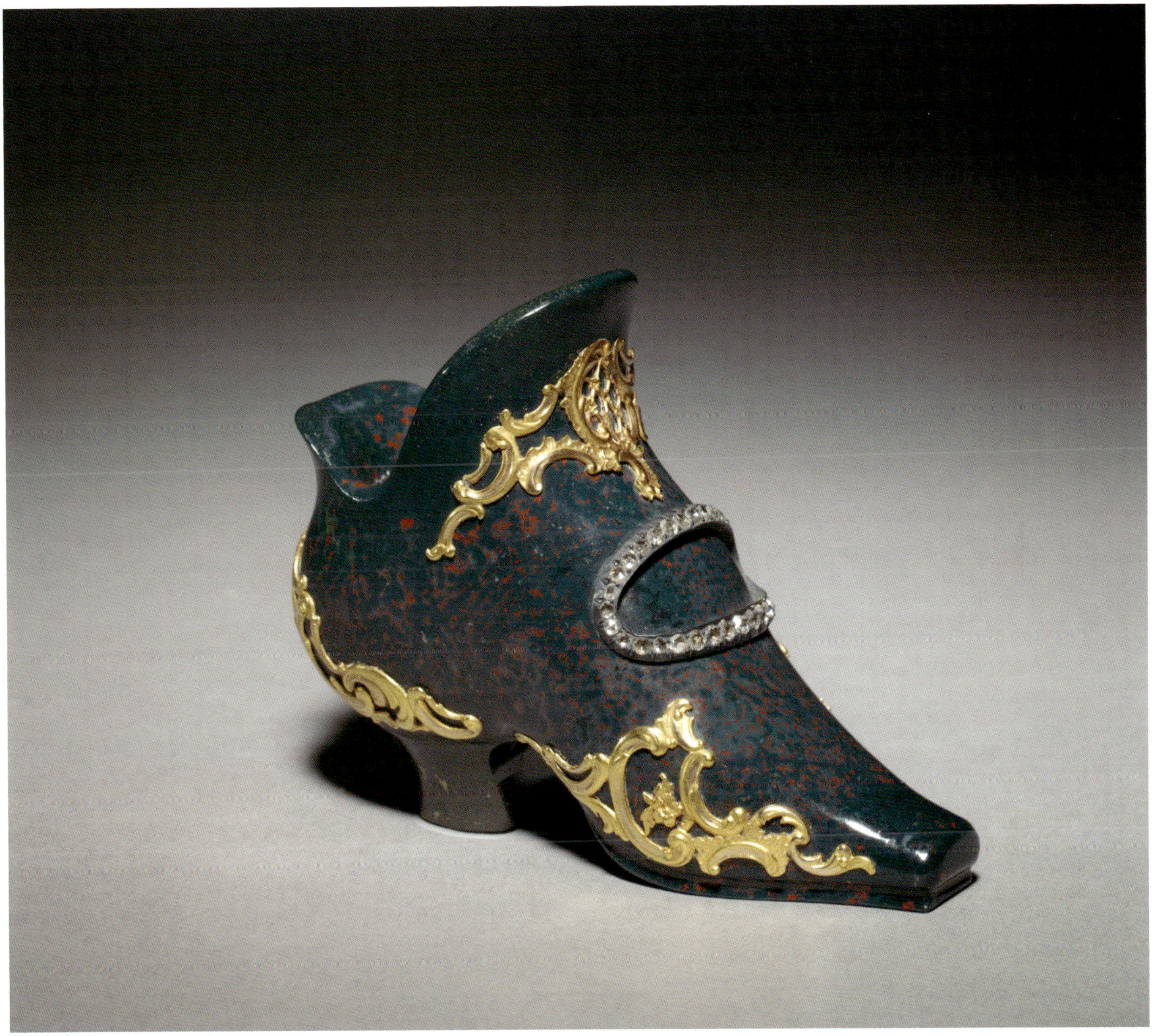

Fabergé miniature shoe, ca. 1890, workmaster Mikhail Perchin. *Courtesy the Cleveland Museum of Art, the India Early Minshall Collection 1966.482*

Previous Page
Two views of the Pine Cone egg. While not made for the tsar, the Pine Cone Egg of 1900 is equally as dazzling. It was one of seven jeweled eggs commissioned by the gold-mining magnate Alexander Kelch for his wife, Barbara, and contained an automaton elephant complete with enameled mahout. © *1989 Christie's Images Ltd.*

The Secret Recipe for Success

Inspired by his triumph with the eggs, Carl Fabergé continued looking to the past. He chose existing historical styles that were popular with the nobility, such as neo-Renaissance, Louis XV and XVI and neoclassic, and began to create a niche market that he would come to dominate. To maintain quality and perfection, he never mixed styles. Fabergé took it one step further. As copies enchanted, so would miniatures. For who doesn't love tiny models, the more intricate the better? He then set out to spot and lure talent capable of realizing these creations.

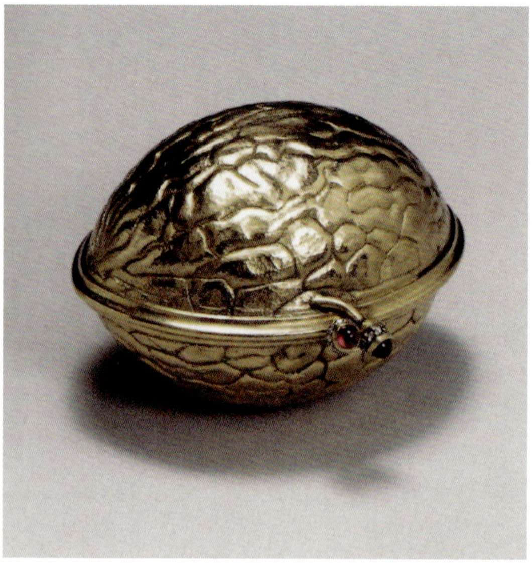

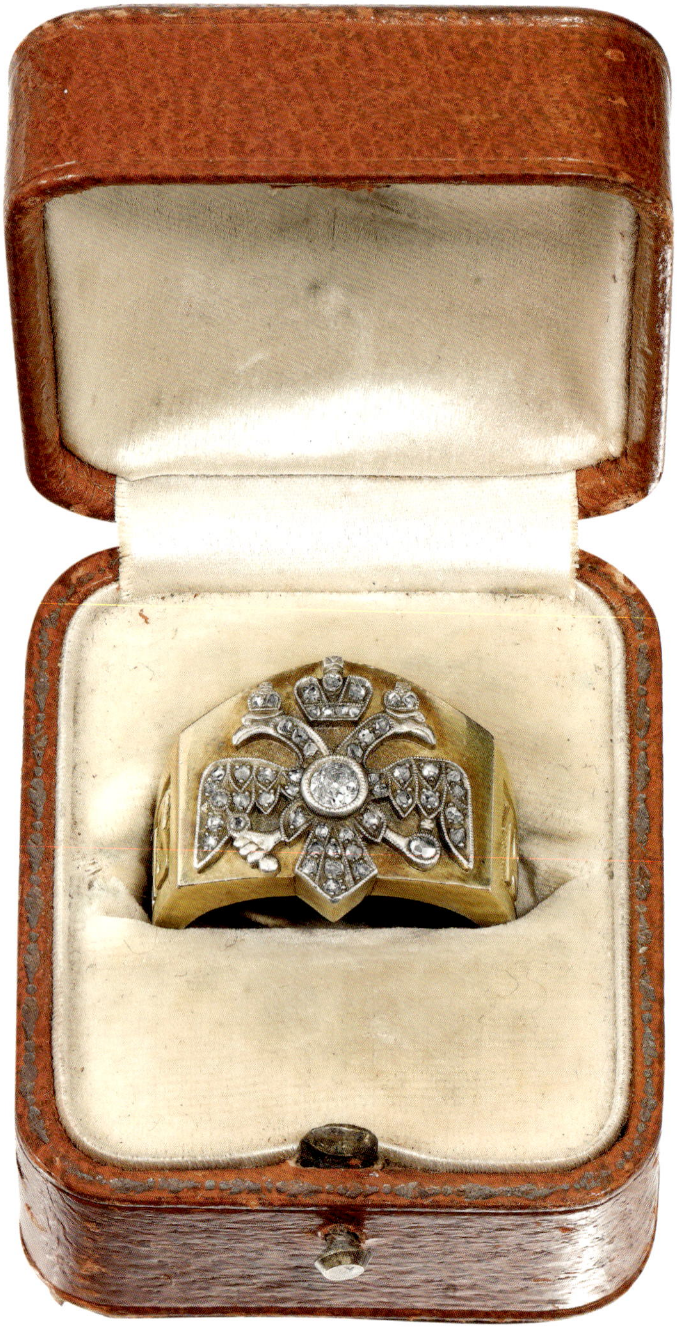

Top artists began to produce miniature paintings of the imperial family, aristocracy, or foreign royalty, or their palaces, each encased in tiny frames. From various workshops, feasts of diminutive replicas materialized, some based on nature, such as hardstone flowers, animals and carvings of local or popular figures, and others on existing themes, in gold and enamel, sometimes set with rose diamonds. These ranged from sedan chairs, sledges, teapots, a rococo lady's shoe, flowers, cannons, picture frames, harps, carved animals and miniature egg pendants, to a spectacular diamond set miniature of the imperial regalia by Holmström.[14] On a pink-quartzite plinth with silver mounts by Julius Rappaport, another Fabergé workmaster, tiny diamond replicas of Catherine the Great's imperial crown by Pauzié, and Empress Alexandra's crown by Carl Hahn, together with minutely detailed orb and scepter, each rested on velvet cushions. To the general public, the original treasures by Hahn and Pauzié were soon eclipsed by the charming miniature renditions Fabergé created.

A diamond presentation ring by workmaster Thielemann displays an imperial eagle for the tercentenary of the Romanov rule in 1913 (*above*), and a miniature gold box in the form of a walnut (*top left*) by Erik Kollin. *© 2002 Christie's Images Ltd. and Courtesy of Sotheby's*

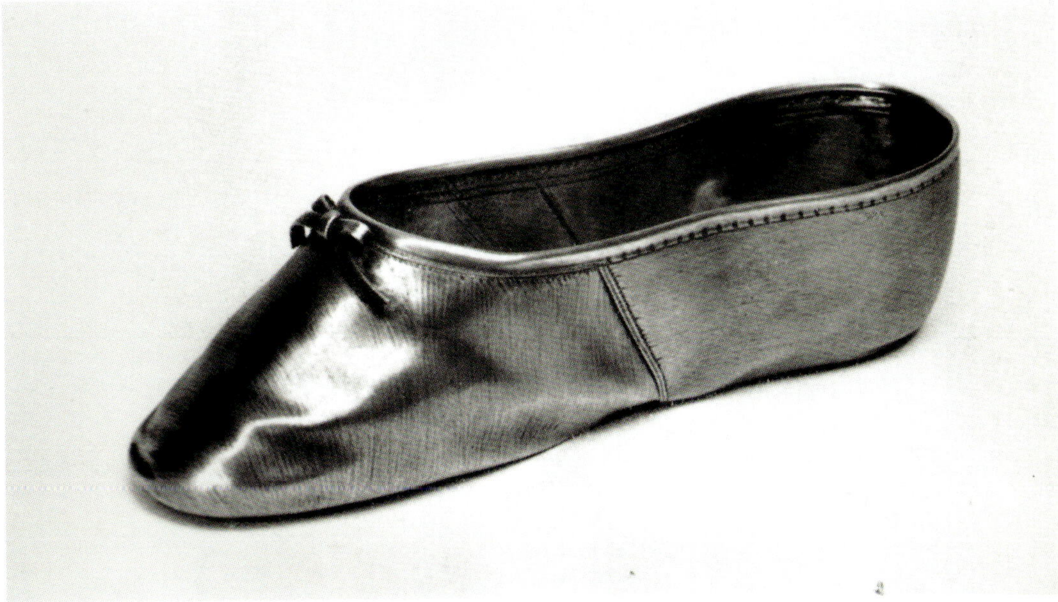

This life-size silver slipper by Fabergé, which no doubt was presented to a ballerina, appeared at auction in the 1960s. It was engraved to simulate satin and the stitching along the sides. *Courtesy of Sotheby's (Sotheby & Co.)*

Paris Exhibition of 1900 and International Fame

At the Paris World Exposition, Fabergé displayed the latest series of imperial eggs, as well as the aforementioned miniature imperial regalia and a host of costly bibelots and jewels. Suddenly everyone wanted enamel objets d'art and accessories from this Russian workshop. Its marketing apparatus, now in full swing, was further fueled by rich foreigners. It became de rigueur to show off the latest trinket acquired from this court artisan. Even the simplest items took on an air of opulence, from cane handles and bonbonnières to belt buckles and enameled bell pushes.

And while the firm repeated designs of cigarette cases and the popular miniature eggs often in different materials and enamel colors, gifts from the House of Fabergé always seemed unique and personalized. Who could resist a present from the famous house carefully chosen by an admirer or a loved one? Articles of curiosity would appeal to a whole range of buyers and, more important, recipients, the way expensive jewels could not.

Carl Fabergé's timing was perfect. Among the royal houses of Europe, many of whose families were related to each other, it became fashionable to give presents by Fabergé for every occasion, be it a wedding, anniversary, or birthday or Saint's Day, or at Christmas or Easter. Word of mouth spread from royal circles to the Russian, English and European aristocracy, and overseas to moneyed American magnates. While jewelry was the domain of other goldsmiths such as Bolin, a bibelot by Fabergé became the gift of choice for crowned heads of Europe. The jeweler's reputation even spread to Siam, as well as Persia, India and China.[15]

Fabergé built his empire by propelling this gift-giving tradition to frenzied new heights in St. Petersburg during the reign of the last two tsars. Recording these gifts in personal albums appealed to several members of the imperial family. Nicholas II himself, like his sister, Grand Duchess Xenia, kept detailed drawings in his own hand of gifts received. In both cases the quality of design is high, indicating a fascination with adornments, from jeweled egg pendants and cuff links to lavish diamond rivières and tiaras. The empress also kept an album of hundreds of miniature eggs she received from family and friends from 1897 to 1906, not all by Fabergé.[16]

Presentation was key, both to appeal to the gift giver and recipient. Anticipating the thrill of discovery in all of us, Fabergé encased each creation in a fitted box to enhance the element of surprise, as those hidden in imperial eggs. Four box-making

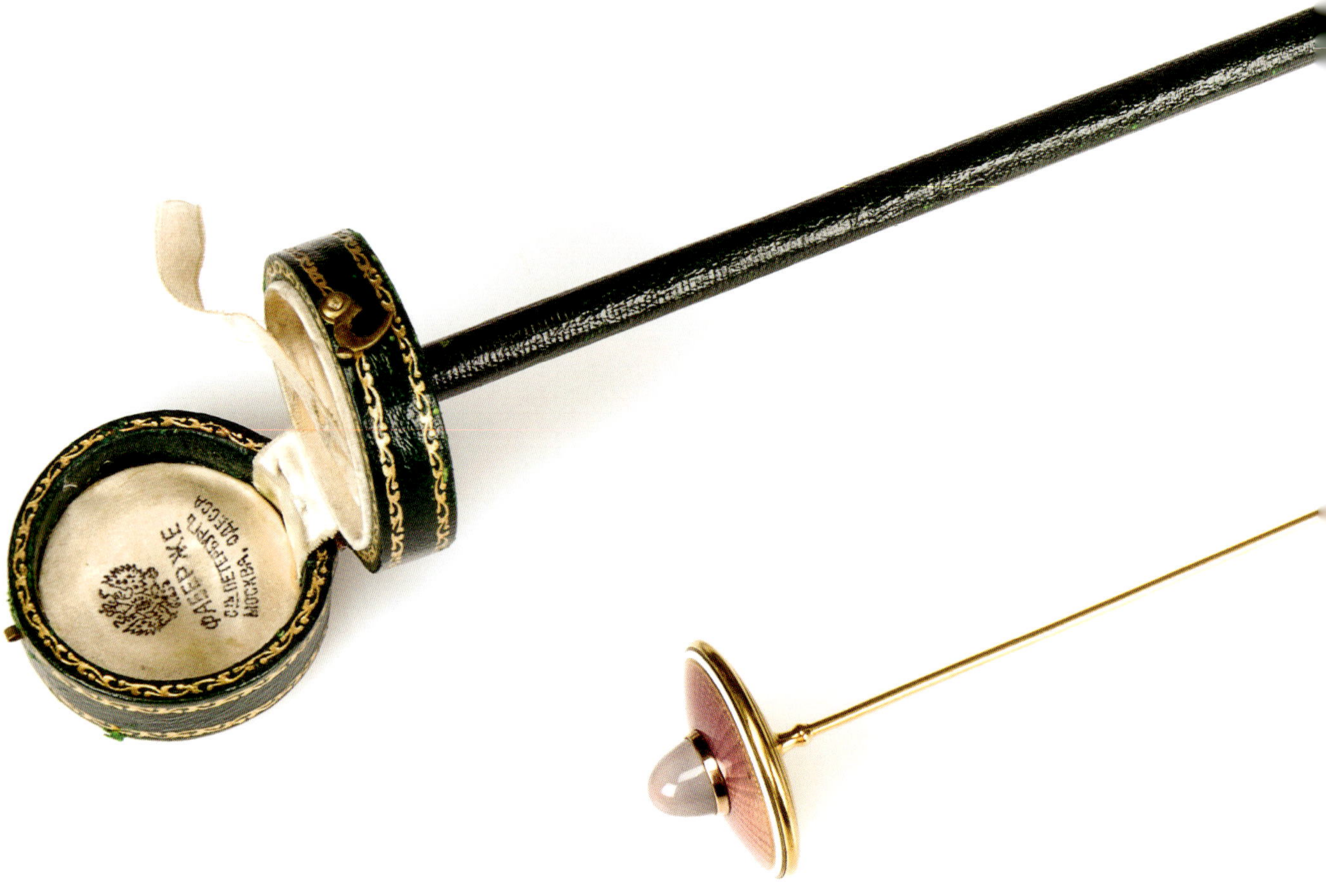
ФАБЕРЖЕ
С.П.ПЕТЕРБУРГЪ
МОСКВА, ОДЕССА

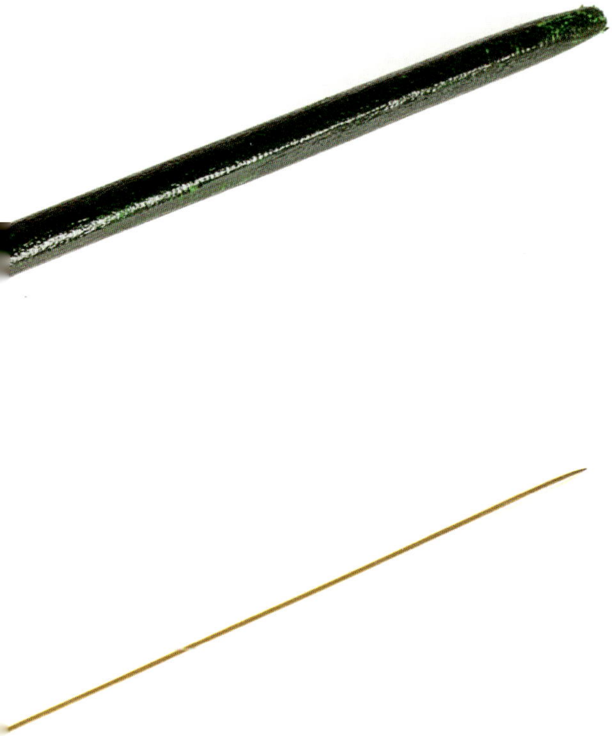

Even hatpins had their own fitted cases fashioned by one of the box-making workshops solely dedicated to this skill, one of which was installed after 1900 on the same premises as the Fabergé St. Petersburg flagship store at 24 Bolshaia Morskaia Street. *Courtesy of Bonham's*

workshops in St. Petersburg, mostly run by Finns, operated full time to fulfill this task, albeit not all just for Fabergé [17] One exception is the firm of Käki, which after 1901 was installed in the courtyard of the Fabergé headquarters, to be in close contact with workmasters as they completed their creations. Cases covered in red or black morocco for the imperial family always bore an applied or imprinted Romanov double-headed eagle on its cover.[18] Others were of cloth, velvet, leather, or, most commonly, palisander or birchwood. Each was silk-lined with the imperial warrant and name of the master jeweler on the lid's interior. Today, these fitted cases are prized almost as much as the objects themselves and add substantial value if still preserved.[19]

Expansion

By 1914, the firm numbered some 700 workers and had added four branches: Moscow (1887), Odessa (from 1900), Kiev (1906–10) and London (from 1903), the latter well patronized by the sister of Marie Fedorovna, Queen Alexandra, and her husband, King Edward VII. For the British monarch, Fabergé produced a series of replicas of the royal menagerie in Sandringham in hardstone. This delighted the king until he learned that copies of these animals commissioned by him were being sold in the London shop, after which he stipulated that only one of each kind would be made, and then only for him.[20]

The Moscow workshop generated a great deal of business, producing massive quantities of silver and accessories for the rich merchant class. This workshop's creations were not always unique. Like those of his fellow artisans, the wares Fabergé

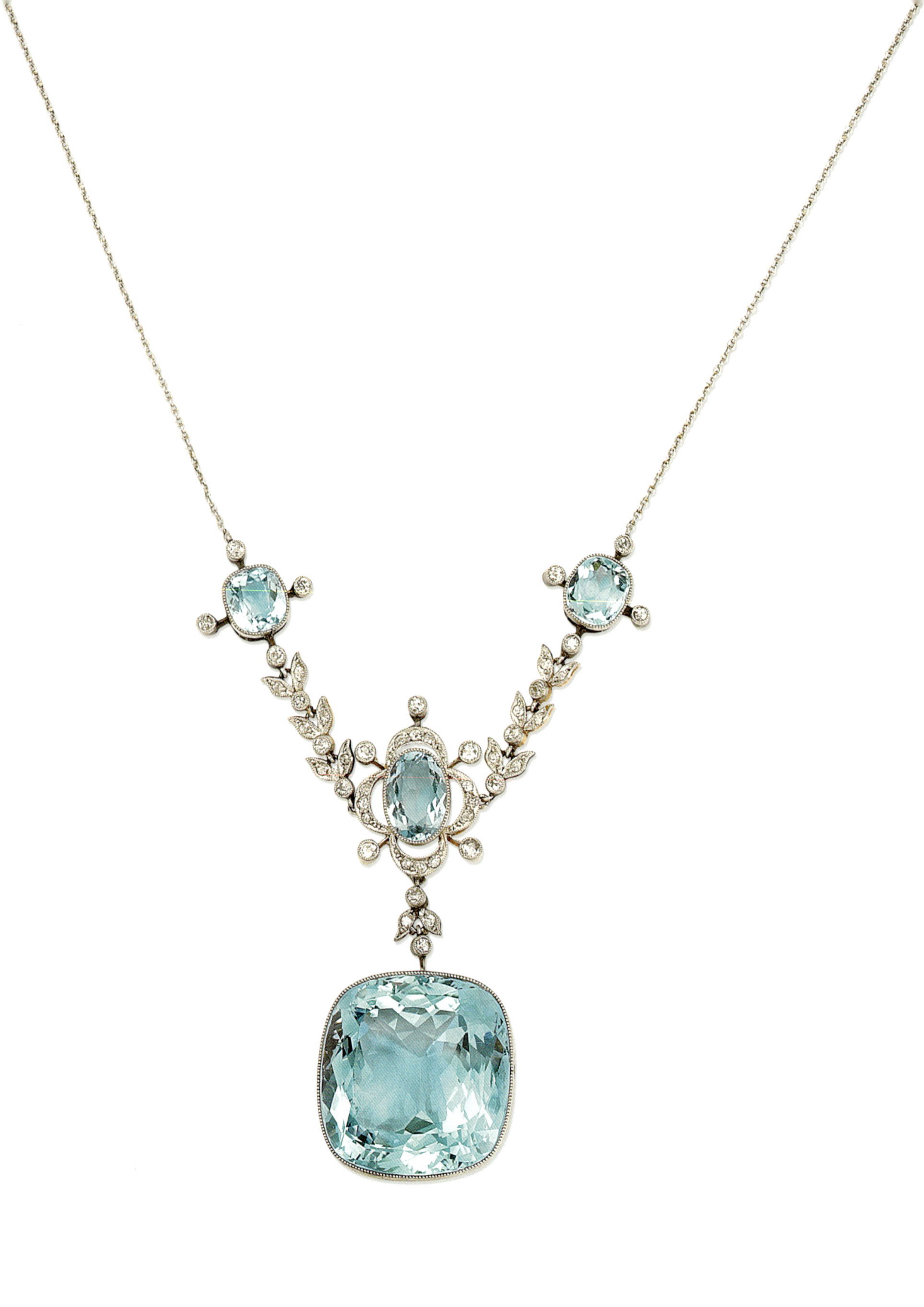

An aquamarine and diamond pendant in the Belle Epoque style made in the Moscow workshop, ca. 1900. Many but not all of Fabergé jewels are stamped; some, like this example, bear only an inventory number. *© 2011 Christie's Images Ltd.*

created in the ancient capital reflected current fashions. Many silver-mounted, cut-glass decanters, centerpieces, punch bowls and kovsh by Fabergé are indistinguishable from those of other silversmiths. Figural silver of bogatyrs (medieval Russian warriors) and peasant women wearing kokoshniks were not the sole domain of Fabergé, but themes pioneered and perfected by Sazikov and Grachev. Guilloché design in fact started with Sazikov, when he bought the first such engine-turning machine in the mid-19th century.

Some of the finest enamels also came from Fabergés' Moscow ateliers, although unlike in St. Petersburg, they were never signed by the makers. Perhaps the most famous Fabergé enamel piece from Moscow was a cigarette case given to King Edward VII by his last mistress, Mrs. Alice Keppel (now in the collection of HM Queen Elizabeth). Of striking translucent royal blue enamel, the case is enveloped by a sinuous diamond-set serpent.

Imperial patrons of the Moscow workshop included Grand Duchess Elizabeth Fedorovna, wife of Grand Duke Serge, the Moscow governor general who was assassinated by terrorists in 1905. After this tragedy, the grand duchess took the veil and had all her family jewelry restyled by the Moscow workshop to give as presents to her friends. Like Tiffany in America, and Marshak of Kiev, Fabergé produced illustrated catalogues to advertise its merchandise to the buying public. A republished 1893 Moscow catalogue reveals a variety of jewelry in all price ranges, from gold brooches for 3 rubles, 50 kopeks, to a diamond necklace for 35,000 rubles.

Like many astute businessmen, Fabergé lured away talented masters from other firms. Many who trained in competing workshops ended up with the jeweler, more so than the other way around. One exception is Samuel Arnd, who worked for Fabergé from 1902 to 1906 and then for Carl Bock.[21] Among those who honed their skills in other ateliers before joining Fabergé were Robert Bach (1859–1933), a talented sculptor and former director of Nicholls & Plincke, Konstantin Linke (1865–after 1917) and Wilhelm Wilhelmovich Goetz (b. 1883), both from Bolin.[22]

While the story of Fabergé is well published (in over 500 sources), that of his artists, designers, miniaturists and enamelers is much less so. They were the soul of the company. Who were the artisans behind the fabled name? We know of head workmasters Michael Perchin, Henrik Wigström, Erik Kollin, August Holmström, August Hollming and Julius Rappaport. They had their own workshops and hallmarks and worked exclusively for the firm. However, many more worked in obscurity. Thanks to two recent publications, *The Era of Fabergé* and *Fabergé: A Comprehensive Reference Book*, this is beginning to change.

Gem merchant Ilia Margolin was rarely mentioned in early books on Fabergé, yet he was the imperial cabinet's most important source of precious stones and pearls. Along with Carl Hahn, Margolin supplied gems for Fabergé snuffboxes and brooches for the 1896 Coronation of Tsar Nicholas II.[23] In St. Petersburg, Vasilii Vasilievich Boitsov can take credit for making Fabergé enamels famous.[24] Others include Peter Nikolaevich Popov, who excelled in Byzantine style enamels, and Nikolai Aleksandrovich Petrov, chief enameler of the House of Fabergé from 1895 to 1917. We see an image of him as a young man in front of a hot brick oven, whose workshop was located in the basement of Fabergé's house. Now recognized as one of the greatest Russian enamelers, he died of malnutrition and stress in 1918.[25]

Carl Fabergé sought to capitalize as much on his fame and royal connections as he could. When the Great War broke out in 1914, the firm shifted from one market to another as the political climate dictated, turning its sights on the Siamese royal family, which was unaffected by the turbulence. But this would go only so far. World War I brought the end to many of Europe's reigning houses. Yet, the St. Petersburg workshop continued operating, producing four more imperial eggs for the tsar, all despite a restricted workforce: 89 employees from the St. Petersburg firm were called up to fight or work in munitions factories, and in Odessa, only three remained out of 35. London closed. Ironically, the demand for gifts even rose during the war.[26]

Despite his fame, Carl Fabergé shunned the spotlight. Shy and reclusive, when orders from wealthy Moscow financiers outpaced those from His Majesty's Cabinet, he was pleased. The newly moneyed were more willing to accept his designs and prices. It was customary for some members of the imperial family to dictate not only costs, but designs, especially for special occasions. Birnbaum mentions that the tsarina imposed her own drawings

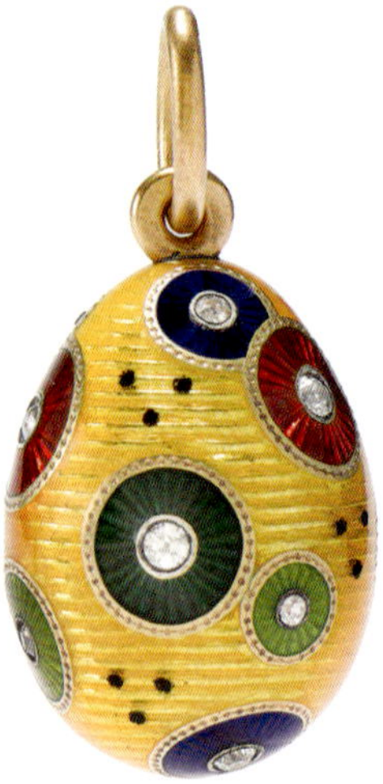

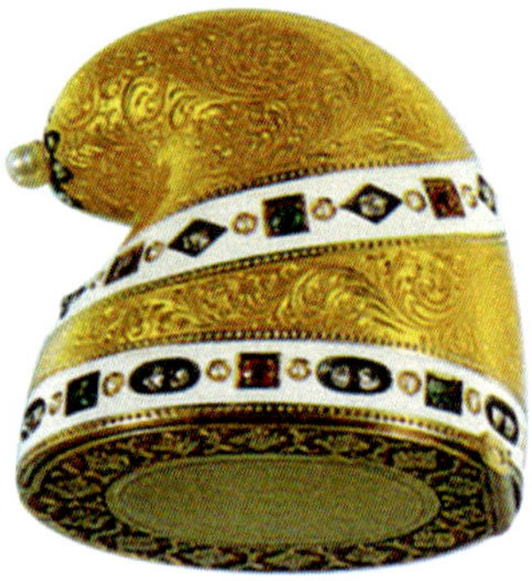

Inspiration for Fabergé creations ranged from Renaissance style to aesthetic movement, as seen in this miniature egg pendant and box in the form of a doge's hat, each rendered in exquisite enamel and gold. *Courtesy of Sotheby's and © 1984 Christie's Images Ltd.*

for items ordered for the Romanov tercentenary in 1913. For the wedding of Grand Duchess Olga in 1901, Dowager Empress Maria Fedorovna rejected Fabergé's design for a *surtout de table* (centerpiece), deeming it unattractive, and ordered it to be redone. Archives indicate that eight years later, new drawings by Fabergé for the ornament still lingered for approval, and only in 1911 did the imperial cabinet finally pay Fabergé 50,000 rubles for this item.[27] The court purveyor disliked approaching the imperial cabinet, since it was altogether staffed by bureaucrats and retired generals, and he soon stopped going there in person.[28] Fabergé tended to avoid client contact, even royalty. In London, when Queen Alexandra expressed interest in meeting him, he evaded the royal visit by leaving England.[29]

In 1918, the shop was taken over by the Russian state. Carl Gustavovich fled to Latvia, then to Wiesbaden. He died in Lausanne, Switzerland, two years later. His sons Agathon and Alexander were imprisoned in Russia. Agathon was released to appraise the contents of the crown jewels and precious medals confiscated by the Bolsheviks and was returned to prison until 1927.[30]

A NEW LIGHT

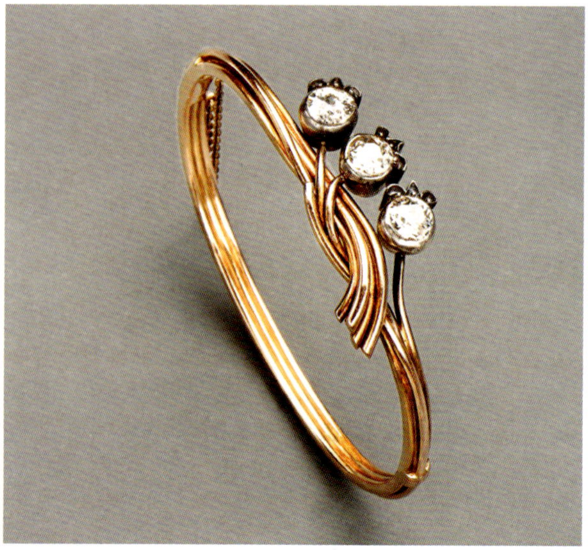

Between 1891 and 1917, the House of Fabergé produced some 200,000 items, five times more than from 1842 to the mid-1880s.[31] In 1910, the estimated turnover from the workshops was one million rubles.[32] As a single enterprise it far eclipsed every other goldsmith in Russia. Even then, though, at its peak this represented only about 14 percent of jewelry and silver production in Russia for that year. Foreign competitors accounted for a slightly lower amount, while some 70 percent came from other Russian artisans.[33]

Fabergé: A Comprehensive Reference Book (Fabergé et al. 2012) has finally shed light on these obscure artists. Yet, they are classified in a confusing way as "partners," "associates," and "competitors," both foreign and Russian, of Fabergé. Even here, jewelers, silversmiths and artisans are seen not on their own merits but through the prism of Fabergé and their relation to that firm. Of 54 enterprises listed under "partners," the vast majority were independent workshop owners. Sculptors, silversmiths, stonecutters, jewelers and even the Hahn workmasters Blank and Treiden make the cut, thanks to having at one time, or perhaps steadily, collaborated with Fabergé. Partner implies joint ownership of a firm or shop, which is not likely here. Famous silver enterprises such as I. E. Morozov, whose turnover was second only to Fabergé, and Grachev, founded in 1866, are included. These firms supplied a whole roster of retailers and private clients, imperial and otherwise, over the decades, and not just the House of Fabergé. The list is based on the memoirs of Carl's son Eugène, which comprised 31 names, some of which are not repeated in the expanded list.

Previous page, bottom:
One of the few surviving jewels made by Oscar Pihl, Fabergé's head of the jewelry workshop in Moscow. Pihl, who favored the lily-of-the-valley motifs set with diamonds, died in 1897 age 37. *Marie Betteley, photo by Noel Allum*

IMPERIAL CRAFTSMAN

Carl Fabergé preferred design over precious gems.[34] In truth, he also probably felt outclassed by compatriots such as Bolin and Hahn, whose single diamond necklaces would sell for four times the average price of an imperial egg. Or by Boucheron, Cartier and Chaumet of Paris, favored by the grand dukes and the Yusupovs. Of course, when the court demanded jewels, as it did throughout his tenure, the goldsmith delivered and always in a traditional style, but he was but one of many suppliers of jewelry and gifts to the imperial family. The year 1911 is a case in point.

For his journey around Russia and Crimea that year, Tsar Nicholas II chose several Russian jewelers to create presentation gifts. The firms of Tillander, Ivanov and Morozov and Zheverzheev received between one and seven orders from the imperial cabinet for items costing from 250 to 3,240 rubles. Carl Fabergé invoiced the cabinet for four jewels at 510 rubles. The watchmaker Pavel Buhré, however, netted an astonishing 62,122 rubles, or $800,000 in today's currency, for over one thousand pocket watches in gold and silver with the imperial crest.[35] Many other archival entries from 1890s to the early 1900s show similar patterns. Eager to support the native goldsmith trade, the imperial family was always careful to patronize a host of Russian jewelers for these official occasions. Bolin, Grachev, Hahn (for diamond decorations and rivières), Köchli, Morozov and A. D. Ivanov were favorites.

This disdain for high-quality gems, however, did not prevent Fabergé from bidding one million rubles with Bolin for a collection of unmounted precious stones in 1906. The imperial cabinet was selling them to replenish reserves, which had been depleted by the Russo-Japanese War.[36] His favorite stones, however—aquamarine, chalcedony, amethyst and moss agate—were native to Russia and not costly. Here too he was not the first. A century and a half earlier, Jérémie Pauzié had dazzled the court with Russian gems upon the discovery of mines in Siberia and the Urals, which began during the reign of Catherine the Great. Fabergé delighted in using unusual materials such as crocodile, calf skin, or cork to show off his designs, as well as porcelain, Gallé and Tiffany glass, Baccarat crystal, pottery and hardstone made by other factories, which his workshops would then finish in silver and gold.

NOTES

1. Fabergé et al, *Fabergé: A Comprehensive Reference Book*, 21.

2. Brigitte de Montclos, "Fabergé, Fournisseur Officiel de la Cour," in *Moscou: Splendeurs des Romanovs*, ed. Emma Cavazzini (Monaco: Grimaldi Forum Monaco, 2009), 161. Spiegel's mentor and father was none other than the great Swiss court jeweler Carl Emanuel Seftigen.

3. One of Gustav's jewelers was an Estonian-born nephew, Wilhelm Reimer. His father, Heinrich Reimer, married Gustav's sister, Carolina. Others included the Latvian Johann Eckhardt (d. 1869) and the Swiss-born Johann Gunst. *Fabergé et al., Fabergé: A Comprehensive Reference Book*, 109, 177.

4. Tillander-Godenhielm, *Jewels from Imperial St. Petersburg*, 224.

5. His children Albert and Hilma and niece Alma Pihl excelled in intricate diamond jewels. Holmström's diamond and platinum pendants, some enhanced with distinctive sepia enamels, would become a trademark of Fabergé and, with the spectacular Winter Egg of 1913, give rise to its phenomenal success.

6. Fabergé et al., *Fabergé: A Comprehensive Reference Book*, 33.

7. In Rome, the Castellani brothers had already perfected these goldworking techniques based on Etruscan, Greek, and Roman jewels and sold them as early as 1855, first in Italy, then Paris and London.

8. Franz P. Birnbaum, "Gemstone Carving, Jewellery and Gold and Silver Work of the House of Fabergé," in Birnbaum, *The History of the House of Fabergé*, 8.

9. Tatiana Muntian, "The Art of Fabergé," in Muntian, *The World of Fabergé*, 76.

10. The Kremlin Egg of 1906, however, was most likely completed by 1904, at the outbreak of the war with Japan. No egg invoices exist for 1904 and 1905. Muntian, "The Art of Fabergé," 74–75.

11. With the opening of Russian archives and other discoveries, some of the egg dates have been revised. For the most up-to-date chronology of Fabergé eggs, see www.wintraecken.nl.

12. Muntian, "The Art of Fabergé," 80. The Hermitage in St. Petersburg houses a striking solid-platinum inkwell that stands even taller than the 1910 Fabergé egg, which was presented to Tsar Alexander I in 1824 upon the discovery of platinum deposits in the Urals.

13. Olle Villumsen Krog, ed., *Ruslands Skatte: Kejserlige gaver* (Copenhagen: Den Kongelige Sølvkammer, 2002), 191; and Muntian, "The Art of Fabergé," 61.

14. Made 1/10th to scale.

15. When I was working at Christie's my parents received a royal summons that most only dream of—a private invitation by Her Majesty Queen Sirikit of Thailand to view and catalogue the incredible Royal Thai Collection of Fabergé, which had been stored unseen in the palace attic for decades. Alas I was not invited. See Krairiksh Busaya, ed., Fabergé (Bangkok: Office of Her Majesty's Private Secretary, 1983).

16. Empress Alexandra's album is preserved in Moscow Kremlin State Museum. Akin to a catalogue of gifts, the drawings are colorful but sketchy, with the donor's name next to each jewel.

17. Tillander-Godenhielm, "The House of Fabergé," in Saloniemi, *The Era of Fabergé*, 176.

18. The imperial cabinet ordered 20 boxes in red morocco by Käki with eagles for pearls as imperial gifts in 1905. The cost per box was 75 kopeks. RGIA, f 468, o 8, d 885, l 4.

19. Untouched for decades, many items in the Royal Thai Collection were still in their original boxes. Some even had retail labels from the St. Petersburg shop still preserved.

20. Wendy Bonus, *The Fabergé Connection: A Memoir of the Bowe Family* (New York: iUniverse, 2010), 39.

21. Fabergé et al., *Fabergé: A Comprehensive Reference Book*, 39.

22. Ibid., 133, 173.

23. Ibid., 70.

24. Matti Klinge, "Nicholas II and His Era," in Saloniemi, *The Era of Fabergé*, 36.

25. Fabergé et al., *Fabergé: A Comprehensive Reference Book*, 238,

26. Muntian, "The Art of Fabergé," 16.

27. RGIA, f 468, o 8, d 648, l 2. While the design still exists, the item has disappeared.

28. Habsburg, *Fabergé Revealed*, 6–8.

29. Bonus, *Fabergé Connection*, 41.

30. Ibid., 121.

31. Fabergé et al., *Fabergé: A Comprehensive Reference Book*, 425.

32. Ibid., 99. While Morozov and Khlebnilov averaged 700,000 each, and Bolin 600,000 rubles.

33. Fabergé et al., *Fabergé: A Comprehensive Reference Book*, 99.

34. In an oft-quoted interview for a 1914 St. Petersburg society magazine, the goldsmith, then at the peak of his fame, stated this preference. *Stolitsa i usadba* 5 (January 10, 1914): 9.

35. RGIA, f 468, o 8, d 1189, 1190.

36. Geza von Habsburg, "Fabergé and His Russian Competitors," in Habsburg, *Fabergé Revealed*, 46.

8

History

THE TALE OF TILLANDER

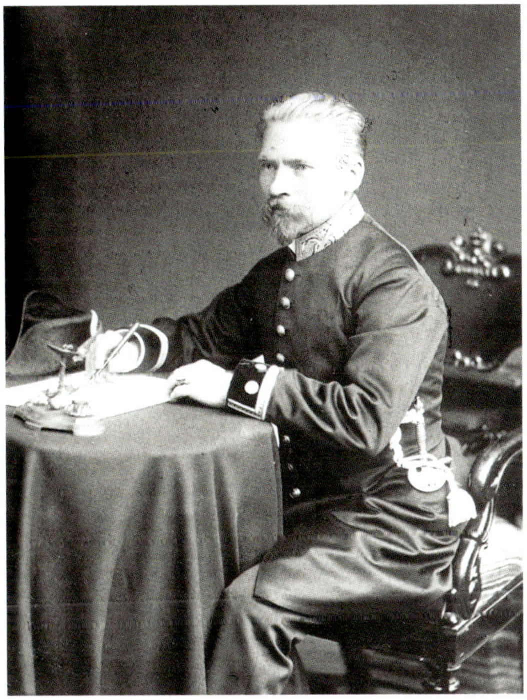

The firm of A. Tillander, by 1917 one of Russia's most successful, provides a perfect example of how a vibrant network of St. Petersburg jewelers sustained its members through close connections and trading. Founded by Peter the Great in 1703, the city grew under the reign of his niece, Empress Anna Ioannovna (r. 1730–40), to include three grand streets forming a crow's foot radiating from the Admiralty, the Navy's headquarters, bordering the Neva. Spanning out like a fan, two of these thoroughfares, the Nevskii Prospect and Gorokhovaia Street, maintained a thriving culture of jewelry and silver manufacturers. The church and respective guilds kept their foreign members, the Swedes, Germans, Finns and Swiss united, as did the proximity of individual workshops. Another street intersecting the other two, the famous Bolshaia Morskaia (or Great Maritime) Street, where Fabergé set up shop, became known as the "Diamond Row" in the 19th century.[1] These three streets defined the jewelry district in St. Petersburg.

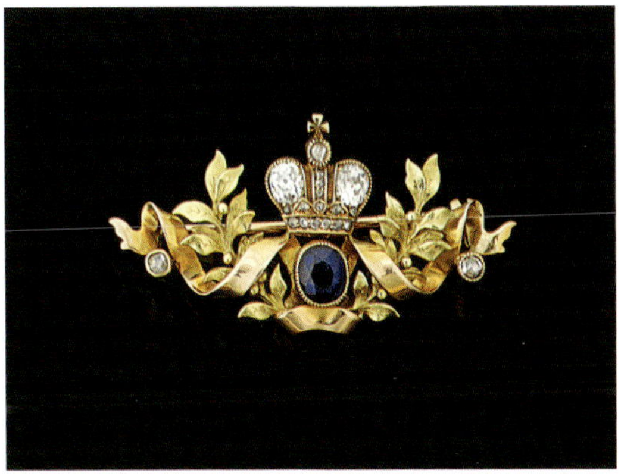

Founder Alexander Edvard Tillander (1837–1918) and a Tillander jeweled imperial presentation brooch commissioned by Tsar Nicholas II. *Courtesy of Ulla Tillander-Godenhielm, © 2011 Christie's Images Ltd.*

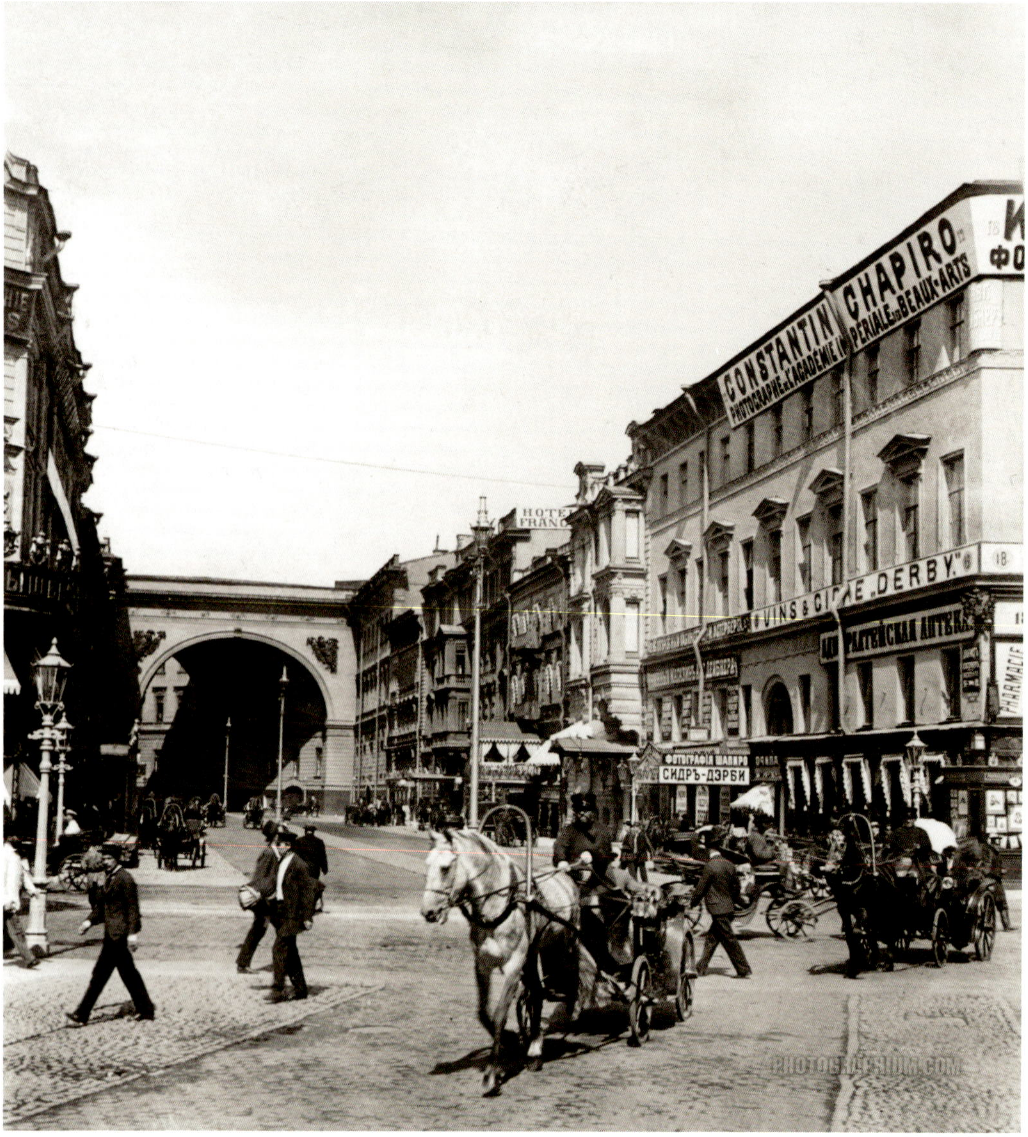

A view of Bolshaia Morskaia Street, the "Diamond Row," leading to the Admiralty Arch and the Palace Square. *Source: Wikimedia Commons*

Opposite page:
The interior of the Tillander shop and workshop in 1906. *On the left*, a well-coiffed customer considers a diamond brooch while Theodor Tillander stands by. The showcase displays row upon row of fitted boxes for each jewel offered for sale, a requirement at the time. *Courtesy of Central State Archive of Film and Photographs in St. Petersburg*

This is the story of how, by working at the heart of the imperial capital for five decades, the firm of Tillander prospered.

Alexander Edvard Tillander (1837–1918), the son of a Finnish farmer, arrived in St. Petersburg in 1848 at the tender age of 11. Scores of teenaged boys from the Grand Duchy of Finland made the same voyage in search of work, particularly in the jewelry field. Some 40 years later, Finnish nationals would rise to fame in the workshops of Fabergé on Bolshaia Morskaia Street.[2] By the mid-19th century, of the over 300 jewelers employing 3,000 workers in St. Petersburg, one-fourth were Finnish.

Like young Jérémie Pauzié when he arrived from Geneva a century earlier, Alexander spoke no Russian but counted on his older brother, Gustaf Adolf, a shoemaker's apprentice, to put a roof over his head. Alexander knew he wanted to study jewelry and soon landed an apprenticeship at Tsarskoe Selo at the workshop of a Finnish jeweler. He fit the profile of many St. Petersburg jewelers—foreign born, of limited means, who would quickly rise from eager apprentice to master goldsmith with hundreds of clients, including the Russian imperial family.

After 1856, following the dictates of the guild, he trained as a journeyman with two noted St. Petersburg jewelers of German descent, including Carl Reinhold Schubert (active 1844–80). Schubert, a skilled and respected jeweler, had learned his craft from his father, Johann Heinrich Schubert, in the early 19th century. His workshop stood on Gorokhovaia Street, a prime location for the young Tillander to immerse himself in the vibrant jewelry-making culture. Later, he and, no doubt, his son kept in touch with Schubert's son, Edward Karlovich, who by repute became chief jeweler of the renowned House of Bolin and an active member of the Union of St. Petersburg Jewelers.

When Alexander Tillander opened a workshop as independent jeweler in 1860, he was 23 (Carl Fabergé was just 14 then, and studying in Dresden). By creating gold chains, bangles and small jewels at his workbench in a rented room he shared with two others, Alexander became part of what would become the reigning network of St. Petersburg goldsmiths. In the 1870s, even before Carl Fabergé, Tillander was making copies of Scythian gold treasures found in recent archeological excavations in the Crimea.

Thrilled at his new location, Tillander could count numerous jewelers both east and west of his small workshop, on the corner of Bolshaia Morskaia and Gorokhovaia Streets, and he knew this would strengthen his business. Bolshaia Morskaia bustled with activity. Extending from the Triumphal Arch of the General Staff, built by Carlo Rossi to commemorate the victory over Napoleon in 1812 and leading to the Winter Palace, to St. Isaac's Cathedral by Montferrand, the fabled *ulitsa* became home to jewelers because of its proximity to the Nevskii Prospect and the largest Gostinyi Dvor (indoor market) in Russia, built by Catherine the Great. By the mid-19th century, it was the haute monde's go-to district for jewels and luxury goods.

Bolshaia Morskaia Street boasted a *pléiade* of famous jewelers. Diamond coronation crown maker Julius Otto Seftigen, already by 1859 a purveyor to the imperial court, lived at no. 16 (see chapter 9, "The Seftigens: Illustrious Swiss Court Jewelers"). Next door, at no. 14, the renowned silver and jewelry concern Nicholls & Plincke plied their wares to Russian grand dukes and the aristocracy. The shop of Carl Fabergé's father, Gustav Petrovich, stood at no. 11, along with the ateliers of Michael Perchin, Wilhelm Reimer and other early Fabergé workmasters. Andreas Römpler, forefather of the city's most famous jeweler, the House of Bolin, had purchased this very building in the 18th century, when it housed the diamond fund of the imperial court. At nos. 17 and 25, court jewelers Karl Julius Albrecht and Friedrich Daniel Butz created treasures for the tsars. Silver firms such as Ovchinnikov from Moscow, famous for its enamels and massive silver settings in the Old Russian style, occupied no. 35, while another Moscow supplier to the imperial court, Valentin Sazikov, son of Russia's foremost silversmith Ignatii Sazikov, occupied no. 39. Alexander was in good company. Even the last shop of the great Carl Fabergé, which would open in 1900 at no. 24, had previously housed the workshops of Jean Paul Ador (whose treasures are now in the Hermitage) in the 18th century, followed by the famous Duval brothers in the next.

Like Carl Bock, Alexander Tillander showed a keen entrepreneurial spirit and an inquiring mind. He traveled widely, absorbing design ideas from abroad, and sourced gemstones in the Urals. Business tended to come his way through diligence, honesty and hard work. His son, Alexander Theodor, having joined the firm at age 15, showed equal if not greater promise by training with fine jewelers in Paris, London and Dresden, then spreading his wings in St. Petersburg, while maintaining contact with his European counterparts. In 1895, he opened an agency selling demantoid garnets from Ekaterineburg to European houses. He sold jewels and antiques on behalf of wealthy clients. And he also represented a Parisian firm at the French Exhibition of Applied Arts in Moscow.

By the 20th century, Tillander, now run by Alexander Theodor, received a steady stream of orders from the Russian imperial family, such as the Dowager Empress Maria Fedorovna, Grand Duchess Olga (the tsar's sister) and many of the Russian grand dukes, including all the family members of Grand Duke

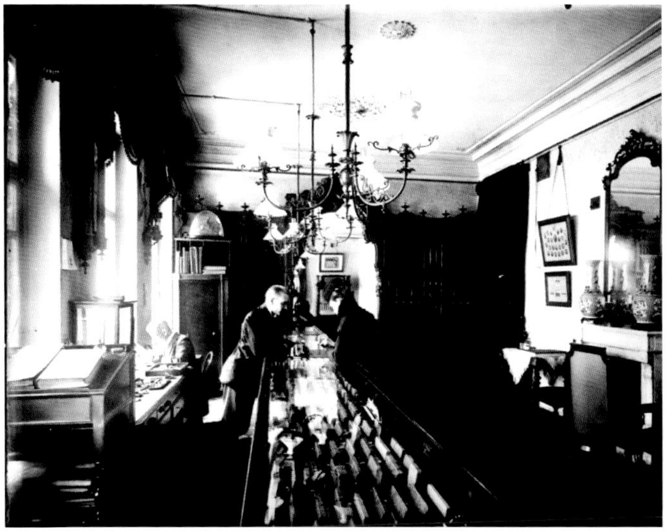

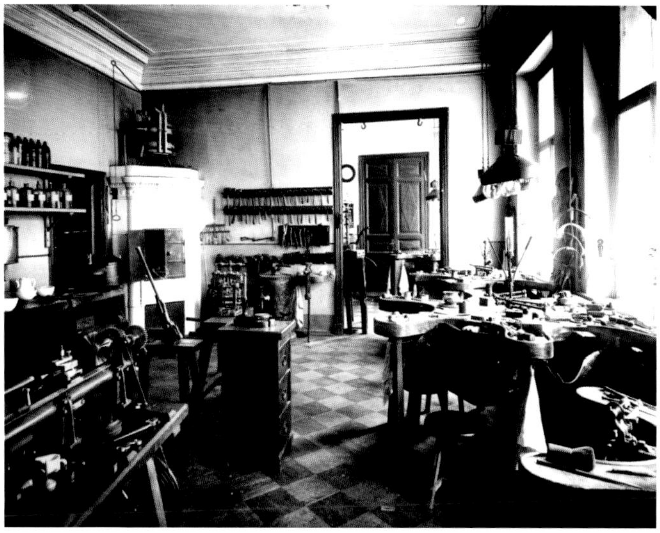

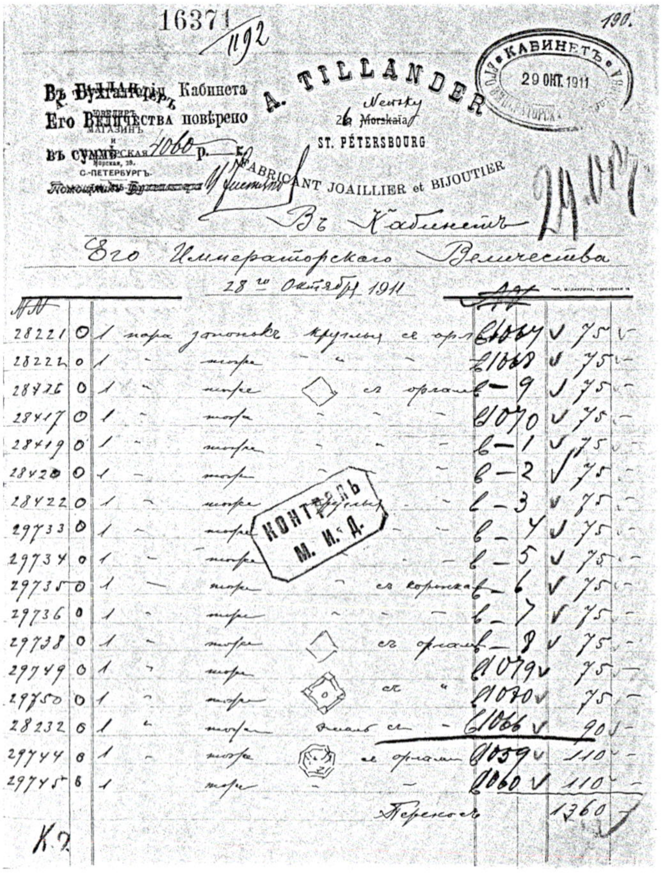
16371

Въ Бухгалтеріи Кабинета Его Величества повѣрено въ сумму 1060 р.

A. TILLANDER Nevsky 26 ST. PÉTERSBOURG FABRICANT JOAILLIER et BIJOUTIER

КАБИНЕТЪ 29 ОКТ. 1911

Въ Кабинетъ Его Императорскаго Величества 28го Октября 1911

КОНТРОЛЬ М. И. Д.

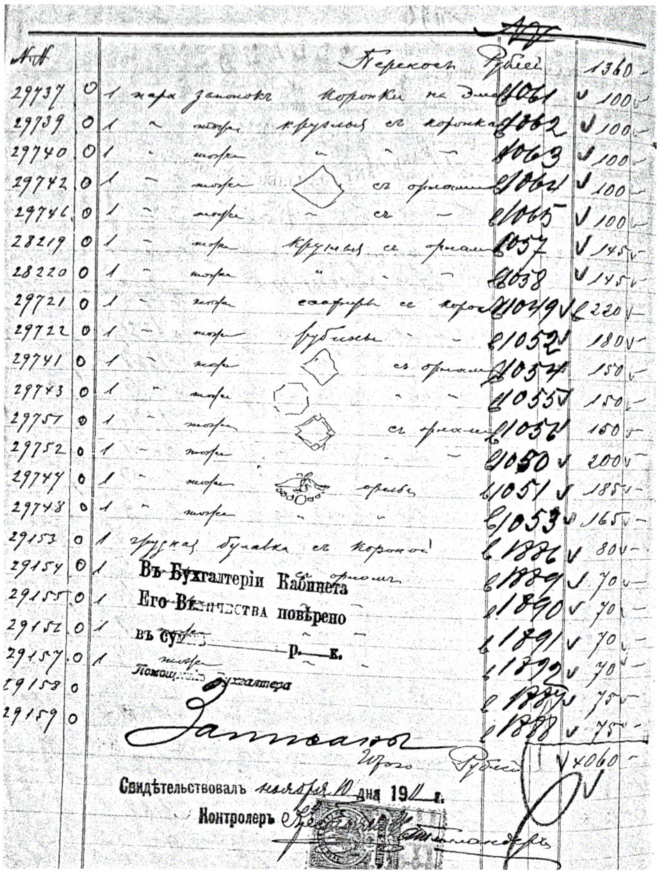
Въ Бухгалтеріи Кабинета Его Величества повѣрено въ сумму р. к.

Помощникъ бухгалтера

Свидѣтельствовалъ ноября 10 дня 1911 г.

Контролеръ

Boris Vladimirovich (1877–1943), third son of Grand Duke Vladimir Aleksandrovich. Tillander's invoices dated 1911 detail numerous cigarette cases in gold and silver, cuff links and tiepins that were sold to the imperial cabinet for 46 to 280 rubles. The Yusupov family and other titled nobility patronized the jeweler as well. Tillander produced many small presentation jewels for the Romanov tercentenary in 1913, all in custom-made red leather boxes by the Finnish box maker Ampuja.[3]

A stopgap measure that kept trade in the city strong was buying out the leases and inventory of dealers closing shop. Tillander benefited from this, especially in 1911. Sadly, this occurred following tragedies. When the venerable Hahn shop had to close (see "Carl August Hahn: The Diamond King") after the sudden death of Dmitri Hahn in 1911, Tillander purchased his lease for 12,000 rubles. The new premises at 26 Nevskii Prospect, St. Petersburg's most illustrious commercial street, raised the firm's visibility and increased profits. That same year, due to a crime that destroyed Boucheron's Moscow branch, when two of its representatives were murdered while carrying goods from a show in Baku, Tillander bought their entire Russian stock. By 1917, Tillander's annual output had risen to an astounding four million rubles, a 40-fold increase since 1904.

Tillander closed his St. Petersburg shop in September 1917, on the eve of the Bolshevik coup. Alexander Sr. died in December 1918 after having been attacked by a group of brigands the previous month. Luckily, Alexander Theodor had managed to transfer funds and jewels to Finland and to flee there himself, where he continued the business. By hiring the son of Finnish Fabergé workmaster Oscar Pihl Jr. as chief designer, a position he would maintain until 1953, the tradition of St. Petersburg jewelry lived on in the Finnish capital.

In 1911 on behalf of the tsar, the imperial cabinet purchased from Tillander 32 pairs of cuff links, seven tie pins, five gold cigarette cases and eight silver cigarette cases, some of which are listed here. *Courtesy of RGIA*

Opposite page, top:
Russian charm bracelet with charms by different St. Petersburg jewelers: an 18-karat gold chain (stamped 72) by Vladimir Solovev, a gold heart pendant by Finikov of Bolin, a purpurine and gold swan egg by Erik Kollin, a triangular reverse crystal toadstool diamond set pendant by unknown master and a moss agate gold-mounted egg by Alexander Tillander. *Courtesy of Sotheby's*

Opposite page, bottom:
Alexander Theodor Tillander (1870–1943), son of the founder Alexander Edvard Tillander. *Courtesy of Ulla Tillander-Godenhielm*

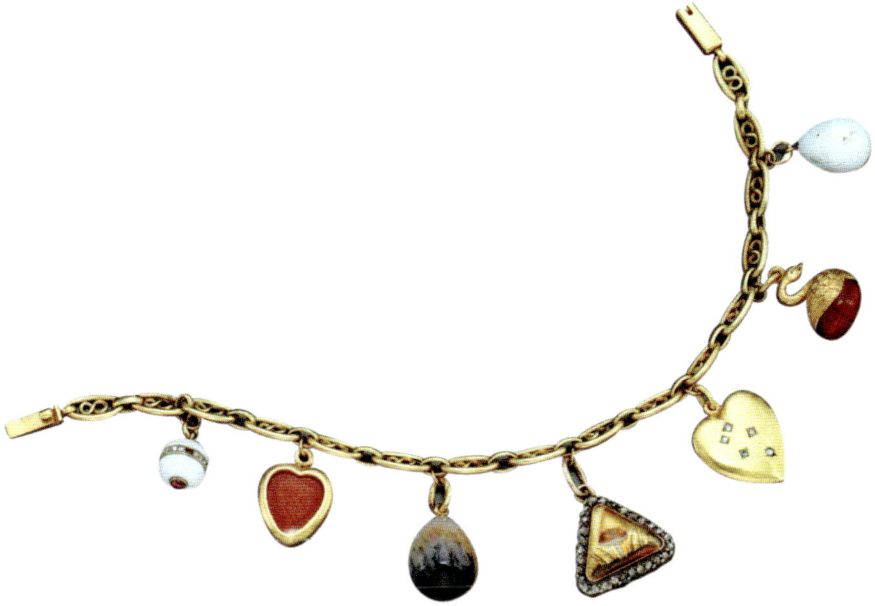

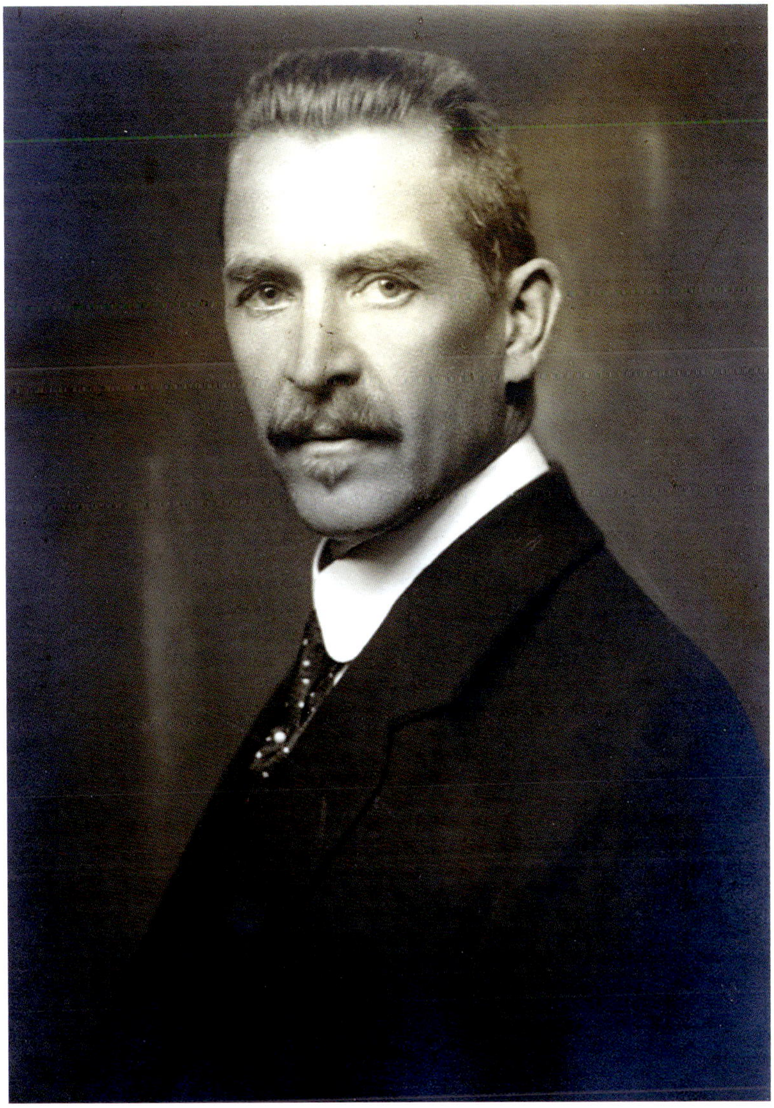

NOTES

1. Viacheslav Mukhin, *The Diamond Row of St. Petersburg* (Washington, DC: Fabergé Arts Foundation, ca. 1995). We wish to thank the founder and staff of the Fabergé Arts Foundation (1990–2010), Mary Ann Allin, Liudmilla Bakayutova, Marina Lopato, and Viacheslav Mukhin, for this information.

2. Most of the information in this chapter comes from Tillander-Godenhielm, *Jewels from Imperial St. Petersburg*, 254–65. Alexander Theodor kept diaries beginning in 1900 describing his life as a jeweler in St. Petersburg, which his granddaughter Ulla Tillander-Godenshielm intends to publish.

3. Tillander-Godenhielm, "Tillander," in Snowman, *The Master Jewellers*, 122.

9

History

THE SEFTIGENS: ILLUSTRIOUS SWISS COURT JEWELERS

The Seftigens[1] were prominent court jewelers during the reigns of Tsar Nicholas I and Alexander II (1825–81), but their history as goldsmiths had begun much earlier in Switzerland. According to family records, a travel permit dated May 14, 1835, with a seal from the tsar, gave master jeweler Carl Seftigen leave from the court to revisit his homeland. Keen on retracing his family history, Carl researched its origins back to medieval Switzerland in Bern. Descended from a wealthy family that boasted two mayors in the 14th century,[2] the family was already an established jeweler by 1748.

Portrait badge of Emperors Alexander II and Alexander III by Leopold Seftigen. *Courtesy of the State Historical Museum in Moscow*

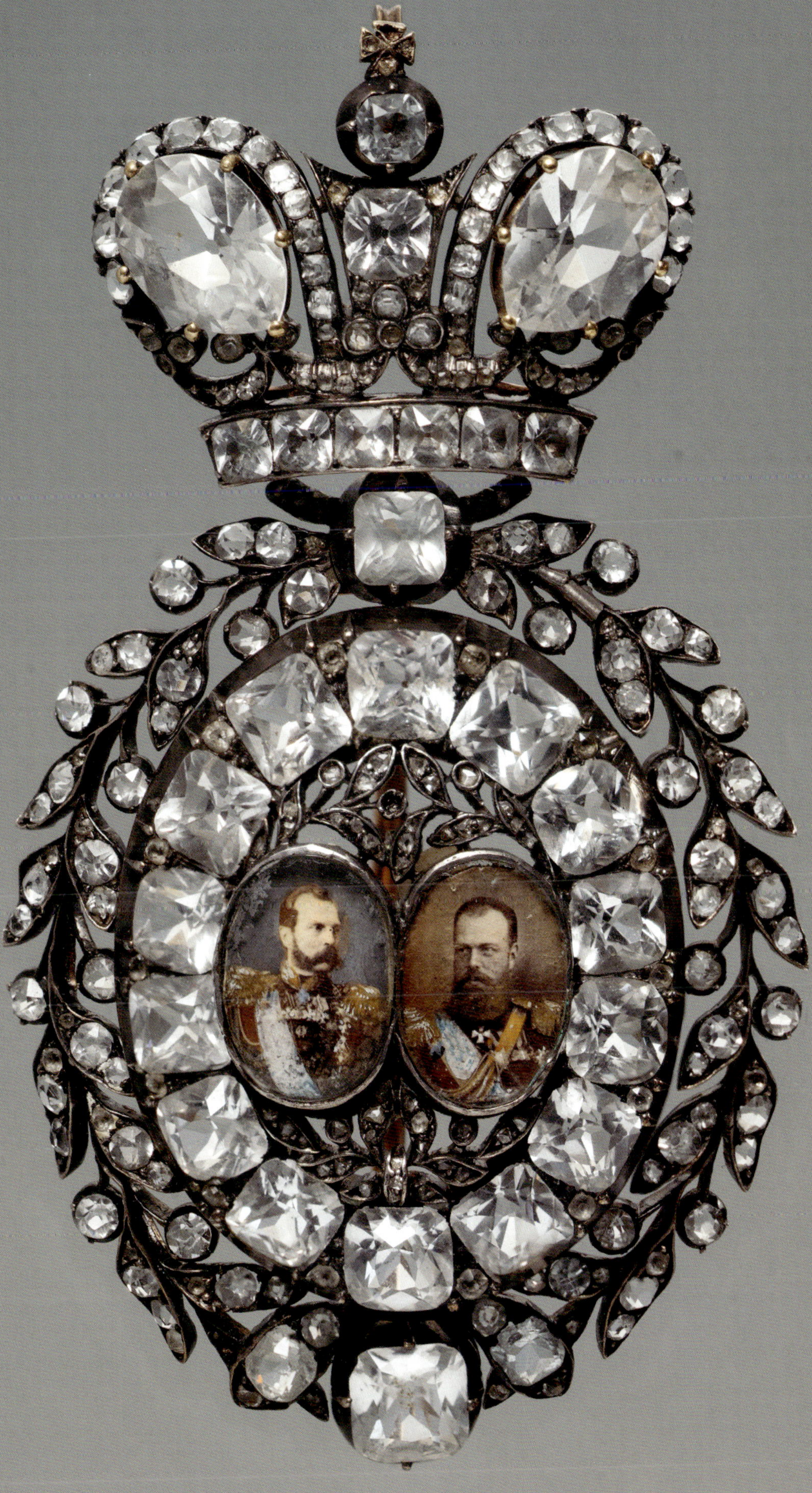

His sons, Adolf Leopold and Constantin Friedrich, continued the jewelry business. Adolf (Leopold Karlovich) Seftigen established his own workshop in St. Petersburg and was a member of a guild by 1849. Ten years later, he became purveyor to the imperial court, rising to Jeweler to His Imperial Majesty in 1869, a title he held until his death. At the same time, Leopold was also appointed appraiser to the court along with Butz and Bolin. His firm created snuffboxes. In the prevailing taste of the period, Seftigen boxes feature gold embossing and cobalt-blue enamel reserves, on which are set portrait miniatures or diamond ciphers. Along with other prominent jewelers and silversmiths in the capital, he received hereditary honorary citizenship. In the 1860s Seftigen shared the building at 16 Bolshaia Morskaia Street with diamond merchant Valerii Zaionchkovskii, who ran Gustav Fabergé's workshop from 1860 to 1872. As early as 1854 Gustav was registered in that building (then numbered 18 Bolshaia Morskaia Street).[3]

By the mid-19th century, Seftigen had joined forces with Wilhelm Kämmerer, a Nevskii Prospect court jeweler who specialized in diamond orders. The partnership was a success. As exhibitors in the Crystal Palace Exhibition of 1851, the firm won the Council Medal (the highest prize) for a diamond and emerald bryony wreath and currant necklace. In keeping with the Victorian taste for naturalism and botany, the intricate tiara featured pavé-set diamond leaves accented with uncut pear-shaped emeralds. These could be taken apart to form other jewels. The wreath was set with 2,836 rose diamonds, 129 brilliants and 12 emeralds.[4] The necklace also caused a sensation. The jurors gushed that

> [it] . . . formed of bouquets of currant-branches in diamonds, the fruit formed of polished uncut rubies . . . its effect is excellent. . . . The importance of the articles in this collection, the superior taste in composition, and, above all, the perfection of the settings, not excelled by the works of any Jeweler in the Exhibition.[5]

Out of 380 Russian exhibitors, the only jewels from their country illustrated in the official catalogue were those by Bolin & Jahn and Kämmerer & Seftigen. The latter also displayed two large diamond and turquoise convolvulus sprays and a stomacher brooch set with cabochon rubies, likewise to great acclaim. Leopold also exhibited in the St. Petersburg Exhibition of 1870 along with fellow jeweler Samuel Arnd.

The legacy continued. Constantin Friedrich (Constantin Karlovich), Leopold's brother and a precursor of the court jeweler Carl Hahn, produced many diamond orders, jeweled

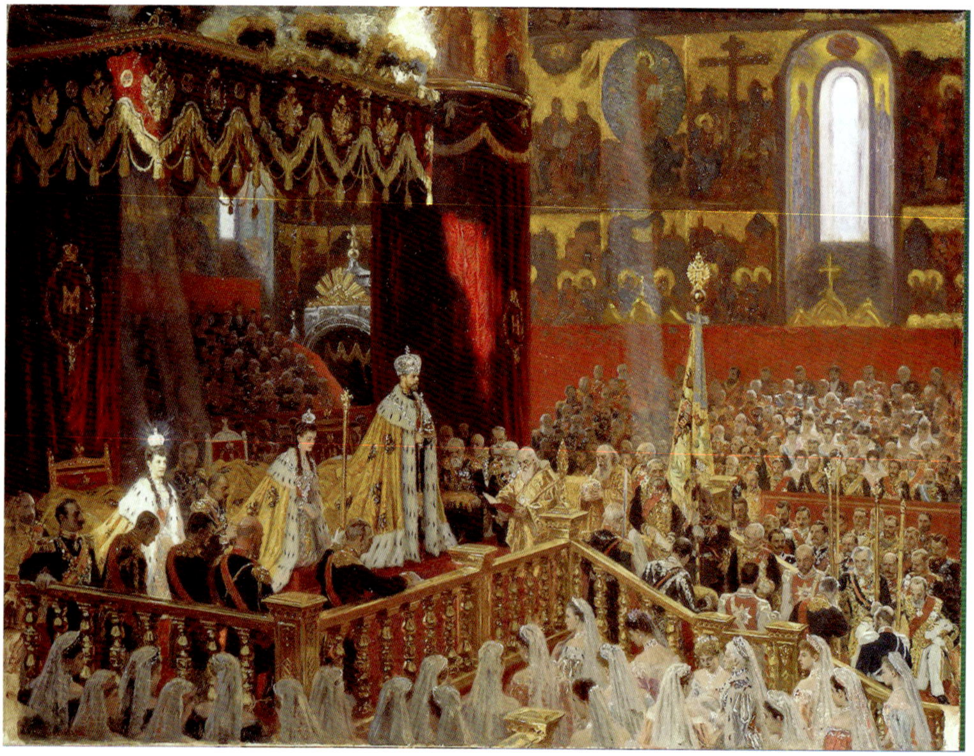

snuffboxes, chamberlain keys, jeweled swords and field marshal batons. Seftigen also made an important diamond portrait badge combining the miniatures of Tsars Alexander II and Alexander III, now in Moscow's State Historical Museum.[6] Julius Otto continued the trade of his father, Leopold.

But it was père Leopold who was responsible for the firm's most famous creation: the coronation diamond crown of Maria Aleksandrovna, consort of Emperor Alexander II in 1855. Still preserved in the Diamond Treasury Fund of the Moscow Kremlin Museum, it also graced the head of Empress Maria Fedorovna during her coronation in 1883 and again at that of her son, Nicholas II, in 1896 (see "The Fate of the Russian Crown Jewels," image on page 237).

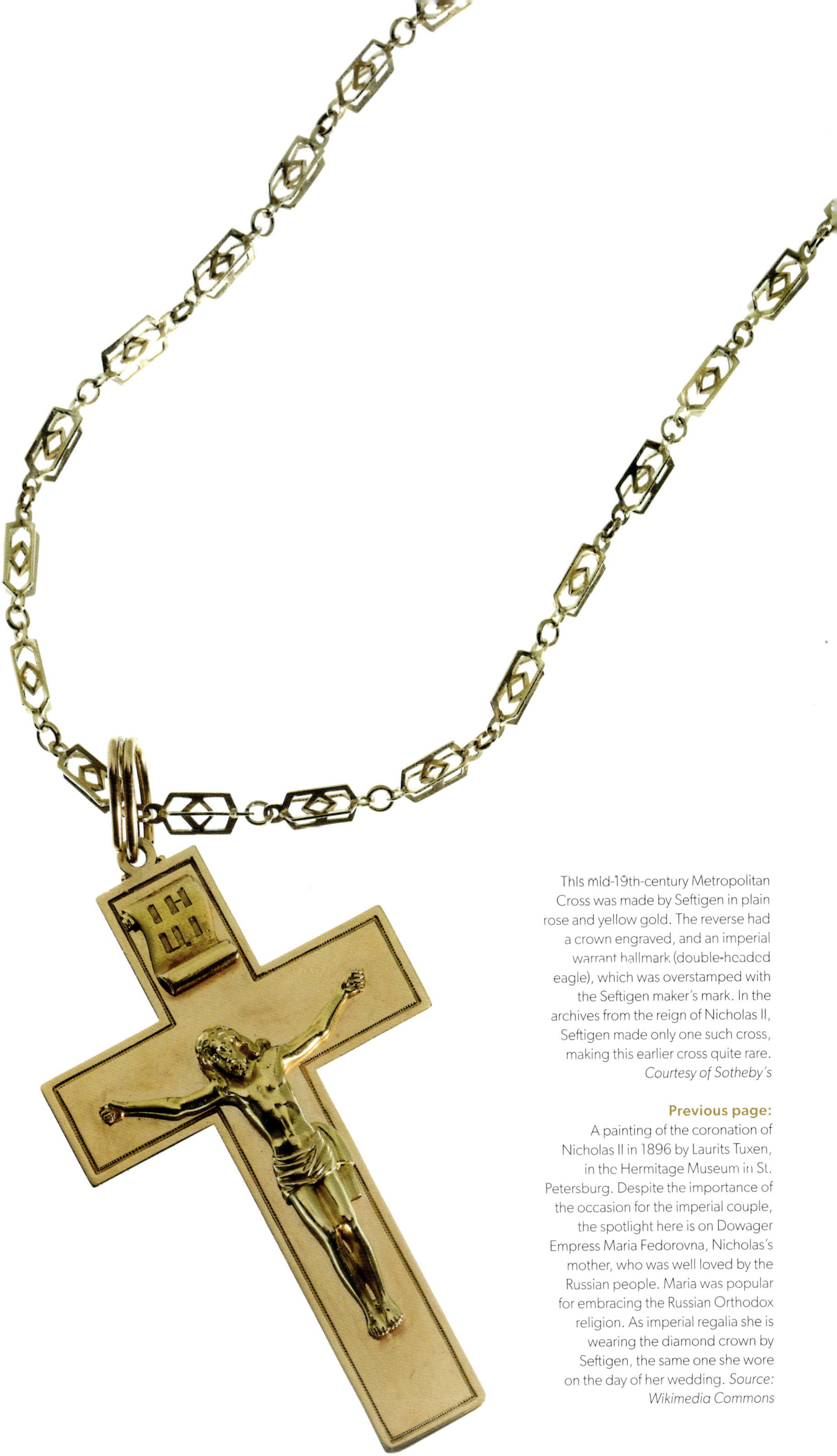

This mid-19th-century Metropolitan Cross was made by Seftigen in plain rose and yellow gold. The reverse had a crown engraved, and an imperial warrant hallmark (double-headed eagle), which was overstamped with the Seftigen maker's mark. In the archives from the reign of Nicholas II, Seftigen made only one such cross, making this earlier cross quite rare. *Courtesy of Sotheby's*

Previous page:
A painting of the coronation of Nicholas II in 1896 by Laurits Tuxen, in the Hermitage Museum in St. Petersburg. Despite the importance of the occasion for the imperial couple, the spotlight here is on Dowager Empress Maria Fedorovna, Nicholas's mother, who was well loved by the Russian people. Maria was popular for embracing the Russian Orthodox religion. As imperial regalia she is wearing the diamond crown by Seftigen, the same one she wore on the day of her wedding. *Source: Wikimedia Commons*

NOTES

As exhibitors at the Crystal Palace Exhibition of 1851, Seftingen and Kämmerer won the Council Medal (the highest prize) for a diamond and emerald bryony wreath and currant necklace.

1. Various spellings include Saefftigen or Zeftigen.

2. Wealth seemed to remain in the family until the revolution. By the early 20th century, the magazine Russkii iuvelir lists Seftigen as the richest jeweler in St. Petersburg.

3. Seftigen is linked to Johan Aleksandrovich Gunst, another jeweler working for Gustav Fabergé. The Swiss goldsmith, said to have "laid hands on" Gunst's inventory after his death, was tried but was acquitted in court. Fabergé et al., *Fabergé: A Comprehensive Reference Book*, 159, 177, 490.

4. Great Britain, Commissioners for the Exhibition of 1851, *Reports by the Juries on the Subjects in the Thirty classes into Which the Exhibition Was Divided* (London: Spicer, 1852), 515.

5. Great Britain, *Reports by the Juries*, 515.

6. This was presented to Chancellor Prince Alexander Gorchakov in 1881 at a cost of 11,350 rubles. The diamonds have since been replaced by pastes. Tillander-Godenhielm, "Russian Imperial Award System," 151 and 505, n. 16.

CARL BOCK: JEWELER ENTREPRENEUR

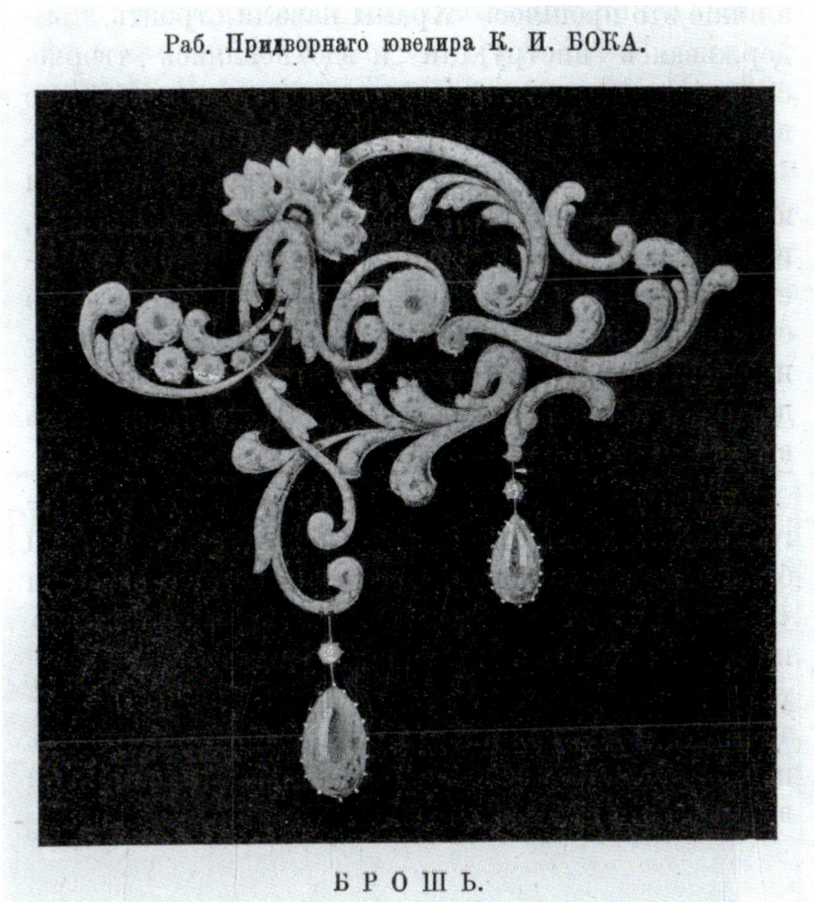

Diamond brooch by Carl Bock as illustrated in the jewelry periodical *Ruskii iuvelir* (Russian jeweler), which was published from 1912 to 1914.

In 1874, 24-year-old Carl Bock opened his St. Petersburg workshop at 9 Bolshaia Morskaia Street, on the corner of bustling Nevskii Prospect. Not far from the Winter Palace, this was right next door to Gustav Fabergé's original location.[1] In fact, the workshop Bock bought that year had once belonged to the goldsmith Johann Eckhardt, who had worked for the elder Fabergé in the 1840s. Eckhardt's manager and fellow jeweler Christian (or F.) Buhler acquired the shop upon his death and later sold it to Bock. Carl retained both names on invoices and fitted retailers' boxes, as he would do with Arnd, which he also later purchased.

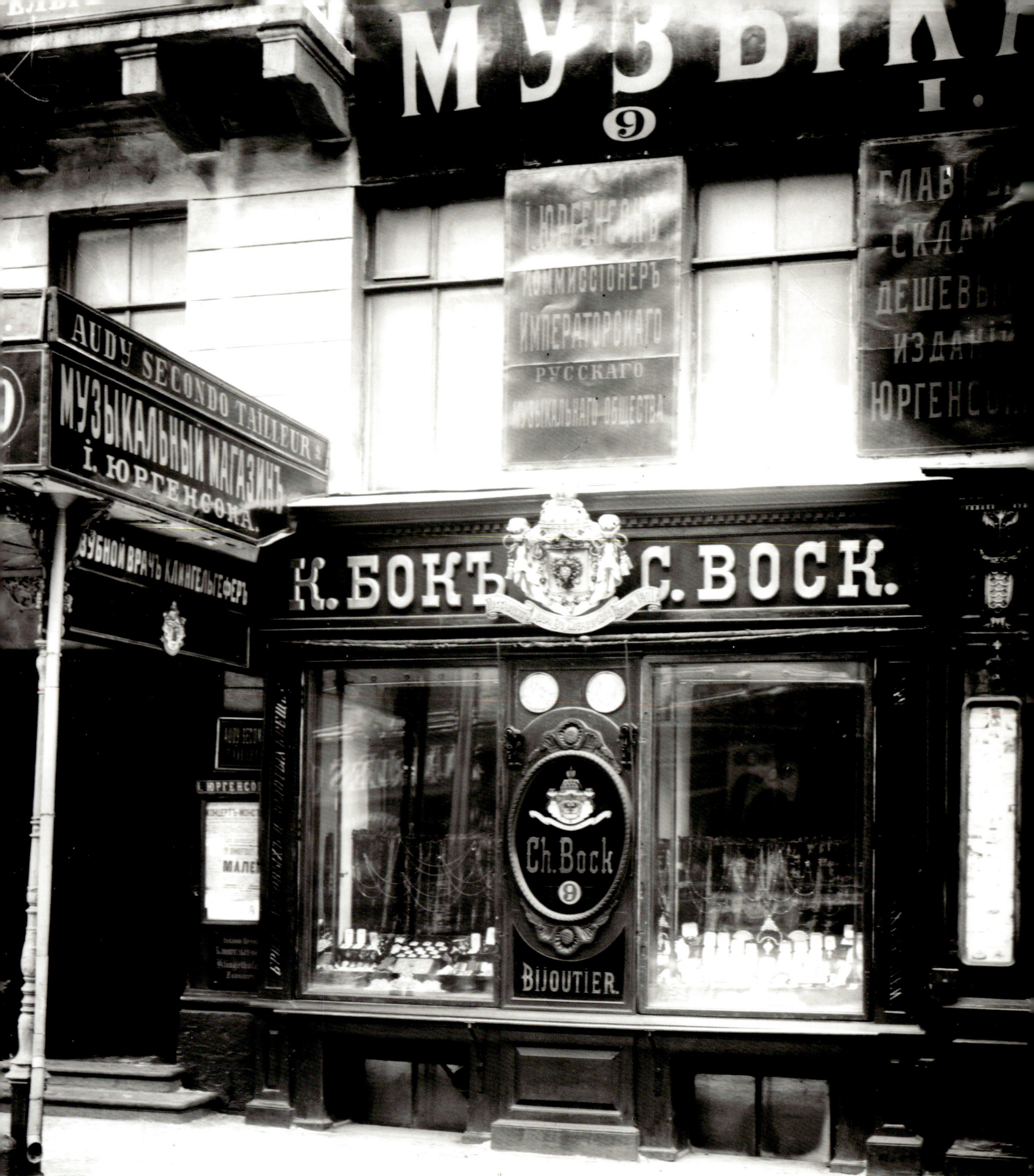

Bock storefront at 9 Bolshaia Morskaia Street, St. Petersburg, 1914. *Courtesy of Central State Archive of Film and Photographs in St. Petersburg*

Opposite page:
Guilloché-enameled cigarette case in a sunray pattern by Carl Bock, ca. 1890. Its original box is stamped C. Bock, formerly Buhler, with his address in St. Petersburg and Moscow. © *1994 Christie's Images Ltd.*

An enameled thimble in original Bock box. © *AuktionenNagel*

Carl was active in the jewelry community and must have been well known around town. He became a merchant of the Second Guild in 1887. That he chose to retain the original owners' names on his letterhead even as late as 1898 indicates either a sense of modesty (his own name is much smaller) or a desire to capitalize on his predecessor's reputation. However, this did not keep his firm from earning several distinctions, including gold medals at both the Nizhnii Novgorod All-Russian Exhibition in 1896 and, like his contemporary Carl Fabergé, at the 1900 Exposition Universelle in Paris.[2] In 1901 the firm received the imperial warrant. In the early 1900s, along with Bolin, Bock supplied imperial gold buttons for the court, ranging in price from 80 to 115 rubles.[3] Documents indicate the jeweler also supplied the court of Grand Duchess Xenia Aleksandrovna.[4]

Bock also opened a store in Moscow, on Kuznetskii Most, where he joined Bolin, Lorié and other fashionable retailers. But it was in St. Petersburg that he carved a niche. By the early 20th century he had acquired the illustrious Arnd enterprise, which was founded in 1832 and was famous, along with Keibel, for its superb imperial decorations. Johann Arnd, perhaps not as astute a businessman as artisan, saw his firm change ownership several times, from Dimitrii Osipov to A. C. Adler, before finally ending up with Bock in 1908. Another Bock acquisition was the famous English-based enterprise, also on Bolshaia Morskaia Street, Nicholls & Plincke.[5] Initially called the Magasin Anglais, it had been founded during the reign of Alexander I by two British silversmiths (see "Nicholls & Plincke: Silver Purveyors to the Tsars").

Carl took an active role as cochair in the St. Petersburg Society of Russian Jewelers, which published a review, *Ruskii iuvelir*, from 1912 to 1914. His shop employed 25 workers and three apprentices. Fedor Afanasiev is said to have worked for Bock from 1888 to about 1907 before joining the Fabergé firm.[6] His son, Alexander Bock, continued the business until 1918 and, along with Agathon Fabergé, helped catalogue the Russian crown jewels for the Soviets in 1922.

Bock diamond jewelry is traditional in style, with garlands and scrolls in the French taste. A 1914 photograph of the storefront in St. Petersburg shows row upon row of fitted cases below a grand emblem of the Romanovs. The firm made large silver trophies with imposing double-headed eagles, as seen in archival images, as well as an impressive cylindrical trophy for Count Ilarion Ivanovich Vorontsov-Dashkov (1837–1916), governor general of the Caucasus.[7] The atelier excelled in gold and guilloché enameled cigarette cases, jeweled brooches and buttons, gentleman's jetons, gem-set cuff links and numerous other jewels for its sophisticated clientele. In purchasing so many firms and their stock both of Russian and foreign jewels, it is assumed the collection offered at Bock was eclectic and far ranging.

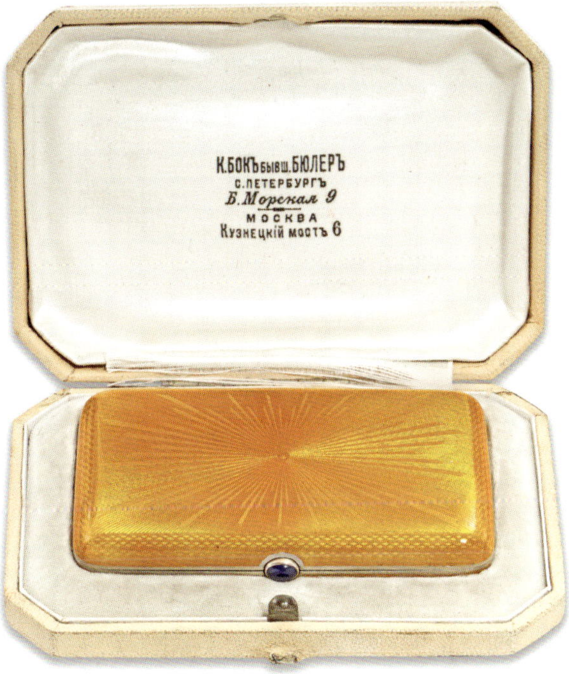

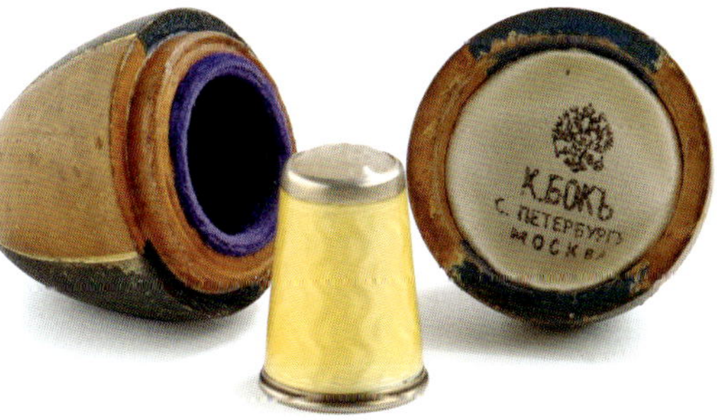

NOTES

1. Only the House of Bolin, across the street, and Eduard Thielemann's workshop on 18 Nevskii Prospect were as close to the palace.

2. Fabergé et al., *Fabergé: A Comprehensive Reference Book*, 105.

3. RGIA, f 468, o 43, d 999, ll 5, 6, 45.

4. Illustrated invoice is from Alexander Nikolaevich Ivanov, *Gold and Silversmiths in Russia (1600–1926): A Guide for Art Experts*, vol. 1 (Moscow: Russkii natsionalnyi muzei, 2002), 122.

5. Fabergé et al., *Fabergé: A Comprehensive Reference Book*, 105.

6. Habsburg, *Fabergé Revealed*, 39.

7. Fabergé et al., *Fabergé: A Comprehensive Reference Book*, 105; and Ivanov, Gold and Silversmiths, 2:293.

11

History

NICHOLLS & PLINCKE: SILVER PURVEYORS TO THE TSARS

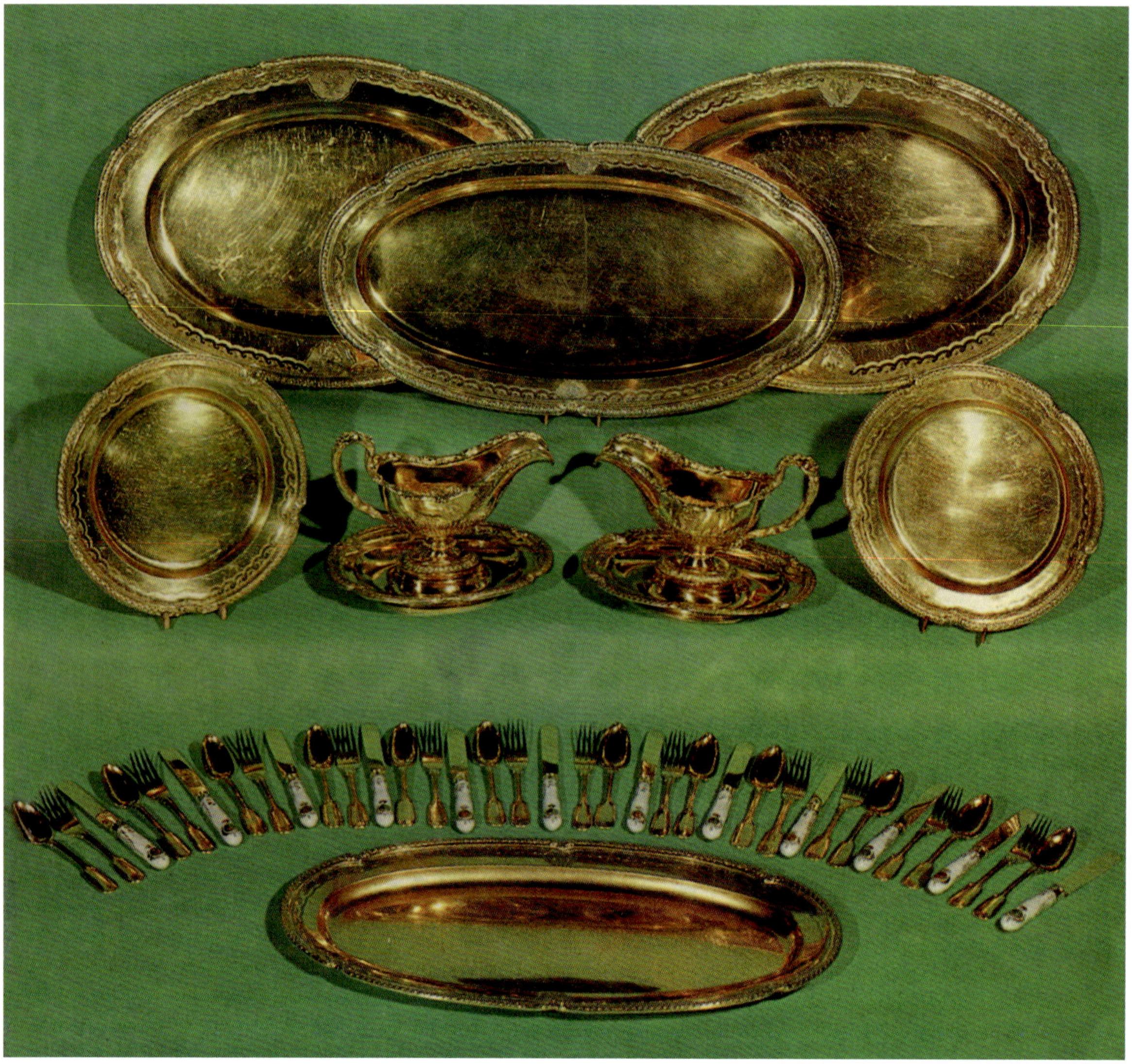

For the first half of the 19th century, Nicholls & Plincke was the most prominent gold and jewelry firm in St. Petersburg. It became famous primarily for selling and importing English silver and wares, as well as making copies in Russia in the English taste. It was initially called Magasin Anglais, until the Crimean War forced a name change, since, as one of Russia's enemies, the English fell from favor.

Oval gilded silver platters, dinner plates and sauce boats, mostly by Tegelsten and Nicholls & Plincke, ca. 1850. *Courtesy of Sotheby's*

Englishmen Constantin Nicholls and William Plincke founded the firm in 1829, although a workshop had existed as early as 1815.[1] Both became Russian citizens and received honorary hereditary citizenship status in 1808.[2] The enterprise was favored by Tsar Nicholas I, received the imperial warrant during his reign, and attracted numerous commissions from the imperial cabinet. The emperor turned to this firm for the dowries of his three daughters, Grand Duchesses Olga, Maria and Alexandra,[3] and for the wedding service of his son Grand Duke Michael Nikolaevich in 1857, when he married Princess Cecile of Baden-Baden (see page 144).

The venerable silver dealers also produced the Orlov Service for the tsar, based on an original set ordered by Catherine the Great from French silversmiths for Prince Gregory Orlov in 1770. The St. Petersburg craftsmen added a Romanov eagle to its design. Since the Russian court also enjoyed close ties to the British silver trade, the tsar ordered the London Service by R. & S. Garrard, the famous British crown jewelers, in 1844. This comprised 1,680 pieces, including large candelabra, girandoles and seven sculptural groups, the bases of which were made by Nicholls & Plincke. In 1852, the Magasin Anglais produced 40 lavish silver tea-and-coffee services as imperial gifts.[4]

Popular with the St. Petersburg aristocracy and no doubt the English, the store was a huge success; even its owners—despite their status as merchants—were considered part of that haute monde. Lady Londonderry was surprised to see Constantin Nicholls at a dinner party hosted by Lord Durham, the British ambassador.[5] The firm's success lasted for decades, until the 1880s.

Workmasters of Nicholls & Plincke

The master goldsmith Samuel Arnd, as well as the silversmiths Carl Tegelsten, Robert Kokhun and Johann Friedrich Falk (1799–1845), worked for Nicholls & Plincke, although little is known about the last two.[6]

Samuel Arnd was quietly plying his trade in St. Petersburg by 1849, selling gold and silver. Arnd & Company at 18 Nevskii Prospect specialized in badges, decorations, gem-set and guilloche-enameled gold works and silver tableware. Samuel was possibly related to other Arnd goldsmiths of Estonian or German origin in the imperial capital. Nicholls & Plincke, for whom Arnd would work many years, was at some point right next door at 16 Nevskii Prospect.

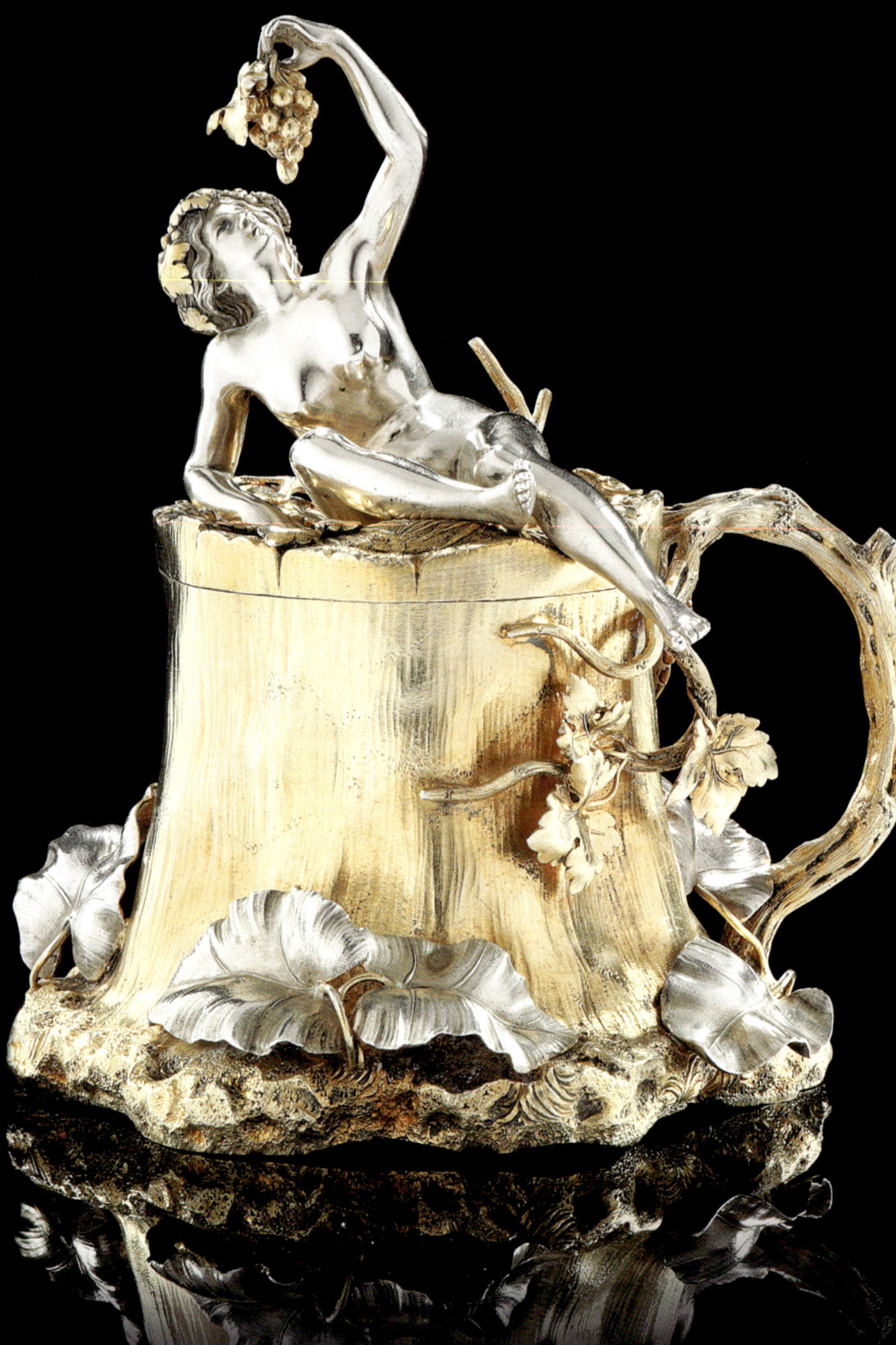

Trompe l'oeil silver tankard by Arnd, St. Petersburg, 1857. *© 2011 Christie's Images Ltd.*

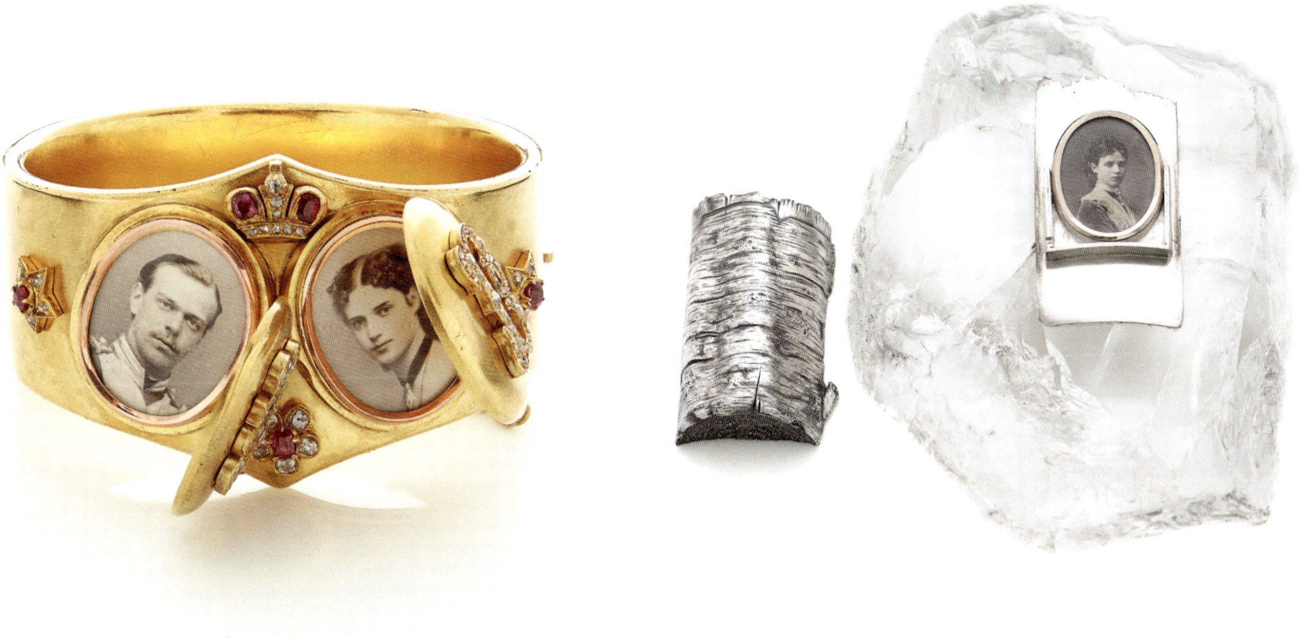

This gold bracelet depicting Grand Duke Alexander Aleksandrovich (future Tsar Alexander III) and Grand Duchess Maria Fedorovna was made by Arnd for their wedding on November 9, 1866. Years later, still a favorite of the dowager empress, Arnd produced a rock-crystal-and-silver paperweight with a photo of the young princess. *Bracelet courtesy: the Royal Danish Collection, Amalienborg and paperweight courtesy: Her Majesty the Queen of Denmark. Photo by Iben Kaufmann.*

Two Arnd items in the Royal Danish Collection reveal the jeweler's importance to Maria Fedorovna. One is a gold bracelet containing portraits of the grand ducal couple at their wedding, while another is an unusual rock crystal paperweight containing an earlier photo of Princess Dagmar, as she was first known. The lid, in the form of a trompe l'oeil silver trunk, fits over the image, which is set into an unpolished slab of rock crystal. To accentuate the roughness of the *crystal de roche*, Arnd left the upper border of the frame unfinished.[7]

Arnd goldwork is distinctive and, like Köchli's, appealed to Russian aristocracy. He was a favorite of Grand Duke Vladimir Aleksandrovich and Maria Pavlovna, whose collection was auctioned in 2009. Two personalized Arnd cigarette cases, one in gold and the other silver, from the 1870s, were inscribed *Marie* for the grand duchess, and numerous pairs of Arnd cuff links were offered in that sale. One pair, adorned with miniature enameled orders of Saint Vladimir, seemed unique to the jeweler, as did links in the form of gold ice skates. For years he also supplied the firm of Nicholls & Plincke.[8] A group of expressive silver stirrup cups in the form of wild animal heads surfaced in New York in 2001, each with the hallmark of both. Arnd was also known, along with Erik Kollin, for producing religious gold and enameled icon pendants, which opened by way of a central pushpiece into six-pointed star shapes.

The firm changed hands several times. From 1890 to 1900 it was owned in part by Dimitrii Osipov, in 1902 by Andre Adler, and then by Carl Bock after 1908.[9] Arnd was married to Sophia Tegelsten, the daughter of silversmith Carl Tegelsten, who also worked at Nicholls & Plincke and owned a bronze factory.[10] The other important silver master who worked for the firm, whose name has recently come to light, was Robert Kokhun (see page 296).

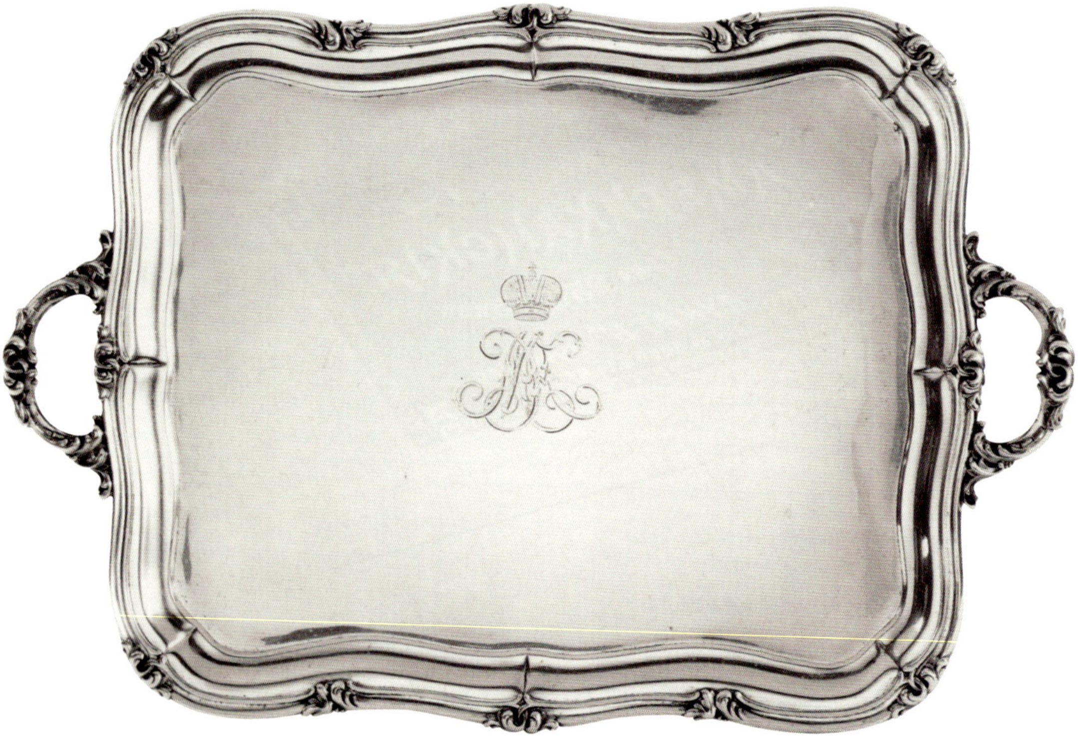

Large silver tray from the Grand Duchess Maria Nikolaevna Service retailed by Nicholls & Plincke. *Courtesy of Sotheby's*

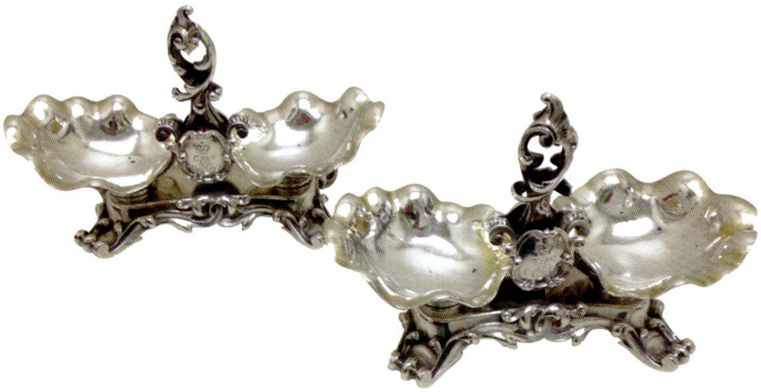

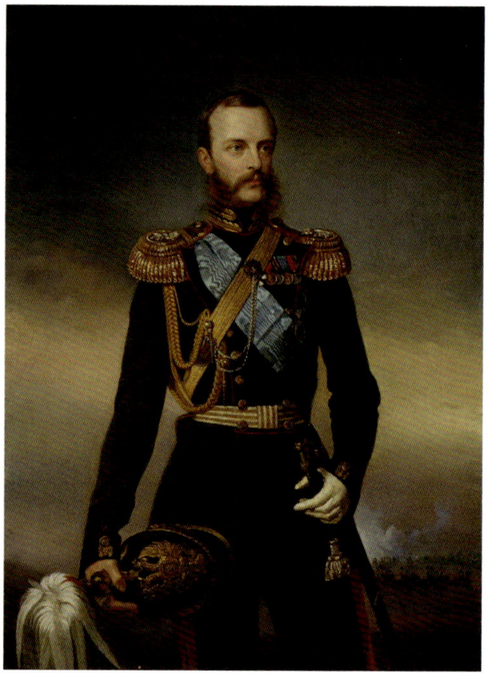

This pair of Russian silver double salts in the Rococo style were made by Arnd for the wedding of Grand Duke Michael Nikolaevich (1832–1909). Each is engraved with the initials *MN* beneath the imperial crown and an imperial eagle. Grand Duke Michael of Russia (1832–1909), pictured, the youngest son of Tsar Nicholas I, married Princess Cecily August of Baden (1839–91) on August 28, 1857. She adopted the Russian name Olga Fedorovna. *Sources: Marie Betteley and Wikimedia Commons*

NOTES

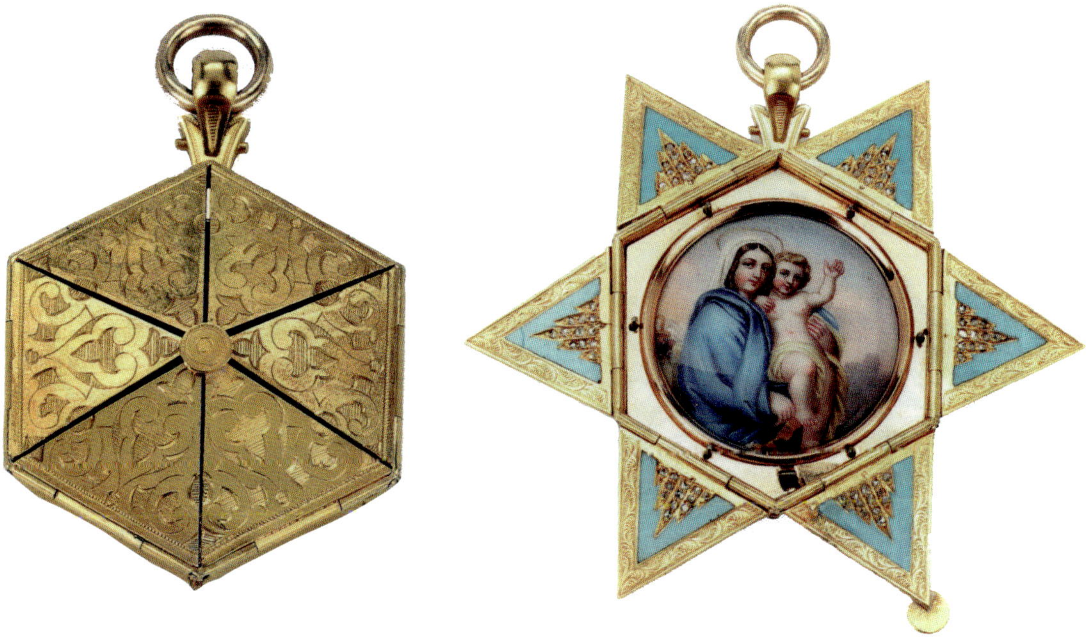

A jeweled enameled gold icon pendant by Samuel Arndt, opened and closed. *Courtesy of Sotheby's*

1. Solodkoff, *Russian Gold and Silverwork*, 200.

2. Tillander-Godenhielm, *Jewels from Imperial St. Petersburg*, 288.

3. Nicholls & Plincke's best silversmith, Carl Tegelsten, made the wedding services of all the grand duchesses, since his mark is found on pieces of each service that survive. Maria Nikolaevna (1819–76) married Maximilian, Duke of Leuchtenberg, in 1839; Olga (1822–92) married Crown Prince Carl of Wurttemberg in 1846; and Alexandra (1825–44) wed Prince Fredrik William of Hesse in 1843 but died in childbirth a year later. In 2015, the Peterhof State Museum Reserves held an exhibition of Grand Duchess Olga's dowry at the Grand Palace ballroom. The "Olginskaia" silver collection consisted of over 80 items, including a recently acquired Nicholls & Plincke silver tea and coffee service.

4. Solodkoff, *Russian Gold and Silverwork*, 200.

5. Ibid.; and Lady Frances Anne Vane Londonderry, *Russian Journal of Lady Londonderry, 1836–7,* ed. W. A. L. Seaman and J. R. Sewell (London: John Murray, 1973), 97.

6. Johann Henricson (b. 1802) is also mentioned as a Nicholls & Plincke silversmith. Tillander-Godenhielm, *Jewels from Imperial St. Petersburg*, 288.

7. Anni Nørskov Mørch, ed., *Fabergé: The Tsar's Court Jeweller and His Association with the Danish Royal Family* (Kolding, Denmark: Museum of Koldinghus, 2016), 109, fig. 87; 110, fig. 92; 111.

8. Confusingly, another Arnd, Johann Samuel, is said to have worked for Nicholls & Plincke, with a hallmark of JA. He may have been Samuel's brother. Ivanov, *Gold and Silversmiths*, 1:77.

9. From 1902 to 1906, Arnd also worked for Fabergé. *Fabergé et al., Fabergé: A Comprehensive Reference Book*, 39.

10. Tillander-Goldenhielm, *Jewels from Imperial St. Petersburg*, 156.

12

History

THE GRACHEV BROTHERS: A DYNASTY OF SILVERSMITHS

The Grachev brothers produced some of the best enamels in Russia. Located in St. Petersburg rather than Moscow, Grachev created masterworks of cloisonné and plique-à-jour enamel in the Old Russian style. This appealed both to Tsar Alexander III and his son Nicholas II, especially as a source of gifts to foreign dignitaries. Vivid enamel colors usually associated with the ancient capital reflected the Russian Empire's ancient ties to Byzantium. This was combined in the hands of this workshop with refined silver craftsmanship of the highest quality. Grachev rose to the challenge on numerous occasions and became principal supplier to the imperial court. By 1910, the firm had a turnover of 300,000 rubles and, after Fabergé, was the leading producer of enamel and silver objects in St. Petersburg.[1]

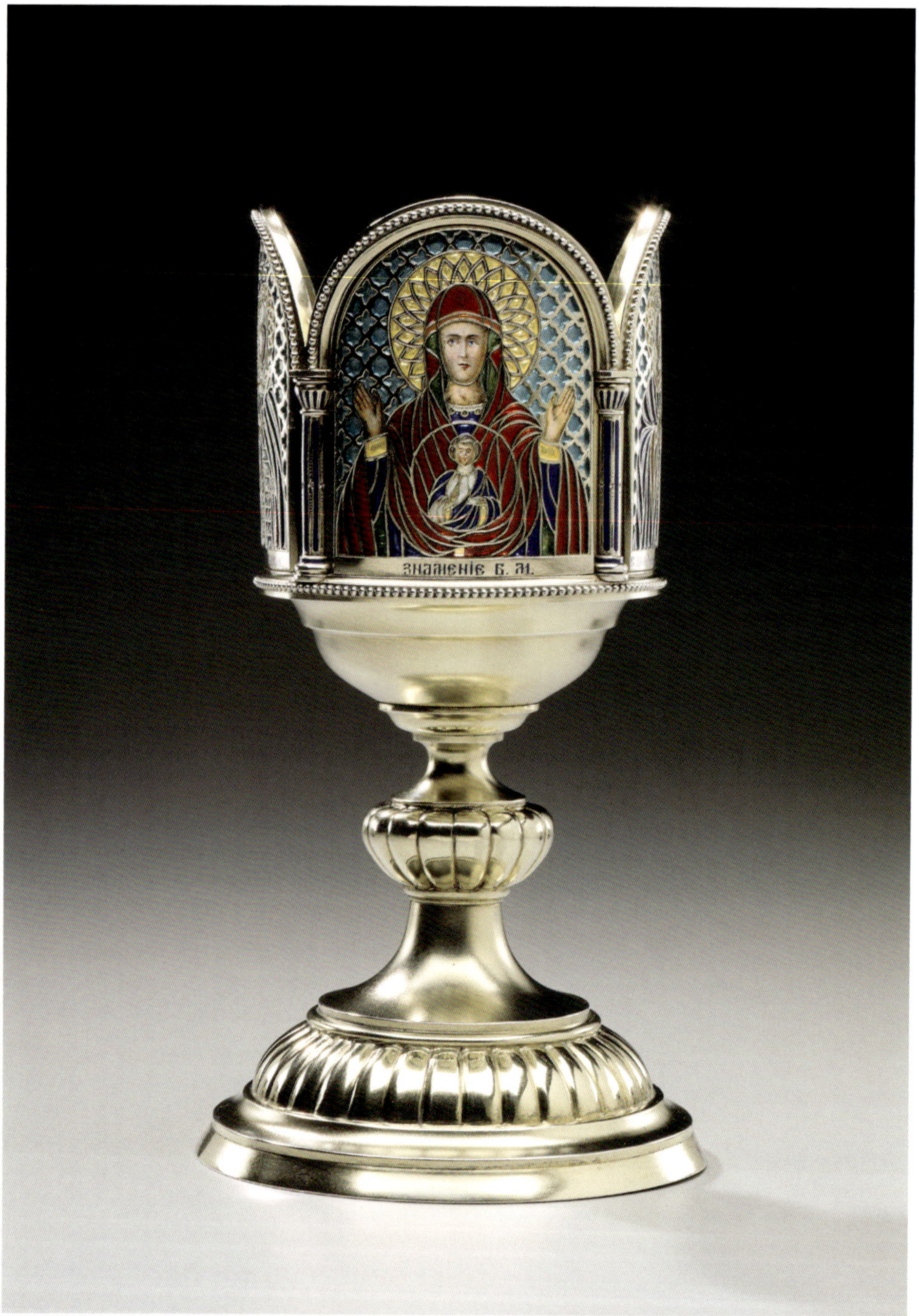

A plique-à-jour enamel silver-gilt sanctuary lamp by the Grachev Brothers, St. Petersburg, late 19th century. *Courtesy of Hillwood Estate Museum & Gardens*

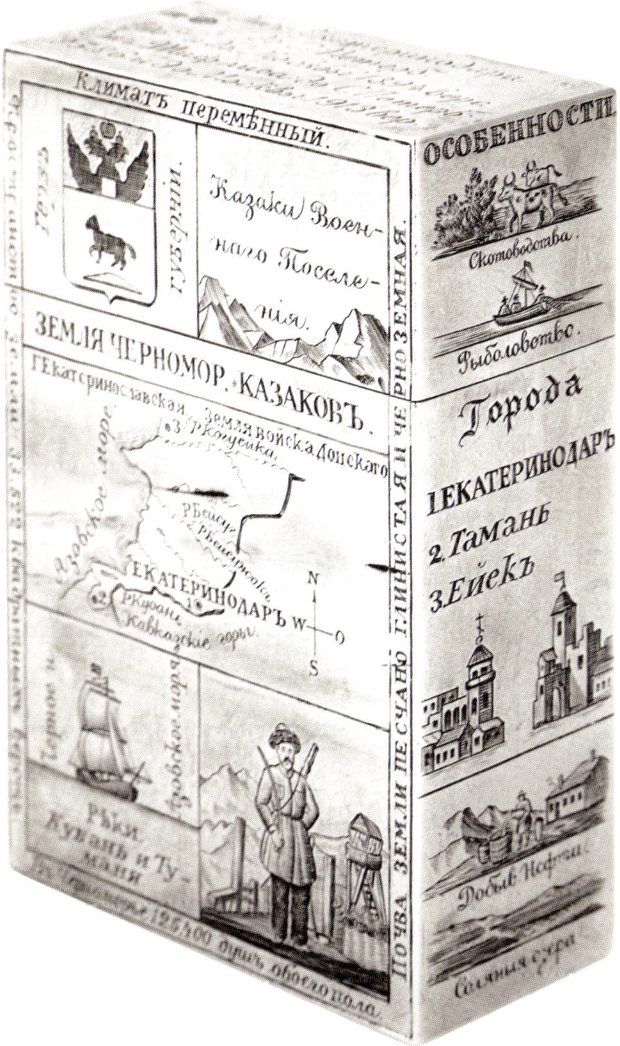

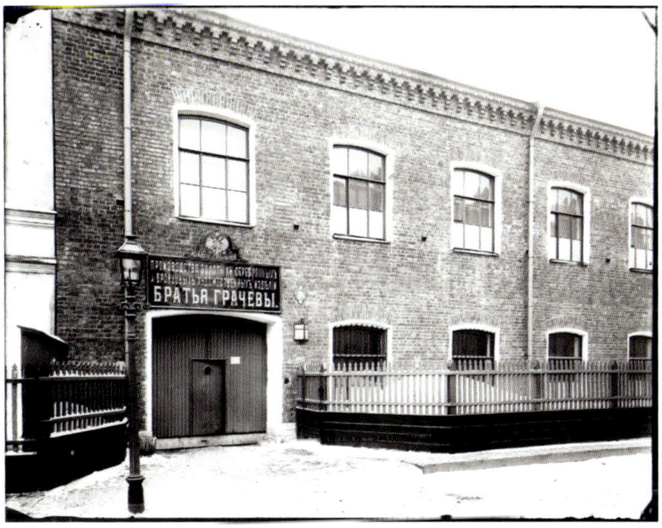

Left:
A silver cartographic card case by Grachev's workmaster Johan Olsonius, St. Petersburg, 1886. Finely engraved, these were designed to show the geography of a particular Russian region in the tsarist era. Each had the coat of arms, a map of the region, major towns, industry, rivers, climate, soil description and inhabitants depicted in local dress. This one depicts the "Land of the Black Sea Cossacks" (now Ukraine. Other Olsonius card cases depict the regions of Kiev and Yakutia). *Courtesy of Doyle Auctioneers and Appraisers*

Right:
Grachev Factory, ca. 1900. The sign reads "Manufacturers of Gold, Silver, and Bronze Artistic Objects, Grachev Brothers." *Courtesy of Central State Archive of Film and Photographs in St. Petersburg*

Silversmith Gavrill Petrovich Grachev founded his namesake firm in 1866. He had apprenticed with a St. Petersburg goldsmith named Gasse,[2] but little more is known about him. Upon his death in 1873, the business passed on to his talented sons. By 1881, the eldest, Mikhail, aged 17, had joined the merchants' guild, while his seven brothers—Grigorii, Alexis, Simeon, Nikolai, Gavrill, Petr and Ivan—would eventually join the firm.[3] Like Sazikov and Fabergé, in 1895 Grachev built his own factory in the capital. Located across the Neva at 14 Pevchevskii Lane, it employed 87 workers and manufactured bronze, silver and gold works. For some time, the firm's silver was stamped with workmasters' initials only, rather than the company name in Cyrillic. The *Grachev* mark appeared in the 1880s, often along with the Latin initials *J.O.* for Johan Olsonius, master jeweler and merchant of the second guild, or with a Cyrillic stamp of *A.P.*, whose identity is not known.

By 1896, the company had earned the title of court supplier of His Imperial Majesty and a year later was renamed Grachev Brothers. While Grigorii and Simeon managed the workshop and factory, Mikhail, as the eldest, carried the torch of creativity and received many prizes. In 1888, he won a gold medal on a St. Stanislaus ribbon in the International Exhibition in Copenhagen. His compatriots there included Chichelev, the master Moscow enamelers Ovchinnikov and Khlebnikov and Carl Fabergé. Just four years later, Mikhail

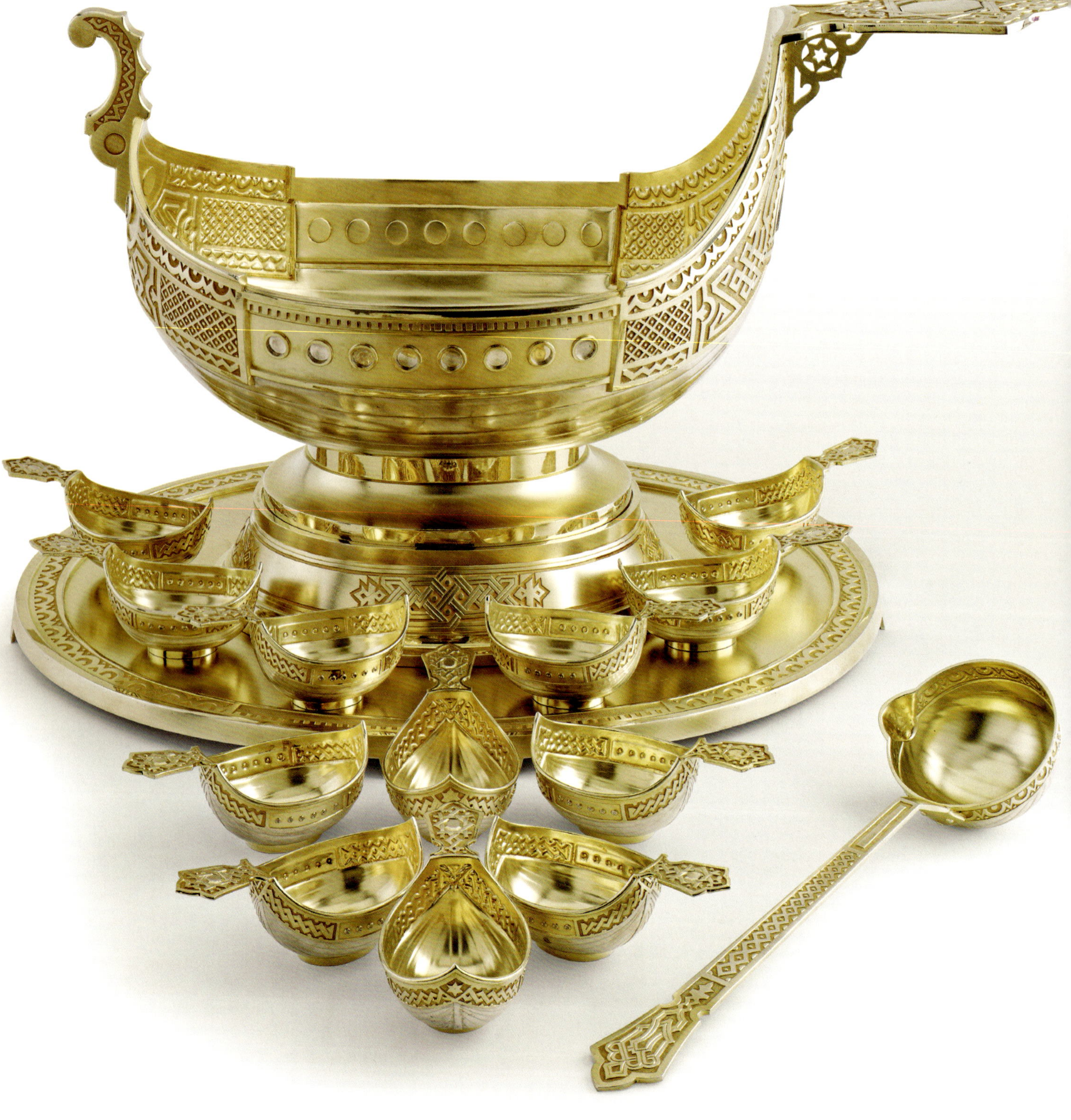

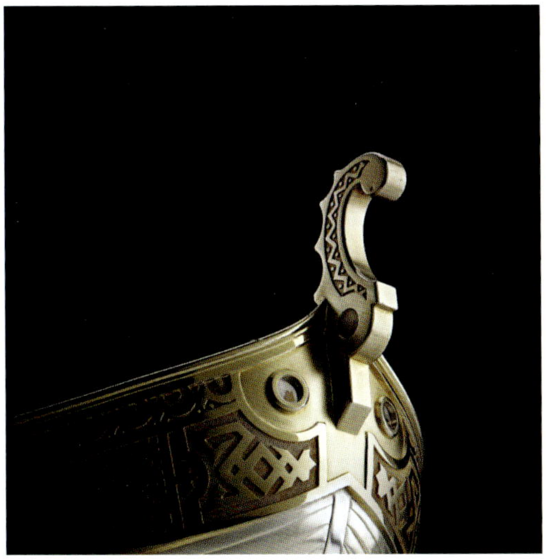

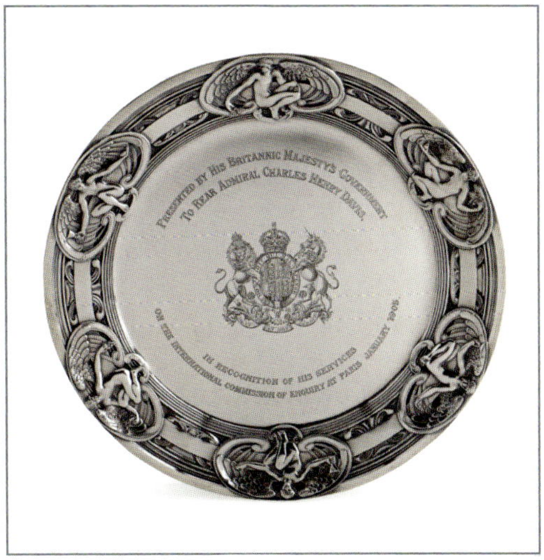

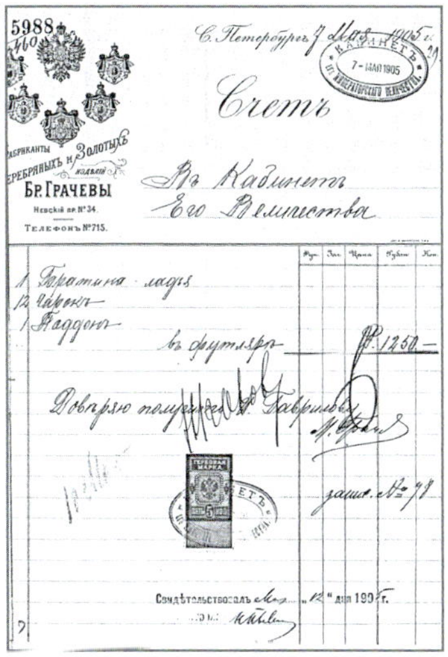

The Russian and British governments presented these gifts to Rear Admiral Charles Davis Jr. for his role in defusing the Dogger Bank Crisis of 1904. He received the Grachev service (previous page) from the Russian government. Detail of the kovsh (top left) and Grachev's receipt (top right). The British government gave him a silver presentation covered cup and sideboard dish (top center) made by the London crown jewelers R & S Garrard & Company. *Courtesy of Lyon & Turnbull and RGIA*

received the coveted title of imperial court appraiser. Earlier that year, the artisan had created a silver service as a gift from Tsar Alexander III to the sultan of Turkey.[4]

The firm participated in the All-Russian Industrial Fairs and received prizes in international exhibitions, including the Paris World Exhibition of 1889 and the Columbian Exposition in Chicago of 1893. In the latter, listed under his own name, Mikhail exhibited chased and enamel wares, including vases, goblets, cigar boxes and flatware, and was already reported to have an annual turnover of 500,000 rubles.[5] In 1900, Grachev Brothers participated in the International Paris Exhibition, along with Carl Fabergé, Friedrich Köchli, Carl Bock and Iosif Marshak.

Hosts of Russian grand dukes and grand duchesses also patronized Grachev. Along with Ovchinnikov in Moscow and the bronze manufacturer K. F. Woerfel, Grachev Brothers had the highest number of grand ducal warrants, as evidenced by its invoices and stamps on fitted boxes. By 1888, the company was purveyor to the grand ducal courts of Michael Nikolaevich (1832–1909), son Tsar Nicholas I and four of Tsar Alexander II's children: Grand Duchess Maria Aleksandrovna and Grand Dukes Serge, Alexis and Vladimir Aleksandrovich. To these sons and daughters of emperors, as highly selective buyers and connoisseurs, Grachev stood out, perhaps more than Fabergé, for the quality of its silver masterpieces. In 1892, Grachev would add another one of the tsar's sons and the most important to his roster of clients when Tsar Alexander III became a customer.

Grachev excelled in figural silver that was popular at the time: salts in the form of rooster and hen, cornucopia-shaped scent flasks with putti, tea-glass holders decorated with an eagle amid repoussé twigs and leaves, silver cigar-cutters in the form of miniature samovars and my favorite, a silver pencil shaped as a miniature hunting rifle. Like Fabergé, the firm collaborated with various Russian factories to produce unique works of art, such as the Kuznetsov porcelain factory in Moscow, and the Imperial Glass Factory in St. Petersburg.[6]

The Grachev Brothers made impressive imperial presentation objects for foreign dignitaries and heads of state, including an enameled charger with the Romanov eagle crest for the French president Felix Fauré in 1897 (see illustration, page 291) and, in 1905, a distinctive silver service for American rear admiral Charles Henry Davis Jr. for his diplomatic role in defusing the Dogger Bank incident during the Russo-Japanese War.[7] A letter to Baron Vladimir Freedrickzs, minister to the imperial court from the foreign minister, Count Vladimir Lamsdorf, reveals that while both the Austrian and French admirals were to receive the Imperial Orders of St. Alexander Nevskii from Russia, Davis, who as an American was forbidden to accept decorations from foreign governments, would be presented this Grachev service, which took the form of a magnificent punch bowl designed as a Viking ship, twelve cups en suite, a ladle and a circular tray.[8]

In 1911, Grachev Brothers created a silver scepter for the Italian ambassador, as well as a silver presentation vase with the tsar's cipher, the state crest and the Imperial Navy's arms for its minister, Ivan Grigorovich, on September 20.[9] The factory closed in 1918.

NOTES

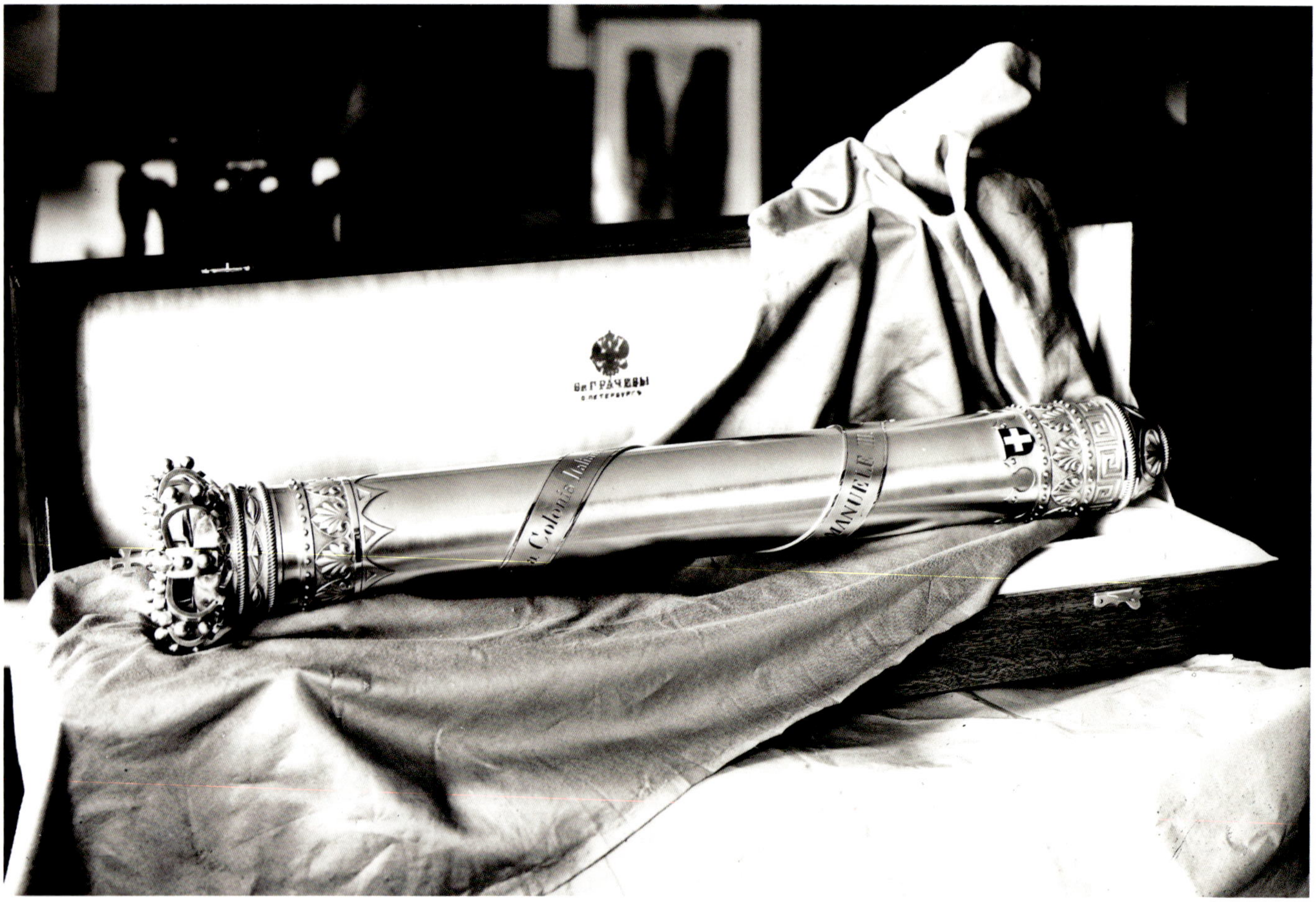

This Grachev silver scepter was presented to the Italian Ambassador, c. 1911. *Courtesy Central State Archive of Film and Photographs in St. Petersburg*

1. Fabergé et al., *Fabergé: A Comprehensive Reference Book*, 99.

2. Or Hasse. Mentioned in 1849 as operating in the Russian capital on Sadovaia Street, although a workshop on Nevskii Prospect is listed elsewhere.

3. At this point the brothers already lived and worked in the rectory of the Catholic Church at 32–34 Nevskii Prospect. This would become their main retail location.

4. RGIA f 468, o 8, d 47, dated January 21, 1892. The set comprised a kettle on burner, coffeepot, teapot, sugar bowl, creamer, bread basket, cup, tea and coffee spoons, lemon fork, sugar tongs, tea strainer, and tray. It cost 3,300 rubles.

5. *Catalogue of the Russian Section, World's Columbian Exposition, 1893, Chicago* (St. Petersburg: Imperial Russian Commission, Ministry of Finances, 1893), 192.

6. Christie's London, November 28, 2011, lot 354; and Christie's New York, May 20, 2015, lot 207.

7. In October 1904, a Russian fleet in the North Sea mistook a British trawler for the Imperial Japanese Navy and fired on it, killing several sailors. The event, also called the Dogger Bank incident, almost led to a war between Russia and Great Britain. This was averted thanks to an international inquiry in Paris in January 1905 in which Davis took part.

8. RGIA, f 468, o 8, d 900, l 23, 26. Davis also received a silver presentation gift by the London crown jewelers R. & S. Garrard & Co. from the British government. Both the Grachev and Garrard services were sold at Lyon & Turnbull in Scotland in 2009.

9. RGIA, f 468, o 8, d 1193, l 10.

IVAN MOROZOV: JEWELER AND SILVERSMITH TO THE TSAR

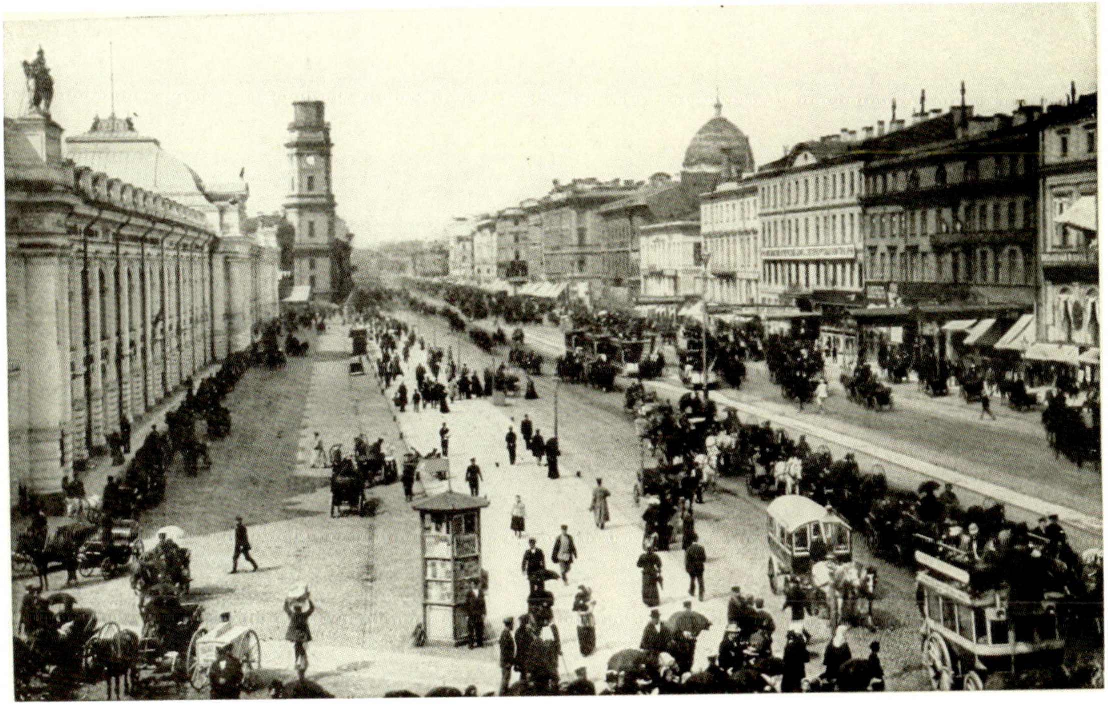

Considered one of Russia's finest, the Morozov workshop was supplier to the imperial court already by 1884. And by 1910, Morozov was a leading jeweler and silversmith in Russia, second only to Fabergé.[1]

Gostinyi dvor (left) on Nevskii Prospect, St. Petersburg's bustling main street. First built in the 18th century, the shopping center housed Morozov's shop, along with many other retailers. *Wikimedia Commons*

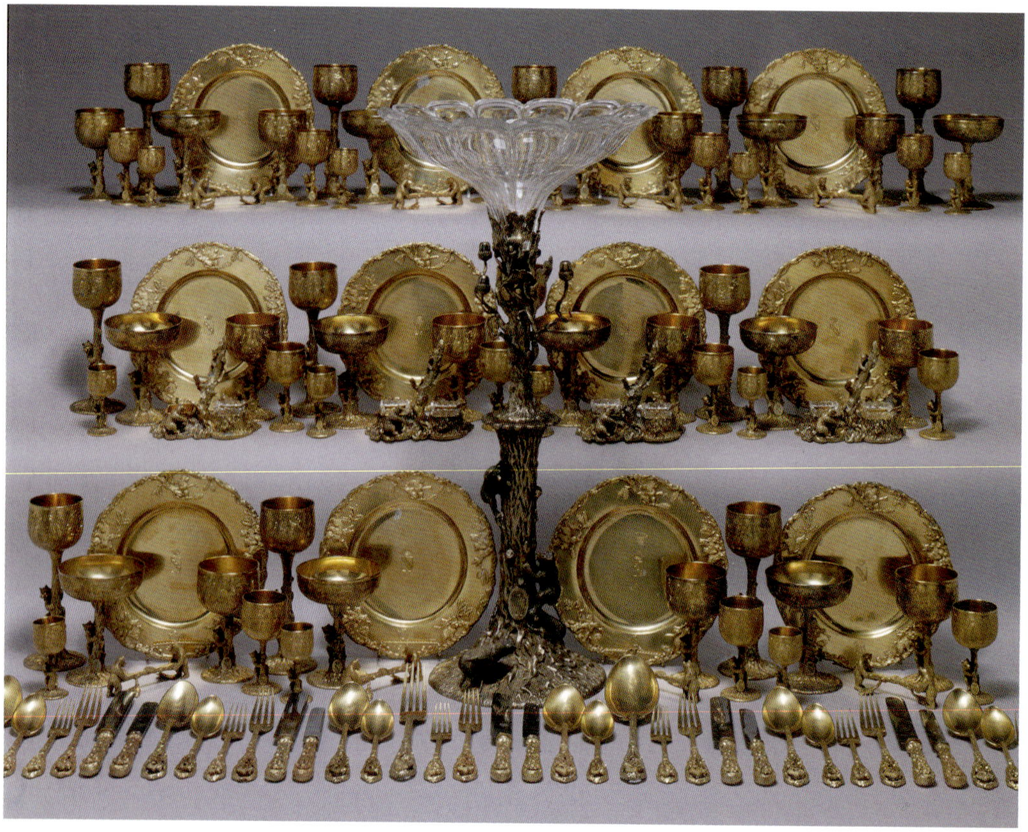

Founded in 1849 by gold workmaster Ivan Ekimovich Morozov (d. 1885), I. E. Morozov occupied three addresses: nos. 85, 86 and 87 in St. Petersburg's Gostinnyi Dvor. A famous shopping gallery, the Gostinnyi Dvor was built during the reign of Catherine the Great. Like Hahn and Blank, Morozov supplied diamonds to embellish imperial snuffboxes for the court. After his death, the firm thrived under his eldest son, Vladimir, and received many imperial commissions until it closed in 1917. Vladimir was one the founders of the Union of St. Petersburg Jewelers. Another son, Sergei, owned S. I. Morozov, a trading house only steps away at 31 Nevskii Prospect, part of the Silver Row. According to Eugène Fabergé, both firms produced items for House of Fabergé.[2]

Trading at Morozov ended with the Russian Revolution. In the 1920s, when Vladimir was eking out a living as a guard at a nearby café, he tried unsuccessfully to retrieve some valuables from the old shop. Four decades later, during a renovation of Gostinnyi Dvor, two female workers unearthed a cache of solid gold weighing 114 kilos at the very location of the old Morozov store.[3]

An extensive silver-gilt dinner service by Morozov, St. Petersburg, 1908–1917. *Courtesy of Doyle Auctioneers and Appraisers*

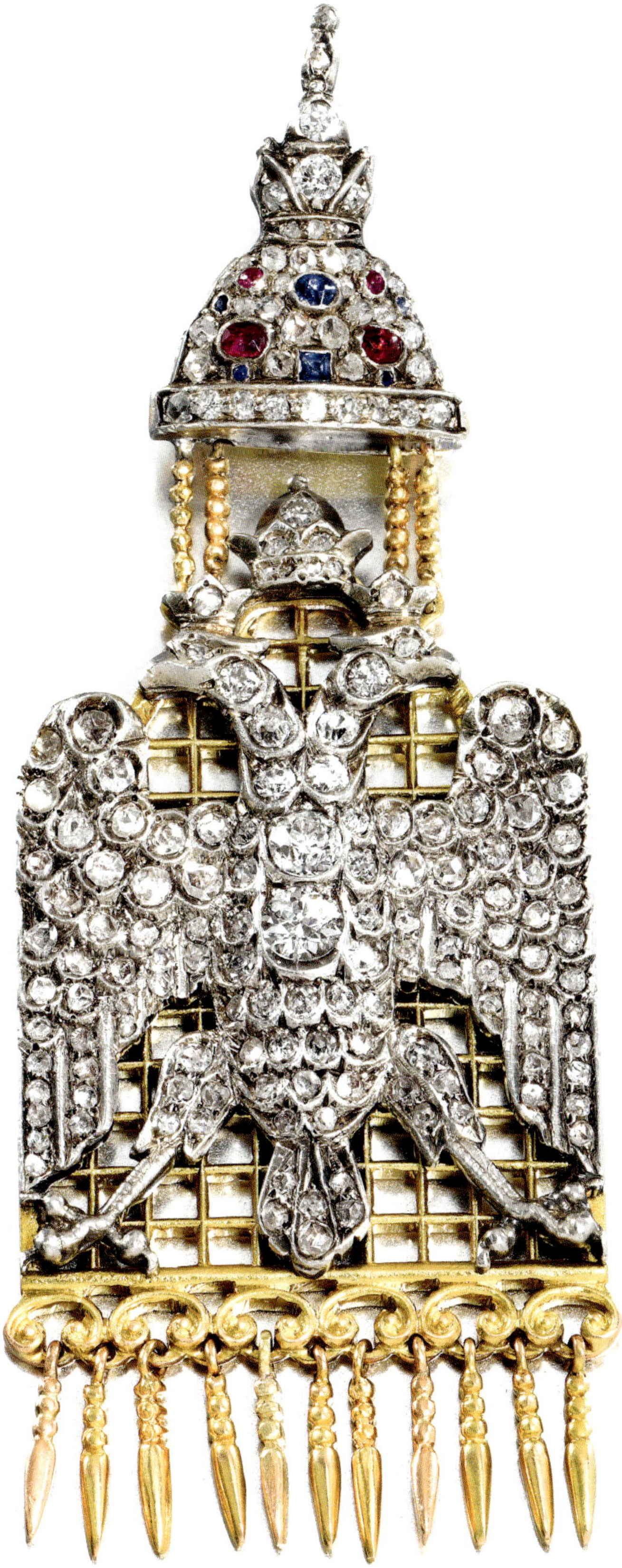

This diamond eagle suspended from a gem set Monomach Crown recalls the era of the first Romanov emperor Tsar Michael (1596–1645) and was made to commemorate the Romanov Tercentenary in 1913. *Courtesy of Sothcby's*

History

While Moscow silversmiths tended to be Russian born, in 19th-century St. Petersburg, foreign craftsmen still prevailed. Ivan Morozov was one of the few native Russian goldsmiths with the imperial warrant working in the capital. Little is known about the master goldsmith himself, other than he ran a prosperous business in a prestigious row of galleries.

I. E. Morozov was known as a large retailer of other makers' wares, and the firm's own production had strong artistic merit. One of its foremost designers was Ivan Mikhailov, a founder of the Russian Industrial Art Society in 1904 and teacher and graduate of the Stieglitz School of Technical Design. Elegant neoclassicism and Russian medievalism embodied the Morozov style.

Extensive silver dinner services and elaborate centerpieces were its stock in trade. One of the few services to surface in the West appeared at auction in New York in 2006. Weighing just under 1,000 troy ounces, the 180-piece set features a large centerpiece of naturalistic design enhanced with oak motifs and bears, and appeared to be complete (see illustration, page 152).

Early-20th-century advertisements boast an on-premises silver and bronze workshop and feature imposing bronze candelabra and chandeliers. The firm also sold enameled cigarette cases, salt cellars, sets of teaspoons and the like by Moscow makers such as Maria Semenova, Fedor Rückert and the 11th Artel. Jewelry also most likely figured prominently in the Morozov storefront, and a few jewels survive in Morozov boxes. Gold and jeweled crosses destined for the clergy, enameled picture frames in 18-karat gold and medals were also sold.

But the workshop's claim to fame was the cigarette case. It produced hundreds of imperial ones. In gold and silver and of all different textures, these were applied with an eagle with or without diamonds, to indicate a gift from the tsar. The eagle took different forms. Some were with downturned wings, a neoclassical emblem from the reigns of Alexander I and Nicholas I, while others were fuller with upturned splayed wings, symbolic of the reigns of Alexander III and Nicholas II. A third was used to commemorate the Romanov tercentenary and had a distinctive pre-Petrine look, surmounted by the Monomakh crown to celebrate the 300th anniversary of the Romanov dynasty in 1913. Empress Alexandra Fedorovna presented a similar gem-set eagle attributed to Morozov to her lady-in-waiting, Baroness Buxhoeveden, but in the form of a pendant.[4]

Tsar Nicholas II often turned to Morozov for this essential accessory. On October 26, 1911, the imperial cabinet ordered from the goldsmith 14 gold cigarette cases and seven silver ones for a total of 2,780 rubles. The gold ones cost 125 to 1,200 rubles, while those in silver cost 35 to 45 rubles. The invoice lists a five-digit number next to each entry, probably an internal stock number.[5]

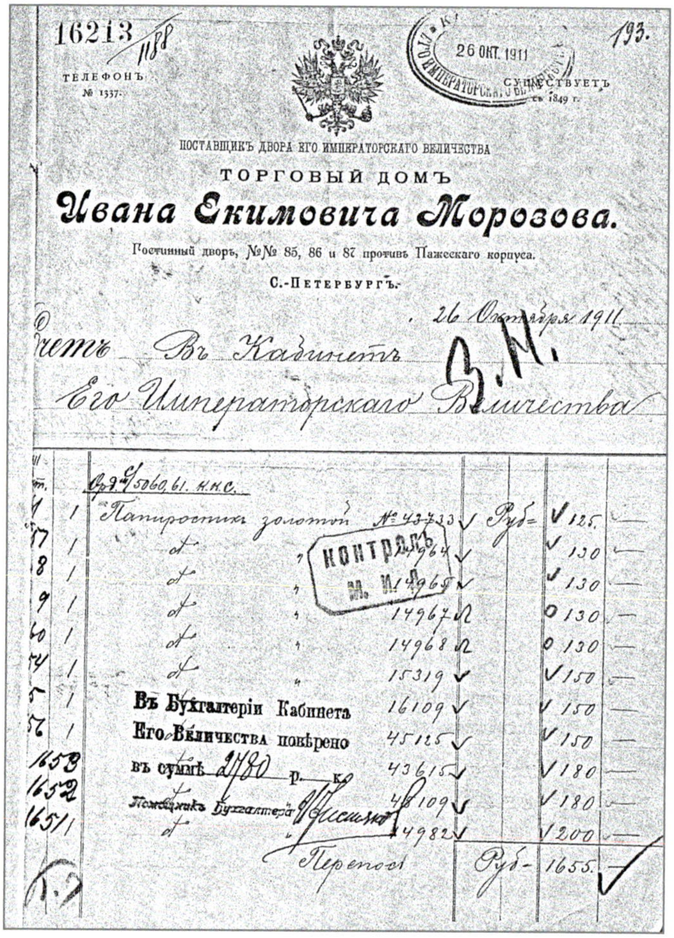

16213 1188 193.

ТЕЛЕФОНЪ № 1337.

26 ОКТ. 1911

ПОСТАВЩИКЪ ДВОРА ЕГО ИМПЕРАТОРСКАГО ВЕЛИЧЕСТВА

ТОРГОВЫЙ ДОМЪ

Ивана Екимовича Морозова.

Гостинный дворъ, №№ 85, 86 и 87 противъ Пажескаго корпуса.

С.-ПЕТЕРБУРГЪ.

26 Октября 1911

Счетъ Въ Кабинетъ Его Императорскаго Величества

Папиросница золотая № 43733 Руб. 125

14964 130

14965 130

14967 130

14968 130

15319 150

16109 150

45125 150

43615 180

48109 180

14982 200

Переносъ Руб. 1655

КОНТРОЛЬ

Въ Бухгалтеріи Кабинета Его Величества повѣрено въ суммѣ 2780 р. к.

Помощникъ Бухгалтера

The Morozov invoice lists a number of cigarette cases ordered by the Imperial cabinet in 1911. *Courtesy of RGIA*

Right:
A Morozov Great War Silver Kovsh, St. Petersburg, 1908–17. *Private Collection, photo by Noel Allum*

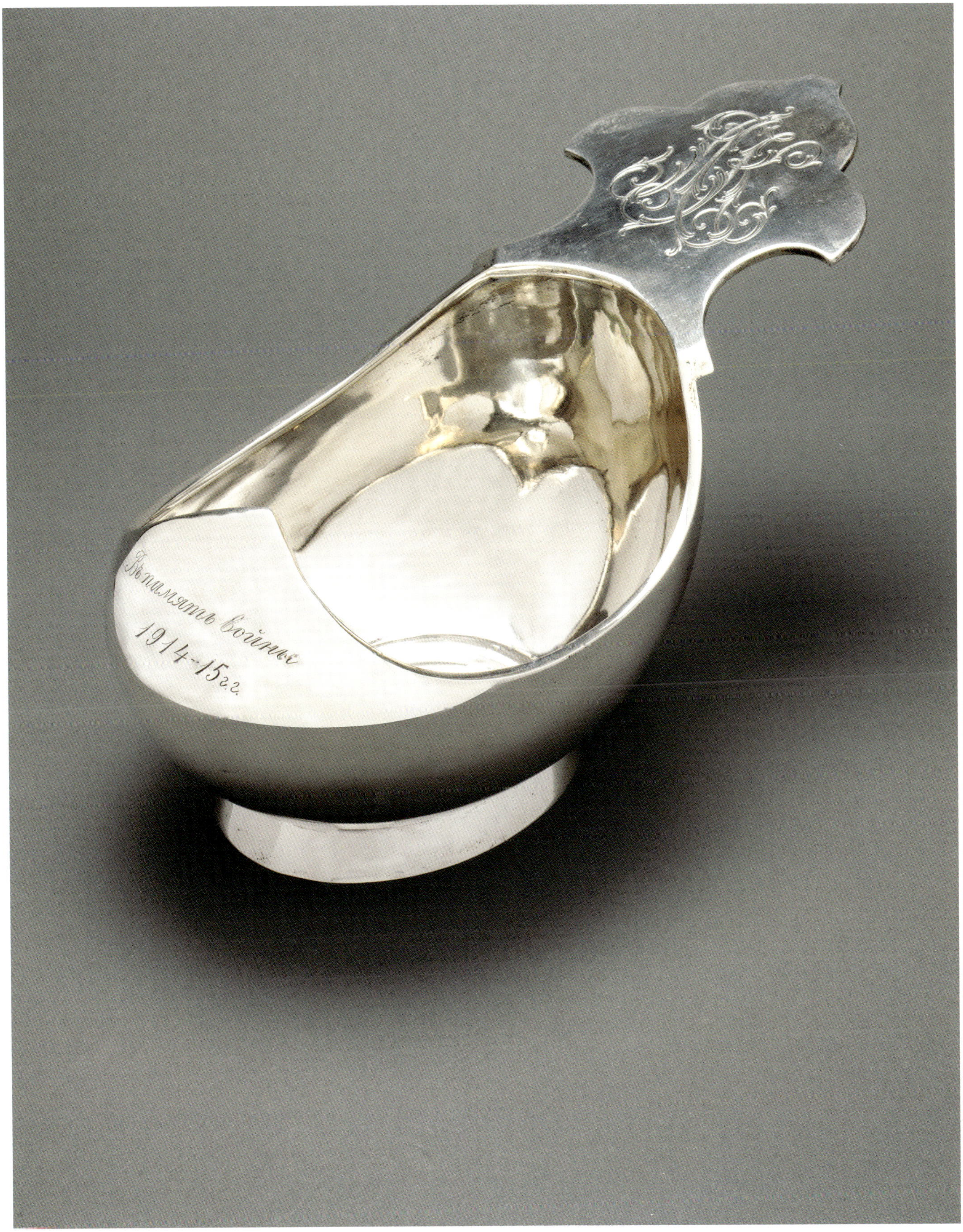
Въ память войны
1914-15г.г.

NOTES

1. Fabergé et al., *Fabergé: A Comprehensive Reference Book*, 99. The total output for the year: Morozov 750,000 vs. Fabergé one million rubles.

2. Fabergé et al., *Fabergé: A Comprehensive Reference Book*, 38.

3. Ibid., 52.

4. Prince Michael of Greece, *Jewels of the Tsars* (New York: Vendome, 2006), 134.

5. RGIA, Fond 468, Opus 8, File 1137, 11.

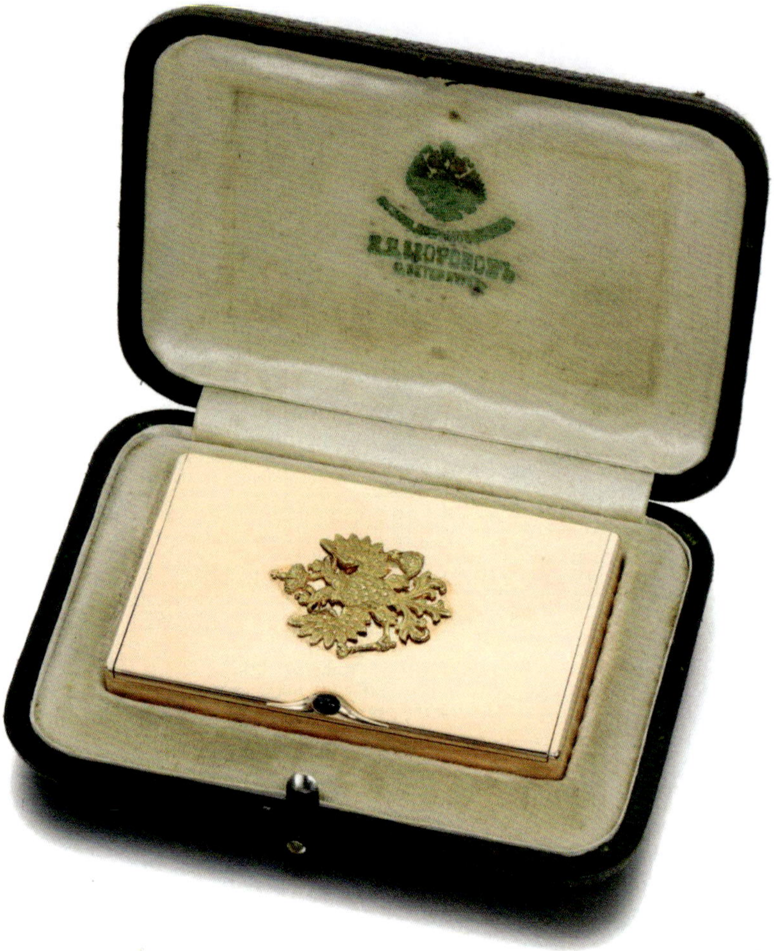

Morozov two-color gold presentation cigarette case. *Courtesy of Sotheby's*

JEWELERS OF ST. PETERSBURG UNITE!

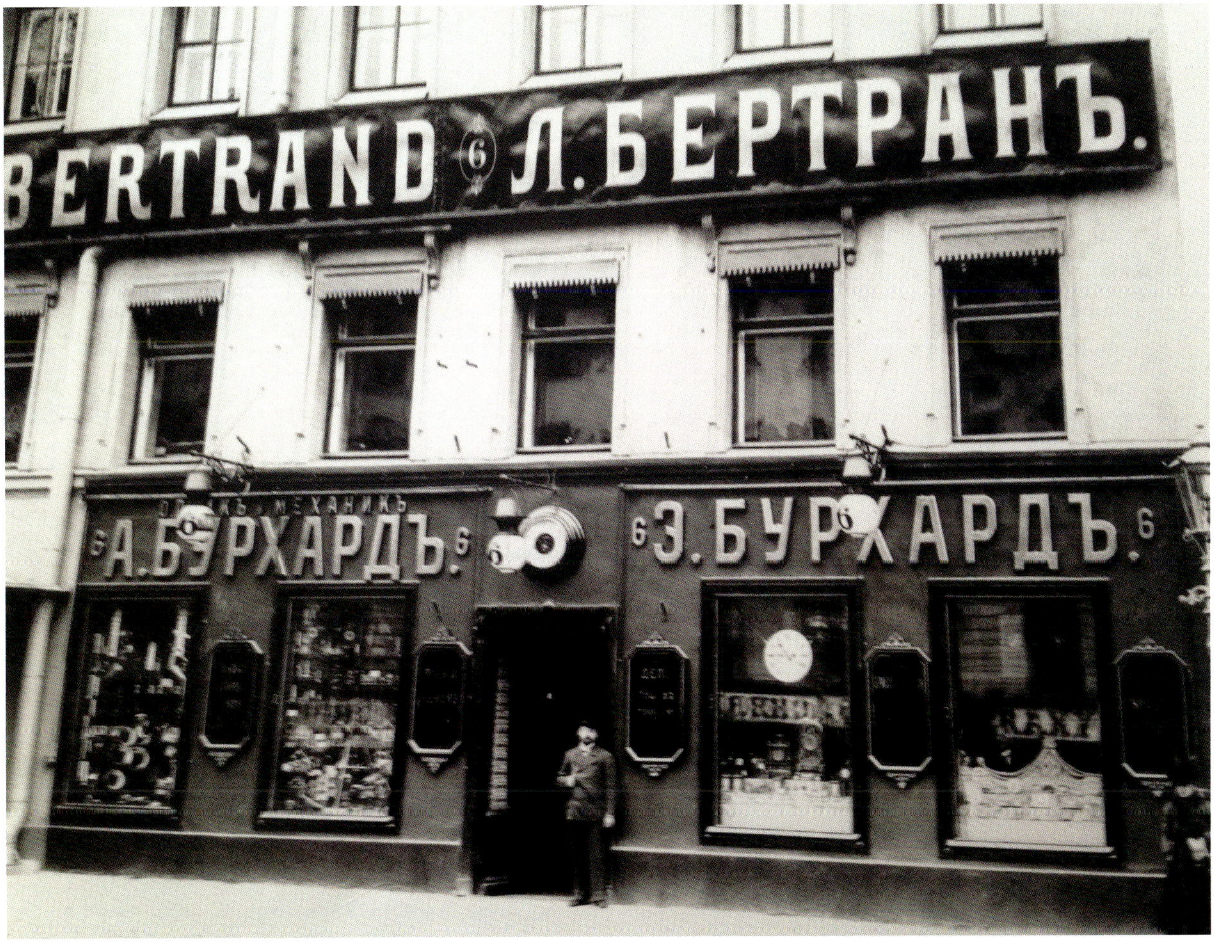

The Burchard storefront at 6 Nevskii Prospect in St. Petersburg. Edward Burchard was an active member of the Union of St. Petersburg Jewelers and sold jewels, watches and clocks. Burchard also sold all manner of optical devices, which are displayed to the left of the entrance. *Courtesy of Central State Archive of Film and Photographs in St. Petersburg*

By 1910, Europeans enjoyed a 14 percent market share of all St. Petersburg jewelry production. Although matched by the output from the House of Fabergé that year, this still represented a major worry for native Russian jewelers. Foreigners were now seen as compromising their business revenues.[1] The worst offenders were the French, who had managed to make inroads since the 19th century, not only as purveyors to the Russian grand dukes, but also to the tsar and his family. The biggest blow came with the successful purchase of Russian imperial jewels from the treasury of the imperial cabinet by the French gem merchant Georges Sachs in 1906. And despite the continued patronage of Empress Alexandra Fedorovna, who favored the Russians, as did some of the empire's most illustrious families, such as the Yusupovs, Shuvalovs, Narishkins and Stroganovs, the Russians felt the need to take action.

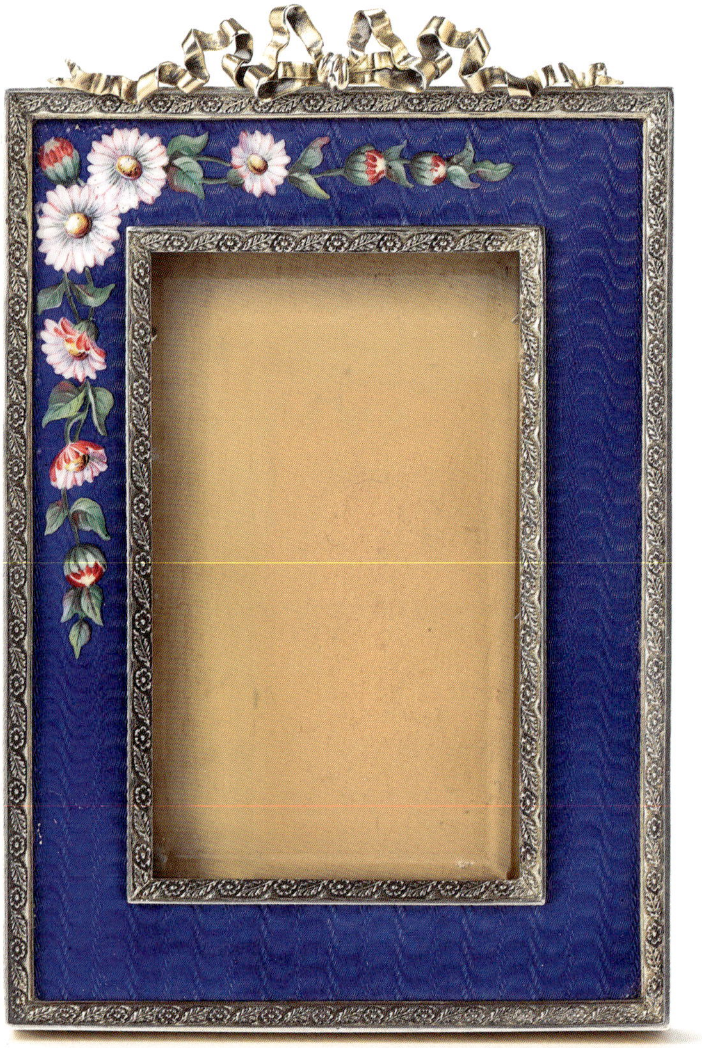

To create a united front against the French, a number of St. Petersburg goldsmiths formed a syndicate in 1912. The Union of St. Petersburg Jewelers offered its members a voice through a monthly publication: *Russkii iuvelir* (The Russian Jeweler). Editorials and advertisements increased the visibility of smaller houses such as Bock, Butz, Utkin and Schubert, although the circulation is not known. The journal covered the market and was aimed at dealers rather than the general public.

At its peak, the union had an estimated 150 members. These included the then-prominent names of Adler, Linden, Denisov-Uralskii, Bolin workmaster Finikov and Kortmann. Participation in the union indicated solidarity of sorts among tradesmen. While many member jewelers are unknown in the West, others are famous, such as Carl Fabergé and Vladimir Morozov, one of the founders. The two would later spar in a lawsuit described below.

Russkii iuvelir was also a platform for news of the trade in the Russian imperial capital, some of it unsavory. Vandalism, thefts, strikes, lawsuits and complaints about foreign competitors and discord among dealers are covered in detail. The January 1913 issue, for example, reported that workers' strikes disrupted various ateliers, including those of Bock, Fedorov, Eduard and others. This apparently led to high tension and unruly meetings the following month. Covering a meeting of striking workers among goldsmiths in February, on page 7, one reporter was shocked by their raucous and disorderly behavior:

> Just returned from the extraordinary meeting of the St. Petersburg Society of Jewelers . . . and rightly I am at a loss as to describe what it was. A nightmare, bad dream or reality . . . The meeting bore a random, undefined and scattered character. . . . If only the striking workers could see what a lot these are.

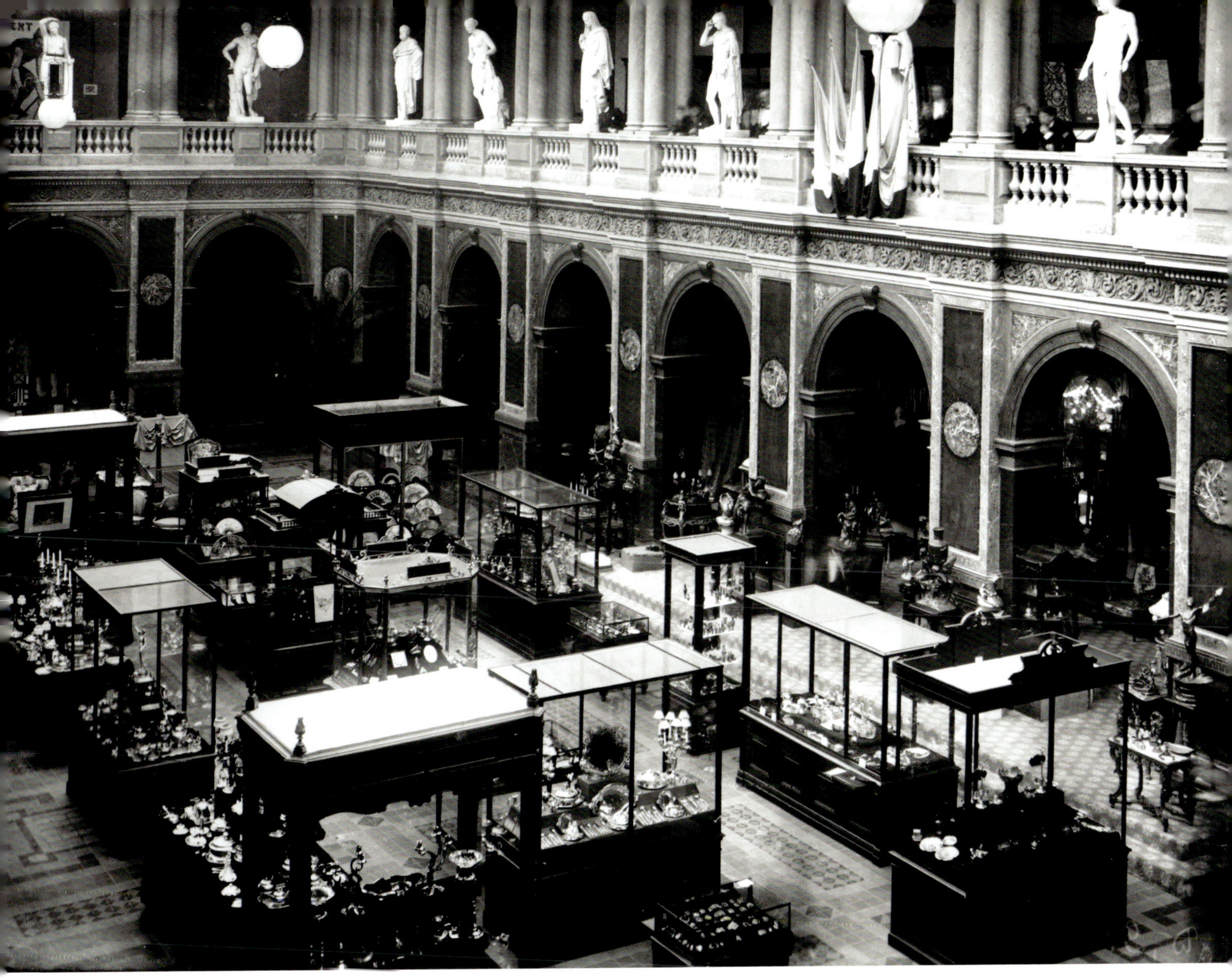

The magazine also featured the memoirs of court jeweler to Empresses Elizabeth Petrovna and Catherine II, Jérémie Pauzié (translated into Russian from the French). The first issue of *Russkii iuvelir* included an article by Baron von Fölkersam about St. Petersburg gold and silversmiths from 1714 to 1814, which had also been published in *Starye gody* in 1907.[2]

The real bane of these jewelers' existence was revealed early on in the second issue: "On foreign jewelers in St. Petersburg creating unfair competition." In an article two months later, the judges (*konkursnoe upravlenie*) described the transactions of the Parisians Chaumet and Cartier as an "affront to our dealers right before Easter with the sale of gold, silver and jewelry from a disreputable debtor." And in June, a report complaining that three-quarters of goods supplied in the market were of foreign origin, the number of firms serving the internal market was gradually diminishing, and even imports of furniture increased.

This exhibition of French goldsmiths in St. Petersburg, which included the Parisian Houses of Boucheron, Gustave Sandoz and the fan maker Duvelleroy, was held at the renowned Stieglitz School of Applied Arts. *Courtesy of Central State Archive of Film and Photographs in St. Petersburg*

Previous page:
The floral enameled picture frame was made by the goldsmith Eduard, whose widow, Vera, was a member of the Union of St. Petersburg Jewelers. *Courtesy of Sotheby's*

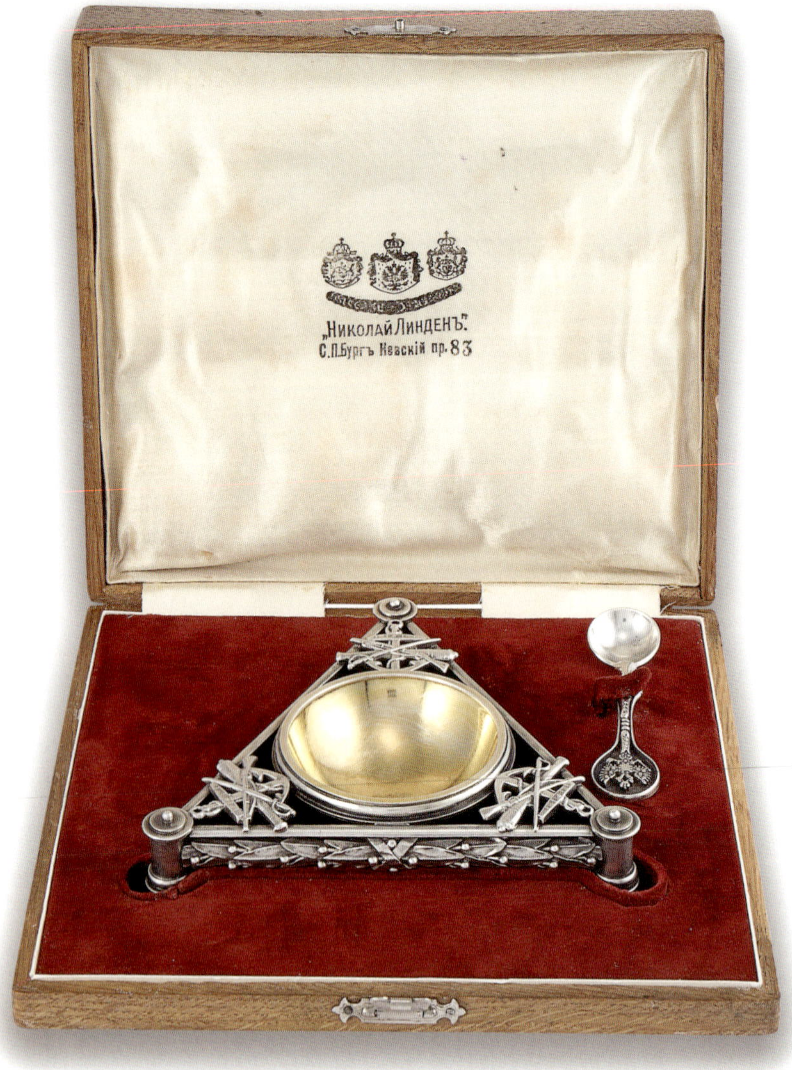

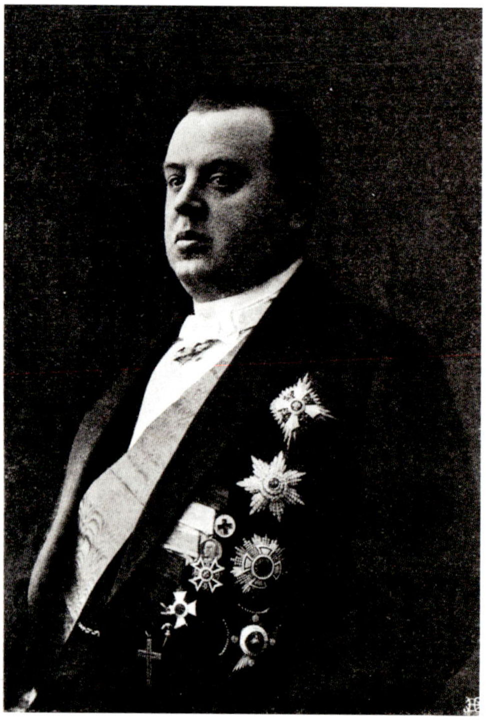

A photo of Nikolai Linden wearing his medals as councilor of state from the August 1912 review, , and a silver salt cellar with spoon by Linden. *Courtesy of Doyle Auctioneers and Appraisers.* Linden advertised in *Ves Petersburg,* the imperial capital's "yellow pages," as selling, among other items, diamonds, gold, silver, watches, and *znaki* (badges). The store was located at 83 Nevskii Prospect, near Znamenskaia (now Vosstania) Square, and down the street from Hahn and Grachev. *Source:* Russkii iuvelir *8 (1912).*

Discord within the ranks reached the highest echelons. The first two editions of 1914 describe a court case between Carl Fabergé and Vladimir Morozov, initiated by Fabergé in 1908. The celebrated goldsmith was suing Morozov for 90,000 rubles, claiming the latter took four items without paying him. Morozov countered by claiming he had paid 11,900 rubles to Fabergé. Fabergé lost the case.

Nikolai Gustavovich Linden

Nikolai Linden was another active and somewhat colorful member. From 1883 onward, his workshop, Nikolai Linden & Company, made jewels, watches, jetons of organizations and institutions and silver and church plate. It is said that early on, Linden's storefront was misleading, since it displayed a royal Montenegran coat of arms similar to that of the Romanov imperial eagle, which gave the impression the jeweler had the Russian imperial warrant.[3] The two double-headed eagles resemble each other, with the main difference being the central shield. Linden's logo, which appears on the interior and exterior of his fitted boxes, featured two other crests and a host of medallions below, reflecting those the jeweler won in Russian fairs. By 1912 Linden had legitimately gained the title of purveyor to the Russian imperial court.[4]

Three Pages from *Russkii iuvelir* (the Russian Jeweler)

The journal's raison d'être was to recognize and support local goldsmiths, many of whom worked in obscurity and subsisted on word of the mouth from the trade network. The short-lived periodical brought to life little-known jewelers of the imperial capital by adding personal details of their lives and careers.

What follows are three excerpts from the journal of jewelers who tried to make their mark in the imperial capital: Nikolai Lazarev, who owned a workshop on Gogol Street; M. I. Drozhin, saluted on his firm's 45th anniversary; and the aristocrat goldsmith Leonard Tatishchev. In his obituary, penned by fellow jeweler Edward Burchard, he was hailed for his creativity upon his early death of a heart attack in 1914.

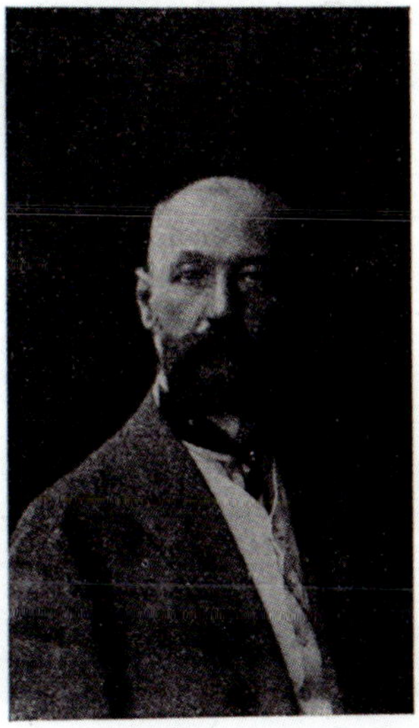

Н. П. Лазаревъ.
Къ тридцатилѣтію его дѣятельности.

Николай Петровичъ Лазаревъ, одинъ изъ самыхъ популярныхъ въ Петербургѣ золотыхъ дѣлъ мастеровъ, въ теченіе 5 лѣтъ работалъ у извѣстнаго тогда мастера Эд. Бера и затѣмъ въ 1883 г. записался въ цехъ мастеромъ и открылъ собственную мастерскую. На-дняхъ исполнилось 30 лѣтъ его дѣятельности. Теперь мастерская Н. П. Лазарева помѣщается на улицѣ Гоголя, 5, въ томъ же помѣщеніи, гдѣ была мастерская Эд. Бера и гдѣ Лазаревъ провелъ свои ученическіе годы. Въ теченіе послѣднихъ 23 лѣтъ Н. Лазаревъ состоитъ цеховымъ выборнымъ и съ самаго начала функціонированія Общества ювелировъ—кандидатомъ въ члены Правленія.

При организаціи Общества распространенія художественно-ремесленнаго образованія г. Лазаревъ первый записался членомъ Общества и состоитъ кандидатомъ въ члены Правленія.

Translation:

Nikolai Petrovich Lazarev, one of the most popular St. Petersburg goldsmiths, who worked for five years with the then-famous craftsman Ed. Ber [Eduard Bähr, located on the Moika Canal, no. 49] and then, in 1883, was registered in the guild of masters and opened his own workshop. His workshop has been operating for 30 years. It is now located on Gogol Street 5, in the same building where Ber's workshop was situated and where he did his apprenticeship. Over the past 23 years, N. Lazarev has been elected to the guild and, since the very start, was a candidate for its board.

With the organization of the Society for the Promotion of Art and Crafts Education, Mr. Lazarev was the first to register as a member of the society and is a candidate for its board.
Russkii iuvelir 12 (1913)

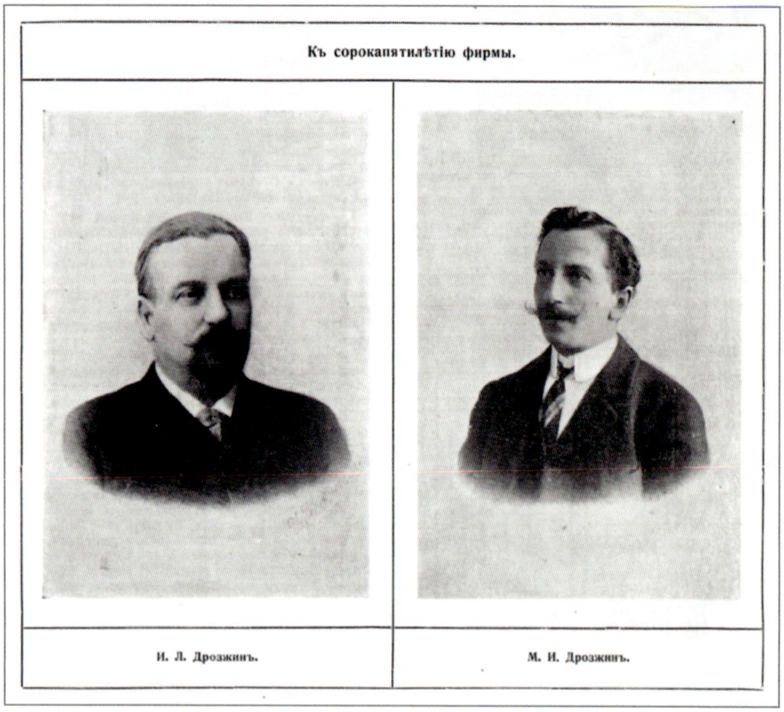

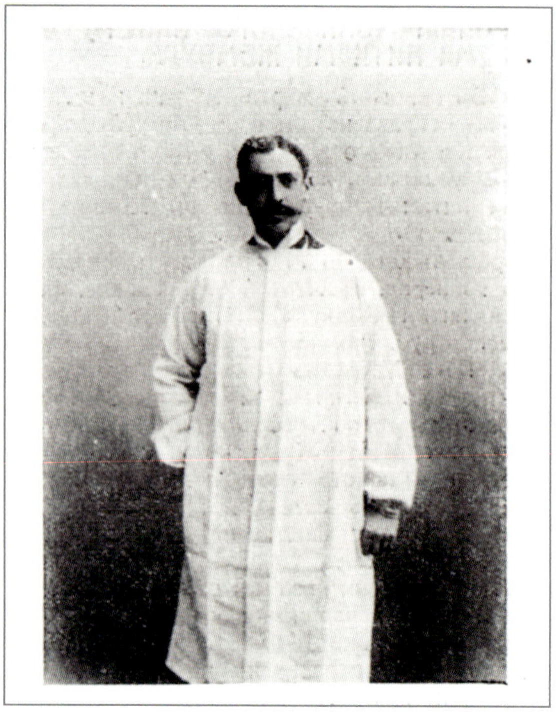

Left:
The 45th anniversary of the M. I. Drozhin firm.

On September 14 a modest ceremony took place—the 45th anniversary of the founding of the gold, silver and diamond dealer I. L. Drozhin. The founder was the late father of the current owner M. I. Drozhin, the founding chairman of the society of jewelers, gold, silver and watch masters and dealers in Petersburg. E. Burchard, one of the oldest St. Petersburg masters, M. I. Lazarev, B. Maseev, G. Utkin and others presented M. I. Drozhin with a gold-framed portrait of the former and current owners of the firm. M. I. Drozhin is no stranger to the society's affairs, serving the young association (whose founder he was) as its first secretary during the first year of its existence.

Russkii iuvelir 10 (1912)

Right:
[cross] L. L. (Leonard Leonardovich) Tatishchev died on April 18 from a heart attack. He was known as the "aristocrat jeweler." L. L. hailed from an ancient noble lineage and had been educated at the Corps de Pages, and according to his origins this aristocrat dedicated himself to the art of jewelry, which he felt was his special calling and to which he devoted many years; he was particularly drawn to precious stones. He drew inspiration for his precious objects from nature; nature for him was an endless book, from which he got beautiful ideas. To study nature, he traveled throughout Europe, sparing neither effort nor expense, as long as it might create beautiful objects. All of his objects were infused with meaning and were often displayed at exhibitions, where they were admired for their deep meaning, originality and beautiful execution.

The late jeweler was blessed with poetic talent, and his pen created many beautiful poems. In his private life he was a supremely kind and sympathetic man; he was endowed with rare spiritual qualities and was universally loved and respected. He died in the flower of his life, having been buried at the age of 45.

May this dear and unforgettable colleague rest in peace.
E. Burchard, Russkii iuvelir 12 (1913)

Following page:
Tatishchev's studio workshop. *Photo courtesy of Central Archive of Film and Photographs*

A gold samorodok cigarette case retailed by Burchard. *Courtesy of Sotheby's*

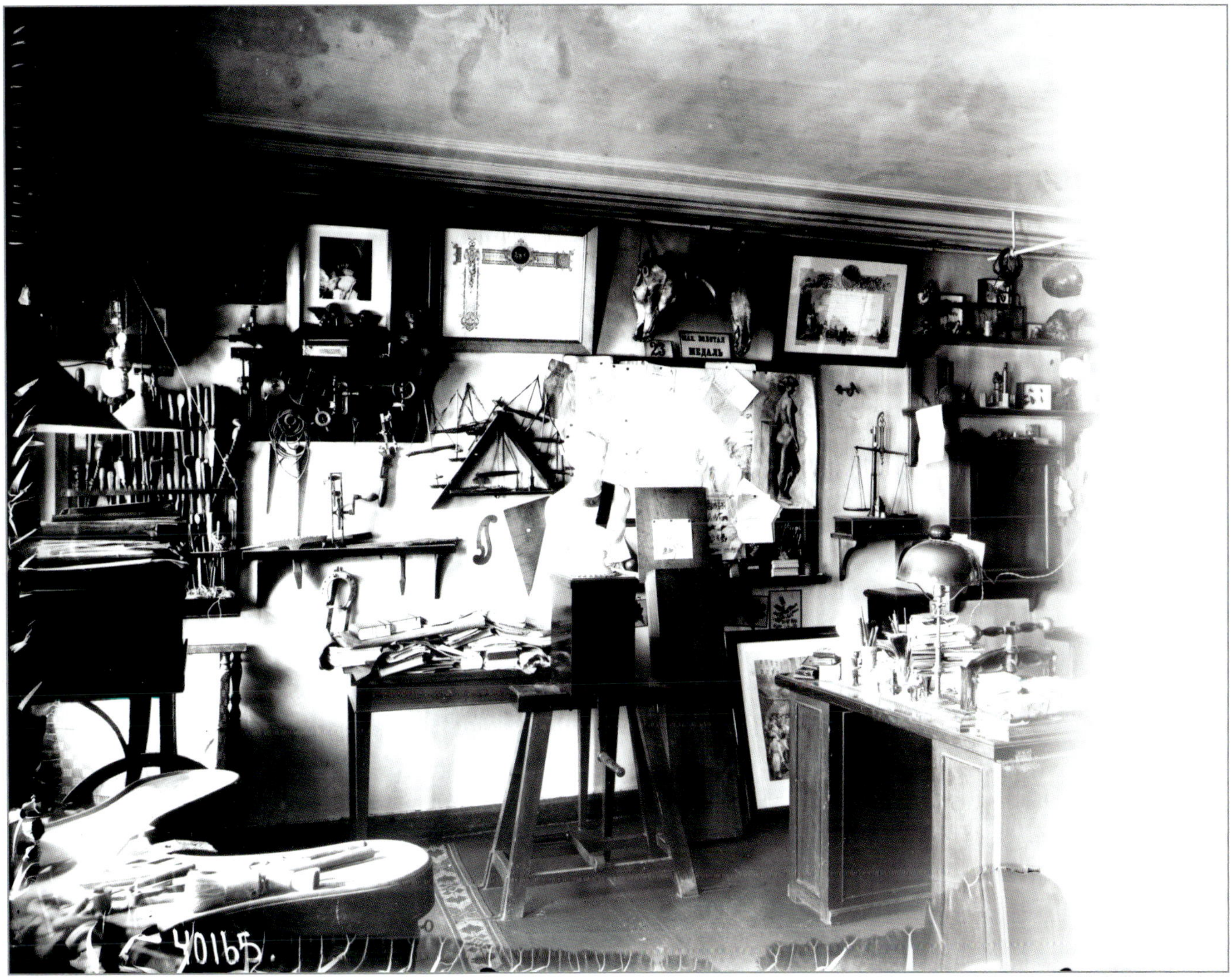

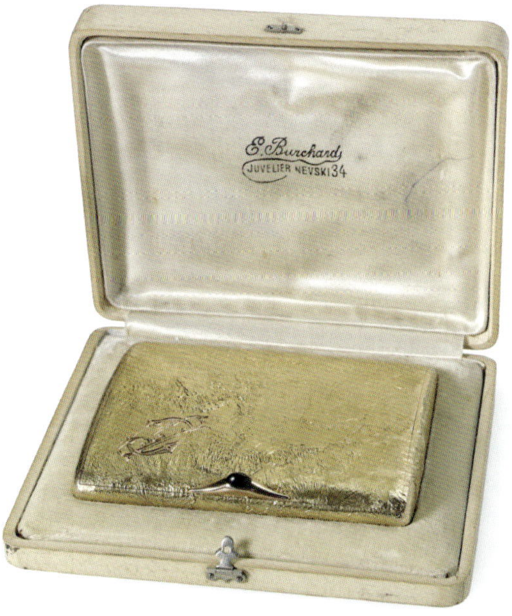

NOTES

1. Fabergé et al., *Fabergé: A Comprehensive Reference Book*, 99.

2. Fölkersam's work was the only reference source for Russian jewelry before the 1970s. Baron Armin von Fölkersam, *Alfavitnyi ukazatel k S-Peterburgskikh zolotykh i serebrianykh del masterov, graverov i proch.: 1714–1814* (St. Petersburg: Starye gody, 1907).

3. Fabergé et al., *Fabergé: A Comprehensive Reference Book*, 49.

4. Valentin Skurlov, "Spisok vedushchikh Peterburgskikh firm i masterov," http://skurlov.blogspot.com/2012/08/blog-post_2565.html.

15

History

OLD RUSSIA REBORN: THE MOSCOW SILVERSMITHS AND ENAMELERS

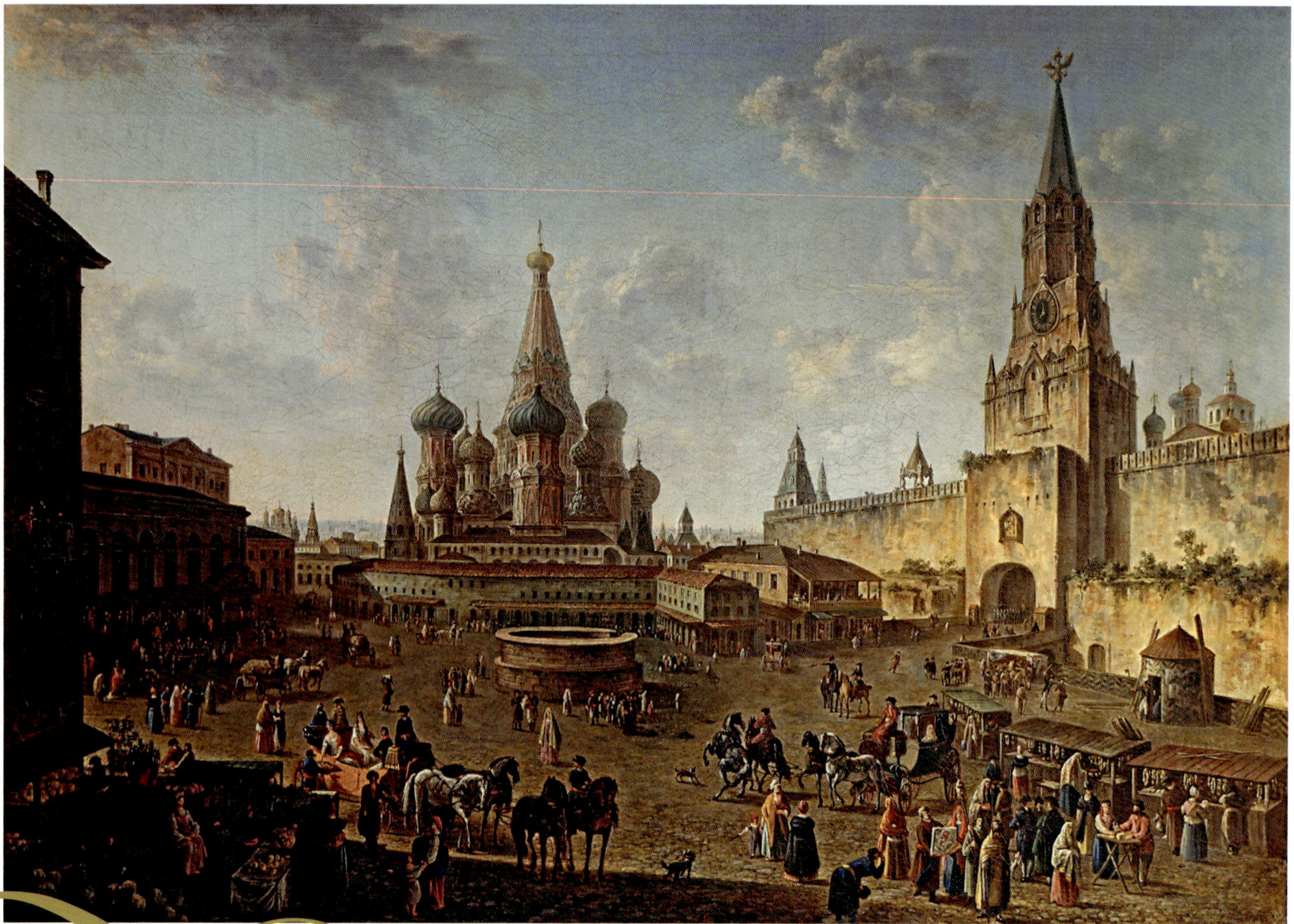

If St. Petersburg was the empire's window on the West, Moscow looked into Russia's soul. In the Imperial era, the metropolis on the Neva River was home to government officials, intellectuals and clerks, while the more traditional nobility, merchants and Old Believers dominated Moscow, the ancient city of "forty times forty churches." To this day, the "two capitals" retain distinctly separate identities.

Previous page:
F. F. Alekseev. *Moscow. Red Square*, ca. 1800. *Source: Wiki Commons*

Below:
Kuznetskii Most, ca. 1900. A fashionable shopping street in Moscow that housed a number of jewelers' shops. The storefront of the silversmith I. P. Khlebnikov, together with a sign "Purveyor to the Imperial Court," are in the left corner.

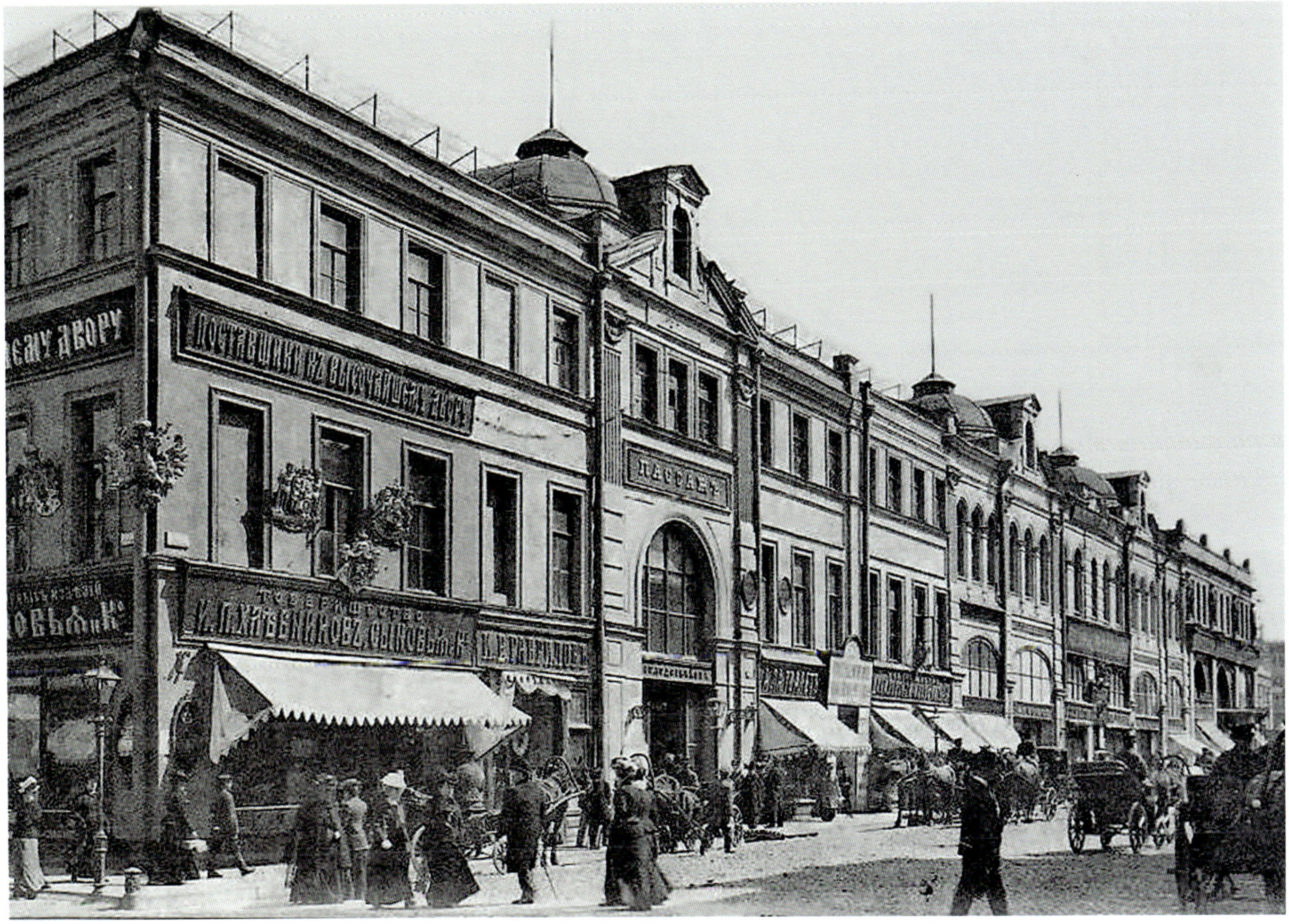

Despite its austere beauty, Peter's progeny, "the most abstract and intentional city in the whole world" according to Dostoevsky,[1] seems an alien import. Imposed by an Age of Reason autocrat on an inhospitable marsh at Russia's western extremity, St. Petersburg's neoclassical architecture and rectilinear prospects reflect the intellect rather than the heart.[2] Moscow, by contrast, appears more organic. Unlike the former's starkly geometrical geography, maps of the old city show its natural growth over the past eight centuries, from the Kremlin outward like the concentric circles of a tree's trunk.

The jewelers' art expressed this great urban rivalry. While the craftsmen of Bolin, Fabergé, Tillander and St. Petersburg's other distinguished houses drew their inspiration from the West, Moscow's silversmiths proudly celebrated their pre-Petrine heritage.[3] The return to bygone years was hardly unusual. In the Romantic Age, many Europeans looked to their ancient past as they sought to commune with their national spirit. This nostalgia for an often-imagined paradisical yesteryear was expressed in the arts throughout the continent, from William Morris's textile designs and Eugène Viollet-le-Duc's architecture to Richard Wagner's operas.

In the rest of Europe, Romantic nationalism was partly a reaction to the mechanized uniformity of industrialization.

Russia, by contrast, was still predominantly agricultural. Here the movement was largely inspired by growing fears about the baleful influence of the Romano-German West.[4] As the historian Nikolai Karamzin famously put it, "We became citizens of the world, but ceased, in some cases, to be citizens of Russia."[5]

If its intellectual variant, the Slavophile movement, was limited to a relatively small circle in Moscow, the cultural impact of this turn to a purer past was broader. Thus, in the 1830s Emperor Nicholas I ordered ladies to wear traditional dress at court. At the same time, he commissioned the composer Aleksandr Lvov to replace "God Save the King," the national anthem his predecessor had imported from England, with a proper Russian hymn, "God Save the Tsar."

Nicholas also enthusiastically patronized Fedor Solntsev, an artist who produced photographically accurate designs of old Russian artifacts.[6] Born a peasant's son, whose talent won him admission to the Imperial Art Academy as a youth in 1815, Solntsev proved an excellent student. And his abilities convinced the school's president, Aleksei Olenin, to take him directly under his wing. Olenin's passion for Russian antiquities led him to send his pupil to the Kremlin Armory in 1830 to make reproductions of its extensive collection of medieval sabers, helmets, shields, liturgical items and other treasures.

Over the next 25 years, Solntsev also traveled to other ancient towns, eventually producing over 3,000 illustrations. The tsar had 500 them reproduced from his own purse at considerable expense in a six-volume collection, *Drevnosti Rossiiskogo Gosudartsva* (Antiquities of the Russian State), beginning in 1846, decreeing "that all historical material and archeological items worthy of attention by scholars and artists be accurately copied, described and see the light of day."[7]

One artist who paid attention right away was Pavel Sazikov, who, as we will see, faithfully used the book as a reference for his prize-winning silver sculpture of the 14th-century Battle of Kulikovo at London's Crystal Palace Exhibition in 1851. He wasn't alone. Solntsev's magnum opus was a major stimulus to the Style Russe that would dominate the decorative arts in Moscow over the coming decades.

Like the various historical trends earlier in the 19th century, the Style Russe did not necessarily strive for exactitude in drawing on the past. Rather, as Evgenia Kirichenko put it, the new fashion sought "an inspired, creative reinterpretation of it."[8] Thus, Moscow's silversmiths fashioned improbably lavish imitations in precious metals of ancient drinking vessels, such as the birdlike *kovsh* and *bratina*, as well as bread and salt trays for the traditional welcome offering symbolizing hospitality. More-modern implements, such as *podstakanniki* (tea-glass holders) and desk sets, also incorporated motifs from bygone days.

Colorful enamels played an important part in the Style Russe.[9] Nearly a thousand years earlier, artisans in Kievan Rus had imported the difficult technique of fixing molten colored glass to metals from Byzantium, although the skill had fallen into disuse when Batu Khan's hordes ravaged the land in the 13th century. While the craft was revived three centuries later, albeit in different form, Solntsev's books and other sources of medieval designs encouraged Moscow's leading silversmiths, such as Ovchinnikov and Khlebnikov, to decorate their creations with bold and bright enameled hues.

Drawing on pre-Petrine designs, themselves a rich fusion of the various Eastern and Western cultures with which Russians had long been in contact, the Style Russe satisfied the yearning among many for a distinctive national style. Nowhere was this desire stronger than among Moscow's proud citizens.

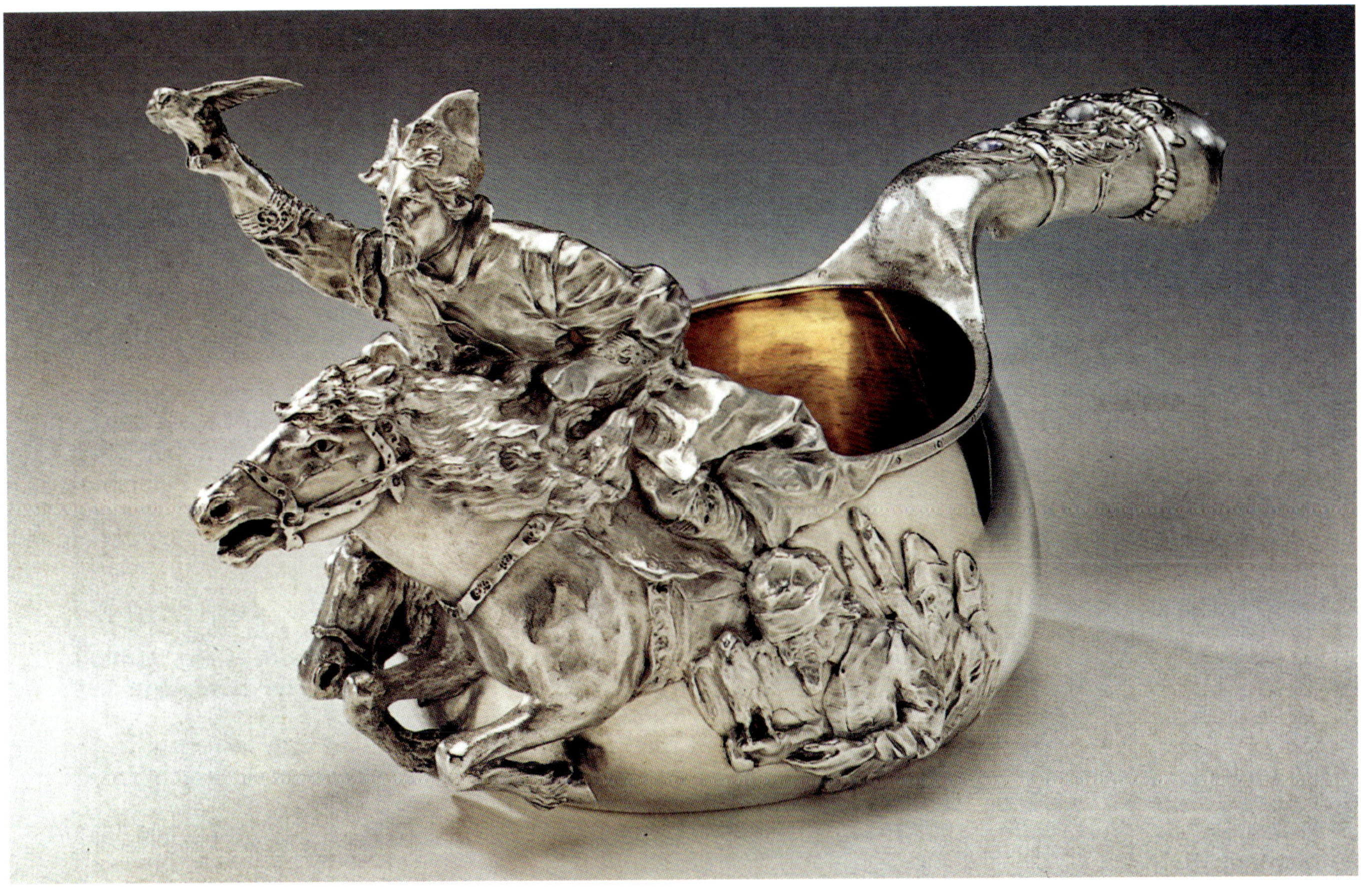

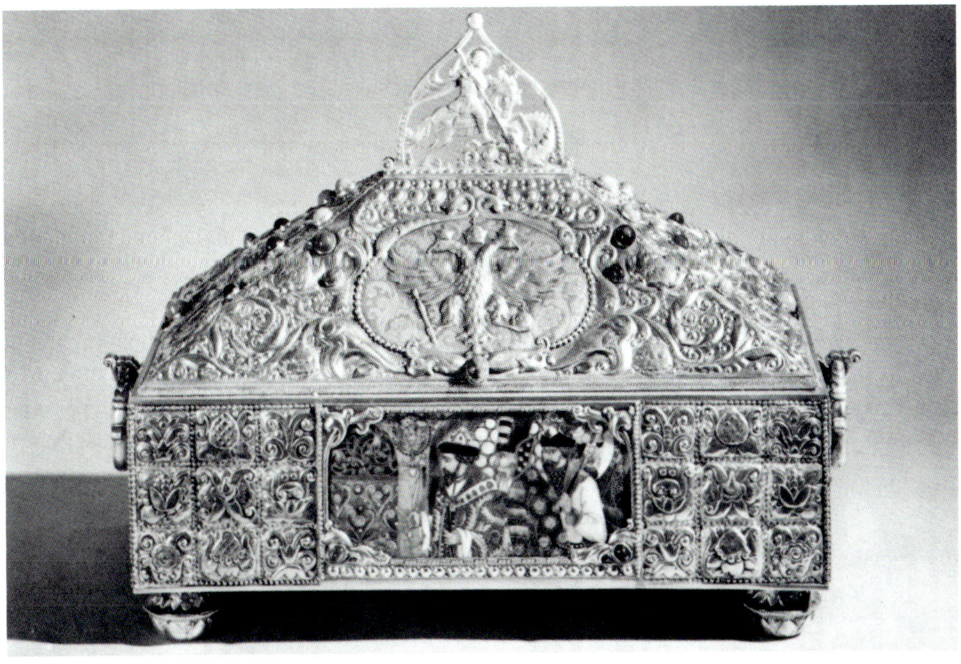

Above:
Silver Style Russe kovsh by Fabergé Moscow, 1908–17. The kovsh, a traditional drinking vessel, was a popular motif in Style Russe presentation pieces. *Courtesy of Sotheby's*

Left:
Style Russe silver box by Khlebnikov. *Courtesy of Sotheby's*

NOTES

1. F. M. Dostoevskii, *Polnoe sobranie sochinenii*, ed. V. G. Bazarov et al., 30 vols. (Leningrad: Nauka, 1972–90), 5:101.

2. The "silver age" poet Andrei Bely captures the imperial capital's artificiality well in his hallucinogenic novel, *Petersburg*, trans. Robert A. Maguire and John E. Malmstad (Bloomington: Indiana University Press, 1978).

3. Nadezhda Iurevna Ivanova, "Iuvelyrnoe iskusstvo Moskvi kontsa XIX—nachala XX veka," candidate's dissertation, Moscow State Academic Art Institute, 2006.

4. Kirichenko, *Russian Design*, 35.

5. In Lindsey Hughes, "Attitudes towards Foreigners in Early Modern Russia," in *Russia and the Wider World in Historical Perspective: Essays for Paul Dukes*, ed. Cathryn Brennan and Murray Frame (Basingstoke, UK: Macmillan, 2000), 11.

6. Cynthia Hyla Whittaker, ed., *Visualizing Russia: Fedor Solntsev and Crafting a National Past* (Leiden: Brill, 2000). See especially the introduction by Wendy Salmond and Cynthia Hyla Whittaker.

7. G. V. Aksenova, "Fedor Solntsev—Sozdatel' 'arkheologicheskoi zhivopisi," www.portal-slovo.ru/history/35459.php; and Fedor Solntsev, *Drevnosti Rossiiskogo Gosudartsva*, 6 vols. (St. Petersburg: Tip. Aleksandra Semenova, 1846–53).

8. Kirichenko, *Russian Design*, 80.

9. Cynthia Coleman Sparke, *Russian Decorative Arts* (Woodbridge, UK: Antique Collectors' Club, 2014), 45–75; and Anne Odom, *Russian Enamels: Kievan Rus to Fabergé* (Baltimore: Walters Art Gallery, 1996), 107–109.

SAZIKOV: THE PIONEERS

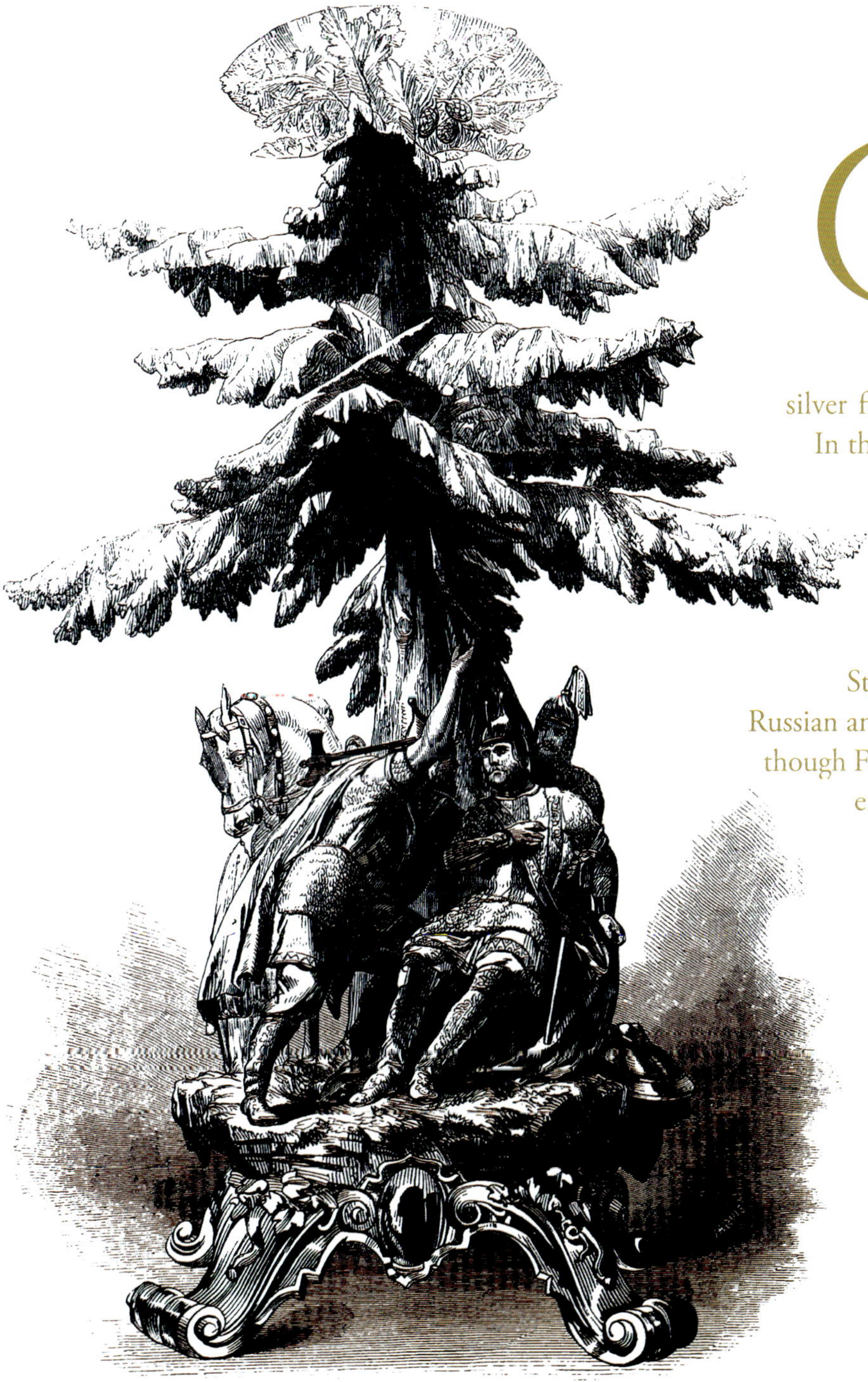

Founded during the reign of Catherine the Great in the center of Moscow, Sazikov was one of the earliest silver firms in Russia and one of its best. In the 1820s Sazikov introduced historicism in Russian silver by producing objects with motifs from the past or imitating ancient styles. Decades before Fabergé, the firm excelled in the Style Russe and won great acclaim in Russian and international exhibitions. And although Fabergé is synonymous with guilloché enameling, it was Sazikov who introduced the *tour à guillochage*, an engine-turning machine made in France, to Russia in the 1840s. Sazikov brought technical perfection of silver to a new level in Russia, also introducing machines for rolling and polishing during the reign of Tsar Nicholas I.[1]

This silver sculpture of a pine tree by Sazikov was shown at the Crystal Palace Exhibition in London in 1851, the world's first international fair. Great Britain, *Catalogue*. III, fig. 194.

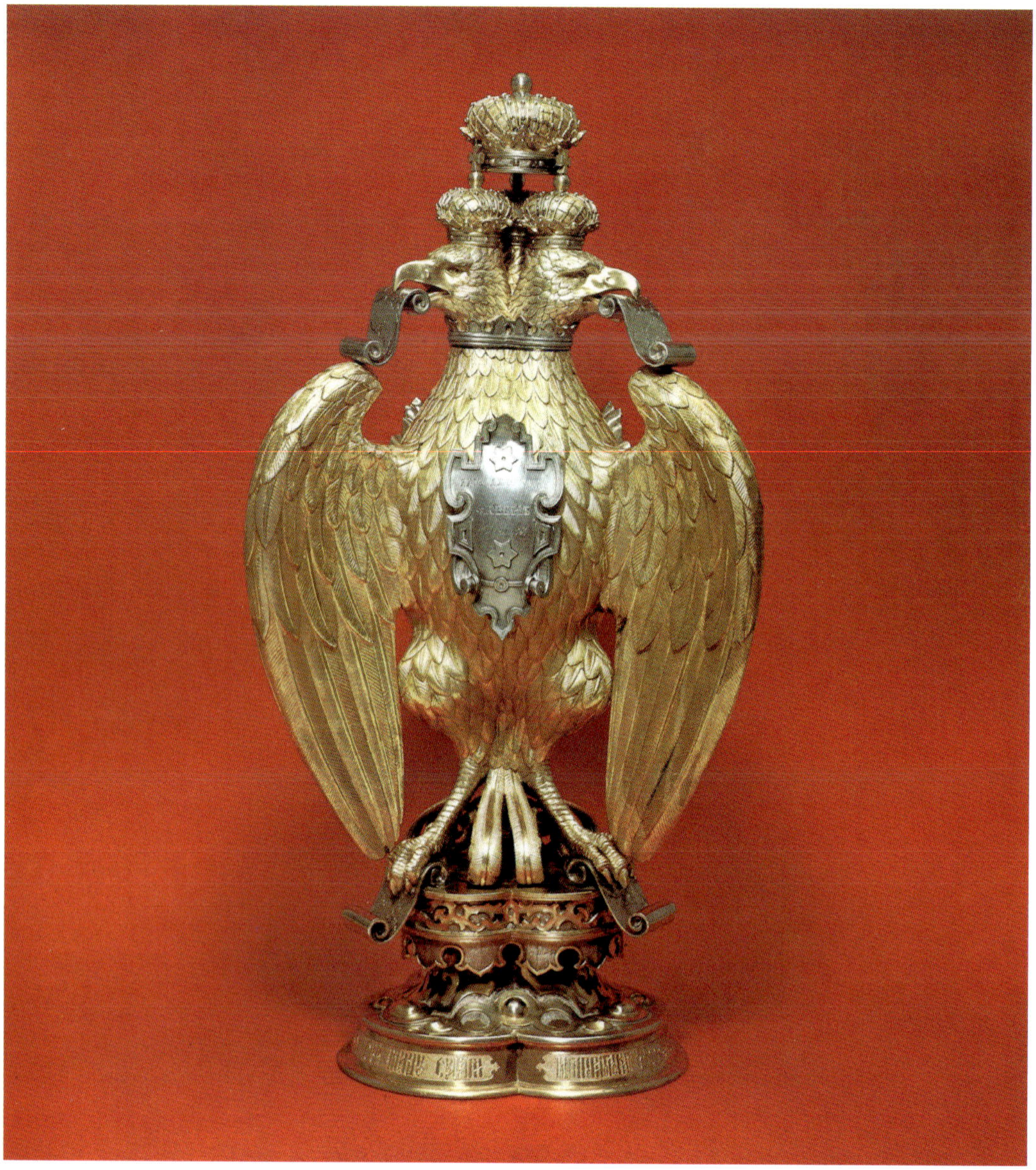

The silver engraver Pavel Fedorovich Sazikov (d. 1830) founded the workshop in Moscow in 1793. Like most of the top craftsmen in the ancient capital, he was of Russian, not European, descent. By 1810, Pavel's modest workshop had already become a factory, which continued to flourish after his death under his son, Ignatii Pavlovich (1793–1868). Sazikov *fils* was a virtuoso silversmith in his own right, and during his tenure the firm excelled both in output and quality. In 1837, Tsar Nicholas I awarded him the imperial warrant. Five years later, Ignatii opened a branch in St. Petersburg, first on the Nevskii Prospect, then at 29 Bolshaia Morskaia Street.[2]

Ignatii Sazikov was an artist, whose designs inspired other leading Moscow silversmiths, such as Gubkin, Ovchinnikov and later Fabergé.[3] An innovator, he invited painters and sculptors to join the firm to experiment with different ideas and techniques. In 1845, he founded a school of goldsmiths and silversmiths, one of the first in Russia. His firm also produced nielloware (blackened designs on precious metal) but was better known for its trompe l'oeil silver. Simulating materials such as wood, fabric, or fur in textured silver, this technique became a hallmark of Russian silver from the 1840s through the 1880s. Sazikov was one of the first to produce truffle dishes imitating peasant napkins, which were exhibited in the 1849 All-Russian Exhibition of Arts and Industry.[4] The Russian historical themes won great acclaim and helped rekindle an interest in Russia's past.

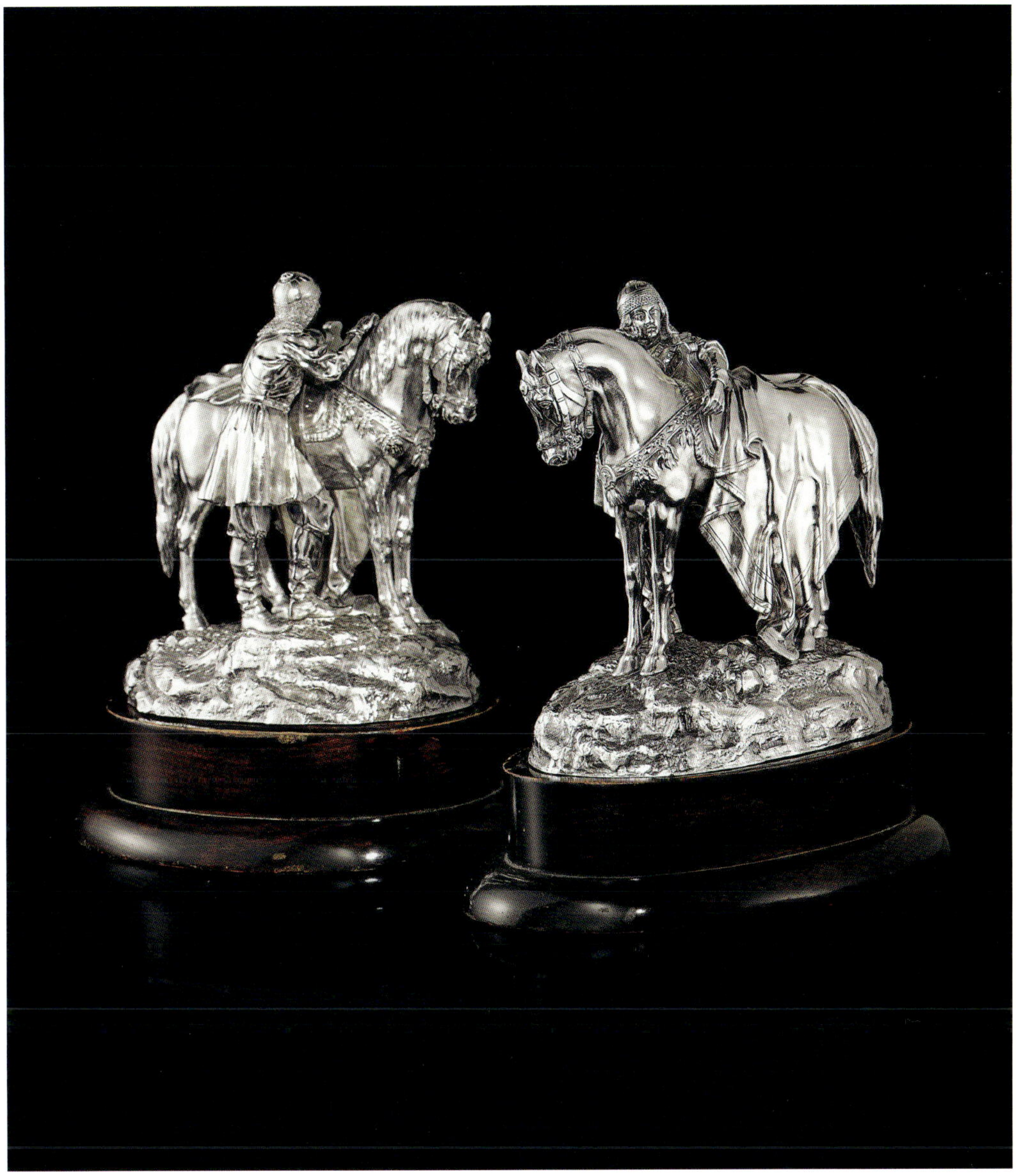

Above:
Two small-scale models of the imperial monumental sculpture group by Sazikov, Moscow, dated 1859. *© 2009 Christie's Images Ltd.*

Previous page:
This monumental yacht-racing trophy by Ignatii Sazikov was awarded to the winner of the Imperial St. Petersburg Yacht Club sea race in June 1851. Its three imperial eagle heads, facing east, west and north below a single Romanov crown, signify the Russian Empire's vast domain under Tsar Nicholas I, while the scrolls are engraved with maps of Russia, America and the South Pacific. *Courtesy of Sotheby's*

In 1852, Tsar Nicholas I commissioned massive Russian sculpture groups for the London Service in the Winter Palace. For this endeavor, he chose the best, Ignatii Sazikov. Eight years earlier, the famous British crown jewelers R. & S. Garrard had produced an extensive imperial service for the emperor. Russian silversmiths added to it, including Samuel Arnd of Nicholls & Plincke, and later Morozov and Fabergé. But Sazikov had the most important role by creating massive centerpieces of unparalleled quality of solid silver weighing 20 kilograms. The monumental group, now in the Moscow Kremlin, recalls ancient Muscovy and was meant to evoke patriotism at the imperial court. "Vitiaz v dozore (Knight on Patrol)" featured a warrior prince and his steed on naturalistic ground. Inspired by design elements in Solnstsev's *Antiquities of the Russian State*, its transformation into sculptural silver in the hands of Sazikov was nothing short of masterful.[5]

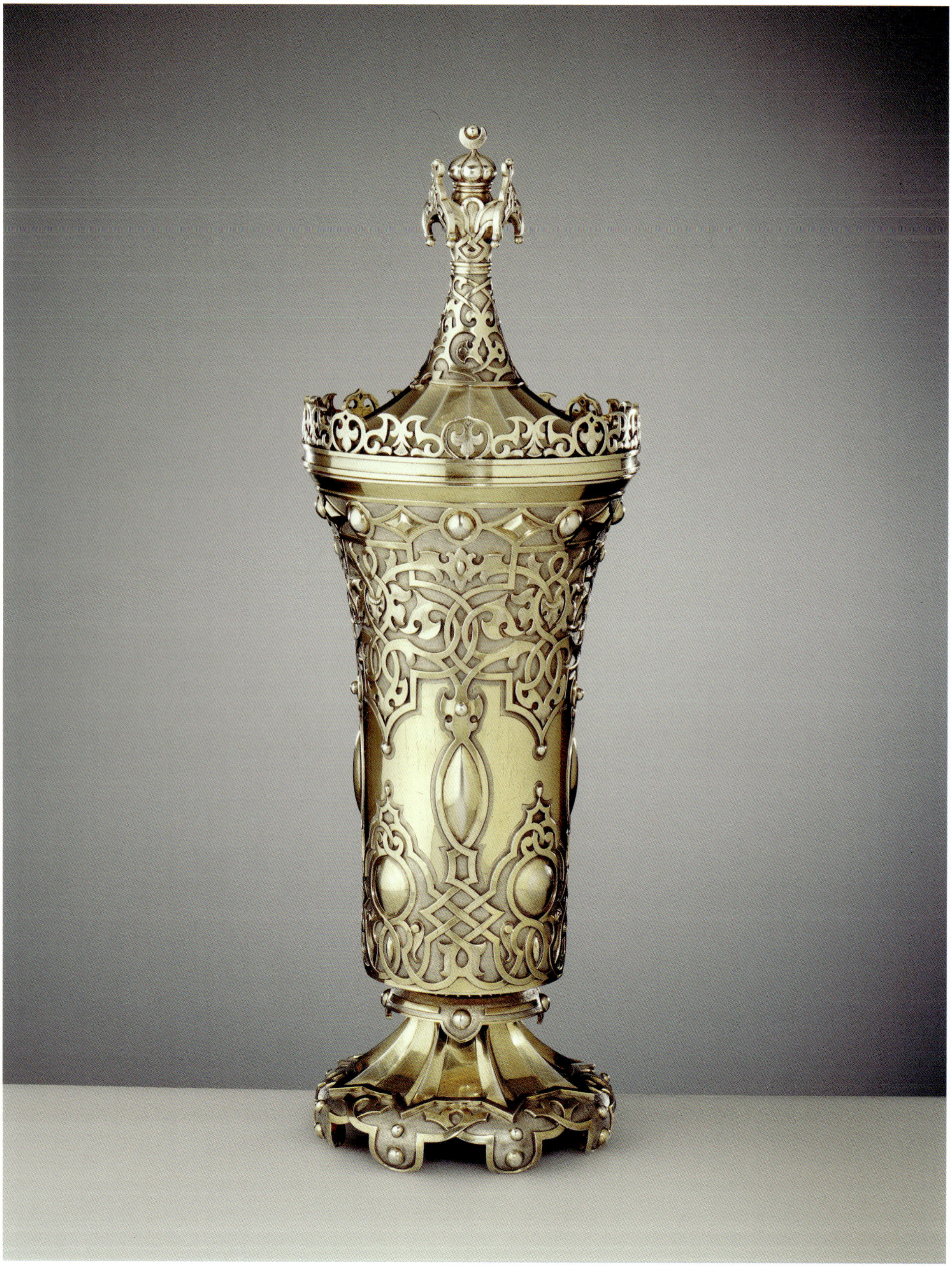

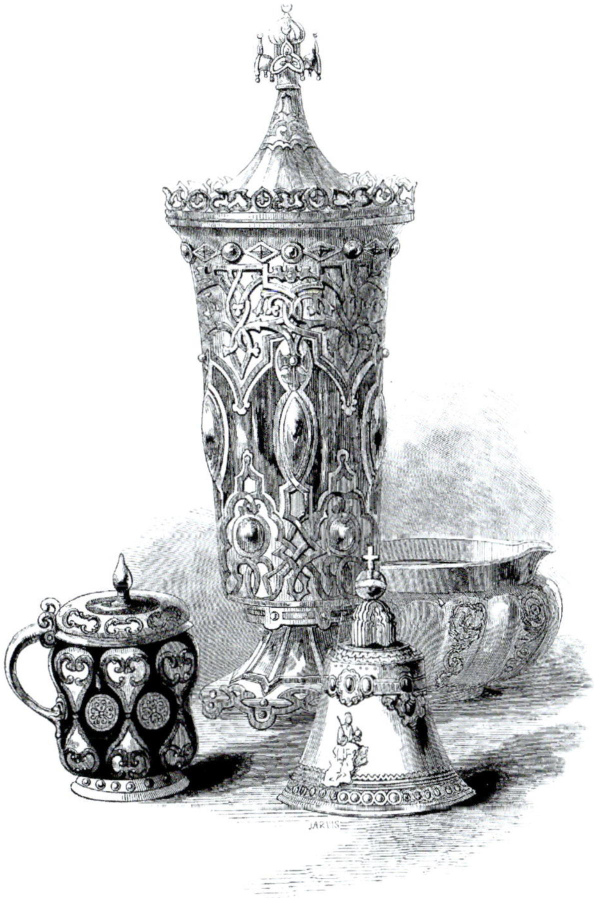

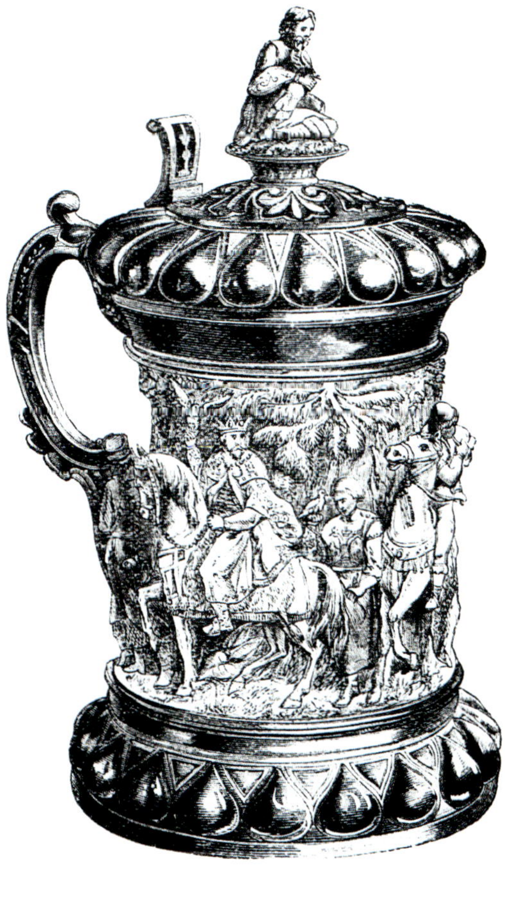

The firm also exhibited in numerous world fairs, including the Crystal Palace Exhibition in 1851 and the 1867 World Exhibition in Paris. In London, Sazikov won the highest award and created a sensation even with royalty. Queen Victoria, who visited the Russian exhibits first, marveled at the monumental malachite vases, impressive furniture and "specimens of plate and some beautifully tasteful."[6]

The jury praised the firm's display of "very elegant statuettes in cast silver" and a large centerpiece of a fir tree, "at the foot of which the grand Duke Dmitrii Donskoi," who, "sitting wounded, is learning from his soldiers that he has gained the victory," a reference to the Russian defeat of the Mongols at the Battle of Kulikovo in 1380. This won the highest prize, a council medal. Sazikov favored Eastern over Western historical motifs, as seen in a pair of massive Byzantine style candelabra, while animal or human figures set off against natural backgrounds adorned goblets, tankards and other vessels, alluding to popular pastoral and genre themes.[7] Silver by Ignatii Sazikov was recognized for its excellent chasing, careful execution and creativity.[8]

In Paris, the firm also won first prize for its composition "Adoration des Bergers," an impressive silver group no doubt made specifically for the exhibition. Its sober ornamentation, sculptural qualities and engraving detail caught the attention and admiration of the Parisian judges. An inkwell was deemed "plain but in perfect taste," high praise indeed from the French.[9] By the time Sazikov, now run by Ignatii's sons Sergei, Pavel and Valentin, exhibited in Vienna, the firm was listed as having 175–200 workers with an annual turnover of 600,000 rubles.[10]

Previous page:
American heiress Marjorie Merriweather Post bought this covered cup by Ignatii Sazikov one hundred years after its creation. It was illustrated in the Official Exhibition Catalogue as one of 39 Sazikov silver objects. *Courtesy of Hillwood Estate Museum & Gardens, photograph by Edward Owen*

Top:
The covered cup by Sazikov was also exhibited at the Crystal Palace Exhibition together with his other gold and silver items. *Great Exhibition, Catalogue. III, fig. 206.*

Left:
Sazikov exhibited this tankard at the Paris Exhibition of 1867. The event enhanced the firm's reputation as a leading Russian silver master equal to its competitors from around the world. Eugène Rimmel, *Recollections of the Paris Exhibition of 1867* (London: Chapman & Hall, 1868), 215.

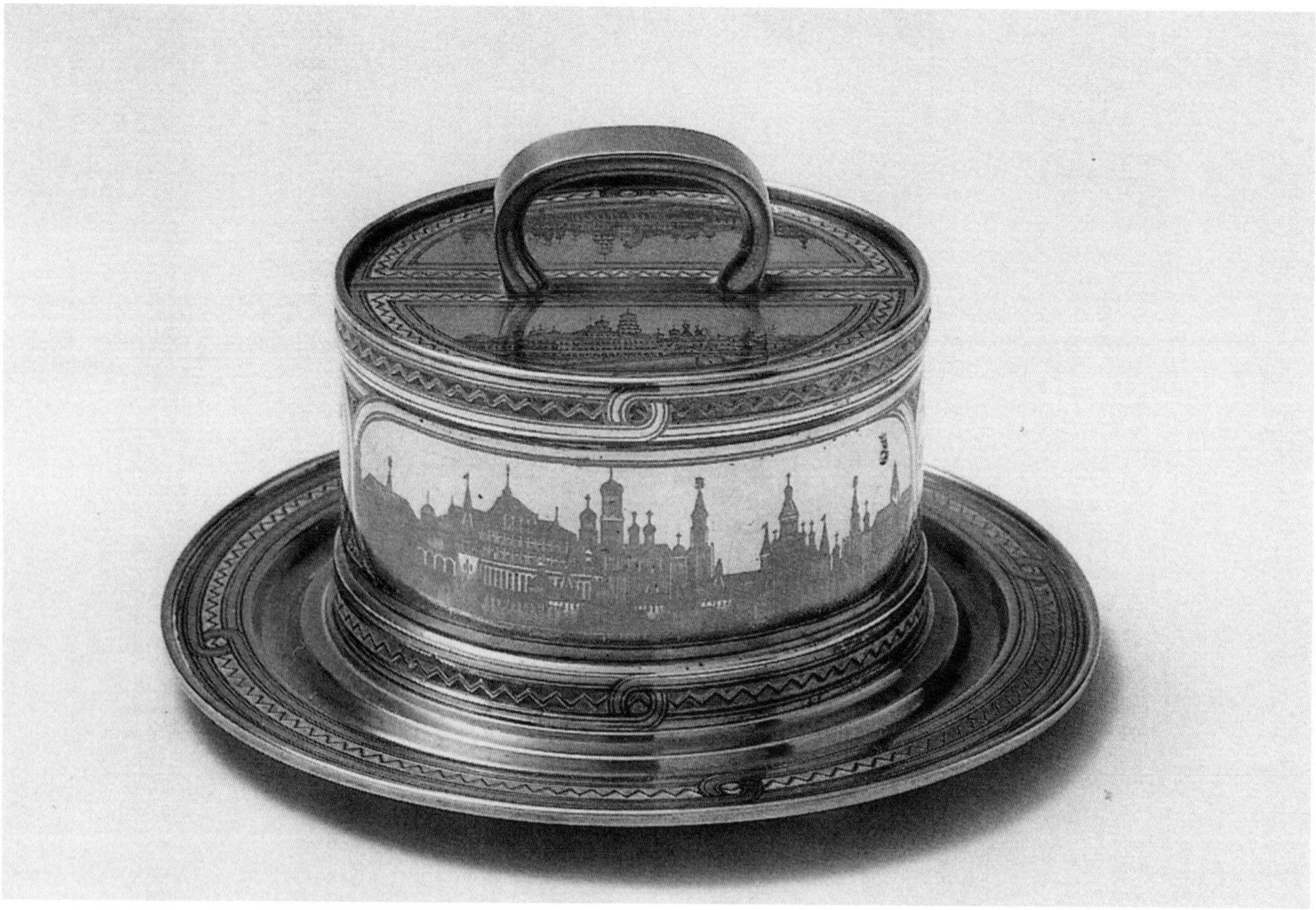

A Russian nielloed caviar pot by Sazikov, 1882. *Courtesy of Sotheby's*

By the 1860s, Sazikov had attracted a large Western clientele with its Style Russe, which, in the second half of the 19th century also proved very popular in Europe through its exposure in international fairs. Unlike the predominantly Western historicism and neoclassicism espoused by Fabergé, the silversmith turned toward ancient Muscovy for inspiration and represented the national style of silver. Since the firm produced works only of the highest quality throughout its tenure, it managed to hold on to its imperial warrant through successive generations until it closed, an unusual feat for any enterprise that catered to the changing whims of the Romanovs.

Carl Fabergé could credit the House of Sazikov not only with the engine-turning machine, but with a steady stream of trained employees. Several artists, sculptors and silversmiths employed by Fabergé were originally trained at Sazikov. The jeweler Johan Gunst (1830–72) first worked for Sazikov, then for Carl's father, Gustav Fabergé. Master silversmith Aleksandr Barshchevkii (d. 1912) had his own workshop on the Fontanka in St. Petersburg and worked for both houses, as did Artemii Aubert (1843–1917), a sculptor from the Imperial Academy of Arts.[11] Trained by Sazikov, Stefan Väkevä (1833–1910) went on to create silver masterpieces for Fabergé.[12]

While some say the firm was sold to Khlebnikov in the 1880s, later dated items stamped "Sazikov" exist. Russian archives indicate that Sazikov produced gifts for the state visit of President Emile Loubet of France to St. Petersburg in 1902.[13] Put in perspective, from the period of Catherine the Great to the twilight of the Romanov era, the House Sazikov led the way in silver production, much like Bolin did for imperial jewels. Pavel was the forefather of all the major silver workshops in Russia and built an enterprise that served each succeeding Russian tsar until its demise, a solid record unmatched by any other imperial silversmith.

NOTES

1. Scott Ruby, "The Crystal Palace Exhibition and Britain's Encounter with Russia," in *A People Passing Rude: British Responses to Russian Culture*, ed. Anthony Cross (Cambridge, UK: Open Book, 2010), 94.

2. Lopato, *Iuveliry starogo Petersburga*, 131–32.

3. Ibid., 132.

4. Ibid., 133–34.

5. In 2009, two reductions (small-scale models) of the famous Sazikov figure group, measuring only 6 inches high, were auctioned for $35,000 and $40,000 in New York. Christie's, April 24, 2009, lots 117 and 118.

6. C. H. Gibbs-Smith, *The Great Exhibition of 1851* (London: H.M.S.O., 1964), 21; and Ruby, "Crystal Palace Exhibition," 92.

7. Great Britain, Commissioners for the Exhibition of 1851, *Official Descriptive and Illustrated Catalogue*, 3 vols, plus supplementary vol. (London: Spicer, 1851), V:1384.

8. Great Britain. *Reports by the Juries*, 515.

9. M. Beagrand, *Rapport sur les Orfèvres et Bijoutiers de L'Exposition de 1867* (Paris, 1868), 75.

10. *Catalogue Spécial de la Section Russe à l'exposition de Vienne en 1873* (St. Petersburg: Imprimerie de l'Académie impériale des sciences, 1873), 102.

11. Fabergé et al., *Fabergé: A Comprehensive Reference Book*, 131, 134, 177.

12. Ibid., 278.

13. Ibid., 459.

Sazikov attracted a large Western clientele with its Style Russe. Unlike the predominantly Western historicism and neoclassicism espoused by Fabergé, the silversmith turned toward ancient Muscovy for inspiration and represented the national style of silver.

FEDOR RÜCKERT: THE ALSATIAN MUSCOVITE

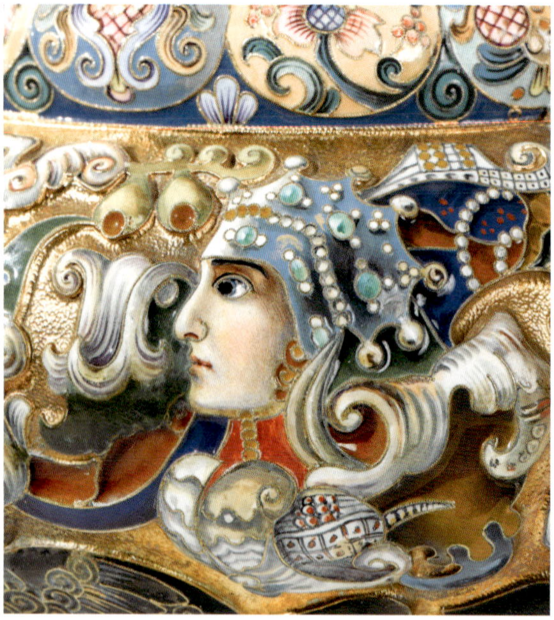

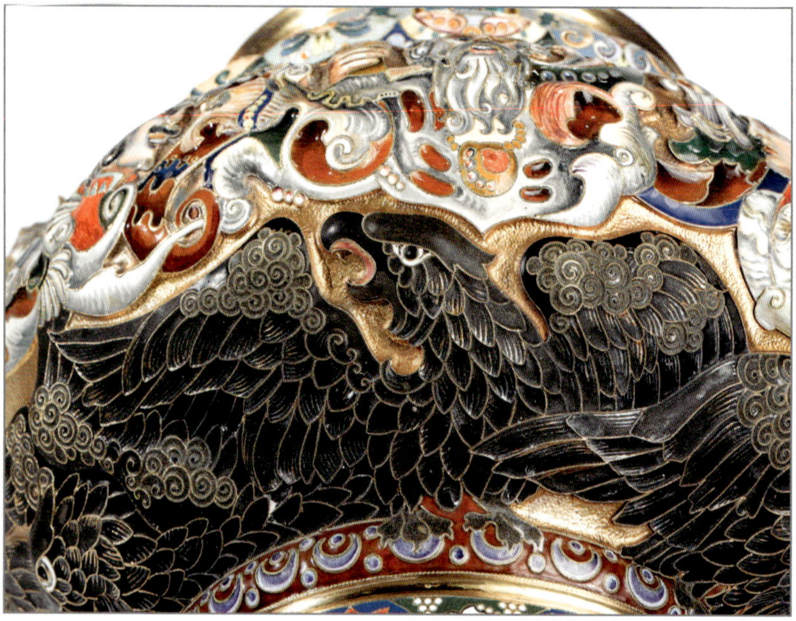

Fedor Rückert (Friedrich Mauritz Rückert), of German descent, was born in Alsace Lorraine in 1840, when it was still part of France. From 1887, when he started collaborating with Fabergé in Moscow, to the Bolshevik Revolution, Rückert brought the art of cloisonné enameling to new heights in the ancient capital of Russia. His style and technique were unique and unrivaled. While many St. Petersburg enamelers were European—either German, Swiss, or Finnish—in Moscow, the field was dominated by Russians. Despite his foreign birth, he perfected the Old Russian style like no other, in some ways surpassing his Muscovite competitors by concentrating on this style alone, and later on Art Nouveau. His bold use of geometric and abstract motifs also foreshadowed Art Deco, which would flourish in Paris in the 1920s. A true artist, he led a workshop of 40 employees, which would include his four sons and a daughter.

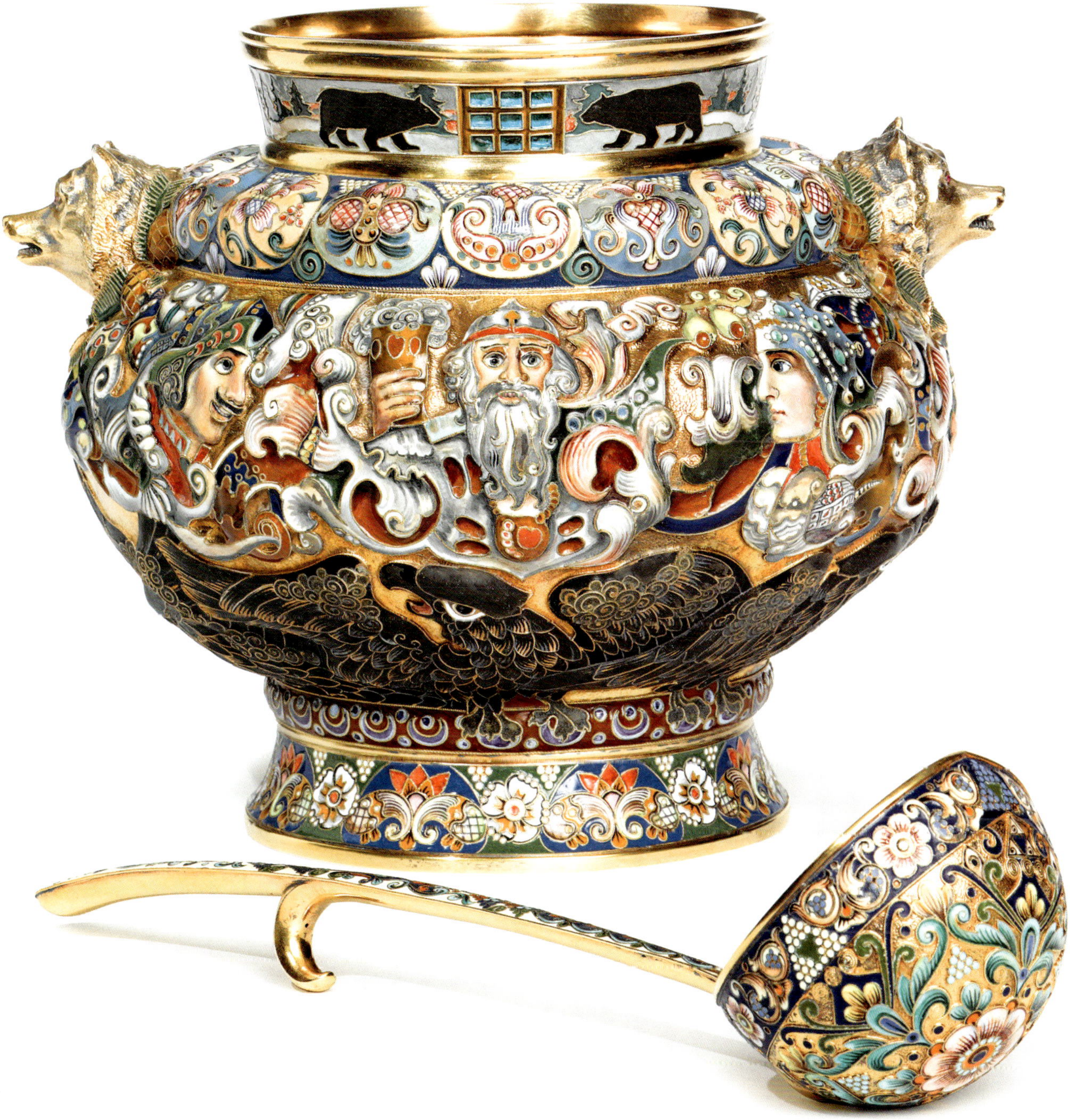

This colorful enameled punch bowl and ladle by Rückert has characteristics of a later personal style (post-1908) in which he experimented with darker colors such as browns, deep grays and black and utilized the cloisons, or silver wires, to further enhance designs. This set him apart from the other Moscow enamelers, although the 11th Artel (a cooperative of skilled enamelers) would come close. *Courtesy of Sotheby's*

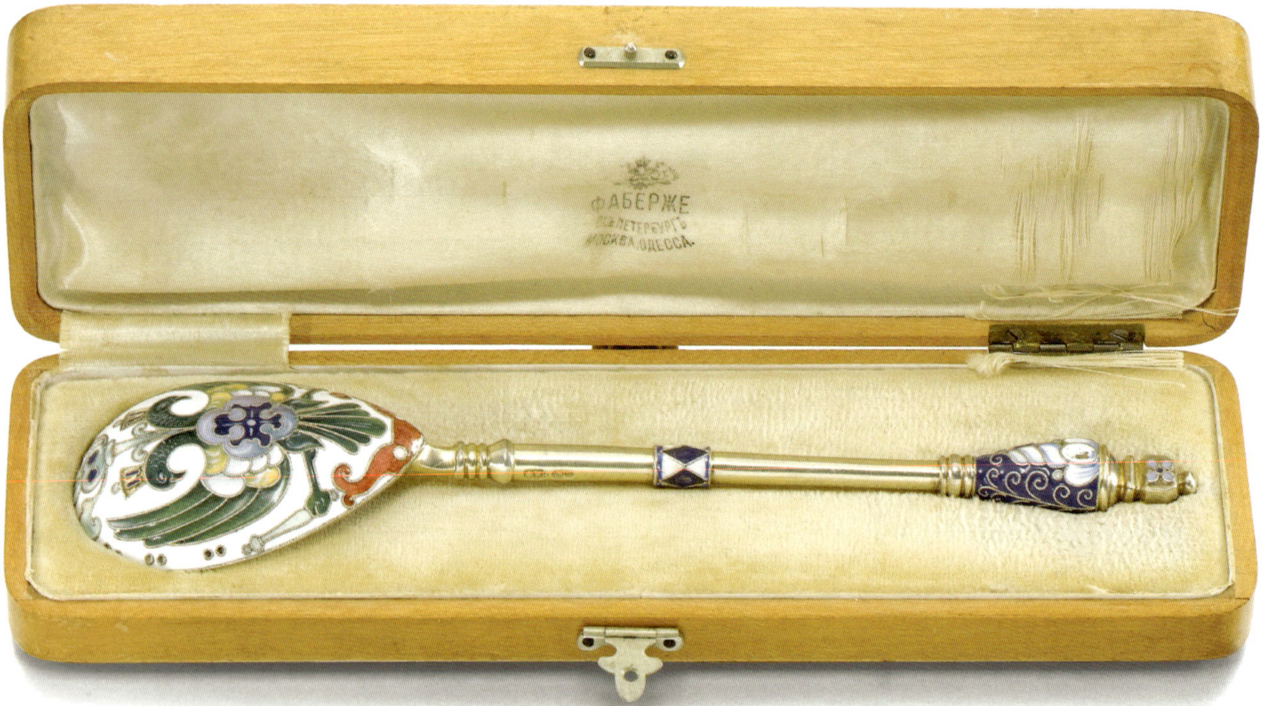

Rückert spoon retailed by Fabergé.
Courtesy of Sotheby's

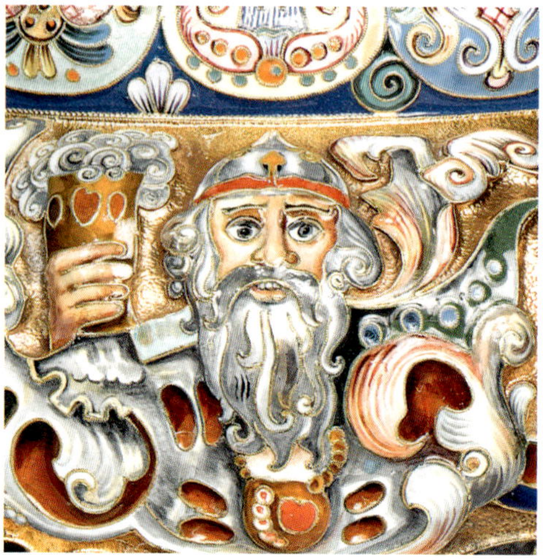

Unlike Ovchinnikov and Khlebnikov, who embraced various forms of enameling, Rückert chose to master only two: cloisonné and en plein (painted enamels in miniature). By combining both, he set a trend that brought the fine and applied arts together. He introduced enamel figures either within the cloisonné or as en plein vignettes inspired by famous Russian paintings by Victor Vasnetsov and Constantine Makovsky. To delight the eye, he created patterns of enamel motifs with distinctive wiring and colors to match perfectly the painted scenes. He later delved into the art nouveau, sometimes combining it with Style Russe and adding his own personal twist: darker, novel colors such as violet and moss green, matte finishes and filigree flourishes such as coils and petals to enhance design. His training at Moscow's Stroganov Institute of Industrial Arts played a major role in forming his taste for ancient Russian designs, religious manuscripts and folk motifs.

His eldest sons and one daughter, all born in Moscow, apprenticed at their father's shop. Yet, this Russian birth did not prevent the children from being expelled from their native land when the war broke out. To the Russians, they were considered Germans and unwelcome in 1914 (Alsace was then under German control as a result of the Franco-Prussian War of 1871). Fedor, at age 74, was allowed to stay in Moscow. Despite these personal difficulties, the Silver Age proved a prolific time for Rückert: many of his finest works were produced between 1900 and 1914.

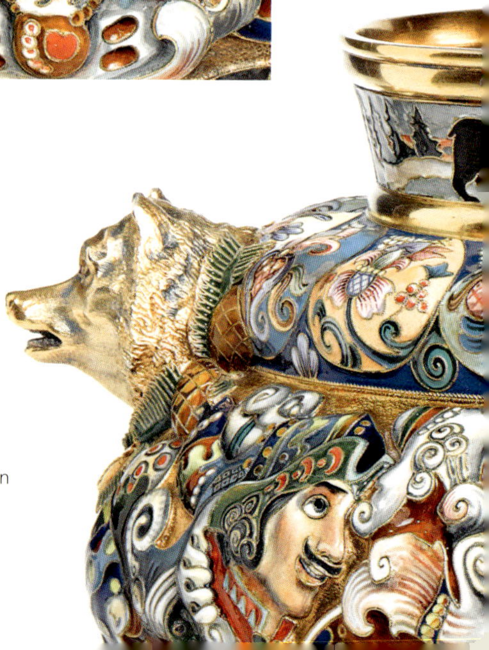

Details of punch bowl on previous page

18

PAVEL OVCHINNIKOV: FROM SERF TO SILVERSMITH

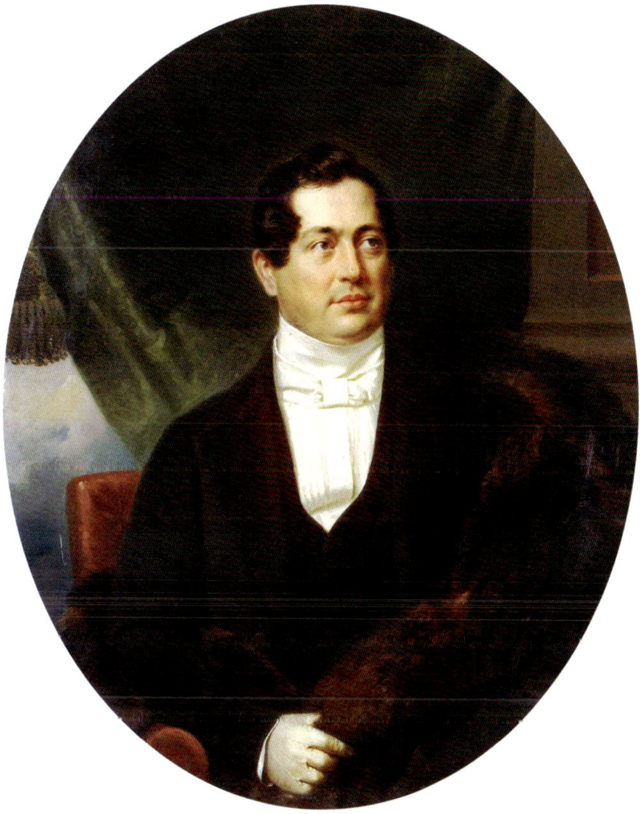

Portrait of Prince Dimitrii Volkonskii by Franz Krüger (1805-59). *Source: Wikimedia Commons*

The story of Pavel Ovchinnikov is incredible. Born into serfdom in the Moscow provinces in 1830, Pavel Akimovich's master was none other than Prince Dimitrii Volkonskii (1805–59), the Russian army's commander and a nobleman of ancient Kievan lineage. Perhaps sensing his servant's innate talents, the Prince sent Pavel, age 12, to Moscow, as draftsman for his elder brother Andrei, a goldsmith. As with Marshak (see "Iosif Marshak: The Cartier of Kiev"), the young apprentice had nothing but promise and his wife's dowry. With that, and issue of four sons, Pavel built a silver dynasty that by 1881 was the largest in the Russian Empire.[1]

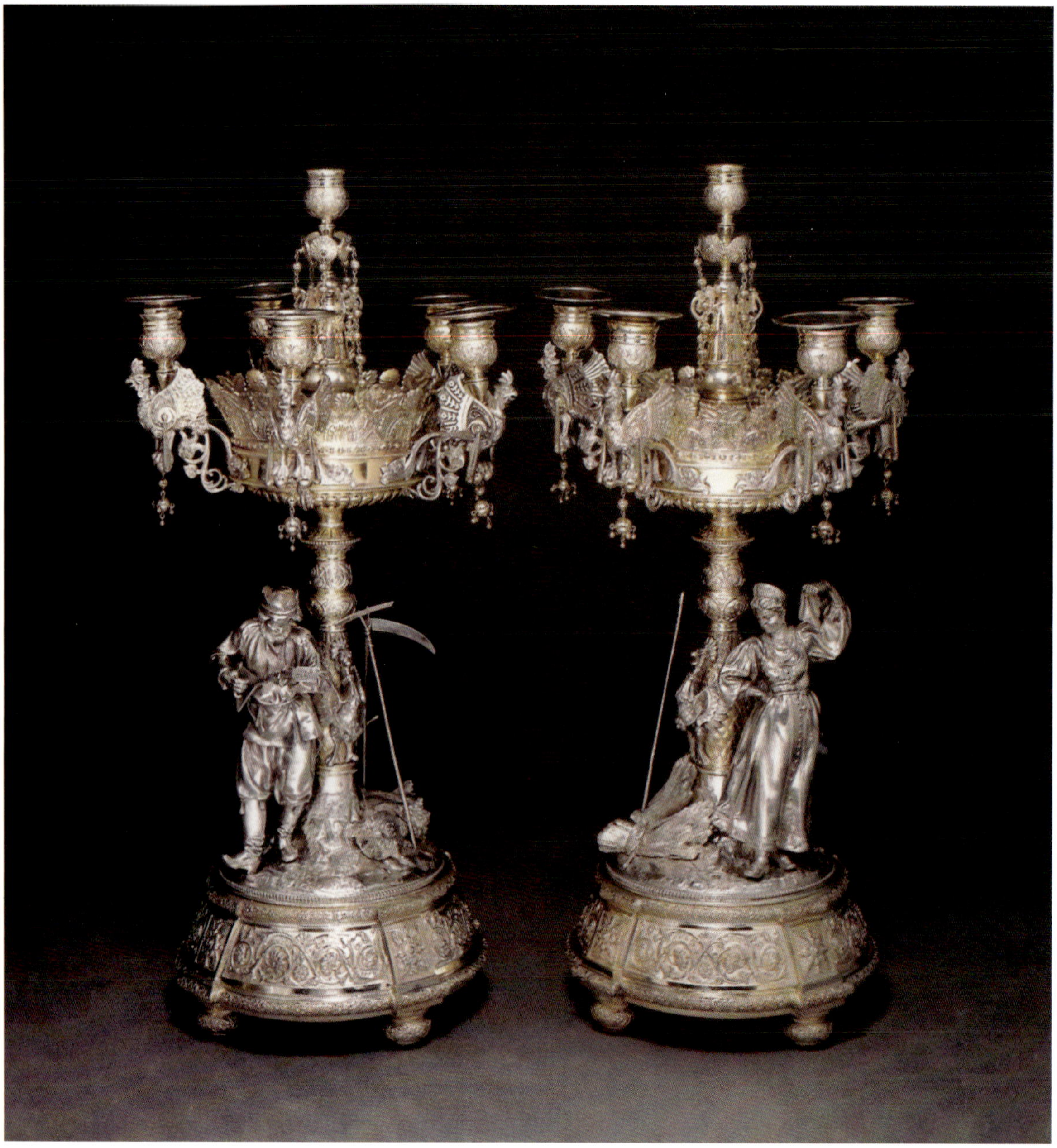

Above:
This pair of silver six-light candelabra is adorned with free standing peasant figures and stylized cockerels, which was all the rage in Moscow from the 1850s to the 1880s. *Courtesy Sotheby's*

Following page:
In 1910, Ovchinnikov was commissioned to create a silver memorial wreath for the funeral of King Chulalonkhorn of Siam. This is the top of the invoice for the order by the imperial cabinet. *Courtesy of RGIA*

Pavel opened a workshop in 1853, during the reign of Tsar Nicholas I. In short order, he bought out his brother's firm, employed 90 workers into specialized workshops and produced an annual turnover of 250,000 rubles. Only one year later, in 1854, this figure had quadrupled to over a million rubles.[2]

In 1865 he won a gold prize at the Pan Russian Exhibition in Moscow and became purveyor to the imperial court. The honor was again granted to his sons both in 1881 and 1896, a testament to the popularity and the high quality of Ovchinnikov silver and enamel. Crowned heads of Europe bought from the Muscovite firm and bestowed on it their own royal warrant, including that of King Victor Emanuel of Italy, King Christian IX of Denmark and King George I of the Hellenes. Grand Duke Michael Nikolaevich was an avid collector of Ovchinnikov.

Outside of royalty, one might conclude Ovchinnikov silver appealed only to Russians, given its robust nationalistic forms, patriotic wares and colorful and very Slavic style. However, to the outside world, this was both exotic and enticing. Large silver vessels (or bratinas), kovshs and massive bread-and-salt platters enlivened with brightly colored enamels in *champlevé*, cloisonné, en plein and more no doubt evoked romantic visions of Russia's past to many foreigners who knew little about the empire.

Sensing this, Pavel marketed his brand by exhibiting in almost all the world fairs, including Paris (1867 and 1900), Vienna (1873) and Chicago (1893). Emblazoned along the top of his letterhead are the many prizes he won at home and abroad—proof of his excellence and creativity. Pavel received the coveted Legion d'honneur from France, and in Vienna, the Order of the Iron Cross. Much is said about Tsar Alexander III's buying from Fabergé at a show in 1885, but the emperor also bought directly from Ovchinnikov, and no doubt other Russian artists in Moscow. Thereafter, the firm received many commissions from the Romanovs for imperial presentation gifts to be bestowed not only on Russian but foreign dignitaries. The court also called upon the firm to design less expensive gifts for its staff on holidays, thereby confirming the fair prices of its ever-popular wares.

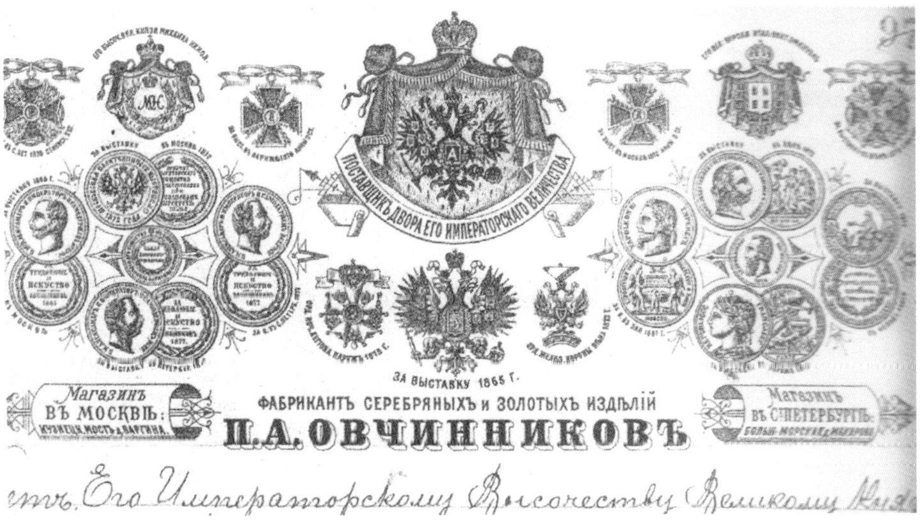

Some designs were international, with a preference for the Far East. Chinoiserie and Japonisme prevailed, as well as colorful enamels recalling the palette of ancient Byzantine wares. Far from insular in its focus, the firm hired various outside designers and artists, including the sculptor Evgenii Lanceray and the Italian Mangetti. In 1871, Pavel founded a school within the factory to train 130 apprentices in the art of enameling and goldsmithing, among other skills. The year of Pavel's death, in 1881, perhaps as a dying wish, Ovchinnikov published a guide for his students and employees. Few such published sources exist; this one may have inspired Carl Fabergé to reorganize his father's shop in St. Petersburg a year later, as well as in 1900. Indeed, already by 1873, Ovchinnikov had opened a branch in St. Petersburg, only steps away from the House of Fabergé.

The quantity of Ovchinnikov silver must have been astounding, since still today it far outnumbers that by any other Moscow silversmith on the market in the West. The one unifying aspect of these items is scale. Unlike the European sensibility and appreciation of miniature and delicate enamels associated with Fabergé in St. Petersburg, Ovchinnikov enamels tend to be large, robust and some even colossal (see "Ovchinnikov Market").

Along with Khlebnikov, the firm led in the production of enamelware in Russia, reintroducing and popularizing not only the nationalistic style from the 16th century, but also a type of painstaking enamel process from the Byzantine era called *plique-à-jour*. In this technique, enamels lacking a silver backing are separated in individual compartments or cloisons, which when held to the light resemble stained-glass windows. Grachev in St. Petersburg also excelled at this, but to a lesser degree and at a later date. Together with his compatriot, Sazikov in St. Petersburg, Ovchinnikov competed with the finest European houses and helped make enamels fashionable on the Continent. According to some, the firm's distinct Russian style helped throw off "the yoke of western European dominance."[3]

NOTES

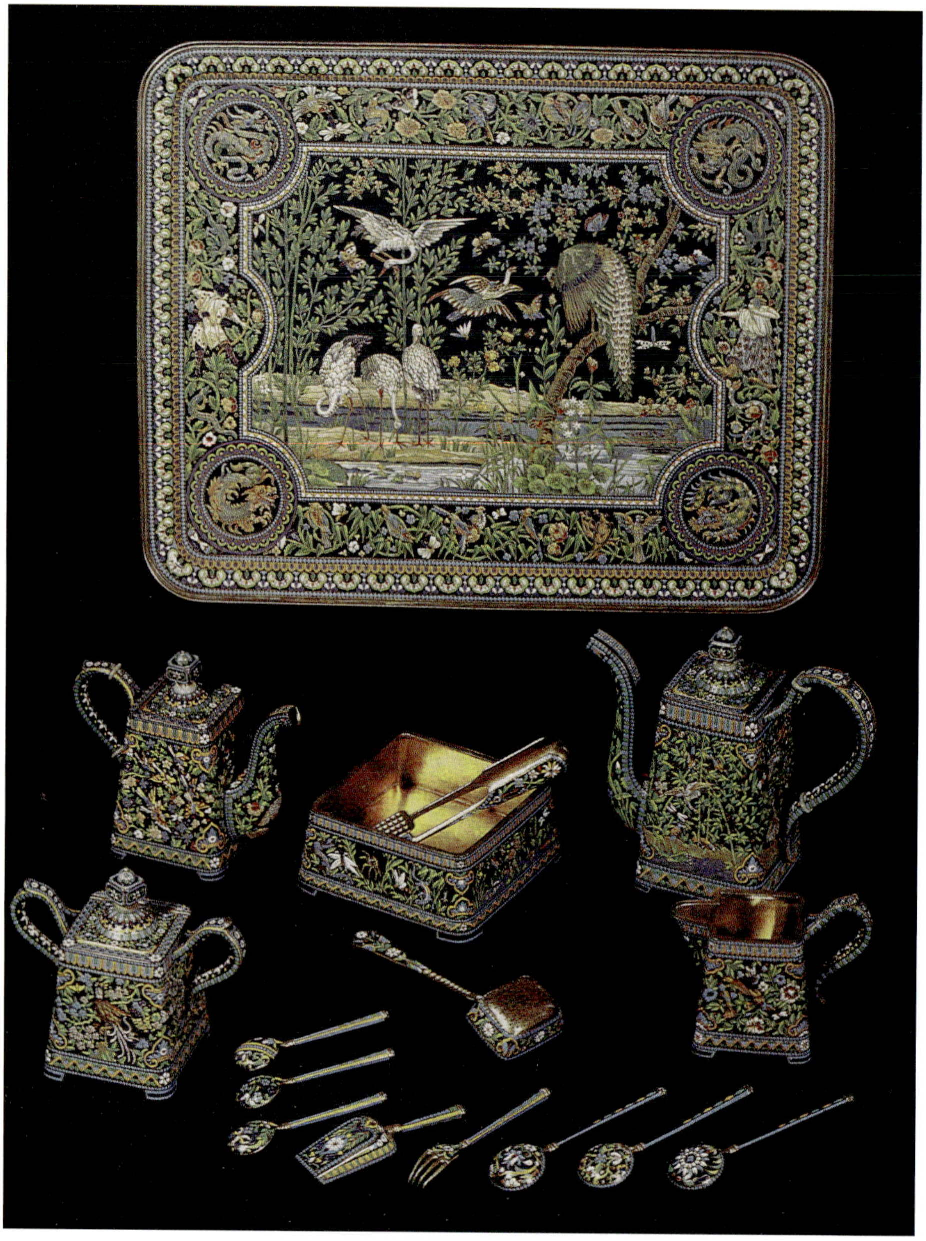

1. Literature still refers to Pavel Ovchinnikov as "contemporary" of Carl Fabergé, even though the former died in 1881. Fabergé had not yet opened a workshop in Moscow and had yet to attract the attention of the tsar.

2. Skurlov, "Spisok vedushchikh Peterburgs firm i masterov."

3. Sotheby's, London, November 25, 2014, lot 447.

Above:
Ovchinnikov also perfected the chinoiserie style, as seen in this tea and coffee service, which was entirely covered in champlevé enamel.
Courtesy of Sotheby's

Following page:
Iconostasis by Khlebnikov in the Kremlin's Cathedral of the Annunciation. *Source: Wikimedia Commons*

IVAN KHLEBNIKOV: ENAMELER TO THE TSARS

If Pavel Ovchinnikov had a soulmate in the trade, it was Ivan Khlebnikov. The two silver patriarchs certainly knew each other, since they exhibited in fairs together, had flagship stores on the same street in Moscow, and shared illustrious clients. Almost exact contemporaries—only 11 years separated them, and both died in the 1880s—the two masters' works are barely distinguishable, so high is the quality of the enameling of each. Ovchinnikov had a larger factory, employed more workers, and produced more silver. However, items associated with Khlebnikov are, like those of his compatriot, always of the finest workmanship. Khlebnikov may have produced more champlevé enamel than Ovchinnikov, at least judging from what's on the market today.

Of the two, Khlebnikov received a higher number of imperial commissions for religious wares, which played an essential role in Russia's cultural heritage. In 1910, for example, of all the empire's production of silver and jewels, 25 percent of it was for the clergy. Khlebnikov was a true master of this. The court and church kept it busy by ordering enormous quantities of icons, liturgical silver, church plate (including utensils) and the most spectacular, iconostases, or icon walls, which separate the nave from the sanctuary in a Russian Orthodox church. In 1896 the enterprise created a magnificent iconostasis in the Annunciation Cathedral and was entrusted with decorating the interiors of the Kremlin cathedrals. In 1912, the firm created another iconostasis along with a chandelier for the church of St. Fedorov in Tsarskoe Selo, the tsar's summer palace near St. Petersburg. Finally, for the 300th anniversary of the Romanov dynasty in 1913, Khlebnikov astounded the world with its exquisite works in the Assumption Cathedral—chased silver icons, metal coverings of tombstones of metropolitans and patriarchs, and yet another iconostasis in the cathedral's side chapel of St. Dmitrii Solunskii (Demetrios of Thessaloniki).[1]

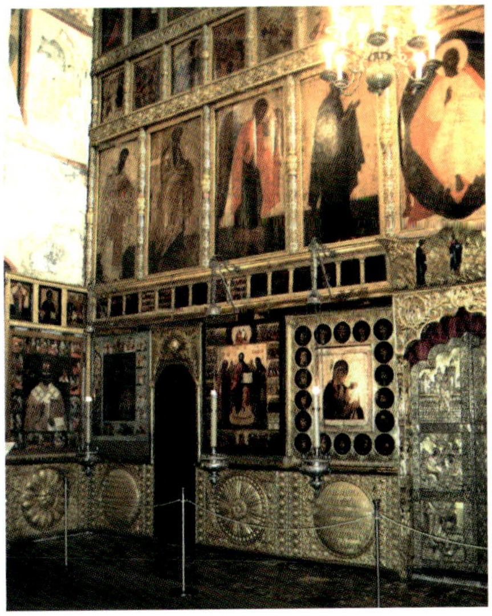

Little is known of Ivan Khlebnikov's early life. During the reign of Alexander II, he worked as a silversmith in St. Petersburg until 1867, and, like his father, Petr (dates unknown), became a merchant of the first class (see "The Tsar's Jewelers"). Sources mention 1840 as a start date for jewelry production for Khlebnikov but omit a location. In 1877, the workshop moved to the Records Bank building on the Nevskii Prospect, a prime location near the Winter Palace, and the palace of his new patron, the vastly wealthy Grand Duke Vladimir Aleksandrovich. The company traded in pearls, watches, jewels and fine silver.

Khlebnikov silver from St. Petersburg is rare. The maker is more closely associated with the ancient capital of Moscow, where, in 1869, Ivan established a jewelry firm. His very family name and that of another Moscow silversmith bespoke ancient

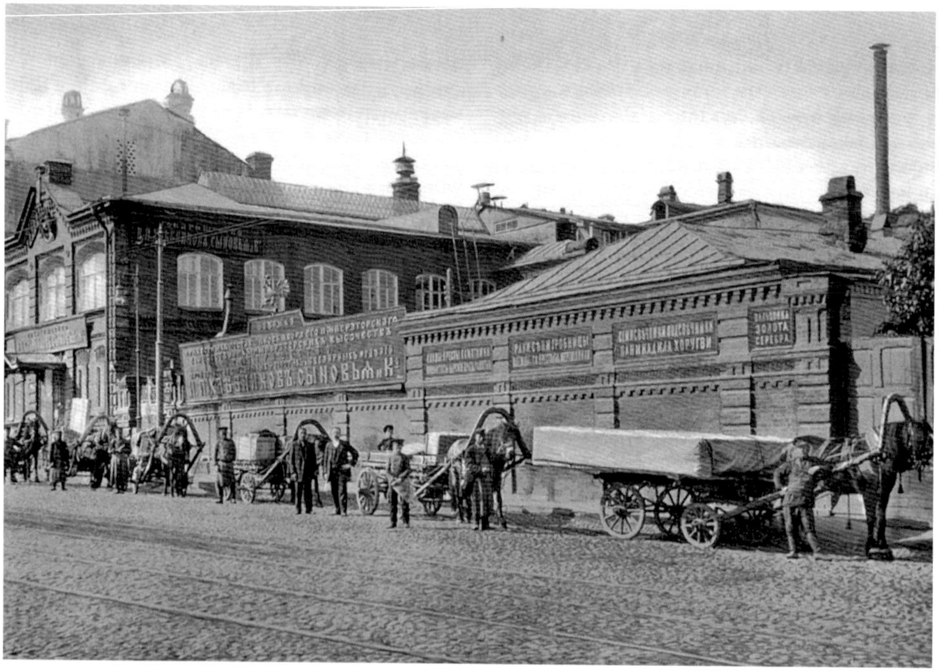

A view of the Khlebnikov factory in Moscow.
Courtesy of Central State Archive of Film and Photographs of St. Petersburg

Russia: Khlebnikov is derived from the Russian word for bread vendor, *khlebnik*. That, together with the silversmith Saltykov, whose name suggests salt, epitomized an old Muscovite tradition. Boyars would greet guests at the threshold with bread and salt. The prominent nobleman, wearing his *shapka gorlatnaia* (a tall cylindrical fur hat) and lavishly embroidered kaftan (robe), would proffer a loaf of bread on an embroidered cloth draped over a large platter to the visitor. Many of the Moscow silversmiths recalled this tradition by creating silver trompe l'oeil loaves of bread, basket-woven trays draped with enameled patterns simulating embroidery and salt chairs with hinged lids. In Moscow, Ivan Khlebnikov avoided the European aestheticism so closely linked to Fabergé—he had no market for it. His clients bought Style Russe in droves, however.

Khlebnikov pioneered the so-called Cockerel style. Admired today as uniquely Russian, at the time of its greatest popularity in the 1870s, St. Petersburg critics dismissed it as primitive and lacking refinement. Based on folk motifs, chickens and the ever-popular roosters appeared everywhere, often in brilliant colors rendered not only in enamel but porcelain and glass.[2] That many items in that signature style survive today in the West is a testament to its wide popularity and commercial success. It also appealed to the Russian aristocracy and the imperial family. By the 1870s Khlebnikov could count Empress Maria Fedorovna and Austria's emperor Franz Joseph as patrons, although the title of purveyor to the imperial court of Tsar Alexander II would come only late in the decade. The firm also supplied the courts of the Danish, Dutch and Serbian kings. A perfect example in silver by Khlebnikov is a lavish tea service in the Royal Danish Collection, which Grand Duchess Anastasia Mikhailovna gave to her daughter Alexandrine in 1897. Claw feet, stylized wings and ruby-set rooster's-head spouts, together with engraved design recalling the fretwork of wooden peasant houses, characterize this truly Russian form.[3] Other silversmiths such as Alexander Sokolov from St. Petersburg perfected this style, but Khlebnikov led the way.

In 1879, after being denied once, the firm received the imperial warrant of Tsar Alexander III. Applying for the right to use the Romanov court of arms was an arduous procedure, but well worth the effort. Once granted, fortunes of the enterprise

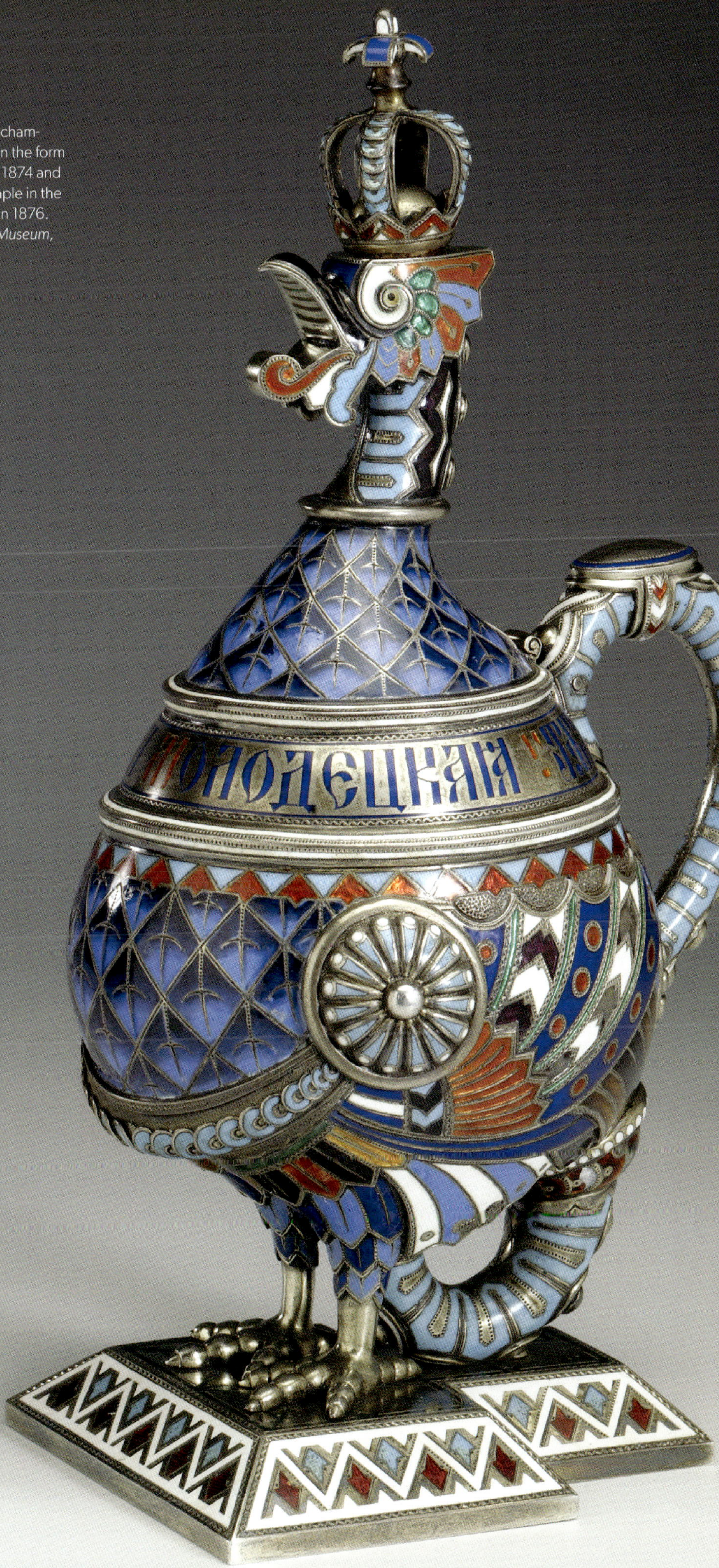

Khlebnikov created this champlevé-enameled carafe in the form of a griffin in Moscow in 1874 and displayed a similar example in the Philadelphia Exhibition in 1876. *Courtesy of Walters Art Museum, Baltimore*

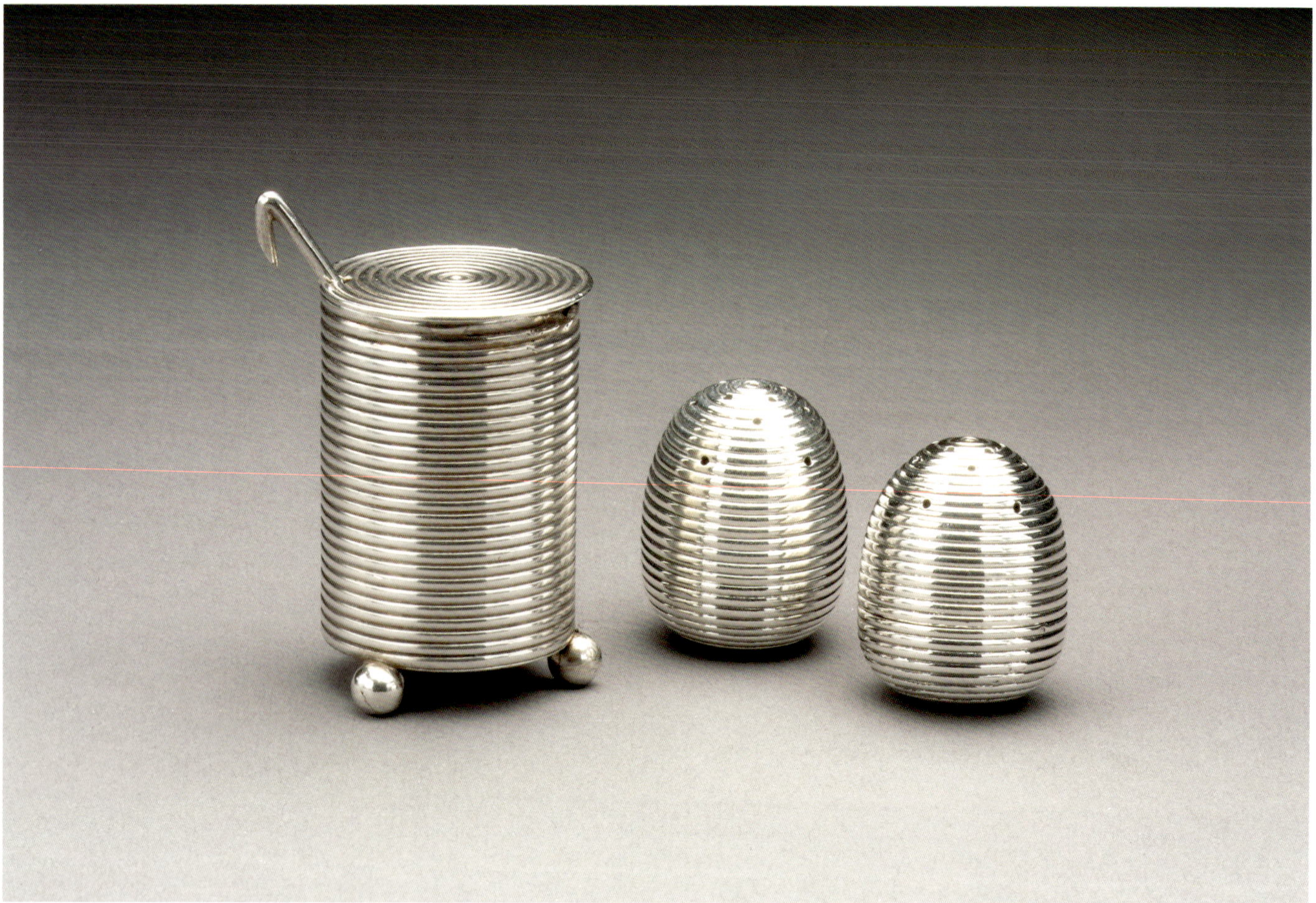

could skyrocket. Displaying the Romanov emblem on its storefront, letterhead and advertisements; at international exhibitions; and on the inside of each and every fitted case was coveted as a true measure of success. For Khlebnikov, the rise to fame was steady and encouraging. In 1882, the annual turnover reached 300,000 rubles, and by 1910 it had more than doubled to 700,000 rubles, just after Morozov and Fabergé. Like Ovchinnikov, Khlebnikov had four sons who carried on the business. Renamed Khlebnikov, I. P. and Sons, the firm won numerous awards in Russian and international fairs, including Philadelphia (1876), Paris (1879), Moscow (1882), Nice (1884) and Copenhagen (1888). Having achieved world renown by 1900, and no doubt kept busy with imperial commissions, the company focused on sales within the empire. Along with Olovianisnikov, it specialized in the historical style, which it produced in quantities of table ware and decoration, in silver, brass and enamel and its production of imperial church plate, especially oklady, for the Romanovs.

One of Khlebnikov's sons-in-law, Orest Kurliukov, went on to open his own workshop producing superb shaded enamel

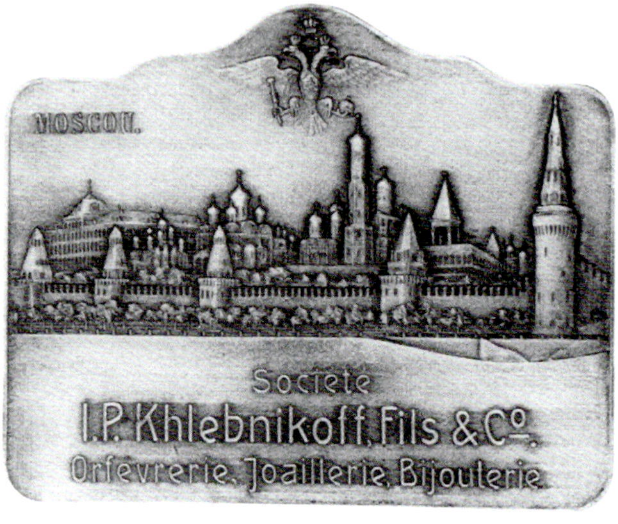

The Moscow silver master made this modernist salt shaker and mustard pot set in 1888, perhaps for the Copenhagen exhibition. The top of each shaker is pierced and screws on to the base, which is weighted with solid silver, enabling the shakers to remain upright to minimize spills. The bronze plaque may have served as a sign for the Khlebnikov store in Moscow. These were often in French to attract international clientele. *Marie Betteley, photo by Noel Allum, courtesy of Sotheby's*

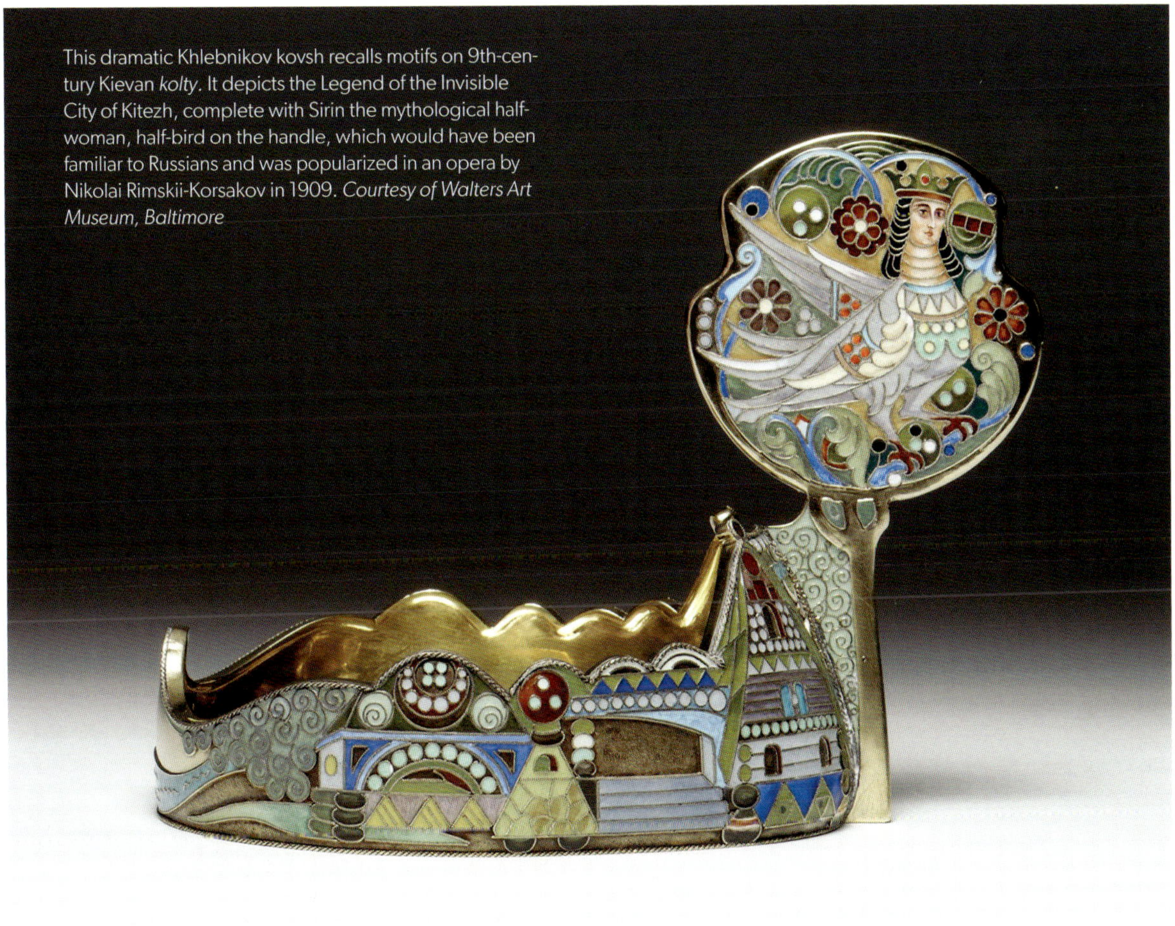

This dramatic Khlebnikov kovsh recalls motifs on 9th-century Kievan *kolty*. It depicts the Legend of the Invisible City of Kitezh, complete with Sirin the mythological half-woman, half-bird on the handle, which would have been familiar to Russians and was popularized in an opera by Nikolai Rimskii-Korsakov in 1909. *Courtesy of Walters Art Museum, Baltimore*

table services. Another, V. A. Mikhailov, was president of the board, reinforcing the close family ties of the founder's employees. Some say the firm bought out Sazikov in both St. Petersburg and Moscow in 1886, although later-dated items have appeared with the Sazikov stamp. If this is true, Khlebnikov may have continued using the latter's hallmark, a practice not unheard of with jewelers. Others claim it was Ovchinnikov who occupied the old Sazikov premises at 29 Bolshaia Morskaia Street in St. Petersburg between 1900 and 1910.[4] There is no evidence that the two collaborated, so the fate and exact closing date of Sazikov and its association with the famous firm of Ivan Khlebnikov bear further research.

NOTES

1. "Torgovyi dom I. P. Khlebvnikova sinov'ia i Ko," https://toptigki.livejournal.com/54189.html.

2. Odom, *Russian Enamels, Kievan Rus to Fabergé*, 110.

3. *Fabergé: The Tsar's Court Jeweler and His Association with the Danish Royal Family*, exhibition held May 12–September 25, 2016, Exhibition catalogue 96, no. 59.

4. Skurlov, "Spisok vedushchikh Peterburgs firm i masterov."

IVAN GUBKIN: MASTER OF THE TROMPE L'OEIL

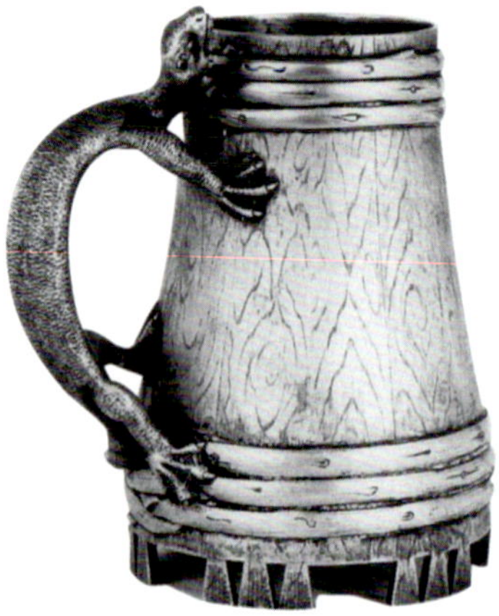

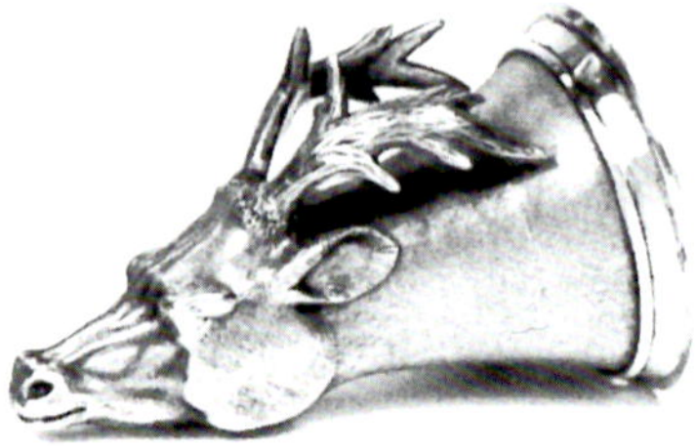

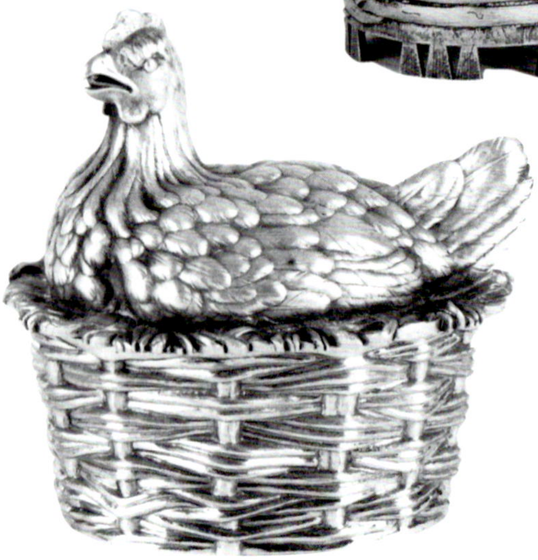

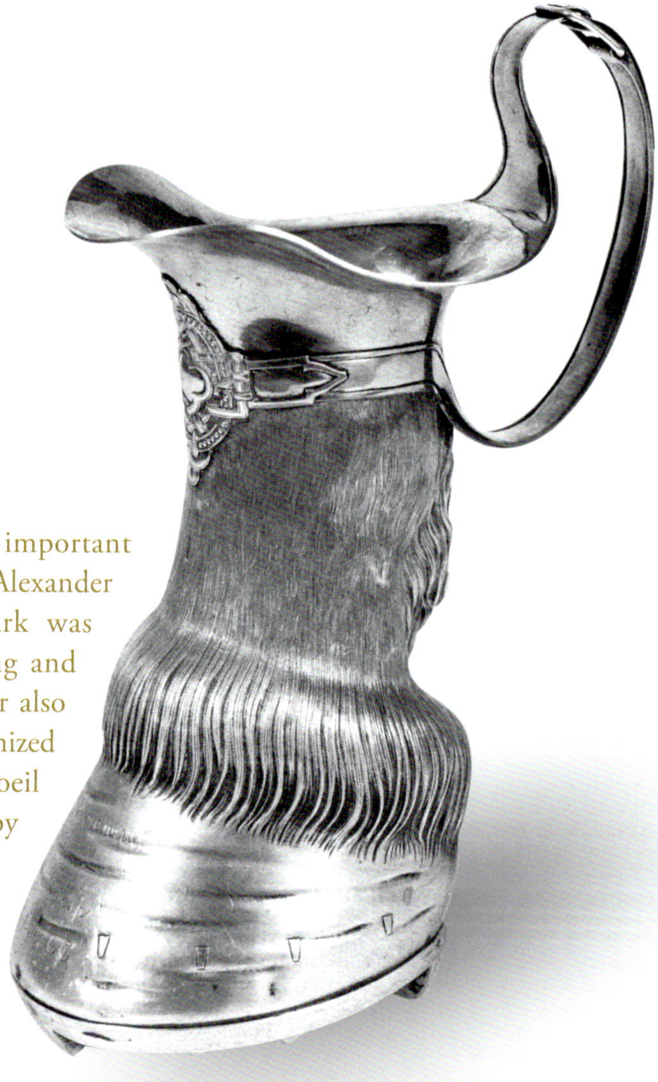

Ivan Semenovich Gubkin (d. 1867) was an important Moscow silversmith to the imperial court of Alexander II. Founded in 1841, his firm's trademark was originality of design as well as silver chasing and casting in the neo-rococo style. Gubkin silver also retains a distinctly Russian flavor. The silversmith is now recognized as having initiated and mastered the technique of trompe l'oeil silver in Russia, which was copied in the 1880s and '90s by Khlebnikov, Sazikov, and others.

Becoming purveyor to the imperial court in 1855, the master excelled in figural silver, especially in that decade, producing salamander-handled tankards, horse's-hoof-shaped carafes, stag's-head stirrup cups and melon-formed hinged boxes on foliate bases. Rising to prominence in the 1860s, by then the factory had an annual output of 500,000 rubles, employed a staff of 88, and exhibited in major fairs in Moscow, St. Petersburg and London. Ivan's sons, Sergei and Dimitri, continued operations until the 1880s.

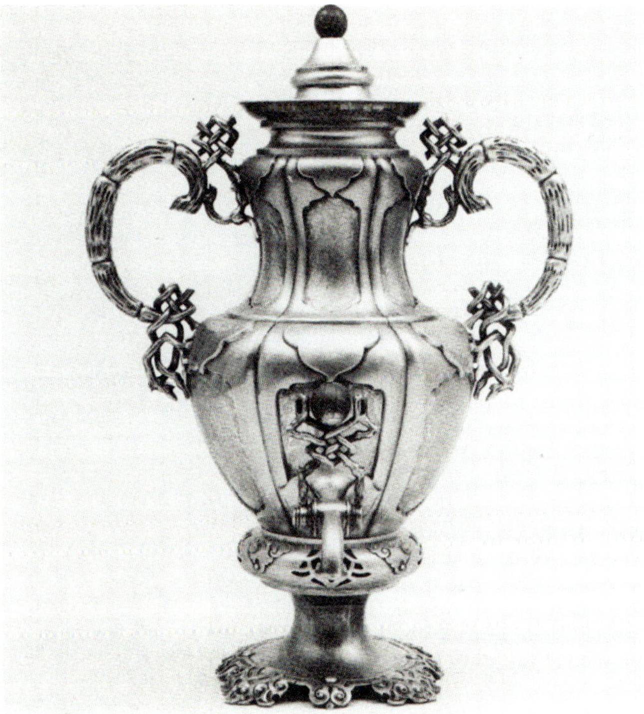

A silver samovar dated 1850 was exhibited at Hillwood Museum & Gardens in the 1980s. *Courtesy of Sotheby's*

Previous page:
Silver Gubkin figural items, all from the 1850s. *Clockwise from upper left:* a silver salamander tankard, a stirrup cup, a horse's-hoof ewer, and a nesting hen. © *1979, 1983, 1998, courtesy of Christie's Images Ltd.*

OREST KURLIUKOV: MAESTRO OF THE MAGICAL

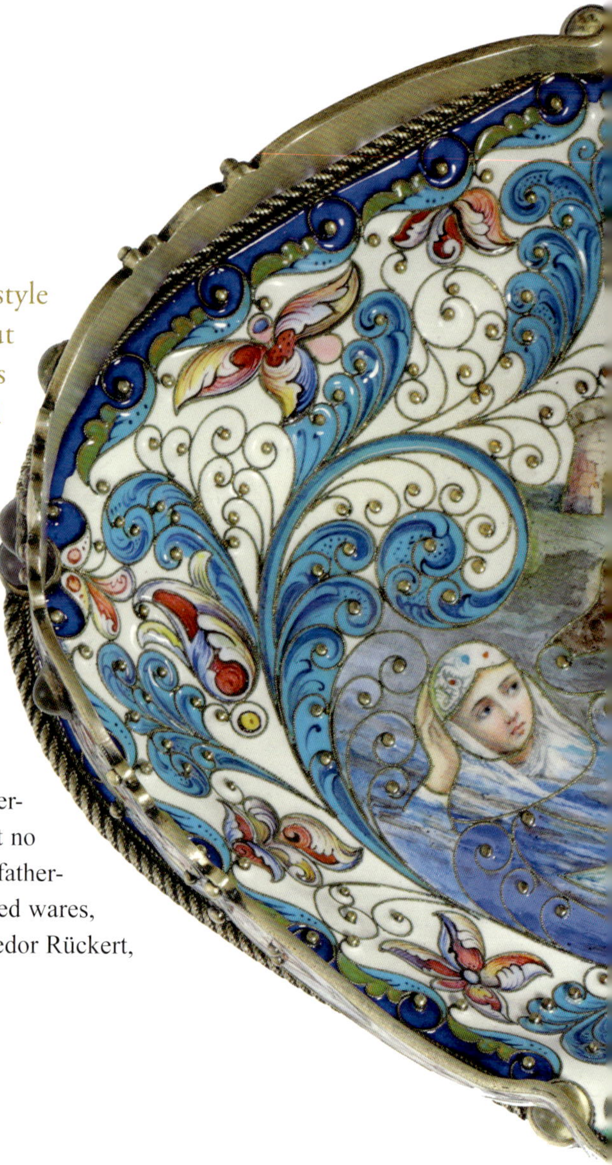

Orest Kurliukov's rich enamels compare in quality and style to those of Fedor Rückert and Ivan Khlebnikov but have a magical quality not always present in those of his colleagues. Replete with graceful swans, firebirds and legendary Russian figures, the palette is soft yet vivid, as seen in the Sadko tray. He favored pastel shades on cream-colored ground. Those dating from around 1900 not only evoke the Russian folkloric past but also have an art nouveau quality of movement, undulating forms and scrolling foliage. Both Fabergé and Tiffany & Company retailed the magnificent enamels and silver of Orest Kurliukov.

Born in 1845, Orest Fedorovich Kurliukov was an active Moscow citizen, merchant and enameler from 1884 to 1916. It is not clear when he set up shop, but no doubt he received his training in the Moscow workshop of Ivan Khlebnikov, his father-in-law. In the 1890s, he won the Finance Ministry award for his brightly colored wares, headed the Merchants of Moscow Association and started collaborating with Fedor Rückert, Carl Fabergé and Tiffany in New York.

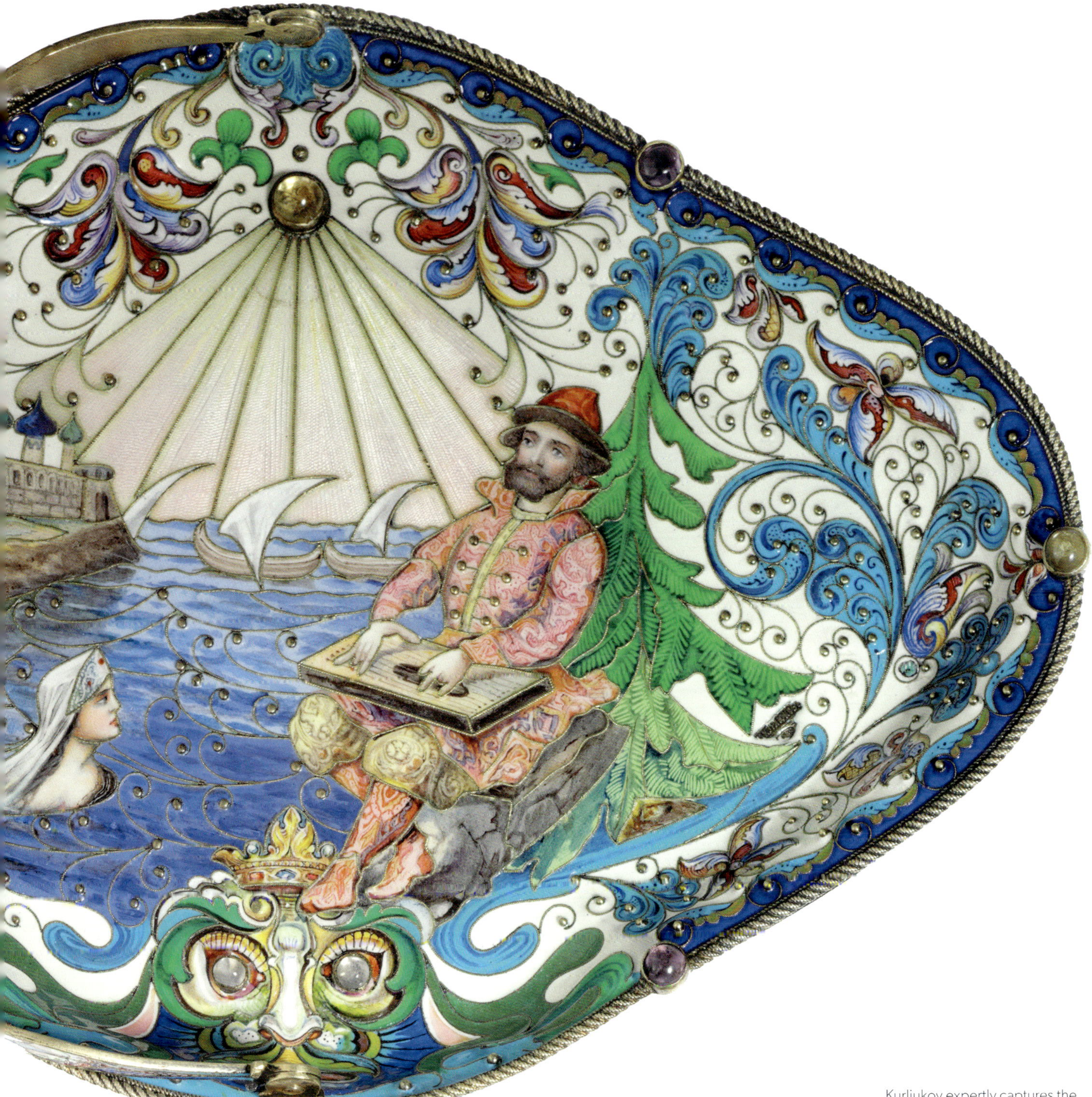

Kurliukov expertly captures the Novgorodian fairy tale of Sadko in this delightful tray. The adventures of the Novgorodian musician were well known by Russians of all ages in paintings, literature and music. © *2012 Christie's Images Ltd.*

22

History

IOSIF MARSHAK: THE CARTIER OF KIEV

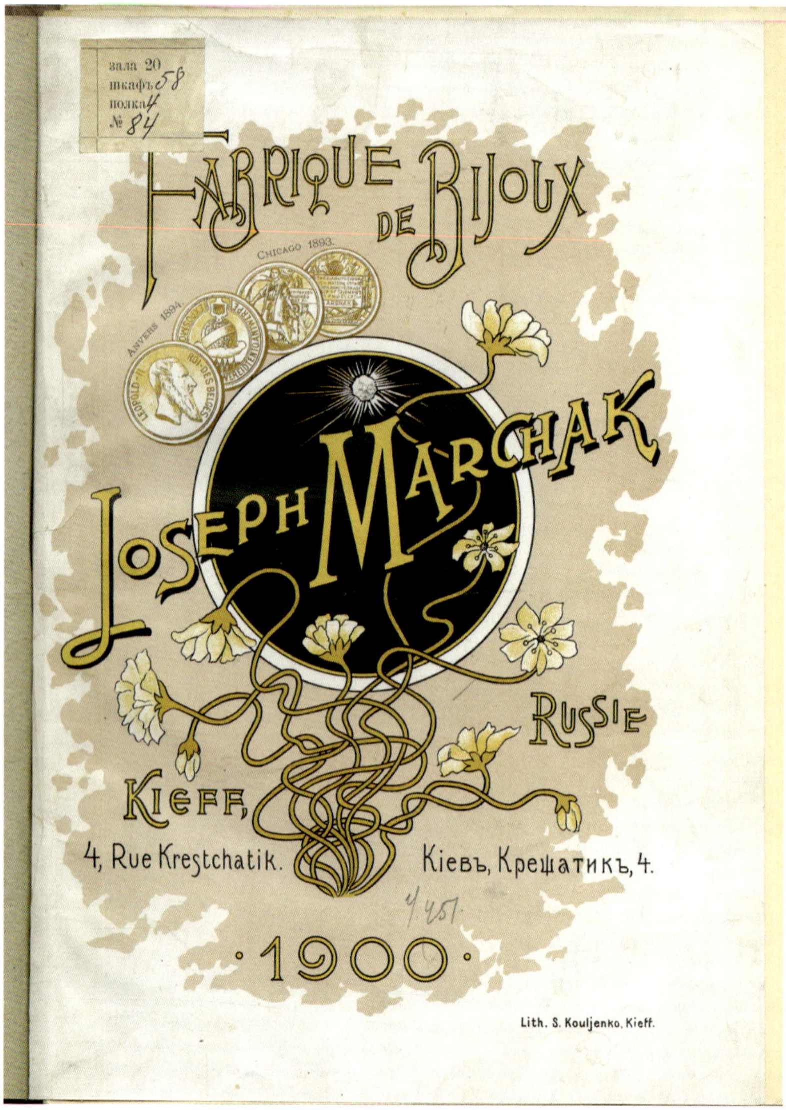

The cover of Marshak's catalogue of 1900 shows its international clientele and stylish Art Nouveau design.

Following page: Silver commemorative plate presented to Iosif Marshak by his workers on May 9, 1890, at the inauguration of the new workshop. *Courtesy of Marchak, Paris*

In a dimly lit room separated by a curtain, Iosif Abramovich hunched over his workbench, making gold chains, link by link. Each was pristine, since he had perfected his skill as an apprentice to a goldsmith on the Kreshchatik, Kiev's principal thoroughfare. His father had sent him there at age 13. It was a good move. Born into a poor family in a shtetl, the Marshaks had few prospects, but Kiev held great promise for his eldest son, Iosif's father, Abraham Isaakovich, felt.

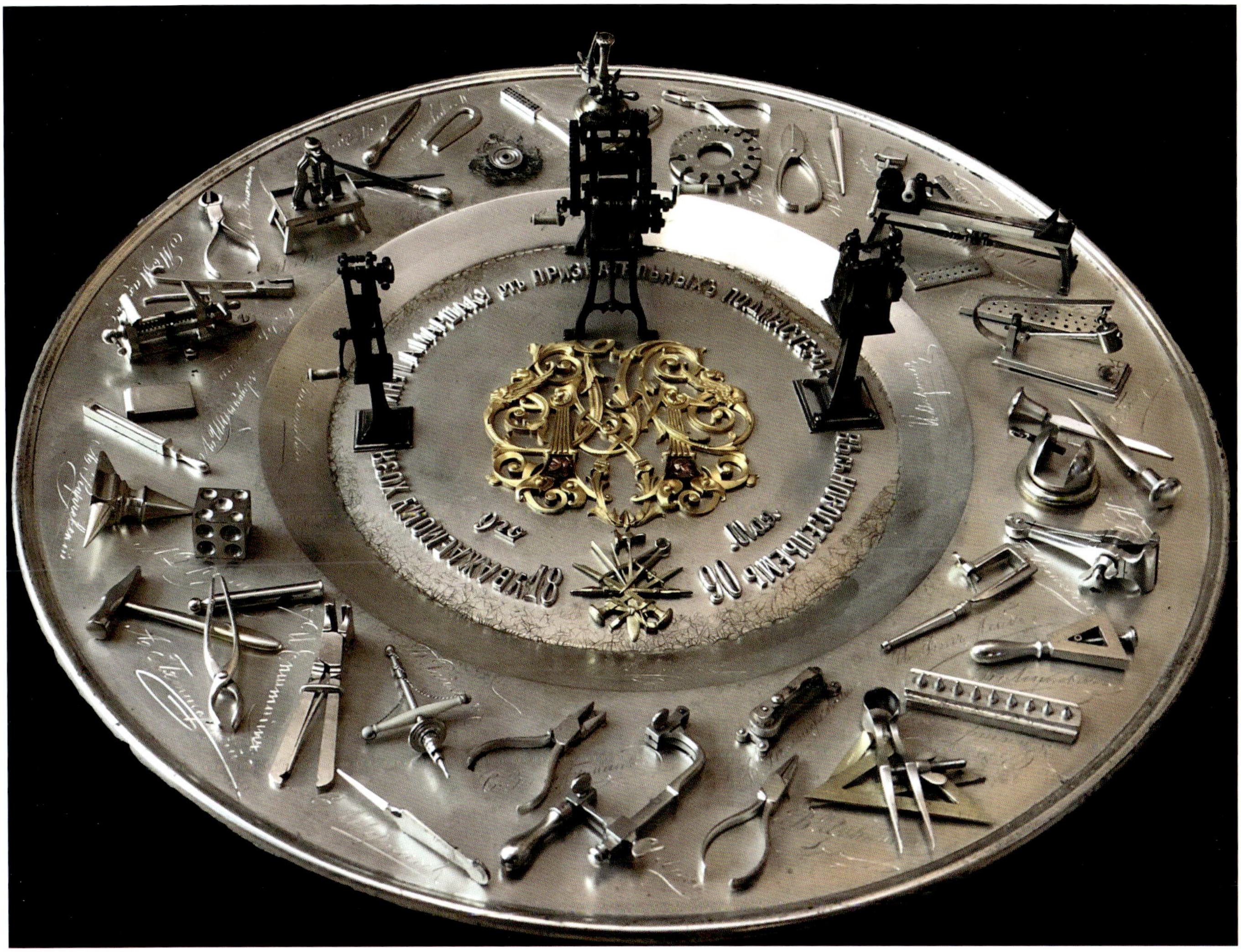

Iosif experimented by fashioning different *fermoirs* or clasps. The links had French names too: "Figaro," "mille anneaux," "Breguet." He mastered them all. Nearby his wife, Elisaveta, helped him.[1] On the other side of the curtain stood a stove, a bed and a table. It was their life, but a happy one. With 100-ruble dowry, they had rented this one-room flat in Podil, Kiev's historic center of trade. As a newly minted master jeweler at age 19, Iosif felt invincible. He would soon be able to fashion his own hallmark, *I. Marshak*, in Cyrillic letters. The future looked bright. An ancient bedrock of the jewelry trade, by the 1870s Kiev was a thriving metropolis. The imperial capital seemed far away, but this was of no concern to Iosif. He was focused on Kiev and the boundless opportunities that beckoned. The timing was perfect. As the seat of Ukraine's largest enterprises and sugar capital of the empire, Kiev's population would triple by the 1890s.[2]

Iosif Marshak started with little but soon made history. In 1878, he opened a workshop in Podil and within a year had moved to the courtyard of 4 Kreshchatik, joining dozens of other talented goldsmiths. From there he launched his dream: I. Marshak, which in three decades grew into the most important gold and silver enterprise in Ukraine. But Marshak never forgot his humble origins and, like Sazikov of St. Petersburg, he opened an artisan school for poor children and established thriving workshops with the latest equipment, employed women as apprentices and jewelers and provided healthcare. His ateliers produced artistic virtuoso silver centerpieces and jewels that compare in quality to works by Carl Fabergé. Marshak would go on to win numerous awards in All-Russian and international exhibitions and create magnificent gifts for the tsar.

From Poverty to Prosperity

Thanks to the memoir of his eldest son, Alexander Marshak (1892–1975), and to the recent research of Valentin Skurlov and Natalia Sapfirova in Russia,[3] we have a clearer picture of Marshak's life. His success continued unabated. By 1885,

Marshak employed 20 workers, and orders were pouring in. Nothing seemed to stop Iosif, not even a fire that destroyed the entire workshop in 1889. Instead, he took the opportunity to modernize, expand and travel to Paris and Germany. In 1890, he opened new premises. To show their loyalty, his workmasters, even those injured in the blaze, presented their boss with a silver platter on which were applied numerous miniature gold tools of the trade, with their signatures and the opening date of the new workshop. Alexander took this dish with him to Paris when he escaped Kiev in 1918 (illustrated).[4] By 1897, the firm employed 72 workers with a turnover of 227,717 rubles.[5]

Supplier to the Romanovs

Despite his firm's distance from the imperial capital, Marshak created numerous presentation objects for the court, beginning with the coronation of Tsar Nicholas II in 1896. When the emperor visited Kiev in August that year, Marshak produced an impressive labradorite bread-and-salt platter mounted in intricate Gothic-style silver. Now in the Hermitage Museum and adorned with the symbol of Kiev, the Archangel Michael, the gift was bestowed on the emperor by the Kiev nobility for the consecration of the Saint Vladimir Cathedral. The presentation dish was one of several. According to Alexander Marshak, "Each platter was made according to a special drawing with rich silver finish, often with enameled crests of the provinces or repoussé emblems of a city."[6]

On the same visit, Emperor Nicholas II and Empress Alexandra Fedorovna also received a Marshak silver-mounted dedication album on behalf of the Dnepr River Steamboat Society (see illustration, page 196). When the tsar traveled to Kiev in 1911 to unveil a monument to Tsar Alexander II for the 50th anniversary of the liberation of the serfs, and again to celebrate the Romanov tercentenary of 1913 in Moscow, Marshak delivered gifts, including one of the most striking objects for presentation to his heir, nine-year-old Tsarevich Alexis: an inkstand in the form of a freestanding silver model of the Kiev Museum of Education, complete with a miniature allegorical frieze and gold trim. The year also marked a celebration of the firm's 35th anniversary and the publication of its jubilee album.

Despite these lavish presentation gifts, perhaps because of his Jewish faith, the coveted title of purveyor to the imperial court eluded the Kievan jeweler. He had applied for it in 1911 but received no response from the imperial cabinet.[7] This did not prevent the firm from attracting an increasingly august clientele, including the Romanovs, the Yusupovs and other Russian and European aristocracy, not to mention rich merchants from Kiev, Moscow and beyond. As his dynasty expanded, so did his reach. In 1891, Marshak sent 5,300 jewels worth about 40,000 rubles mostly to Poland and other Russian territories. He often journeyed to Moscow to recruit talent, get ideas for his business and purchase inventory.[8]

The King of Kiev

But Marshak's domain was Kiev. Having been born, raised and trained in Ukraine, he knew the clientele and their tastes, aspirations, culture and wealth. His birthplace had a rich cultural and trade history dating back to medieval times, and Marshak was well aware of its storied past as the capital of Kievan Rus nearly 1,000 years earlier. The city's first goldsmith was documented as early as 1384. Jewelry arts in the Ukraine flourished during the reign of Tsar Fedor I (1557–98), son of Ivan the Terrible. Lvov, in western Ukraine, was the main center of jewelry making by the late 16th century, with

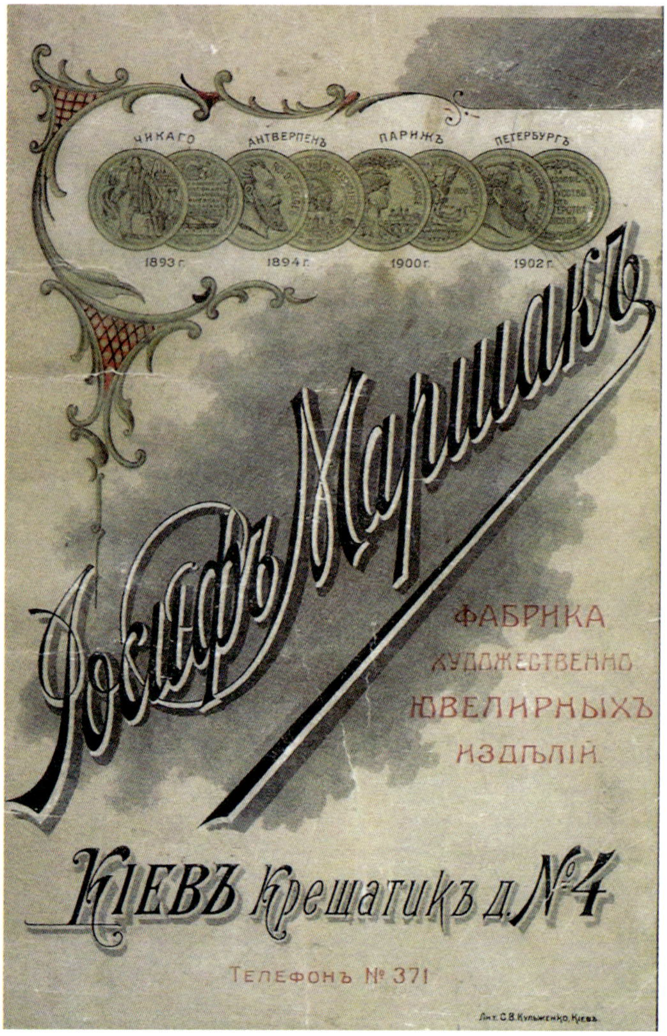

Cover of the Marshak sales catalogue, 1897.

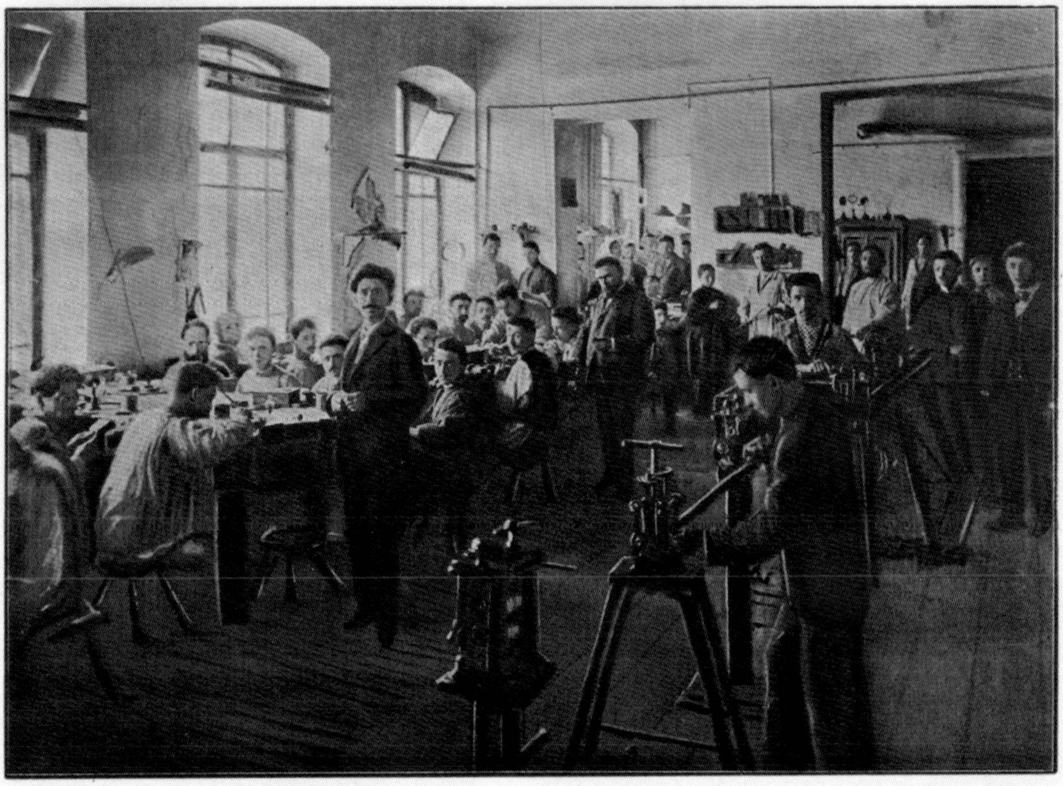

Часть главной ювелирной мастерской. ☆ Partie de l'atelier principal de joaillerie.

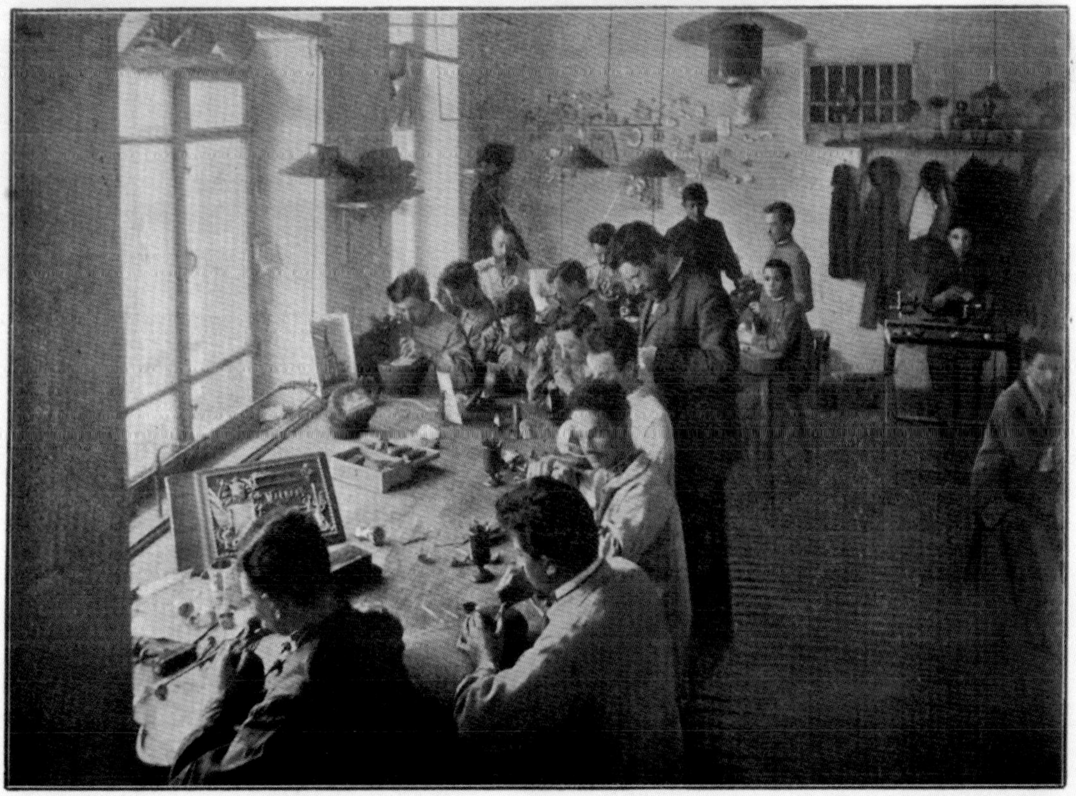

Граверный отдѣлъ. ☆ Section de gravure.

Marshak's main workshop in Kiev. *Iubileinoe izdanie Fabrika Iuvelira Iosifa Marshaka* (Kiev, 1913)

Engraving section, Marshak workshop. *Iubileinoe izdanie Fabrika Iuvelira Iosifa Marshaka* (Kiev, 1913)

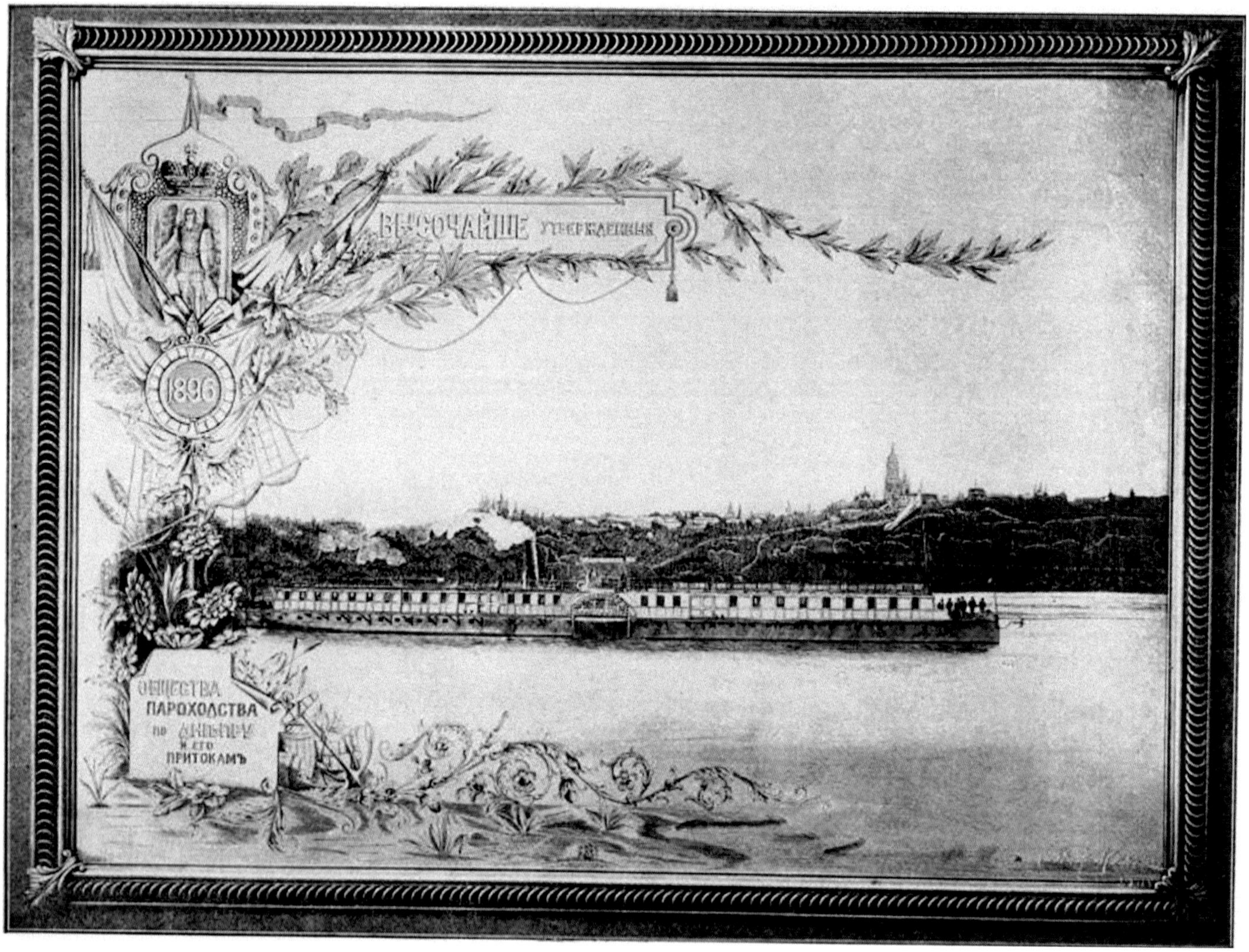

This silver cover was made by Marshak for an album the Dnepr Steamship Company presented to Tsar Nicholas II for his coronation in 1896.

30 goldsmiths plying their trade there. Hallmarking was instituted in 1600, and the Lvov town mark of a standing lion in a field was adopted in 1678. A goldsmith's guild had already been formed in Kiev in 1503, long before Peter the Great's guilds in St. Petersburg. By the 18th century, Kievan goldsmiths began marking their wares with Cyrillic or Latin letters, along with the town mark: Archangel Michael with a sword.[9] Against this backdrop, Marshak thrived in a city he knew and cherished.

In short order, Marshak cultivated a vast network of suppliers both locally and abroad. He viewed master jewelers and craftsmen as partners, not competitors. Working closely with fellow Kievans, Marshak offered wares by the two main artels and by the ingenious Israel Rokhumovskii of Odessa.[10] He sold items by Fabergé in his shop,[11] as well as creations by the famous houses of Grachev, Ivan Britsyn, Vladimir Finikov (Bolin workmaster), Fedor Rückert, the Third Jewelry Artel, the Moscow artels, Ovchinnikov and Kurliukov.

As Marshak flourished, so did its own artistic brand. From Moscow, Iosif recruited Israel Tsivkin, who specialized in monograms and commemorative medallions, first as engraver, then designer and then head of operations. Nikolai Viktorovich Khokorev and Mikhail Stepanovich Zavelskii joined as jeweler and sculptor, respectively. Renowned Russian sculptors Naoum Aronson (1872–1943), who was based in Paris, and Prince Pavel Trubetskoi (1866–1938) also worked for Marshak. Like Carl Fabergé, Iosif hired his younger brother, Israel, to lead the gemstone department.[12]

In the new workshop, masters worked in groups by specialty:

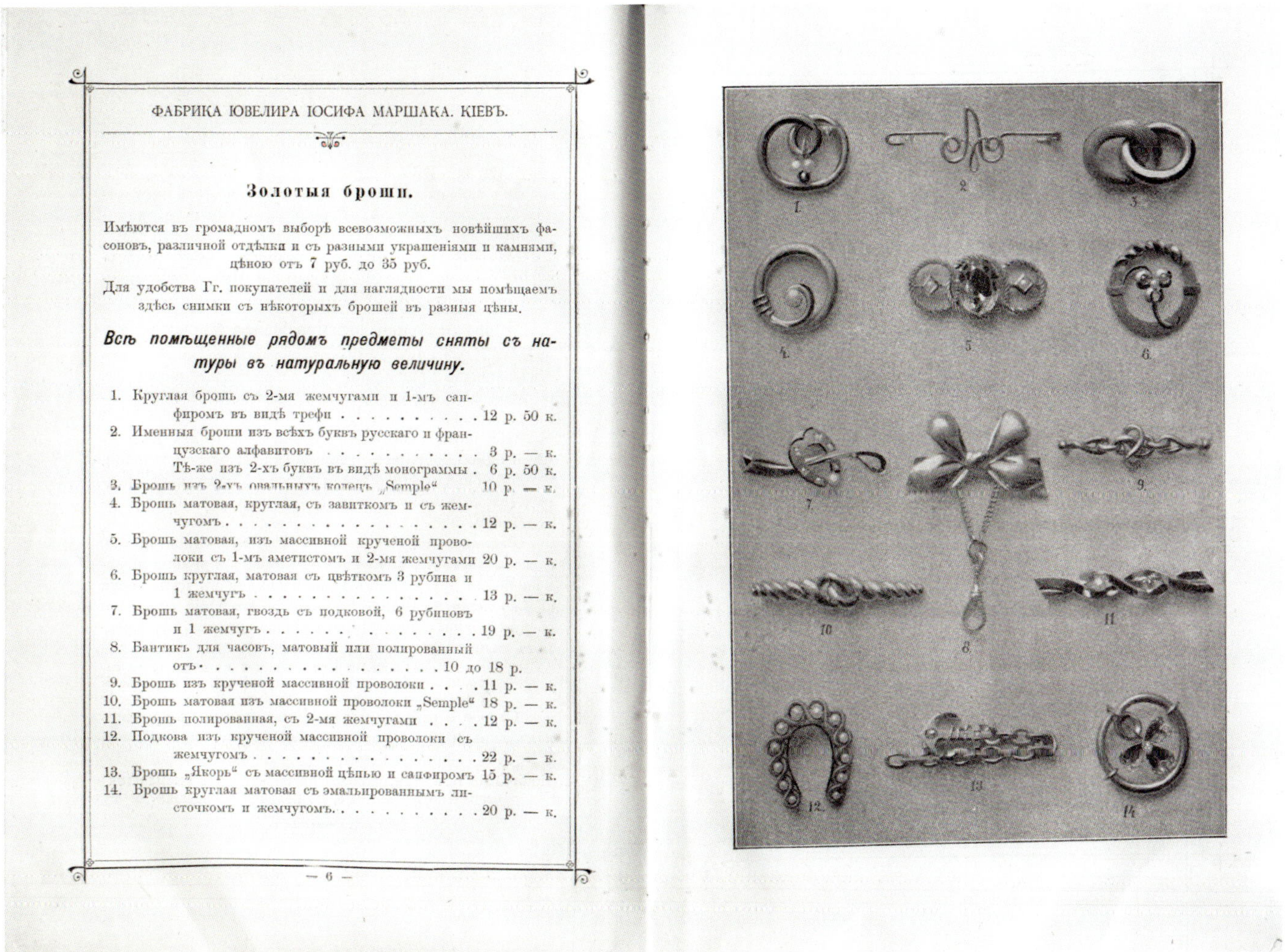

ФАБРИКА ЮВЕЛИРА ІОСИФА МАРШАКА. КІЕВЪ.

Золотыя броши.

Имѣются въ громадномъ выборѣ всевозможныхъ новѣйшихъ фасоновъ, различной отдѣлки и съ разными украшеніями и камнями, цѣною отъ 7 руб. до 35 руб.

Для удобства Гг. покупателей и для наглядности мы помѣщаемъ здѣсь снимки съ нѣкоторыхъ брошей въ разныя цѣны.

Всѣ помѣщенные рядомъ предметы сняты съ натуры въ натуральную величину.

1. Круглая брошь съ 2-мя жемчугами и 1-мъ сапфиромъ въ видѣ трефи . . . . 12 р. 50 к.
2. Именныя броши изъ всѣхъ буквъ русскаго и французскаго алфавитовъ . . . . 3 р. — к.
   Тѣ-же изъ 2-хъ буквъ въ видѣ монограммы . 6 р. 50 к.
3. Брошь изъ 2-хъ овальныхъ колецъ „Semple" 10 р. — к.
4. Брошь матовая, круглая, съ завиткомъ и съ жемчугомъ . . . . 12 р. — к.
5. Брошь матовая, изъ массивной крученой проволоки съ 1-мъ аметистомъ и 2-мя жемчугами 20 р. — к.
6. Брошь круглая, матовая съ цвѣткомъ 3 рубина и 1 жемчугъ . . . . 13 р. — к.
7. Брошь матовая, гвоздь съ подковой, 6 рубиновъ и 1 жемчугъ . . . . 19 р. — к.
8. Бантикъ для часовъ, матовый или полированный отъ . . . . 10 до 18 р.
9. Брошь изъ крученой массивной проволоки . . . . 11 р. — к.
10. Брошь матовая изъ массивной проволоки „Semple" 18 р. — к.
11. Брошь полированная, съ 2-мя жемчугами . . . . 12 р. — к.
12. Подкова изъ крученой массивной проволоки съ жемчугомъ . . . . 22 р. — к.
13. Брошь „Якорь" съ массивной цѣпью и сапфиромъ 15 р. — к.
14. Брошь круглая матовая съ эмальированнымъ листочкомъ и жемчугомъ. . . . . 20 р. — к.

— 6 —

Two pages from Marshak's sales catalogue, 1897.

jewelers and stone setters, sculptors and silversmiths, engravers and chasers, polishers and enamelers, etc. were separated by department, each of which included students. The latter would pursue a five year course, with pay by the beginning of the second year.[13] There was also a drawing school where students would gather for lessons three times a week. Iosif was generous with his employees and even provided health insurance and medical care. This would be repaid in loyalty and long service. On the 25th-anniversary jubilee celebration of the business, Iosif awarded each workmaster and employee a gold commemorative pendant engraved with recipient's name, some with small diamonds, as well as a briefcase with cash and an extra monthly bonus proportional to his or her salary.[14]

Like any successful merchant, Marshak paid attention to his customers. Ever enterprising, he published sales catalogues to be distributed at the shop and by mail. Judging from these publications, the earliest of which seems to date 1897, Kievan buyers favored Old Russian motifs, trompe l'oeil and neoclassical and art nouveau in silver, as well as Marshak silver-mounted luxury crystal by Baccarat of Paris.

In the 1897 catalogue the jewels—brooches, necklaces, earrings, rings, bracelets and pendants—were meant for the general public and priced accordingly. Prices start at three rubles for a gold letter pin and 16 rubles for a gold bangle. Diamonds were popular, but aside from one or two showstoppers, they play a minor part. One exception is a striking *collier d'esclavage* (diamond necklace) that can be separated into earrings, a brooch and a rivière for formal occasions. The price is 4,200 rubles, while an impressive emerald and diamond brooch fermoir is priced at 2,500 rubles. Like other Russian jewelers, French was the language of choice, as these captions attest. In 1905, the firm published a grander catalogue. Perhaps aware of Fabergé's impending arrival in Kiev (he opened a branch there in 1906), the Marshak catalogue featured more important jewels. Of note is a

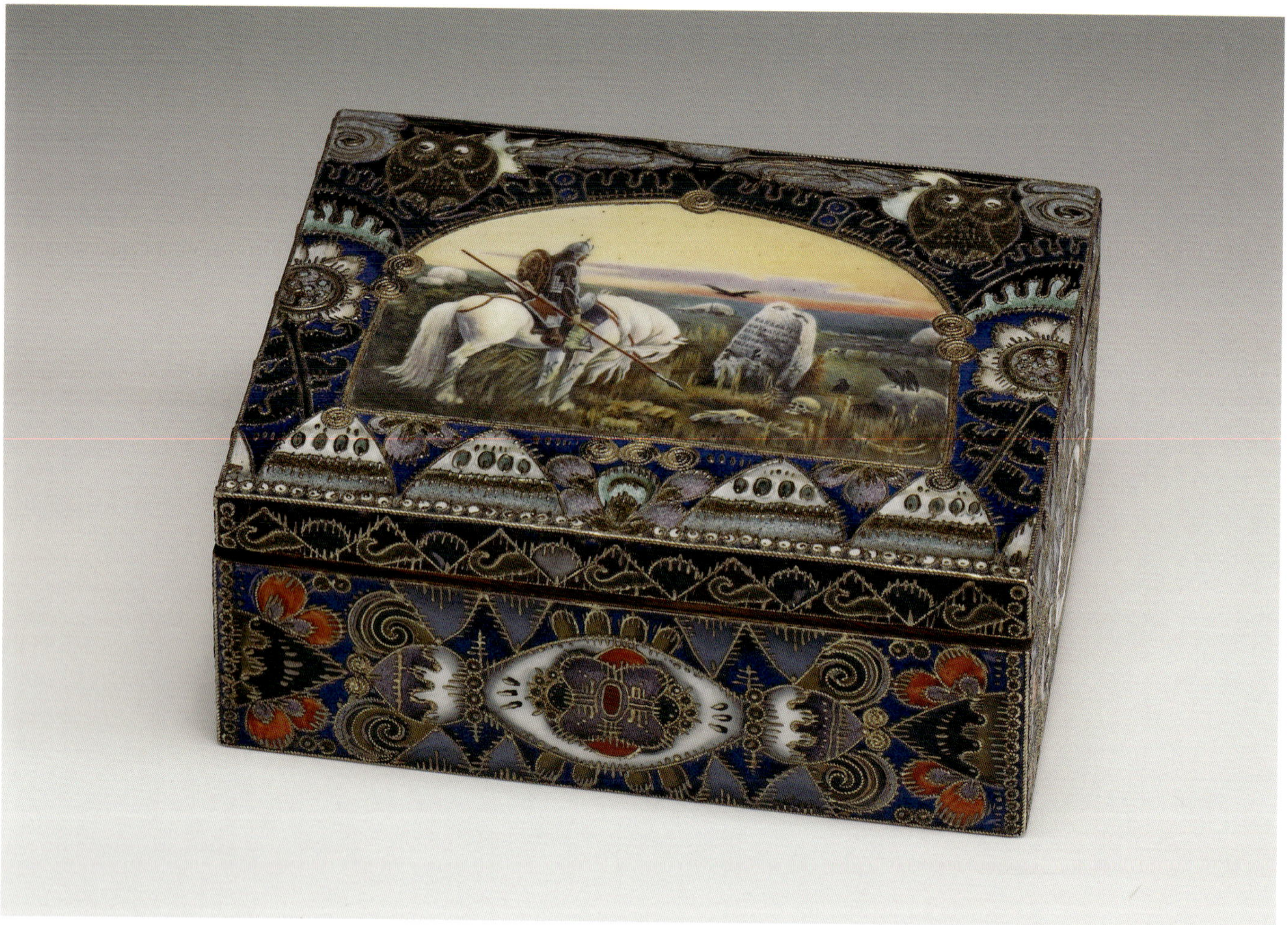

necklace of "very elegant workmanship" with 16 large diamonds and smaller diamonds for 18,000 rubles, followed by a pair of diamond earrings en suite for 7,500 rubles, and a five-strand oriental pearl necklace with an engraved emerald and diamond clasp for 8,000 rubles.[15]

World Fame

Like Carl Fabergé, who was eight years older, Iosif Marshak participated in international exhibitions, including the World's Columbian Exposition in Chicago on 1893. Although joined by Mikhail Grachev, a silversmith from St. Petersburg, and the enamelers Gustav Klingert and Ovchinnikov from Moscow, judging from the exhibition catalogue the intrepid Marshak seemed to have been the only goldsmith from the empire. True, crossing the Atlantic was no small feat at the time, even more so laden with an expensive and cumbersome inventory, a prospect that may have seemed daunting to the average Russian jeweler or silversmith. Still, where were Fabergé, Bolin, or Sazikov?[16] In Chicago, Marshak received an honorable mention. The firm displayed a meticulous silver model of a steamer—this is possibly Silver Model of the Ship *Derzhava*, intended as a desk set, which weighed 20 pounds,[17] and a "velvet blotting book with silver ornaments, Silver dish and Gold Scotland Skeleton."[18] The latter refers to an intricate gold pendant by Israel Rokhumovskii (see "Israel Rokhumovskii and the Case of the Counterfeit Crown").

Marshak went on to receive gold and silver medals in Antwerp, Paris and St. Petersburg between 1894 and 1902, a Grand Prix award in Liege in 1905 and the highest prize in the All-Russian exposition in Kiev in 1913.[19] Images of these medals

This enameled cigar box by Fedor Rückert, Warrior at the Crossroads, based on a painting by Victor Vasnetsov, was retailed by Marshak. *Courtesy of Walters Art Museum, Baltimore*

would grace the covers of sales catalogues, price lists and the inside lids of fitted Marshak boxes. It was in that year, 1913, that Marshak opened an art school for poor children, which trained over 300.[20]

Fabergé Folds

In 1906, Carl Fabergé opened a branch in Kiev, steps away from Marshak, at 25 Kreshchatik. Indeed, Kiev was the biggest commercial center in the Russian Empire's Southwest, and by 1902 it boasted 92 gold and silver workshops.[21] Fabergé's Moscow branch, which opened in 1887, was proving a resounding success, even more than that of the imperial capital. Odessa was humming along. Why not Kiev? After all, Louis Cartier, the famous Parisian jeweler, had conducted business there.[22]

But the future bode ill for the great Fabergé in the Ukrainian capital. In spring 1906, a parcel filled with precious jewels from either Moscow or St. Petersburg on its way to Kiev went missing. Meanwhile, Fabergé proved no match for the mighty Marshak of Kiev, despite an impressive St. Petersburg workforce and world fame.[23] Vanquished by a native son, the most successful goldsmith in history found himself struggling on the Kreshchatik.

Did they do business together, or even talk to one another? Although Marshak offered Fabergé items in his shop, did Fabergé do the same for Marshak? One imagines Iosif as outgoing, while Carl was more reclusive, or perhaps dismissive. The two must have crossed paths many times, since their shops lined the same street. The great Moscow enameler Fedor Rückert worked for both houses. Both exhibited in the Paris Exposition Universelle in 1900. According to Valentin Skurlov, Marshak would visit Fabergé's shops in Kiev and Odessa for inspiration, and Fabergé lost no time in going to the Winter Palace in 1911 to view Marshak-made gifts to the tsar, freshly arrived from Kiev.[24] That was also the year Fabergé closed shop in Kiev.

Iosif's customers remained loyal to the end. They admired this self-made jeweler who rose from nothing through diligence, honesty and an unflagging spirit of enterprise. From that single workbench in a divided room to Ukraine's most successful jewelry and silver dynasty, this spoke to the people. They also liked his personal touch, as the many tributes in the Kiev Tribune (*Kievskaia mysl*) attest upon his demise. In 1918 the twin fatal blows of Marshak's death and the Bolsheviks proved its downfall. Iosif's close-knit family, children and grandchildren were gathered around him for months as he lay ill at home and in his dacha. His granddaughter Nelli Ptashkina (1903–20), whose own life would end in tragedy, wrote, "We are all very sorry for him. Saddened that he will suffer a lot and soon will die; what a horrible world! Despite all this, life goes on, as always; even more, everyone is living life!"[25] Iosif Abramovich died on August 12, 1918, mourned by many.

In 1919, Alexander Marshak fled to Paris, where he opened a shop on Rue de la Paix. The firm, renamed Marchak, became a leading jewelry house in Paris while maintaining Iosif's legacy for excellence of design and superb workmanship, a tradition that continues today.

A MYSTERIOUS MONUMENT BY MARSHAK

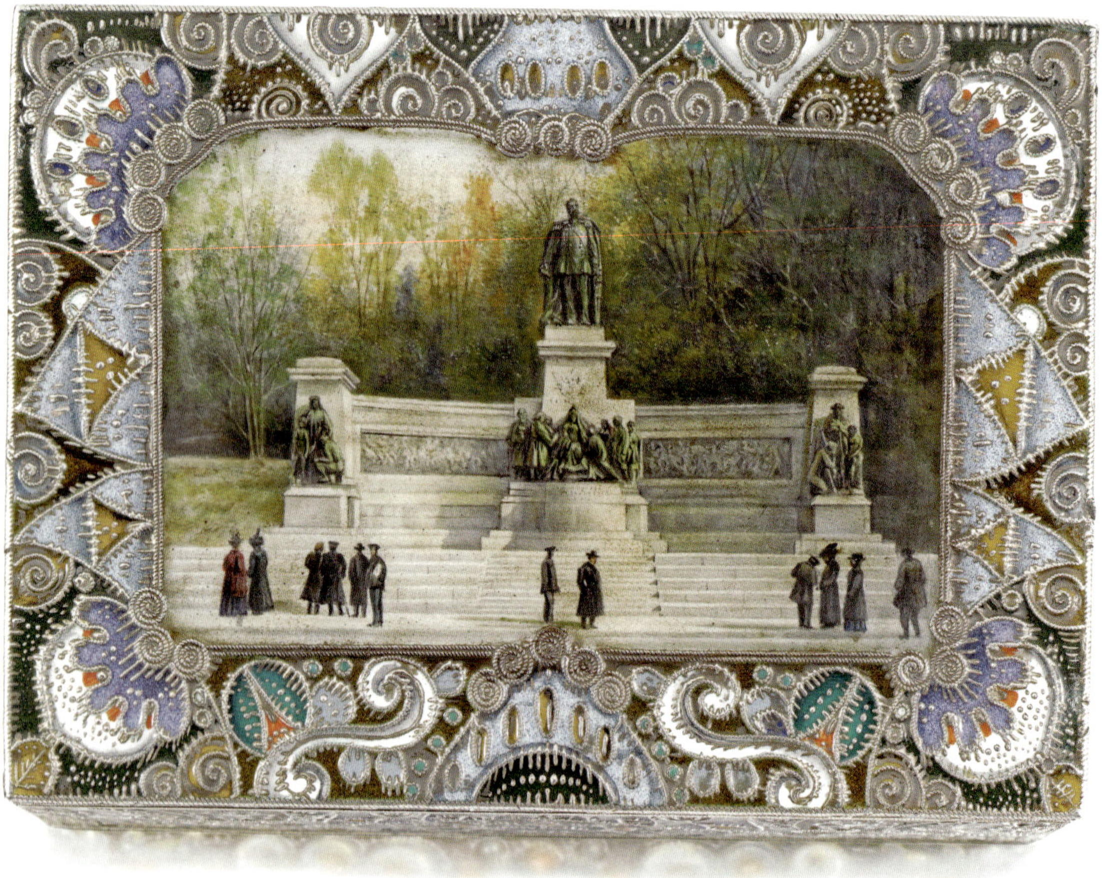

A rare Marshak box by Fedor Rückert depicting the inauguration of the monument in Kiev to Tsar Alexander II, to honor the 50th anniversary of the Liberation of the Serfs. *Courtesy of Sotheby's*

At first, it stumped the experts. A Russian enameled box retailed and stamped by Marshak and made by the famous Moscow enameler Fedor Rückert. That much was clear, but what was the scene on the cover?

Against autumn foliage the en plein enamel painting featured a monument with an imperial-looking figure raised high on a pedestal. It looked huge and dwarfed the bystanders below.

A search for Russian monuments proved futile, but since Marshak was based in Kiev, by googling *Kiev* and *monument*, the mystery fell away.

This massive edifice was erected in 1911 in the Ukrainian capital to Tsar Alexander II, to commemorate the 50th anniversary of the liberation of the serfs. In fact, it was the largest monument dedicated to the tsar liberator in the entire Russian Empire. No one knew about this impressive creation today, because it was torn down by the Bolsheviks in 1920, only nine years later.

Created by the Italian sculptor Ettore Ximenes (1855–1926), the monument was unveiled on August 30, 1911, to great fanfare. This was a historic event, attended by Tsar Nicholas II and his family. Fittingly for Marshak, it stood at the head of the Kreshchatik, the famous boulevard in Kiev, along which his enterprise was located. It is said Marshak spent a year preparing for this event.

Although its recipient is unknown, Marshak may have created this box for presentation to one of three personages: the Russian tsar himself, the sculptor Ettore Ximenes, or perhaps the tsar's prime minister, Petr Stolypin, who only days later was assassinated at the Kiev Opera House in front of the emperor and his two eldest daughters, Grand Duchesses Olga and Tatiana.

NOTES

1. Elisaveta Fedorevna, a hairdresser's daughter, would soon learn to polish and prepare gold for her husband's workshop. Aleksandr Marshak, "Istoriia fabriki moego otsa," in *K. Faberzhe i Iosif Marshak*, eds. Valentin Skurlov, N. Sapfirova, and Tatiana Fabergé (St. Petersburg: Tipografiia "NP-Print," 2015), 34–35. Much of the information on Marshak in this chapter comes from this source.

2. Marshak, "Istoriia fabriki moego otsa," 34–35.

3. Alexander Marshak immigrated to Paris and opened a shop on rue de la Paix. Now known as Marchak, the firm still exists today in Paris. It is said Alexander also worked for Fabergé et Cie in Paris in the 1930s. Fabergé et al., *Fabergé: A Comprehensive Reference,* 511. Marshak originally gave his handwritten notes to Professor M. M. Postnikova-Loseva, author of a seminal book on Russian hallmarks, *Zolotoe i serebrianoe delo XV–XX vv: Territoriia SSSR* (Moscow: Edition Nauka, 1983), in 1978. These memoirs were published in Russian in 2003 by her successor, A. K. Afanas'ev, chief scientist of the Russian Historical Museum in Moscow, and excerpted in 2004 edition of *Antiquariat* magazine. The diary of Marshak's granddaughter Nelli Ptashkina (who died at 17 in a tragic fall in the Alps), published in Paris in 1922, also provides a glimpse of Iosif Marshak's final days and of the hardships endured during the Bolshevik takeover of the firm. Nelli Ptashkina, "Dnevnik Nelli Ptashkinoi, 1918–1920 gg.: Poslednie gody sem's Marshaka na rodine," in Skurlov, *K. Faberzhe i Iosif Marshak*, 66–68.

4. Marguerite de Cerval, "l'Heritage," in *Marchak* (Paris: Éditions du Regard, 2006), 57, illus. 60.

5. N. Sapfirova, "Antikvarnyi rynok: Predmety fabriki khudozhestvenno-iuverlirnykh izdelii Iosifa Marshak i drugikh iuvelirnykh prepriiatii Kieva kontsa XIX-nachala XX vv.," in Skurlov, *K. Faberzhe i Iosif Marshak*, 29.

6. Marshak, "Istoriia fabriki moego otsa," 34–35

7. Sapfirova, "Antikvarnyi rynok," in Skurlov et al., *K. Faberzhe i Iosif Marshak*, 22–23.

8. Cerval, *Marchak*, 58–59.

9. Museum of the Historical Treasures of Ukraine, https://Mihu.org.ua/en/jewelry_art_in_ukraine_16th_20th centuries.html.

10. A gold skeleton pendant as a gift from Rochoumovksy to Marshak was no doubt for display only. It was exhibited in Chicago in 1893.

11. Skurlov et al., *K. Faberzhe i Iosif Marshak*, 28–29

12. Marshak, "Istoriia fabriki moego otsa," 34–35.

13. Ibid.

14. Ibid.

15. *Fabrika Khudozhestvenno-Iuvelirnykh izdelii Iosifa Marshaka* (Kiev, 1897); and *Fabrika Khudozhestvenno-Iuvelirnykh izdelii Iosifa Marshaka* (Kiev, 1905).

16. There were just under 1,100 Russian exhibitors out of 70,000 from around the world.

17. Skurlov et al., *K. Faberzhe i Iosif Marshak*, 32–33.

18. *Catalogue of the Russian Section, World's Columbian Exposition*, 1893, Chicago, 194.

19. Sapfirova, "Antikvarnyi rynok," 29.

20. Ibid., 29.

21. Skurlov et al., *K. Faberzhe i Iosif Marshak*, 28–29.

22. Cerval, *Marchak*, 60.

23. By the end of the 19th century, Fabergé employed 700 workers in both St. Petersburg and Moscow, compared to Marshak's 125. However, Marshak had a greater selection of goods that appealed to local clientele. Unlike Fabergé, Marshak also offered an impressive array of pocket watches to suit all tastes and budgets. Taking a cue from the imperial watchmaker Pavel Buhré, Marshak bought out the inventory and the premises of the neighboring Swiss watchmaker Verlet in 1909.

24. Skurlov et al., *K. Faberzhe i Iosif Marshak*, 28–29.

25. Ptashkina, "Dnevnik," 66–67.

23

History

ISRAEL ROKHUMOVSKII AND THE CASE OF THE COUNTERFEIT CROWN

Unlike his friend Iosif Marshak, Israel Rokhumovskii (1860–1934) shunned the spotlight. While Marshak prospered in Kiev, in Odessa to the south, Rokhumovskii struggled to make a living. Generous with his time and talent, he would help jewelers complete difficult commissions.[1] He probably did not charge them for this service. Rokhumovskii's modest workshop had no sign, and he had no credentials.[2] It is not known whether he ever even apprenticed with a jeweler. What is clear is that he was a genius at goldsmithing, his brilliance innate. According to some, he could fashion gold like no one else.[3]

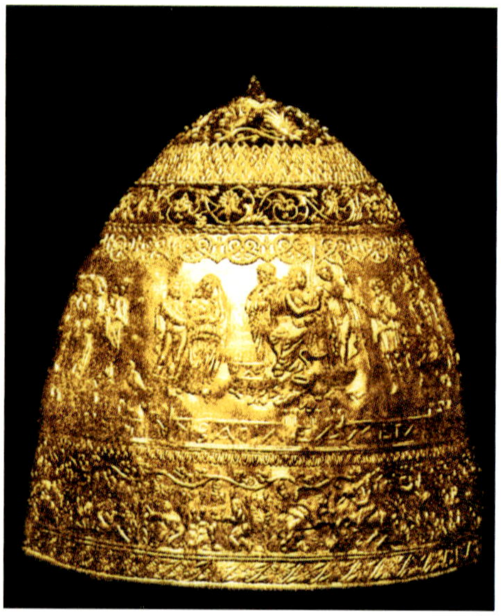

The Crown Tiara of Saitapharnes that fooled the Louvre. *Source: Wikimedia Commons*

Marshak recognized his extraordinary gift, as did the Hochmann brothers, two notorious dealers who would pass off his remarkable 24-carat-gold creations as ancient Scythian treasures to none other than the Louvre in Paris. One such case caused a huge *scandale* in the City of Light in 1903.

Born in 1860 in Mozyr, Belarus, Rokhumovskii loved art and engraving. As a boy, he made perfect wooden models. The Kievan engraving workshops to which his parents sent him at age 13 had nothing to teach him, so he left.[4] In 1892, Rokhumovskii obtained a work permit in Odessa, but where he made his living and what he did up to that point is a mystery.

This coincided with important archeological excavations near the Black Sea. Suddenly throughout Europe, gold antiquities were all the rage. Western museums vied for items from this hoard to compete with the Hermitage's magnificent collection (see "Russian Jewelry over the Ages"). The shifty-eyed Hochmann brothers from Ochakov, a Ukrainian town near Crimea, were well aware of this craze. Quick to pounce on Rokhumovskii's undiscovered talent, they commissioned several gold artifacts in the ancient Scythian style from him.

The most striking, and one that would live on in history, was a pure-gold conical crown known as the Tiara of Saitapharnes. Named after the third-century BC Scythian king, to whom it was given by the citizens of Olbia, as the story goes, its surface depicted intricate engraved and repoussé scenes of the Trojan War, Scythian nomadic horsemen, archers, animals and birds. To ensure its historical accuracy, the brothers provided drawings from a reputable and renowned source: *Antiquités de la Russie méridionale* by Count Ivan Tolstoi, Nikodim Kondatov and Salomon Reinach (published only a few years earlier in Paris).[5] Rokhumovskii received 2,000 rubles for the tiara, no doubt only upon completion. It was a labor of love on which he spent a year or more.

The Tiara Triumphs

The tiara secured, the brothers scurried first to Vienna on March 4, 1896, to offer it to the Viennese Imperial Museum. Its agents were not quick enough to pay, so the following day, Leo Hochmann, along with two Viennese accomplices, headed for the Louvre in Paris. Somehow, they had the foresight to gather French experts beforehand for this much-anticipated meeting. The director marveled at this magnificent treasure, as did the cognoscenti. The asking price was 200,000 francs (thousands of times its cost!). Hands flew up in the air. *C'est impossible!* But the swindlers would not budge on the price. They even tried to raise it to 300,000 francs and demanded immediate payment. Unwilling to let this go, the director of the Louvre approached Reinach himself (the coauthor of the book cited above) and another patron for funds that same day, which were later reimbursed when the sale was passed by the French National Assembly.[6]

On April Fool's Day 1896, the Louvre announced its purchase. To great acclaim, the tiara was unveiled to the world in the Louvre's hallowed halls. Almost immediately, experts challenged its authenticity.[7] Ernst von Stern, director of the Odessa Archaeological Museum, having presumably seen more reproductions than his French counterpart, reported on the existence of a network of secret salesmen trading in forged art, which included the Tiara of Saitapharnes.[8] Berlin scholar Adolf Furtwängler also panned it. Stern accused Rokhumovskii of trading in fakes. The goldsmith pleaded innocence in a letter to the *Journal des Debats* in 1897.[9] Then silence. Finally, in 1903, a Russian jeweler living in Paris claimed he had seen his friend Rokhumovskii make the tiara in Odessa.[10] Rokhumovskii was loath to enter into the fray, but when other jewelers began saying they had made it, he agreed to set the record straight.

Thus, for the first time in his life, Rokhumovskii left Odessa for Paris. On April 5, 1903, he arrived at the Louvre and, before an astonished panel of French specialists, curators and scholars, and a horde of reporters, re-created with the tools of his trade a portion of the tiara before their very own eyes. The international press devoured him. This reclusive goldsmith from Belarus had duped the Louvre! That same year he was awarded a gold medal at the Salon Exhibition of Decorative Arts for a gold skeleton (see page 339), and a miniature of the tiara. France, however, felt affronted by this blow to the reputation of her distinguished experts. So she hid the tiara from view (it's now at the Musée des Arts Décoratifs).[11] When Rokhumovskii returned to Odessa, he finally received the title of master jeweler and set up shop at 36 Uspenskaia but could not make ends meet. The goldsmith returned to Paris with his sons in 1910 and worked as a restorer at the Louvre. Evidently, there were no hard feelings. He died, some say in poverty, in 1934, but his gravestone indicated he was a happy man.[12]

NOTES

1. According to his memoirs, Rokhumovskii helped a colleague make a miniature gold skeleton, now in the Museum of Historical Treasures in Ukraine, but felt he could do better, and did. Sotheby's footnote, New York, *A Treasured Legacy: The Michael and Judy Steinhardt Judaica Collection*, April 29, 2013, lot 291.

2. Fellow jewelers were envious of his talent. Some did their best to prevent him from becoming a master jeweler, since they preferred to put their own hallmarks on his work. Ivanov, *Gold and Silversmiths in Russia*, 19.

3. Ivanov, *Gold and Silversmiths in Russia*, 17.

4. Ibid., 18.

5. Mark Jones, Paul T. Craddock, and Nicholas Barker, eds., *Fake? The Art of Deception* (Berkeley: University of California Press, 1990), 166. Sometimes the brothers would instruct jewelers to include fragments of original gold treasures to enhance its "authenticity."

6. Ivanov, *Gold and Silversmiths in Russia*, 23.

7. Jones et al., *Fake?*, 33.

8. Ivanov, *Gold and Silversmiths in Russia*, 26.

9. Sotheby's, New York, *A Treasured Legacy: The Michael and Judy Steinhardt Judaica Collection*, April 29, 2013, lot 291.

10. Jones et al., *Fake?*, 33.

11. The tiara was exhibited in the Israel Museum in Jerusalem in 1997 as the focus of its exhibition *The Secret of the Golden Tiara: Works by Israel Rouchomovsky*.

12. Ivanov, *Gold and Silversmiths in Russia*, 27. The tombstone read in part, "I loved my work, my wife, and my home / Even after my death my spirit will prevail / As the work of my hands that I have left behind." Sotheby's, *A Treasured Legacy*, April 29, 2013. Catalogue note from the jeweler's memoirs.

Market

24

Market

EXHIBITIONS IN RUSSIA AND ABROAD

Exhibitions in Russia

National exhibitions were held in Russia beginning in 1829 as a way for jewelers, silversmiths and manufacturers to advertise their businesses to the wider public. Some also chose to market their companies in the print media, such as *Sankt-Peterburgskia vedomosti* (the St. Petersburg News), *Severnaia pchela* (the Northern Bee) and *Illiustratsiia* (Illustration).[1] Already in 1809, G. von Reimers published his *Address and Guidebook*, which would be followed by a number of directories during the 19th century.[2] The most comprehensive, *Ves Petersburg* (All Petersburg), was issued annually from 1902 to 1914.[3] Today these are useful guides for finding information about types of goods sold and the location of businesses during a certain period of time, since many firms changed addresses over the years.

But for many merchants the big break came by securing a stand in the All-Russian Industrial Exhibitions in Moscow and St. Petersburg. Organized by the Russian state to boost national industry, these became a regular feature of the bustling jewelry trade after 1831 and were held every two years in either city, as well as in Warsaw, and the last one took place in 1896, in Nizhnii Novgorod.

In the St. Petersburg All-Russian exhibition of 1839, renowned jewelers showed their polished or glittering wares to mostly positive acclaim. Exhibitors included Ignatii Sazikov, Otto Koenig and Johann Wilhelm Keibel, who needed no introduction. Keibel (1788–1862) had restored the coronation crown for Tsar Nicholas I and taught Gustav Fabergé (Carl's father) the trade, allowing him to open shop in 1842. Yet, it was a little-known Vologda silversmith, Sakerton Skripitsyn, who not only won gold in this show but gained the empire's most illustrious client, Tsar Nicholas I, for his nielloed table service with views of Vologda and St. Petersburg.

Throughout the 19th century, Pan-Slavic expositions continued to attract stellar exhibitors of international renown, such as Bolin and Sazikov, as they solidified their client base at home and brought more-well-heeled customers to their shopfronts, many from the highest aristocratic circles. Bolin's shop at 10 Bolshaia Morskaia Street, for example, was located only 100 steps from Palace Square, close to the Winter Palace, home of the imperial family, and adjacent to the sumptuous palace of enormously wealthy Grand Duke Vladimir Aleksandrovich and Maria Pavlovna, among Russia's most prolific fine jewelry and decorative arts buyers.

Long before Fabergé drew notice in Paris in 1900, international exhibitions in several capitals had a Russian presence. The Ministry of Finance chose applicants carefully, selecting the finest to represent Russia . . . Once chosen, a handful of intrepid Russian goldsmiths and artists agreed to cross Europe's borders and brave the English Channel and even the Atlantic Ocean to exhibit their newest creations.

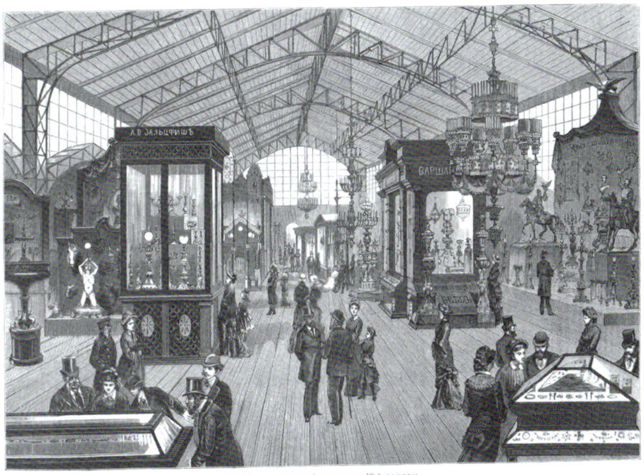

Общій видъ главной галлереи VI-й группы

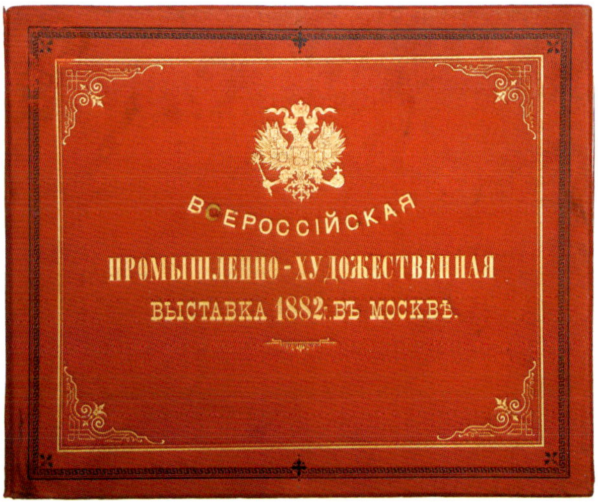

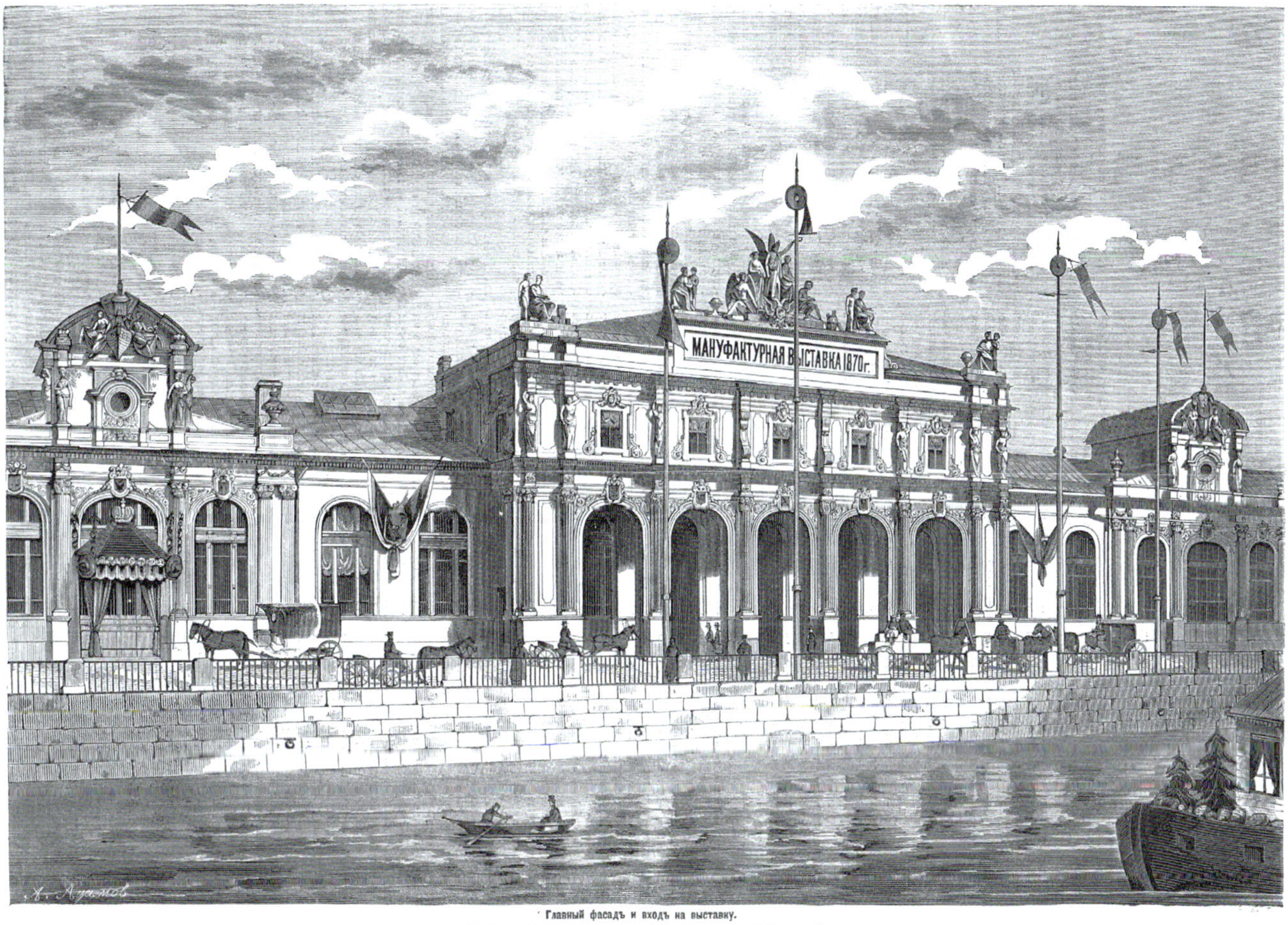

Главный фасадъ и входъ на выставку.
(Съ фотогр. Фелиша, рисов. на дер. А. О. Адамовъ, грав. Ф. Герасимовъ).

Left & right:
Visitors admire the offerings at the 1882 All-Russia Industry and Art Exhibition in Moscow. Exhibition catalogue illustration. *Right*, the cover of a photo album of the exposition.

Bottom:
The facade of the All-Russian Industrial Exhibition of 1870, which took place in St. Petersburg, just north of the Mikhailovskii Palace on the Fontanka River. *Source: "Manufakturnaia vistavka" supplement to* Vsemirnaia illiustratsiia *1–2 (1870): 4*

St. Petersburg 1870

The All-Russian Industrial Exhibition of 1870 took place in the salt storehouses (Solianoi District in St. Petersburg), just north of the Mikhailovskii Palace on the Fontanka River. Along these banks, Peter the Great would conduct naval drills every Sunday at the turn of the 18th century. This building, which still stands, is located near the baroque Church of St. Panteleimon the Healer and the Stieglitz Museum of Decorative and Applied Arts.

The 1870 St. Petersburg exhibition drew top silversmiths and jewelers from around the empire. In total, 17 silver masters displayed their wares: six from St. Petersburg, five from Moscow, five from the Caucasus and one from Warsaw. Sazikov, who had won many accolades some 20 years earlier at the London Great Exhibition in 1851, continued to do so here, while the Muscovite Pavel Ovchinnikov attracted high praise for the originality of his Russian designs and trompe l'oeil silver, and less so for designs based on foreign models. All three catalogue illustrations of silver are Ovchinnikov works, including one of a lady's *nécéssaire* in the form of a silver cat perched on a pillow, playing with a ball of yarn. It is not clear whether the illustrations were paid for by the dealers or chosen by the jury panel.

Twelve of the empire's finest goldsmiths participated in 1870. Winning first prize, Russia's most famous, Carl Edvard Bolin of St. Petersburg, dazzled visitors with the beauty, technical perfection and price of a diadem simulating leaves of ivy in diamonds, while young Ivan Chichelev, the Moscow-based jeweler to King Victor Emanuel of Italy, fresh from a successful stint at the Paris Universal Exhibition of 1867, took second. He and compatriot Fedor Fulda, court jeweler to Tsar Alexander II, garnered acclaim for intricate naturalistic designs, which were still fashionable in Russia, with two jeweled headdresses styled as lilac leaves and a gem-set butterfly ensemble, respectively. The jury also praised Friedrich Köchli.

Moscow 1882

Superstars Ovchinnikov, Sazikov and Bolin continued to lead the pack in Moscow at the Artistic Industrial Exhibition of 1882. Ovchinnikov displayed a stunning silver centerpiece of a triumphant medieval warrior on horseback, designed by Evgenii Lanceray père, that commemorated the Liberation of the Slavs, a reference to the Russo-Turkish War of 1877–78. Sazikov unveiled a monumental cistern in the European rococo taste, designed by the German-born August Karlovich Spiess (see page 306), while Bolin sold to Grand Duke Vladimir Aleksandrovich a magnificent pearl drop and diamond fringe tiara, similar in style to another one Bolin had created for him for his wedding in 1874 to his bride, Duchess Marie of Mecklenburg-Schwerin. Unlike the latter, which today forms part of the British crown jewels, the one purchased in 1882 resold at auction in 1978 at Sotheby's and was then dismantled. Carl Fabergé also exhibited at this show but was not yet well known. It was here, however, that he first met Tsar Alexander III, when he sold the monarch a simple pair of gold cicada cuff links in the ancient style. This small sale would lead to a series of magnificent egg creations three years later and catapult the European-trained goldsmith to international fame (see "Fabergé in Perspective").

Other, smaller Russian exhibitions were held both in the capital and Moscow, including one ordered by Alexander III in 1883 to display his private collections of Russian porcelain and silver in the Winter Palace, and two others of imperial decorative arts in 1901 and 1904.[4] The Stroganov Central School for Technical Drawing organized shows of 17th- and 18th-century Russian silver for their students, many of whom would go on to work for Moscow jewelers, while the Stieglitz School of Design played a similar role in St. Petersburg.

Expositions Abroad

London

Long before Fabergé drew notice in Paris in 1900, international exhibitions in several capitals had a Russian presence. The Ministry of Finance chose applicants carefully, selecting the finest to represent Russia to cast a favorable light on its artistic and industrial achievements. Beginning in 1862, for example, only the paintings of prize-winning artists from the Academy of Arts were eligible.[5] Once chosen, a handful of intrepid Russian goldsmiths and artists agreed to cross Europe's borders and brave the English Channel and even the Atlantic Ocean to exhibit their newest creations. Sometimes lasting over 200 days, this was a major undertaking that often required months of preparation. Eager to make a brilliant impression on the world, the organizing committee may have had to exert extra pressure on its selected dealers to accept the challenge. For the first and largest exposition, the Great Exhibition of the Works of Industry of all Nations of 1851 in London (also known as the Crystal Palace Exhibition), several of Russia's most renowned artisans heeded the call, as did smaller enterprises ready for their big break.

To westerners, Russia was a great unknown. Fascinated by the land of the tsars, visitors flocked to have a look at its exotic and

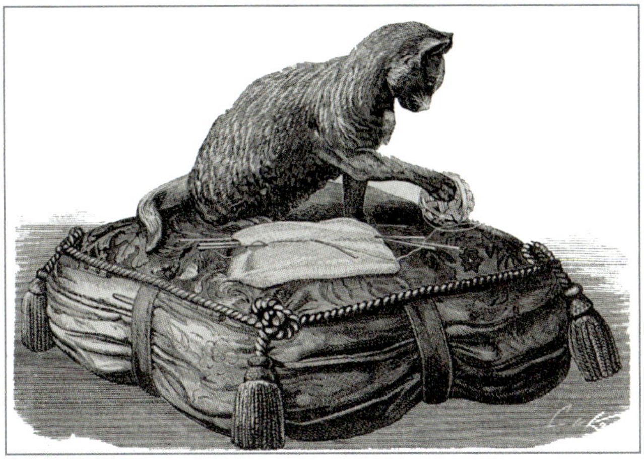

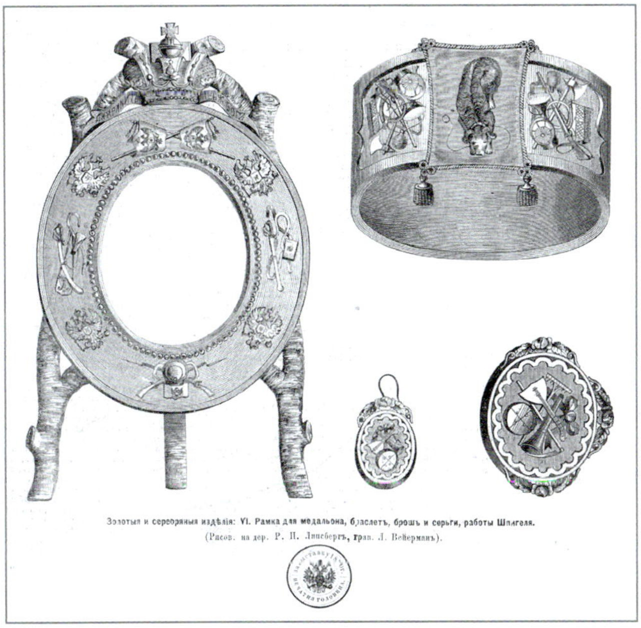

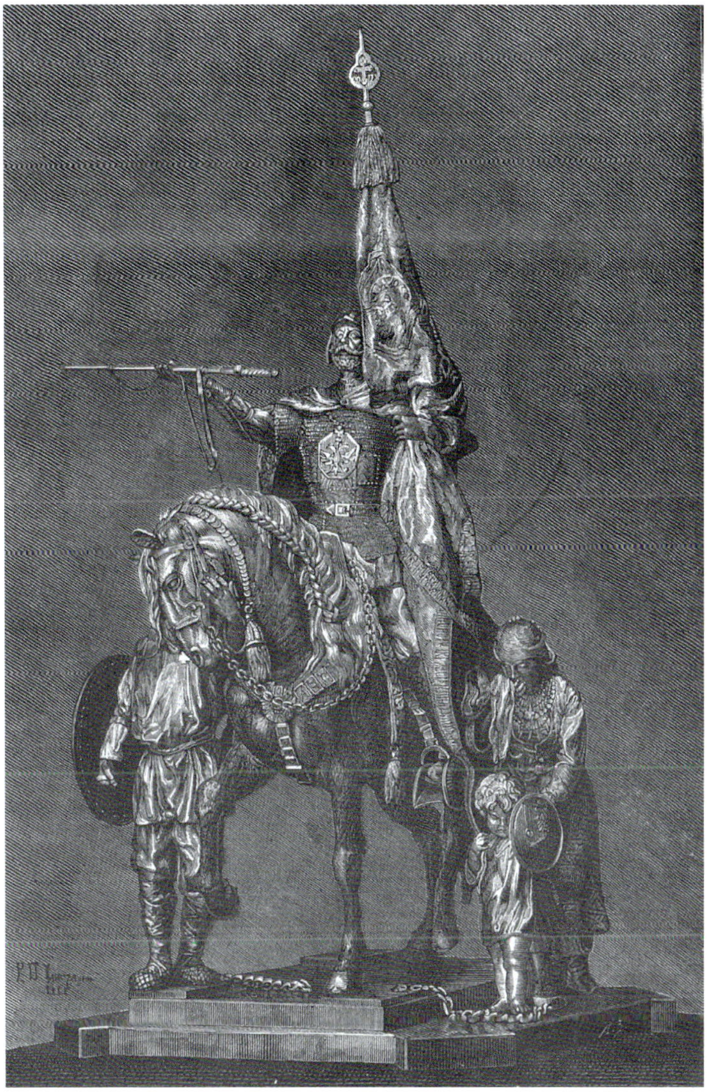

Top left:
Ovchinnikov displayed this trompe l'oeil silver box of a cat at the 1870 exhibition. *Source: "Manufakturnaia vistavka" supplement to* Vsemirnaia illiustratsiia *76 (1870): 12*

Bottom left:
The exhibition also featured a suite of gold jewels and picture frame on birchbark legs by Petersburg goldsmith Annette Spiegel. *Source: "Manufakturnaia vistavka" supplement to* Vsemirnaia illiustratsiia *13–14 (1870): 56*

Right:
This monumental Ovchinnikov figural centerpiece highlighted the Russian silver section and the 1882 exhibition. *Source: "Khudozhestvenno-Promyshlennaia Vistavka" supplement to* Vsemirnaia illiustratsiia *8 (1882)*

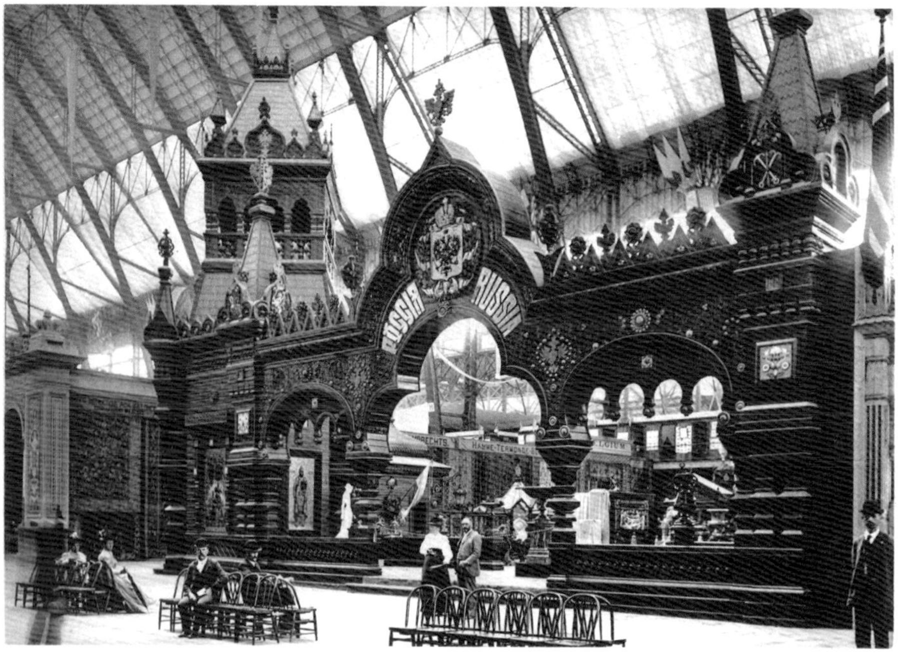

The Russian pavilion at the Chicago World's Fair in 1893. Marshak and Grachev sold silver there, as did the Moscow enamelers Klingert and show veteran Ovchinnikov. This may explain why so many of their wares have surfaced on the market in America. *Source: Wikimedia Commons*

often-spectacular displays.[6] Queen Victoria herself headed straight there upon arrival and remarked on its "very fine . . . vases in malachite, specimens of plate and some beautifully tasteful and very lightly-set jewellery."[7] Except for the raw materials, the Russian section of some 380 participants impressed both press and public. Visitors admired monumental urns by the Prince Demidov Lapidary Works and Imperial Stonecutting Factories, grand both in scale and detail, as well as delicate "bouquet of diamonds of singular beauty" by the St. Petersburg jewelers Kämmerer and Seftigen. Bolin's bryony wreath diadem was deemed "exceedingly beautiful." The jury proclaimed Russia's glittering gems "of great splendour and worth,"[8] and best appreciated for their brilliance under the sun at high noon.[9]

Massive decorative objects carried the day by evoking the sumptuous palaces of the Romanovs. Towering malachite, jasper, or porcelain vases on enormous pedestals extended twice the height of viewers, as did a spectacular 14-foot brass candelabrum. A carved gate and "superb suite of furniture in malachite and or-molu" attracted the most interest, while imposing figures of Russian warriors lent the display a distinct Slavic pre-Petrine exoticism.[10] Silver by Sazikov was no less impressive. Noted for its exquisite hand-chased creations in the neo-Byzantine style, these included impressive historical centerpieces, goblets, tankards, bowls and a bell, 11 of which were chosen for illustrations in the official catalogue.

Paris

Eager to emulate London, in 1855 Paris held its first international exhibition, followed by others in 1867, 1878, 1889 and 1900. Russian participation was strong in all of them, with exhibitors ranging in number from 831 in 1889 to 3,179 in 1900.[11] French reviews were for the most part favorable, particularly with regard to Russian silver mastery and originality of design. In *L'Exposition universelle de 1867 illustrée*, on the 1867 fair, a Parisian reviewer, Prosper Poiterin, discusses tongue in cheek the relative merits of the two Moscow jewelers Chichelev and Fulda, and recounts the convoluted misadventures of a pin lost in a flowerpot, then recovered by its owner, Fulda, upon a tardy arrival to the show. Poiterin compliments Chichelev for winning a silver medal for fine work on unspecified jewels, while suggesting the jeweller be awarded one of lead for his butterfly pin, which he deemed of heavy design. *Quelle surprise* should that one ever "fly" out of the showcase![12] Undaunted, Chichelev went on to exhibit in Vienna in 1873, winning praise for his spectacular gem-set tiara. Sazikov and Ovchinnikov won gold medals in Paris in 1867, while Ivan Khlebnikov and Adler won silver. It must be noted that medals were widely distributed, with a little over half of the exhibitors receiving one in 1889. But to all businesses, this international prize—whose image dealers could display on their storefront, on their letterhead and in advertising—bestowed many benefits, including an increase in sales and a higher company profile.

The Exposition Universelle of 1900, celebrating a century of achievement in Paris, featured the firms of Ovchinnikov and Alekseev from Moscow; Grachev, Bock, Köchli, Dietwald and

Fabergé from St. Petersburg; Marshak from Kiev; and the silversmith M. Yusupov from the Caucasus. Both Friedrich Köchli and Carl Fabergé served as members of the jury. It was here that Fabergé, displaying the latest series of imperial eggs and the miniature imperial regalia by Holmström, attracted widespread acclaim that would mark the beginning of his spectacular rise to fame and fortune.

The United States

The two most important 19th-century shows in America for Russia were the 1876 Centennial International Exposition of Philadelphia and the World's Columbian Exposition in Chicago of 1893. After Britain and the United States, Russia had the largest exhibit in Philadelphia. Praised as "uncommonly elegant . . . the most attractive portion of the display," Russian jewelry and silver drew the highest praise. In silver, Sazikov and Ovchinnikov once again triumphed, for "the Adoration of the Magi," a massive, "beautifully finished" sculptural centerpiece, and a magnificent enameled and gilded silver punch bowl set, respectively, among many other articles of distinction.[13] Seventeen years later, Russia sent over 1,000 exhibitors to the Chicago World's Fair, but only about one-tenth represented fine and decorative arts, including seasoned and established silversmiths Mikhail Grachev of St. Petersburg, Iosif Marshak of Kiev and Gustav Klingert and Ovchinnikov of Moscow. The St. Petersburg court jeweler Carl Hahn, celebrated for his stunning diamond creations for Alexander III and Nicholas II, appeared abroad for the first time, with gold cigarette cases, cups and various articles of gold and enamel, joining fellow St. Petersburg gem dealer Sumin, who displayed cut and uncut precious stones.

From the Revolution to World War II

In 1928 Alexander Polovtsov organized the first exhibition of Russian art held abroad, in Brussels, which was followed by a show of Russian porcelain at Sèvres in France that included over 600 tsarist items from imperial and private factories. In 1933 Armand Hammer exhibited his wares in "A Century of Progress International Exposition" in Chicago, a world's fair celebrating that city's centennial. However, the largest and most important show in the West was the 1935 Exhibition of Russian Art in London, also curated by Polovtsov. It attracted keen interest from a public that knew even less about the field than their predecessors in the 19th century, since the Soviets had led a campaign of denial of the Romanov legacy and the riches long associated with that era.[14] Designed by Mstislav Dobuzhinskii, famous for *Ballet Russe* stage sets, one imagines the show featured stunning, colorful backdrops bringing to life in each room glorious displays of Russian icons, textiles, paintings, porcelain and ballet designs, as well as enamels, silver and jewelry.

Published only 18 years after the Russian Revolution, the catalogue provides valuable information about which treasures survived and who still (or now) owned them. Despite short descriptions and few images, the high quality of the offerings can be gleaned from the illustrious owners whose names are listed under many entries. Lenders included Queen Mary, the King of Sweden, the Queens of Spain and Romania, the Princess Royal, Grand Duchess Xenia, Zinaida Yusupov, the Galitzines and the Gagarins, among other famous members of the British, French and Russian aristocracy.

It would be difficult today to find these items to exhibit. Over half of the 84 silver entries, including kovshs, bratinas, wine tasters, beakers, plates, spoons, goblets and bowls, dated back to the 17th century, while most of the enamels were from the 18th century and are now exceedingly rare. The jewelry section of 171 displays consisted largely of Fabergé objects and carved animals (29 elephants, 5 imperial eggs). Other rare treasures include the Order of the White Eagle by Johann Wilhelm Keibel, a Catherine the Great gold gem-encrusted chalice by Buch (now at Hillwood Museum) and numerous gold medals and coins dating from the era of Peter the Great. Already then, lavish jewels by Russia's finest goldsmiths seemed dwarfed by Fabergé and occupied only a single case. To dazzle the viewers, the display featured Princess Zinaida Yusupov's historic Azra black pearl, which Catherine the Great had given to Potemkin in 1783, and a turquoise-and-diamond necklace and pendant presented by the same empress to the Walpole family, lent by the Countess of Marlborough.

NOTES

1. Larissa Zavadskaya, "Gold and Silver in St. Petersburg 1830–50," in Habsburg, *Fabergé: Imperial Craftsman*, 49.

2. G. von Reimers, *Adresnaia i spravochnaia kniga na rus., nem., i frants. iazykakh* (St. Petersburg, 1809).

3. Renamed *Ves' Petrograd* from 1914 to 1925.

4. Anne Odom, *Russian Silver in America* (Washington, DC: Hillwood Museum and Gardens Foundation, 2011), 178–79.

5. Anna Zavyalova, "Russian Fine Arts Section at the World's Columbian Exposition 1893: Notes on Organization and Reception," *MDCCC 1800* 6 (2017): 119–30, http://edizionicafoscari.unive.it/media/pdf/article/mdc-cc-1800/2017/1numero-monografico/art-10.14277-2280-8841-MDCCC-6-17-9.pdf.

6. According to Scott Ruby, the empire "conjured up images of Barbaric people living in arctic cold and ruled by tyrannical despots—a view established by English travel accounts of the 16th century." Ruby, "Crystal Palace Exhibition," 87.

7. Victoria, Queen of England, "The Queen's Exhibition Journal," in C. R. Fay, *Palace of Industry, 1851: A Study of the Great Exhibition and Its Fruits* (Cambridge, UK: Cambridge University Press, 1951), 59.

8. "Russia," in Great Britain, Commissioners for the Exhibition of 1851, *Official Descriptive and Illustrated Catalogue of the Great Exhibition of the Works of Industry of All Nations*, part 5:1361.

9. James Tennant, "On Gems and Precious Stones," in *Lectures on the Results of the Great Exhibition of 1851: Delivered before the Society of Arts, Manufactures and Commerce* (London: David Bogue, 1853), 334; and Judy Rudoe, "Jewellery at the Great Exhibition," *American Society of Jewelry Historians Newsletter* 20 (May 2003): 14.

10. "Russia," in *Official Descriptive and Illustrated Catalogue*, 1361.

11. Brigitte Schroeder-Gudehus and Anne Rasmussen, *Les Fastes du Progrès: Le Guide des Expositions Universelles, 1851–1992* (Paris: Flammarion, 1992), 114, 134.

12. Prosper Poiterin, "Un papillon perdu dans les fleurs," *L'Exposition universelle de 1867 illustré 29* (1867): 450.

13. "Exhibit of the Russian Empire," in *Centennial Exposition Described and Illustrated*, ed. J. S. Ingram (Philadelphia: Hubbard Bros., 1876), 470–76.

14. In her book *A Concise History of Russian Art*, Tamara Talbot-Rice helped shed light on this obscure world of fabled imperial possessions. Various museum experts and dealers contributed chapters about their chosen fields, including Alexandre Benois, the artist and former picture gallery curator of the Hermitage, and Parisian dealers Alexander Popoff and Léon Grinberg, on 18th-century art, porcelain, and enamels, respectively.

25

Market

THE TRADE: AN OVERVIEW

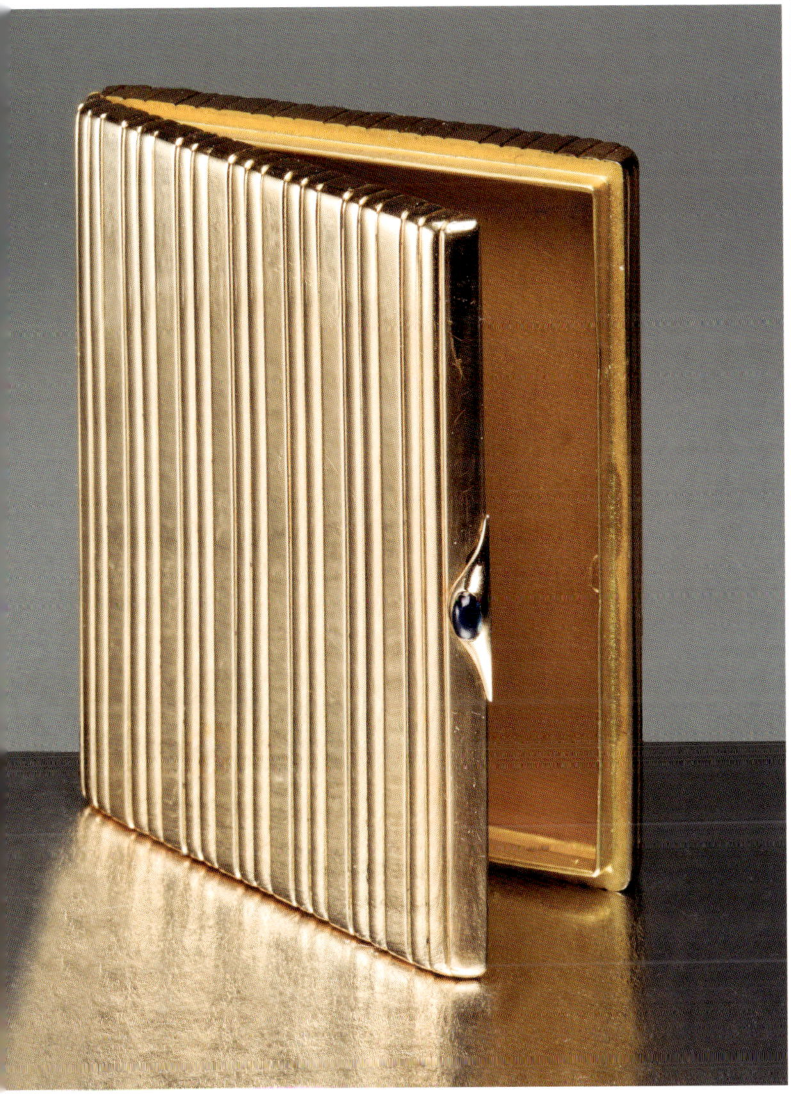

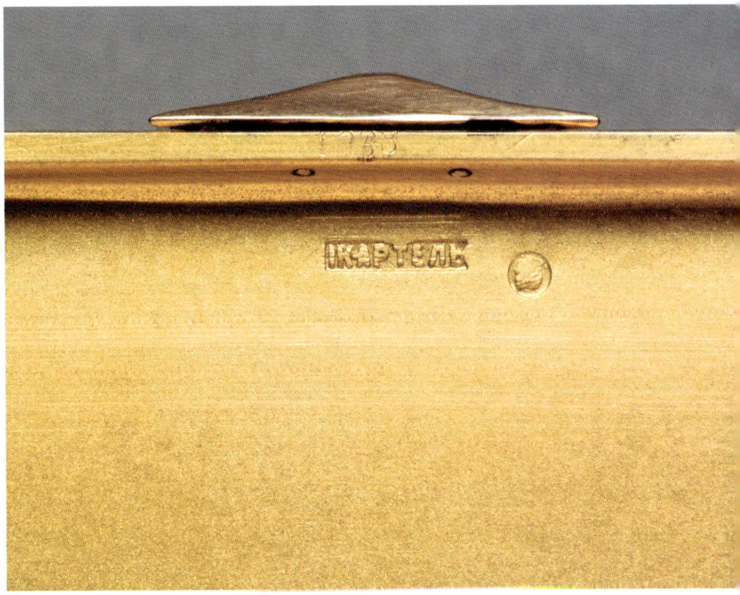

A reeded rose-gold cigarette case made in the 1st Kiev Artel, stamped with the maker's mark in Cyrillic, and the kokoshnik (Russian headdress) for Kiev, 1908–17. This workshop produced items for the House of Fabergé in Kiev and was located at the same address. *Marie Betteley, photo by Noel Allum*

The Russian art market emerged in the West after the revolution and drew its share of interesting merchants. Stories of gem and Fabergé tradesmen across generations can be as intriguing as those of the masters themselves. As in all commerce, family ties often prevailed. Many dealers, both in Europe and America in the 20th century, like the jewelers whose wares they plied, tended to be related to one another or otherwise had ties to an established firm.

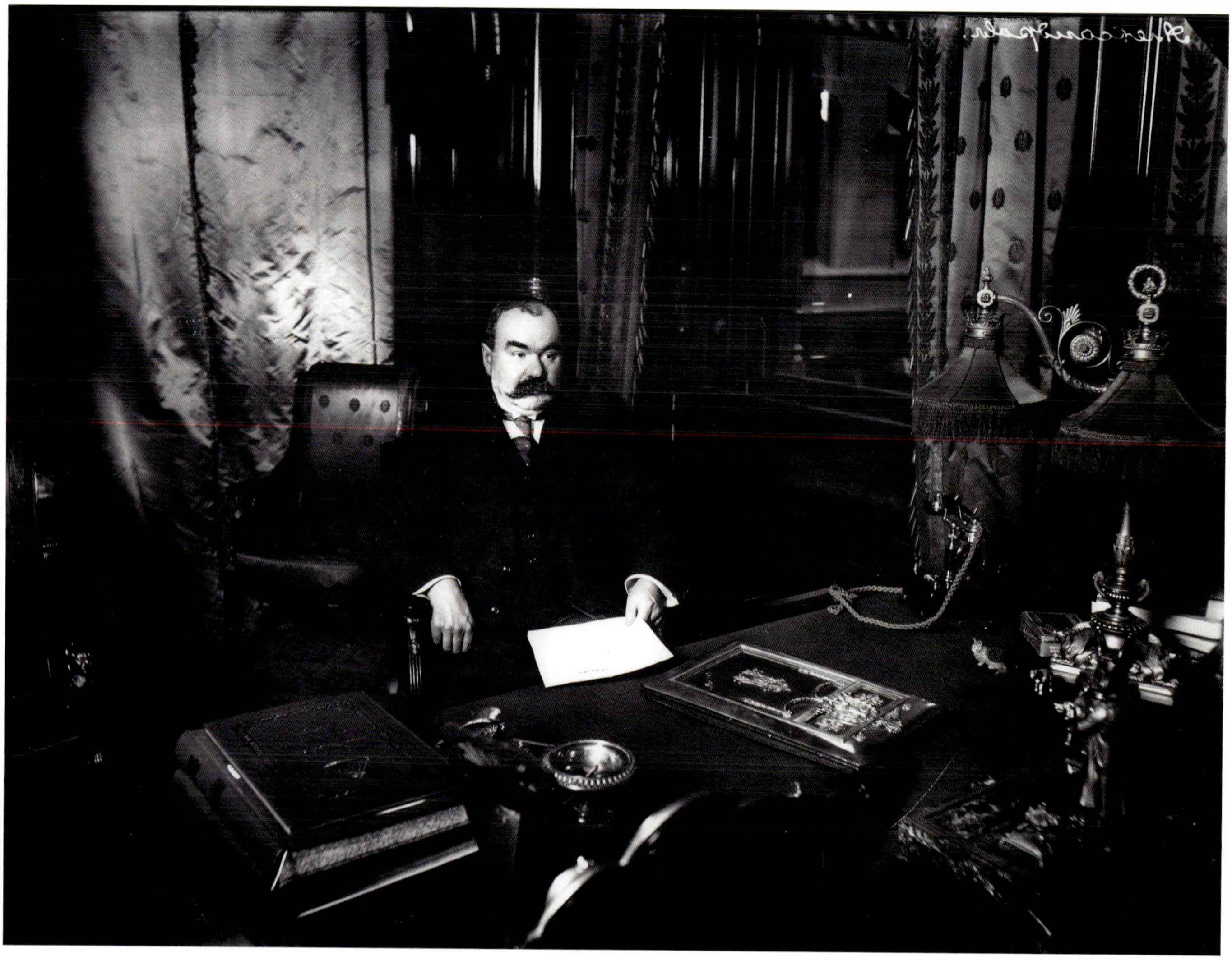

Alexander Fernandovich Kelch at his desk in his house on Sergeevskaia Street in St. Petersburg in 1913. Kelch provided raw materials and supplies to all the jewelers in town. *Courtesy of Central State Archive of Film and Photographs in St. Petersburg*

Following page
Interior of Tiffany & Co., Union Square store showing Russian silver goods (1896). Photograph Collection. *Copyright of Tiffany & Co. Archives, 2019.*

One well-known example of the latter was an exiled Hungarian soccer player, Alexander Schaffer, who had been a buyer for the Paris-based house of A la Vieille Russie. Founded by Iakov Zolotnitskii in Kiev in 1852, the firm reopened in Paris after the revolution, where it operated until the Second World War.

Schaffer, who owned the Schaffer Collection of Russian Imperial Treasures in Rockefeller Center, had worked with Zolotnitskii and Grinberg. As war clouds gathered over Europe, he sponsored their immigration to the United States, and they closed their shop in Paris. When Schaeffer moved his shop to Fifth Avenue in 1941, he also took over the name of A la Vielle Russie.[1]

I first encountered Zolotnitskii's name and that of his nephew, Léon Grinberg, in the 1980s, when researching the Kelch Fabergé eggs. In 1920, newly ensconced in Paris, the Kievan jeweler purchased six large Fabergé eggs, apparently from another Parisian jeweler for $3,300, and resold them for triple to an American buyer seven years later.[2] Did it really take that long to sell them? In fact, Fabergé in 1927 was out of fashion, and rumor has it the eggs were sold "under the table."

After decades in California, four of the eggs resurfaced at Christie's in the late 1980s when I headed its Russian department: the Pine Cone Egg of 1900, the Apple Blossom Egg of 1901, the Bonbonnière Egg of 1903 and the Nobel Ice Egg. All these Fabergé creations, except the last, were made for the gold-mining magnate Alexander Kelch, whose wife, Barbara, from 1898 to 1904 obtained eggs as lavish as those made for the tsar, presumably for her mansion on 28 Sergeevskaia (now Chaikovskii) Street in St. Petersburg. Fabergé also sold her an enormous silver table service (now lost), which cost far more than an egg: 125,000 rubles.[3] In a cruel twist of fate, Alexander died penniless in Siberia, while Barbara, having moved to the City of Light after the revolution, continued to live in splendor and purchase enormous quantities of precious gems from Frédéric Boucheron, founder of the legendary jewelry house on Place Vendôme. Negotiating like a shrewd dealer, she had the jeweler refashion her parures on over 50 occasions into new styles set with rubies, diamonds, sapphires, emeralds and pearls.[4] One wonders what led Barbara to sell her eggs in Paris for so little. Perhaps to erase the memory of her husband, to whom she was never close? Grinberg also knew Alexander Fabergé (Carl's son), who identified the eggs as belonging to Kelch in 1922. Still active in the trade, the former helped catalogue the 1935 Exhibition of Russian Art in London and provided a chapter on metal work and enamels in its catalogue.

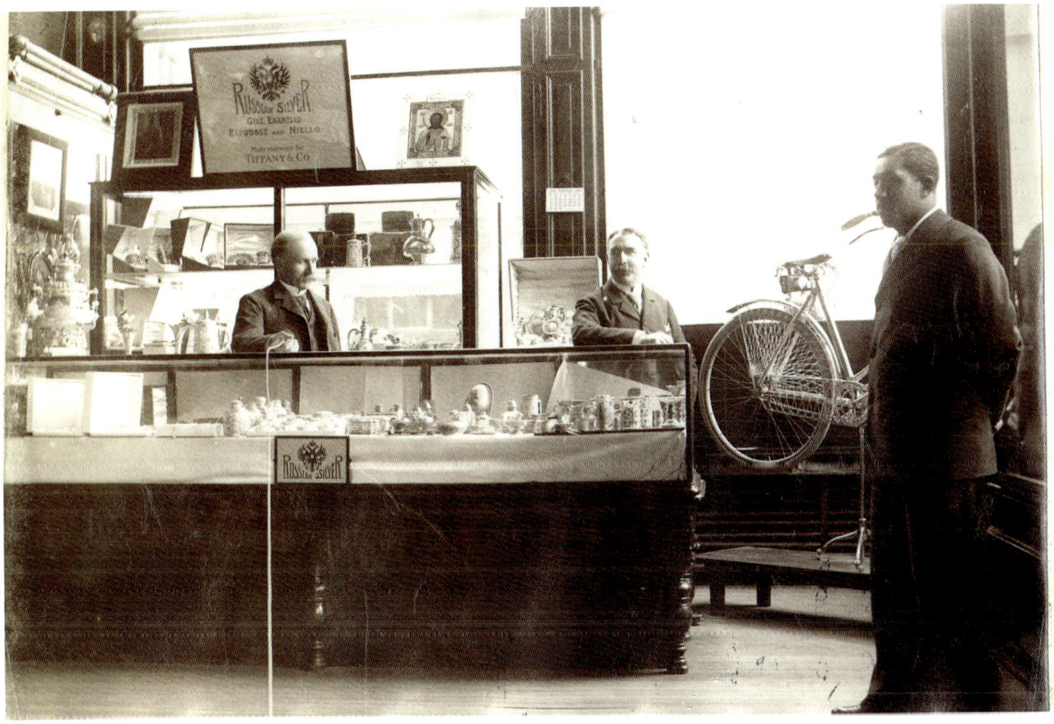

The first owner of Wartski, the London-based dealer of Fabergé, also hailed from Ukraine. Its founder, Morris Wartski, was from Galicia, in southwestern Ukraine. Having moved to Great Britain, he first started selling wares in Bangor, Wales, in 1865. His son-in-law, Emmanuel Snowman, opened the London branch in 1911.

Alexander A. Polovtsov (1867–1944) was another prominent dealer of Russian art in Europe and America. A diplomat and museum curator before the revolution, Polovtsov played an important role in forming the collection of Henry Walters (1848–1931), founder of the Walters Art Museum. The son-in-law of Baron Alexander von Stieglitz, and former curator of the Stieglitz Museum in St. Petersburg, Polovtsov helped save Pavlovsk, an 18th-century Russian imperial residence Catherine the Great had built for her son, Grand Duke Paul, after the revolution and before moving to Paris. Coming from a wealthy and artistic background, he was well respected in the art world. Curiously, few bills of sales exist from his numerous transactions with Walters. Did they conduct business on a handshake? We may never know. However, an exhibition catalogue from the Walters, *Fabergé and the Russian Crafts Tradition: An Empire's Legacy*, provides an excellent account of his prominent role in the Russian art market and his dealings with the American collector.[5]

Some Western dealers had no family ties to Russia but caught the buying bug when living there or visiting it frequently. Ralph Sylvester Bartlett (1868–1960), a well-traveled lawyer from Boston, is a perfect example. Bartlett began collecting after trips to Russia in 1911 and 1912. He opened a shop called "Old Russia" on Arlington Street in 1928 and ran it until 1939, specializing in 18th-century Russian silver and liturgical objects, of which we see little today. In 1958 Bartlett bequeathed the entire collection to his alma mater Dartmouth College's Hood Museum. Marjorie Merriweather Post purchased an early Empress Anna teapot when the college sold part of the Bartlett collection in 1963.[6]

Tiffany & Company played a major role in bringing Russian silver and enamels to the United States. The firm began trading in Russian objects after hiring Henry W. Hiller (1838–1926), a former Siberian-based US consul under President Lincoln, to buy goods in Russia, where he lived for 25 years. That same year, Tsar Alexander III bestowed the highly coveted Russian imperial warrant upon the American firm, adding to its rich

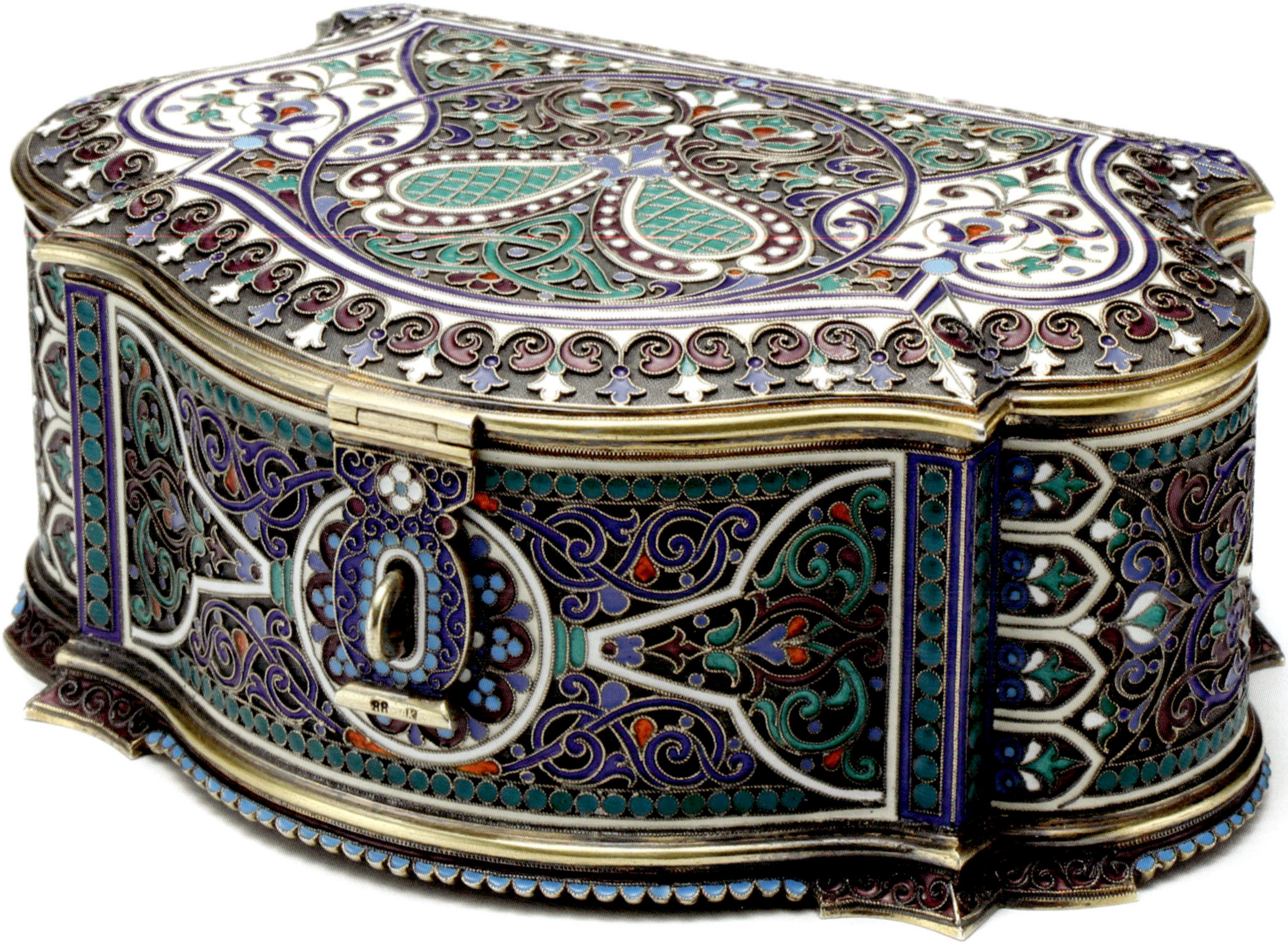

A Russian enamel box by Antip Kuzmichev, retailed by Tiffany & Co.
Copyright of Tiffany & Co. Archives, 2019

Opposite:
Scene of a Russian viewing at Christie's New York.

client roster of crowned heads of Europe. In Paris, the wealthy Grand Duchess Maria Pavlovna also patronized Tiffany, along with Alexis Aleksandrovich, the tsar's brother, although it seems likely the imperial family bought non-Russian items from the American retailer. Around 1885, Tiffanys opened a Russian shop on Union Square in New York, which operated into the 1900s. The store sold numerous enamels and silver and nielloed wares, as well as bronzes and porcelain. Today, Russian enamels in the Tiffany & Company Archives are mostly by Antip Kuzmichev and carry the stamp *Made for Tiffany & Co.*, along with the usual prerevolutionary Moscow hallmarks.[7]

In the 1930s, department stores including Marshall Fields in Chicago and Lord and Taylor in New York sold Russian prerevolutionary wares. The dealer Armand Hammer, acting as broker to the Soviets, supplied these venues with scores of Russian icons, eggs, jewels and Romanov memorabilia over several years, all accompanied by certificates of authenticity, many with fanciful provenances. In 1928, the trade commissar Anastas Mikoyan had asked Hammer to act as an agent to sell Russian works of art abroad, although the dealer claimed it was his own private collection. Americans loved Romanov history, and some heiresses such as India Early Minshall and Marjorie Merriweather Post became avid clients. When the Cleveland Museum of Art deaccessioned India Early Minshall's collection of Russian memorabilia in 1988, many Hammer items still had the original certificates, adding interest to the pieces for future buyers. A controversial figure, it is said that before 1921 Armand Hammer lived in the former Fabergé Moscow shop for four months at a cost of $12 a month and took the Fabergé punches to hallmark Russian silver and even new silver items from Paris.[8]

BAPTISM BY FIRE

"Go downstairs and have a look," my boss Alice told me on my first day in the Russian department at Christie's. Someone had brought in a "Fabergé" item and was waiting for an appraisal at the front counter. Would it pass muster? I knew about Fabergé from living at Hillwood Museum. But fresh out of university, the prospect of wading into unchartered waters of the turbulent Russian market hold little appeal.

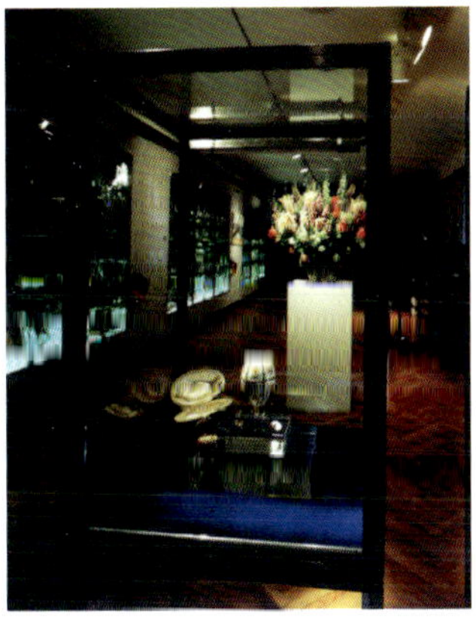

How would I evaluate this piece on the spot?, I wondered in a panic. And in front of the owners, no less. I don't remember what I saw or said that first day but will never forget the thrill of anticipation as I ran down those stairs. Will it be a masterpiece or a monster? I knew one thing: auction was then and still is the chosen testing ground for forgers all over the world and in all art fields, especially with Fabergé. Daily, hapless Russian specialists are thrown into the fray of fakes amid fabulous finds. I was about to join them.

My suspicions were quickly confirmed. With Fabergé, the most famous goldsmith in the world, fakes or "fauxbergés" abound. I learned to treat each item and its story with doubt, and to trust my first instinct. If it looked strange on the whole, I stayed away. If it seemed right, and the marks looked good, there was a second layer of questioning: Had the item been tinkered with at some point, perhaps been re-enameled, or was it "as right as rain"? Were there add-ons, such as a Romanov crown, the "tsar's" initials, or his miniature portrait? Was the hardstone original, or the gems themselves? The only objects above suspicion would be those in original collections formed during Fabergé's tenure (1885–1917). An original fitted box is always nice, especially when the exterior follows the contours of the objects for which it was made, such as an egg-shaped or hatpin-shaped box. No one has managed to copy that kind of thing. However, the inside of original rectangular fitted Fabergé boxes is sometimes retooled to fit around whatever object or jewel someone will try to pass off as right.

Russian Auctions in the West

In 1927, the dealer Jacques Zolotnitskii sold six Kelch Fabergé eggs in Paris to an American collector for $10,750. Ten years after the Russian Revolution, the creations of the storied Fabergé firm languished in storerooms. You could barely give them away.

Then came the landmark Russian crown jewels sale in London on March 16 of that year. It was the jewelry sale of the century, and no other Russian auction has managed to duplicate the magnificence of the gems offered. After all, they were crème de la crème of Romanov treasures (see "The Fate of the Russian Crown Jewels"). Another outlet for Russian art was the Berlin auction house Rudolf Lepke, and other dealers there acting at individuals or syndicates.

It was the best time to *buy* Russian treasures and Fabergé. From a dealer's point of view, paradise prevailed. Although they had survived the revolution, a feat in itself, such goods were plentiful in the West, and still inexpensive. Alexander Schaffer bought many objets d'art, including, along with Armand Hammer, Fabergé imperial eggs. In those days, Russian items were considered "secondhand and outdated," which kept their prices low. Alexander's son Peter, co-owner of A la Vieille Russie, concurs that as dealers at the time, three main conditions all worked in their favor: quality, quantity and price.[8] Cane handles and other Fabergé objects, including miniature eggs, typically sold for less than $50.[9]

By 1936, Antikvariat and Torgsin, two Russian trading organizations, had closed down, as had the Soviet trade mission in Berlin three years earlier.[10] And while literally tons of silver faced the melting pot in that tumultuous time, from large-scale punch bowls to candelabra, commemorative trophies, processional icons, chargers and tea services and more, many Fabergé enameled and hardstone objects were spared. As unwanted items of small intrinsic value, they were easier to pocket.

If Fabergé eggs sold with difficulty in the West in the 1920s, Russian 18th-century silver fared even worse in the 1930s. Part of the problem was ignorance. Russian decorative arts were little known, and the market for it was nonexistent thanks in part to a concentrated push by the Soviets to obliterate it. In 1923, Moisei Lazerson, head of Gokhran, wrote that the Russian silver market had "as good as disappeared, while the foreign market had no knowledge of, showed no interest in, Russian silver."[11]

One of the earliest specialized Fabergé sales was held at Christie's London in 1934. The First Hen Egg of 1885 sold then for £85 ($430) and was not even illustrated in the catalogue, perhaps because of its simple design. However, the Resurrection Egg, which is now no longer considered imperial, was, and it sold for £110 to a private buyer. Both are now in the Fabergé museum owned by the Link of Times Foundation in St. Petersburg, Russia.[12] During the Second World War, Christie's on King Street in London was bombed, and auctions ceased for a few years.

The 1950s marked an increase in Russian sales. A Christie's London catalogue from March 18, 1958, featured property belonging to the Duke of Windsor, among other notable vendors. Fairly typical of the format used at the time, out of 163 lots, only six were illustrated, and those in black and white. A year earlier at Sotheby and Co., Fabergé animal carvings belonging to the King of the Hellenes were paired with portrait miniatures and objects, a tendency that continues to this day. Fabergé hardstone figures attracted interest, even back then, a reflection of the early-20th-century Fabergé retail business in London, since many of the animal carvings are illustrated, perhaps also to please the royal client. Prices started at £10 for a Fabergé miniature hippopotamus in gray agate (one leg missing), to £600 for a larger one in Kalgan jasper.

Across the Atlantic, by the 1950s carved Fabergé animals appeared at auction and were also illustrated in the catalogues. In 1956, these were included in a sale of carpets, tapestries, gold coins, objets de vertu, furniture and decorations. Other Russian

Auctions and the trade have always fascinated me. Ever since I started out at Christie's front counter answering phones, I grabbed every opportunity to peruse auction catalogues of upcoming sales and witness (on my breaks) live auctions. To hear the banter of merchants seated in the back of the room was always a treat. Except when they would break out into fights over a particular rug or a missed bid! Still, I respect these dealers, since I am one of them now.

Auctions are the best barometers of the market. And that's why I've devoted this section to Russian art auctions in the West, beginning with the most spectacular of them all, the sale of the Russian crown jewels in 1927. The rest is devoted to an analysis of top realized prices in public sales of the Russian jewelers and silversmiths covered in the first section. To provide a historical look at the trade, I also include a brief section on dealers of Russian jewelry in America.

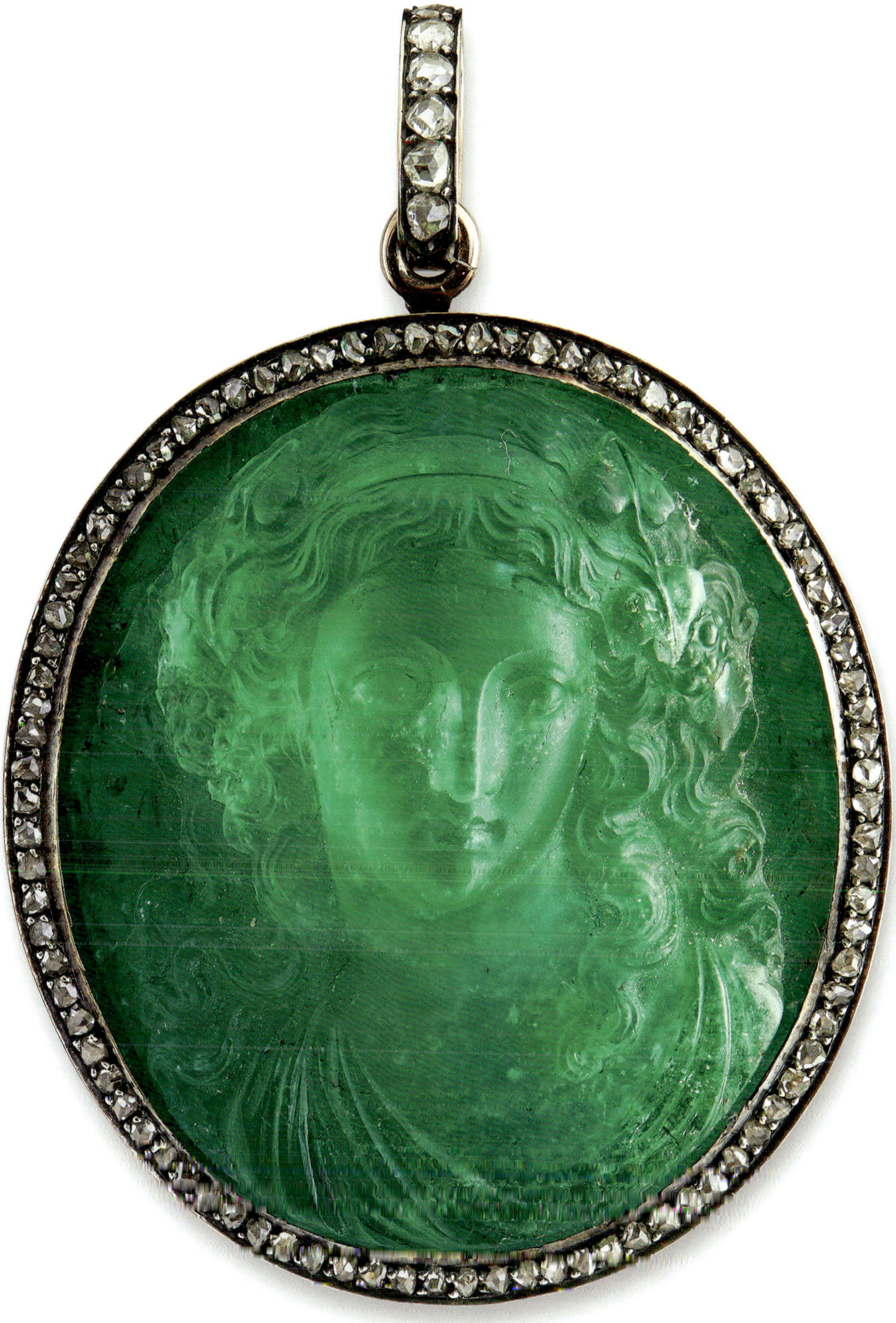

This carved emerald and diamond pendant, which was owned by the fabulously wealthy Princess Vera Lobanov Rostovskaia (1836–1914), first sold in Lausanne in 1920 (in a massive sale of her jewelry collection). It resurfaced in a Bern auction in 1964, then in 2016, still in Switzerland. *© 2016 Christie's Images Ltd.*

GEMS THAT CHANGED MY LIFE

Early on at Christie's New York, François Curiel, the head of its jewelry department, hired me to catalogue gems for upcoming sales. I was studying for my Graduate Gemologist diploma at Gemological Institute of America at the time, which I completed, thanks to François's encouragement.

Working behind the scenes, hunched over a microscope, my role was to examine and test the world's finest precious gems to make certain they passed muster—20-carat-plus D flawless diamonds, Burmese sapphires the size of quail's eggs, rubies to beguile maharajas and Hollywood stars—and also to spot those coveted hallmarks (Van Cleef and Arpel, Cartier, Harry Winston) that would send prices skyrocketing.

It was a rarefied atmosphere if ever there was one. Yet, after a while I realized that a perfect diamond is just that. It was perfect, ideal, nice, but that was about it. Next in line?

My heart skipped a beat when I saw them. There in front of me was a stunning gold bracelet set with the most-amazing cabochon rubies and sapphires, each encircled with antique cut diamonds, then a magnificent ruby and diamond cluster ring, followed by an incredible sapphire and diamond man's ring. Simply beyond belief in beauty. Besides the quality of the gems, the patina of the gold and the way the stones were mounted drew me in.

Of course they were Russian. And from St. Petersburg, the glittering capital of the tsars and the empire's jewelry center. The owner of these precious jewels was none other than Dr. Thomas Wiltberger Evans (1823–97), dentist both of the French empress Eugénie and the Russian imperial family.

I catalogued the lot, describing them in the usual words: carat of gold, cut of stones, length of bracelet, weight. But these descriptions did not begin to tell the story of these treasures.

Who made them? Why? And when exactly? What prompted Evans to buy them in St. Petersburg, or were they a gift from the tsar? I eagerly plowed through Evan's biography, *The Dentist and the Empress*, but it yielded no clues about his Romanov clients. Questions like these raced through my mind, and I discovered a new passion: imperial Russian jewelry.

Evans Collection of Russian jewelry.
© 1983 Christie's Images, Ltd.

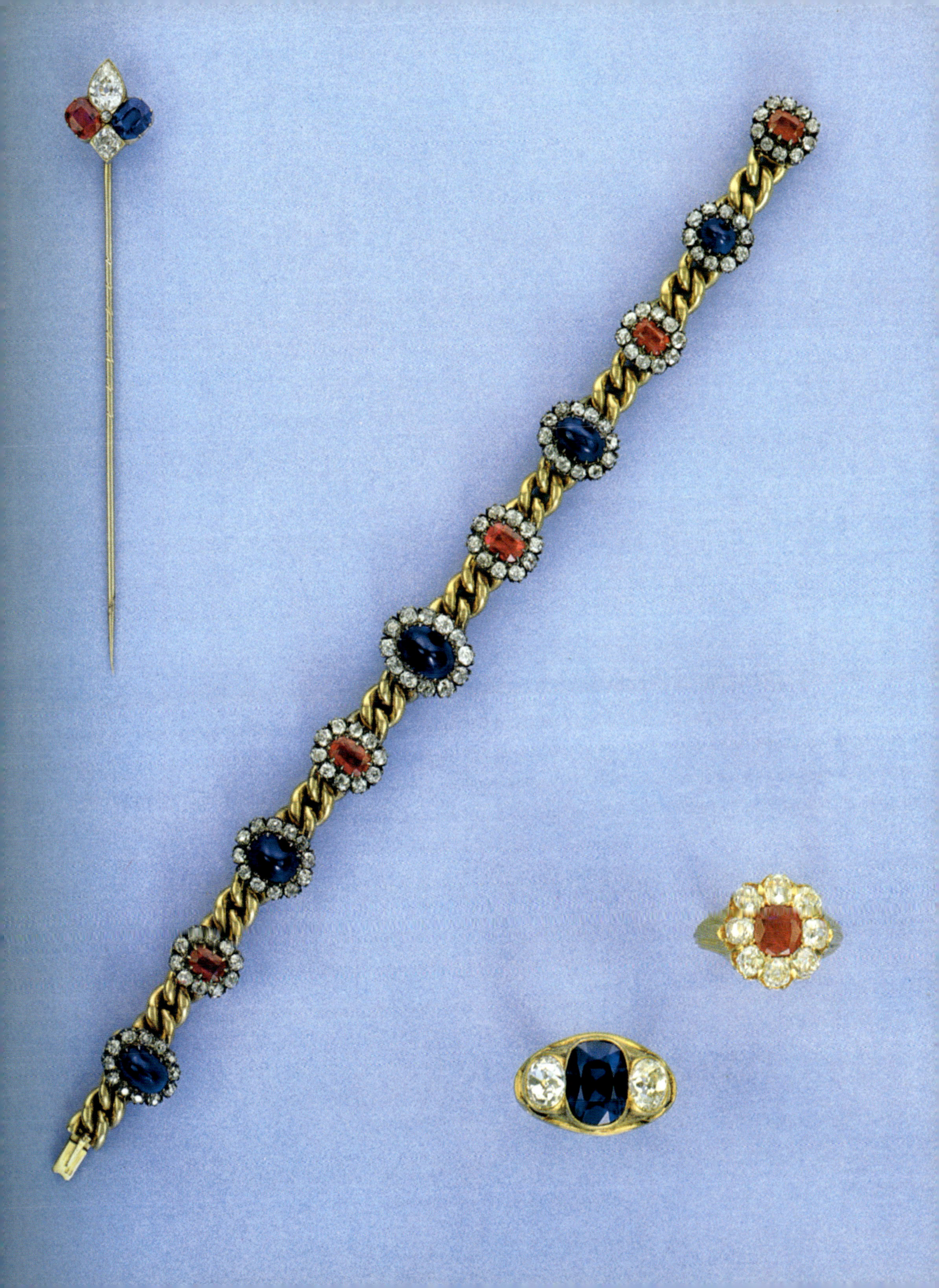

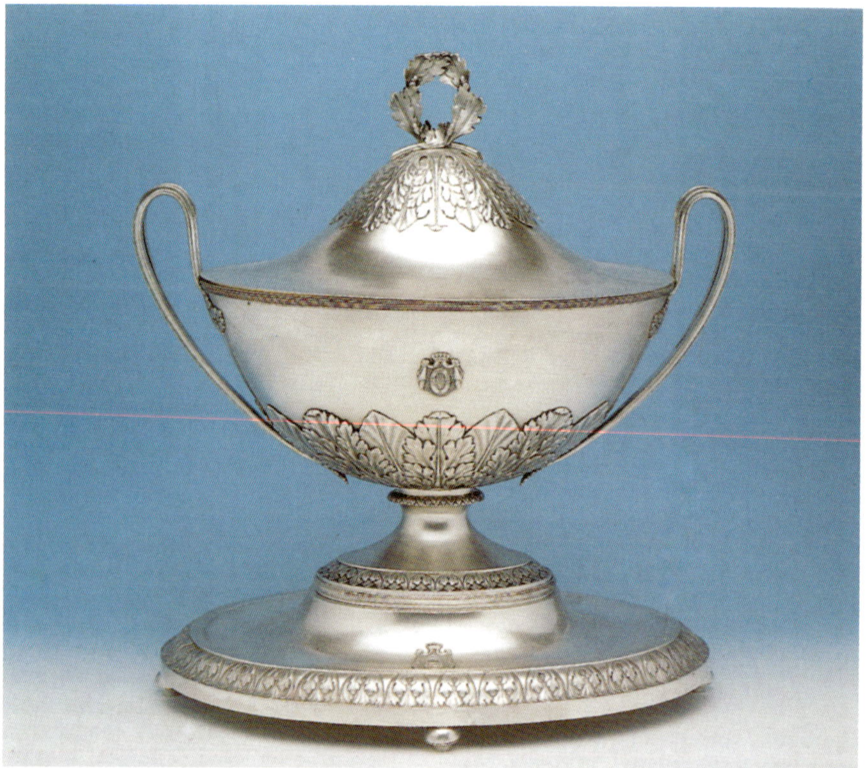

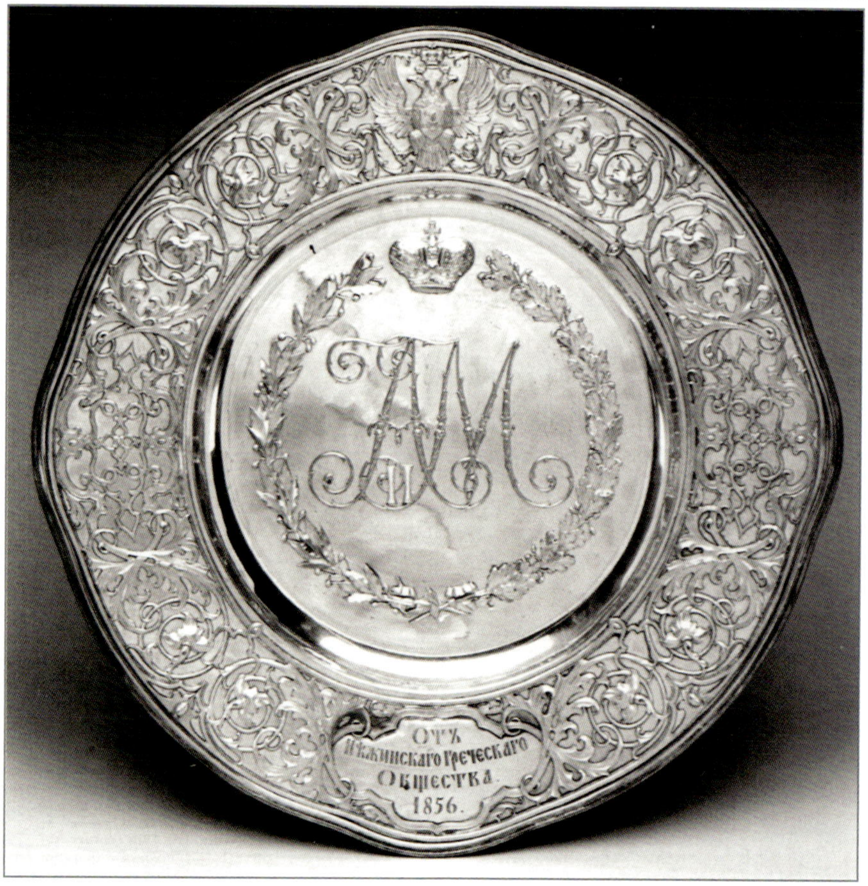
ОТЪ
НѢЖИНСКАГО ГРЕЧЕСКАГО
ОБЩЕСТВА.
1856.

items surfacing at auction then were silver presentation pieces and enamels. An enamel box by Khlebnikov displaying the Boyar wedding brought $650.[13] Enamels would occasionally warrant an image, and makers were sometimes identified, such as Nemirov-Kolodkin and Ovchinnikov, whereas those of plain silver such as samovars were unidentified, unless they were by Fabergé. One exception was a Morozov tea service, unadorned but in interesting triangular shapes,which sold in 1962 for $201, a bargain for a 33-piece set (see page 294).[14] These sales also featured icons, which were illustrated along with the other decorative arts.

By the mid-1960s, sales grew in scope. Catalogues were larger now, and images of objects more numerous and bigger, some taking up an entire page. At the same time, color illustrations began to appear in Parke-Bernet catalogues. Most enamel makers, except for Ovchinnikov, were still unidentified, while icons and carved animals as well as gold and enamel objects by Fabergé continue to sell in mixed or general sales.

Sales became specialized toward the end of the decade. Russian paintings, porcelain, glass and silver makers such as Sazikov begin to appear alongside Fabergé items and icons. The Lansdell K. Christie Sale in 1967 marked one of the first New York auctions, with 66 lots dedicated to Fabergé. Two years later, Russian auctions took off, and the May 1969 sale at Parke-Bernet featured 339 lots. The market continued to grow. In 1971, Christie's offered a collection belonging to Jean Herbette, France's ambassador to the Soviet Union from 1924 to 1930. Jewelry in these sales was scarce, but it began to make a modest appearance in the early '70s. Important pieces usually ended up in major jewelry sales, which is still true today. At the time, Parke-Bernet ruled the roost in America for Russian art (Christie's did not open in New York until 1978).

Moscow enamelers now came to the fore. A massive punch bowl set by Ovchinnikov realized the highest price at a New York sale in December 1969, at $22,000.[15] In Geneva in 1975, a 218-lot sale of Fabergé and Russian works of art was entirely sold, a rare feat in the auction business.

In the 1980s, early Russian silver or silver by little-known makers seemed undervalued. A fine soup tureen made for Prince Demidov by Carl Bredenburg of St. Petersburg brought $4,748, while an 1856 massive imperial silver salver by Greshchnikov from Moscow fetched only $6,435 in London. Still, interest in Fabergé predominated as it still does today. In 1988, of the top-ten highest lots at Christie's, eight were by Fabergé, and one each by Bolin and Bushkovskii.[16]

Today the results of Russian art sales are easily accessible online through art search engines as well as the auctioneers' websites (prices of individual silversmiths and jewelers are discussed in the market chapter). In general, values started spiking in 2004–2005, experienced a dip in 2006, then recovered and surged from 2006 to 2009, before entering into a steep decline that plateaued in 2014, both in lots sold and offered and prices. Prices for enamels and silver of lesser-known makers have come back down to the level of the year 2000. For example, compared to gross sale revenues in one auction house of $46,450,489 on April 15–16, 2008, and of $50,967,260 at another on April 16–17, 2007, on June 2, 2015, it had dipped to $1,738,968. What might this mean to the new collector? Perhaps it's time once again to buy Russian art.

Russian soup tureen and salver from the early to mid-19th century.
Courtesy, © 1987 Christie's Images Ltd. and Sotheby's

PRICE LISTS ARE PRICELESS!

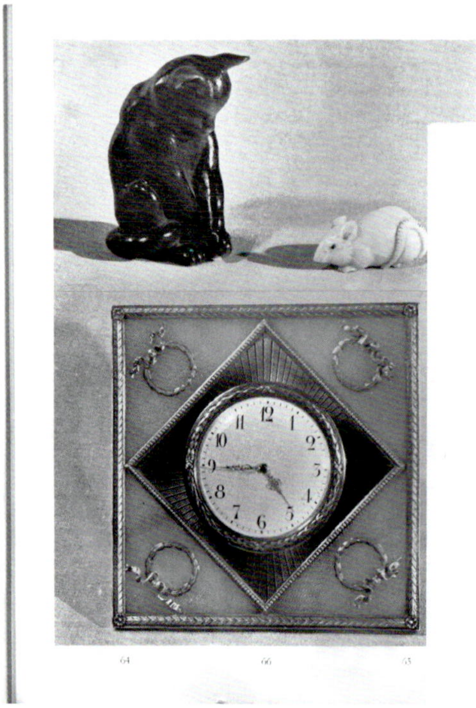

SOTHEBY & Co's

SALE OF

AN IMPORTANT COLLECTION OF

ANIMAL CARVINGS BY

CARL FABERGE

25th November, 1957

PRICES AND BUYERS' NAMES

Lot		£	s.	d.	Lot		£	s.	d.
1	Parsons	6	0	0	37	Ayres	100	0	0
2	Schidlof	7	0	0	38	Kurke	22	0	0
3	Woollett	6	0	0	39	Hakim	36	0	0
4	Woollett	17	0	0	40	Kurke	32	0	0
5	Tite	9	10	0	41	Drager	42	0	0
6	Ashwell	6	10	0	42	Wartski	39	0	0
7	Ashwell	24	0	0	43	Angyalfi	19	0	0
8	Eyles	15	0	0	44	Kurke	24	0	0
9	Tussar	62	0	0	45	Drager	68	0	0
9a	Robinson, R. D.	24	0	0	46	Kurke	28	0	0
9b	Twining	18	0	0	47	Tussar	11	0	0
9c	Cowley	18	0	0	48	Ayres	15	0	0
10	Withdrawn ...	—	—	—	49	Beeson	15	0	0
11	Reid, D. S. ...	14	0	0	50	Weaver	295	0	0
12	Twining	7	10	0	51	Holborn	350	0	0
13	Twining	20	0	0	52	Adamson ...	65	0	0
14	Twining	28	0	0	53	Adamson ...	60	0	0
15	Parsons	34	0	0	54	Donovan ...	210	0	0
16	Cowley	75	0	0	55	Bramwell ...	42	0	0
17	Cowley	100	0	0	56	John	110	0	0
18	Tussar	50	0	0	57	Wartski	38	0	0
19	Tussar	42	0	0	58	Adamson ...	28	0	0
20	Cowley	34	0	0	59	Stapyleton ...	28	0	0
21	Weaver	30	0	0	60	Cowley	44	0	0
22	Robinson, R. D.	310	0	0	61	Cowley	42	0	0
23	Robinson, R. D.	480	0	0	62	Harvey Smythe ...	80	0	0
24	Denton	9	0	0	63	Wartski	220	0	0
25	Woollett	5	0	0	64	Wartski	450	0	0
26	Woollett	11	0	0	65	Phillips, S. J. ...	265	0	0
27	Gardner, M. ...	28	0	0	66	Syles	240	0	0
27a	Bentley, O. ...	26	0	0	67	Tahsin	210	0	0
28	Lavender ...	26	0	0	68	Wartski	200	0	0
29	Allan	9	0	0	69	Wartski	200	0	0
30	Provatoroff ...	11	0	0	70	Cortona	35	0	0
31	Piper	30	0	0	71	Malvern	200	0	0
32	Asprey	34	0	0	72	Tahsin	40	0	0
33	Koblitz	40	0	0	73	Roscoe	10	0	0
34	Bencher	26	0	0	74	Roscoe	52	0	0
35	Ayres	32	0	0	74a	Phillips, S. J. ...	350	0	0
36	Lavender ...	90	0	0	75	Adamson ...	26	0	0

I love both live auctions and collecting vintage Russian sales catalogs. My prized possession is the 1927 Crown Jewels catalogue of the landmark Christie's London sale. As with all dealers, catalogues play a vital role in research and when buying inventory. The key is to have all the price lists, which record the prices of individual lots, what didn't sell, what was withdrawn and occasionally even the buyers' names.

Sale catalogs provide details about the market, hard copies to be consulted. As far as I know, they have not yet all been digitalized, although some libraries may have done so. To me, it's much more satisfying to have them at your fingertips on a shelf in chronological order, to take them down and leaf through them. Early examples from London will often include not only the price list (what the lots sell for in the local currency) but also the name of the buyer. In today's privacy-obsessed world, this never happens. Bidders now often buy anonymously, either by phone, through a dealer, or online. Early auctions were patronized more by dealers than private individuals. The reverse is true now. Prices were closer to wholesale back then, and one would have a better chance of snatching up a treasure in a more or less confidential setting, devoid of private collectors and the internet.

Descriptions of Russian jewels and decorative arts captivate me, either by their well-researched footnotes on individual pieces, or the opposite, by their lack of information. My favorite entry from the 1950s read "A group of oddments." No further details were provided, including the type or quantity. Of course, in those early days, the catalogues were poorly illustrated, if at all. Barring firsthand inspection, it was anybody's guess as to what these objects were.

This current study is of Russian jewels seen through the lens of my personal experience in this specialized market. The accent is on American or the western market, since that is what I know best. The stated prices are mostly from North American sales, or London and Geneva sales, and are sometimes rounded off. I did not delve into the auctions in Russia. This is of interest to me, but it will have to wait until I can devote more time to it.

NOTES

1. Laura Cerwinske, *Russian Imperial Style* (New York: Prentice Hall, 1990), 14–15; and Odom, *Russian Silver in America*, 214.

2. Geza von Habsburg-Lothringen and A. von Solodkoff, *Fabergé: Court Jeweler to the Tsars* (New York: Booth-Clibbon, 1979), 139.

3. Adam Szymański, "Fabergé Silver Service," www.adamszymanski.com.pl/Fabergé-kelch-tableware/. Knives from this service resurfaced on the market in 2016.

4. Vincent Meylan, *Archives Secrètes*, Boucheron (Paris: Ed. SW Télémaque, 2009), 174. Kelch spent the equivalent of €9,600,000 on pearl jewelry alone (p. 279).

5. Margaret Kelly Trombly, ed., *Fabergé and the Russian Arts and Crafts Tradition: An Empire's Legacy* (New York: Thames & Hudson, 2017).

6. Odom, *Russian Silver in America*, 26–28.

7. Ibid, 176.

8. Fabergé et al., *Fabergé: A Comprehensive Reference Book*, 542, and Carl Blumay and Henry Edwards, *The Dark Side of Power: The Real Armand Hammer* (New York: Pocket Books, 1993), 106.

9. Cerwinske, *Russian Imperial Style*, 19.

10. Anne Odom and Wendy Salmond, eds., *Treasures into Tractors: The Selling of Russia's Cultural Heritage 1918–1936* (Washington: Hillwood Museum, 2009), 26.

11. M. J. Larsons (a pseudonym for Moisei Lazerson), *Expert in the Service of the Soviet*, trans. Angelo Rappoport (London: Ernest Benn, 1929), 157, in Odom, *Russian Silver in America*, 210.

12. Fabergé, *Fabergé: A Comprehensive Reference Book*, 587; and Will Lowes and Christel Ludewig McCanless, *Fabergé Eggs: A Retrospective Encyclopedia* (Lanham, MD: Scarecrow, 2001), 19.

13. Parke-Bernet Galleries Inc., New York, February 10 and 11, 1956, lot 282.

14. Parke-Bernet Galleries Inc., New York, February 9 and 10, 1962, lot 57.

15. Parke-Bernet Galleries, December 2 and 3, 1969, lot 286.

16. Christie's, London, November 16, 1988, top sales results published by auction house.

26

Market

THE FATE OF THE RUSSIAN CROWN JEWELS

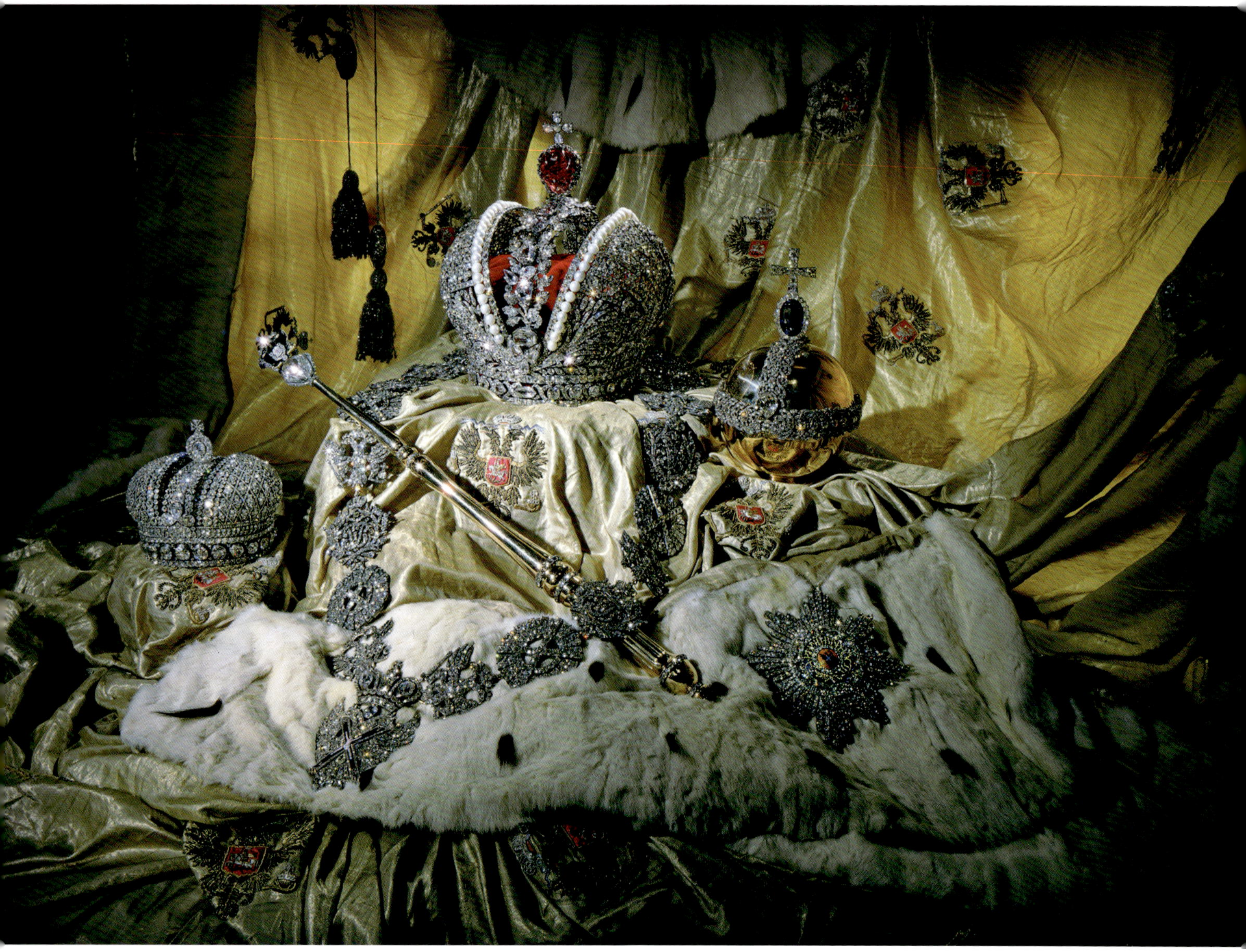

The Russian imperial regalia, mid-19th century. *Collection of the Moscow Kremlin Museums; photo by Nikolai Rakhmanov*

All black-and-white images in this chapter come from the Fersman catalogue of 1925. Appreciative thanks to GIA (Gemological Institute of America) for these images.

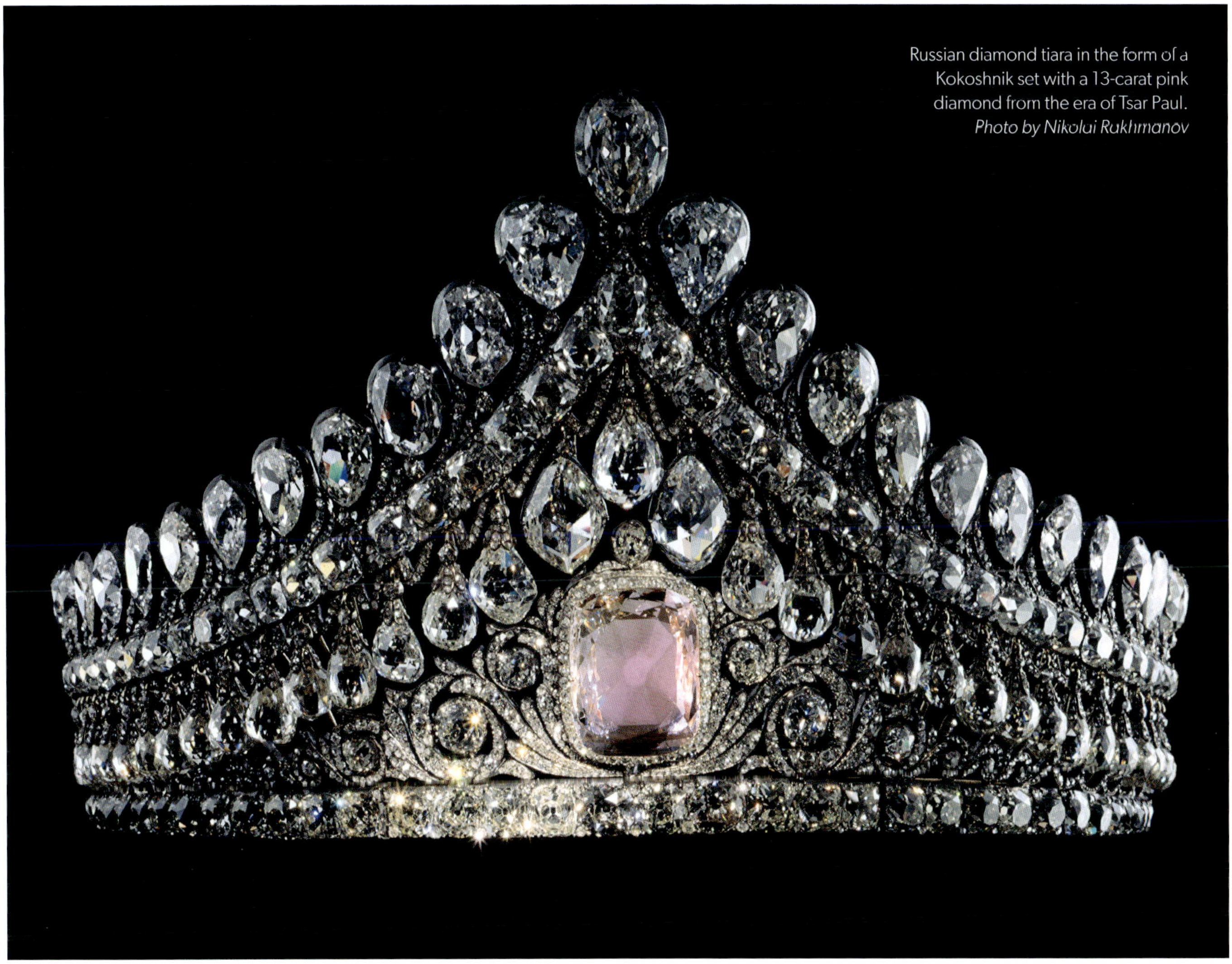

Russian diamond tiara in the form of a Kokoshnik set with a 13-carat pink diamond from the era of Tsar Paul. *Photo by Nikolai Rakhmanov*

Treasures Seized

The demise of an empire raises the awkward question of what to do with its riches. Once they have plundered and confiscated their fill, do the victors destroy all remaining symbols of the despised former realm. Or do they sell them? This dilemma faced the Soviets, newly in power in the early 1920s. Dealing with tsarist silver was straightforward, melt it all down, especially the large church silver, iconostasis and presentation icons, for scrap value—ostensibly, as Lenin had declared, to buy grain to feed the starving people in the Volga region (funds went instead toward tractors, transportation and the Communist movements abroad[1]).

But the Romanov crown jewels? To the Bolsheviks, indignant of these lavish court baubles, the obvious choice was to sell them outright: to foreigners, of course, with poor taste and deep pockets. Yet, some of these treasures must have given them pause. Was really everything to be sold off? Even the imperial coronation regalia, the foremost symbols of the power of the Russian Empire?

Revolution

For centuries, the imperial cabinet had looked after the finest jewels in the land, appointing court appraisers such as Römpler, Bolin, Seftigen, Blank, Grachev and Fabergé to update inventories on a regular basis. With each monarch, contents changed and were often augmented, especially during the reign of Catherine the Great. The cabinet's officials even kept these lists secured under lock and key. State symbols of power as first decreed by Peter the Great in 1719, the crown jewels of Russia were the property of the Treasury, to be passed down to each succeeding ruler. No one except for the appraisers themselves, the imperial family and the court's most trusted representatives knew about the extent of the dynasty's holdings.

This all changed during the Russian Revolution. On July 24, 1914, just days before Germany declared war on Russia, the treasures were packed into eight trunks and moved from the Winter Palace in St. Petersburg to the Moscow Kremlin for safekeeping. Because the enemy advanced deep into the empire during the catastrophic "Great Retreat" of 1915, trainload after trainload of jewelry, paintings and other valuables from Petrograd's (formerly St. Petersburg) imperial palaces and museums continued to make deliveries to the Kremlin Armory. Shortly after the Bolsheviks seized power, they counted over 2,000 boxes and suitcases of valuables in the building.[2]

Until recently, most historians believed that the treasures lay undisturbed until 1922, entirely forgotten amid the chaos of civil war and the conflict with Poland. The actual story turns out to be different. Recent research in the Kremlin's archive by Tatiana Tutova reveals that the new regime was well aware that the Armory held a fantastic trove of Romanov jewels.[3]

Already two days after their coup, Red Army troops demanded an inventory from the committee that the provisional government had appointed to protect the valuables. Amazingly, they meekly turned back when told that the boxes were property of the state and would be released only by direct order of its legitimate government.

On June 1, 1918, an official of the People's Commissariat for State Control urged his superiors to take stock of the mountain of sealed packages in the Armory. As he put it, "This is not just a matter of interest for State Control, but for the entire government. . . . [The valuables] are as important as gold, if not more so."[4]

Lenin's new regime quickly put together an interdepartmental committee to take an inventory. Eager to get their hands on the treasures, various officials tried to have the jewelry dismantled and the precious metals molten down. However, the committee successfully resisted these efforts as they carried out their task, well guarded around the clock. Their initial work was done by July 1919.

Once the committee had completed its basic inventory, it was time to decide what to do with the thousands of valuables in the Armory. Property belonging to museums was returned to their rightful places in Petrograd. Meanwhile, the Bolsheviks set up a new agency, Gokhran, the Russian acronym for the Government Depository of Valuables under the Central Budgetary-Accounting Agency for Narkomfin (the People's Commissariat for Finance). Lenin put it more succinctly: "Gokhran stores, collects, and arranges for sale."[5]

The latter was a challenging task, given the enormous quantity of jewelry, tableware and other precious objects still at the Kremlin. After repeated complaints by those impatient to convert them for hard currency, not to mention the state's rapidly depleting gold reserves, in late 1921 Lev Trotskii took charge of the effort as head of a new commission "to inventory and collect the valuables of the palace administration."

The group consisted of various experts, including jewelers (one of Carl Fabergé's sons, Agathon Fabergé [1876–1951], and Alexander Bock were among them), two museum curators and Dmitrii Ivanov.[6]

Although the latter had been a jurist, Ivanov had long had a strong interest in safeguarding cultural heritage during conflicts, having published an article 1904 for a French journal, "On protecting works of art in times of war."[7]

Their basic job was to decide which objects would be kept for their historical and artistic importance and which could be sold. Beginning in January 1922, the commission's members worked at a frantic pace, at times in temperatures so cold that the contents of their inkwells froze. Within two months, one of the curators had died, and soon thereafter the other had to stop due to ill health. Nevertheless, by September they had sorted through some 7,823 objects, "not counting objects deemed of little value."[8]

Because the Bolsheviks undertook their evaluation of the crown jewels in the strictest secrecy, rumors spread that it had all vanished abroad, sold to the highest bidder. After all, this is what had happened in 1906 with the million-ruble sale of imperial jewels to a French merchant.[9]

To quell the chatter, it was deemed necessary to hold a public display. Let the common man feast his eye on the sheer decadence of the Romanovs, the glittering gems and pearls of empresses and grand duchesses: enormous emeralds, sapphires and rubies set in diamond-clustered mounts or on diadems, necklaces, or devants de corsage, including gem-encrusted parures made for their weddings. Thus, in 1925, for the second time in history and for one month only, the Russian crown jewels were exhibited in Moscow.[10]

On view were over 400 lavish jewels, set with diamonds, sapphires, rubies, emeralds and pearls, with a total weight of 36,360 carats.[11] Spanning the reigns of the Russian emperors Peter I (r. 1689–1725) to Nicholas II (r. 1896–1917), no less than 85 percent dated from between the reigns of Peter the Great and Nicholas I (r. 1825–1855), with 40 percent of those from the era of Catherine the Great and Paul I (r. 1796–1801).[12] The highlight was the imperial regalia, including Pauzié's masterpiece, Catherine the Great's Coronation Crown set with 5,000 diamonds and a spinel of just under 400 carats; the 18th-century solid-gold scepter crowned by the famous Orlov diamond, one of the 10 largest in the world; and the imperial orb surmounted by a 142-carat Ceylon sapphire. The regalia also included a magnificent diamond-encrusted Great Chain of the Order of St. Andrew, Russia's most prestigious knighthood (see page 28). Its splendid collar, set with more than 3,000 diamonds weighing over 1,000 carats, had encircled the imperial mantel of the emperor at every coronation while he took his solemn and sacred vows.[13]

The exhibit was accompanied by the publication of a detailed catalogue in four parts, *Russia's Treasure of Diamonds and Precious Stones*, by the eminent gemologist Professor Alexander E. Fersman

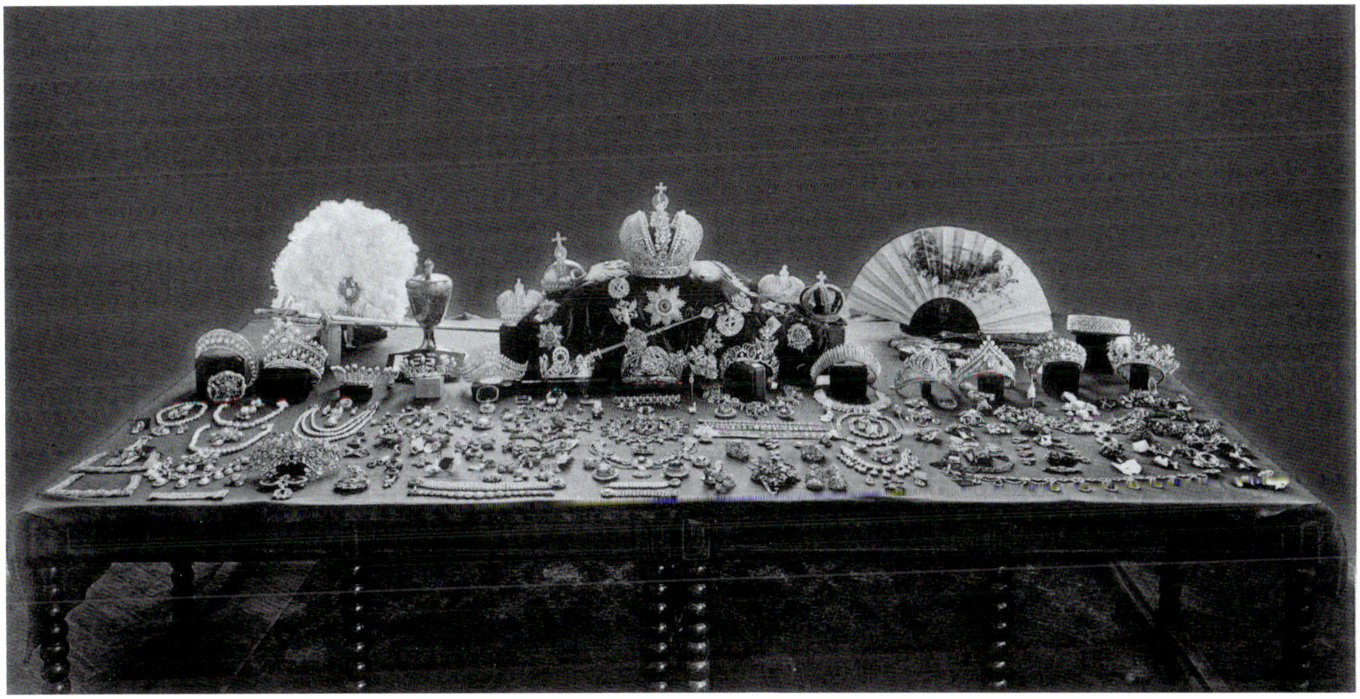

The Russian crown jewels, Moscow, 1922, Fersman portfolio, frontispiece. *Photo courtesy of GIA*

(1883–1945).[14] The catalogue was based on an 1898 court appraisal as well as the one conducted in 1922 (both now lost). Published by Narkomfin in 1925–26 in Russian, English and French, the rare catalogue remains the most complete published inventory of the Russian crown jewels. An invaluable document with 100 photographic plates, it documents each entry, with stones measured, weighed and assessed, and, where known, its provenance.[15]

Let the Sales Begin!

No values were placed on the pieces. Yet, the reason for publishing the collection was to prepare it for sale to help finance Joseph Stalin's First Five-Year Plan to industrialize the Soviet Union. The systematic sale of the Russian crown jewels began in 1927 and lasted until 1936. According to Victor Nikitin (1949–2009), director of the Diamond Fund of the Russian Federation in the 1990s, over three-quarters of them had been listed in the Fersman album. Many of the 228 entries that left Russia contained multiple jewels, including precious brooches, snuffboxes and diamond trimmings. At least 93 percent of the unillustrated entries in Fersman were sold. Nikitin also claimed that by 1936 the Moscow Diamond Fund collection had dwindled to 141 items from 717.[16]

The biggest sale was held in London in 1927. In November 1926, a Hungarian-born dealer named Norman Weisz (d. 1963) and a British syndicate bought about one-third of all the Fersman items for £50,000, the bulk of which they consigned to Christie's London to auction on March 16, 1927.[17] Appropriately titled "An Important Assemblage of Magnificent Jewellery Mostly Dating from the 18th Century. The Russian State Jewels," the landmark sale of 124 lots was entirely sold, realizing £[illegible] (about £4.[illegible] million today), and created a sensation around the world.[18]

Now itself a historic document, the Christie's 1927 catalogue illustrates only 16 lots, or just 13 percent of the Russian crown jewels featured. Of those, several have resurfaced at auction (*see below*). For the rest, since descriptions are short, many reduced to a single line of text, there is little chance of finding and identifying them. One hopes photos exist elsewhere, perhaps with the descendants of the original buyers at the first Christie's sale.

Treasure Hunt

The sell-off included some of the most lavish examples of the jeweler's art:

- **Bolin's Pearl and Diamond Tiered Tiara**, "one of the finest specimens of its kind" according to Fersman,[19] and last worn by Empress Alexandra Fedorovna at the opening of the First State Duma in 1906 (see illustration, page 76)
- **Empress Alexandra's Aigrette** with two large emeralds (weighing together 32 carats and diamonds "of perfect purity" weighing 21 carats (no. 234). As lot 94 in the Christie's 1927 sale, it sold for £4,300.
- **Diamond-encrusted Imperial Orders of St. Andrew**
- **Two diamond rivière necklaces**, possibly by Hahn, the diamonds weighing 473 carats total
- **Elizabethan-era Amethyst Necklace and Aigrette**, deemed "most beautiful jewels" of the 1750s (no. 232). Offered as lot 80 at Christie's in 1927, they sold for £470.
- **Two diamond ceremonial swords**, one purported to have belonged to Tsar Paul I (sold at Christie's as lot 119)

Every jewel was a treasure, since listed amid parures and glittering imperial orders we find snuffboxes, diamond aigrettes, pins, girandole and pendant earrings, a Peter the Great gold fermoire (clasp), rings, necklaces, bracelets and many diamond ornaments or trimmings used as decoration on gowns.

Apart from the official imperial regalia, which was kept in Moscow, officials chose to sell the most magnificent jewels. All but one out of 12 exquisite tiaras, as well as the nuptial crown, now at Hillwood Museum, were sold (see illustration, page 255). Christie's sold two tiaras and the nuptial crown in 1927, but the others have vanished without a trace. In addition, all 19 sumptuous necklaces—except for one that resurfaced in 2005 (illustration 26-26)—have disappeared. Given the enormous value of the gemstones involved, it's likely these were all disassembled once purchased.

What We Know

Fersman identified the makers of only about 10 percent of the listed Russian crown jewels. The imperial coronation regalia and selected treasures are still in Russia, in the Moscow Kremlin's Diamond Fund. As for those that were sold, only a handful have reappeared in the West since 1927. The partial list of crowned jewels below, which includes only those in the Fersman album, is divided by

I. Jeweler
II. Those that were resold at auction since 1927
III. In Western museums
IV. Other crown jewels still at large

I. Russian Crown Jewels Listed by Jeweler

The vast majority of jewels are unattributed, and most unsigned. One reason was the habit of sovereigns to dismantle and restyle older sets, breaking them up and using them in more-fashionable creations or wedding parures. Many smaller coronation crowns, the first of which was made by Louis David Duval in 1797 for Empress Consort Maria Fedorovna for her and Tsar Paul I's coronation, were disassembled and distributed in the dowries

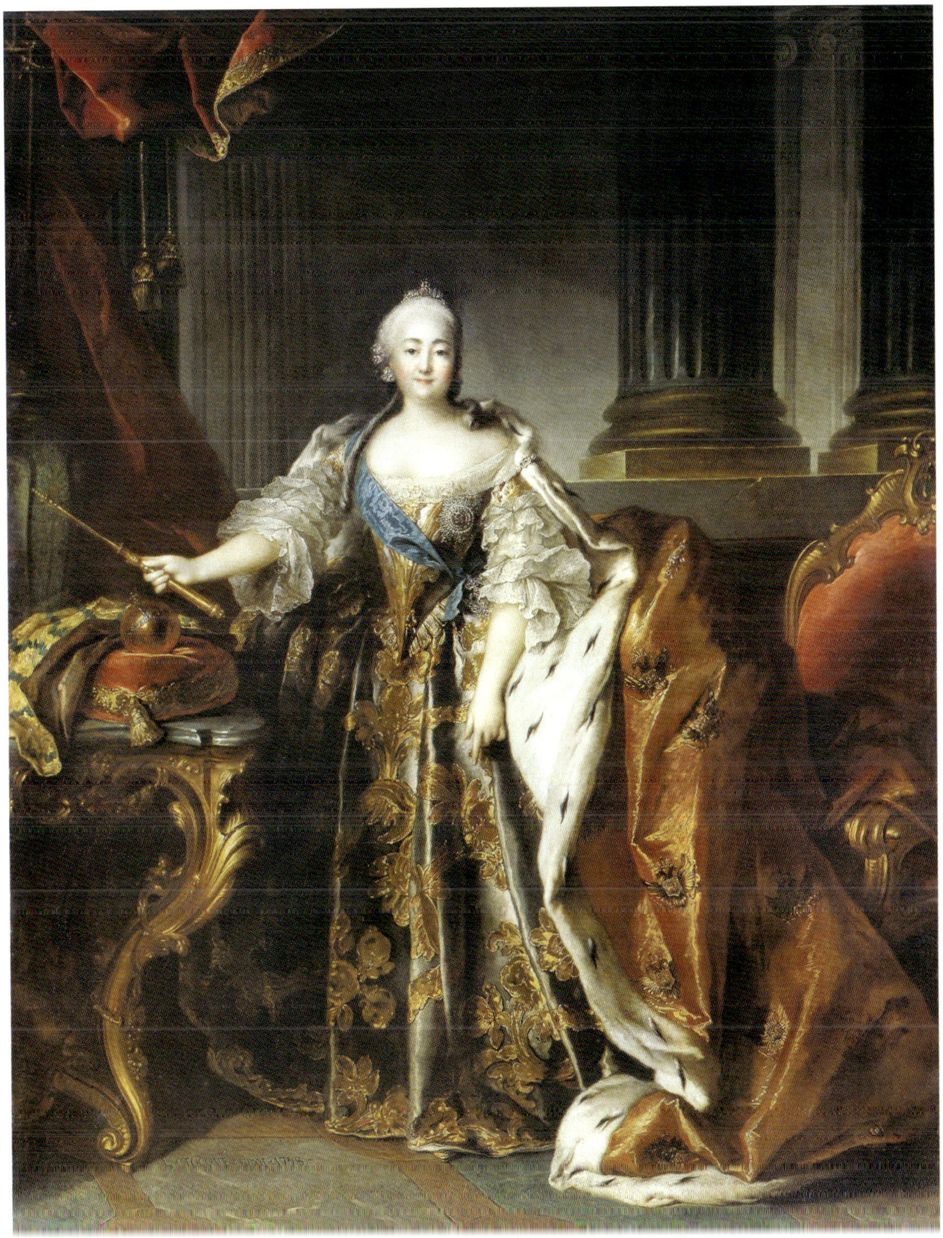

Empress Elizabeth of Russia by Louis Tocqué, 1756.
Source: Wikimedia Commons

of grand duchesses. Duval's original design prevailed in subsequent small diamond crowns. However, while Seftigen's crown for Empress Alexandra Fedorovna (Tsar Alexander II's wife) was preserved, two smaller diamond crowns made for the coronation of Tsars Alexander I and Nicholas I, by court jewelers Jean Francois Loubier and Johann Keibel, respectively, were dismantled. Finally, the diamond crown by court jeweler August Hahn for the last empress consort, Alexandra Fedorovna, has also vanished, having been dismantled by the Soviets.

The reverse, whereby diamonds from parures were reset into crowns, also took place; sometimes only temporarily, to fill a need for an instant coronation-ready crown. Empress Alexandra Fedorovna plucked out 20 solitaires from a necklace to use in Seftigen's crown, which she switched back after the coronation of 1856 and later replaced with diamonds from the treasury. Some 30 years later, Fabergé made a collier d'esclavage (see illustration, page 250) in great haste from old emeralds, diamonds and pearls in the Treasury for the empress at a costume ball.

Although Carl Fabergé has more attributions than most (eight), it is likely that Bolin, Pfisterer and Duval surpassed him in making crown jewels, since the bulk of the treasures date from before Fabergé's tenure. His work was no doubt also more easily identified by his own son, Agathon, who was one of the cataloguers.

Attributions below are based on the Fersman album and various sources, including the Diamond Treasures of Russia, the official Diamond Fund catalogue and Liliia Kuznetsova's research. Fersman's headings are in italics, with plates indicating illustration references and "no." for number of the full description in the album. The entries are formulated as follows:

MAKER (*if known*)

General title

- Description, date and imperial provenance, if known
- Subsequent provenance. Current whereabouts if known

Fersman description and image reference

I. Imperial Coronation Regalia by Known Jewelers

JÉRÉMIE PAUZIÉ *(1716–79)* AND GEORG FRIEDRICH ECKHARDT (*active 1730s–60s*)

Catherine II Coronation Crown

- Dated 1762, with the collaboration of Belgian diamond setter Jean Henroté, this crown has remained unaltered to the present day.
- Diamond Fund of the Moscow Kremlin

Great Imperial Crown, no. 1, plates 2, 3, 4, 5 and 6

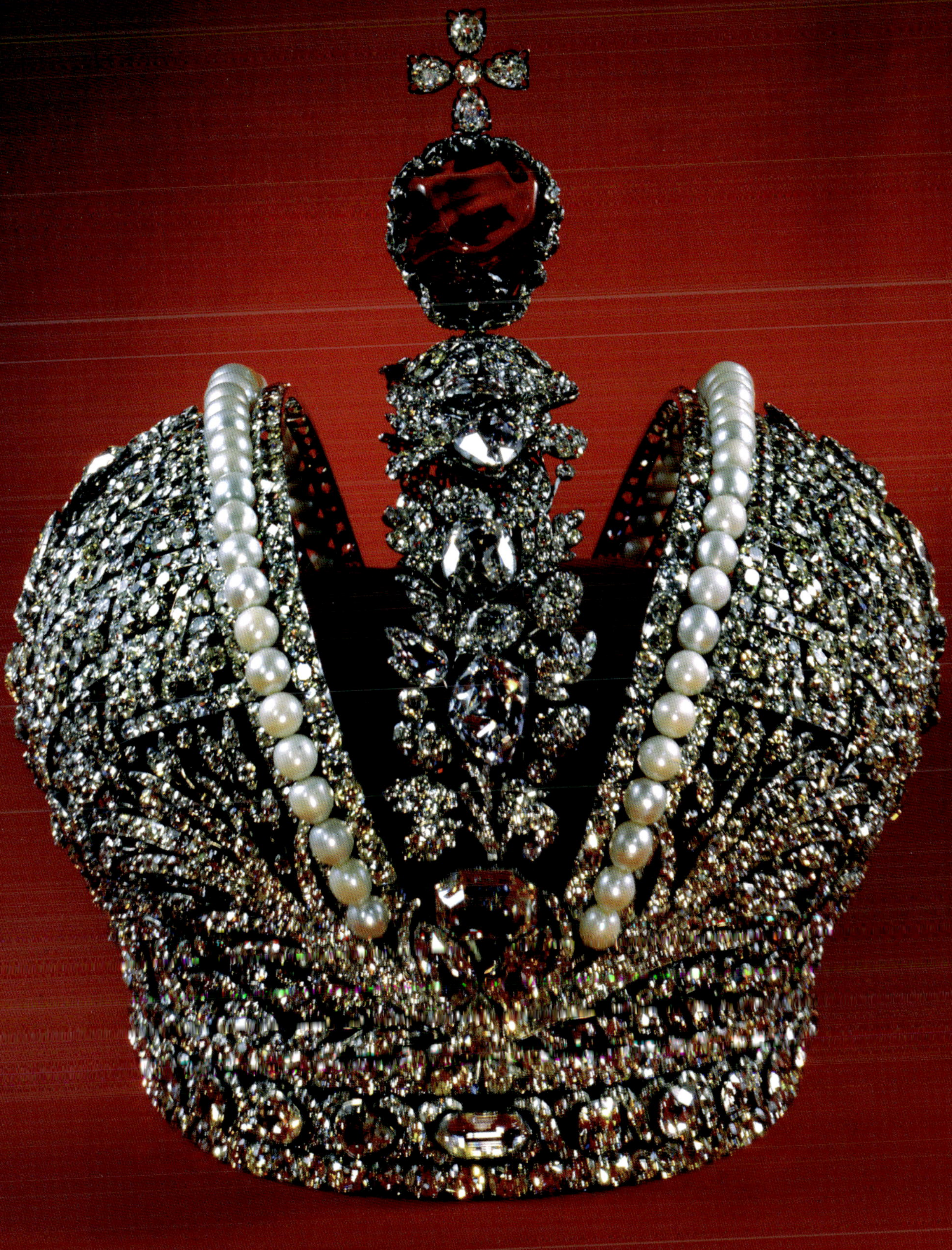

Catherine II coronation crown by Pauzié.
Photo by Nikolai Rakhmanov

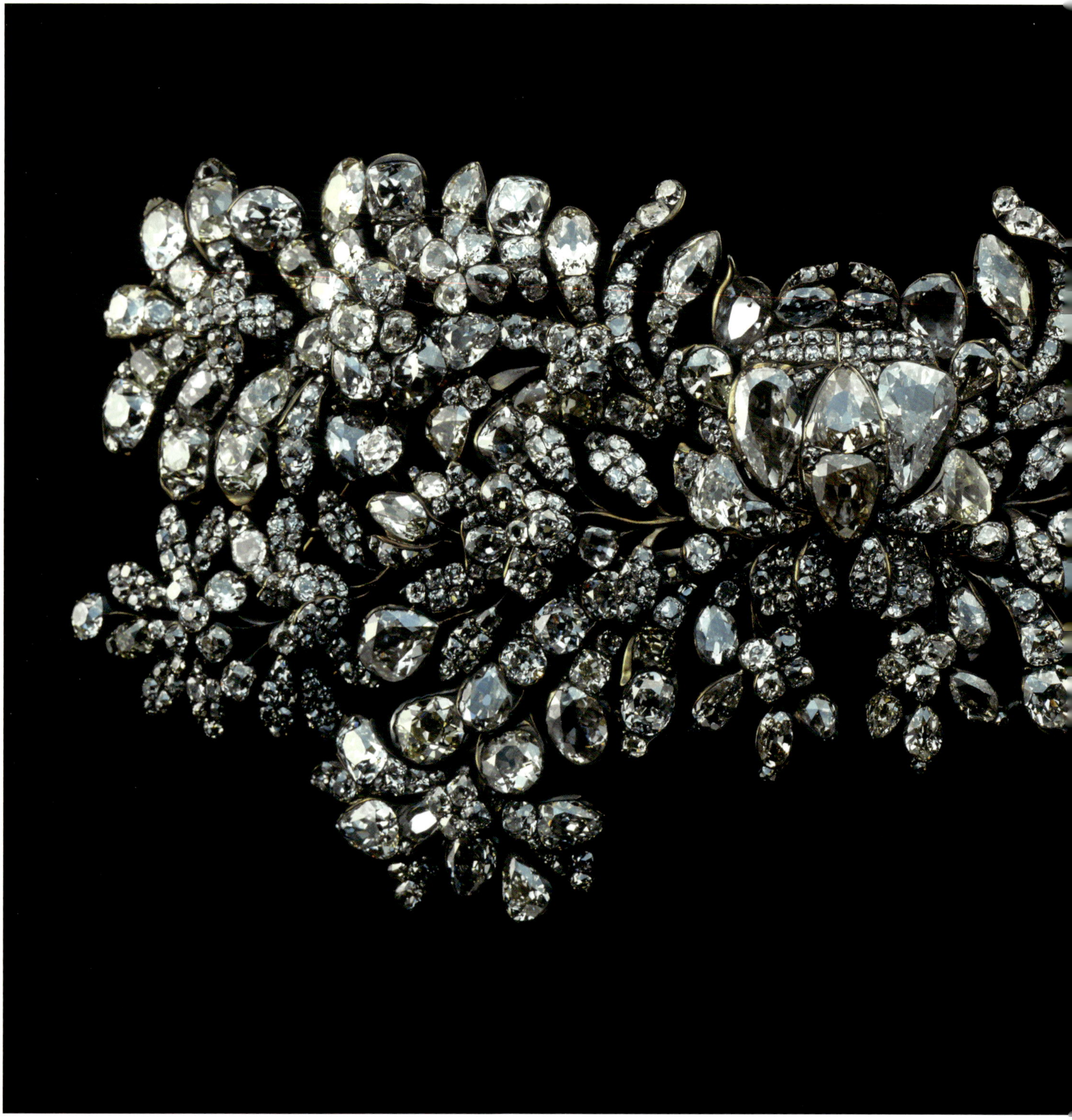

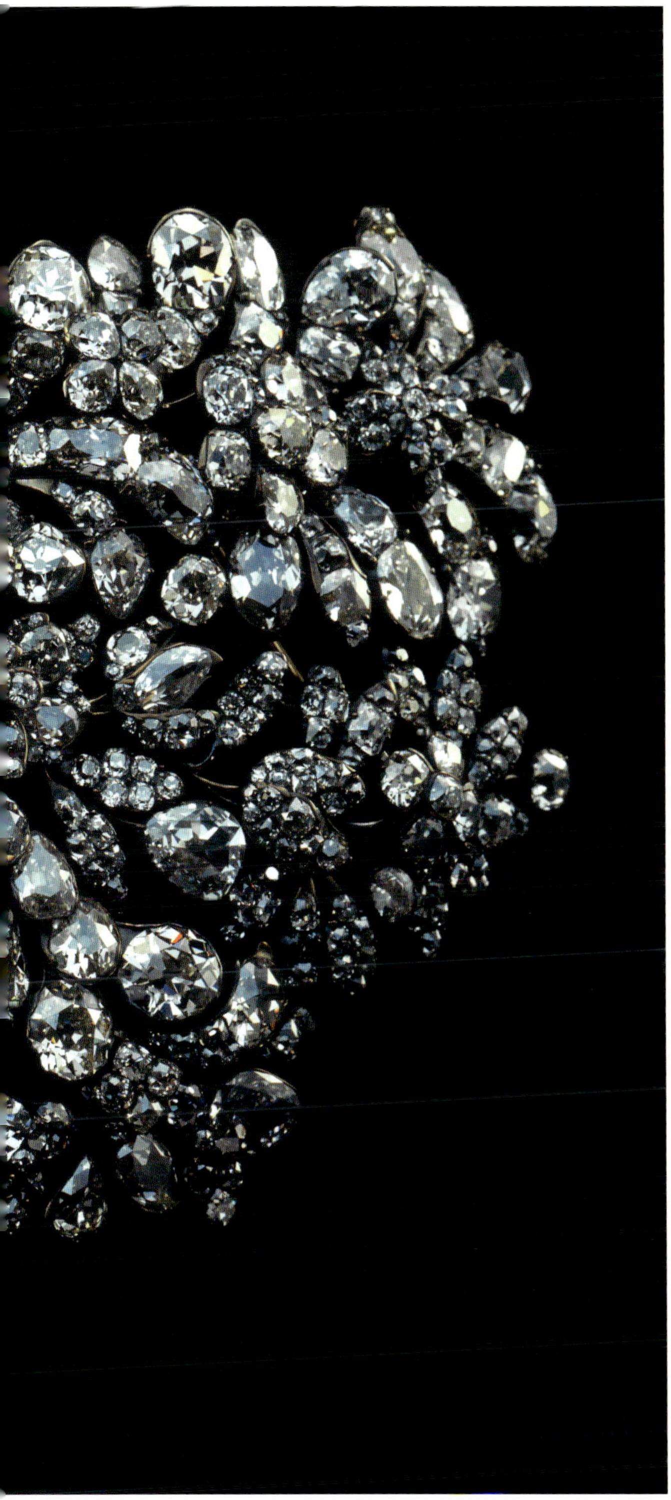

JÉRÉMIE PAUZIÉ (*1716–79*)

Diamond Mantel Clasp

- Used to join the imperial mantel in the front. 1760s.
- Diamond Fund of the Moscow Kremlin

The Mantel Clasp, no. 26, plate 18

Diamond mantel clasp by Pauzié.
Photo by Nikolai Rakhmanov

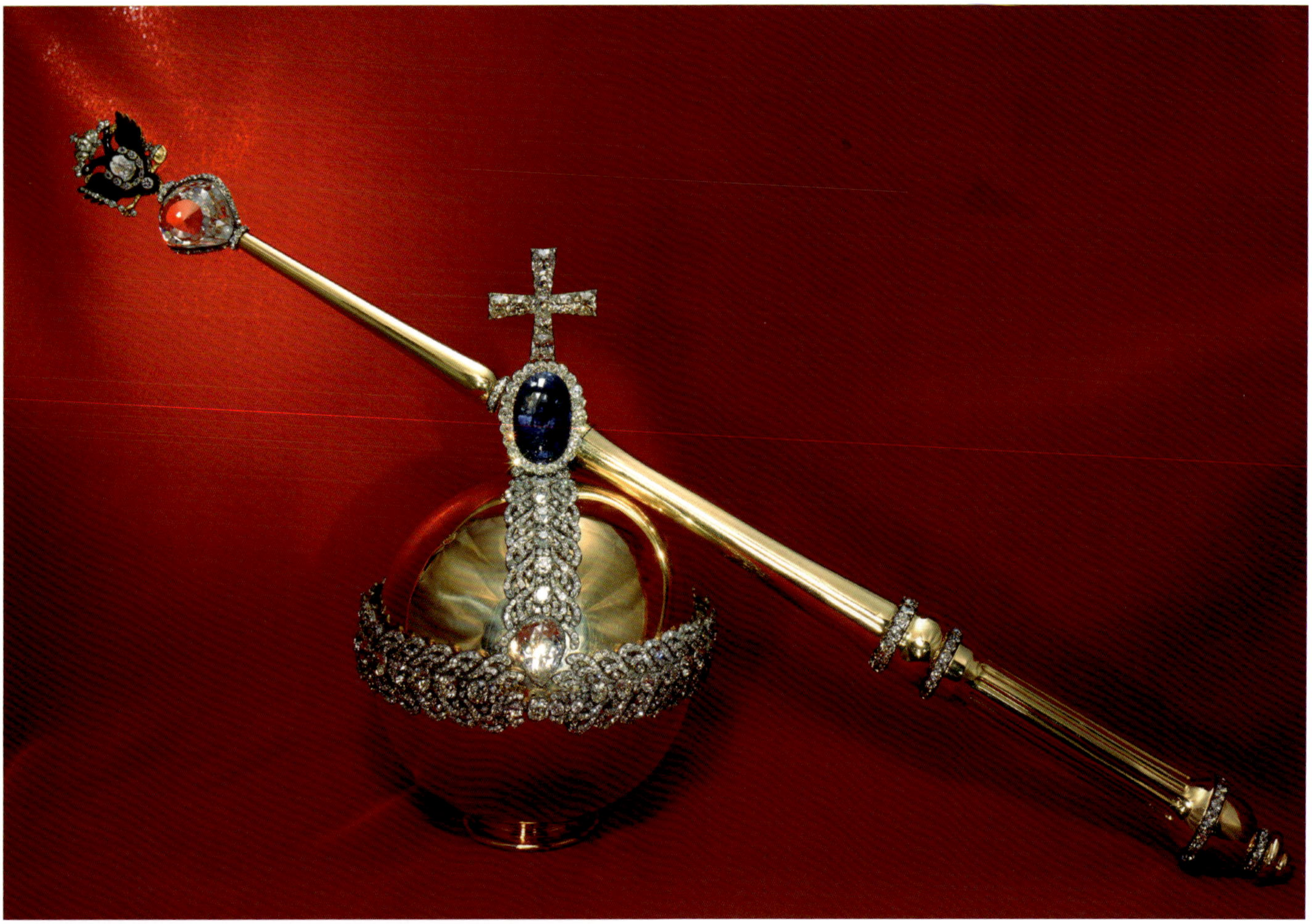

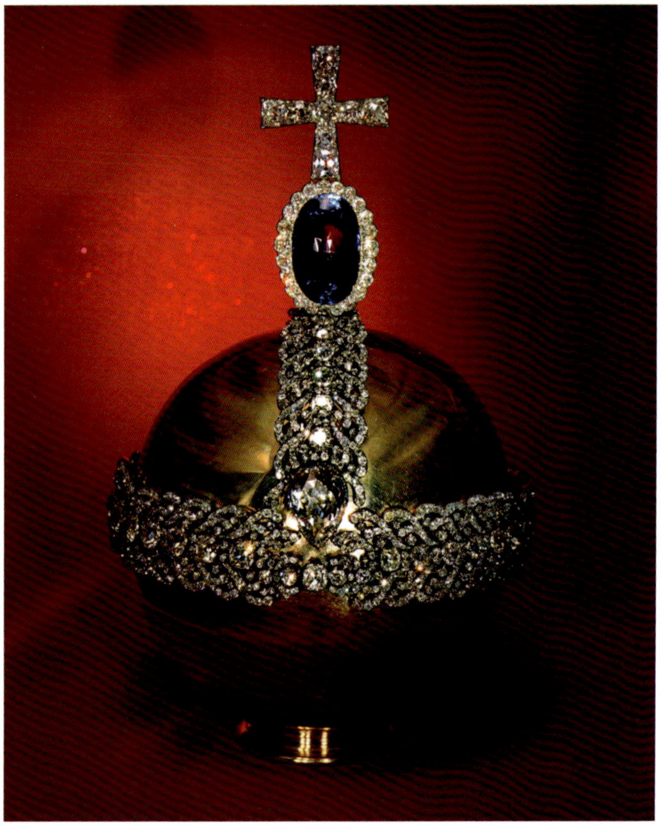

Gold orb by Eckhardt and scepter by Pfisterer.
Photo by Nikolai Rakhmanov

GEORG FRIEDRICH ECKHARDT (*active 1730s–60s*) in part

Gold Imperial Orb

- With Ceylon sapphire weighing 195 carats, added during the reign of Tsar Paul I
- Diamond Fund of the Moscow Kremlin

Imperial Globe, no. 2, plate 7

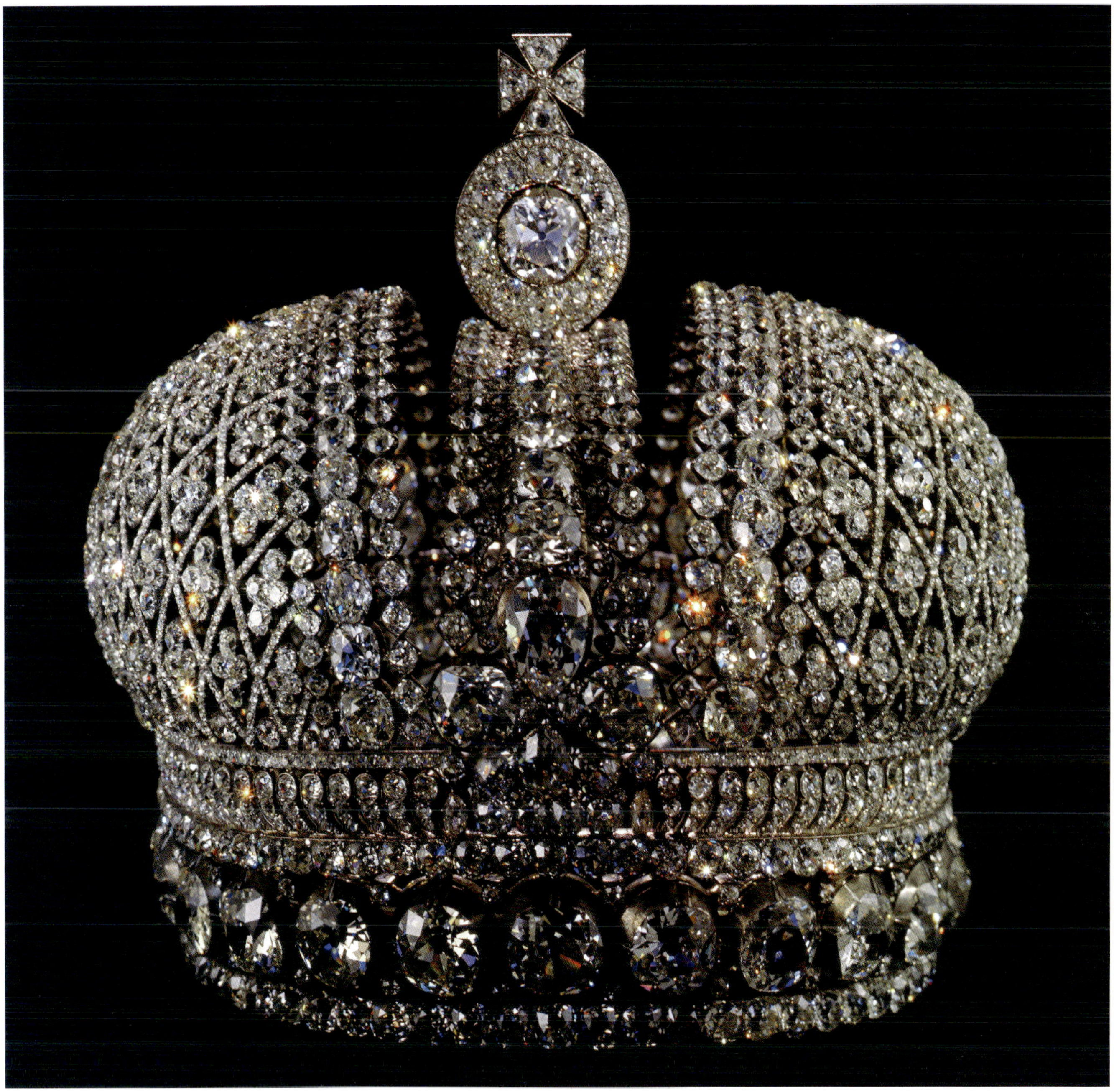

Diamond crown for the empress-consort, by Seftigen. *Photo by Nikolai Rakhmanov*

CONSTANTIN FRIEDRICH SEFTIGEN (*active 1840s–1899*)

Small Diamond Crown for the empress-consort

- Made for the coronation of Maria Aleksandrovna and Alexander II in 1856
- Diamond Fund of the Moscow Kremlin

The Small Imperial Crown, no. 82, plate 51

Imperial scepter by Pfisterer, with Orlov diamond.
Photo by Nikolai Rakhmanov

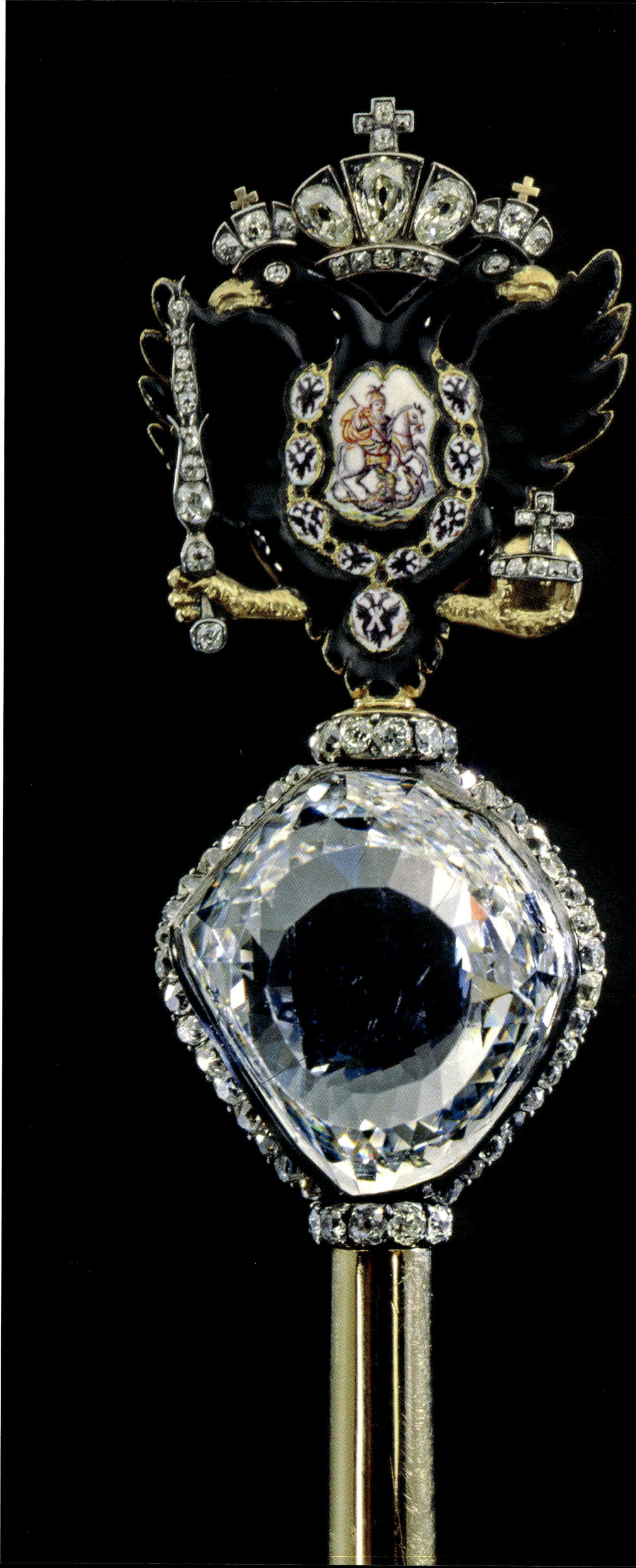

LEOPOLD PFISTERER
(*active 1760s–90s*)

1771, enamel by Ivan Leonovich

- With Orlov diamond weighing 189.62 carats
- Diamond Fund of the Moscow Kremlin

The Sceptre—The "Orlov," no. 3, plate 8

Other Crown Jewels by Known Jewelers

LOUIS DAVID DUVAL (1727–88)

Diamond Cornucopia Pin and Two Diamond Basket Pins

- The first signed "Duval, St. Petersburg," each era of Catherine II
- Diamond Fund of the Moscow Kremlin

Diamond Hair-Pin in the Form of Horn of Plenty, no. 46, plate 32

Diamond Hair-Pin Representing Flower Baskets, no. 47, plate 32

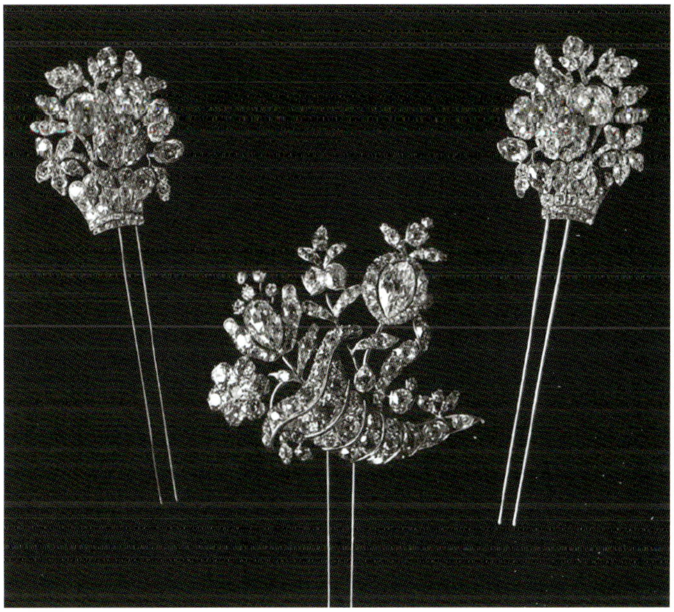

Six Silver Clasps with Diamonds (four illustrated)

- Circa 1780, period of Catherine the Great
- Christie's, 1927, lot 25, for £6,100

Six Silver Clasps with Diamonds, no. 118, plate 61

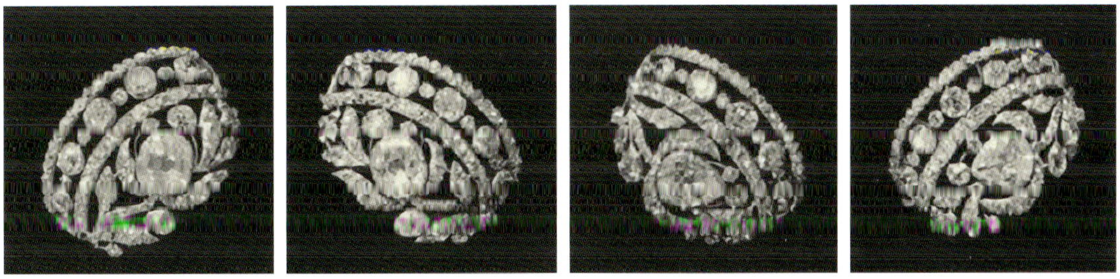

Top: Three diamond pins by Duval. Plate 32.

Bottom: Six silver clasps with diamonds, by Duval. Plate 61.

Two diamond ornaments.
Courtesy of Sotheby's

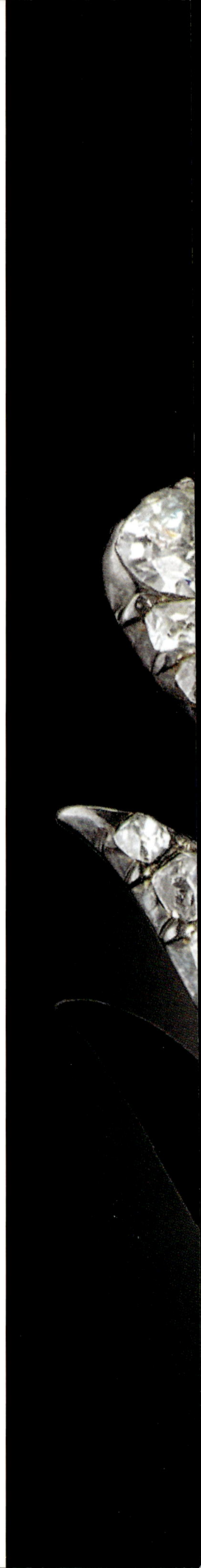

65 Diamond Ornaments

- Circa 1780
- Christie's, 1927, several lots sold, including 31, 32, 33, 34, 35, 36, 37 and possibly 54.
- S. J. Phillips Ltd, London
- Two sold at Sotheby's, 2005, lot 222, for $207,552, which were incorrectly catalogued as corresponding to no. 216 in Fersman

Diamond Trimmings of Different Designs, nos. 106 and 188, plate 58 (tassels) and plate 93 (flower sprays)

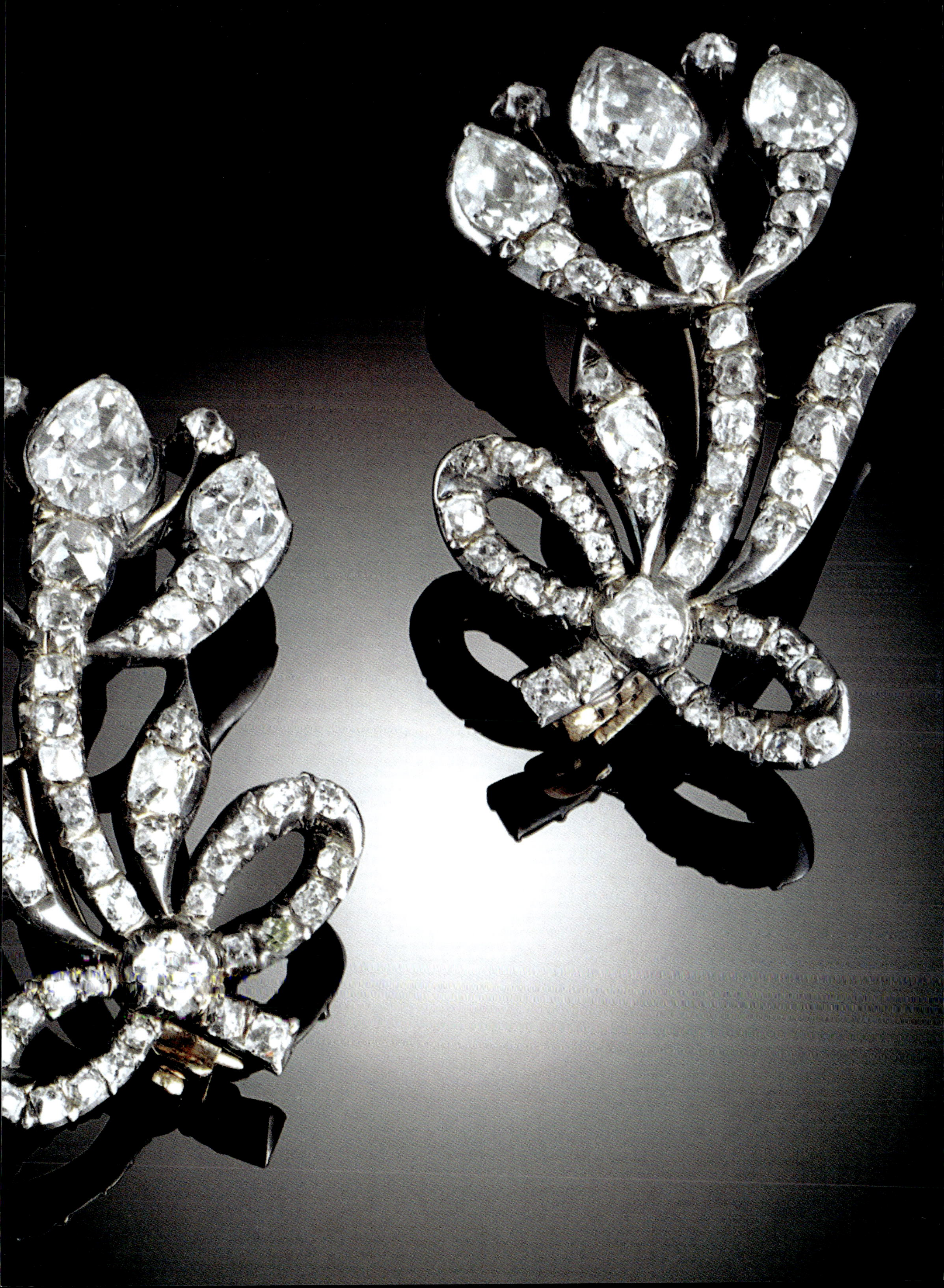

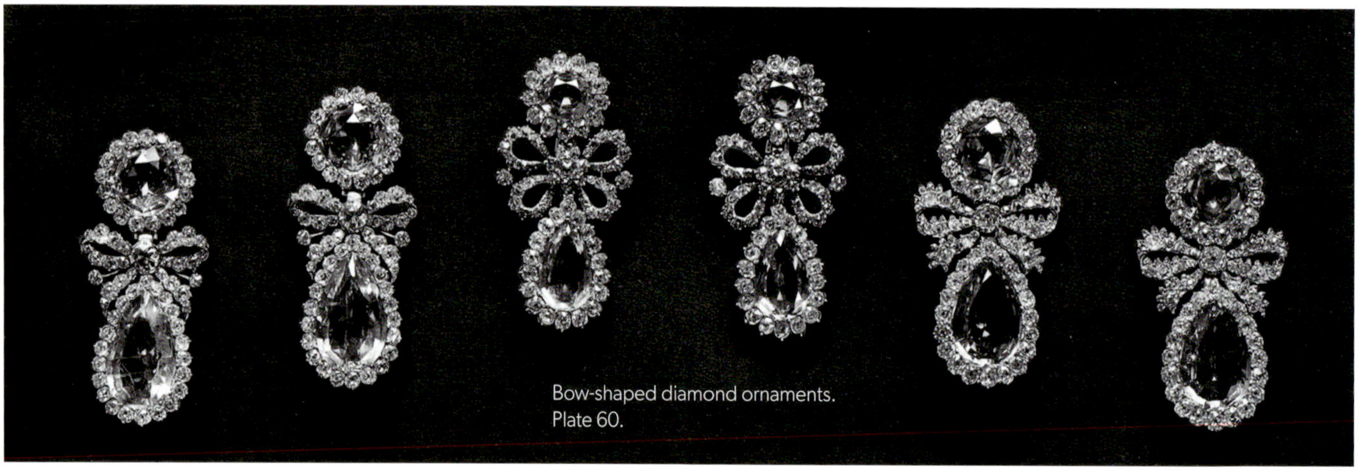

Bow-shaped diamond ornaments. Plate 60.

Bow-Shaped Diamond Ornaments

- Attributed to Duval. Era of Catherine the Great
- Christie's, 1927

Diamond Bow-Trimmings, no. 115, plate 60

Miniature Ruby and Diamond Hat (no photo)

- Probably by Duval, 1763
- Diamond Fund of the Moscow Kremlin

A Doll's Hat, Studded with Precious Stones, no. 296

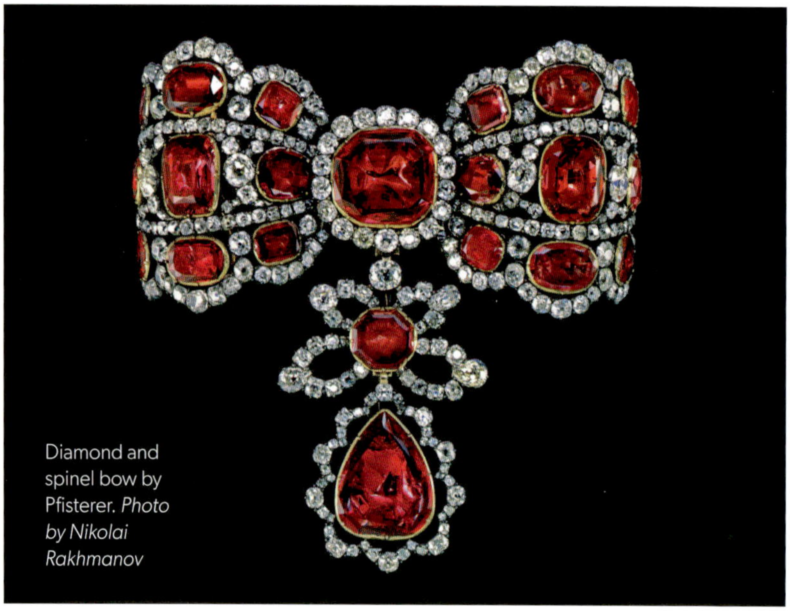

Diamond and spinel bow by Pfisterer. *Photo by Nikolai Rakhmanov*

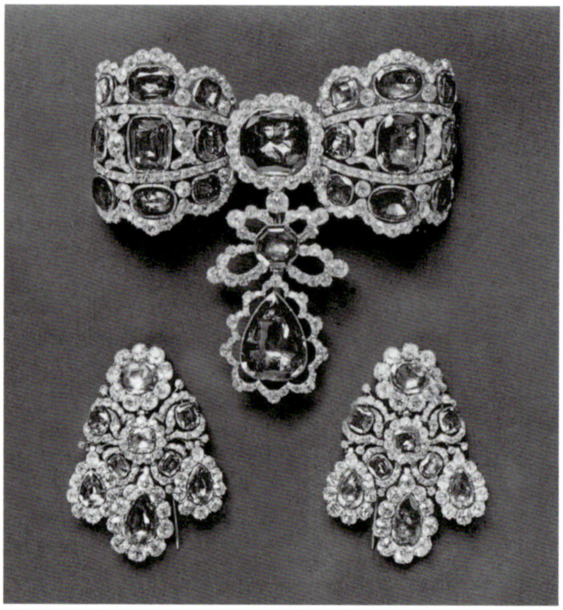

LEOPOLD PFISTERER (*active 1760s to 1790s*)

Diamond Leaf-Shaped Floral Ornaments

- 45 diamond ornaments, catalogued as period of Catherine the Great (no photo)
- Christie's, 1927, lot 92, sold for £1,150 (lists 46 ornaments)
- Lady Jane Corey
- Victoria & Albert Museum

Diamond and Spinel Set

- The bow signed "Pfisterer, April 10, 1764," the earrings "Pfisterer, May 27, 1764"
- Diamond Fund of the Moscow Kremlin

Diamond Bow with Red Spinels, no. 90, plate 53

Earrings with Spinel Ear-Drops, no. 91, plate 53

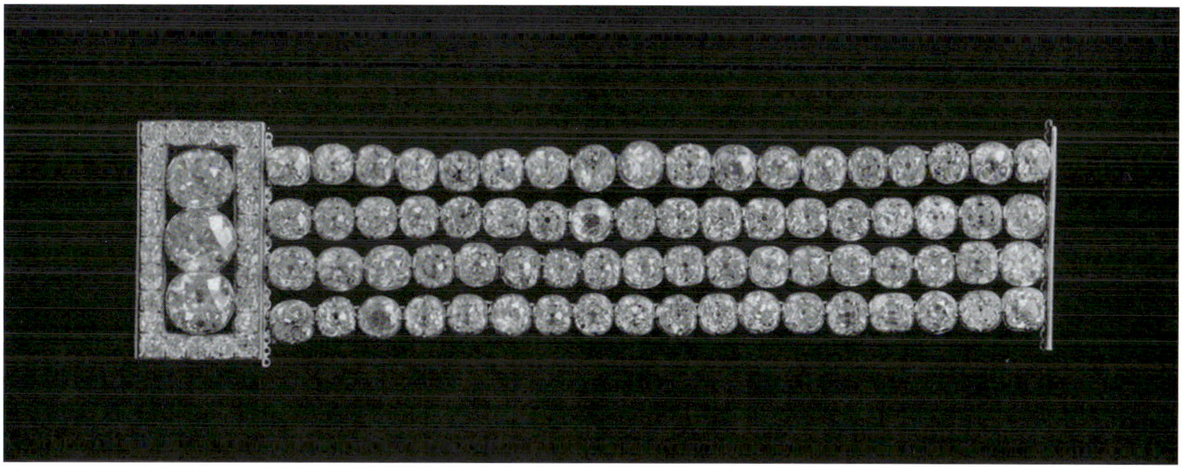

Diamond row bracelet by Keibel. Plate 34.

JOHANN WILHELM KEIBEL (*1788–1862*)

Diamond Row Bracelet

- Signed "K," mid-19th century

Bracelet of Four Rows of Diamonds, no. 52, plate 34

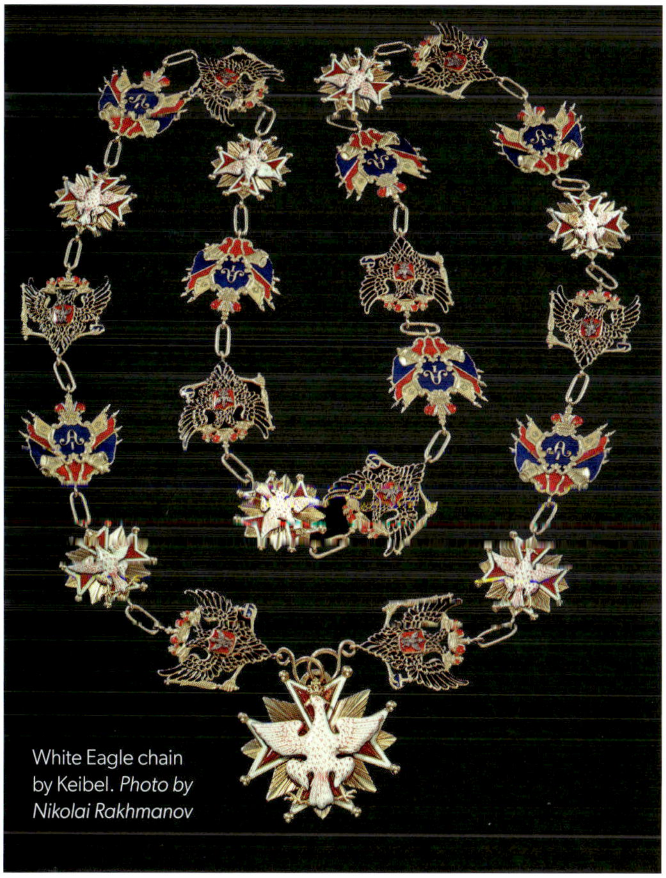

White Eagle chain by Keibel. *Photo by Nikolai Rakhmanov*

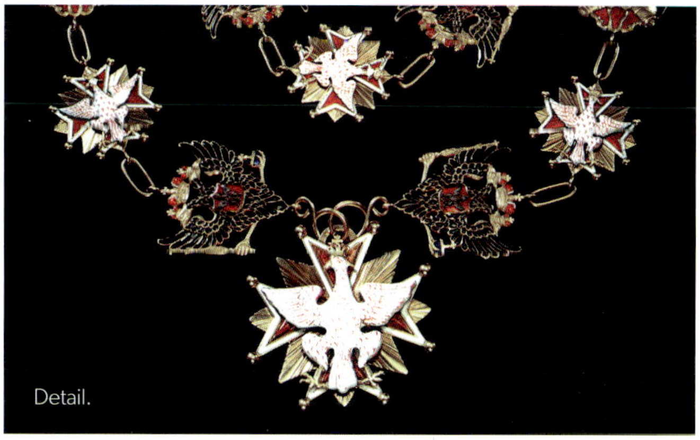

Detail.

Chain of the Order of the White Eagle

- By Keibel, St. Petersburg, 1829
- Diamond Fund of the Moscow Kremlin

Golden Chain of the Order of the White Eagle, no. 177, plate 90

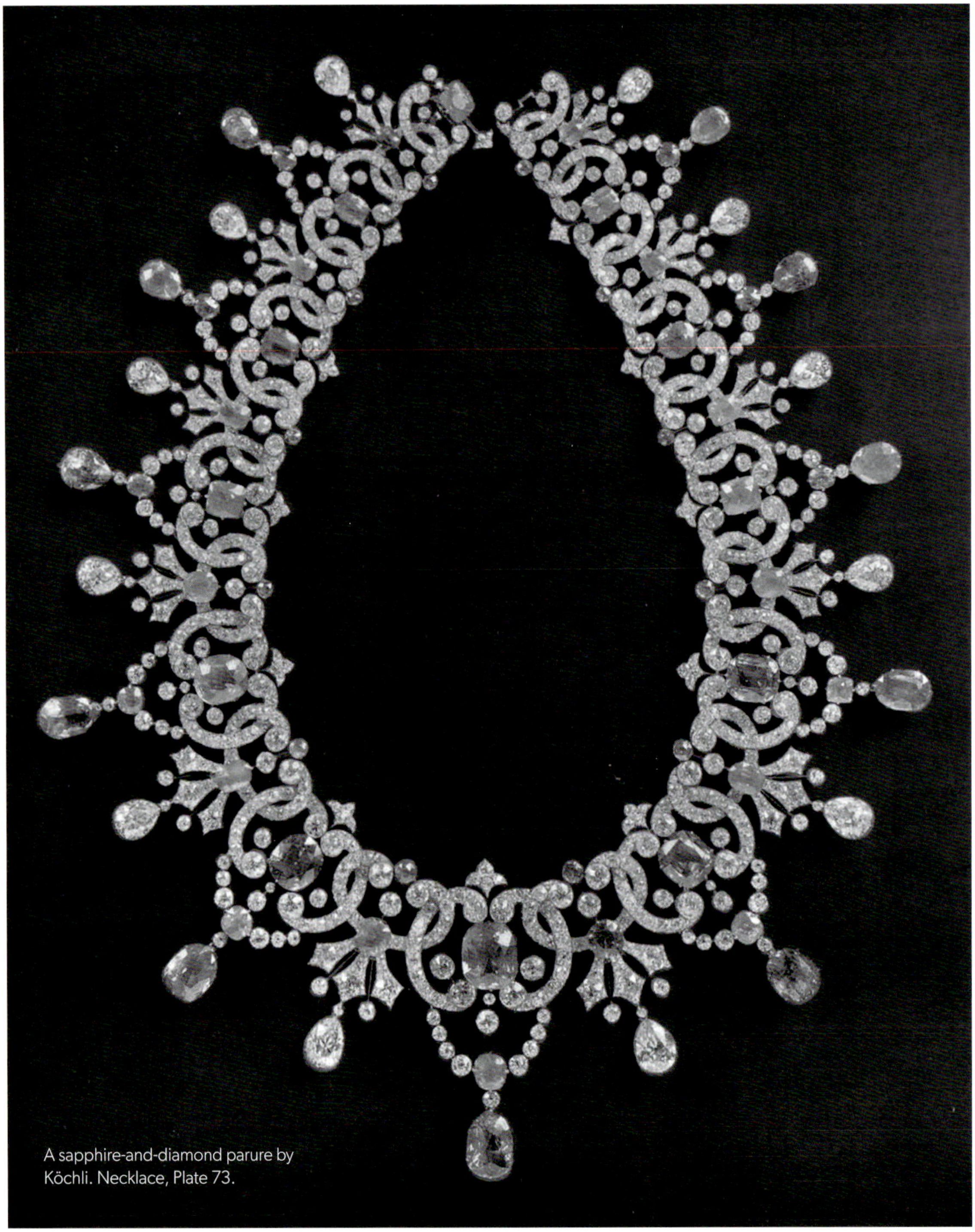

A sapphire-and-diamond parure by Köchli. Necklace, Plate 73.

FRIEDRICH KÖCHLI (1837–1906)

A Sapphire and Diamond Parure including Diadem, Necklace, Brooch and Bracelet (no photo for bracelet)

- Made for the wedding of Empress Alexandra Fedorova, 1894.

Diamond Set with Sapphires, no. 140: Necklace, plate 73; Diadem, plate 74; Brooch, plate 75

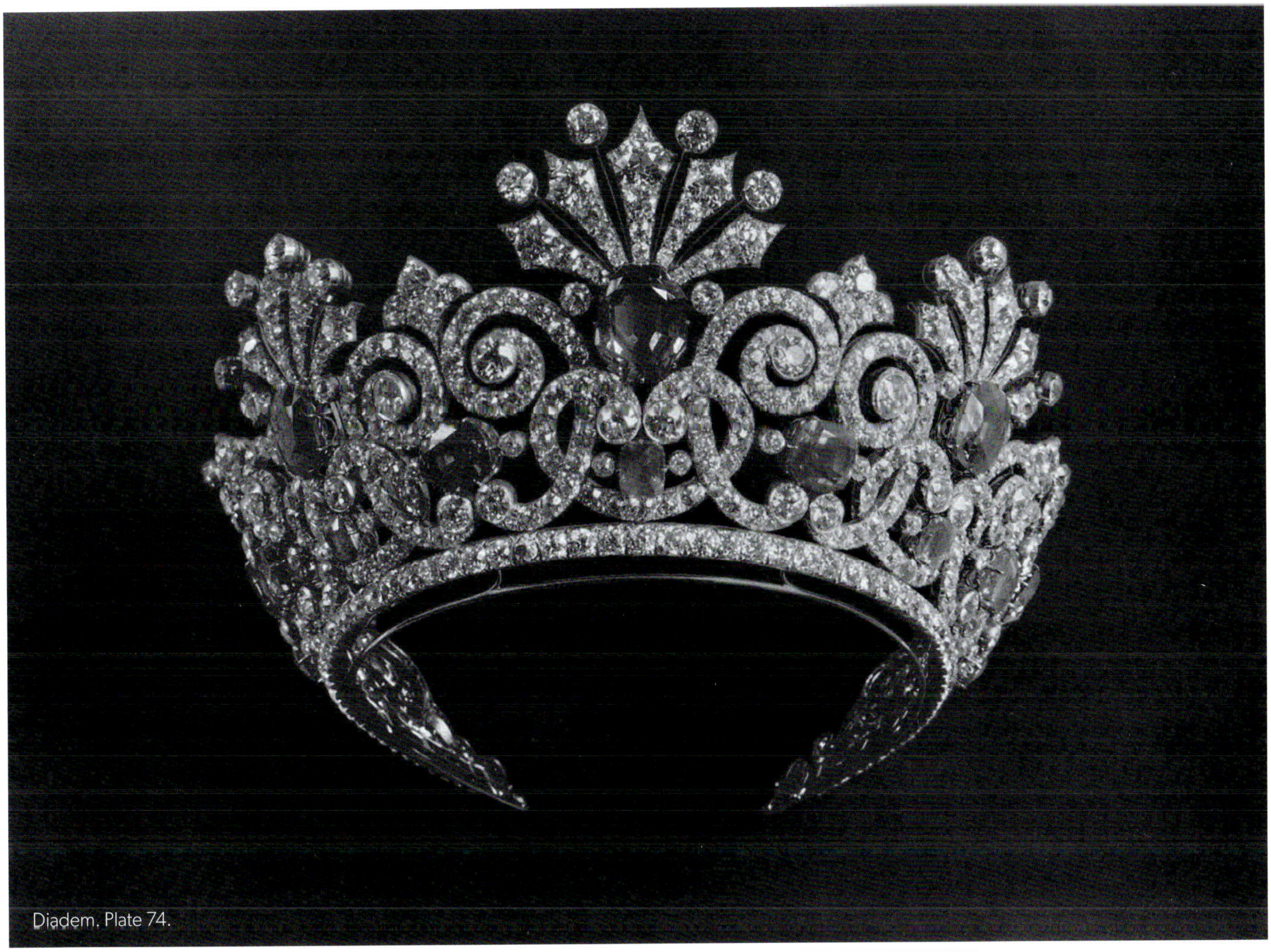

Diadem. Plate 74.

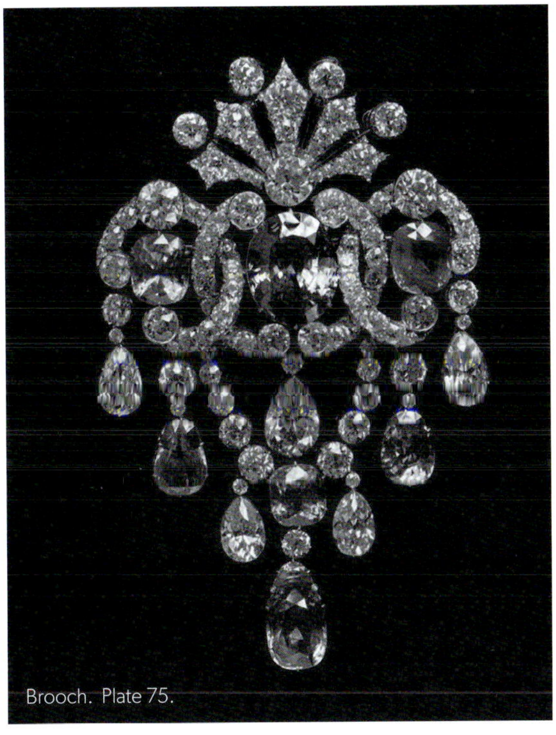

Brooch. Plate 75.

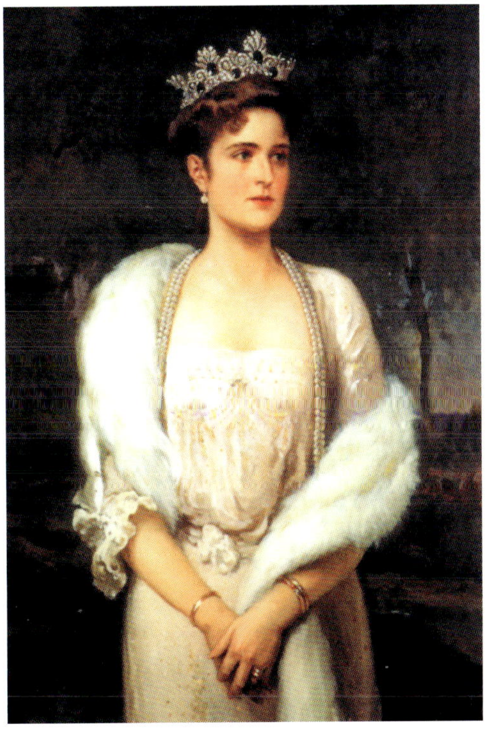

Empress Alexandra of Russia wearing the Köchli crown by Konstantin Makovskii, 1914 (detail). *Source: Wikimedia Commons*

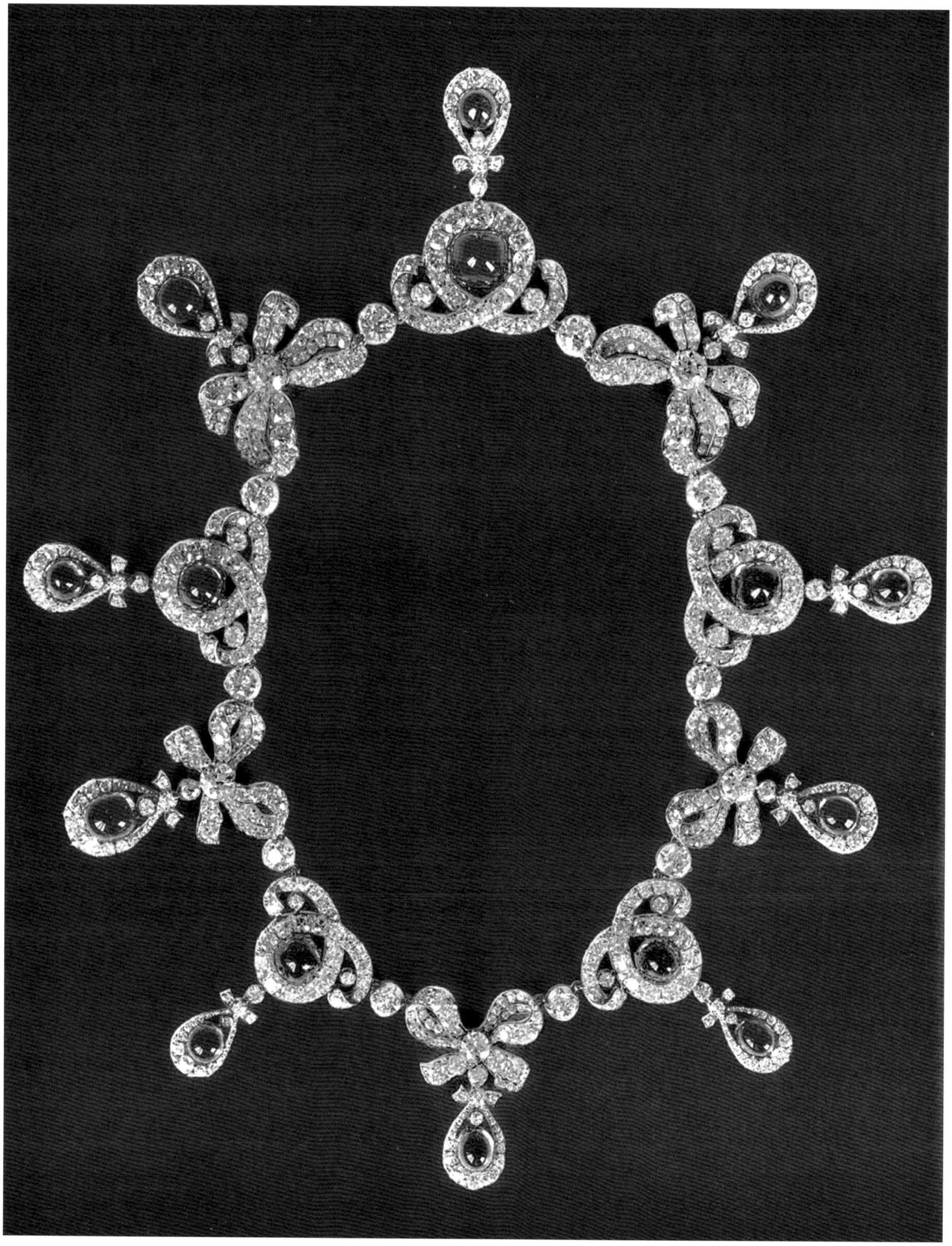

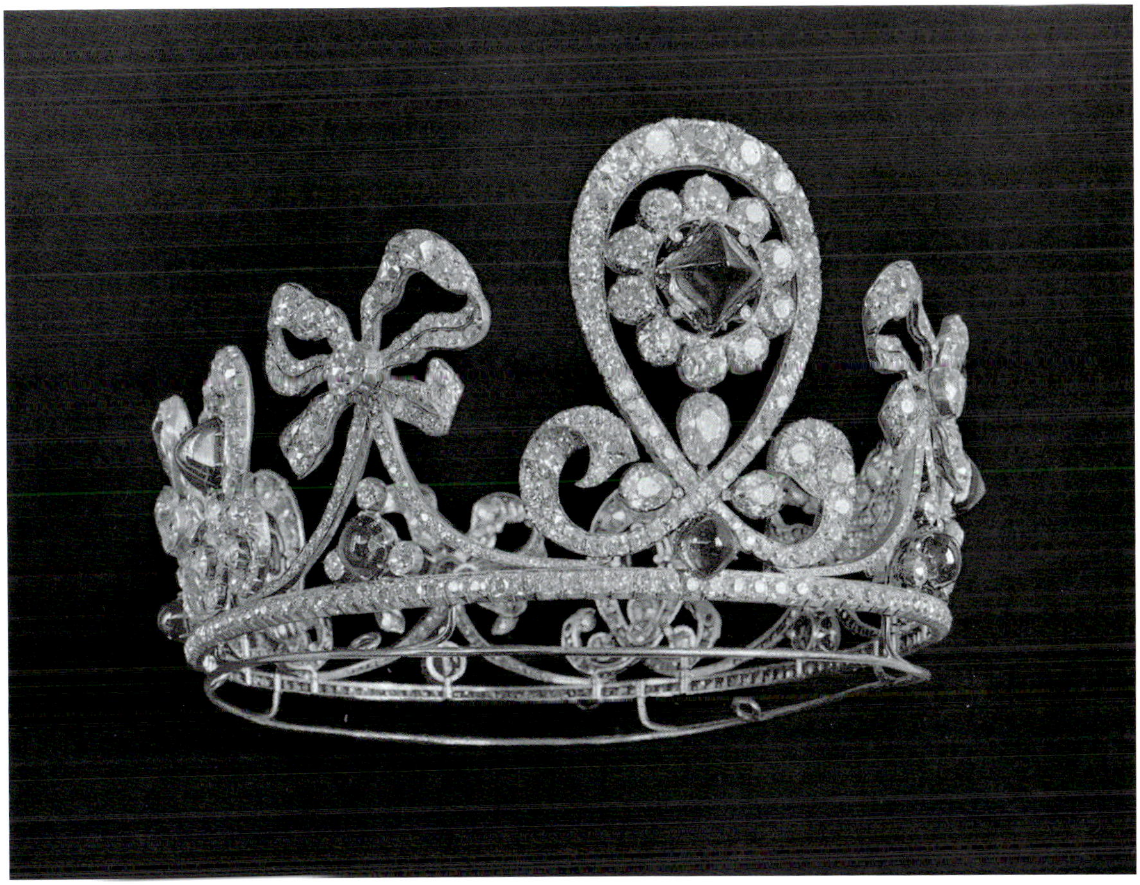

Parure of emeralds and diamonds: diadem by Bolin. Plate 72.

Previous page:
Parure of emeralds and diamonds: necklace by Bolin. Plate 71.

THE HOUSE OF BOLIN (*1830S TO 1917, ST. PETERSBURG*) and THE HOUSE OF FABERGÉ (*1842–1917*)

Parure of Emeralds and Diamonds

- By Bolin and Fabergé, made for Empress Alexandra Fedorovna and Grand Duchess Elizabeth Fedorovna, the necklace by workmaster Robert Swan, signed with his initials

Diamond Set with Large Emeralds: The Necklace; Diadem, no. 139, plates 71 and 72

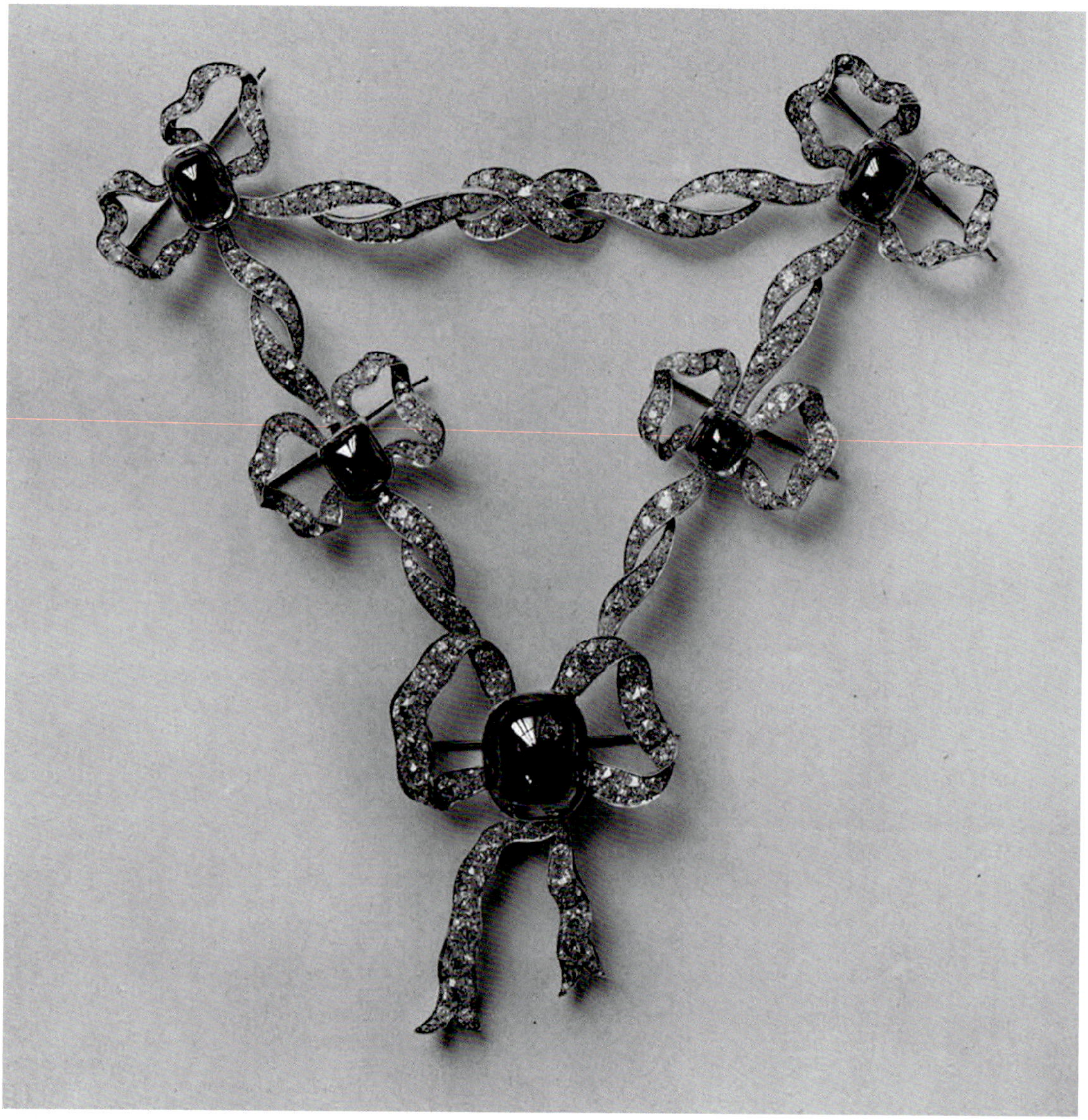

Bodice ornament (plastron) by Fabergé.
Plate 70.

Bodice Ornament (plastron)

- By Fabergé, Moscow workmaster Oscar Pihl, signed with his initials
- A copy was made in 1985 for the Diamond Fund of the Moscow Kremlin.

Plastron, no. 139, plate 70

Diamond and Turquoise Diadem and Brooch

- By Fabergé, catalogued as circa 1895

A Diamond Brooch with an Oriental Turquoise, no. 153, plate 81

A Diamond Diadem with an Oriental Turquoise, no. 154, plate 81

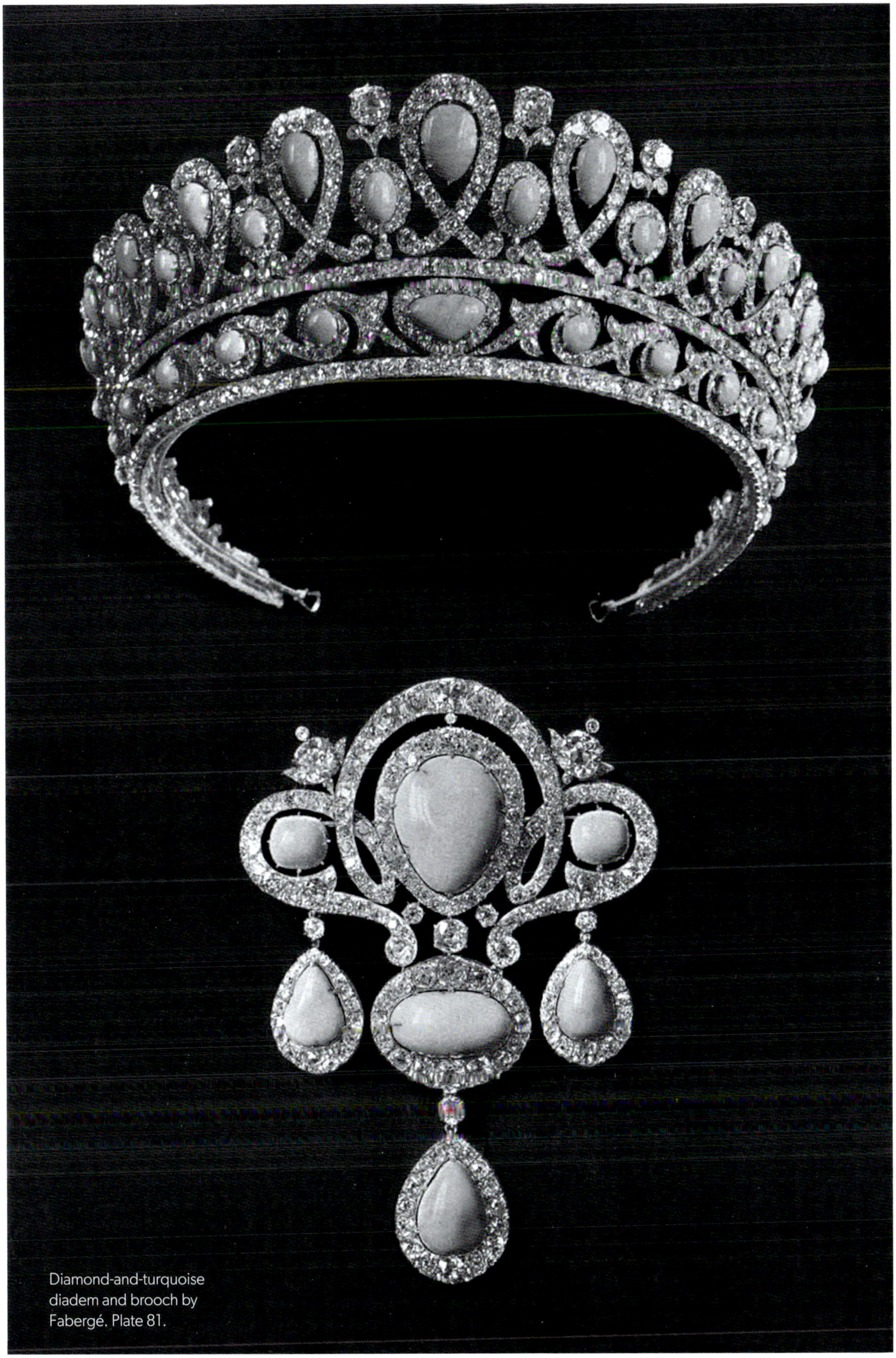

Diamond-and-turquoise diadem and brooch by Fabergé. Plate 81.

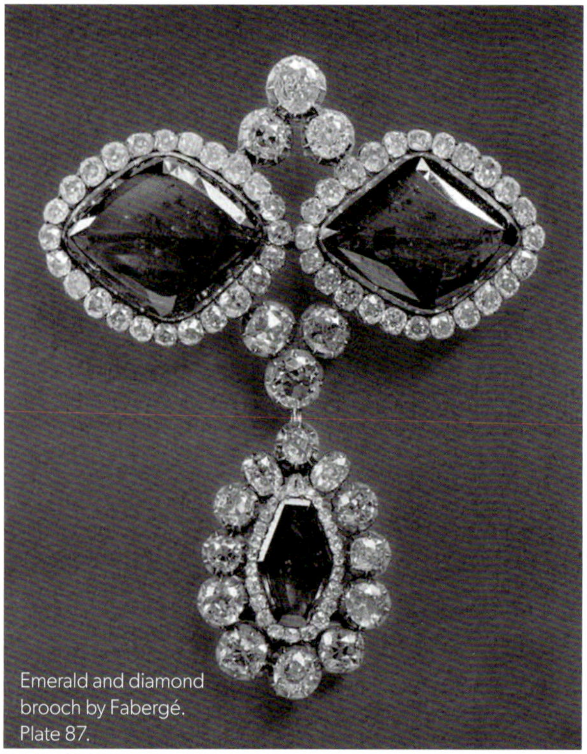

Emerald and diamond brooch by Fabergé. Plate 87.

Emerald and Diamond Brooch

- By Fabergé, catalogued as 1898, made in haste for a costume ball with stones selected by the empress from the imperial Treasury

Emerald "Sévigné" Brooch, no. 165, plate 87

Large Necklace

- By Fabergé, catalogued as 1898, made in haste for a costume ball with stones selected by the empress from the imperial Treasury

Necklace Called "d'esclave" Diamonds, Pearls and Emeralds, no. 73, plate 43

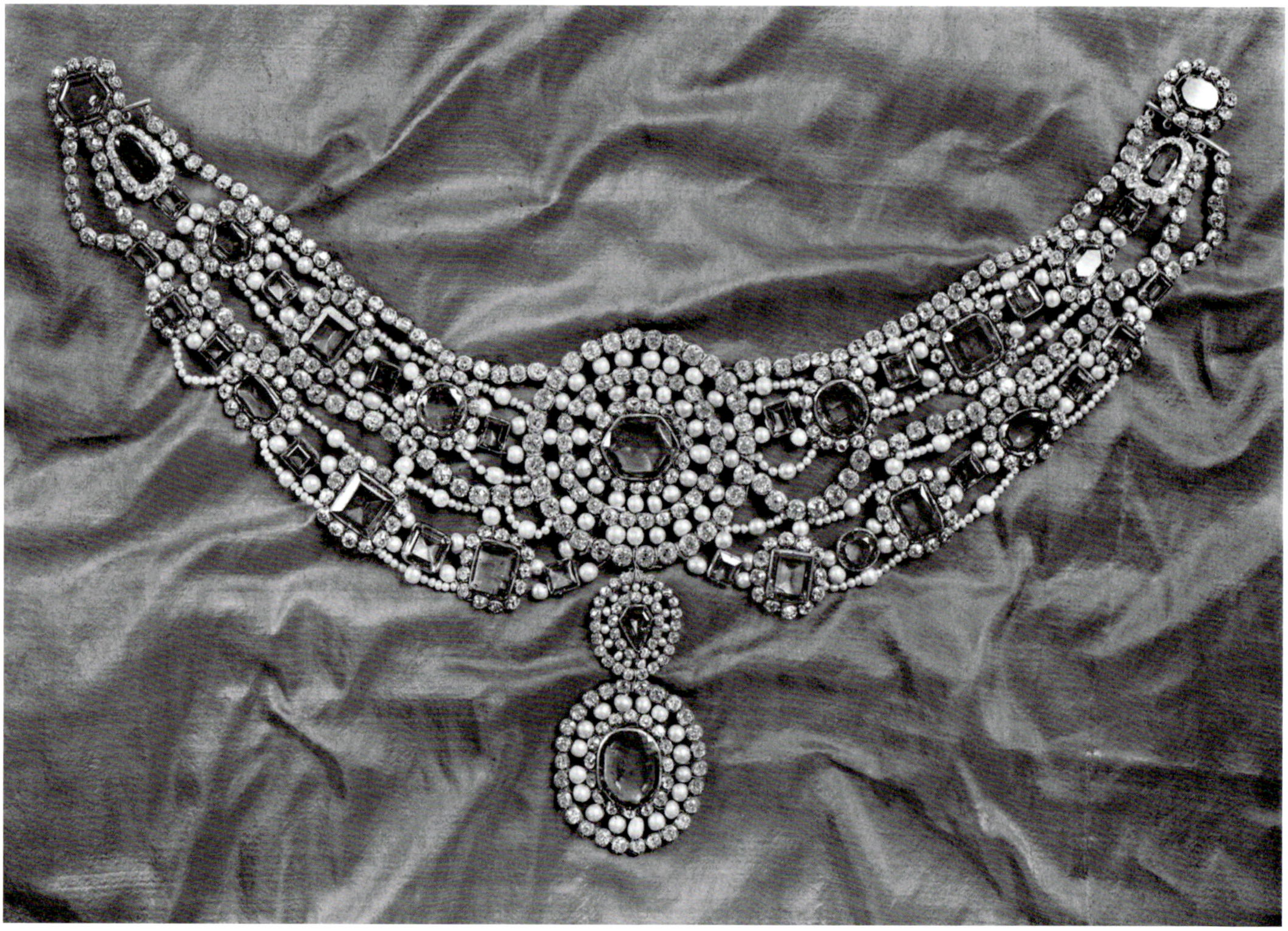

Large necklace by Fabergé. Plate 43.

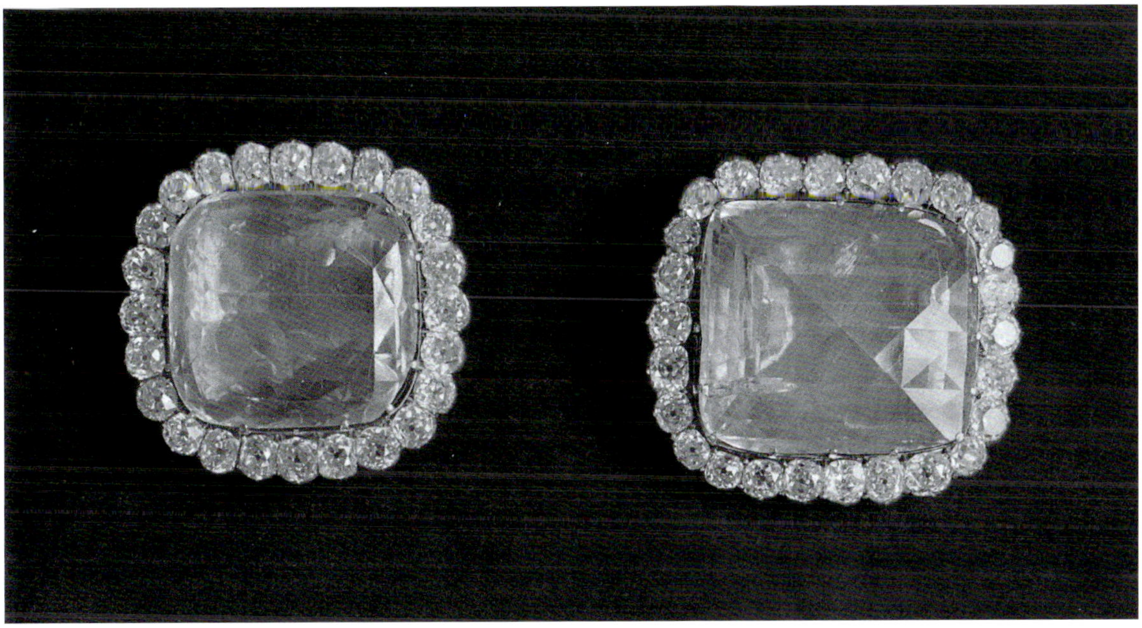

Two sapphire brooches by Fabergé. Plate 86.

Two Sapphire Brooches

- By Fabergé

Two Brooches with Ceylon Sapphires, no. 161, plate 86

Enamel Magnifying Glass (no photo)

- By Fabergé, workmaster Michael Perchin

A Large Magnifying Glass, no. 297

Diamond Rose Brooch

- By Fabergé.
- A similar life-size diamond-set rose, based on sketches by V. V. Nikolaev and consisting of over 1,600 diamonds, was created in 1970 for the Diamond Fund in Moscow.

A Diamond Brooch Representing a Rose with Leaves, no. 49, plate 33

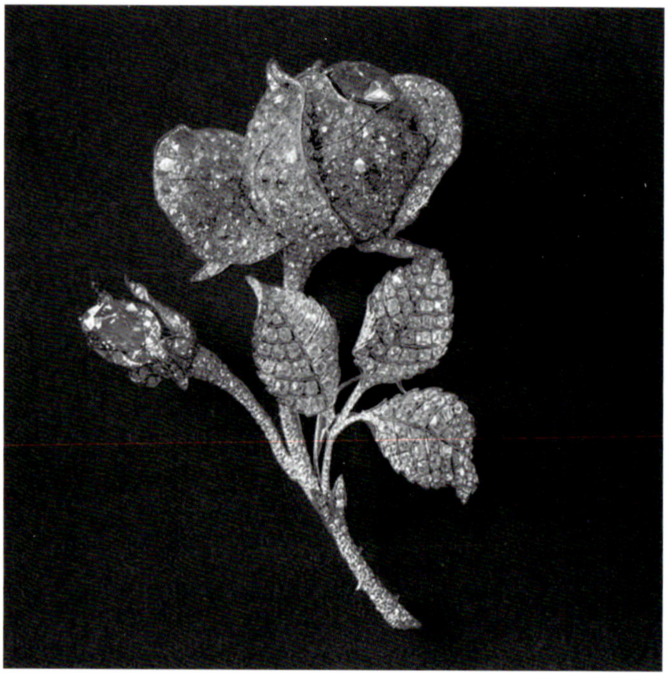

Diamond rose brooch by Fabergé. Plate 33.

II. Russian Crown Jewels Resold after 1927 in the West

Pair of Diamond Bow Bracelets

- Circa 1780, era of Catherine the Great
- Christie's, 1927, lot 44, sold for £3,400
- S. J. Phillips, Ltd., 1980s
- Christie's, 2006, lot 390, only one offered, which sold for $259,082

Two Golden Bracelets Decorated with Diamonds, no. 48, plate 32

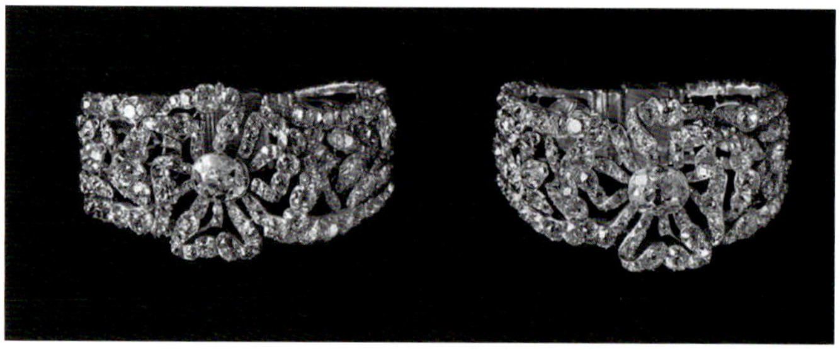

Pair of diamond bow bracelets. Plate 32.

Sapphire, Diamond, Ruby and Emerald Brooch in the Form of an Eagle

- Era of Empress Elizabeth Petrovna (r. 1741–61).
- Christie's, 1927, lot 56, sold for £180 to S. J. Phillips
- Christie's, 2007, lot 268, sold for $129,574

Aigrette Representing a Bird with Natural-Coloured Stones, no. 190, plate 94

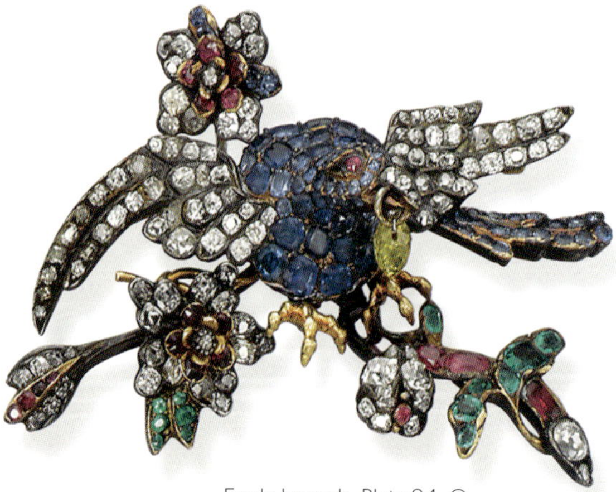

Eagle brooch. Plate 94. © *2006 Christie's Images, Ltd.*

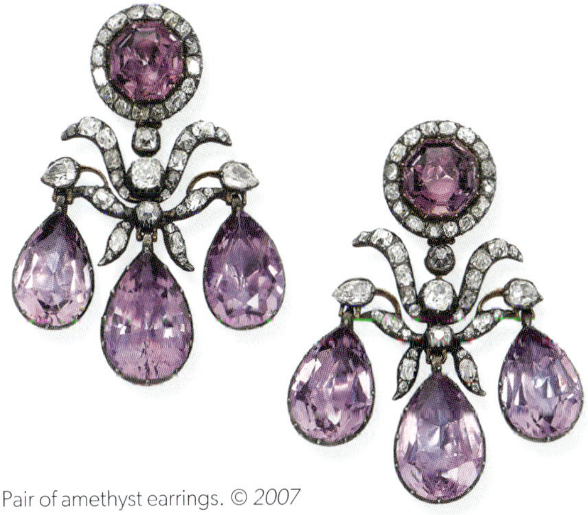

Pair of amethyst earrings. © *2007 Christie's Images, Ltd*. Plate 59.

Pair of Amethyst Girandole Earrings

- Circa 1760
- Christie's, 1927, lot 23, sold for £295 to S. J. Phillips, London
- Christie's, 2007, lot 269, sold for $386,936

Amethyst Earrings, no. 110, plate 59

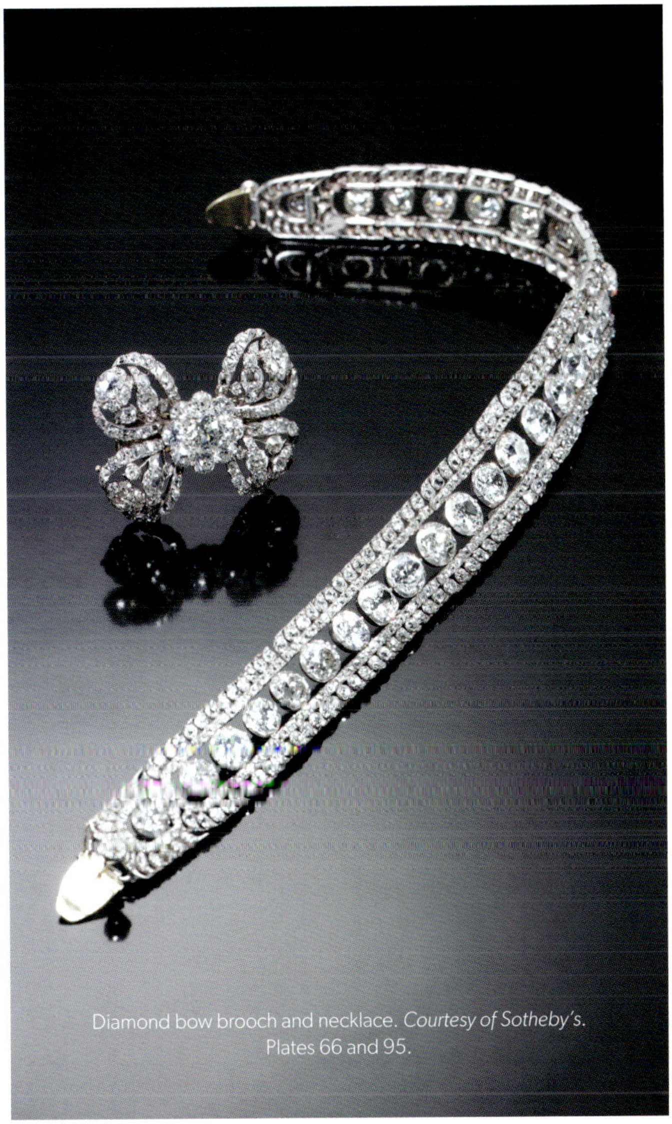

Diamond bow brooch and necklace. *Courtesy of Sotheby's*. Plates 66 and 95.

Diamond Bow Brooch

- Catalogued as 2nd half of the 19th century
- Christie's, 1927, lot 59, sold for £300.
- S. J. Phillips, London
- Sotheby's, 2005, lot 442, now listed as a diamond bow clasp, attached to diamond necklace presumably the one listed below (Christie's, 1927, lot 71). Together, they sold for $1,630,000. Unsold when reoffered in 2016.

Diamond Brooch in the Form of a Bow, no. 128, plate 66

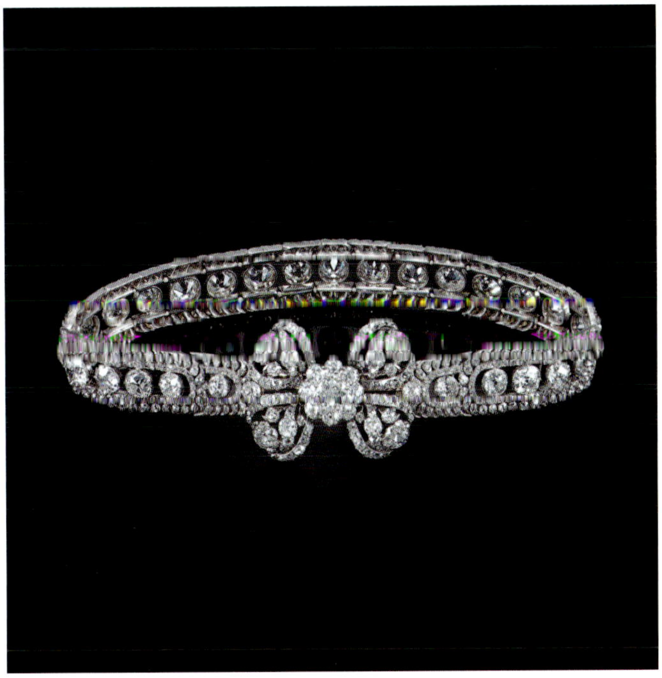

Diamond Necklace (previous page)

- Catalogued as antique stones with 25 big diamonds weighing 60 metric carats, bordered by smaller diamonds
- Christie's, 1927, lot 71, sold for £2,700, illustrated
- S. J. Phillips, London
- Sotheby's, 2005, lot 442, altered to accommodate two jeweled extensions set with two more diamonds, for a total of 27 graduated diamonds, and attached to diamond bow clasp, presumably the brooch listed above. (Christie's, 1927, lot 59). Together, they sold for $1,630,000. Unsold when reoffered in 2016.

Diamond Necklace, no. 195, plate 95

III. In Western Museums

The Nuptial Crown

- According to Fersman, the crown was made around 1840 of "old trimmings of diamonds" from the era of Catherine the Great and kept in a box by Nicholls & Plincke of St. Petersburg, a firm that went out of business in the 1880s. Hillwood dates the crown in 1884, with diamonds from a doublet belonging to Grand Duke Paul Petrovich (future Tsar Paul I). Its late curator emerita, Anne Odom, wrote about finding: "Documentation that the diamonds for the nuptial crown were removed from the treasury in October 1884" and that it was a common practice at the time to dismantle and reassemble crowns according to the new wearer's taste.[20]
- Christie's, 1927, lot 62, for £6,100, illustrated. Purchased by Founés, possibly the furniture dealer Isaac Founés. In the 1930s, Pierre Cartier bought it from an antique dealer in Paris, as recorded in the memoirs of Prince Christopher of Greece.[21]
- Worn by Armi Kuusela, crowned the first-ever Miss Universe in 1952.
- Parke-Bernet, 1966, Estate of Helen de Kay of New York
- Purchased by Henry Levinson, of Levinson's Jewels Chicago, Illinois, who then resold it to Alexander Schaffer of A la Vieille Russie buying on behalf of Marjorie Merriweather Post
- Hillwood Museum, Washington, DC

Imperial Nuptial Crown, no. 37, plate 26

Nuptial Crown. *Courtesy of Hillwood Estate Museum & Gardens. Photograph by Edward Owen.*

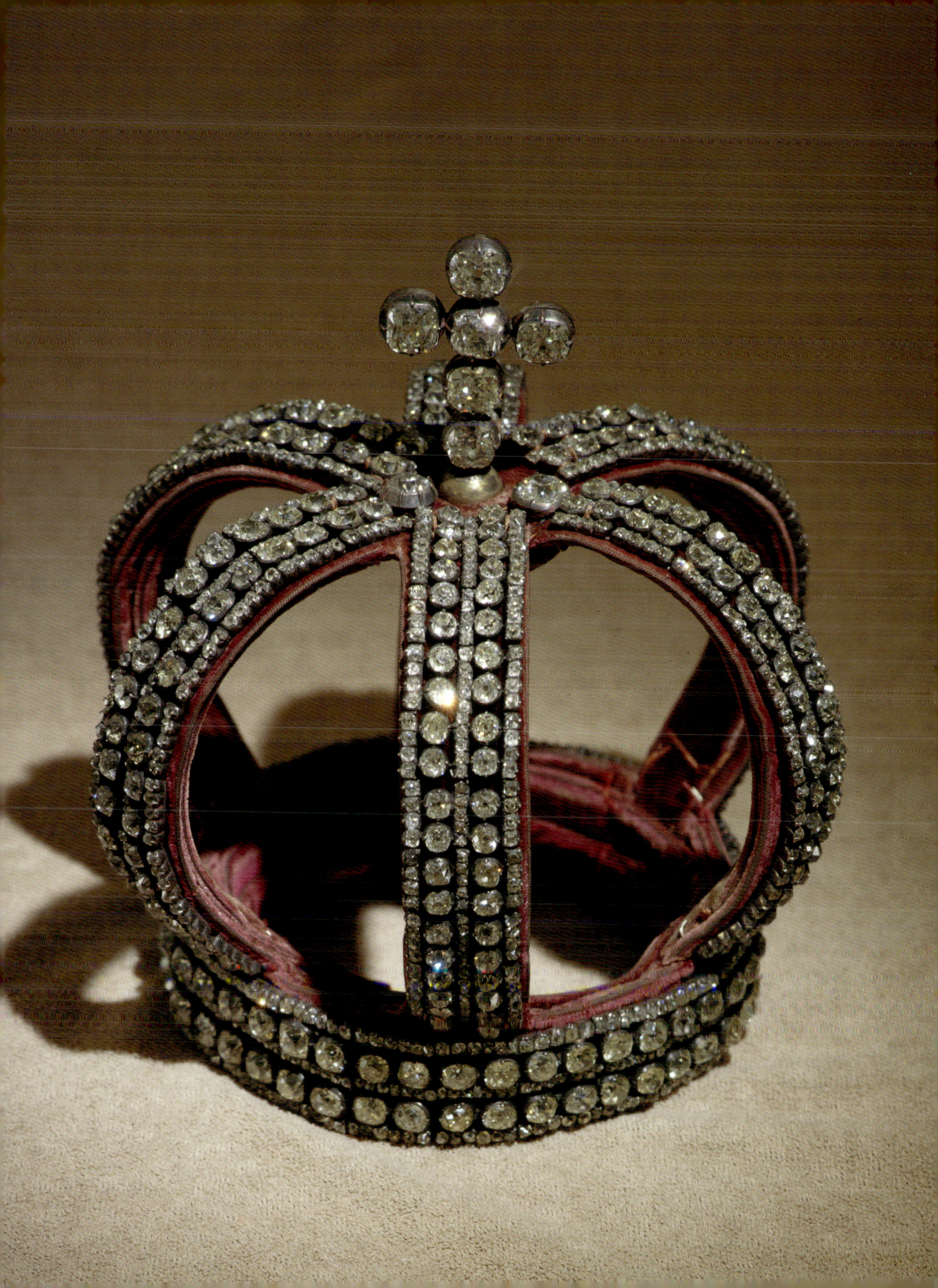

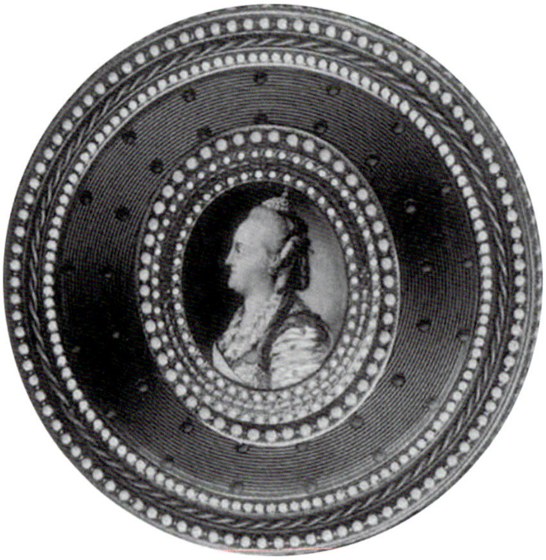

Round gold-and-enamel snuffbox. Plate 96.

Round Gold and Enamel Snuff Box

- 19th century
- Marjorie Merriweather Post
- Hillwood Museum, Washington, DC

Round Snuff-Box with the Miniature of Catherine II, no. 199, plate 96

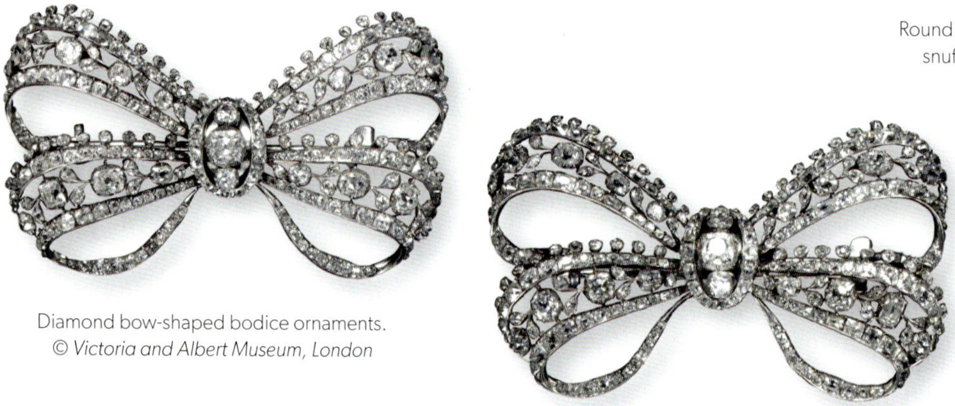

Diamond bow-shaped bodice ornaments.
© Victoria and Albert Museum, London

Diamond bow-shaped bodice ornaments

- Two from a set of three diamond bow-shaped bodice ornaments, possibly by Duval and circa 1760
- According to Dr. S. A. Amelekhina of the State Museums of the Moscow Kremlin, they may have composed part of a set of six listed in the 1865 inventory of the Diamond Room of the Winter Palace (RGIA f 468, o 43, d 1026 and 1027.)[22]
- Lady Jane Corey
- Victoria & Albert Museum, London
- These were not included in the Fersman catalog

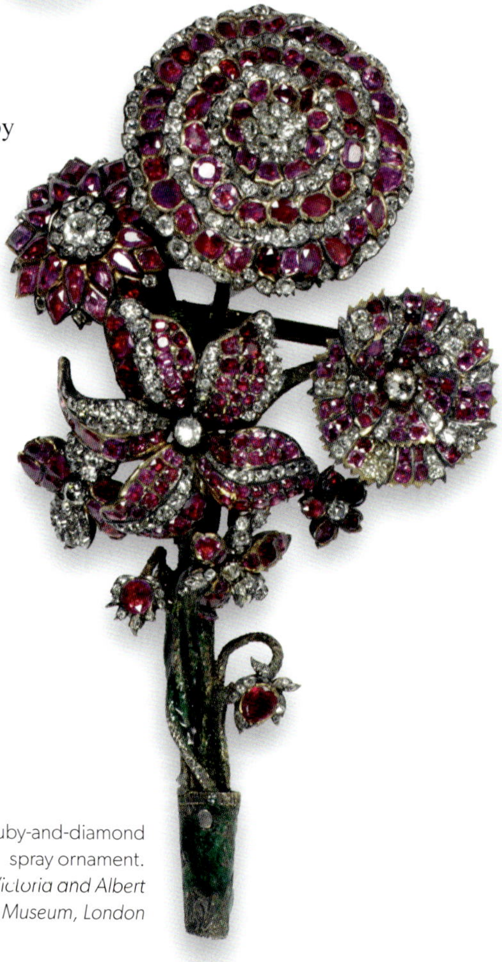

Ruby-and-diamond spray ornament.
© Victoria and Albert Museum, London

Ruby and Diamond Spray Ornament

- Maker unknown. Dated 1750–60.
- Christie's, 1927, lot 83, sold for £370
- Lady Jane Corey
- Victoria & Albert Museum, London

A small nosegay with enameled leaves and ruby flowers, no. 157, plate 83

Diamond Leaf-Shaped Floral Ornaments

- 45 diamond ornaments, catalogued as period of Catherine the Great. Now attributed to St. Petersburg court jeweler Leopold Pfisterer.
- Christie's, 1927, lot 92, sold for £1,150 (£65,000; lists 46 ornaments)
- Lady Jane Corey
- Victoria & Albert Museum, London
- These were not included in Fersman's catalogue.

IV. A Sampling of Crown Jewels Still at Large

A. ILLUSTRATED IN THE FERSMAN CATALOG

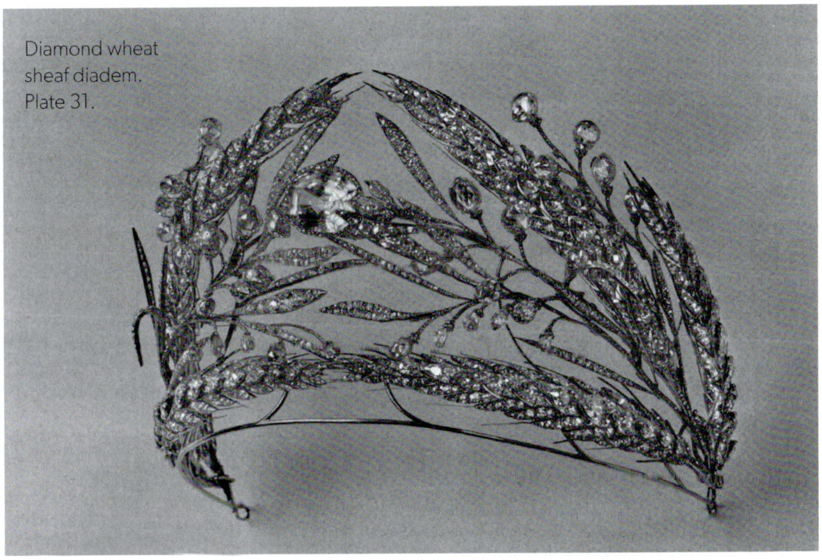

Diamond wheat sheaf diadem. Plate 31.

Diamond Wheat Sheaf Diadem

- First quarter of the 19th century, transferred to the Diamond Fund after the death of Empress Maria Fedorovna in 1829.
- Christie's, 1927, lot 116, sold for £240, illustrated.
- Reproduction in the Diamond Fund of the Moscow Kremlin.

A Full-Eared Diadem with Diamond with a Leuco-sapphire, no. 45, plate 31

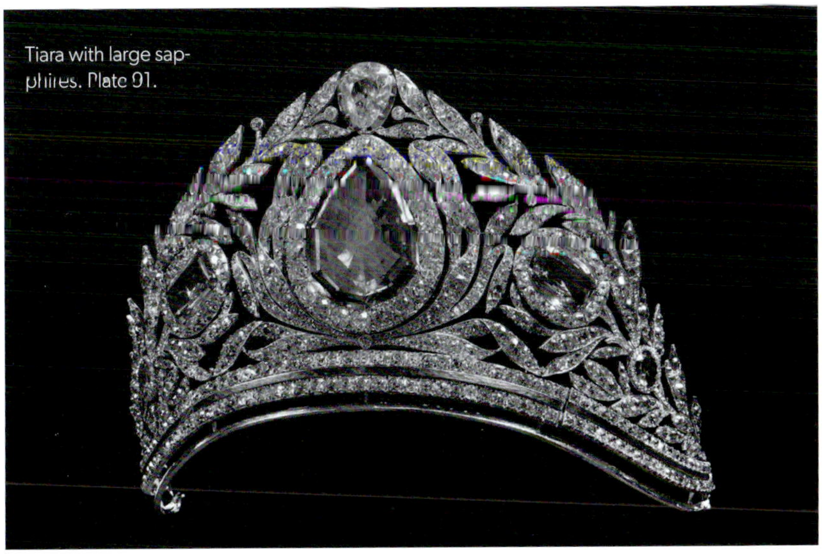

Tiara with large sapphires. Plate 91.

Tiara with Large Sapphires

- Period of Paul I, ca. 1805

Diadem with Large Sapphires, no. 178, plate 91

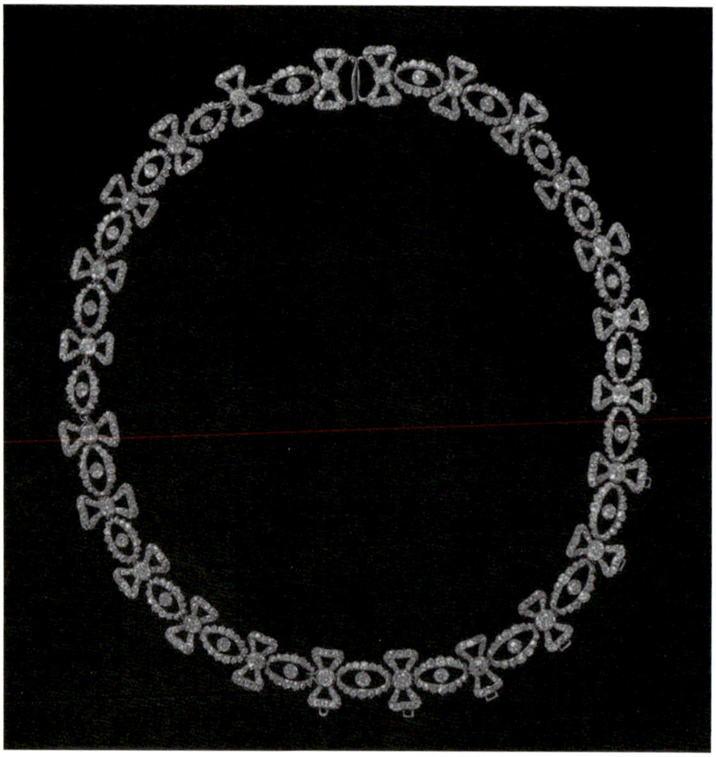

Catherine the Great diamond necklace. Plate 78.

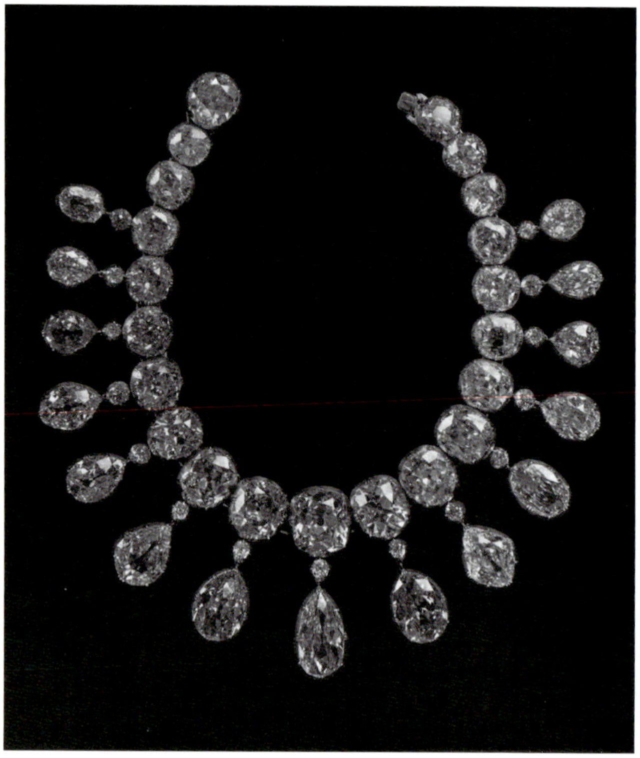

Diamond esclavage. Plate 30.

Diamond Bow Necklace

- In the Louis XVI style, period of Catherine the Great.

Necklace with Diamond-Studded Bows, no. 149, plate 78

Fringe Necklace with Massive Diamonds

- Comprising 36 large diamonds weighing over 475 carats total. Diamond cuts date from 17th to 18th centuries.

Diamond Rivière, the So-Called Collier d'Esclavage, no. 44, plate 30

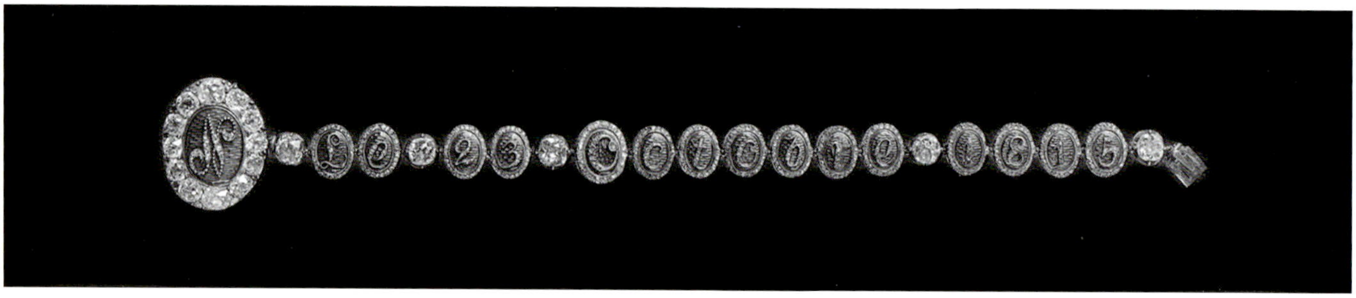

Enamel bracelet with diamonds. Bottom of Plate 95.

Enamel Bracelet with Diamonds

- Set in diamonds on separate links against blue enamel "N le 23 Octobre 1815"
- Christie's, 1927, lot 14, sold for £270

An Enamel Bracelet with Diamonds, no. 196, plate 95

Two Brooches Set with Solitaires

- Not dated. Estimated at 115,000 rubles and weighing over 40 carats, and 200,000 rubles and weighing over 53 carats, respectively, in an early inventory (probably 1898).
- The first sold at Christie's, 1927, lot 100, for £11,800, illustrated

Indian Solitaires Set in Brooches, no. 85, plate 52

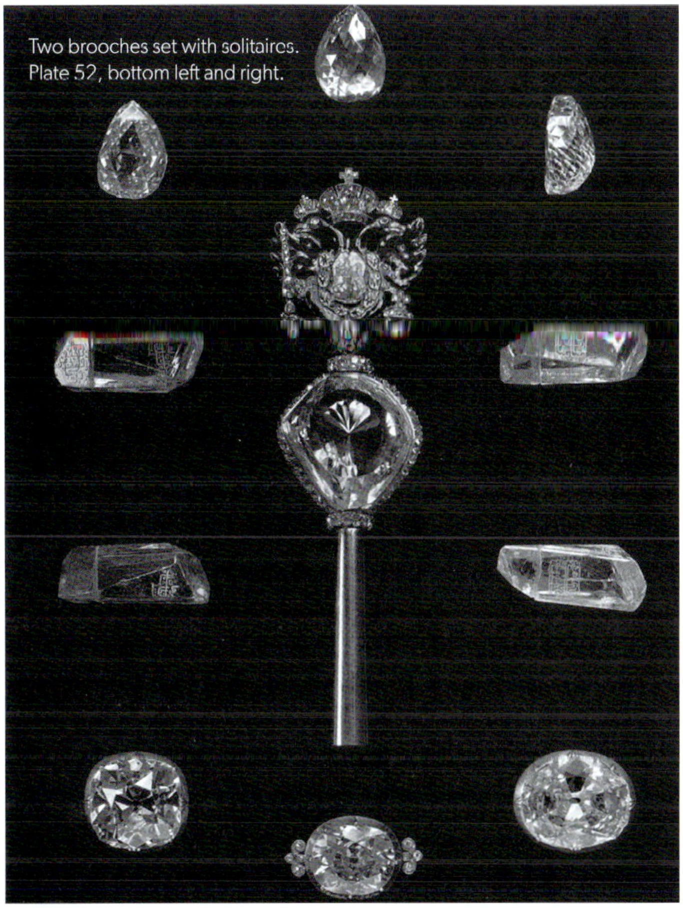
Two brooches set with solitaires. Plate 52, bottom left and right.

Topaz Diamond Mantel Clasp (center) and Seven Gem-Set Diamond Brooches

- The mantel clasp set with red topaz, by repute "the finest jewel wrought in Russia" (Fersman), probably period of Tsar Paul I (r. 1896–1901)
- Six brooches set with spinels, one set with a ruby, each catalogued as belonging to Empress Maria Fedorovna, mother of Nicholas I

Mantel Clasp with Cherry Red Topaz, no. 13, plate 15

Seven Brooches, Large Spinels and Diamonds, nos. 14–20, plate 15

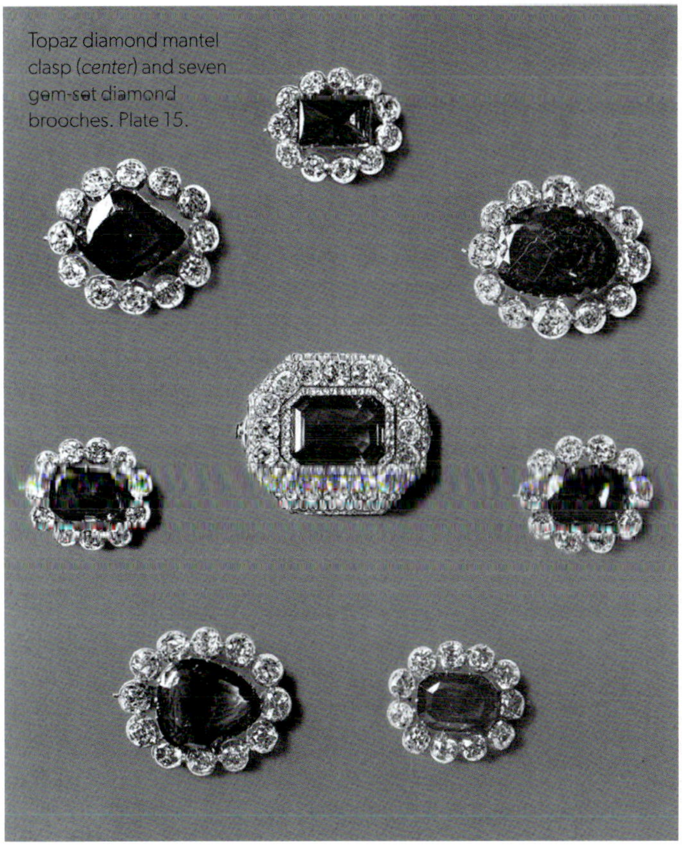
Topaz diamond mantel clasp (*center*) and seven gem-set diamond brooches. Plate 15.

Emerald, Sapphire, Pink Topaz and Diamond Clasp

- "A most beautiful jewel" (Fersman), period of Nicholas I, ca. 1830.

Brooch-Fermoir with Diamonds and Different Natural-Coloured Stones, no. 141, plate 75

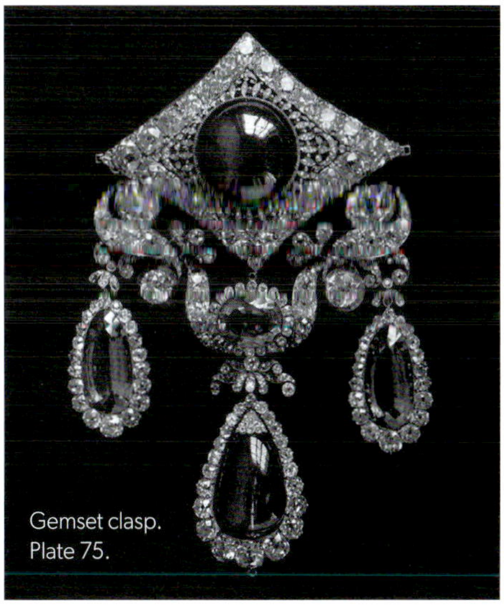
Gemset clasp. Plate 75.

Pearl and Diamond Pin

- Catalogued as 18th century, period of Empress Elizabeth Petrovna
- Christie's, 1927, lot 30, sold for £300

Diamond Pin in the Form of a Flower, with a Pearl Pendant, no. 183, plate 93

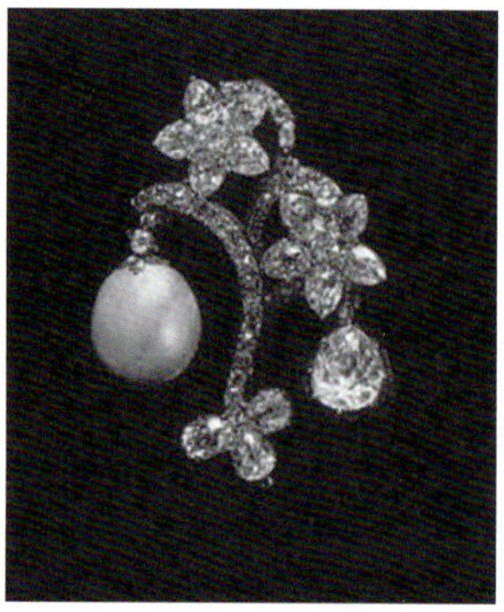

Pearl and diamond pin. Plate 93.

Diamond Aigrette Brooch

- Catalogued as circa 1750, era of Empress Elizabeth
- Christie's, 1927, lot 93, no price, illustrated

Diamond Brooch-Aigrette in the Form of a Branch, no. 185, plate 93

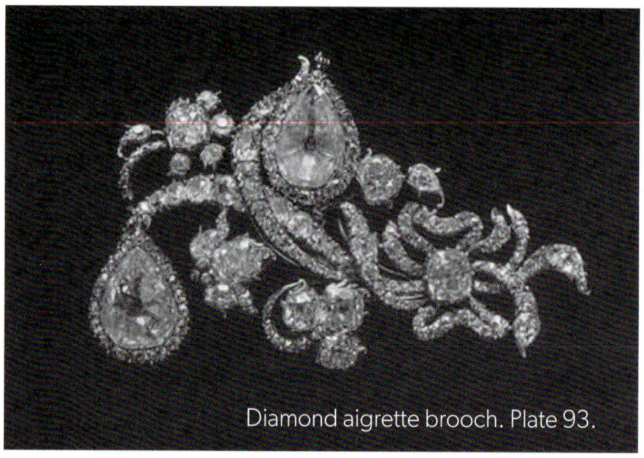

Diamond aigrette brooch. Plate 93.

Two Pairs of Pearl and Diamond Earrings

- Christie's, 1927, lot 55, sold for £240, combined with another pair of diamond earrings, possibly Diamond Earrings, Pearls and "Pendentifs," no. 25, plate 17

Diamond Earrings, Pearls, no. 24, plate 17

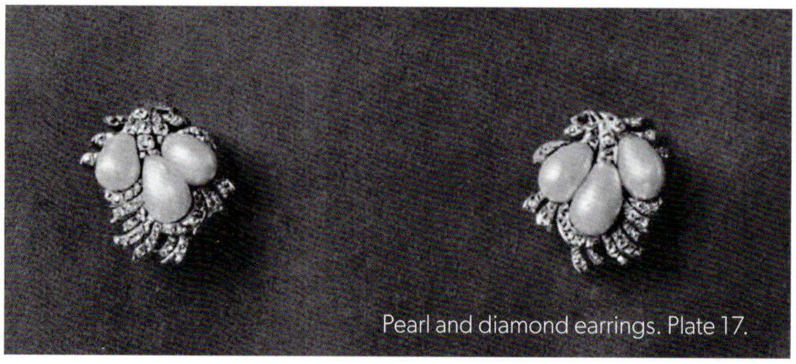

Pearl and diamond earrings. Plate 17.

Diamond and Pearl Brooch with Colored Gemstones

- Catalogued as part late 18th century, with later adjustments
- Christie's, 1927, lot 10?, sold for £175 (listed as a pair of brooches)

Diamond Brooch; Natural Coloured Stones and Pearl Pendeloques, no. 78, plate 44

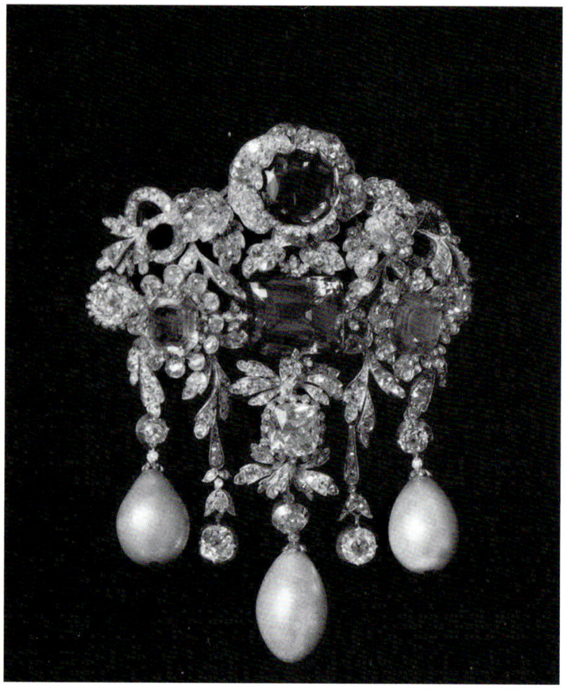

Diamond and pearl brooch with colored gemstones. Plate 44.

Amethyst Necklace and Brooch

- Catalogued as circa 1750, the necklace set with 47 trapezoidal amethysts from the Urals
- Christie's, 1927, lot 94, sold for £4,300, illustrated.

Amethyst Necklace and Aigrette, no. 231

B. WITH NO ILLUSTRATION IN THE FERSMAN CATALOG

Without images, the mystery deepens:

Emerald and Diamond Brooch

- Catalogued as belonging to Empress Alexandra Fedorovna, from the era of Catherine the Great
- Christie's, 1927, lot 80, sold for £470

An Aigrette with Two Large Emeralds, no. 234

Diamond Ring

- Catalogued as early reign of Catherine the Great
- Christie's, 1927, lot 82, sold for £260

Ring with a Large Diamond, no. 242

Two Gem-Set Bracelets

- Catalogued as period of Emperor Alexander I, circa 1820
- Christie's, 1927, lot 18 sold for £310

Two Bracelets with Different Coloured Stones, no. 229

Turquoise and Diamond Forget-Me-Not Bracelet

- Engraved "18 April 1818" (birthday of Alexander I)
- Christie's, 1927, lot 8, sold for £70

Listed under Two Golden Bracelets, no. 230

Chrysoprase Jewels

- Comprising six pins, a necklace and pair of earrings. Dated 1770s, era of Empress Catherine the Great.
- Christie's, 1927, lot 5, sold for £265

Chrysoprase Ornaments, no. 220

Garnet Jewels

- Comprising a long necklace suspending a cross, three other necklaces, a pair of bracelets, three buckles and six clasps. Era of Empress Catherine the Great.
- Christie's, 1927, lots 1 and 4 sold for £58 and £37.

Bohemian Garnet Ornaments, nos. 222 and 223

Smoky Topaz Jewels

- Comprising three gold bracelets, a pair of earrings and 23 hairpins. Circa 1780–90. Era of Empress Catherine the Great.
- Christie's, 1927, lot 2 and 3, sold for £58 and £27

Ornaments of Smoky Topaz, no. 218

Five Sapphire Pins

- Christie's, 1927, lot 97, sold for £380

Sapphire Pins, no. 262

Lost in the tragic turmoil that marked the end of a dynasty, most of the Russian crown jewels have vanished. Given the enormous intrinsic value and the rarity of such treasures, and indeed of each individual gemstone, there is little hope of finding them intact, if at all. In uncertain times, the first thing to be dismantled is jewelry. However, perhaps somewhere in the world, an unwitting owner possesses one of these rare, storied jewels from the former house of the Romanovs.

CROWN JEWELS VS. FABERGÉ EGGS: WHICH WOULD YOU CHOOSE?

Given its astronomical value, finding a missing Fabergé egg would rate high up on anyone's wish list. But to me, nothing could beat the thrill of discovering missing Russian crown jewels. Unlike Fabergé, so little is known about their makers. Whereas most of the imperial eggs have survived and are accounted for, almost all of the massive parures, diamond rivières and bejeweled tiaras have disappeared. We do not see them in the Hermitage, in the Diamond Room, or in the Kremlin's Diamond Fund. Sadly, they were the first to be sold. What a treat it would be to examine the mounts and designs, to say nothing of the unsurpassed size and quality of the gemstones themselves.

Fabergé eggs have appeared and reappeared at auction for decades. Now, fittingly, most of them are back in St. Petersburg, in the Fabergé Museum. But except for a handful of missing eggs, all are well documented, their trajectories known to us via myriads of reference books and museum catalogues. While their surprises tend to go missing—since they were easy to sell separately after the revolution—one is less likely to dismantle a Fabergé egg itself, as one would a gem encrusted diadem. In the rare instance when crown jewels have surfaced at auction (see "The Fate of the Russian Crown Jewels"), unlike Fabergé eggs, they then disappear for good. And why not? Who wouldn't want to cherish and perhaps even wear jewels that crowned the heads of the Russian empresses, adorned their lavish gowns, or rested on Catherine the Great's décolleté. Or, as is unfortunately more the case, reap a fortune by selling, plucked from its sumptuous setting, one historic gem at a time. Then again, I would *not* turn down a missing Fabergé egg should one come knocking on my door.

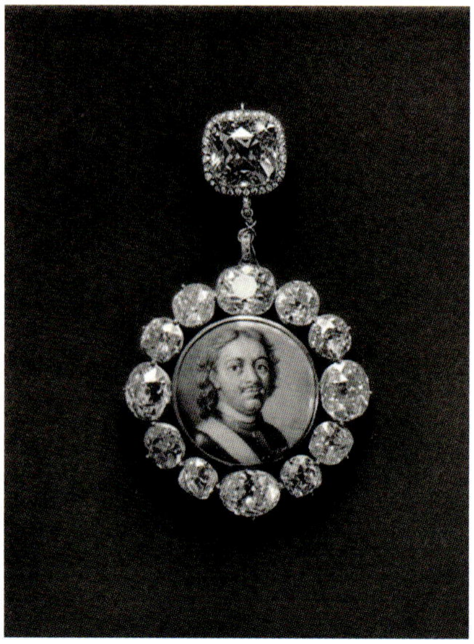

Diamond pendant with enamel portrait of Peter the Great, ca. 1840. Plate 56, Fersman.

NOTES

1. Odom, *Russian Silver in America*, 209.

2. T. A. Tutova, *Sud'ba dvortsovikh tsennostei Rossiiskogo imperatorskogo doma. Zhurnaly raboty Komissii 1922 goda v Moskovskom Kremle v dvykh chastiakh*, vol. 1 (Moscow: Moskovskii Kreml', 2015), 19.

3. Tutova, *Sud'ba tsennostei*. The following paragraphs are largely based on the introduction of Tutova's two-volume publication of the minutes of the committee that evaluated the valuables in 1922.

4. Tutova, *Sud'ba tsennostei*, 19.

5. Tutova, *Sud'ba tsennostei*, 23.

6. On Dmitrii Ivanov, see T. A. Tutova, "Direktor Oruzheinoi palaty D. D. Ivanov i borba za sokhranenie muzeinikh tsennostei v 1922–1929 godakh," in N. S. Vladimirskaia, *Sokrovishcha Rossii: Stranitsy instoricheskoi biografii museev Moskovskogo Kremlia* (Moscow: Moskovskii Kreml', 2002), www.kreml.ru/fi/c5m5/i1208/v14s08_Tutova.pdf.

7. [Ivanov, D. D.] "De la protection des oeuvres d'art en temps de guerre," *Les Arts* 28 (1904).

8. Tutova, *Sud'by tsennostei*, 26–27.

9. Betteley, "A Bid for the Best Backfires," 46–49.

10. The imperial coronation regalia was first exhibited after the coronation of Catherine the Great in October 1762.

11. In metric carats. Fersman, *Russia's Treasures*, 15. Other gems include alexandrites, topazes, amethysts, aquamarines, and beryls, and many more.

12. During the four-year period of 1797 to 1801, the cabinet spent almost 3.5 million rubles on jewelry by leading goldsmiths of St. Petersburg. I. Polynina, *The Diamond Treasures of Moscow* (Moscow, 2011), CD-ROM.

13. These items were preserved in the Diamond Room of the Moscow Kremlin, where they have been exhibited to the public by appointment since 1967.

14. Alexander E. Fersman, *Russia's Treasures of Diamonds and Precious Stones* (Moscow: People's Commissariat of Finances, 1925). The English edition is now also available on the internet: https://archive.org/details/RussiasTreasureOfDiamondsAndPreciousStones.

15. In 2017, a contemporaneous publication (1922) titled *The Russian Diamond Fund* came to light at the American library of the US Geological Survey. Owned by the late gemologist George Kunz, it contains illustrations similar to those in Fersman's album but also lists four additional crown jewels: a sapphire-and-diamond tiara, a sapphire bracelet, an emerald drop necklace, and a cabochon sapphire-and-diamond bow brooch. Three of these items are illustrated in the group photo of the crown jewels displayed above. Both the tiara and brooch were listed in the Fersman catalogue (nos. 204 and 240) but are not illustrated; that was published four years later. Both were sold, and the four are at large. Despite the tiara's illustrious provenance—it was worn by Empress Maria Fedorovna at the wedding of Grand Duchess Maria Aleksandrovna to Prince Alfred, Duke of Edinburg, in 1874—Fersman deemed its design "not very successful." Perhaps this explains why it was not illustrated. Information from Victor Nikitin's compilation "A List of the Russian Crown Jewels" was published in Nicholas Iljine and Natalya Semyonova, *Selling Russia's Treasures: The Soviet Trade in Nationalized Art*, 1917–1938 (New York: Abbeville, 2014), 261, 274, and appendix II: "A List of the Russian Crown Jewels," as well as in *Fabergé Newsletter*, Spring 2013, http://Fabergéresearch.com/newsletter-2013-spring/.

16. Victor Nikitin "A List of the Russian Crown Jewels," 238.

17. For a synopsis of the Fersman portfolio, the events leading up to the sale at Christie's, and the personalities involved in selling the historical gems, see Christel Ludewig McCanless and Annemiek Wintraecken, "Fersman Portfolio—Fabergé Jewels—Nuptial Crown," *Fabergé Research Newsletter*, Fall 2010, http://Fabergéresearch.com/newsletter-2010-fall/.

18. *Fabergé Research Newsletter*, Fall 2010, https://Fabergéresearch.com/newsletter-2010-fall/.

19. Fersman, *Russia's Treasures*, 28, no. 9.

20. Anne Odom and Liana Paredes Arend, *A Taste for Splendor: Russian Imperial and European Treasures from the Hillwood Museum* (Alexandria, VA: Art Services International, 1998), 304–306.

21. *Fabergé Research Newsletter*, Spring 2012, http://Fabergéresearch.com/newsletter-2012-spring-2/.

22. "Bodice Ornaments," http://collections.vam.ac.uk/item/O73807/bodice-ornaments-unknown/.

27

THE MARKET FOR RUSSIAN JEWELERS AND SILVERSMITHS

THE LEADING FIRMS

Bolin

Most of Bolin's Russian pieces on the market are early 20th-century silver items from the Moscow workshop. To the trained eye, some are recognizable purely by style. Art nouveau works by Bolin in silver and enamel are especially distinctive. Fueled no doubt by Russian buyers, prices have surged. A Bolin enamel picture frame that sold for $6,000 in 1992 fetched $75,000 in 2012. Art nouveau boxes by Bolin are also in demand. Hillwood Museum recently acquired one at auction for $56,160. At Sotheby's in 2009, a Bolin *porte cigarette* of peacock design belonging to Grand Duke Vladimir Aleksandrovich went for over $100,000.

Important silver table items also do well. In 2004, Christie's New York sold an art nouveau Bolin centerpiece, circa 1916, for $175,000. With Swedish marks for 1919, it was probably made in Moscow for the opening of the Stockholm branch (see "Bolin: The Brightest Star," on page 86).

Maria Linke of Moscow, an innovative silversmith, was one of the few Bolin designers to work in enamel. Although Linke's silver-mounted glassware attracts collectors, her sleek enamel items, smaller yet more interesting, seem undervalued, especially when compared to the huge prices paid for enamels by her Moscow compatriots Ovchinnikov, Khlebnikov and Rückert. A delightful Linke beaker featuring children playing in the snow circa 1890 fetched $3,800 in 1997, while a champlevé enamel silver bowl dated 1887, retailed by Shanks and Bolin, sold for $4,800 in 2001. In November 2011, a Linke champlevé-enameled box from about the same period, estimated at $12,000–18,000,

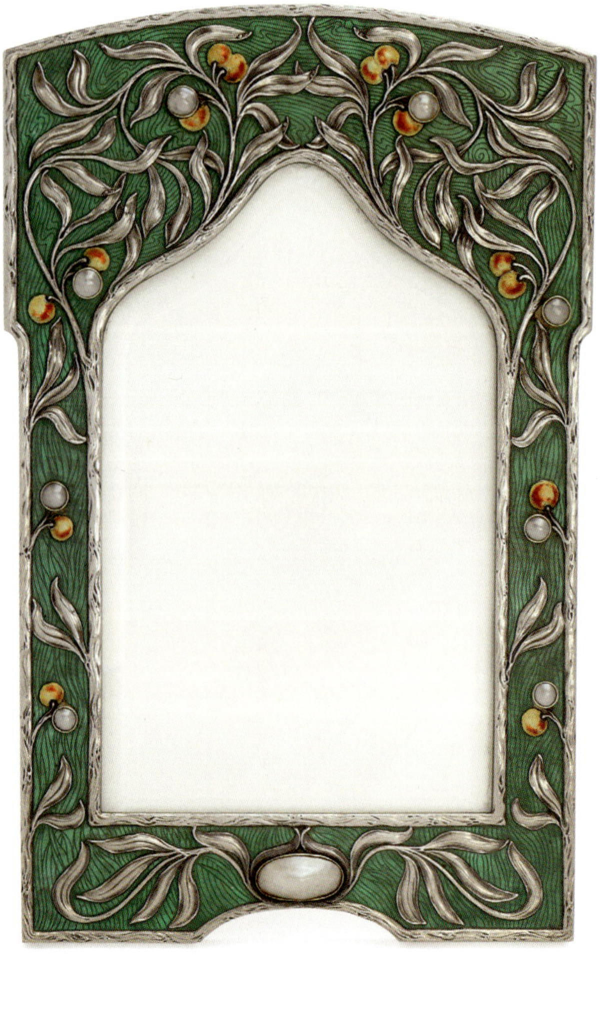

This Art Nouveau enameled Bolin picture frame accented with half pearls first sold in 1983 for $4,620, then in 1992 for $6,082 and finally in 2012 for $75,054. *© 2012 Christie's Images Ltd.*

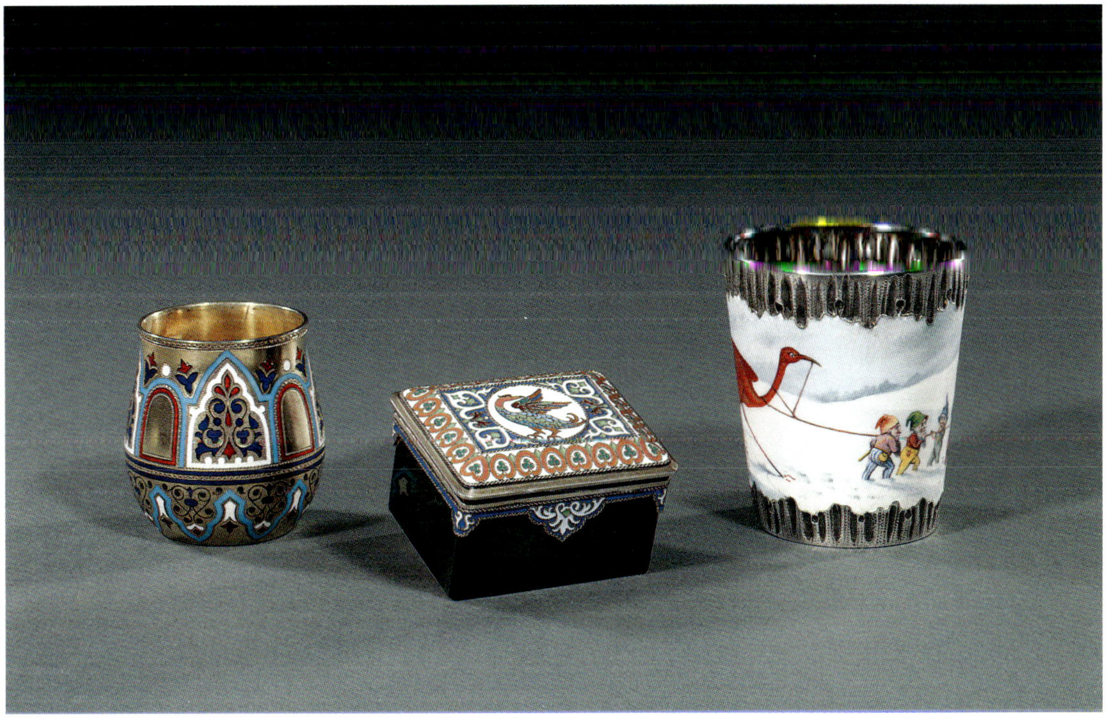

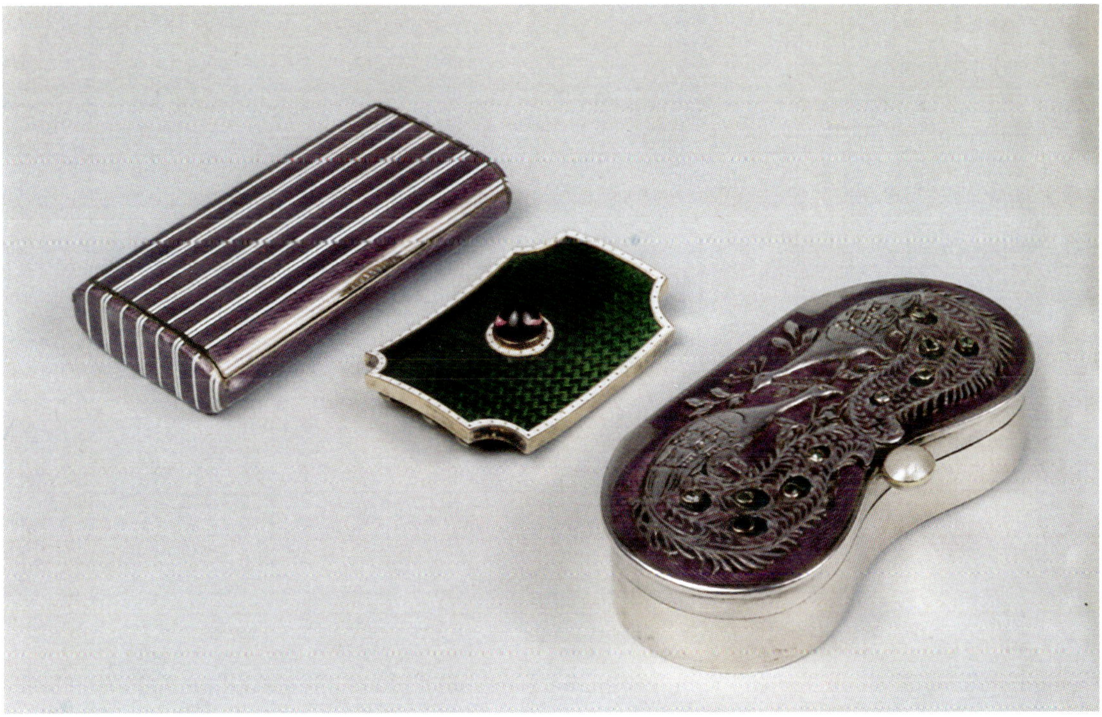

Right side in each image: Two silver and enameled items from Bolin's Moscow shop. The whimsical beaker was by Bolin workmaster Maria Linke while the Art Nouveau enamel box depicting peacocks was stamped *RL* or perhaps *KL* for Konstantin Linke. © *1997 and 1988 Christie's Images Ltd.*

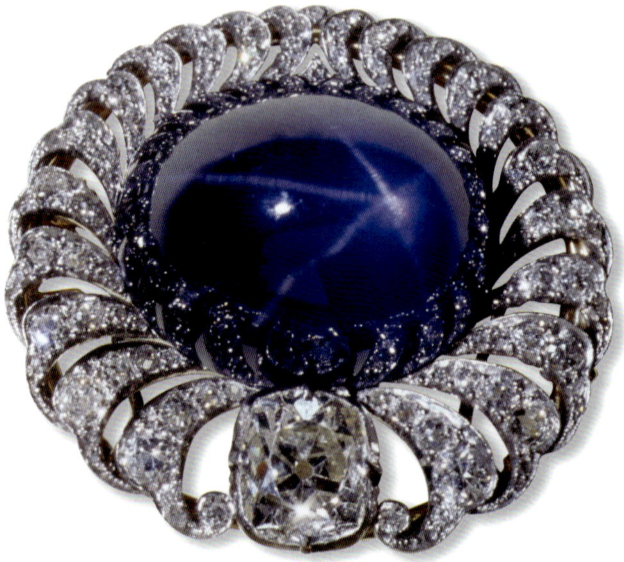

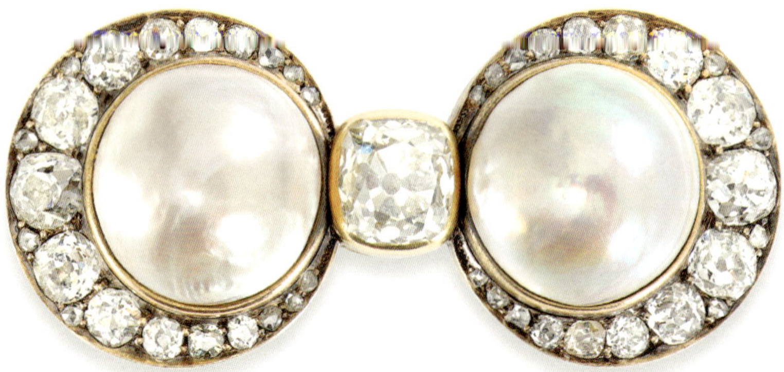

Top:
A star sapphire brooch by Bolin workmaster Sophia Schwan, ca. 1910. *Courtesy of Court Jewellers W. A. Bolin.*

Below:
Bolin workmaster Finikov specialized in exquisite pearl jewelry as seen in this brooch. *@ 2013 Christie's Images Ltd.*

failed to sell. Maria Linke's time is perhaps yet to come. Luckily for westerners, Bolin Moscow silver bears the company's full name in Latin, rather than Cyrillic lettering (see "Glossary of Jewelers and Silversmiths in Russia from the 18th Century to 1917").

Most of the grand imperial presentation jewels by Bolin have vanished, but there are some exceptions. It is exciting indeed when they resurface. In 1966, Sotheby's London sold a Bolin diamond brooch set with a "pigeon egg" sized sapphire that had been commissioned in 1845 by Grand Duke Constantine, son of Nicholas I. In 1969 Parke-Bernet New York offered a jeweled belt buckle by Bolin with diamonds and sapphires.

Even more spectacular was the reappearance of Grand Duchess Maria Aleksandrovna's sumptuous ruby and diamond wedding parure at Christie's Geneva in 1978 (see "Bolin: The Brightest Star," pages 79–82). This is the first and only time I've seen an almost complete imperial Russian parure resurface on the market. And although it was before my time on the Russian scene, it is thrilling to contemplate the excitement this must have created. According to Christian Bolin, as court jeweler and the firm's dignified patriarch, Henrik Conrad Bolin Jr. was often invited to Christie's in Geneva to impart a sort of imperial Russian ambiance to the proceedings. For this momentous occasion, he apparently posed for a family photo, holding the tiara that his forefathers had created. Sold by the descendants of the grand duchess, the tiara was still in its original Bolin box. The necklace sold for about $731,000, the tiara for $274,140 and the 9.19-carat cushion-shaped ruby ring fetched $286,323. The necklace reappeared at auction, and perhaps the tiara as well, but their current whereabouts are unknown, if in fact they are still intact. The tiara was apparently disassembled.

In 1986 in New York, a lavish Kashmir sapphire and diamond Bolin choker, circa 1880, in its original fitted Bolin case, sold for $750,000. More recently, Sotheby's sold a Bolin sapphire-and-diamond demiparure, the brooch by Sophia Schwan, from the collection of Grand Duchess Elena Vladimirovna, daughter of Grand Duchess Maria Pavlovna of Russia, in Geneva for over $473,000.

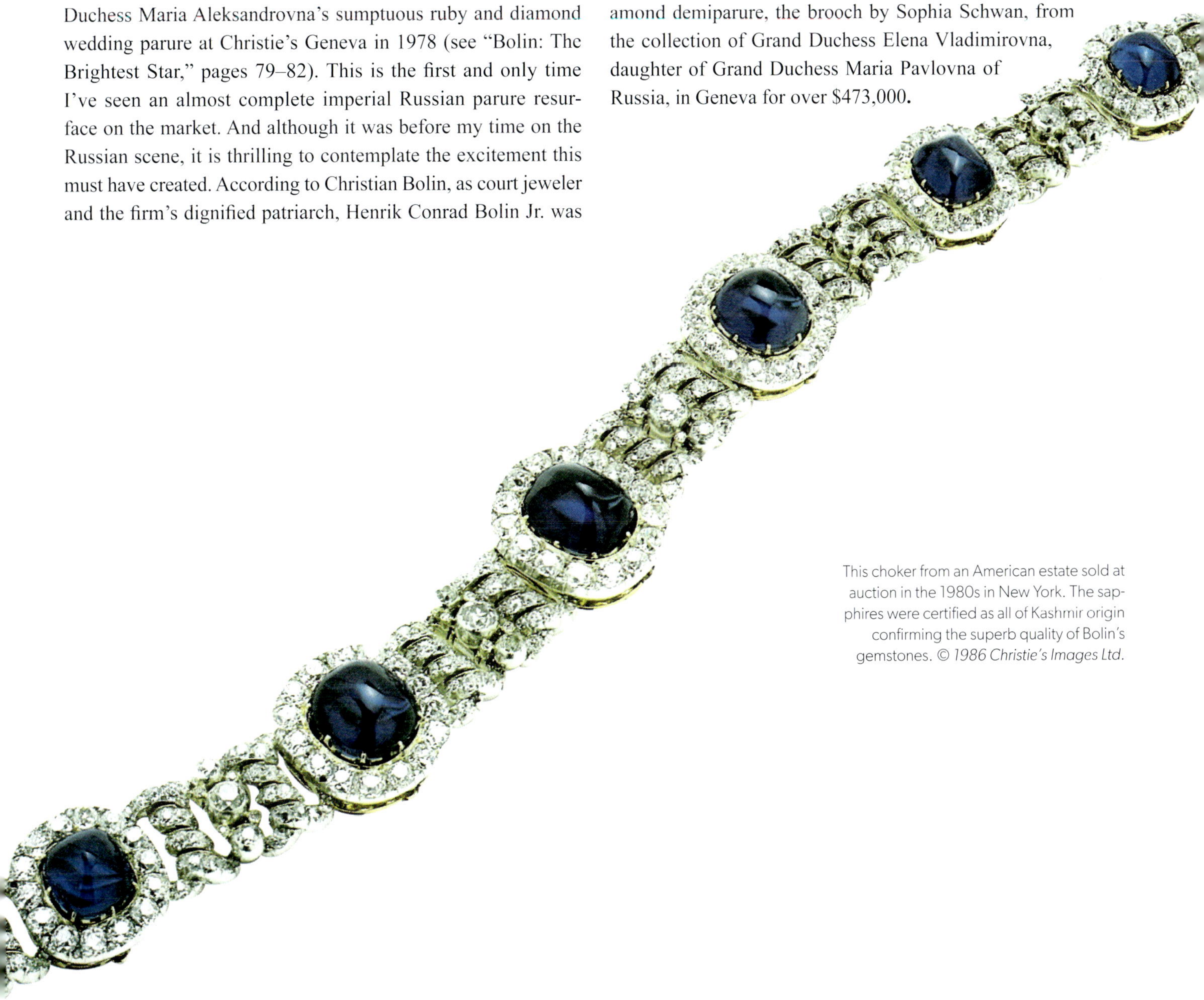

This choker from an American estate sold at auction in the 1980s in New York. The sapphires were certified as all of Kashmir origin confirming the superb quality of Bolin's gemstones. © *1986 Christie's Images Ltd.*

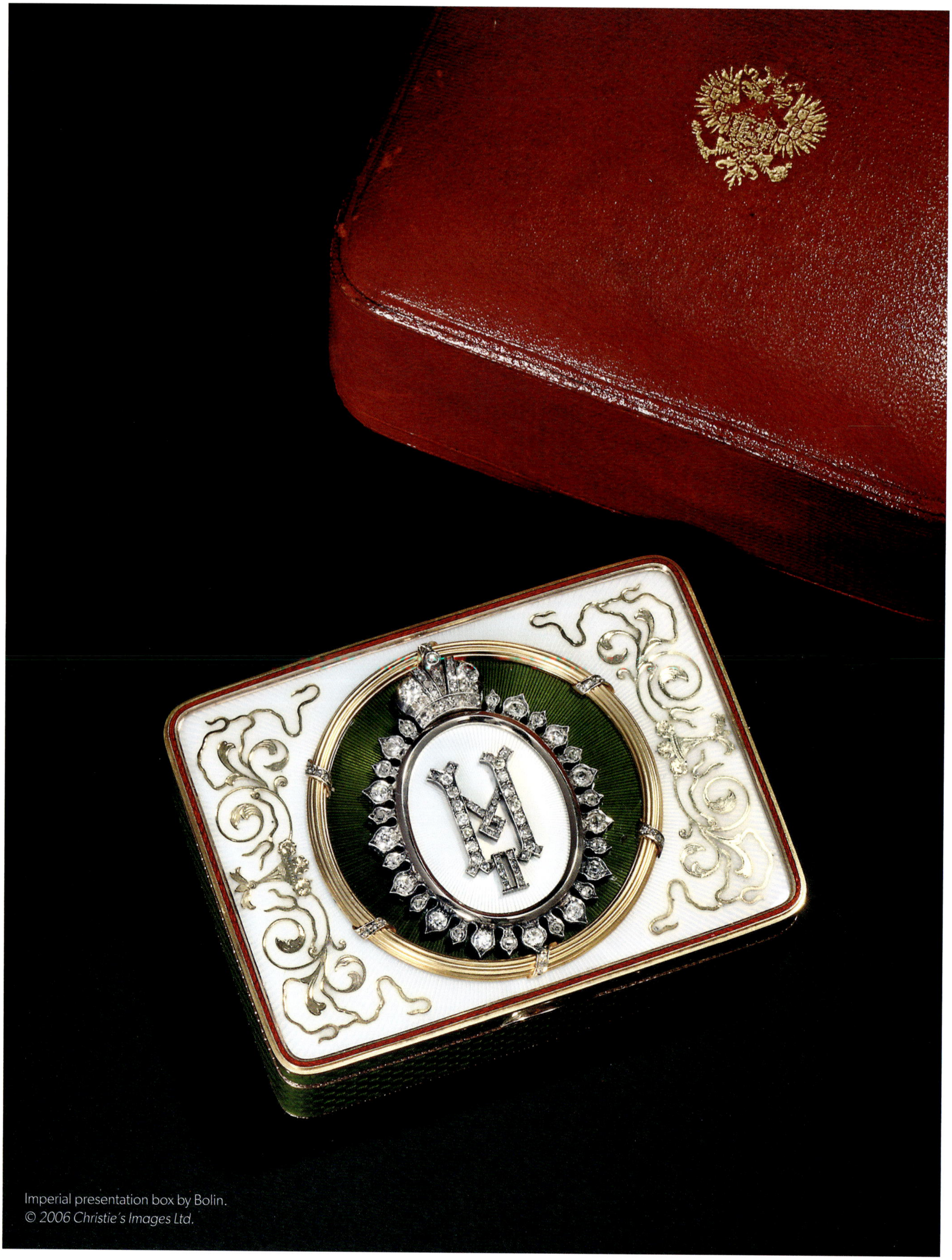

Imperial presentation box by Bolin.
© 2006 Christie's Images Ltd.

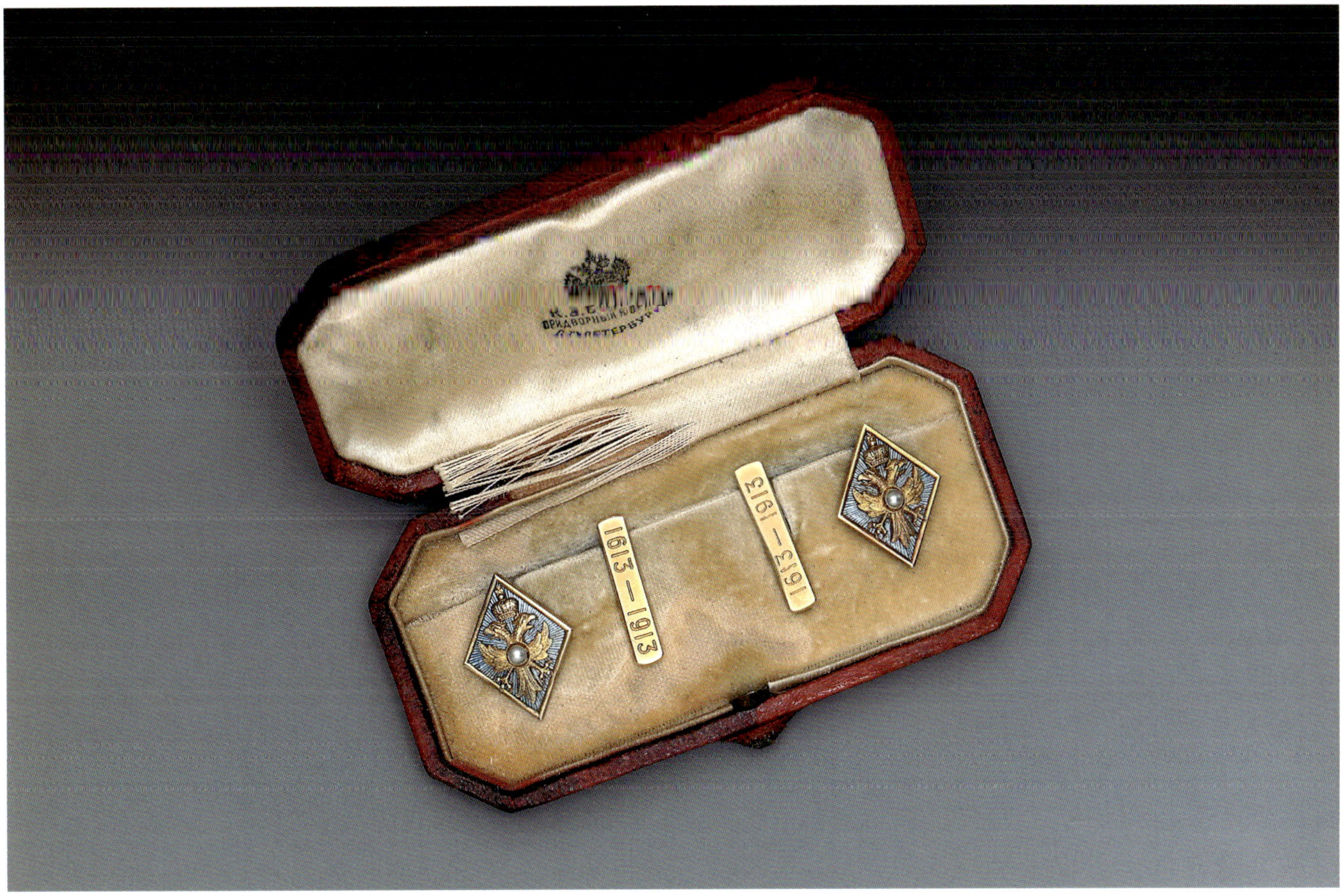

Above:
This pair of enameled Romanov Tercentenary cuff links inscribed with the dates 1613–1913 by the Bolin workmaster Chernokov were probably purchased as a gift to a gentleman to mark the occasion. *© 2005 Christie's Images Ltd.*

Previous page:
This imperial enamel and diamond box by Bolin was ordered by Tsar Nicholas II in 1909 for presentation to a foreign dignitary. *© 2006 Christie's Images Ltd..*

As for imperial presentation objects, Bolin examples are scarce compared to those by Fabergé, even though Bolin made more in the course of its long history. By comparison, earlier Bolin boxes (pre–Nicholas II) seem undervalued. In 2012 Christie's sold a Russian imperial gold snuffbox from the period of Alexander III in its original Bolin fitted case for $78,000. In 1987 the same box sold in Geneva for $18,097. With few exceptions, most surviving presentation gifts by Bolin date from the period of Nicholas II.

A Nicholas II Bolin jeweled and enameled box sold at auction in 2006 for $667,360. A year later, another in nephrite of scalloped outline, with the tsar's cipher in diamonds, fetched $371,830. Compared to Fabergé imperial boxes from this period, Bolin's still bring less than a million dollars.

Yet, prices are increasing. A Nicholas II imperial presentation picture frame in rhodonite and diamonds, which brought $63,000 at auction in New York in 1998, sold for over 10 times more ($691,520) just seven years later.[1]

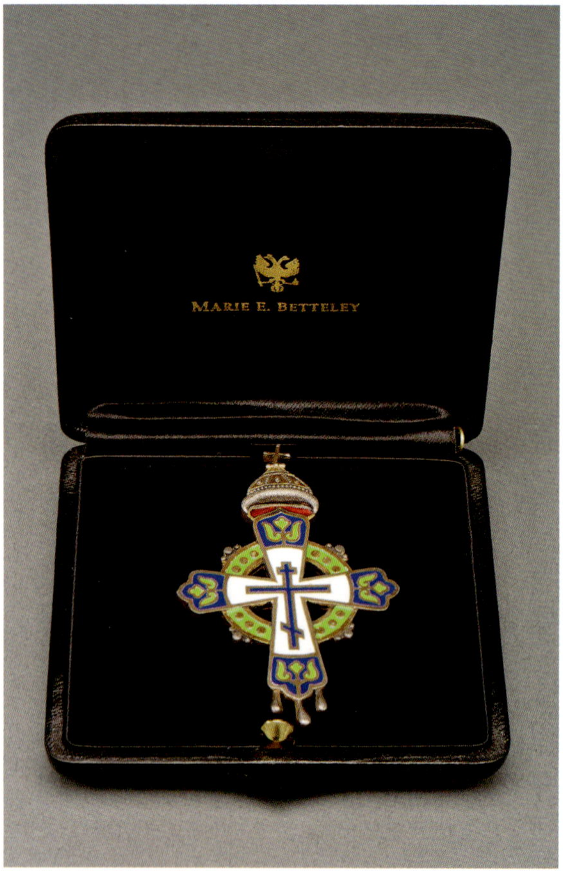

This Romanov Tercentenary cross made in St. Petersburg by an unknown jeweler was presented to Orthodox priests for exceptional merit.

Following page:
A selection of jewels and objects by Carl Fabergé. *Marie Betteley, photos by Noel Allum and Roger Bester*

Interest in Bolin's objets d'art is rising as well. In 2007 a small nephrite pin tray by Nikolai Chernokov sold in London for over $157,000, while in 2008, a circa 1900 jeweled and enameled kovsh or drinking vessel in original fitted Bolin case fetched $217,000.

Without provenance, smaller Russian jewels by Bolin, including cuff links, pendants and brooches, usually bring $5,000 to $18,000 on the market. Earrings are very rare. The highest price for a pair of gold-and-enamel Bolin cuff links in Grand Duke Vladimir's collection was over $22,556 in 2009. Another pair in moonstone and enamel came close back in 2004 ($15,273). This still seems like a bargain compared to Fabergé cuff links, which can fetch more than double. In 2007, a fine art nouveau enameled pin by Bolin workmaster Vladimir Finikov sold for just under $18,000 in Geneva, while at a Swedish auction in 2008, a Siberian amethyst brooch of his, circa 1900, changed hands for $21,840.

Judging from recent sales, jewels commemorating historical events, such as the Romanov tercentenary of 1913, are more in demand. One such brooch in white enamel applied with a diamond-set eagle sold in London in 2010 for $52,586.

Given these rising prices, the possibilities of forgeries increase. It is curious that one or two jewels catalogued as marked by Bolin continue to reappear at auction without selling. It is difficult to pass judgment without having inspected them. But, as with pieces bearing Fabergé hallmarks, it is always wise to buy with caution, particularly as the market for Bolin strengthens. On the other hand, silver and champlevé enamel items by Bolin are so technically difficult to reproduce that one is unlikely to find forgeries any time soon.

Fabergé

"Is it Fabergé?" is a question that is still asked with breathless anticipation. And why not, when the last rediscovered imperial egg by Fabergé is rumored to have fetched £30 million in 2013.[2]

Spectacular prices don't just include the imperial eggs. An oval guilloché-enameled Fabergé snuffbox that sold in 1983 for $15,400 fetched $416,850 in 2009, 27 times more![3] However, the heyday of astronomical prices for typical objets de vertu now seems to be behind us. A bowenite box from the prestigious Kazan collection, which sold in 1997 for $21,850, realized $10,000 less in 2015.[4]

The market for the rest, however, is complicated. Over the decades, Fabergé prices have risen and fallen gently, then plateaued, only to skyrocket and then plummet later on.

The Fabergé market suffers from overexposure. This is because for decades, dealers have speculated by buying in one auction only to flip (dealer speak for resell quickly) in another. As with art in general, objects from private or museum collections that are fresh to the market create interest, which increases prices. But because Fabergé objects have a distinctive design, color, provenance and history, once seen at auction or in museum catalogues, they are remembered. The internet makes this worse. There are dozens of examples of repeats at auction that lost value sometimes by half, with others by not selling at all, simply because of too recent previous market exposure. However, this is not restricted to Fabergé, since overexposure is sure to diminish the value of all items at auction.

In America, Fabergé collections of objets d'art, except when donated or loaned to museums, tend to resurface for sale within 20–25 years. Some collectors seem besieged by buying frenzies,

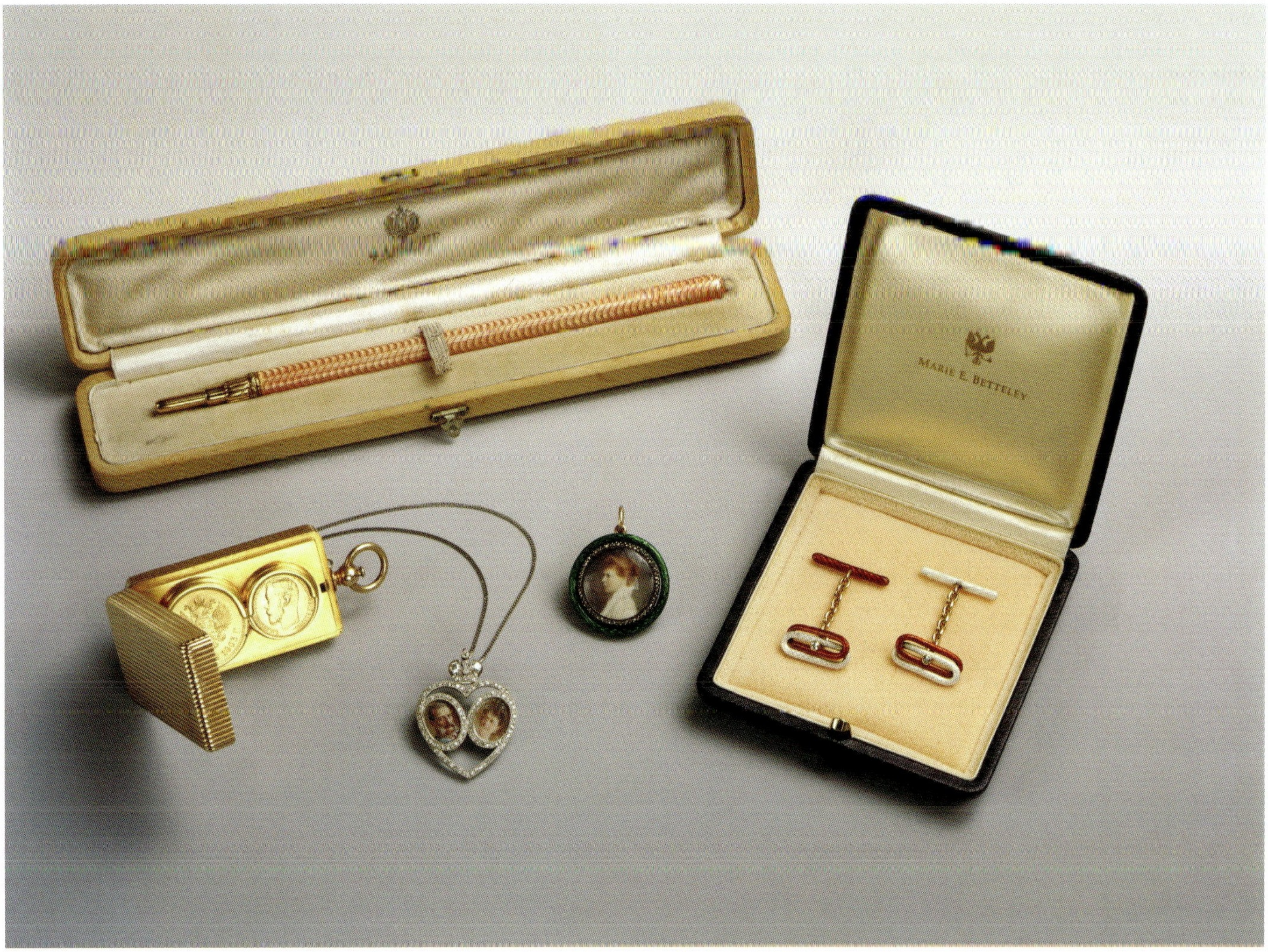

only to let it all go in one fell swoop. The shine of bibelots and objets de vertu either seems to wear off with the original buyer, or for a host of other reasons, with the next generation. This happens more frequently with Fabergé than with other types of Russian objects.

Fabergé jewelry is another matter. Curiously, on the whole it is underpriced.[5] It has never plunged in value but tends not to resurface as frequently as objets d'art.

Compared to objects, jewels that miraculously survived the Russian Revolution without being molten down or dismantled are more likely to be kept and handed down to future generations. Unlike table items, silver centerpieces and enameled cigarette cases, jewelry is wearable, timeless and always valuable. But Fabergé jewelry will not always rise in value, even with minimum market exposure. A guilloché enamel pin by Michael Perchin that sold at Sotheby's in 1995 for $4,300 fetched only $200 more at a Manhattan auction 20 years later.[6]

Who can argue against the beauty and allure of antique-cut stones, especially from the land of the tsars? Those diamond cutters and their techniques are gone, so Fabergé jewels that have survived unaltered are rare and treasured. If I were to buy one Fabergé jewel, it would be a diamond pendant by the workmaster August Holmström.

The frequency with which Fabergé items resurface on the market fuels a fascination. And it allows us to retrace the historical sales paths particular items took over the century since the revolution. I am part of a small but ardent group of Fabergé market followers. With Fabergé appearing at auction as early as the 1930s, the field is very well documented (or misdocumented in some cases). My treasured collection of Russian auction catalogues allows me to trace this trajectory. I can spend hours poring over them. There's that quest for provenance that's so important to collectors and dealers. It is also a prerequisite for a successful sale of items of Russian origin, especially with the number of forgeries that exist today.[7]

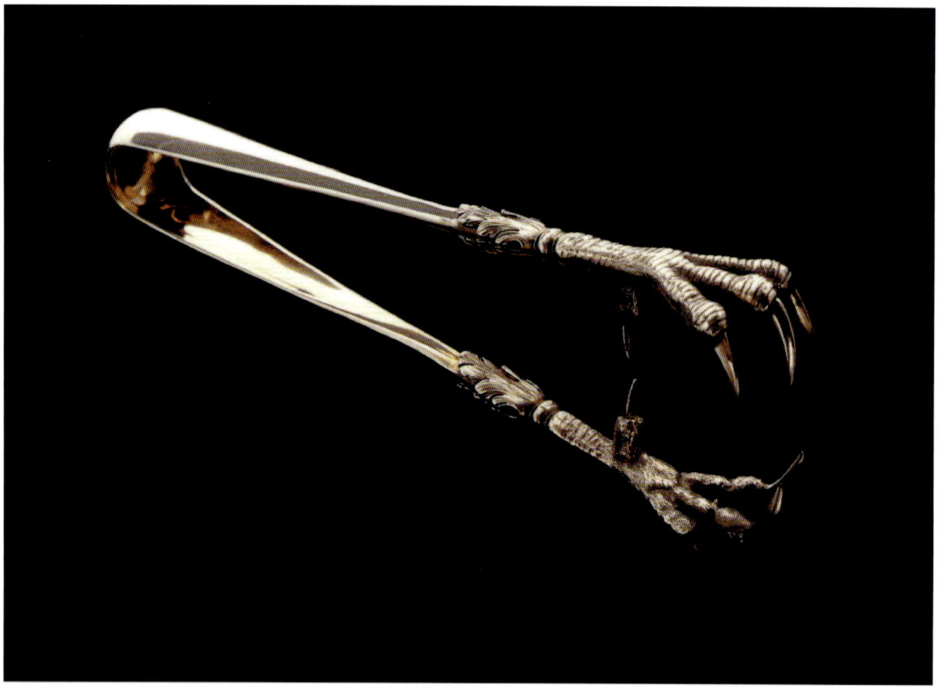

Fabergé silver ice tongs. *Marie Betteley, photo by Roger Bester*

Hahn

Hahn was one of the few Russian jewelers other than Fabergé to be identified at auction in New York before the 1970s. The firm's hallmark tended to be its full name (in Cyrillic), which made it easier for cataloguers. In 1960, Parke-Bernet Galleries in New York offered a magnificent gold triptych by Hahn. It was pictured in black and white in the catalogue, below a smaller gold one by Fabergé (*pictured on the next page*).[8] Catalogues were sparsely illustrated then. In this case, the presence of an object by a more famous maker no doubt justified the illustration of a similar item by one lesser known.

However, as far back as the 1930s, less than 20 years after the Bolsheviks took power, Hahn was considered important enough to fake, as is revealed by two picture frames sold by Armand Hammer bearing false Hahn stamps. The quality of both is so poor that it remains a mystery how the dealer managed to hoodwink his customer, Lillian Thomas Pratt, into buying them. She was not the only one. Although much of his stock was genuine, Hammer was notorious for providing spurious imperial provenances for almost everything he sold, and gullible American heiresses and collectors sometimes fell prey to his fabrications. In fact, the dealer furnished a certificate of authenticity with imperial provenance for most of his Russian inventory.

Sadly, while some of his designs still exist, the sumptuous jewels of Carl Hahn, including his diamond rivières and most gem-encrusted imperial decorations, have all but disappeared. At least for now, we find little trace of them. Given the extraordinary value of the gems, it is unlikely we will see them again. I hope to be proven wrong.

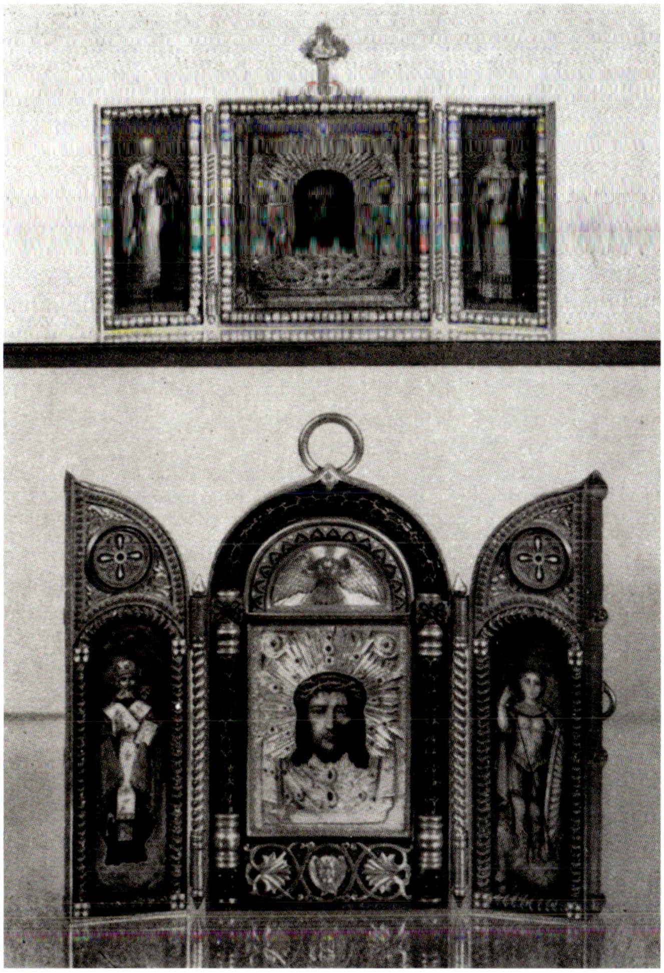

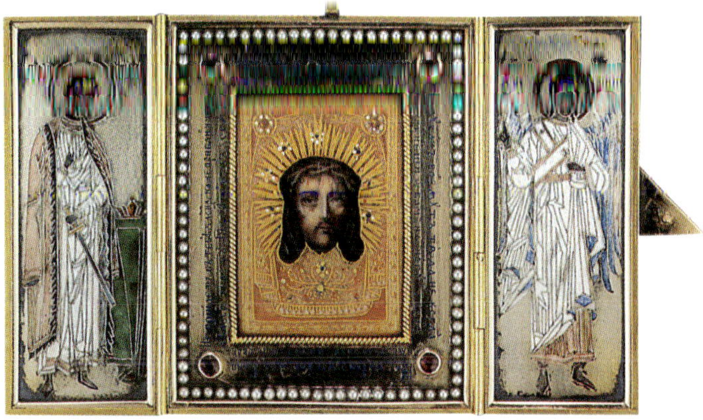

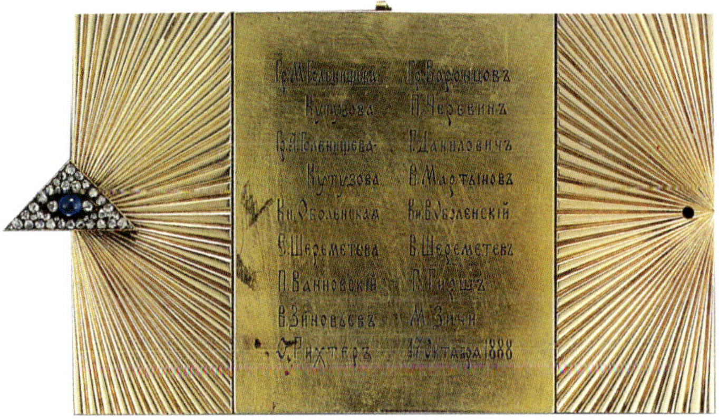

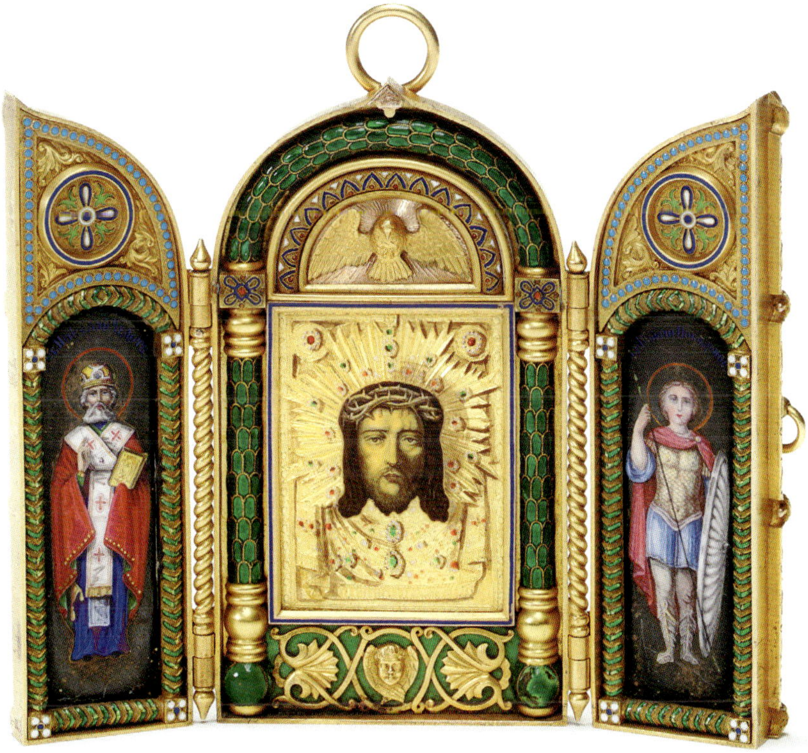

Gold and enameled Fabergé and Hahn icons past and recent. *Top left:* Triptychs (3-paneled icons) by Fabergé (*top*) and Hahn as illustrated in a 1960 New York Parke-Bernet Galleries catalogue, prices unknown. *Top right:* A similar Fabergé triptych (front and back) with imperial provenance sold at Christie's in 1987 for $33,000. *Right:* The same Hahn icon by master enameler Alexander Treiden resold in 2006 for $284,000 in New York. © *1987 Christie's Images Ltd., and Sotheby's*

Several Hahn snuffboxes survived the revolution and have appeared at auction in the West over the decades. Their prices have risen along with those by Fabergé—and in one case even surpassed them. A number appeared in the 1960s. In 1968 Parke-Bernet sold a Hahn Nicholas II presentation box in enamel for $5,250. In 1969, another one by Hahn in gold with diamond-set cipher of Nicholas II fetched the same amount, while another in enamel by Fabergé fetched $12,500. Both were illustrated in color, a rare occurrence at the time. Judging from the size of the catalogue, which contained 422 lots, this was one of the first sales dedicated to Russian works of art in America and marked the beginning of a growing market. By 1970 Parke-Bernet's Russian art sale featured over 700 lots.

The 1980s were lackluster for Hahn items in this category. I spotted only one: a presentation cigarette case, which sold for $10,210 in 1989.[9] Then, in 1998, Sotheby's sold a presentation snuffbox with the tsar's portrait embellished with a diamond wreath and pastes (imitation diamonds) for $135,420. Provenance now makes a stronger appearance, as since 1991 the archives have opened to scholars, and this affects prices. Other Hahn items no doubt crossed the auction block by the end of the 20th century. But the market took off after 2000. Values soared, and many Hahn pieces now see the light of day—over 45 in European and American auctions alone, with prices starting at $5,600 for a pair of guilloché-enameled cuff links in 2009. The name is now recognizable, and his objects are sought after.

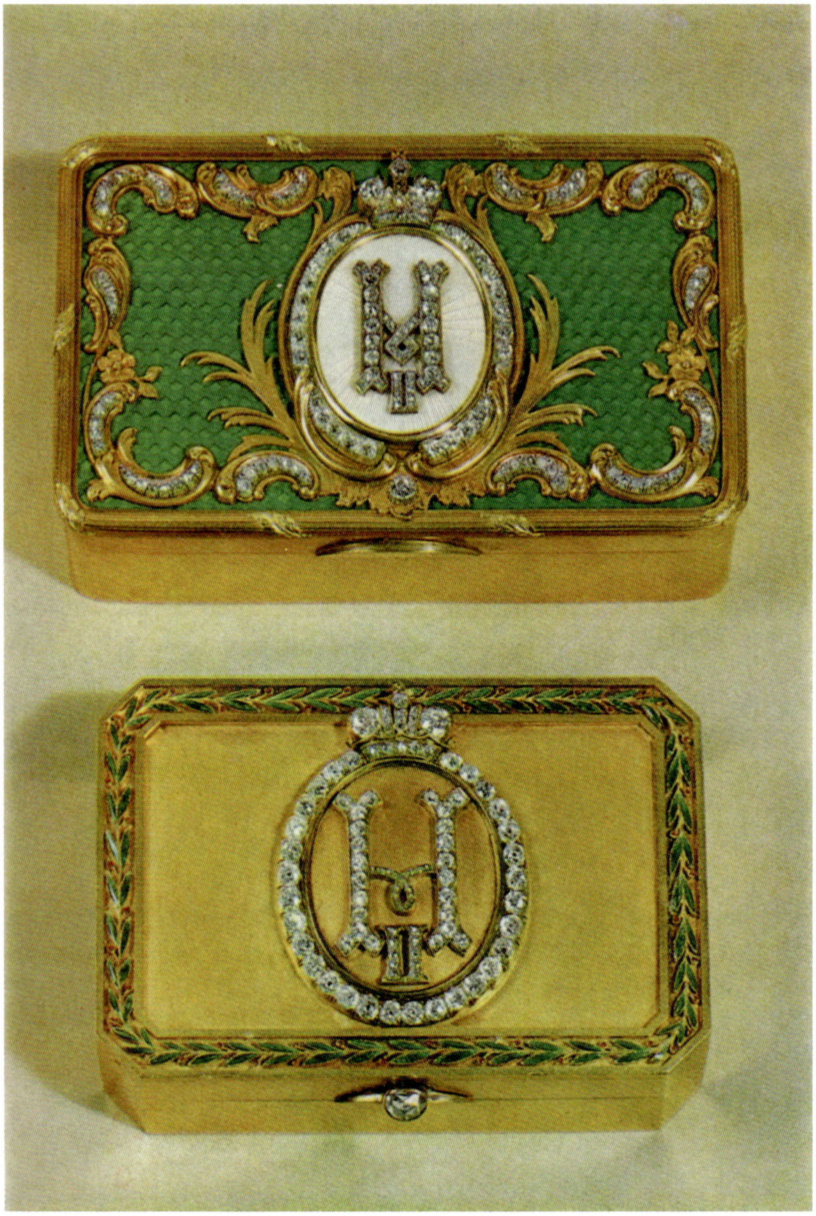

A Fabergé (*top*) and a Hahn presentation box that were sold at auction in December 1969. *Courtesy of Sotheby's*

Following page:
In 2012, this imperial snuffbox by Carl Blank that was presented to a Persian dignitary sold for just under $755,000. *Courtesy of Sotheby's*

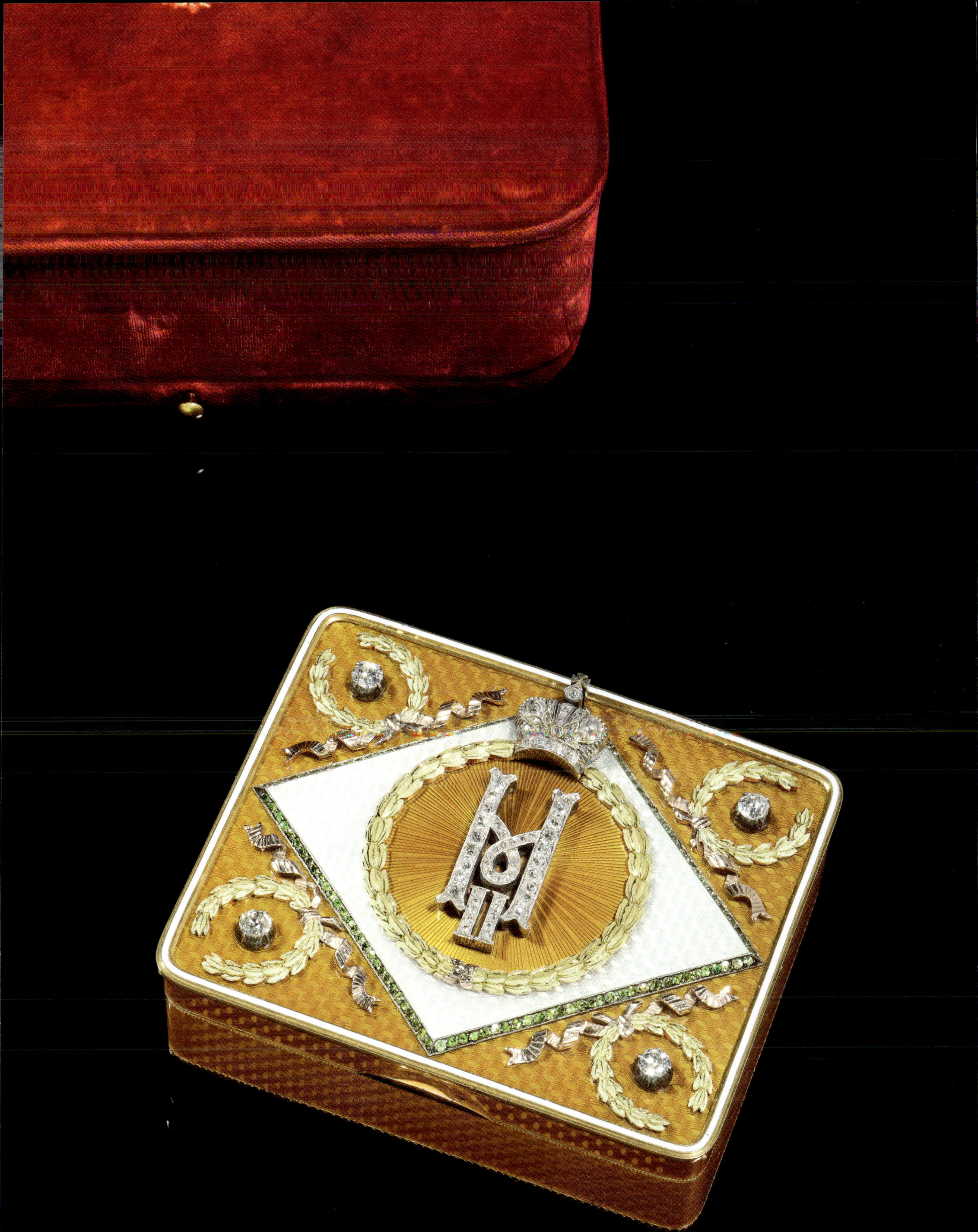

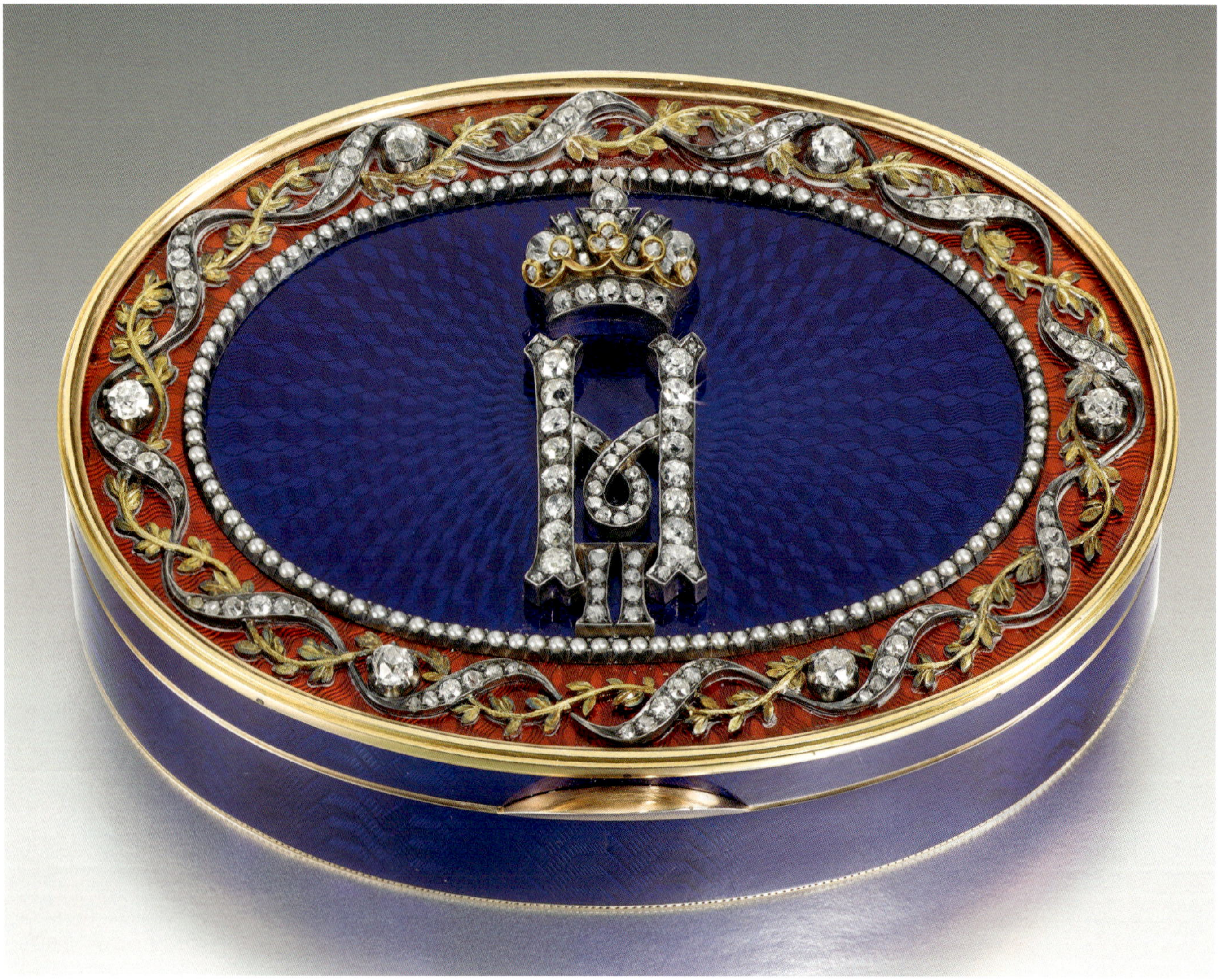

This Hahn presentation snuffbox sold for $641,000 in 2015, outperforming a Fabergé one (*following page*) of the same category of imperial gifts by the tsar in the same sale. *Courtesy of Sotheby's*

Following page:
Fabergé presentation snuffbox.
Courtesy of Sotheby's

Hahn snuffboxes began to skyrocket in value after 2010. One in oval blue enamel commissioned by Tsar Nicholas II that had fetched $14,000 in 1979 and $56,100 in 1992 realized $641,623 in 2015, despite the lack of a provenance in the catalogue. For the first time, this Hahn presentation snuffbox sold for more than one by Fabergé also set with the tsar's diamond initials.[10]

Most of the surviving Hahn boxes are by Carl Blank (see "Carl August Hahn: The Diamond King") and bear both signatures. In 2015, a very rare snuffbox by Blank sold in New York for $665,000.[11] Enameled in pale pink and steel blue, it was one of only five known imperial boxes decorated with a diamond imperial eagle from the last Romanov reign. Tsar Nicholas II presented it to the Bulgarian minister in St. Petersburg, Dmitrii Stancioff, in 1899.[12] While the provenance of the other three boxes is unknown, the fifth (now lost) was made for the Emir of Bukhara in 1906 (page 279), by the jeweler Ivanov. Hahn or Blank upgraded the gift by adding larger and more costly diamonds for this august recipient.

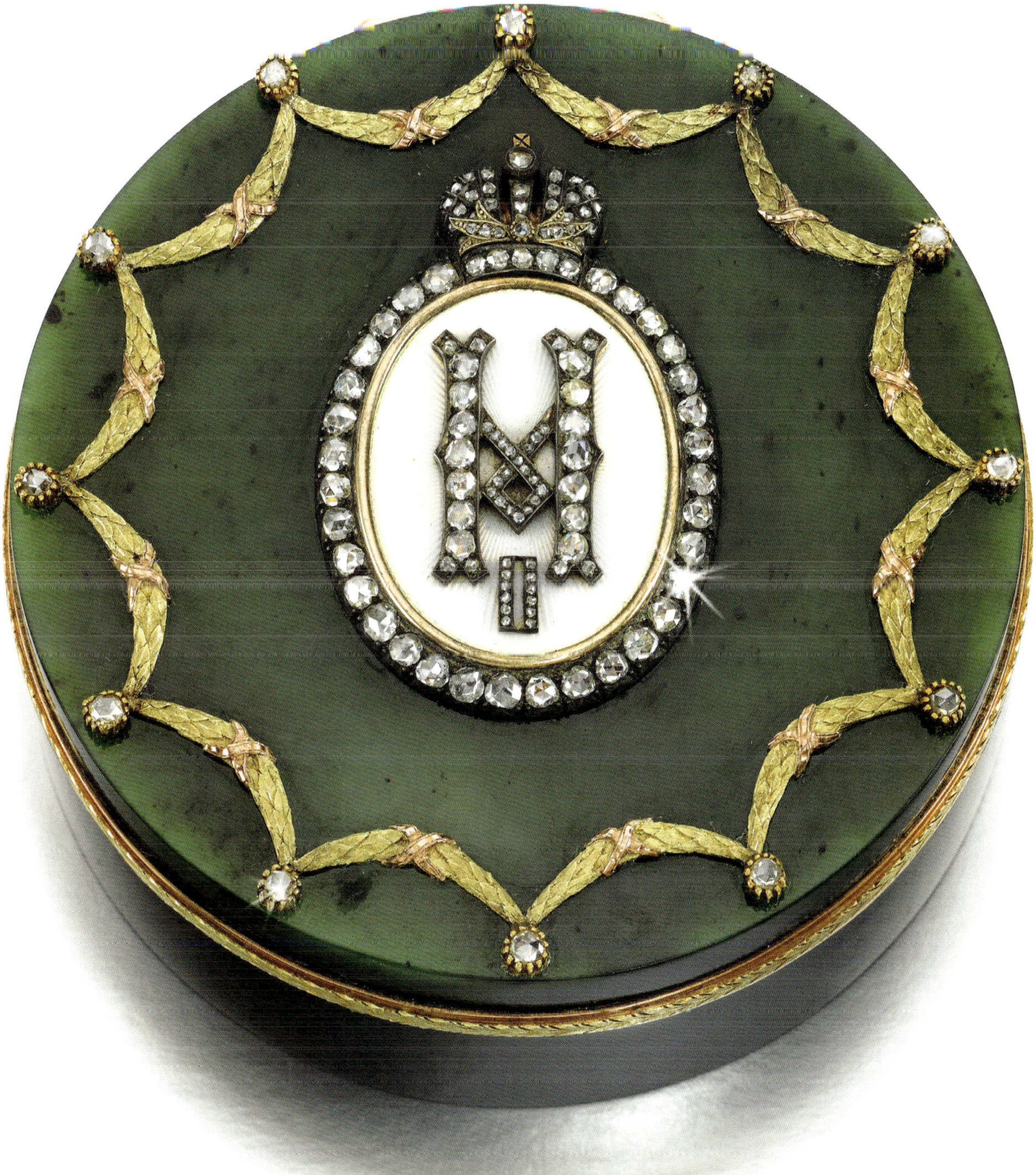

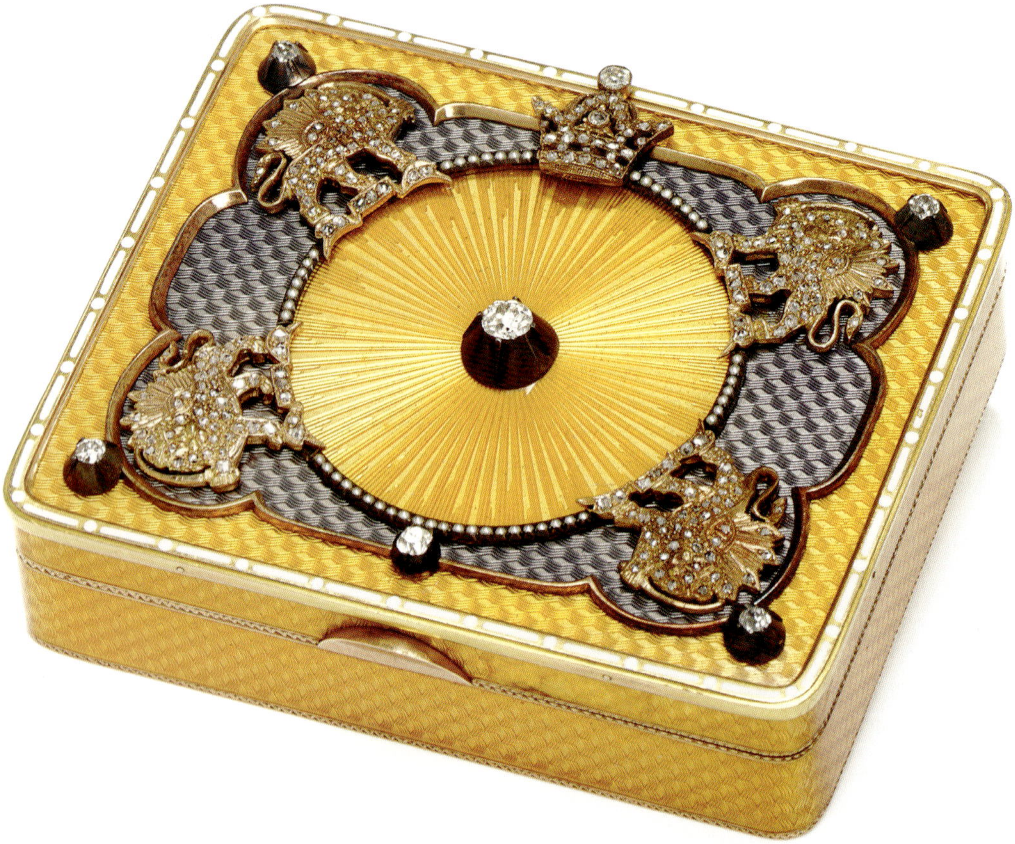

Carl Blank made the bright-yellow box for the imperial Persian court. *Courtesy of Sotheby's*

Following page:
The Emir of Bukhara, Said Mir Mohammed Alim Khan (1880–1944), poses in ceremonial robes. Photograph taken in 1911 by Sergei Prokudin-Gorskii, a pioneer of color photography. *Source: Wikimedia Commons*

A most unusual box of Persian inspiration denotes Hahn's appeal to Middle Eastern clients. Square in yellow enamel, a single diamond set in its center and decorated with the Qajar Dynasty's crown and lion and sun emblem in diamonds, in 1983 it was catalogued in Geneva as a gift from Shah Muzaffar al-Kin to a Persian dignitary, where it sold for $12,600. When it resurfaced at auction in New York in 2006, although its provenance was omitted, the colorful Hahn box fetched $350,000.

The sale of another Hahn presentation box demonstrates the danger of overexposure. It involves a diamond-set box in yellow enamel that the tsar apparently gave to Professor

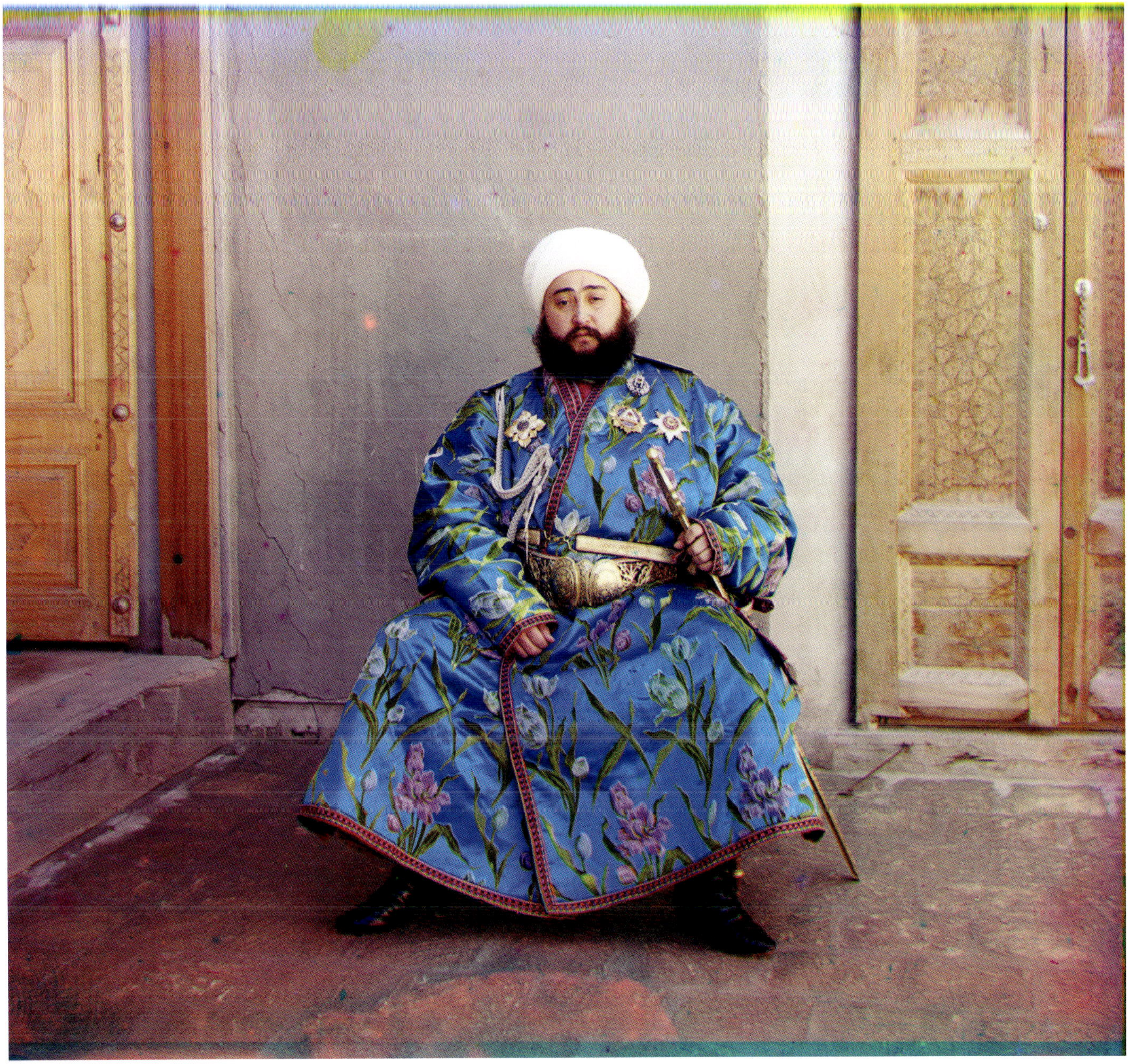

Dmitrii Ott, the imperial accoucheur. It bears a strong resemblance to one in pink that he had received for the birth of Tsar Nicholas's first born, Grand Duchess Olga Nikolaevna, in 1895. When offered in 2005 in New York, the box sold for $90,000, with a mistaken attribution and provenance unknown. Four years later the box reappeared at auction with a correct provenance and sold for just under $300,000, a seemingly hefty profit for the owner. However, it is likely the buyer failed to pay, and the consignor was left with nothing at the time. Six months later the same box reappeared but now only brought in $113,913, almost two-thirds less.[13]

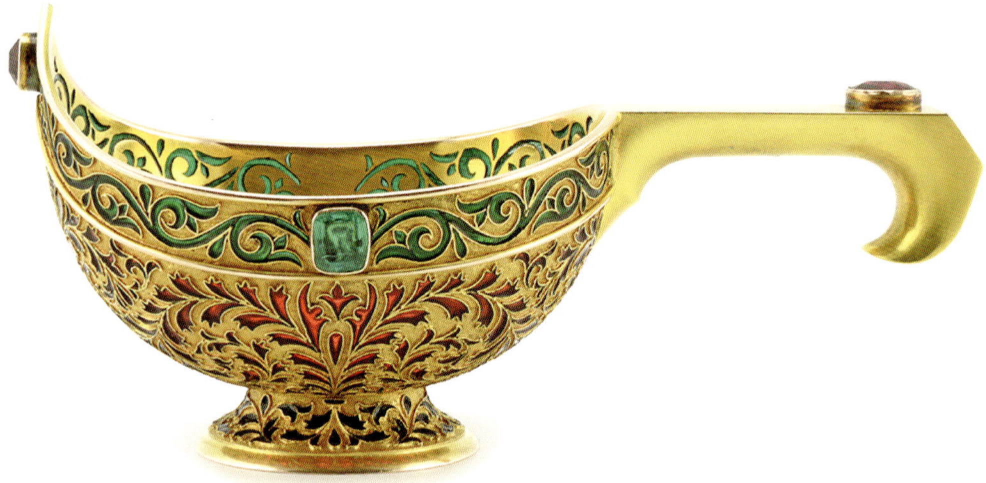

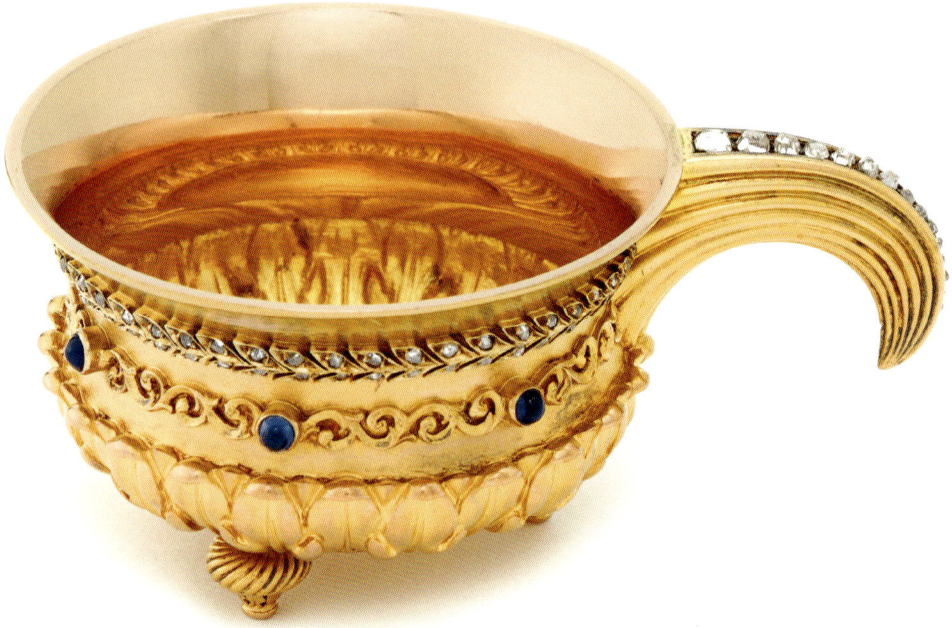

Top:
Plique-à-jour enamel and gold kovsh by Alexander Treiden. *Courtesy of John Atzbach*

Bottom:
Gold and jeweled charka by Alexander Treiden. *Courtesy of Bonham's*

The most interesting items on the market are not presentation boxes—since they were made to strict specifications from the court and thus tend to look the same regardless of maker—but personalized and often whimsical objets de vertu. Here Hahn's originality shines through. The scale is small and the enamel execution is brilliant. A tiny gold spoon pin with diamond center sold in 2002 for $15,535; while a bowl adorned with chicks in gold by Treiden fetched just under $39,000 in 2014. The following year, a plique-à-jour enamel repoussé frame in the original box realized $56,625. And while the original recipients are not always noted, the enameled icons mentioned above were of high quality and no doubt commissioned as personal gifts. The nicest cigarette case I've seen by Hahn was pale-green translucent enamel enhanced with jeweled flies in a pattern. Formerly in the Forbes Collection, it realized $101,575 in 2002.

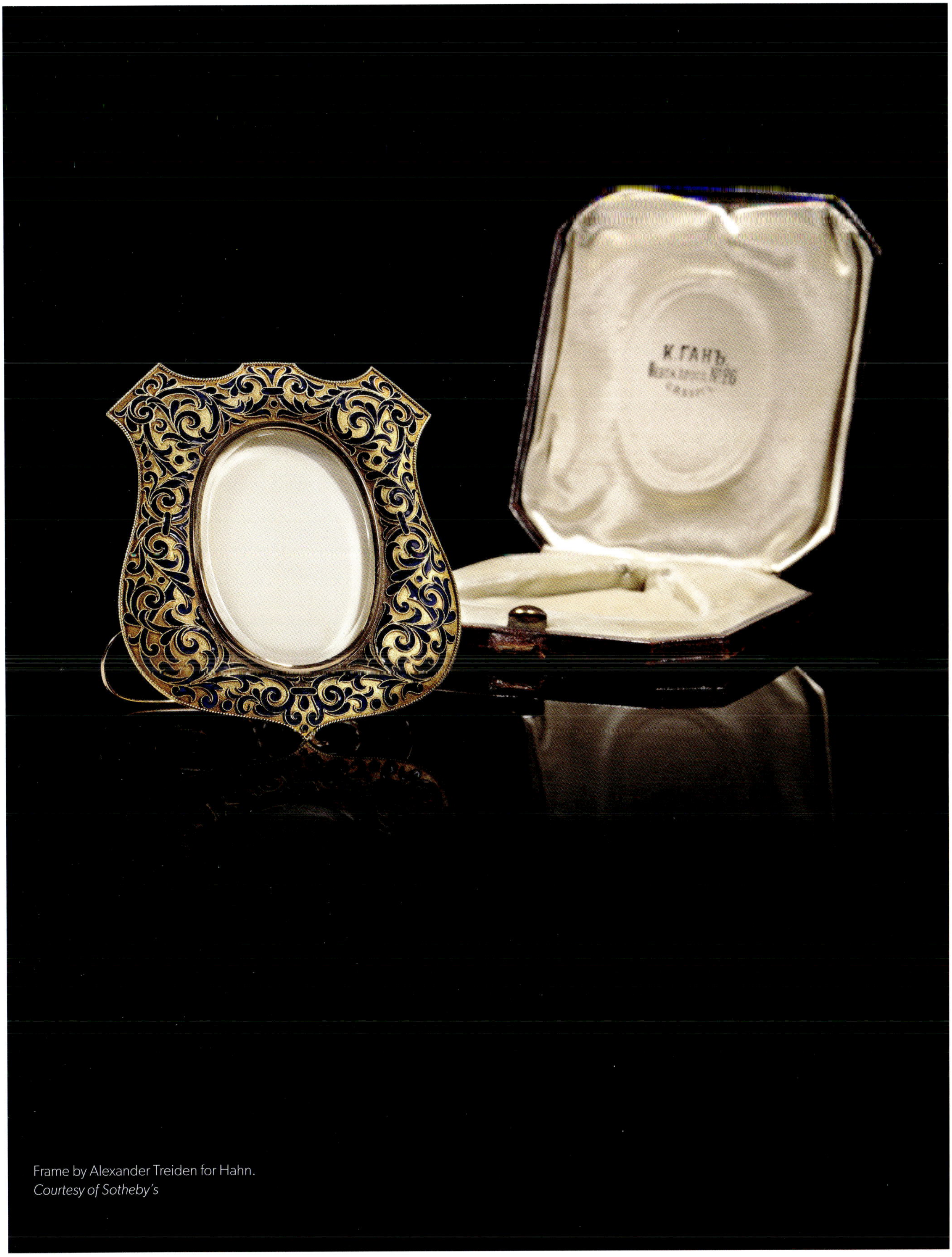

Frame by Alexander Treiden for Hahn.
Courtesy of Sotheby's

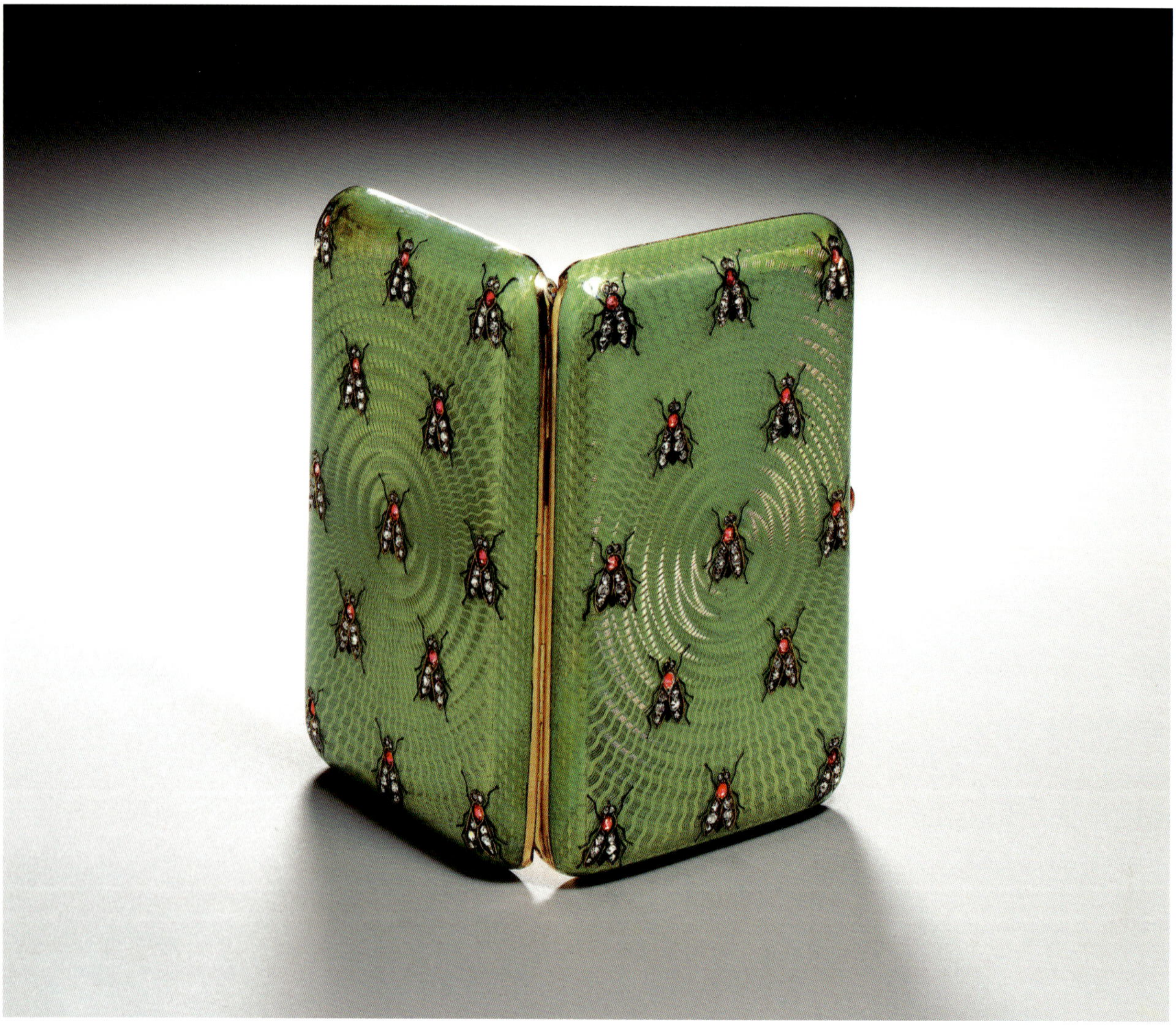

Köchli

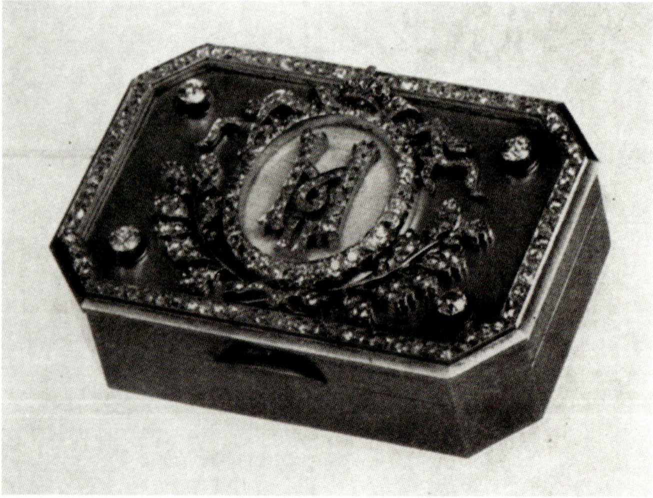

Köchli's creations are not unknown in North America. Armand Hammer traded jewels by the goldsmith, as did Tiffany & Company and the Schaffers in New York.[14] The name appears at least three times in New York auction catalogues in the 1960s, each for imperial presentation boxes commissioned by Tsar Nicholas II. The Latin initials *FK* as a hallmark may have helped cataloguers identify the jeweler, along with the occasional fitted original box. One with the tsar's diamond cipher sold in 1960, and another sold in 1967 for $4,000. Yet another box with a fabulous double-headed eagle etched below the tsar's diamond initials differed from the others in that the Romanov crown was set with cabochon sapphires, a characteristic Köchli touch (something you would rarely see in a Fabergé box). The box was featured as a cover lot at Sotheby's in 1984, and its illustration appeared again

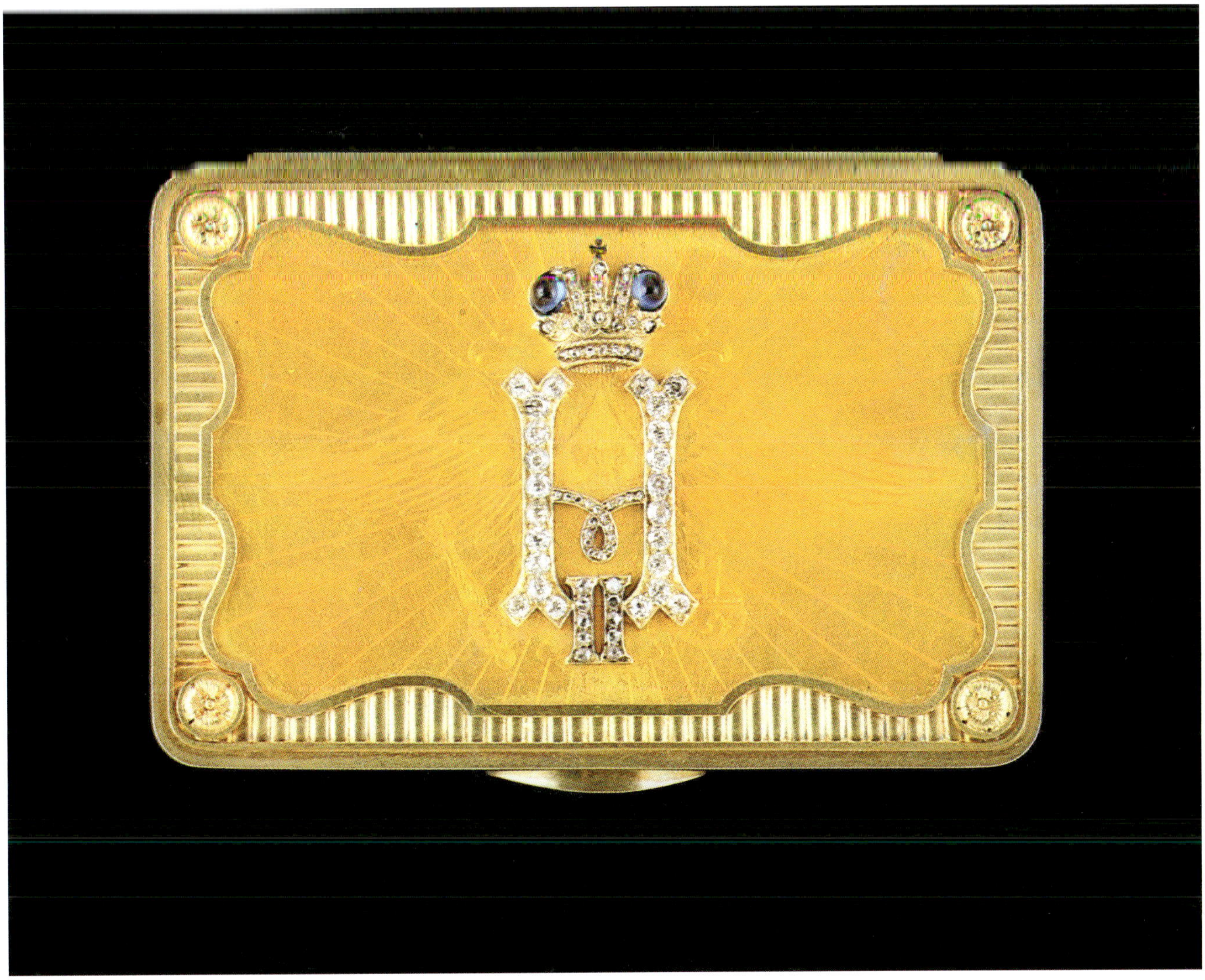

Above:
This Köchli imperial presentation box with the tsar's diamond cipher sold in New York in 1984 for $18,750 and again in Monte Carlo in 2018 for $75,693.
Courtesy of Sotheby's

Previous page, top:
Guilloché-enameled cigarette case adorned with jeweled flies, the symbol of luck, by Carl Blank for Hahn, circa 1900.
© 2002 Christie's Images Ltd.

Previous page, bottom left:
Box by Köchli offered at Parke-Bernet in 1960.
Courtesy of Sotheby's

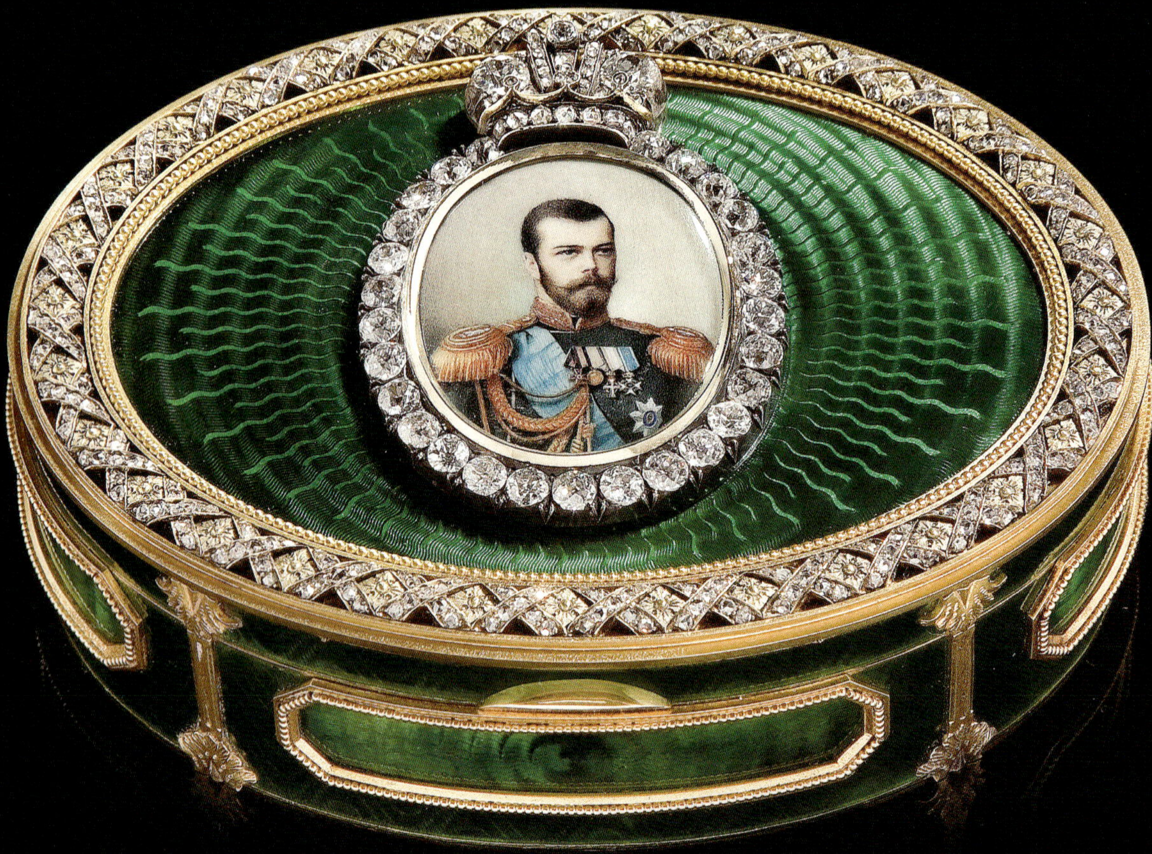

Köchli box.

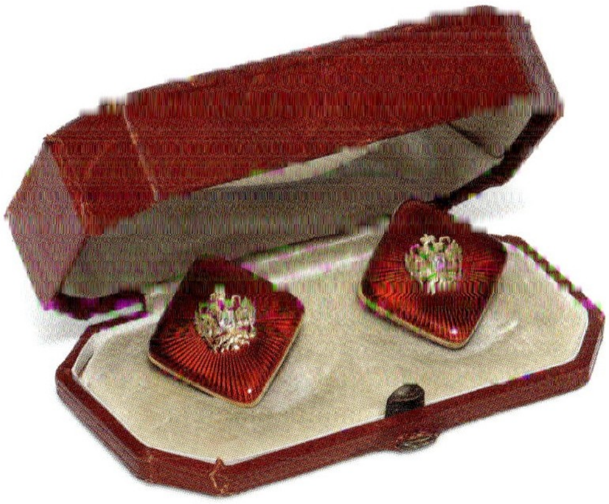

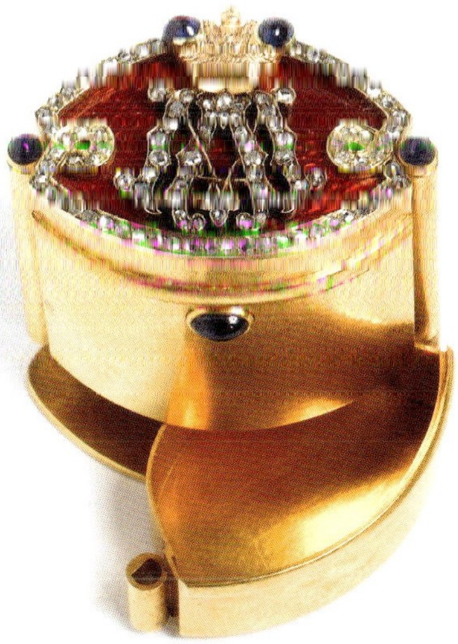

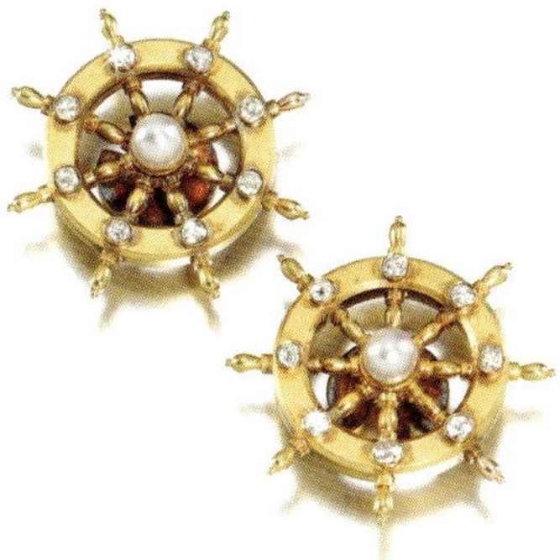

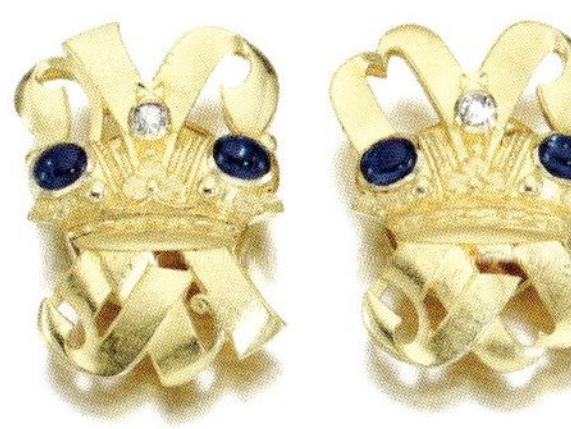

Top left and top right:
A pair of enamel cuff links by Victor Lindroos, said to have supplied Köchli, sold in London in 2016 for $17,928, while a red enameled bonbonnière with Romanov initials by the jeweler fetched $41,000 in 2008. It was made for Grand Duchess Anastasia Mikhailovna of Russia (1860–1922), daughter of Grand Duke Michael Nikolaevich. © *2008 Christie's Images Ltd., Courtesy of Bonham's*

Bottom left and right:
These two pairs of Köchli gold cuff links made for Grand Dukes Vladimir and his brother Serge Aleksandrovich sold in the Romanov Heirlooms sale in 2009. *Courtesy of Sotheby's*

in 2011 in *Fabergé Revealed.*[15] In 1981 Christie's Geneva sold two Köchli cigarette cases, one in a Greek Key pattern in silver and the other in gun metal. Each is applied with a gold imperial eagle set with a single cabochon sapphire.[16]

As with Bolin creations, objects rather than grand parures have survived. The St. Petersburg goldsmith's stock in trade was precious *objets* and small jewels embellished with cabochon gemstones, either rubies or sapphires. Today, we mainly see Köchli's diamond brooches of the typical Russian design of open circles or leaf shaped in yellow gold. Some of these are set with crowned diamond initials or pearls, gold stickpins and cuff links of personal or thematic motifs, such as crowned initials for grand dukes, crystal scent flasks with textured mounts and cabochon sapphires as well as boxes and miniature eggs carved of the finest native hardstones, including nephrite, lapis lazuli and rhodochrosite. The firm also produced crosses and panagias, or small icons for the clergy, as well as pendants and bracelets.

Other than presentation boxes, which were in a standard size specified by the imperial cabinet, the Köchli boxes that survive tend to be either cigarette cases or compact bonbonnières. One of the latter, made in gold for a Russian grand duchess, cleverly opens on the side, its lid in vermillion enamel applied with the diamond initials *AM* below a Romanov crown.

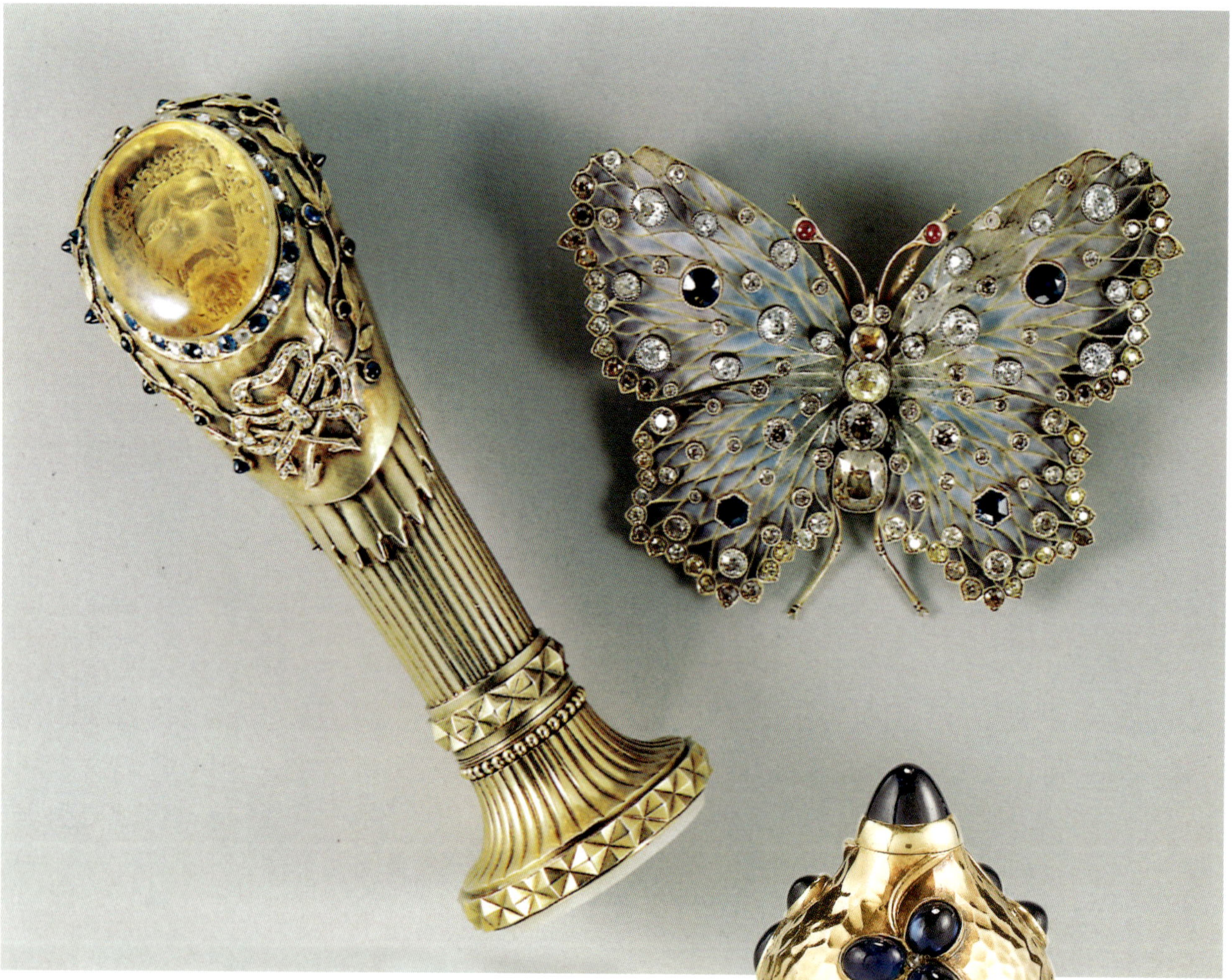

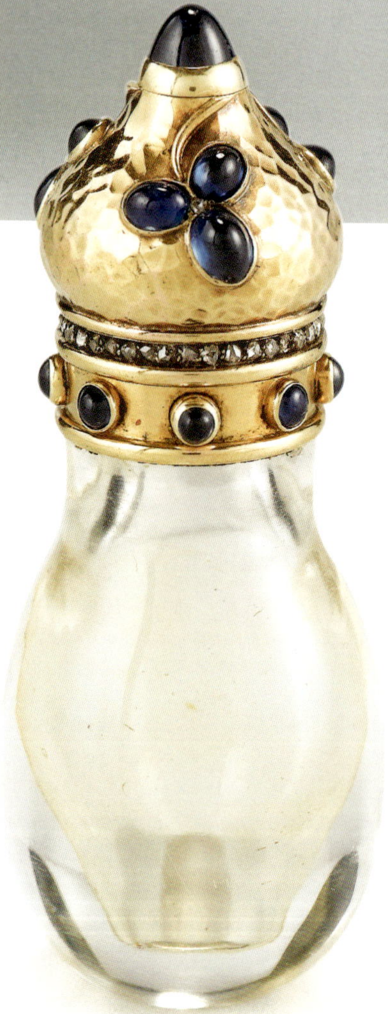

Above:
This gold seal by Köchli is set with a citrine carved with a lion's head, cabochon sapphires and small diamonds. It sold in 1990 for $17,286. *© 1990 Christie's Images Ltd.*

Right:
The hammered gold and cabochon sapphire perfume bottle by Köchli fetched $18,000 in 2013. *Courtesy of Sotheby's*

Following page top:
Calibré-cut (channel-cut) sapphire and diamond cuff links by Carl Bock. *Private Collection, photo by Noel Allum*

Following page bottom:
The Bock rose gold cigarette case came from the estate of the pianist Joseph C. Hoffman, who was a close friend of Grand Duke Serge Aleksandrovich. It sold in 1987 for $4,400. *© 1983 Christie's Images Ltd.*

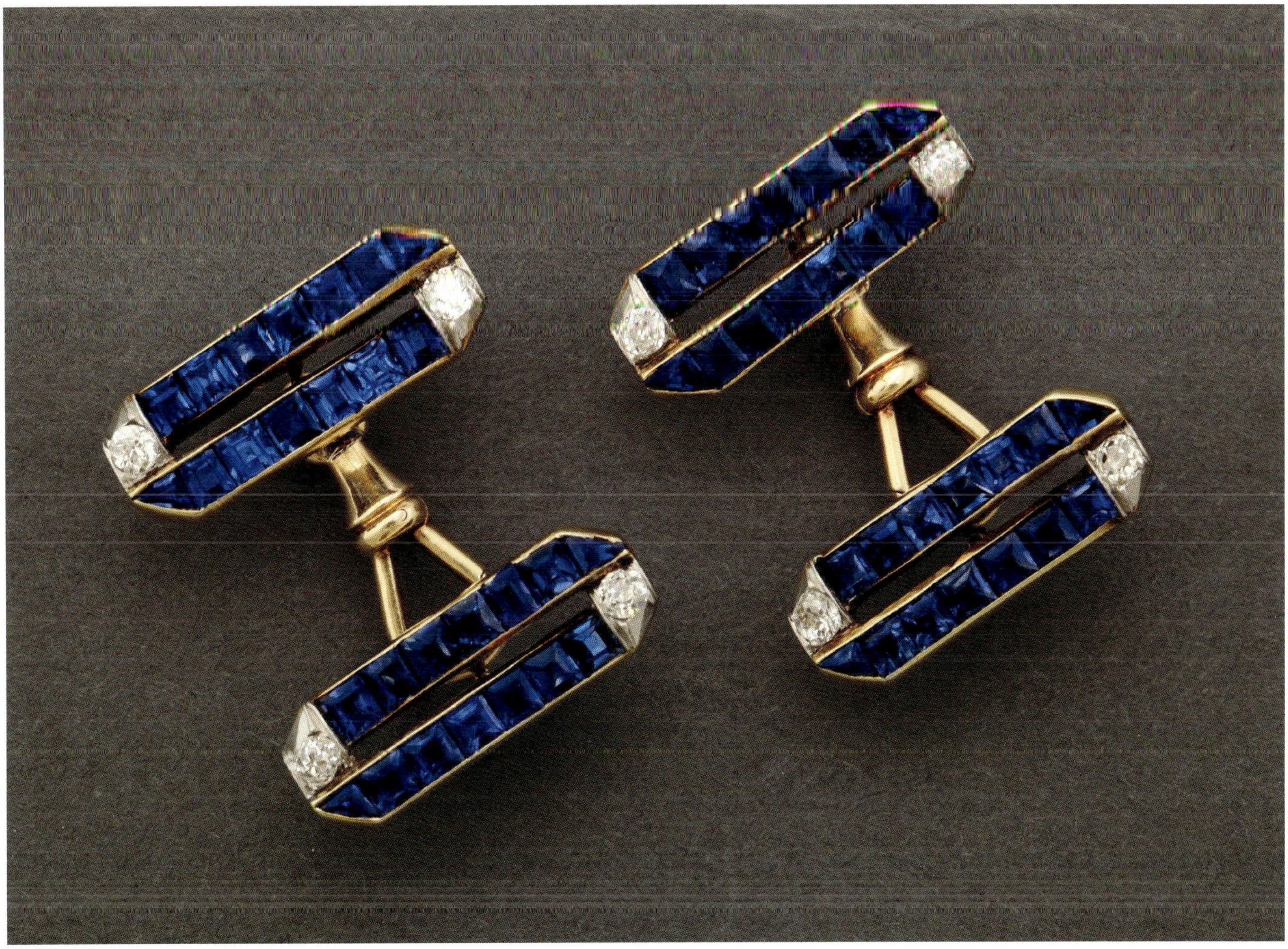

Bock

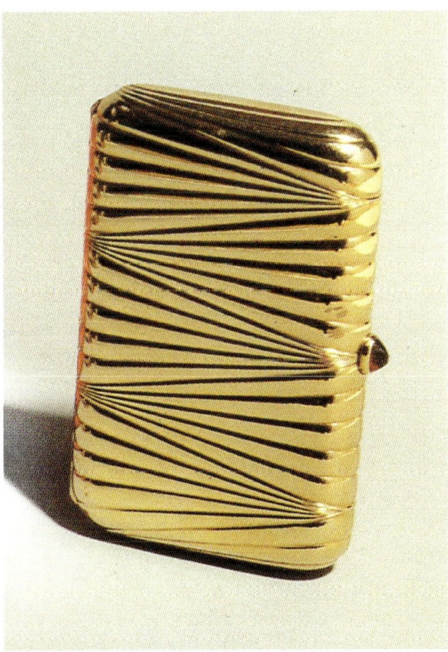

Bock made a beautiful pair of modernist sapphire-and-diamond cuff links that survive. Not many of his items surface on the market, probably as a result of the jeweler's primary role as a business owner rather than jeweler (he bought several jewelry enterprises and was keen, as in the case of Arnd and Buhler, to retain the seller's name).

Russian items sold at auction either made or retailed by Bock in the West include a lozenge-shaped diamond and ruby brooch (1996, $4,895), a silver art nouveau cigarette case from Moscow offered in London (2002, $4,836), a miniature rhodonite hippopotamus in New York (2015, $5,625) and an art nouveau plique-à-jour enamel pendant (2015, $3,058).

Archival images from 1910 attest that Carl Bock created at least two large silver trophies with imposing double-headed eagles, as gifts to be presented by the tsar. According to Alexander Ivanov, these were later erroneously attributed to and accepted as by Carl Fabergé at auction in the West, due to the high quality of silver workmanship.[17] There is no indication the two firms ever collaborated.

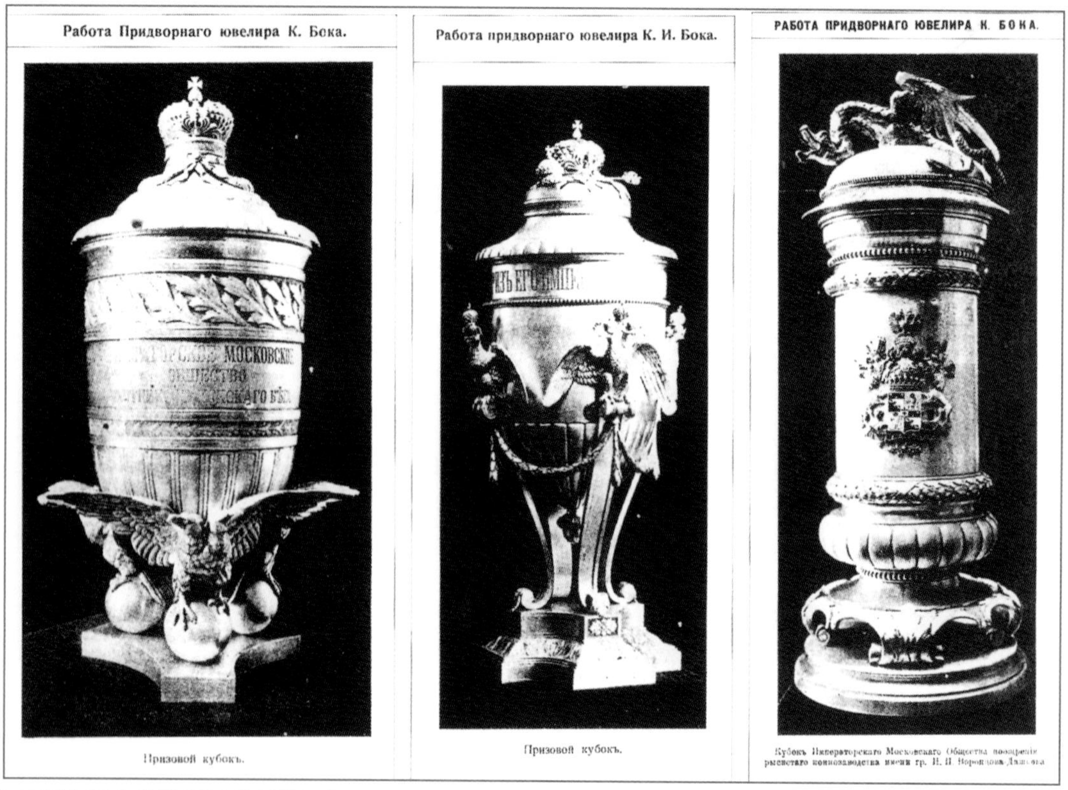

Работа Придворнаго ювелира К. Бока.

Работа придворнаго ювелира К. И. Бока.

РАБОТА ПРИДВОРНАГО ЮВЕЛИРА К. БОКА.

Призовой кубокъ.

Призовой кубокъ.

Кубокъ Императорскаго Московскаго Общества поощренія рысистаго коннозаводства имени гр. И. И. Воронцова-Дашкова

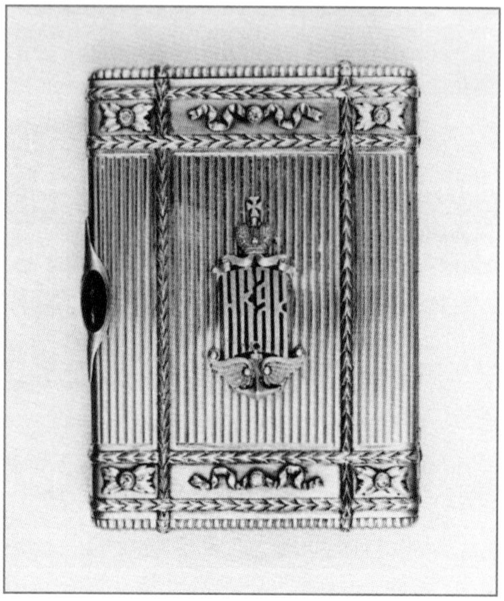

Three silver trophies by Bock, Ivanov, vol. II, p. 293.

This two-colored gold cigarette case by Carl Bock was sold in Geneva in 1983 for $3,378.

THE ST. PETERSBURG SILVERSMITHS MARKET

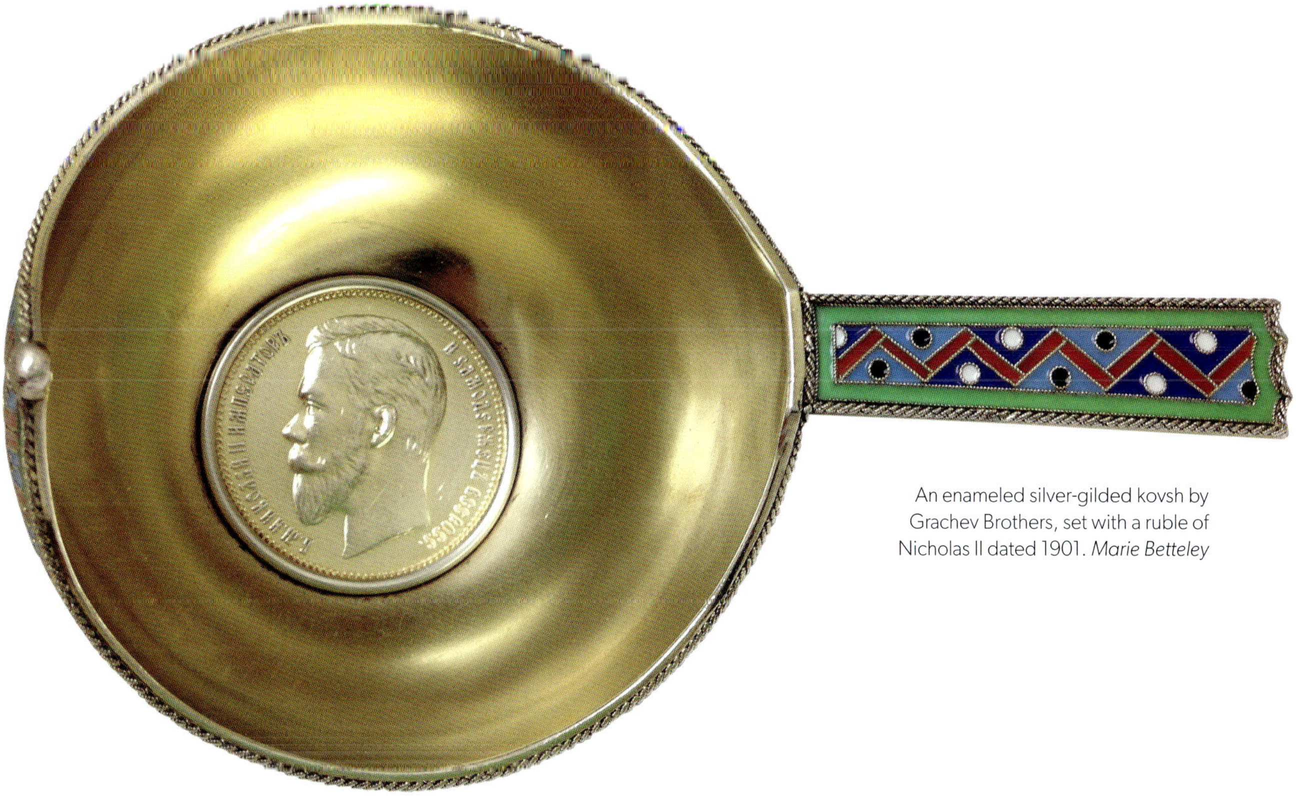

An enameled silver-gilded kovsh by Grachev Brothers, set with a ruble of Nicholas II dated 1901. *Marie Betteley*

Grachev

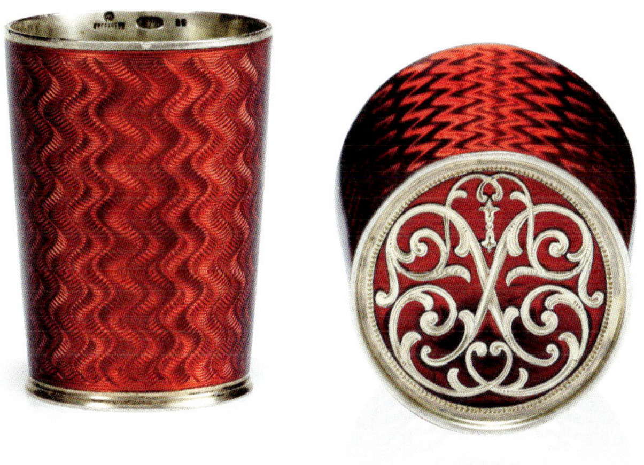

Two views of a Grachev guilloché enameled vodka cup, the base with a cipher of Peter the Great in plique-à-jour enamel. © *2010 Christie's Images Ltd.*

The most interesting Grachev Brothers pieces are those in enameling or trompe l'oeil silver. Grachev enamels are bright, bold and unlike those of Moscow enamelers. The silversmith often used primary colors, vivid reds and cobalt blues in Pan-Slavic designs or pastels in floral designs. Sometimes enamelwork adorns only part of tea and coffee pots or as borders on trays, but the effect is harmonious and pleasing to the eye. A six-piece tea service with enamel in its original fitted case sold at auction in 2006 for almost $100,000. In 2011 a large kovsh by Grachev adorned with a black enamel double-headed eagle prow fetched just under $77,000, its precise history unknown. For the American market, Grachev produced a wonderful champlevé-enameled serving spoon decorated with the Great American Seal, no doubt by special government decree in the 1890s. It sold for $5,625 in New York at auction in 2011.[18] I especially like Grachev enamel vodka cups for their vibrant colors and bold designs.[19] Enamel tea-glass holders by the maker are also in demand and usually sell at auction and through dealers for between $5,700 and $15,000.

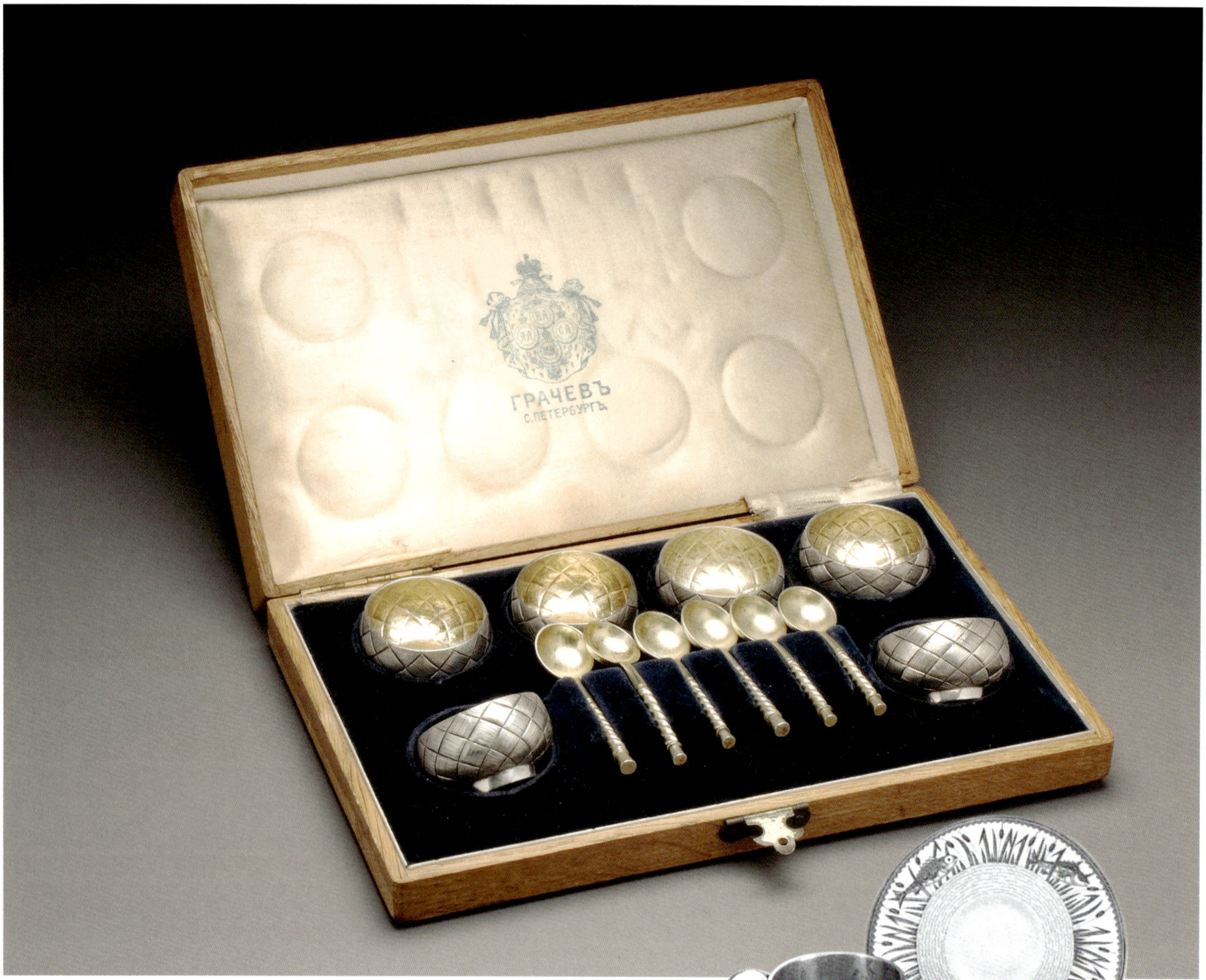

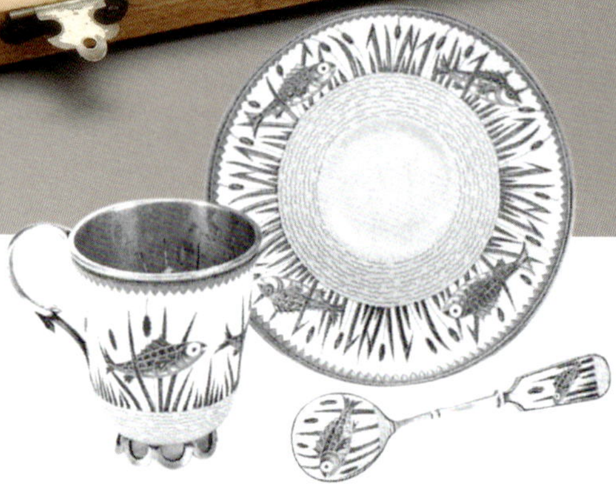

The high quality of Grachev silver is seen in its textured surface, which is meant to simulate another material such as birchwood or basket weave. Russian silversmiths, particularly during the second half of the 19th century, excelled in this technique. The grand masters of this were Gubkin from Moscow, and Sazikov and Grachev in St. Petersburg.

Sets of vessels or salts in original fitted boxes by Grachev are prized as collectors' items and have been for decades. Sotheby's sold a set of 12 enameled vodka cups, each a different design by the maker, in 1983 for $44,000. Individual items tend to fetch less per piece but are no doubt unique. One of my favorites was a pale blue enameled teacup and saucer and spoon, each decorated with plique-à-jour enamel fish swimming amid cattails, which yielded $6,050 in 1982. Silver tea-glass holders, miniature samovars and the like by Grachev tend to sell at auction for between $1,800 and $3,600.

Top:
This set of silver salt cellars by Grachev was presented to Maria Aleksandrovna of Russia (1853–1920) wife of Prince Alfred Ernest Saxe-Coburn, Duke of Edinburgh, and her children. The bases are variously engraved *1888* and *Marie* for HRIH Grand Duchess Marie Alexandrovna, *Alfred* for HRH Prince Alfred (b. 1874), *Marie* for HRH Princess Marie (later Queen of Romania) (b. 1875), *Victoria*, for HRH Princess Victoria Melita (b. 1876), *Sandra* for HRH Princess Alexandra (b. 1878), *baby*, the nickname for HRH Princess Beatrice (b. 1884). *Private Collection. Photo by Noel Allum.*

Bottom:
Pale-blue cloisonné and plique-à-jour enamel cup and saucer. *© 1983 Christie's Images Ltd.*

Right:
Cloisonné enameled vodka cups. *Courtesy of Sotheby's*

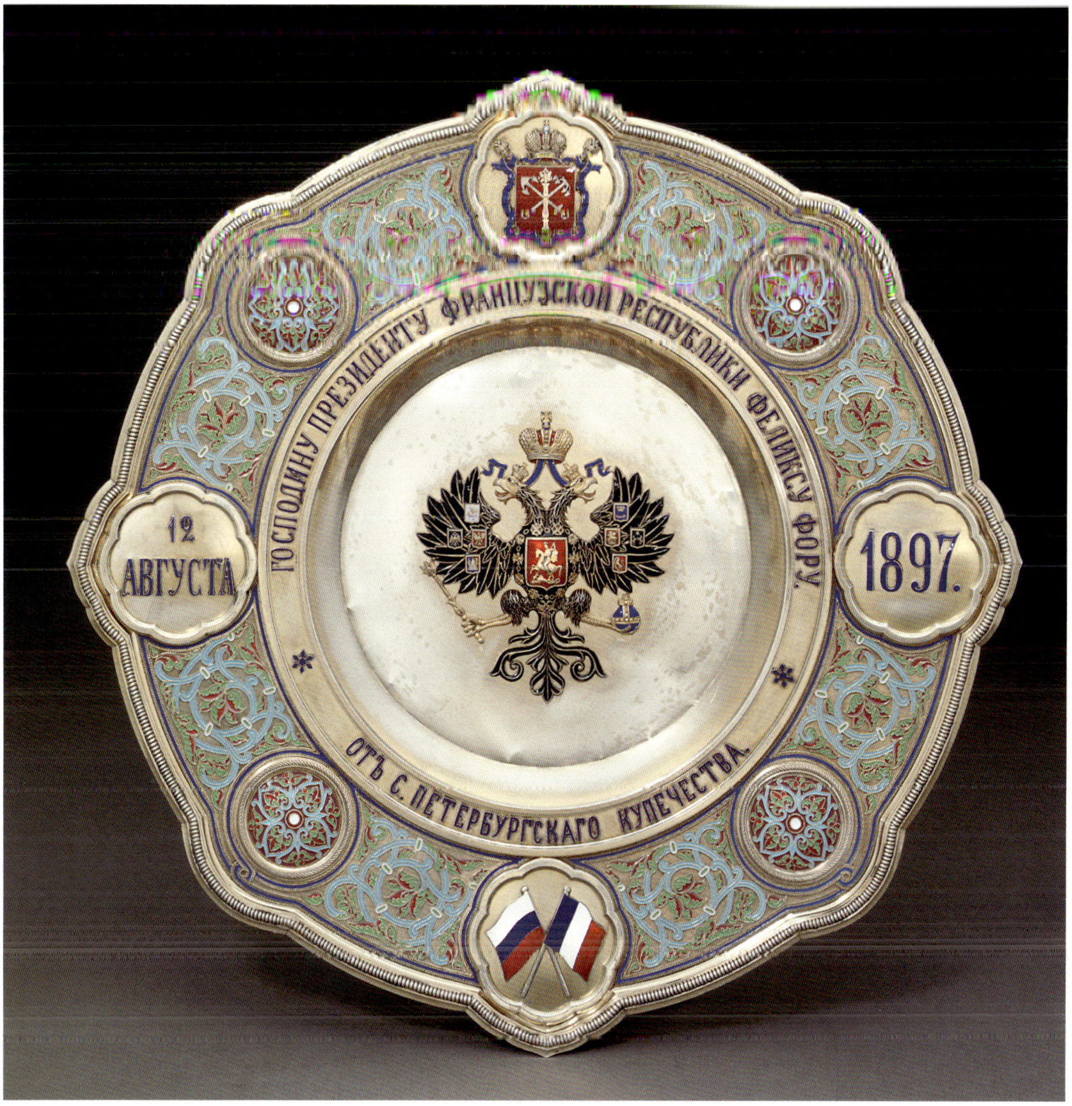

Grachev enameled presentation platter inscribed: "For Mr Felix Fauré, President of the Republic of France, from the St Petersburg Merchantry 12 August 1897." *© 2005 Christie's Images Ltd.*

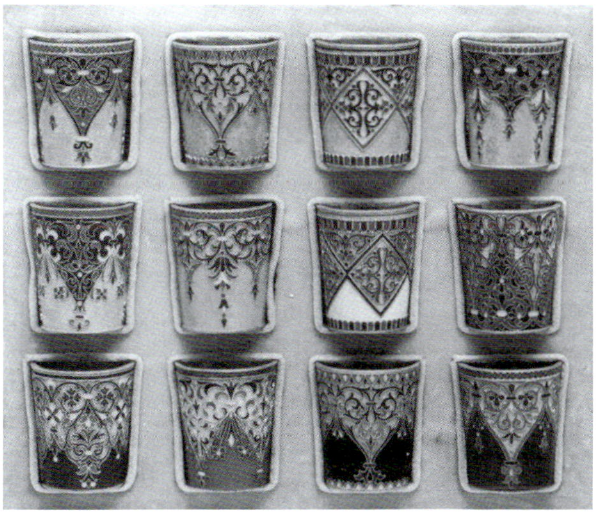

Larger Grachev silver items have enjoyed a steady increase in value, due to the participation of Russian buyers eager to repatriate treasures from their heritage. In 2006, Christie's sold a Grachev figural inkwell in the form of a Russian officer with his horse modeled in silver on a marble base for $144,000. Its original fitted case was stamped Fabergé as the retailer, showing a collaboration between the two firms. The Scottish auctioneer Lyon and Turnbull sold an enameled Grachev kovsh decorated with a rooster's head in 2008 for $75,000, which had sold 25 years earlier in New York for $8,250. A very Russian look, the rooster figures prominently in many enameled designs recalling ancient Muscovy.

The same Edinburgh auctioneers sold another Grachev kovsh in 2009, this one of known provenance. In richly modeled silver, complete with 12 kovsh-shaped drinking cups each of

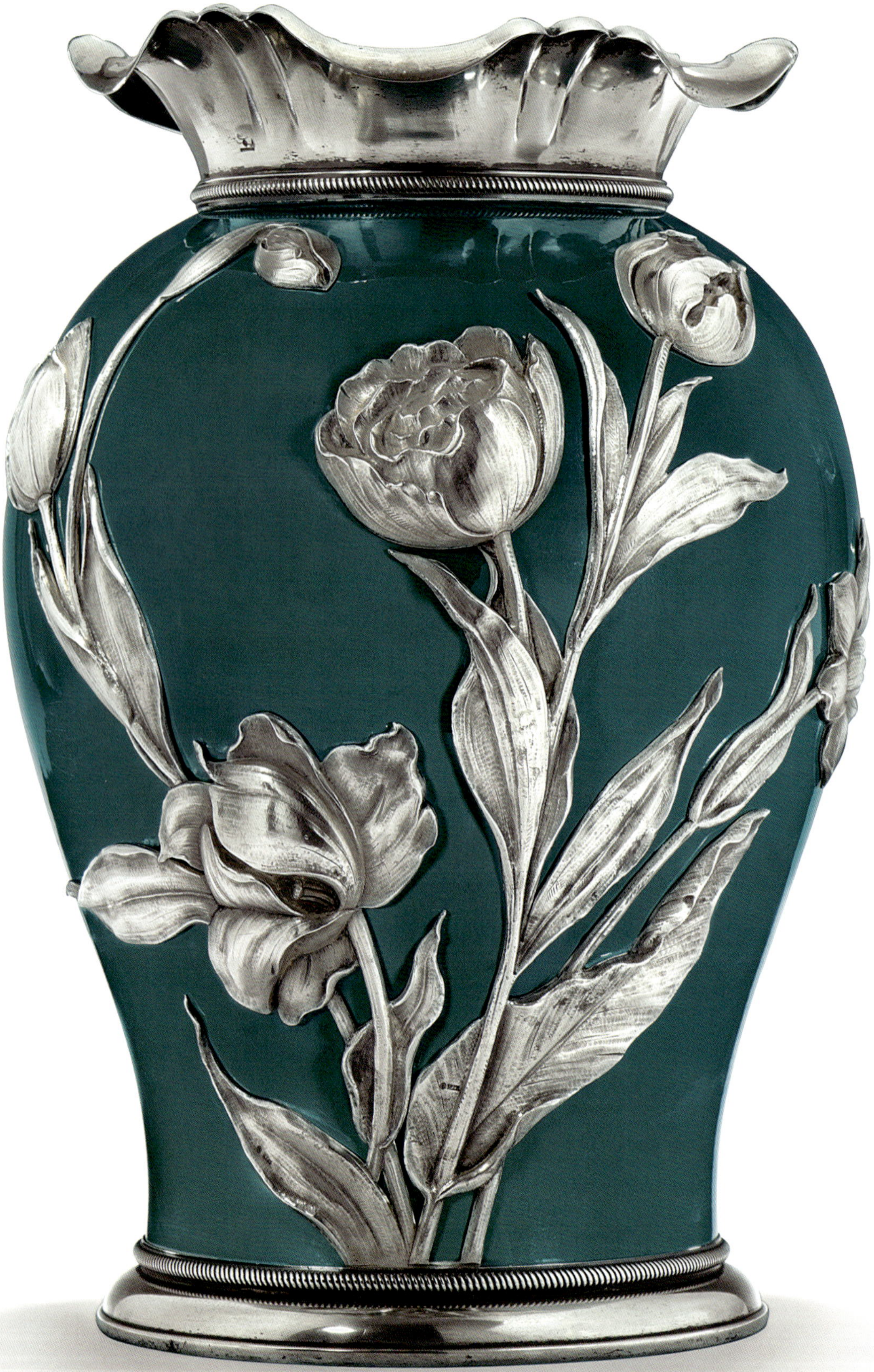

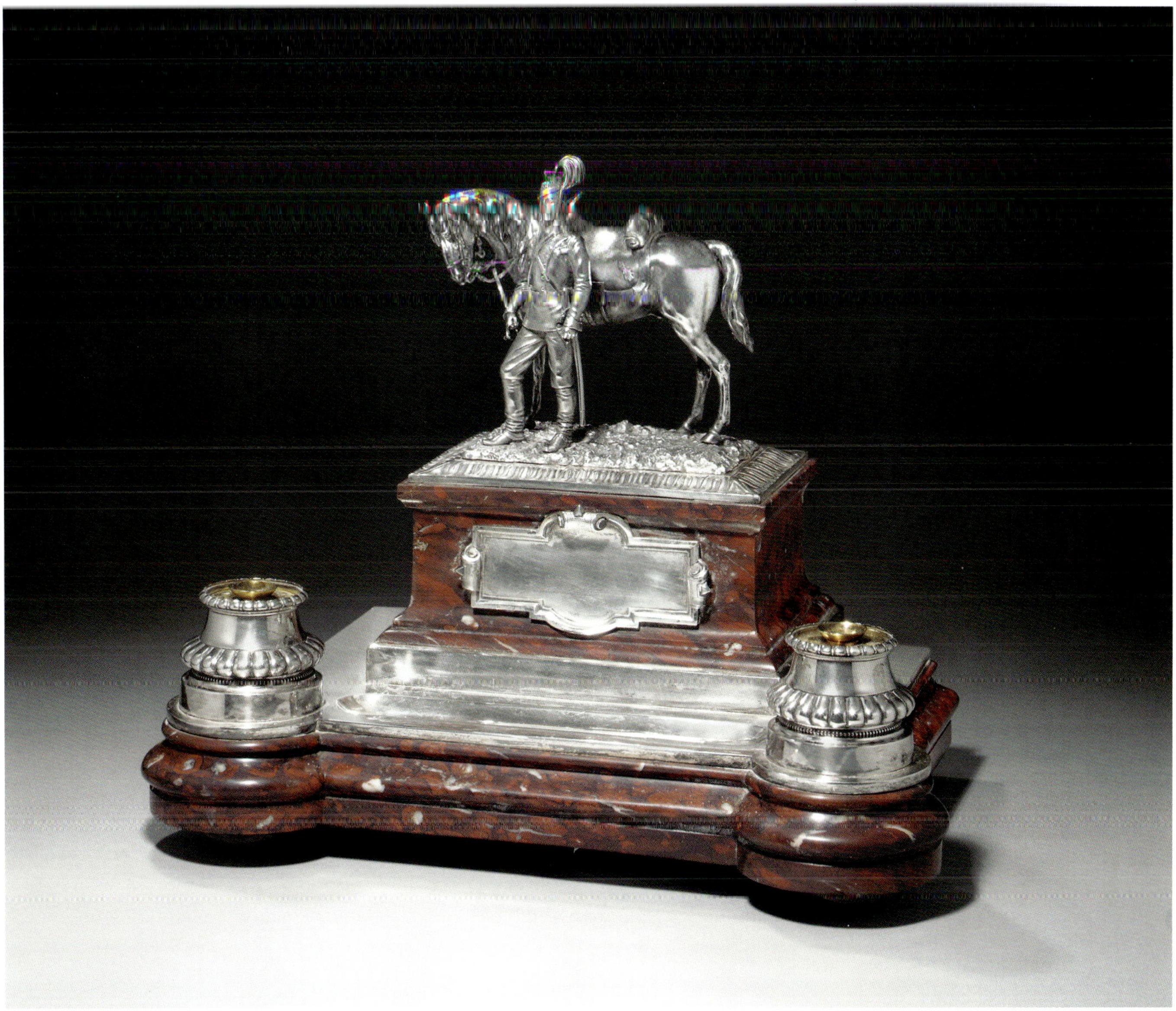

Viking-ship design, as well as a circular tray and ladle, the set was presented to American rear admiral Davis for his diplomatic role in defusing the Dogger Bank crisis during the Russo-Japanese War of 1904–1905 (see "The Grachev Brothers: A Dynasty of Silversmiths"). An English silver trophy also awarded to Davis for the same reason by the British appeared at the same auction. Thus, these two items no doubt appeared on the Western market for the first time. The kovsh set sold for $115,579. Grachev also created a large presentation platter for French president Félix Fauré on his state visit to Russia in August 1897, which resurfaced at a London auction in 2005 (see page 291). Despite these high prices, the market for Grachev items compared to similar Fabergé silver pieces seems undervalued.

Grachev inkwell retailed by Fabergé. *© 2006 Christie's Images Ltd.*

Previous page:
Grachev of St. Petersburg made silver mounts in the Art Nouveau taste for this ceramic vase by the Kuznetsov Factory of Moscow. © *2011 Christie's Images Ltd.*

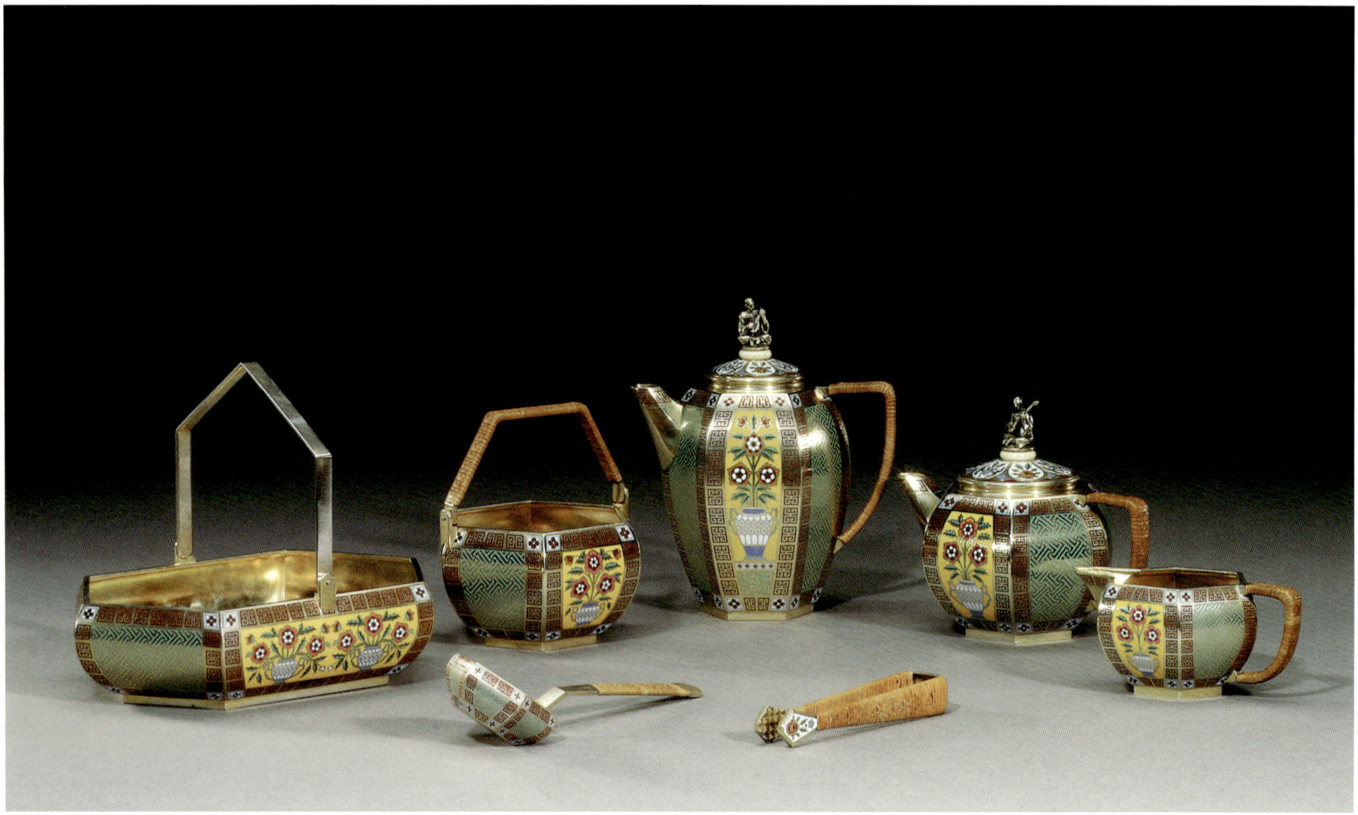

This distinctive Chinoiserie champlevé enamel tea service by Grachev sold for $58,000. *© 1997 Christie's Images Ltd.*

Below:
In 1962 this 33-piece Imperial presentation silver tea service by Morozov complete with samovar and two original fitted wooden cases sold for $210. It had been presented by the Russian tsar to Emperor Menelik of Abyssinia (Ethiopia) and was engraved with the Imperial lion of Judah. *Courtesy of Sotheby's (Parke-Bernet)*

Morozov

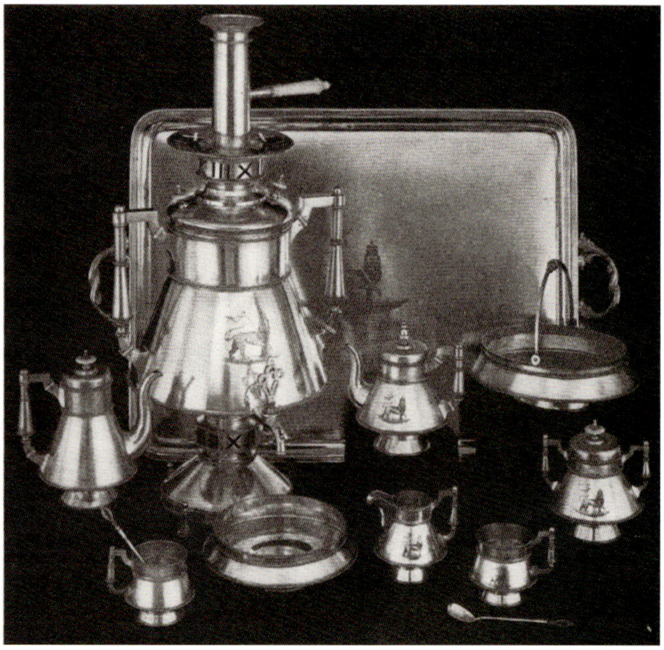

Morozov items are more prevalent in Europe and Russia than in North America. A recent visit to the Moscow Antique Show revealed dozens of large-scale items by the native Russian silversmith, many in fitted wooden cases with a Morozov stamp below the imperial warrant. Some of these boxes are refitted today in Russia and cleverly designed to look just like the old ones. The hallmark varies, with additional initials representing the maker stamped next to the full name in Cyrillic. For Ivan Morozov, the imperial warrant appears above the name; for Vladimir, his son, it precedes it, each within a single stamp (see glossary).

Grand silver ensembles by Morozov rarely appear on the market. However, in 2006, Doyle New York auctioned off a large and very elaborate 180-piece silver gilt dinner service from the estate of an American ambassador. Made by the

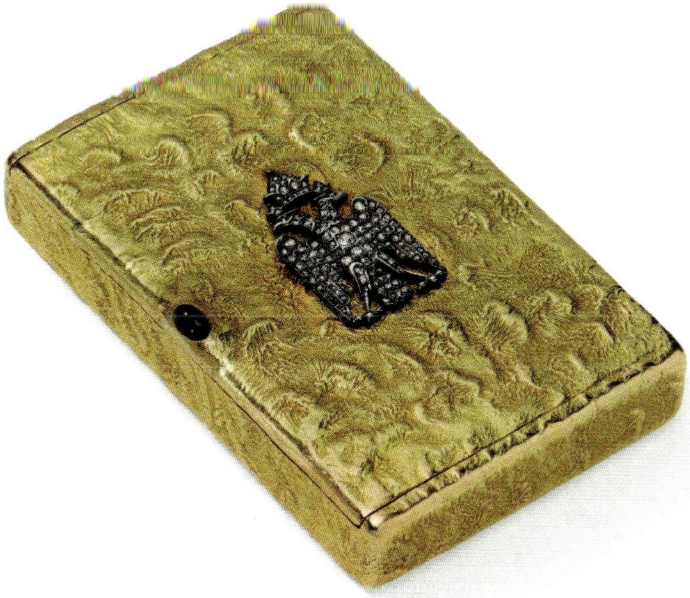

Gold samorodok and diamond cigarette case by Morozov. *Courtesy of Sotheby's*

Morozov workshop from 1908 to 1917, it included a massive centerpiece decorated with frolicking bears and naturalistic trees in the mid-19th-century style, which sold for $912,000 (see page 152).

For the Romanov tercentenary celebrations of 1913, a distinct eagle emerged in jewelry and silver, based on an ancient design. Morozov excelled in this. Pendants, brooches and cigarette cases that bear this striking decoration are usually by this firm. Recent prices for Morozov cigarette cases seem to fluctuate with the value of gold and vary between $7,000 and $17,000. More unusual was a gold pectoral cross by Morozov that sold in 2011 for $21,384.

In the United States, Morozov cigarette cases surface regularly, although not as often as those by Fabergé. That these *porte cigarettes*, the essential accessory for gentlemen at the turn of the 20th century, survived the Russian Revolution is not surprising: easy to conceal and carry across countries, war-torn or otherwise, they were not valuable enough to melt down, and most did not have many gems. Cases varied in texture, but not in other aspects. I sold one that was reeded or

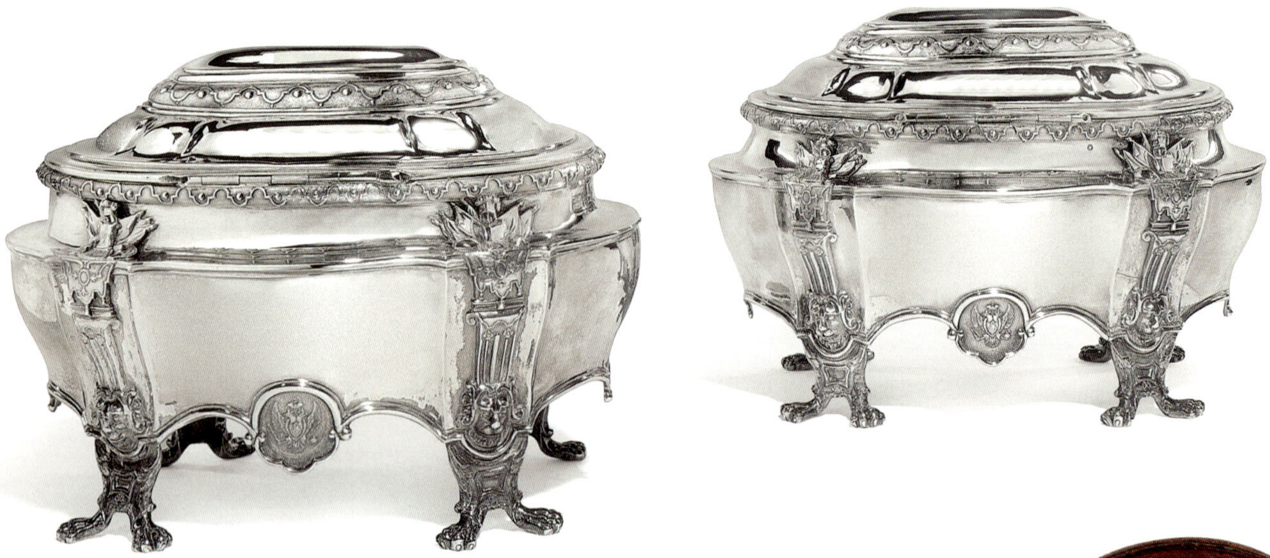

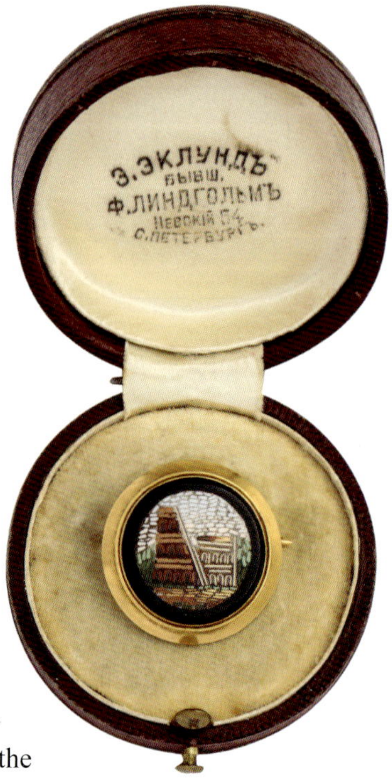

decorated with bands overall, its applied gold eagle set with a central diamond. Others are of a highly reflective polish in rose or yellow gold. Otherwise, Morozov items are surprisingly scarce in North America.

Nicholls & Plincke

The talented master silversmiths and jewelers who contributed to the success of the Nicholls & Plincke firm in St. Petersburg are finally becoming known in the West. The most important were Samuel Arnd, Robert Kokhun and Carl Tegelsten.

Arnd

Arnd goldwork is superb, as is its champlevé enameling, particularly on jetons and decorations. At times, jewels by this goldsmith don't sell at auction, no doubt because his name is unknown to buyers. A distinctive gold bracelet with intricate scrollwork in the ancient tradition, set with a large cabochon garnet by Arnd, failed to sell in 2008 and again later. This is astonishing given the high quality of the workmanship. One also finds smaller gold jewels on the market, pins, pendants, cuff links, tiepins and desk seals. One fabulous seal incorporates a free-flowing design of polished yellow gold and turquoise enamel, a technique unseen in Russian jewelry.

The six pairs of Arnd cuff links that belonged to Grand Duke Vladimir soared at auction in 2009, a function of provenance, novelty and the fact that the entire collection had never been on the Western market. The miniature St. Vladimir Order cuff

Previous page, top:
Two Imperial Russian silver caskets from the Grand Duchess Maria Nikolaevna Service, Carl Tegelsten, retailed by Nicholls & Plincke, St. Petersburg, 1839. *Courtesy of Sotheby's*

Previous page, bottom:
Italian micro-mosaic, Nicholls & Plincke. *Marie Betteley, photo by Josh Gaddy*

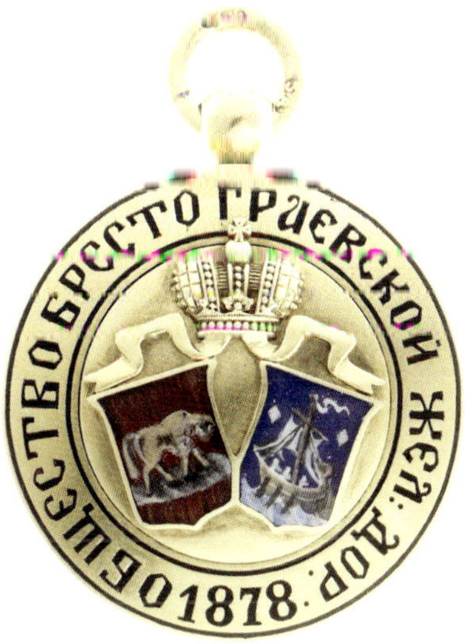

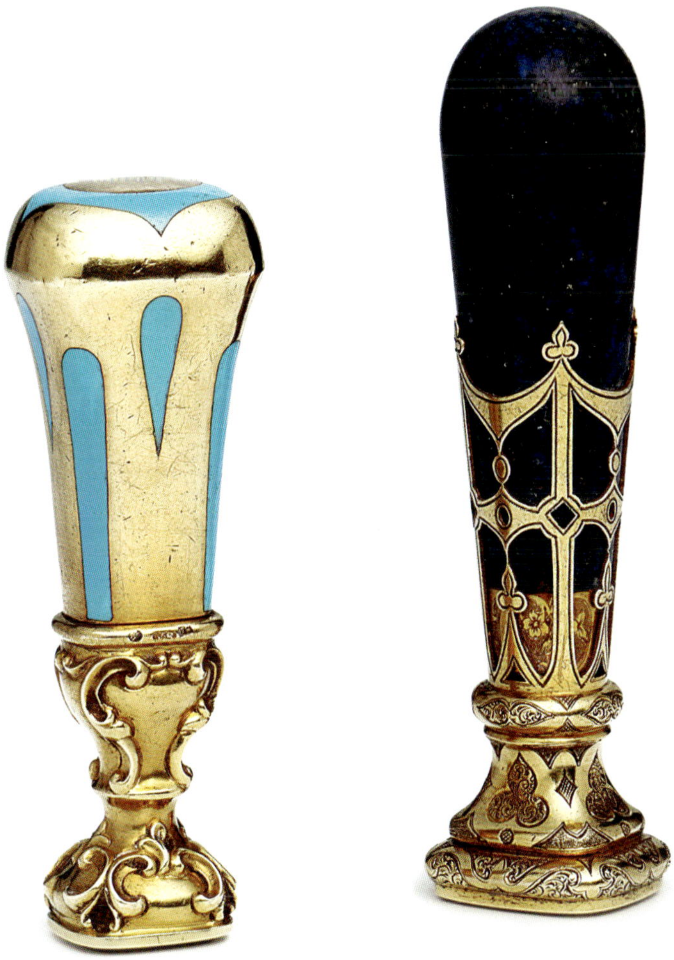

Top:
A gold-and-enamel commemorative jeton. *Courtesy of Bonham's*

Left:
Two gold-mounted hardstone desk seals, each by Samuel Arnd. © *2010 Christie's Images Ltd.*

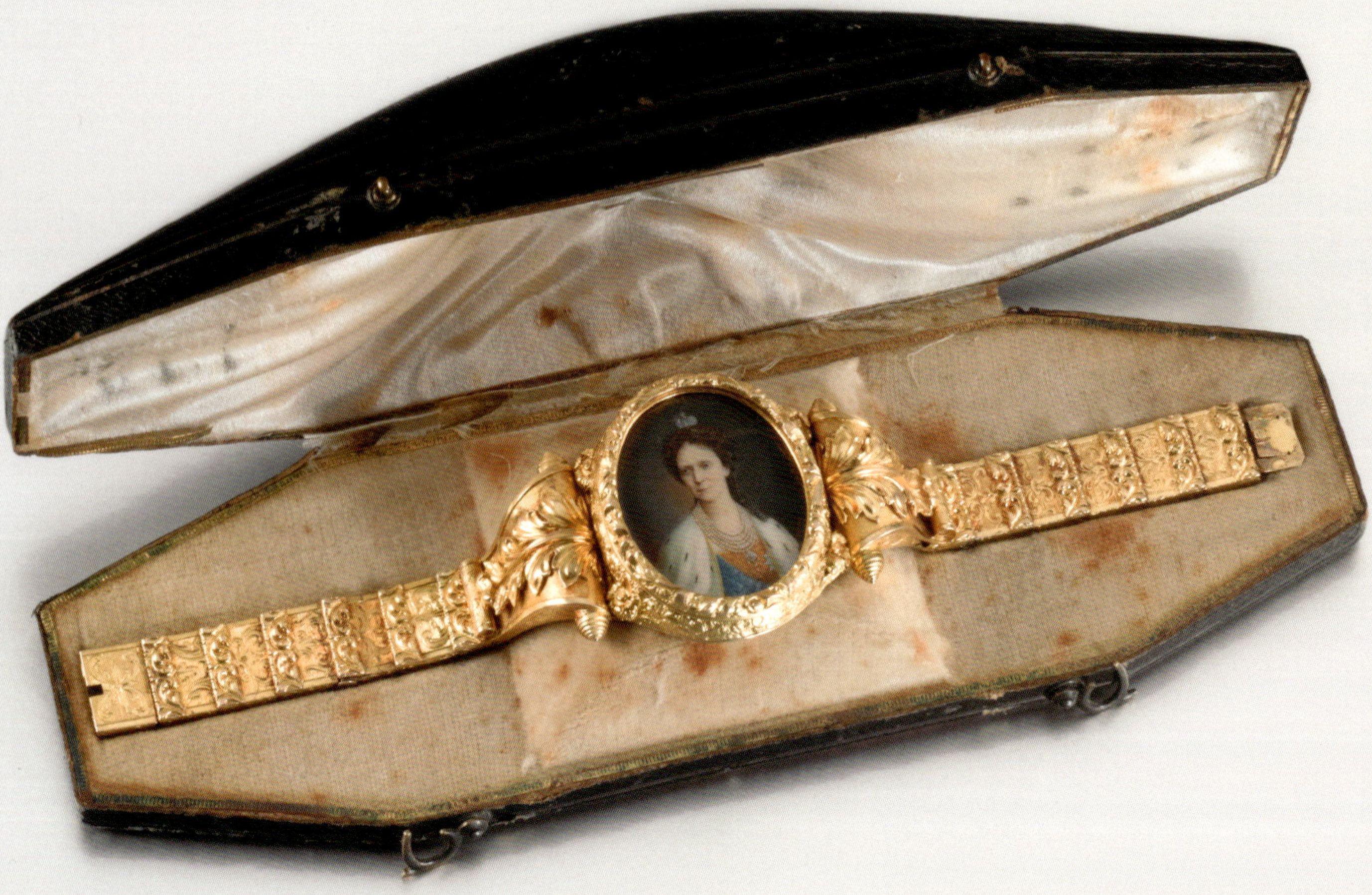

Imperial presentation bracelet with miniature of Empress Maria Alexandrovna (1824–1880), by Samuel Arnd.
Courtesy of Sotheby's

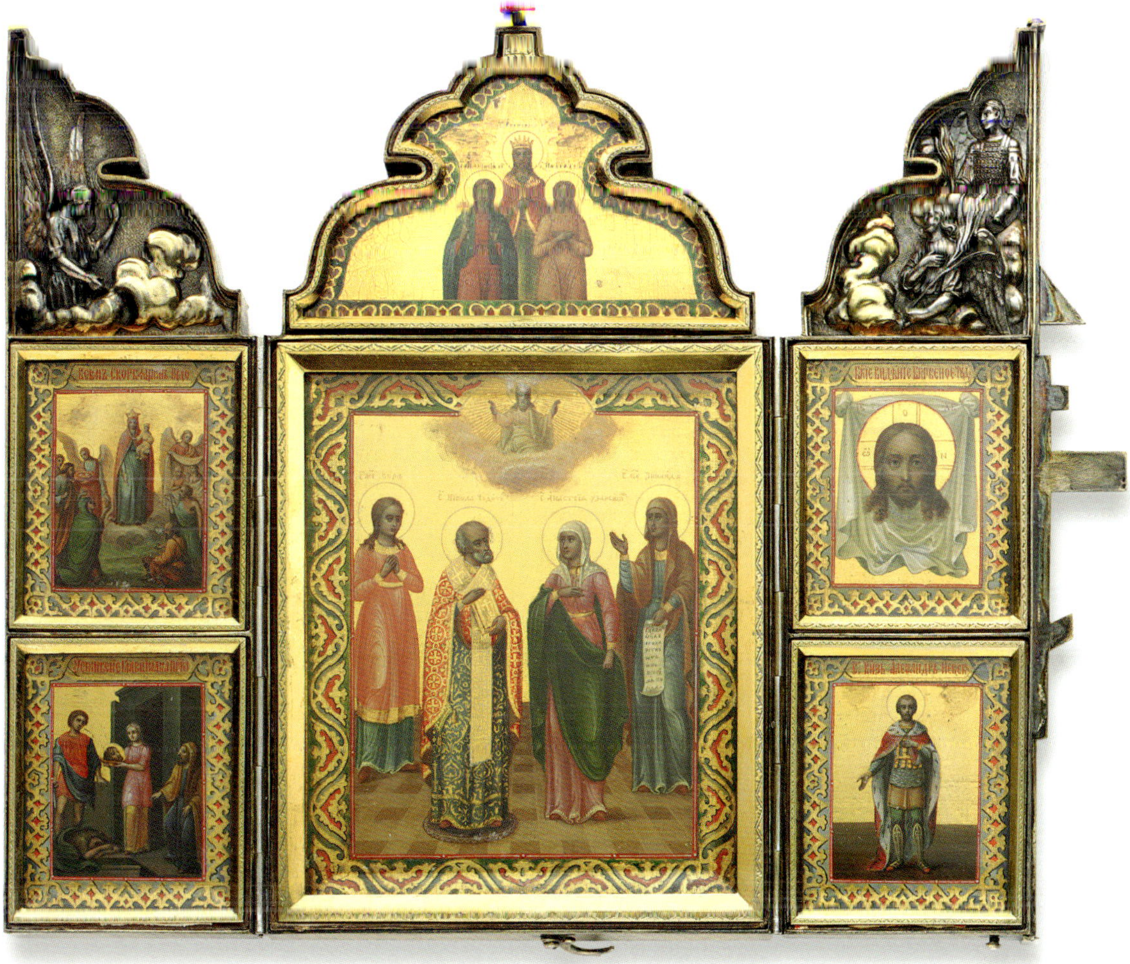

A silver-gilt triptych icon by Samuel Arnd.
Courtesy of Sotheby's

links by Arnd fetched over $45,000, while others with intricate goldwork brought between $12,000 and $28,845, perhaps putting Arnd on the map. Another pair made for the Qajar dynasty in Persia, with enameled portraits and mounts by Samuel Arnd, sold in England in 2014 for $3,354.[20]

A panagia, or icon pendant by the master in gold and enamel, sold in New York in 1988 for $4,180, while a similar one brought $38,000 in 2006.[21] No doubt admired for crisp enamel detail and lettering, miniature dress medals, stickpins and commemorative jetons by the goldsmith sell well at auction.[22]

Bracelets and pendants seemed to be the most popular form of jewelry for the goldsmith, judging from what still survives. The bracelets are all different, some in the form of gold cuffs decorated with diamond-set Cyrillic inscriptions, and others of simple openwork design with a detachable central motif set with richly colored cabochon gems or enclosing a miniature. Rings are scarce, as are earrings. A diamond and emerald brooch by Arnd sold in 2008 for $8,551.[23]

I rarely see Arnd objects and would love to find more, since I admire the firm's goldwork, and its silver is always of the highest quality. Silver stirrup cups by Arnd are extraordinary in detail and have become collectors' items. In 1993, a group of seven stirrup cups from the 1860s by the silversmith brought $36,262, an average price of over $5,180 each.[24] Twenty years later, the price had almost doubled when a group of six sold for $54,650.[25] More recently, an Arnd stirrup cup in the form of a boar's head fetched $13,423.[26] A miniature inkwell in the form of a gold cube with suspension ring fetched $13,271 in 2009.[27] As more previously obscure Russian goldsmiths such as Samuel Arnd become known, the market for their jewels and silver continues to strengthen.

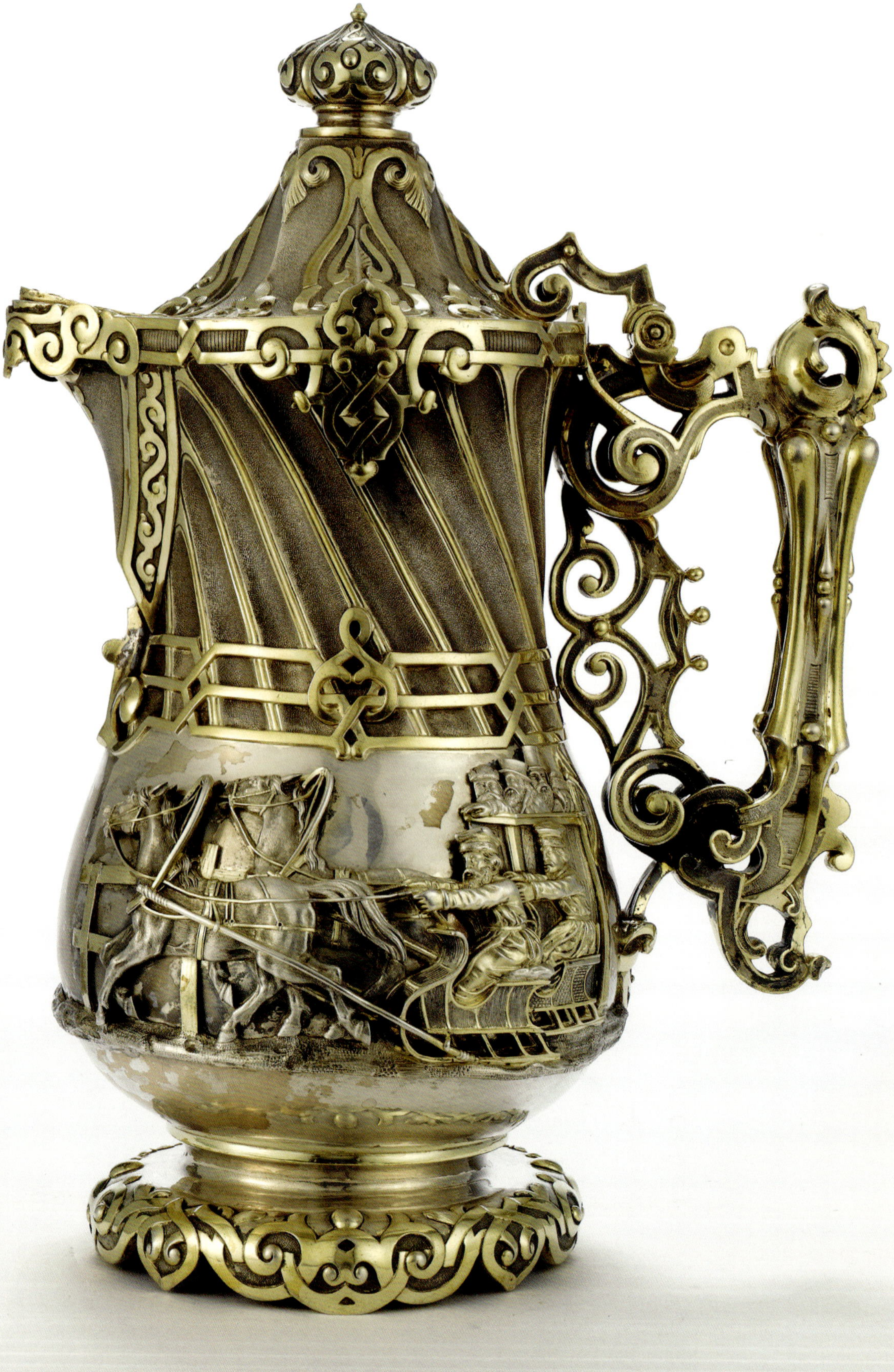

Tankard by Carl Tegelsten.
Courtesy of Sotheby's

Tegelsten

Finnish born, Carl Tegelsten immigrated to St. Petersburg in 1817 and became a master silversmith in 1833. A prolific workmaster of Nicholls & Plincke, he was famous for making the wedding silver services for several daughters of Tsars Nicholas I and Alexander II.[28] The business continued under his widow, Eva Elisabeth Lönnquist, and son Carl Julius Tegelsten until 1855.

Tegelsten silver does well in the West, since most of it has an established provenance. Even without one, buyers are attracted to its high quality. In 2006, Sotheby's sold a pair of Tegelsten silver salt cellars adorned with putti for over $40,000.[29] Four years later, a striking neo-Gothic tankard made the year of Carl's death (1852) fetched over $80,000 in New York.[30]

Silver owned by the grand duchesses of Russia has attracted strong prices. A pair of boxes belonging to Grand Duchess Maria Nikolaevna, the eldest daughter of Emperor Nicholas I (1796–1855), adorned with her crest sold for $43,750 to the trade, thus ensuring an even-higher markup. They came from the Van Cliburn collection, which also included a silver Tegelsten soup tureen that was made for the wedding of her sister, Grand Duchess Olga Nikolaevna, in 1840. This brought $158,500, well above its estimate.[31] Although prices have stabilized within the past few years, in 2014 a smaller Tegelsten box from the same imperial service brought $25,128, ensuring the continuation of a strong market for the Finnish-born silversmith.[32]

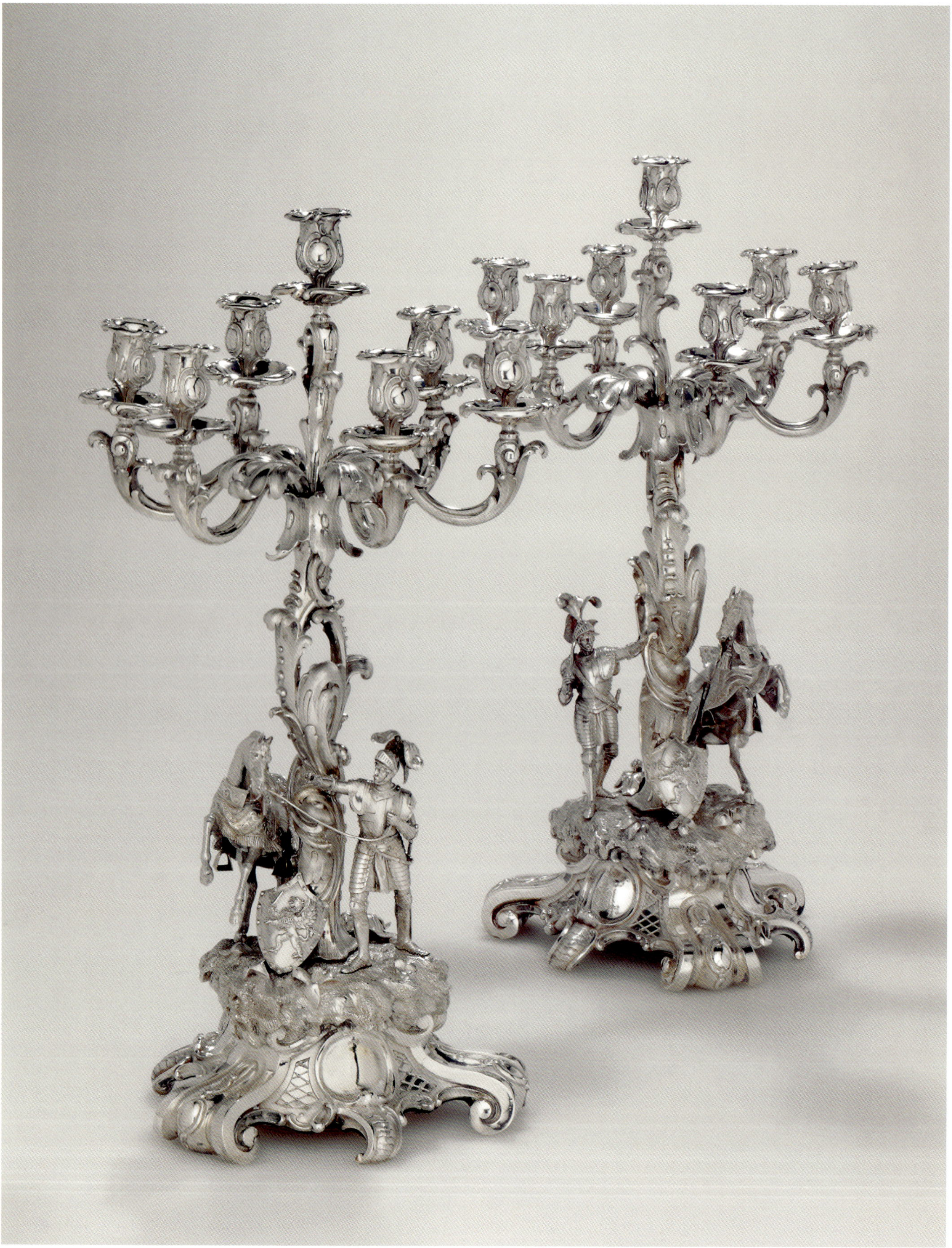

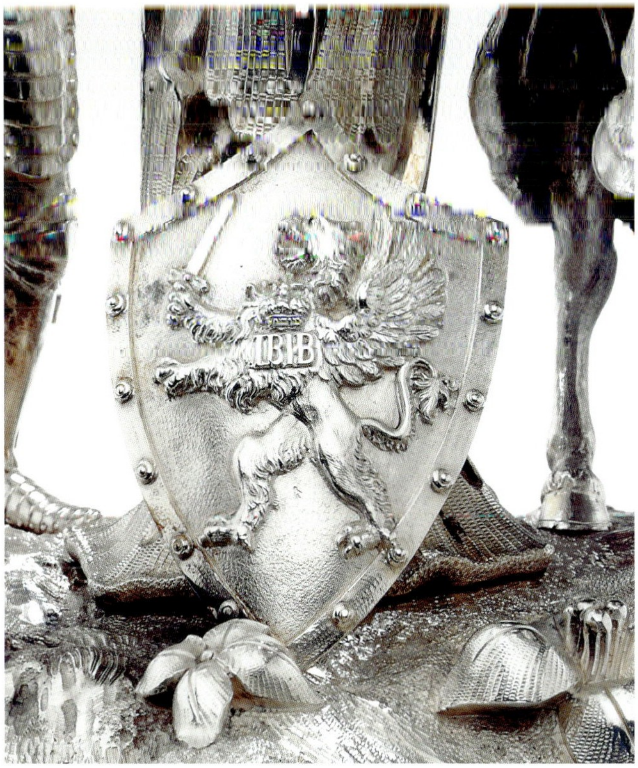

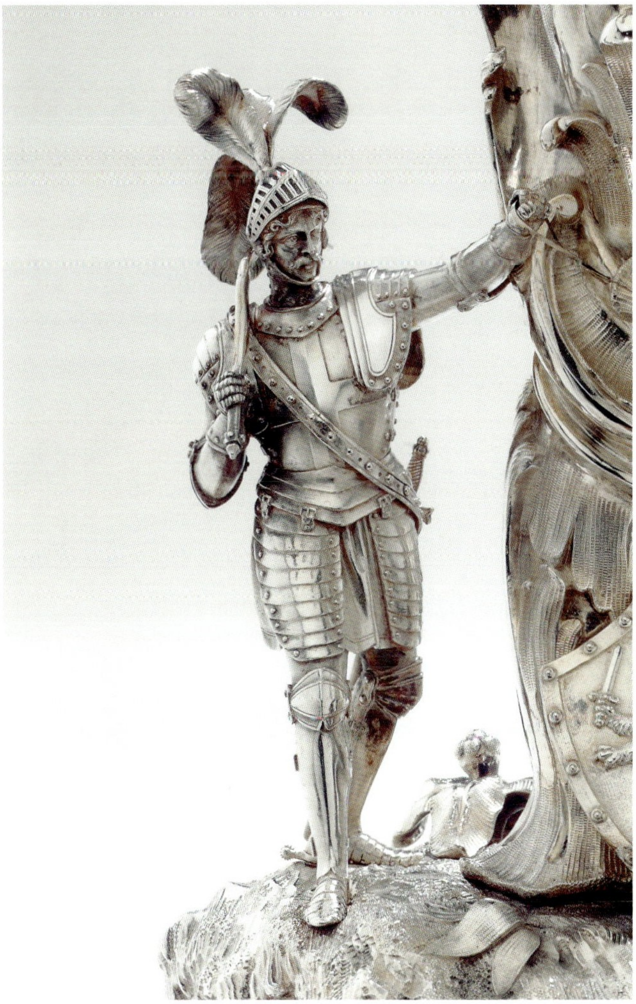

Kokhun

Robert Kokhun (b. 1807) made a striking silver wine cooler retailed by Nicholls & Plincke in 1890. In the naturalistic taste, perhaps on the basis of earlier designs, it features a vine-covered tree trunk enhanced with frolicking putti, and sold in London in 2006 for $123,631.[33] A pair of seven-light candelabra (illustrated) depicting knights on naturalistic ground with the same marks sold for $486,400 that same year.[34]

His forte, along with Arnd, was silver stirrup or hunt cups with realistically chased animals, which were particularly popular in the mid-19th century. A group of five in the form of a moose, owl, lynx, hare and terrier, stamped Cyrillic *PK* (although not identified, but no doubt for Kokhun), sold for $59,308, or $11,862 each on average in 2013.[35]

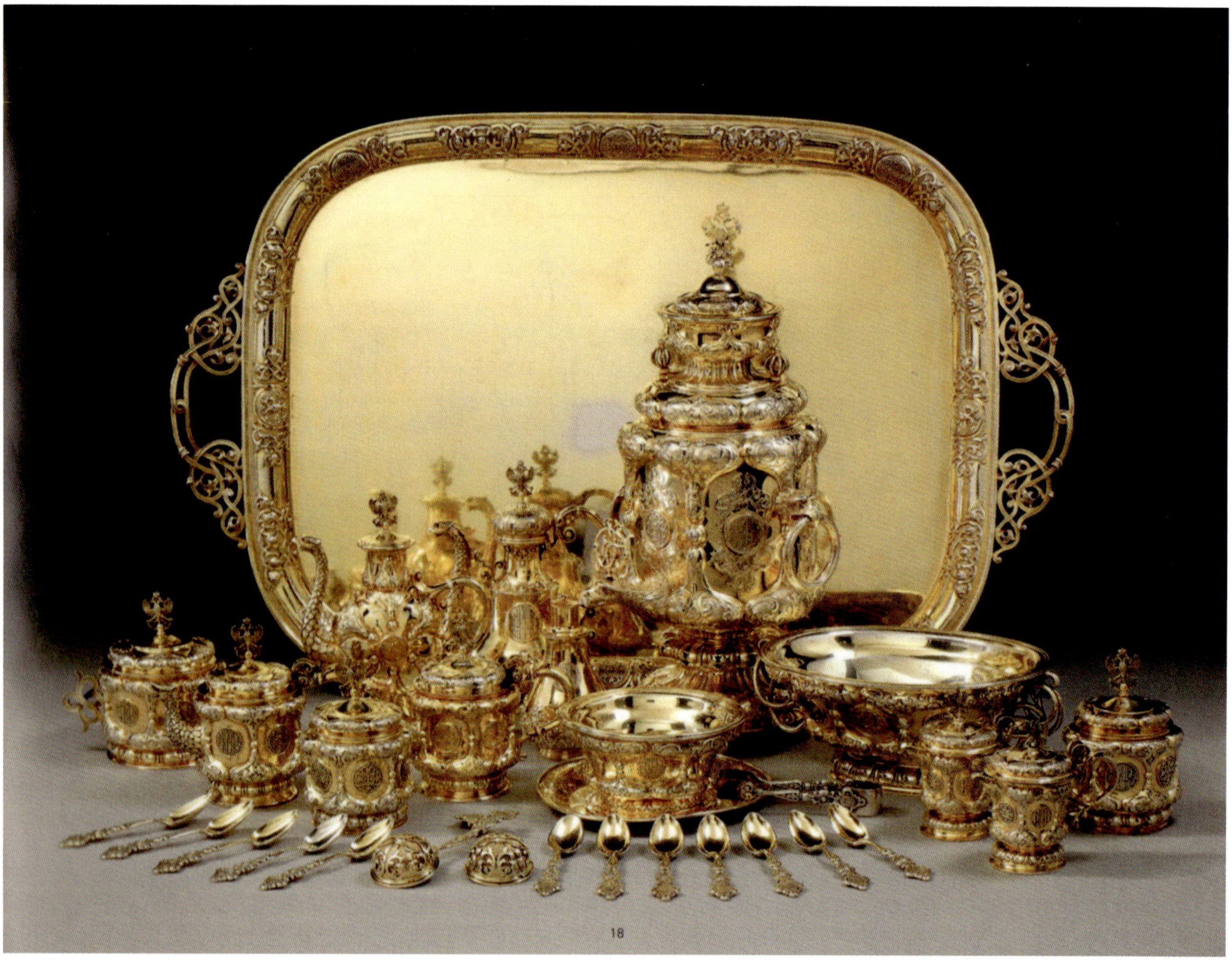

18

THE MOSCOW SILVERSMITHS MARKET

Sazikov

Monumental pieces by Sazikov are scarce. Over the past 50 years, only a handful has surfaced in the West, and when they do, prices soar. In 2005, an extensive gilded tea and coffee service belonging to Grand Duke Constantine Nikolaevich (1827–1892), brother of the Tsar Liberator, Alexander II, sold for over $1 million.[36] Dated 1848, it was made for the 21-year-old grand duke's wedding to Princess Alexandra von Sachsen-Altenburg. In the Old Russian taste and like its porcelain counterpart based on Solntsev's designs, the sumptuous service featured double-headed eagle finials, Pan-Slavic strapwork motifs and roundels enclosing the stylized initials of the Romanov heir.

An impressive Sazikov silver and enameled charger that had been presented to Tsar Alexander III and Tsarina Maria Fedorovna by the Smolensk nobility in 1883 sold at auction in 2011 for just under $300,000.[37] Its center adorned with a crowned Romanov griffin, the platter was bordered by enamel roundels of various cities and villages of the region south of Moscow. Its most impressive feature was the bold, raised Cyrillic lettering in silver with the dedication inscription.

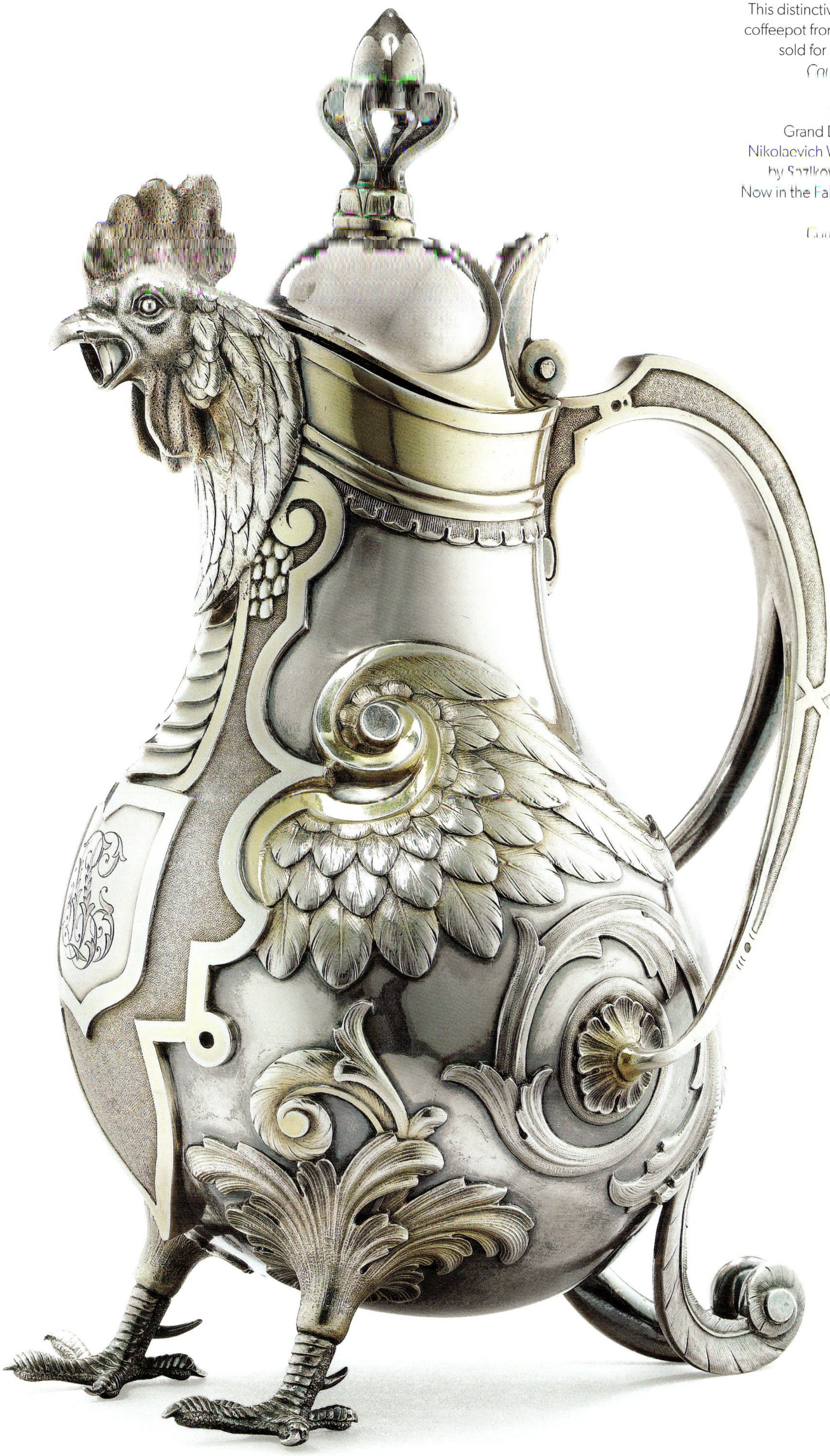

This distinctive Sazikov rooster coffeepot from Moscow, 1883, sold for $92,292 in 2010. *Courtesy of Sotheby's*

Previous page: Grand Duke Constantine Nikolaevich Wedding Service, by Sazikov, Moscow, 1848. Now in the Fabergé Museum in St. Petersburg. *Courtesy of Sotheby's*

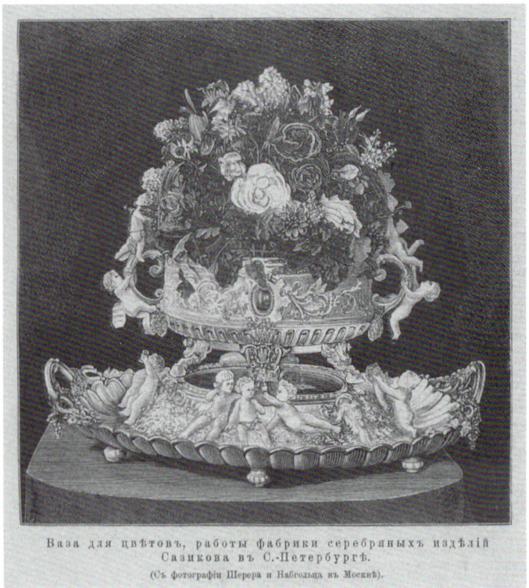

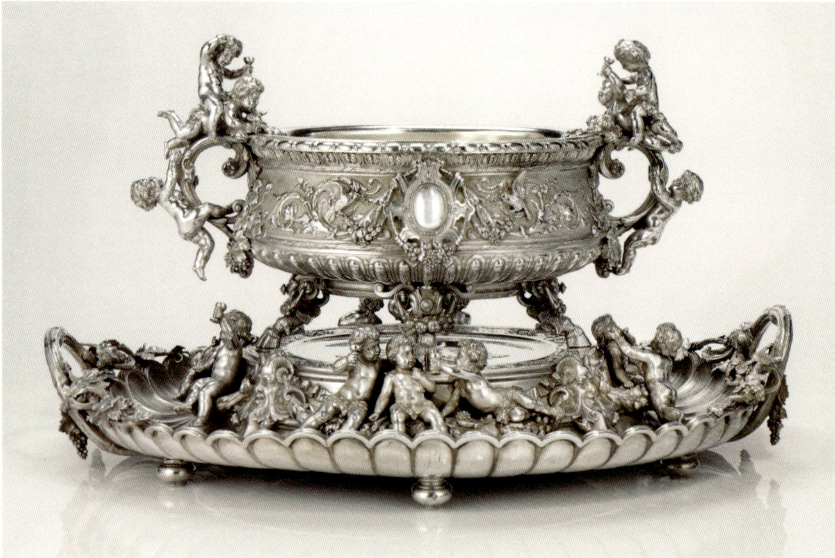

Sazikov wine cistern exhibited at the All Russian Exhibition of 1882. Another, of similar design, sold at auction in 2013. *Courtesy of Sotheby's*

Two years later, a wine cistern by Sazikov realized \$377,000.[38] Ornate and in the rococo taste, it was designed by August Karlovich Spiess (d. 1904), a German-born sculptor from the Berlin Academy of Art, and featured frolicking putti, masks, grape motifs, birds and hoof feet. I found its prototype illustrated in the 1882 All-Russian Exhibition catalogue of Moscow. Filled with flowers and called a *jardinière,* it seemed identical except for the arrangement of the putti. While it predated the Sotheby's cistern by at least eight years, the Romantic style was more in keeping with the mid-19th century, or even the 18th, than the period of Alexander III, which espoused ancient Muscovy over European or Western sensibilities. Spiess was well versed in the imperial tastes, since he had designed for the Winter Palace and the Imperial Porcelain Factory in the 1840s. Despite the tsar's nationalist tendencies, Western fashions still seemed to prevail at court.

A monumental Sazikov figure of a bogatyr and his horse sold in Paris, also in 2013, for \$166,382.[39] This appears to be a larger version of one of the pair sold at Christie's in 2009, which was based on the monumental sculpture group commissioned by Tsar Alexander II for the Winter Palace. The silver of the Paris lot is oxidized, or darkened.

However, even important Sazikov items with historical provenance do not always sell, as evidenced by a massive and richly embellished Pan-Slavic presentation punch bowl service. It first sold for \$56,672 in London in 1989 but failed to find a buyer in 2015.[40] This was probably due to an aggressive estimate (\$500,000), a softening of the Russian market, or both.

Sazikov silver appears regularly at auction. My favorite pieces are the finely rendered trompe l'oeil items. There is always a distinct design quality to them. In my first encounter I was smitten with one such creation, a tiny salt spoon in the form of a trailing grapevine that I catalogued for the India Early Minshall sale. It sold for \$825. I should have bought it myself and will try if it ever comes my way again. Christie's sold a wonderful salt cellar and spoon dated 1851, the bowl in the shape of a fisherman's net, with fish trapped within, and the spoon adorned with a lobster, fish and a seated toad.[41] Other Sazikov trompe l'oeil masterpieces include ornate jugs in the form of roosters, caviar pots chased to simulate oak grain adorned with a sturgeon finial, or ashtrays in the form of *lapti* (birchbark woven shoes), samovars adorned with overlapping bandwork, a burlap-tied top, a pair of peasants astride its handles, and boxes bordered by Old Russian–style silver interlaced mounts.

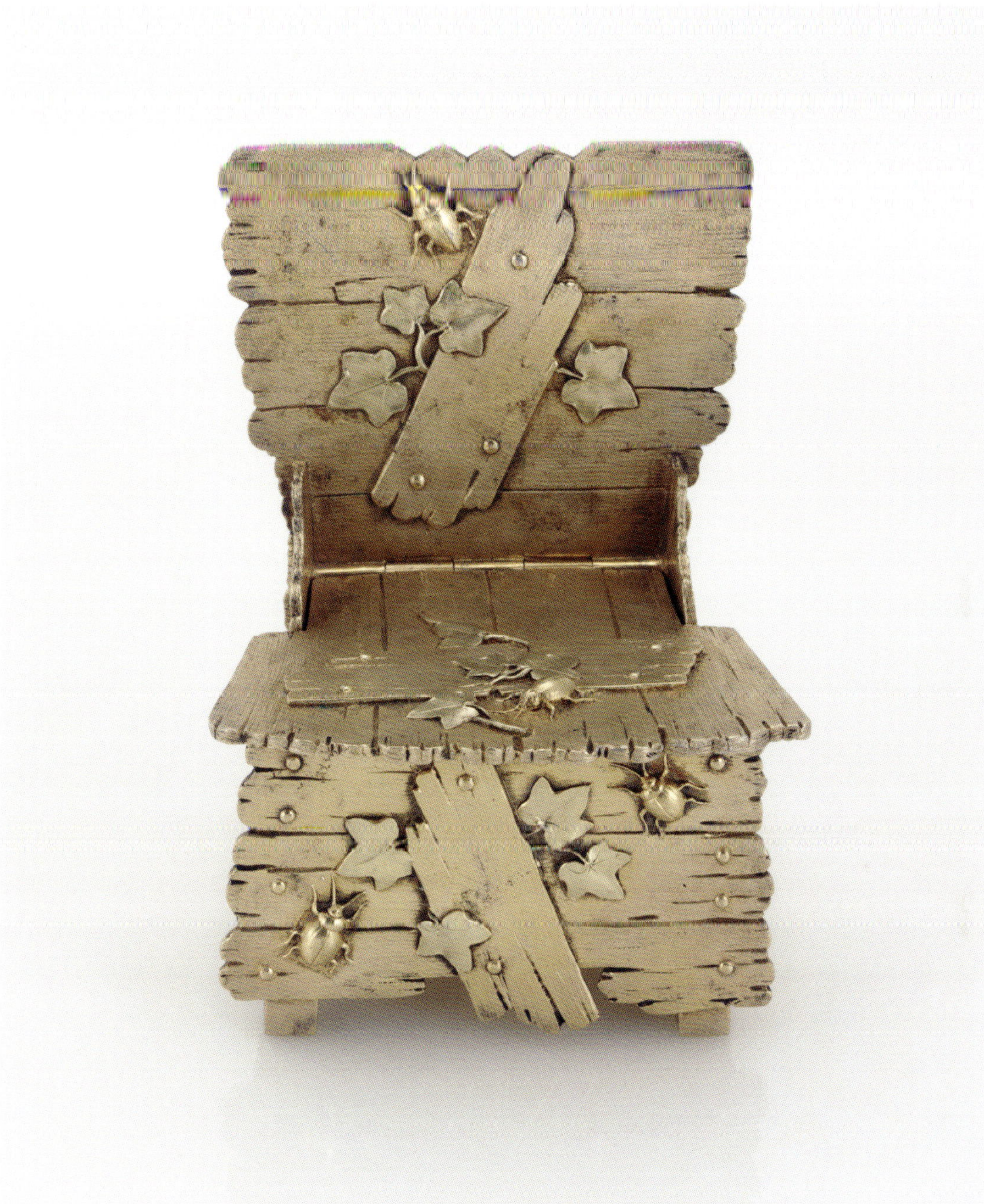

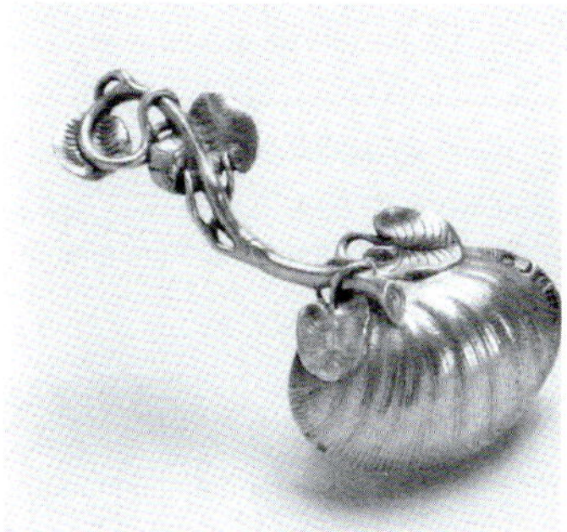

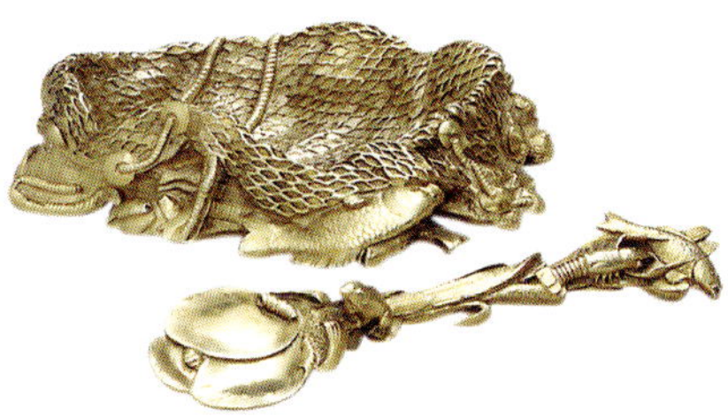

Top:
Rustic salt throne by Sazikov.
Courtesy of Sotheby's

Left:
cellar in the form of a fisherman's net with fish, while the spoon is ecorated with a lobster, a fish and a seated toad. © *2003 Christie's Images Ltd.*

Far left:
Tea caddy spoon.
© *1988 Christie's Images Ltd.*

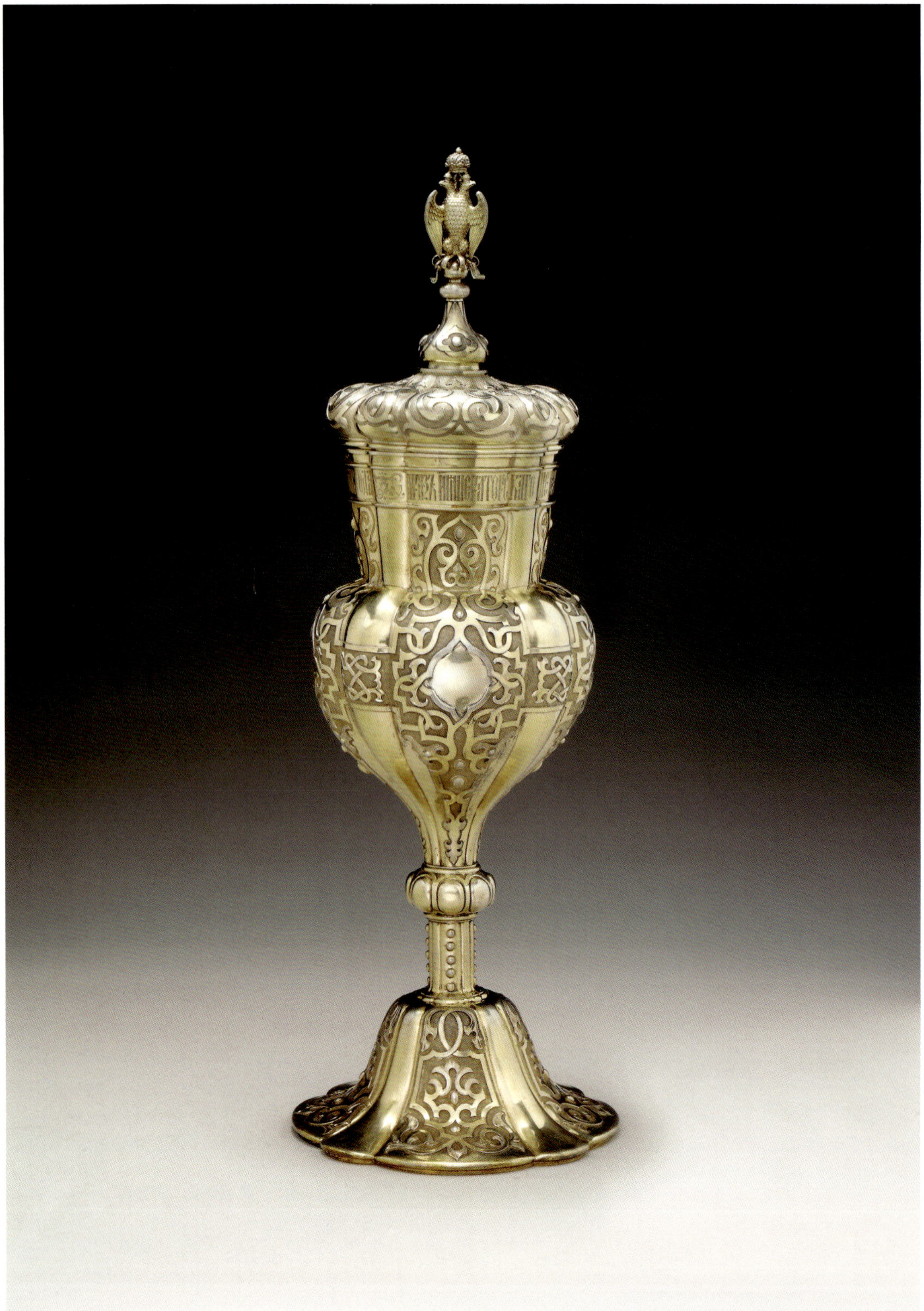

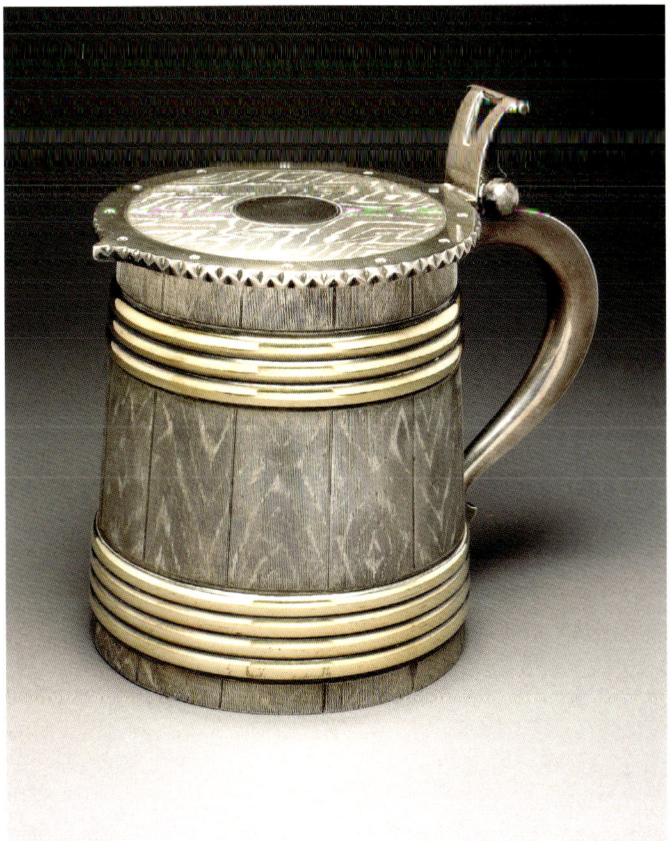

Like many Russian silversmiths, Sazikov made a wide array of tankards, some with Russian peasant figures, and others imitating wooden barrels with smooth concentric bands and rivets.

A trademark of Sazikov silver is smooth overlapping bands to accentuate corners or borders, called strapwork or *entrelac*, and associated with the Pan-Slavic movement in decorative arts beginning in the mid-19th century. The firm mastered ornate silver mountings, as seen in a nephrite glove box that appeared on the market, and a coffeepot that sold at Phillips in 1994, which enclosed a central scene of a Russian sleigh driven by a bearded *muzhik* (Russian peasant). Topped by a double-headed eagle finial, denoting an imperial commission, it was dated 1856.[42]

Sazikov also made several miniature silver models of famous Russian artifacts that likewise recall their rich Slavic roots. A popular table ornament was a silver replica of the *Tsar Pushka* (Tsar's Cannon) of Tsar Fedor Ivanovich (r. 1584–98). The original, which is in the Moscow Kremlin, was cast by Andrei Chokhov in 1586 for the early Russian ruler and measures 17½ feet long. Sazikov's version is 7½ inches. In 1851, the silver firm produced at least two of these in exact detail. I found three more miniature cannons for a total of five in auction catalogues dated 1974 to 2013, some with a warrior figure in front. They sold from between $4,500 and $22,275. Each was on rectangular plinth, two engraved in Russian "Work by the Master Sazikov." It was no doubt Sazikov who laid the groundwork for Fabergé's famous silver replicas by St. Petersburg workmaster Julius Rappaport.

My search for Sazikov stock in trade silver in auction

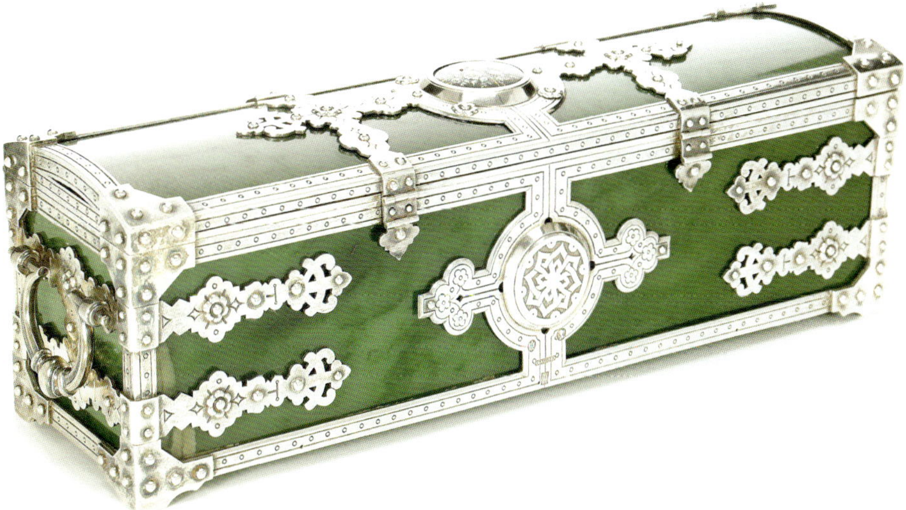

Above:
Sazikov silver tankard.
Marie Betteley, photo by Noel Allum

Right:
A nephrite glove box.
Courtesy of Stockholms Auktionsverk

Previous page:
Imperial presentation Sazikov covered cup.
© 2003 Christie's Images Ltd.

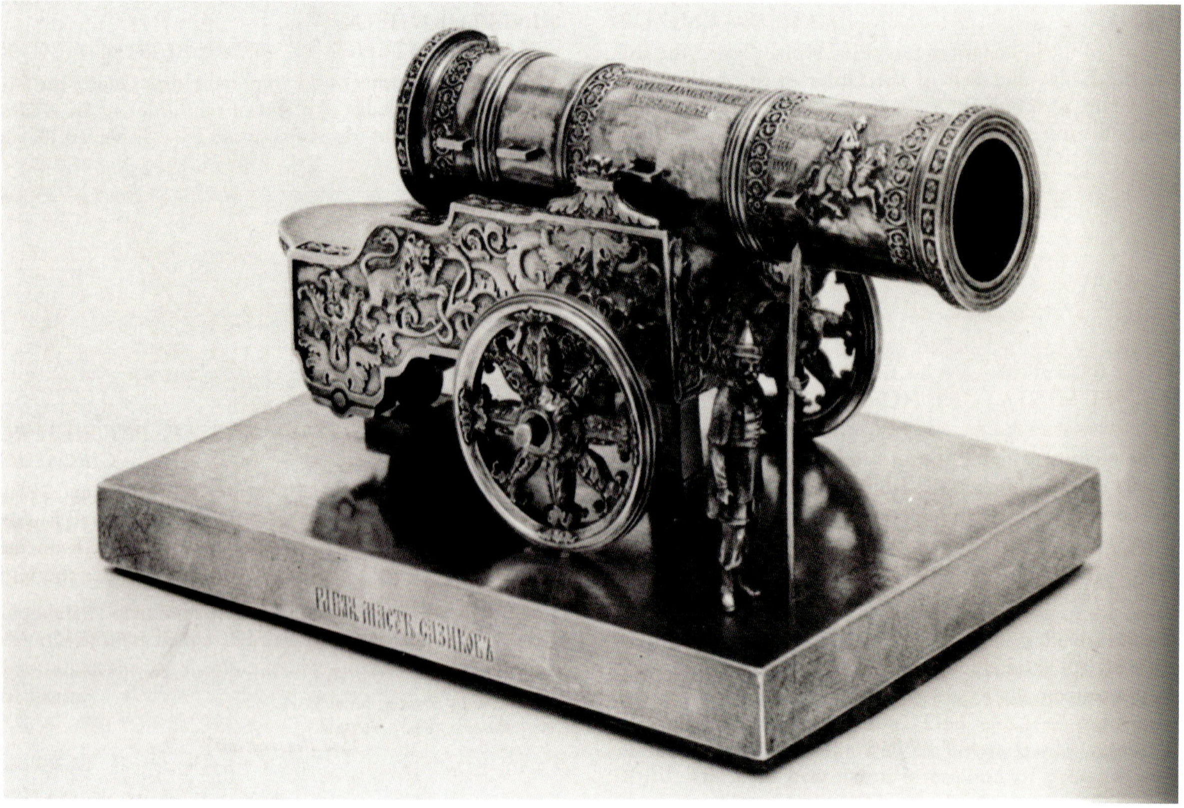

catalogues yielded no fewer than 65 lots. These consisted of beautiful ewers, salt thrones, *kulaks* (traditional loaf-shaped boxes), vegetable dishes, sculptural stirrup cups, samovars, vodka barrels or jugs adorned with dancing peasants or recumbent cows, enameled icons and Easter eggs.

The name "Sazikov" begins to appear in catalogue entries only in the 1980s, although the firm's items may have sold before and were perhaps just not identified. Sotheby's offered a magnificent Yacht Club trophy dated 1851 in the form of a massive gilded triple-headed imperial eagle facing east, west and north (see page 170).[43] A pair of solid-silver 10-light candelabra weighing 20 kilos fetched $11,957 in Geneva in 1983.[44]

The firm produced enamelware and displayed it in both of the All-Russian Exhibitions of 1870 and 1882. It is rare in today's Western market. The ones I've seen were of a religious nature. I catalogued a pair of large enameled Easter eggs on stands by Sazikov for auction above but have never seen them since. In 2008, Sotheby's sold a Sazikov champlevé-enameled presentation hand cross, dated 1874, for $109,000.[45] Triptychs and smaller enameled oval icons have appeared as well.

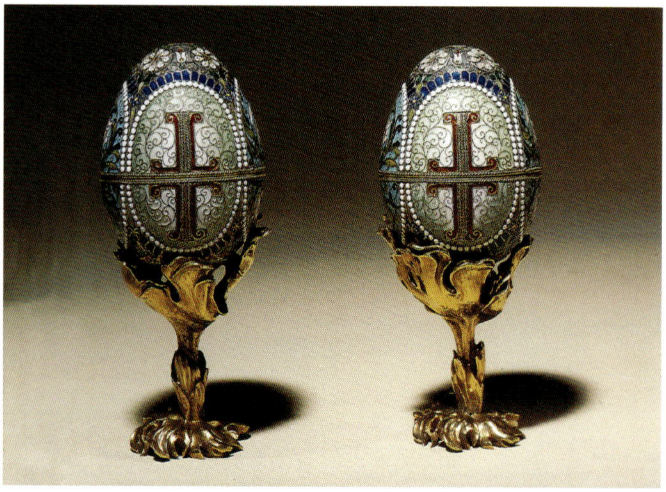

Top:
Sazikov miniature cannon. The plinth is engraved in Russian "work by the master Sazikov." *Courtesy of Sotheby's*

Pair of cloisonné-enameled Easter eggs. *© 1985 Christie's Images Ltd.*

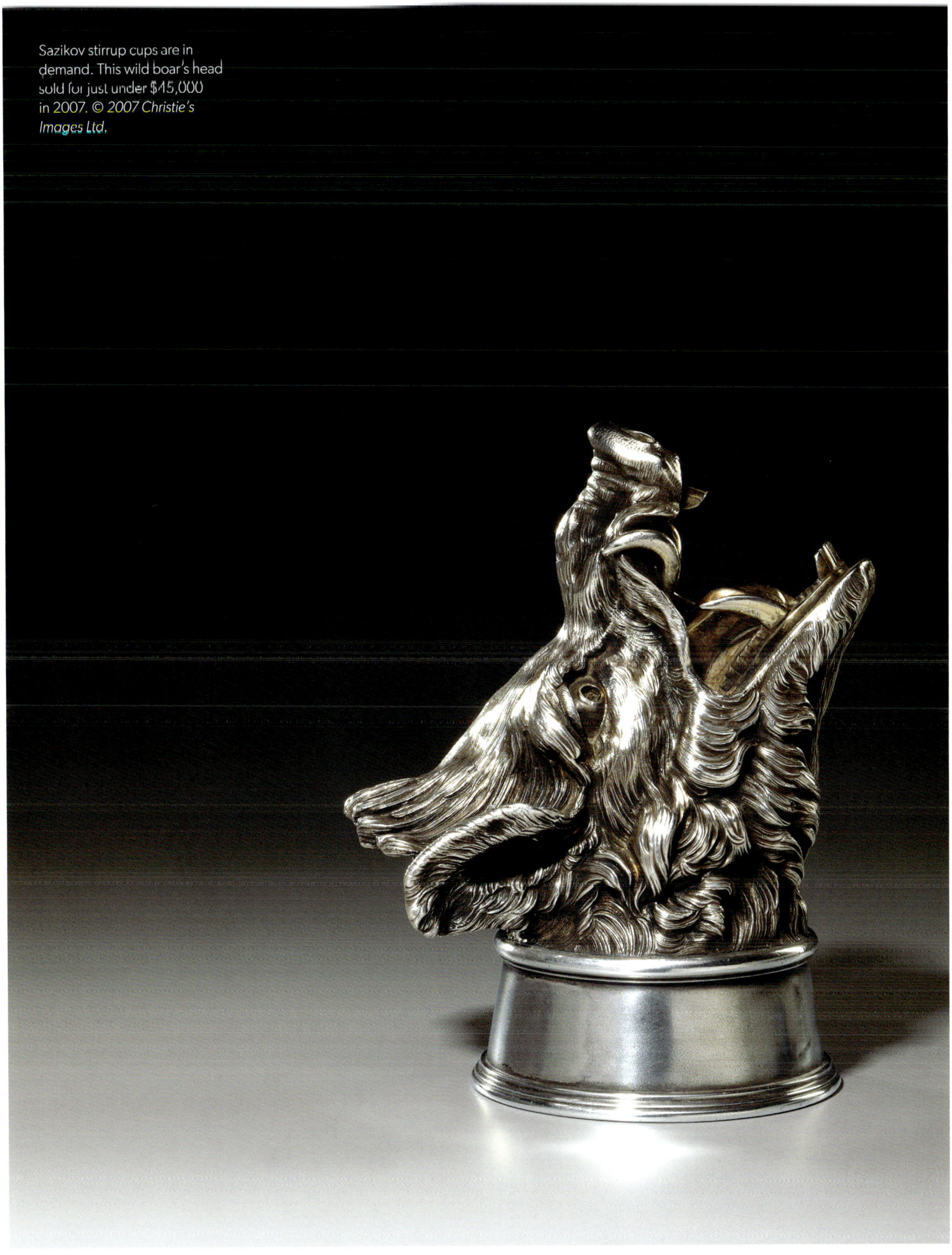

Sazikov stirrup cups are in demand. This wild boar's head sold for just under $15,000 in 2007. *© 2007 Christie's Images Ltd.*

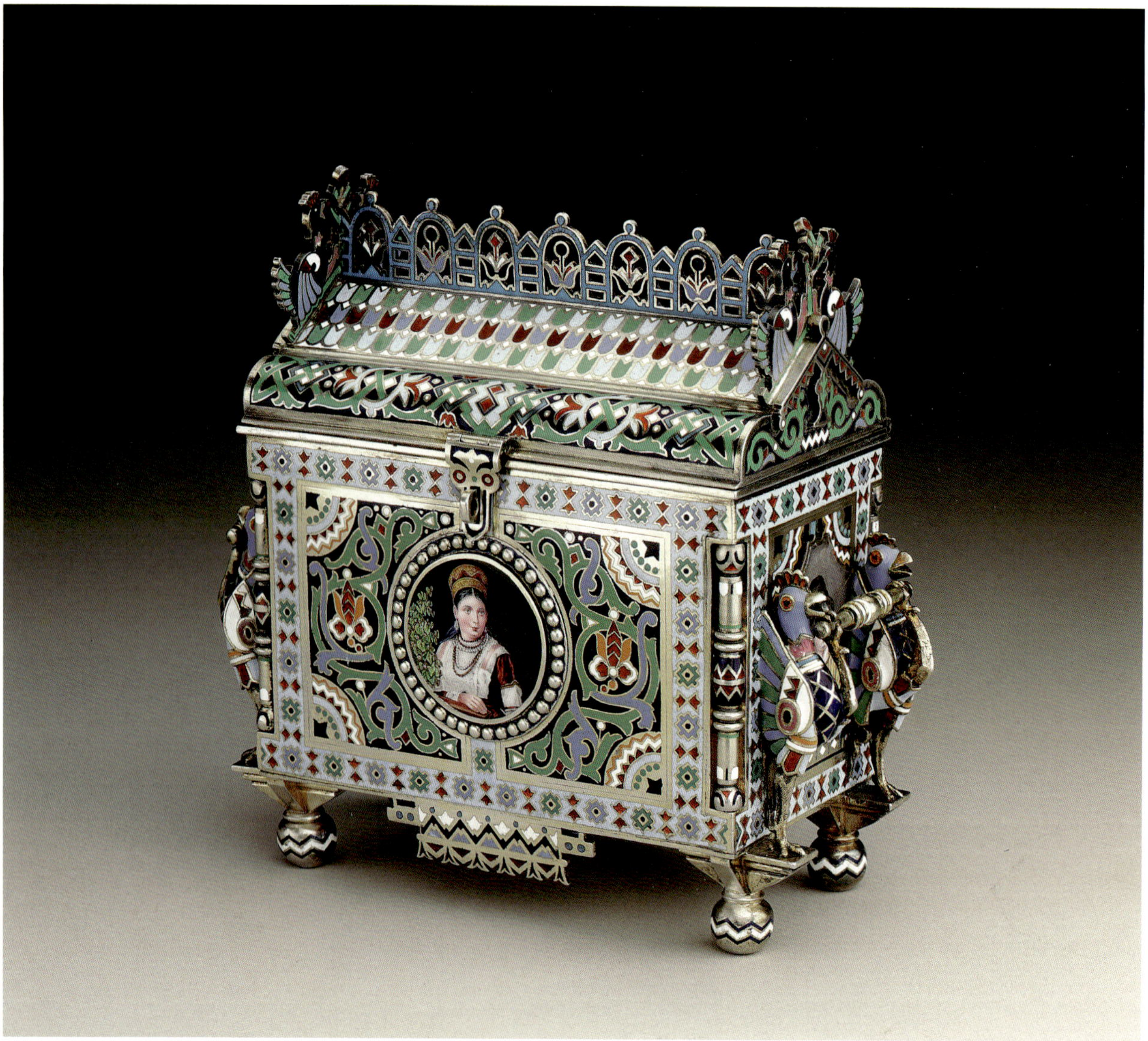

Above:
This enameled jewel casket in the form or a Russian *izba* or cottage epitomizes Ovchinnikov *Style Russe* design. It sold in 1998 for $46,000. *©1998 Christie's Images Ltd*

Following page:
These two platters by Ovchinnikov were coronation gifts presented to Emperor Alexander III and Empress Maria Feodorovna, top, from the Nobility of the Tula Province in 1882, decorated with the profile of the 14th century Grand Prince Dmitrii Donskoi of Russia (sold for $122,542 in 1994) and bottom from the Buryats of the Transbakailian Province ($245,241 in 2014). *©1994, 2014 Christie's Images Limited*

Ovchinnikov

Ovchinnikov, Khlebnikov, Rückert and Kurliukov are top names in the field. Enamels adding color and vibrancy to large Pan-Slavic works realized huge prices at the market's peak around 2007. Russian buyers paid enormous sums for all things Russian then, with Style Russe enamels being the most sought after. Values for works by these four virtuosos soared and seemed to be in direct proportion to size: the bigger and bolder, the higher the price. Once seen, we tend not to forget these creations, even if illustrated only in black in white, whether in the form of a kovsh, platter, or punch bowl set, as was the case in most pre-1970 auction catalogues. With bright colors, or even muted ones, each vessel has a unique design recalling the glories of Russia's storied past. In general, though, since 2006–2008, fewer such objects appear at auction, due largely to a drop both in Russian sellers and buyers.

The public either loves Russian enamel or esteems it not at all. So much of it appeared in New York in the 1980s and earlier that I got enamel fatigue. But masterpieces are always unforgettable. Bidders began to go high then for these enamel showpieces, of which the market is still rich. As in its own day in tsarist Moscow, Ovchinnikov is the most popular maker with Russian buyers.

Ovchinnikov was the king of the imperial presentation charger. These massive silver platters, averaging 22 inches in diameter, were the gift of choice to the tsar from visiting provincial dignitaries of his vast empire, who presented them in an elaborate ceremony held in the Kremlin Palace during his coronation. As was the custom, bread and salt would be placed on these platters, which yielded a tradition of lavish gift giving that began with the coronation of Tsar Alexander II. To house the profusion of ceremonial plates, the tsar had an entire room reserved for them. They were also created for visiting heads of state. In 1902, Ovchinnikov produced a pair of elaborate chargers for presentation to the French president, Emile Loubet, by the citizens of Tsarskoe Selo, the other by the city of Moscow.[46]

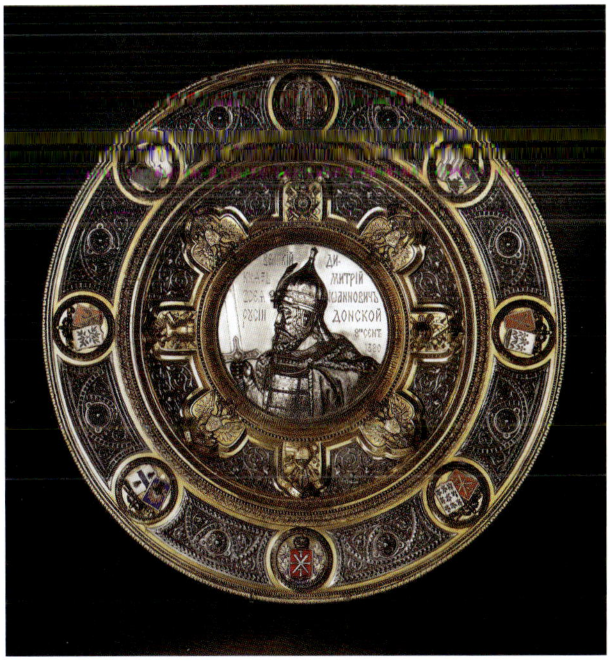

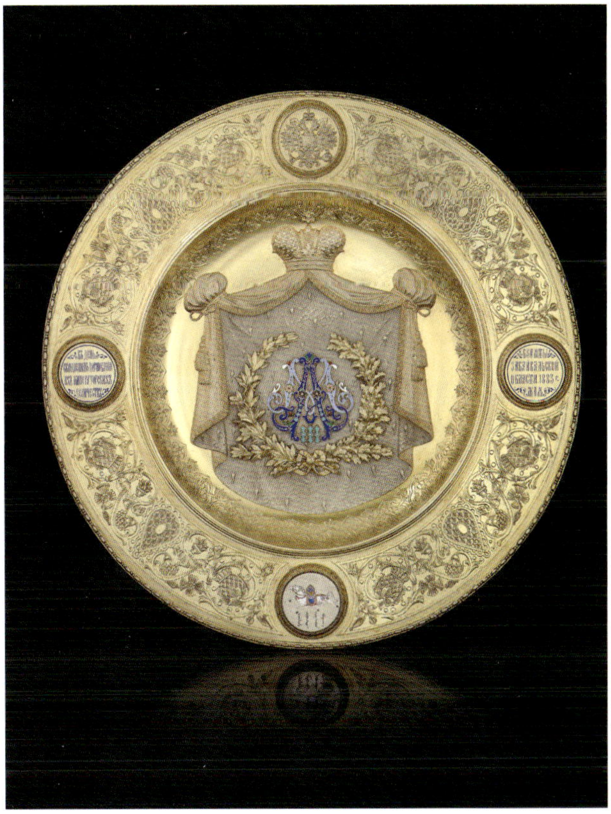

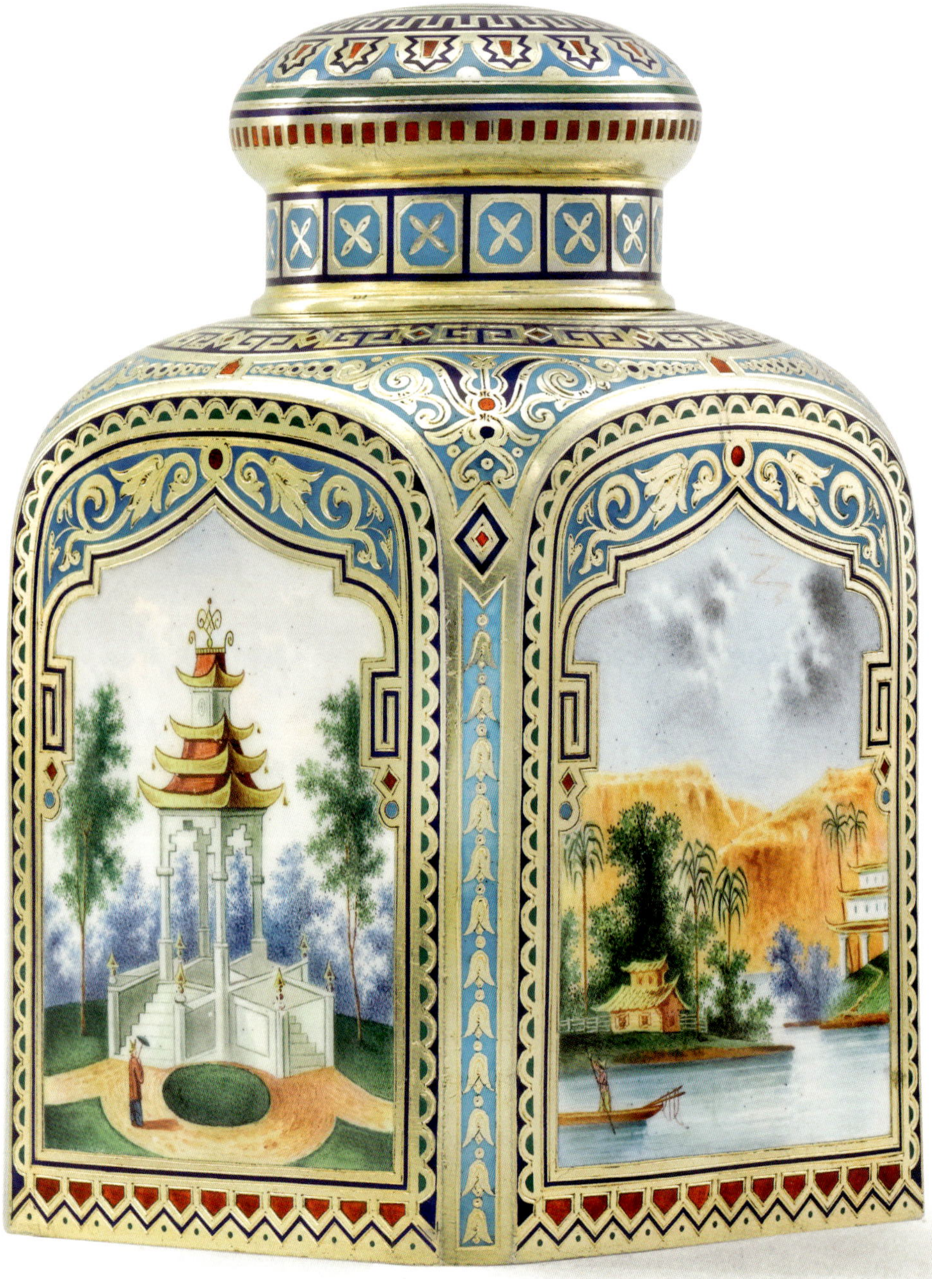

Chinoiserie tea caddy.
Courtesy of Sotheby's

A magnificent chinoiserie champlevé enameled tea and coffee service by Ovchinnikov resurfaced in New York in 2006. A close-up of the tray's glorious enameling graced every inch of the catalogue cover, front and back. The complete set sold for over a million dollars. In Switzerland, it had fetched just under $32,000 in 1977 and $128,000 in 1984 (see page 182). I saw it in person. It was in perfect condition, a purely decorative addition to a wealthy, no doubt Moscow household—never used, only admired and cherished. Tea caddies in this style are also in demand. One in 2015 brought just under $160,000; another of similar inspiration in the same sale, $123,000.

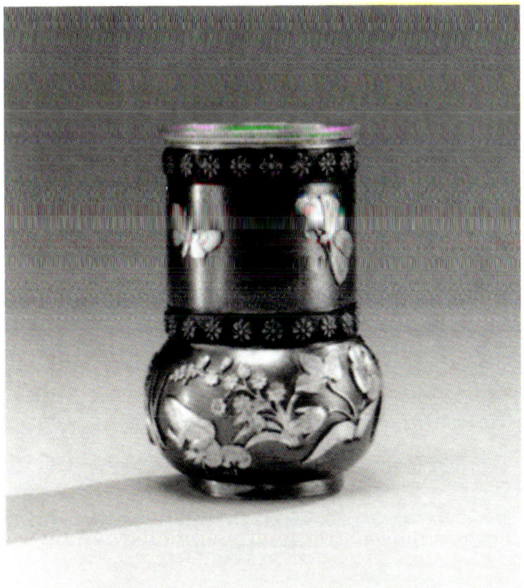

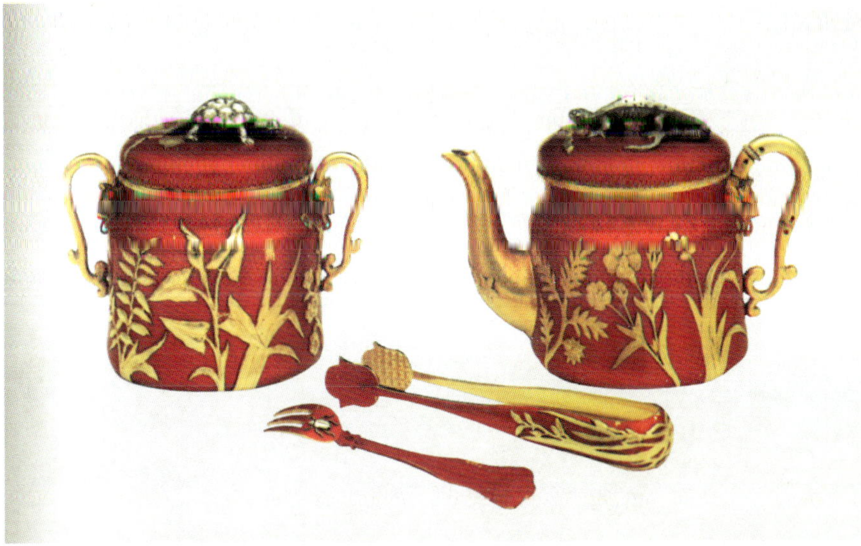

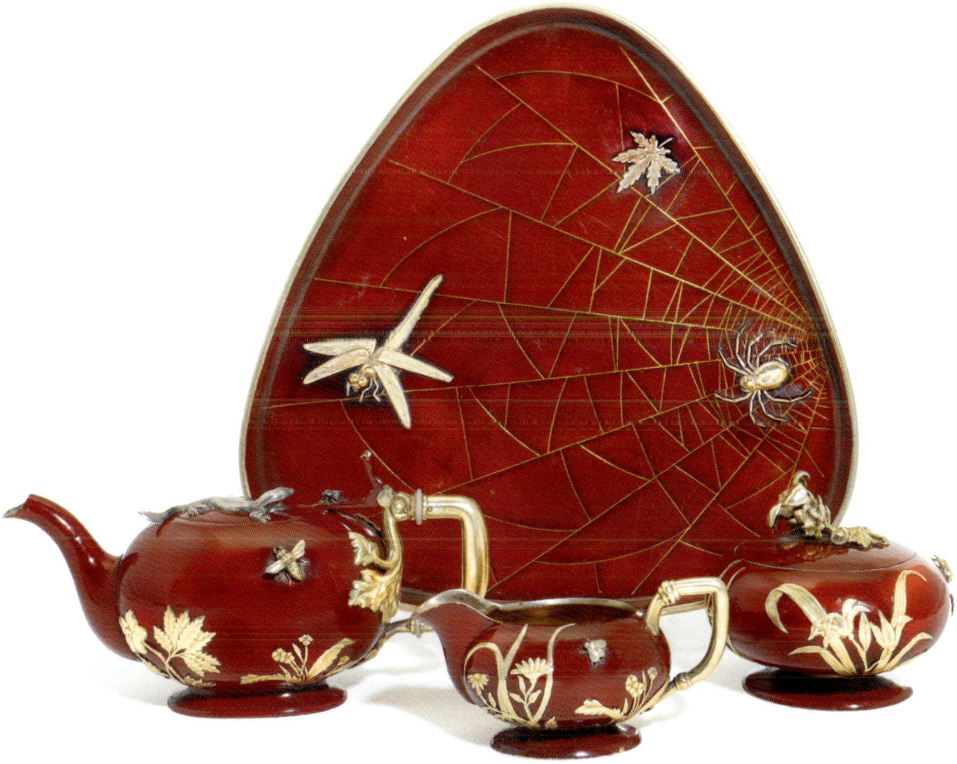

Ovchinnikov excelled in the Japonisme technique of overlaying leaves and dragonflies in gilded silver on a martelé or hand-hammered ground, a style also popularized by Tiffany and Gorham in America. The Russian silversmith made it his own by smoothing out the silver base and adding red lacquer, and he was the only one in Russia to do so. Prices vary over the years. Most Ovchinnikov lacquered items in the 1970s and 1980s sold within modest estimates, despite their rarity.

Examples of Japanese style items made by Ovchinnikov in red lacquer. The vase upper left sold for $1,045 in New York in 1988 and the set on the upper right in 1978 for about $8,000. In 2015, the tea service below, which had brought $13,820 in 1980, sold for $117,002. *Courtesy of Sotheby's, ©1978 Christie's Images Ltd*

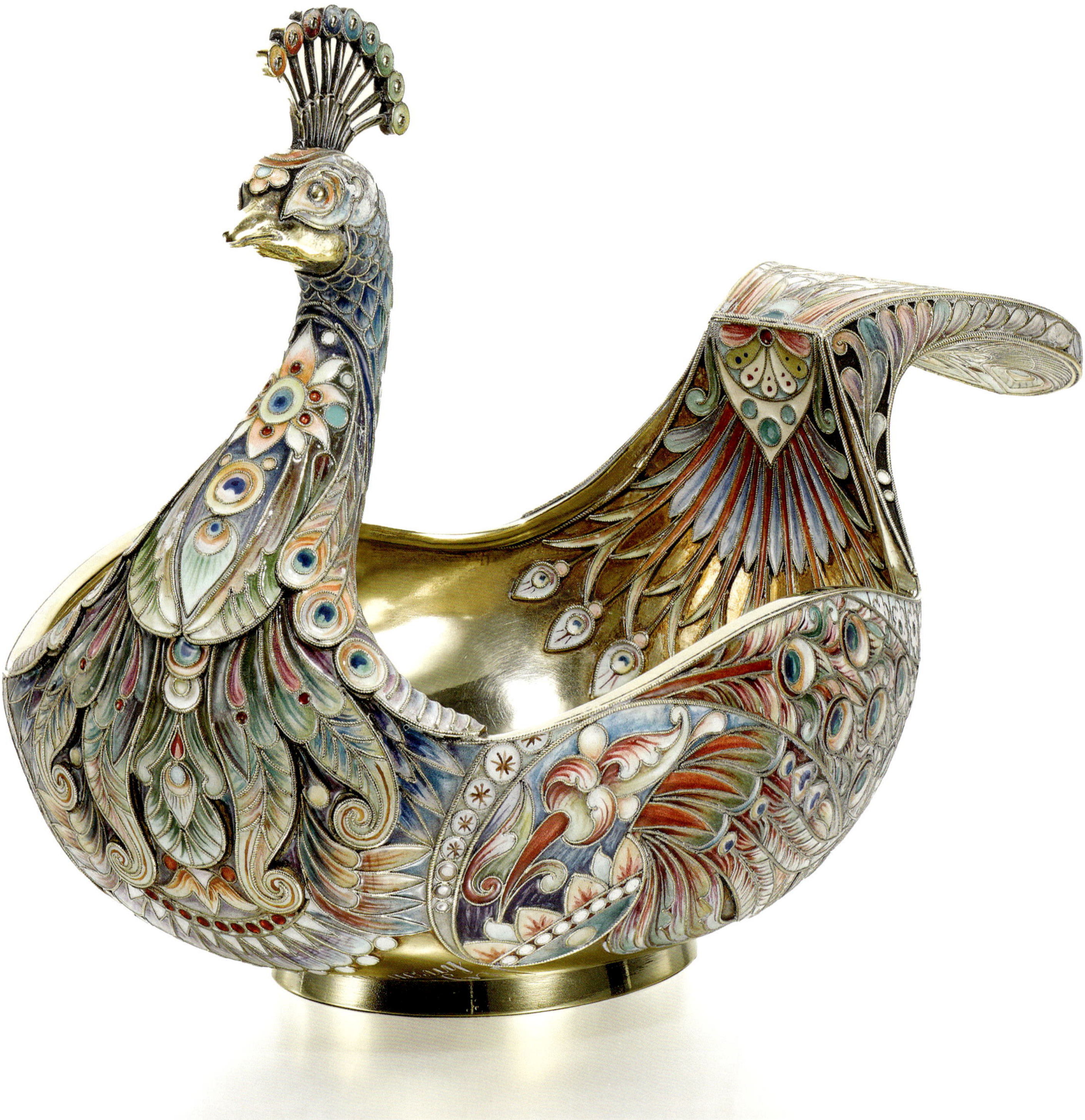

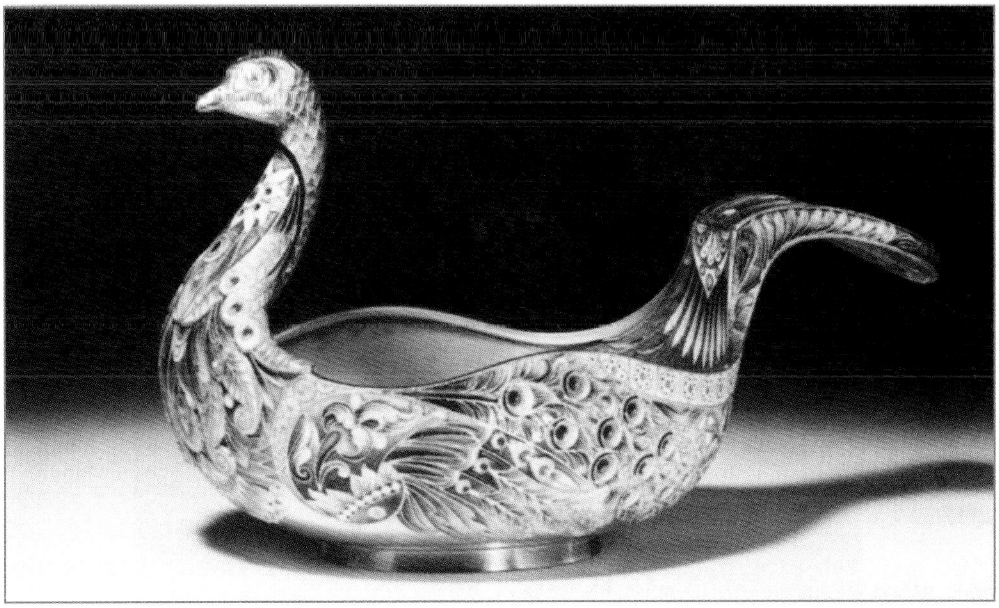

Enameled kovsh was auctioned in 1981 in New York (*above*) for $19,800. In 2002, it fetched only $500 more. However, in 2016 (*left*), with researched provenance and an added crest, the peacock brought $136,041.
Courtesy of Sotheby's

Prices for smaller-to-medium-sized enamels have either held steady or increased dramatically. A curious example is a bird-form enamel kovsh that alighted three times in New York sales, in 1981, 2002 and 2016. What's interesting is not just the recent price escalation, but the addition of an enameled fanlike crest on the bird's head, thereby making it a peacock, which was beautifully done. A dedication inscription on the base, briefly mentioned in the 2002 catalogue, in 2016 (according to Sotheby's) revealed the provenance of a Red Army commander named Filipp Mironov. Was the inscription there in crestless version in 1981? It's possible, since cataloguers made shorter entries in those days. The crest must have been added between 1981 and 1989, since it appears in Gerard Hill's *Fabergé and the Russian Master Goldsmiths*.

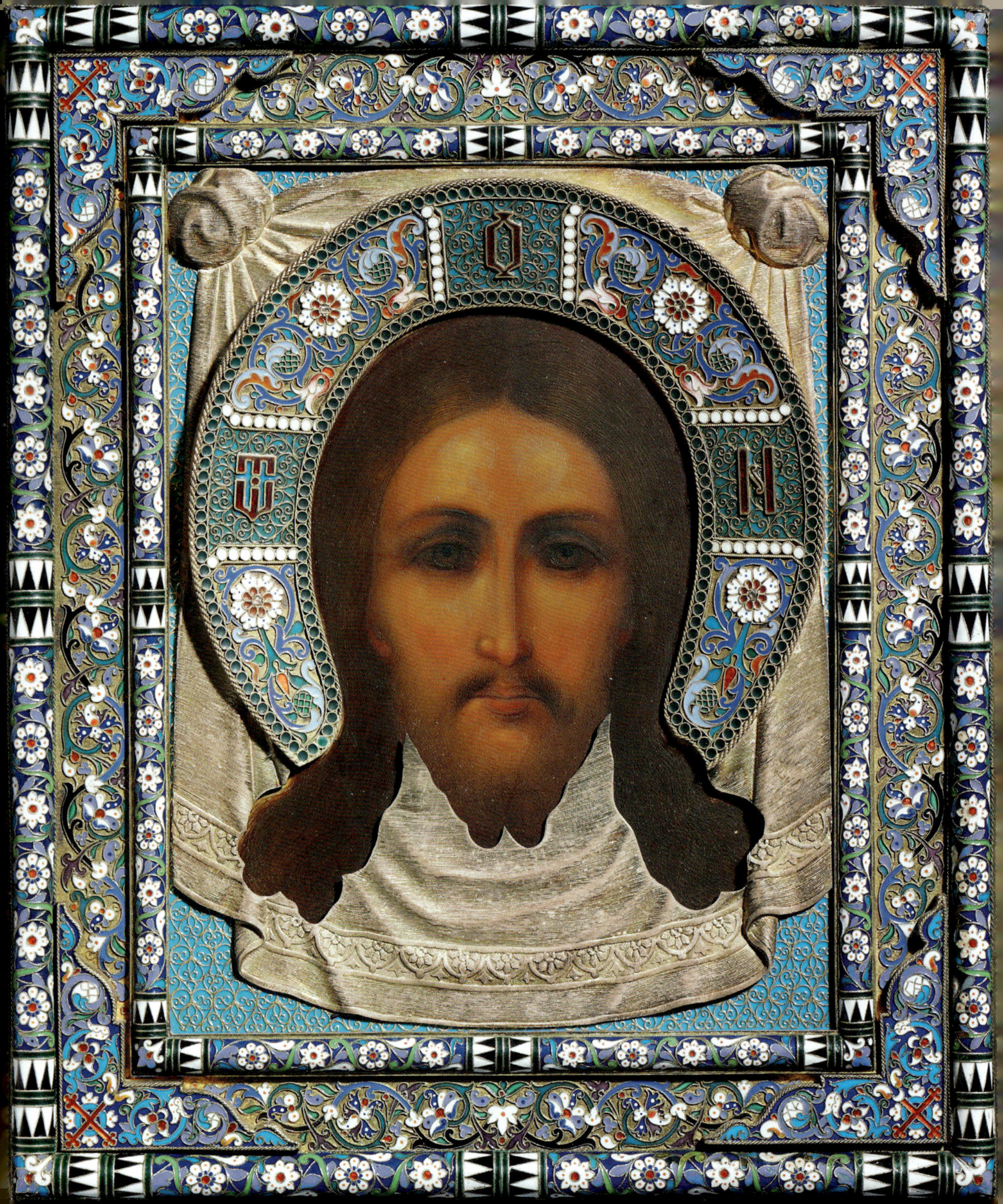

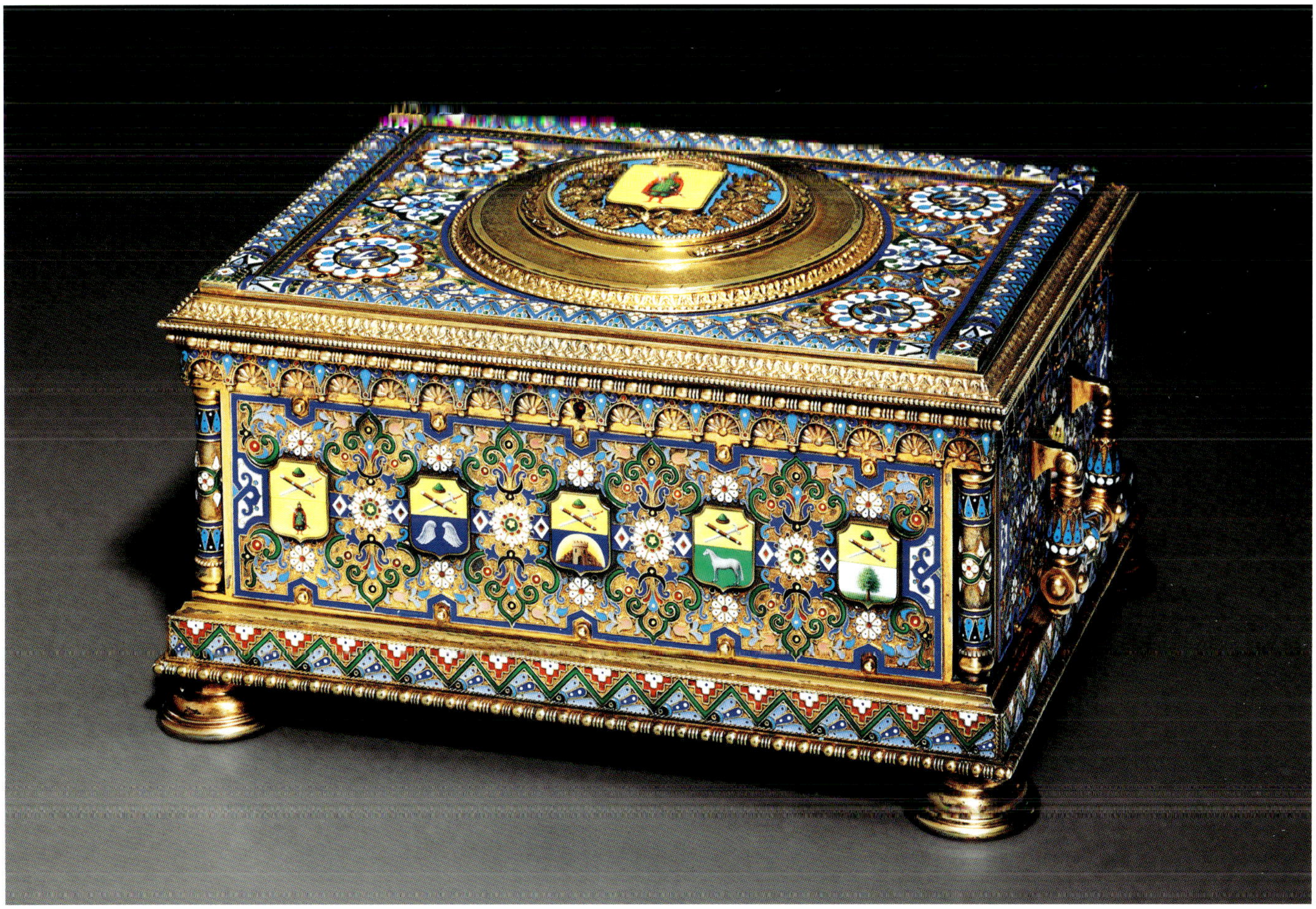

In general, the top two Russian contenders (apart from Fabergé and Rückert, who constitute a separate market), Ovchinnikov and Khlebnikov, have commanded the highest prices at auction in the past 40 years. An Ovchinnikov icon of the Vernicle (the Holy Shroud of Christ), 12½ inches high, fetched over $395,000, with no documented provenance. An impressive enameled casket, which was presented by Riazan Province dignitaries to an unknown recipient and was set with coats or arms of the twelve districts, increased in price nearly threefold, from $82,500 in 2000 to $236,400 in 2007.

Previous page:
An Ovchinnikov enameled icon of the Vernicle.
© 2007 Christie's Images Ltd.

Above:
Presentation box by Ovchinnikov dated 1893.
© 2008 Christie's Images Ltd.

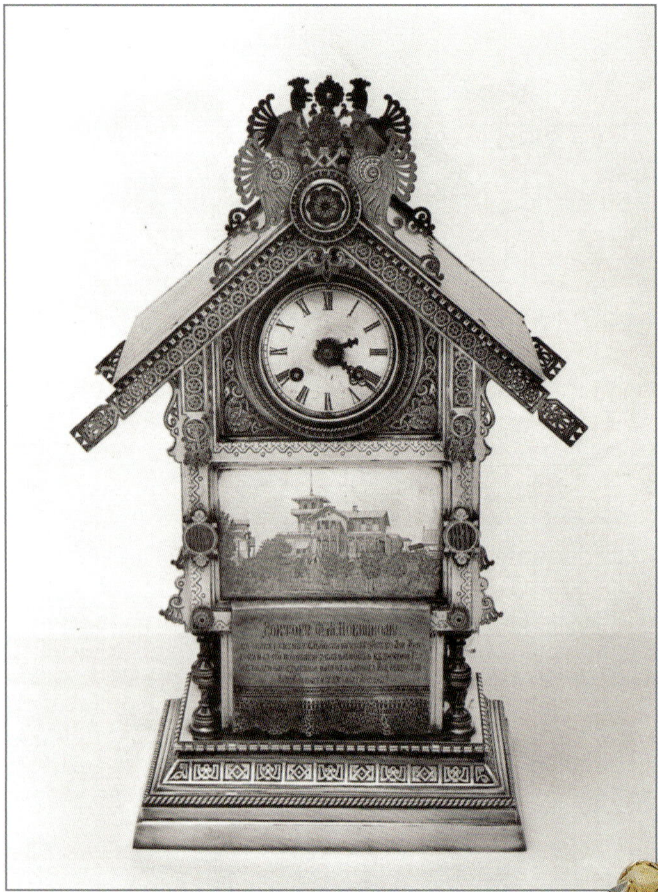

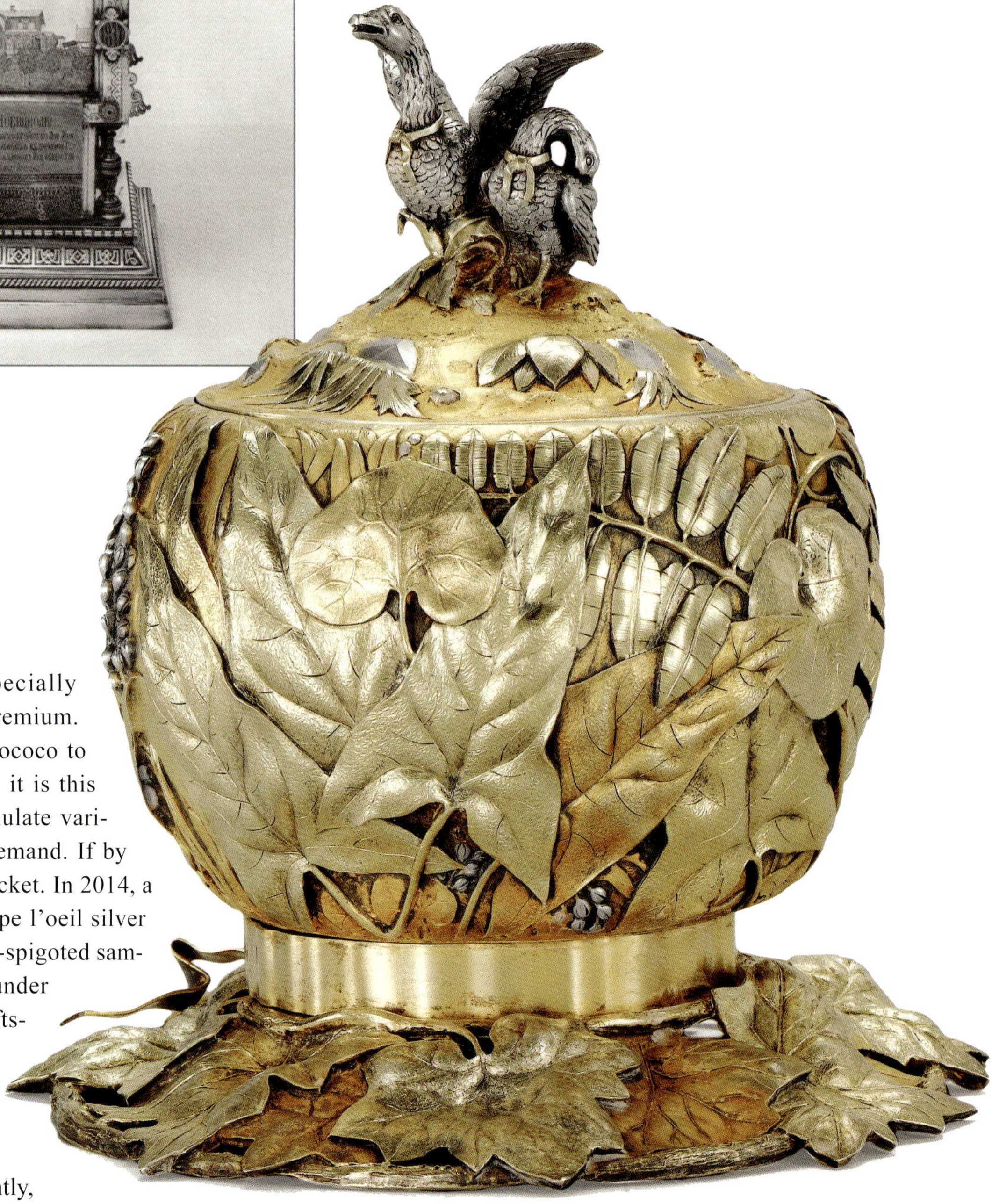

Ovchinnikov clock in the form of a dacha. *Courtesy of Sotheby's*

Wrapped with gilded silver woodland plants, this covered bowl fetched $21,320 in 2011. *Courtesy of Sotheby's*

Following page:
A 10-piece imperial presentation service by Ovchinnikov which included a matching samovar and belonged to Countess Alexandra Karlova Litke was sold in 2014. *Courtesy of Sotheby's*

Figural salt cellar of a marmoset holding a spoon above its head and snarling at a cat, by Ovchinnikov, sold for $1,750 in 1974. *Courtesy of Sotheby's*

Ovchinnikov silver, especially trompe l'oeil, commands a premium. Of all the silver styles, from rococo to neoclassical to style moderne, it is this one, expertly fashioned to simulate various textures, that is most in demand. If by Ovchinnikov, values can skyrocket. In 2014, a magnificent Ovchinnikov trompe l'oeil silver service complete with a rooster-spigoted samovar sold in London for just under $750,000. Its superb silver craftsmanship and high price, despite a weakening market, are a testament to the enduring appeal of this famous Russian silversmith. More recently,

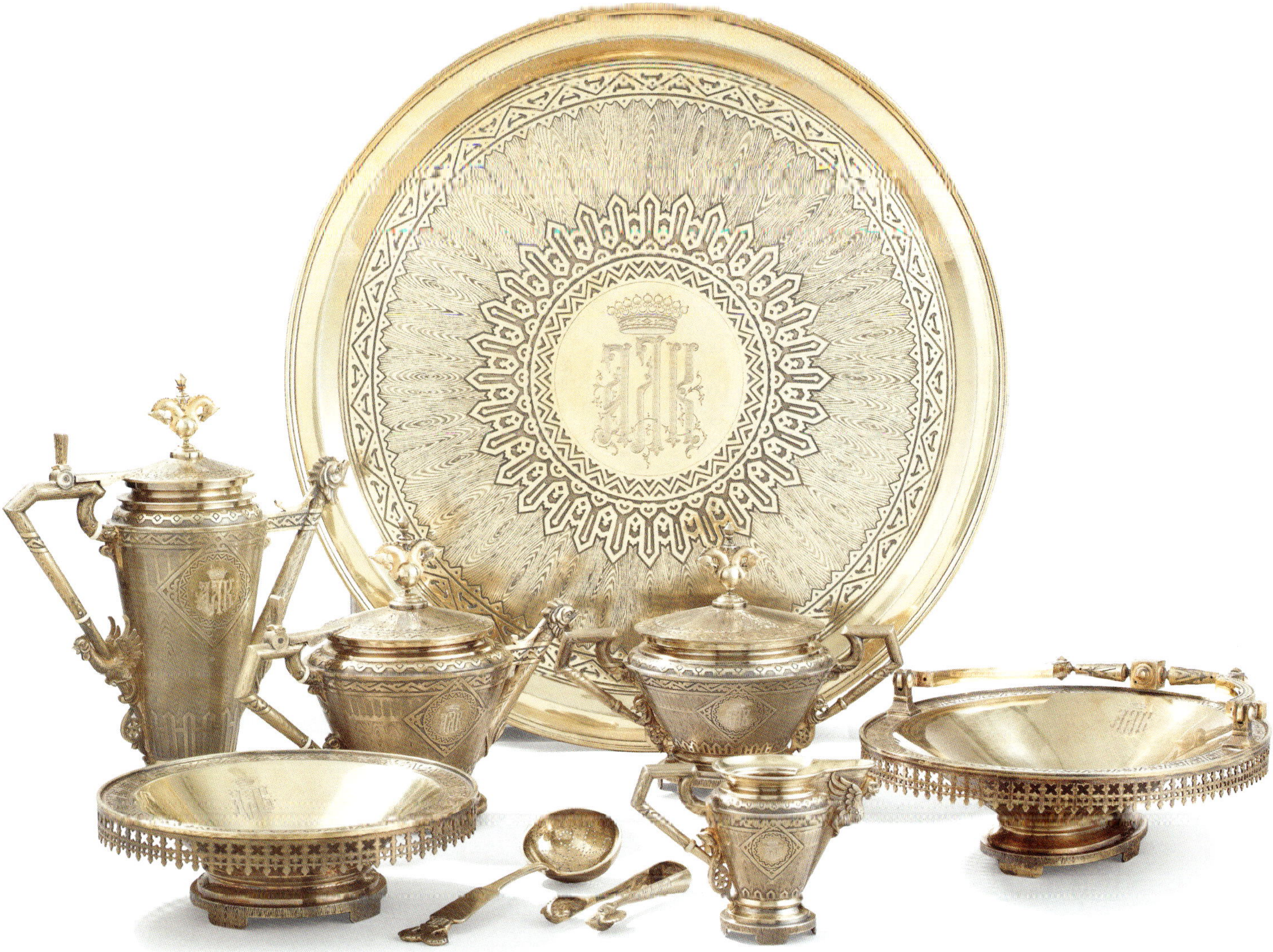

a silver basket with enameled, embroidered details so typical of Russian work sold for $62,500 in 2013. While not as recognizable as Fabergé on the Western market, Ovchinnikov items did appear in America as early as 1950 in an exhibit of Russian art in Ohio.[47]

The company name, fully spelled out in Cyrillic under an imperial warrant as its hallmark, probably became familiar to Russian auction experts, particularly beginning in the 1970s, when enamels took off in price and almost flooded the market. Sometimes the entire name and date were scratched out in order to avoid stiff import duties for Russian items entering the United States. In the 1970s Sotheby's far outpaced Christie's in market share of Russian items in North America, since Christie's had not yet established a branch in New York. Today, Ovchinnikov is world renowned and represented in numerous international museum exhibitions.

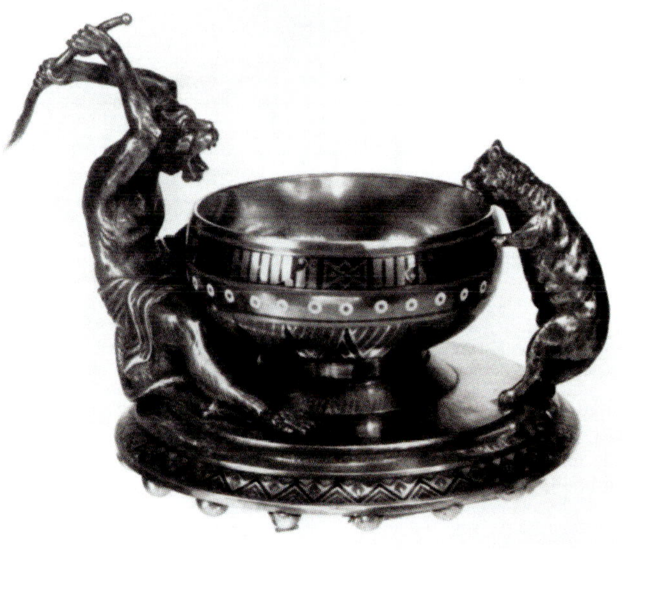

This Khlebnikov enameled triptych was presented to the future tsar, Grand Duke Nicholas Aleksandrovich in 1886 when he was eighteen. As is the Russian Orthodox custom, the central panel featured the recipient's namesake Saint, St. Nicholas, flanked by St. Alexander Nevskii and St. Mary Magdalene, for his parents. It achieved $372,891 in 2015. In 1883 Khlebnikov had made a similar icon for presentation to Tsar Alexander III and Maria Feodorovna on their coronation, now in the Hermitage Museum Collection in Russia. *Courtesy of Sotheby's*

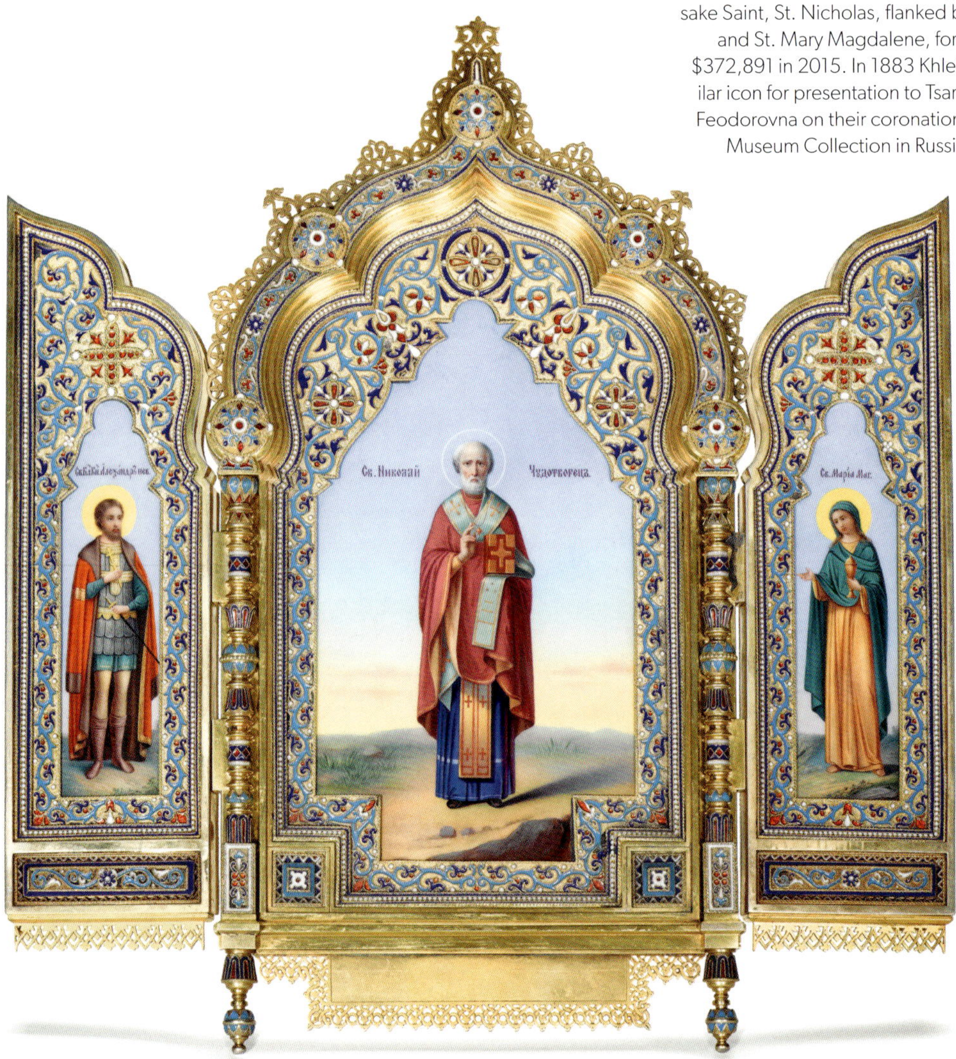

Khlebnikov

We have Torgsin (the Soviet hard-currency stores that catered to foreigners from 1931 to 1936) to thank for the survival of many enamels by Khlebnikov and others after the revolution. Documents from 1933 state that

> It is necessary to conserve exceptionally well-executed articles from the firms Fabergé, Khlebnikov, and Ovchinnikov, etc. Special attention should be paid to the Russian silver gilt of the above establishments with multicolored enamels in the Russian style.

Even Maxim Gorki recognized his country's unique cache of tsarist silver items when he called them antiques worthy of preservation.[48]

In that tumultuous decade, tons of silver made after 1835 faced the melting pot, from large-scale punch bowls, candelabra, commemorative trophies, processional icons, chargers and tea services, to sets of spoons, teacups and saucers, charki, cigarette cases and wine glasses. Although the Bolsheviks suffered few qualms about dismantling or selling enormous volumes of gold and gems, the silver gave some of them pause. But to most Marxist revolutionaries, the end of the Romanovs spelled a welcome death of the plastic arts—skills that would be lost forever and never duplicated.

So high is the quality of these works that few have managed to fake the rich and precise enamels of any of the great

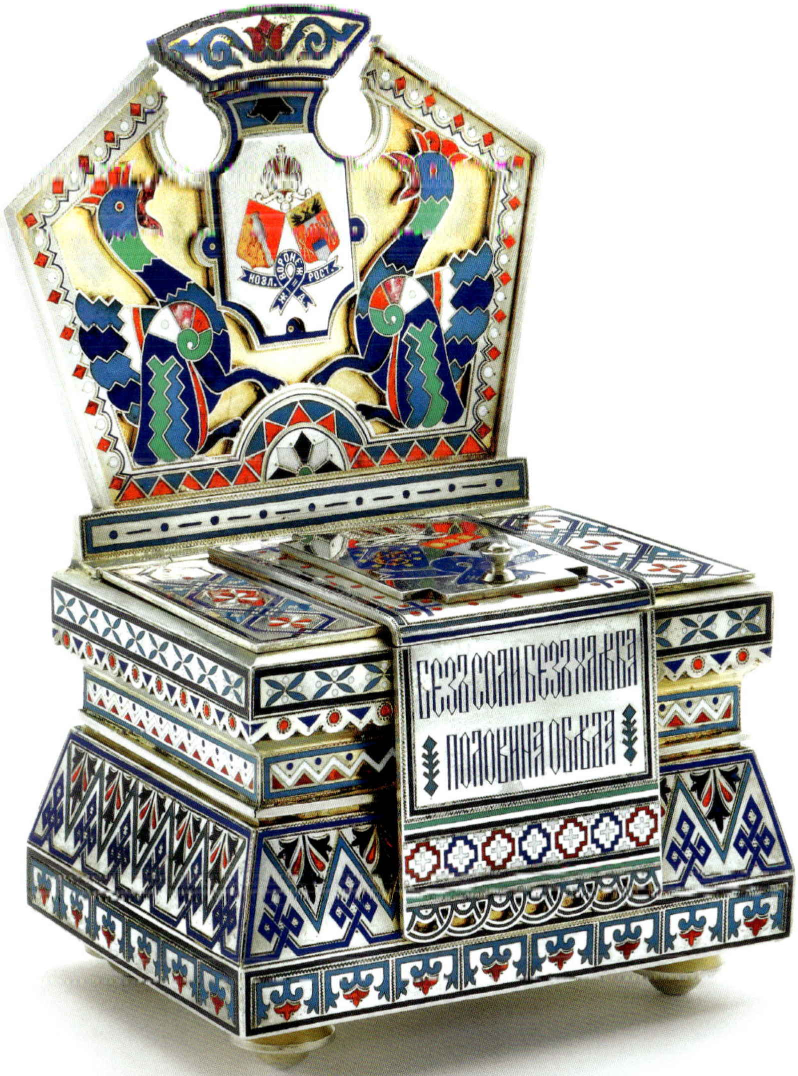

Champlevé-enameled silver item by Khlebnikov. Inscribed with the Russian saying: "Without salt and bread it's only half a lunch." *Courtesy of Sotheby's*

masters from Moscow. While modern guilloché enamels have at times come very close to imitating the work of Carl Fabergé (due to highly skilled jewelers around the world, some with decades of training in enameling), the original creations of Moscow's leading enamelers have yet to meet their match. Plain silver fakes by these modern masters, however, are more difficult to detect, since the items are expertly recast from originals. The hallmarks are copied as well and rendered in precise punches.

The market for Khlebnikov is on a par with that for Ovchinnikov. In 2007 it broke the $1 million barrier with an enamel casket measuring just under 3 feet. As with most Moscow enamels in terms of value, the larger the better. This is true because every inch is beautifully executed. Khlebnikov's lively colors and unique style appeal not only to Russians but to many clients worldwide.

But prices vary, and some seem low. A large, bold wooden presentation charger, bedecked with silver boyars on the rim and St. George slaying the dragon in the center, both medieval symbols of Moscow, sold for only $16,250 in 2009. A charming chinoiserie four-piece tea service, entirely covered by champlevé enamel, brought $20,900, although this was in the 1980s, before prices surged.[49] In 2007 a delightful, bombé-enameled Khlebnikov ink throne achieved the same price. A punch bowl set, of similar outline, which included six kovsh and a ladle, realized $240,690 in 2012. With only traces of enameling, the look was big, bold and bombé, a winning combination.

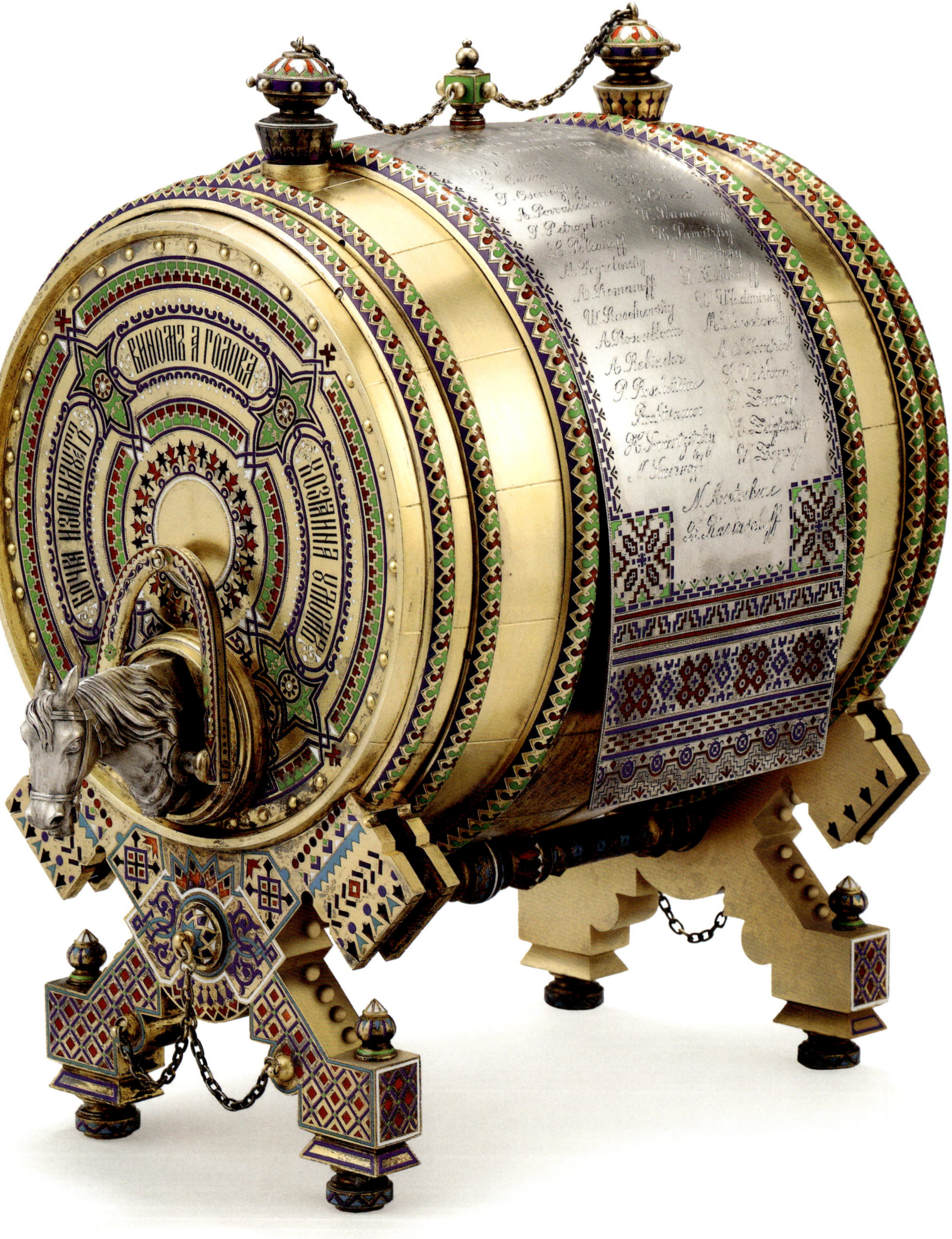

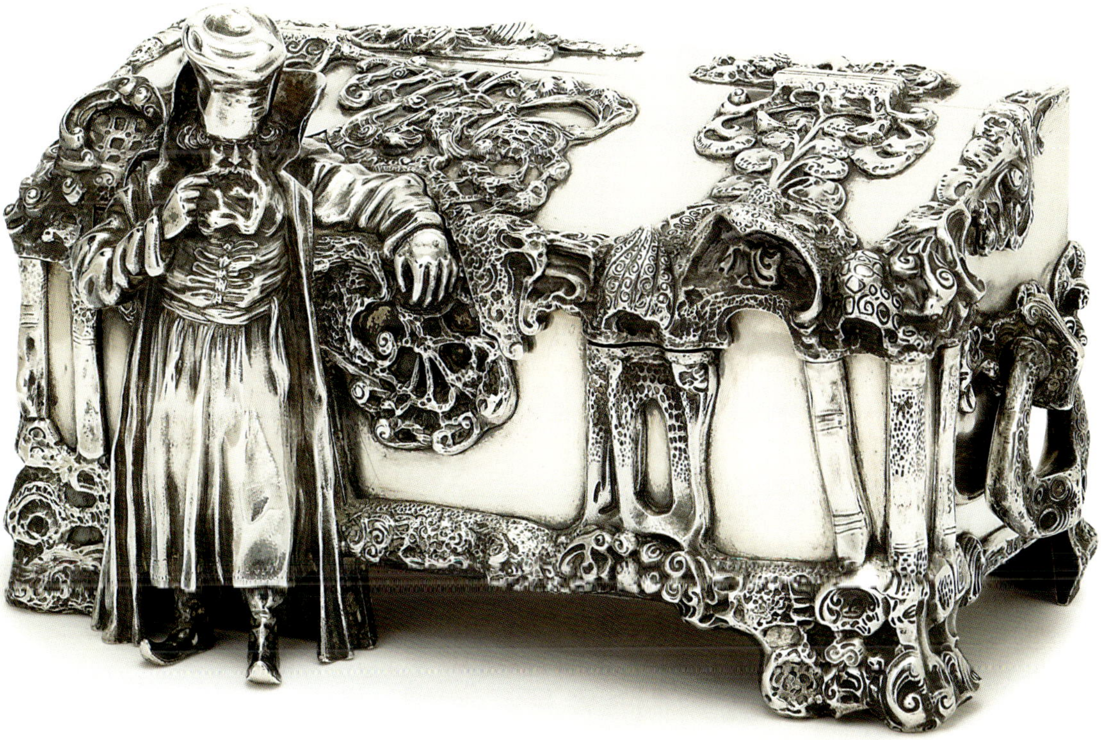

The dramatic Boyar box in silver by Khlebnikov which measured 12 inches realized $470,710. *© 2007 Christie's Images Ltd.*

Previous page
This barrel-shaped cask brought $470,191 in London in 2012. The presentation plaque in the form of a cloth overlay, which was added later on, features the names of the Russian civil engineers who presented it to their French colleagues in 1889. The front is inscribed with a drinking adage in Russian: "The barrel overflows with wine and the owner's head with wit." *Courtesy of Sotheby's*

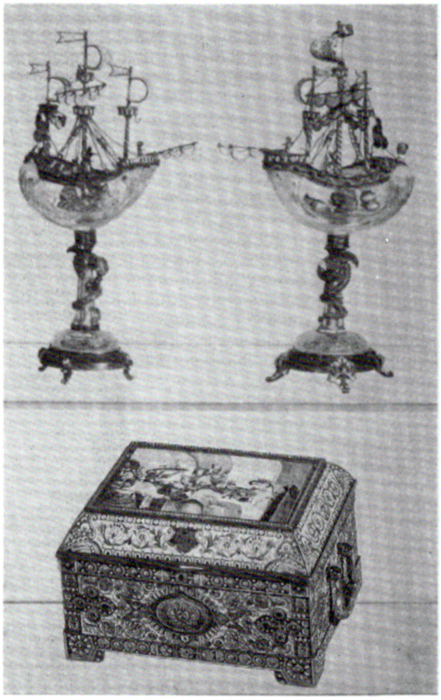

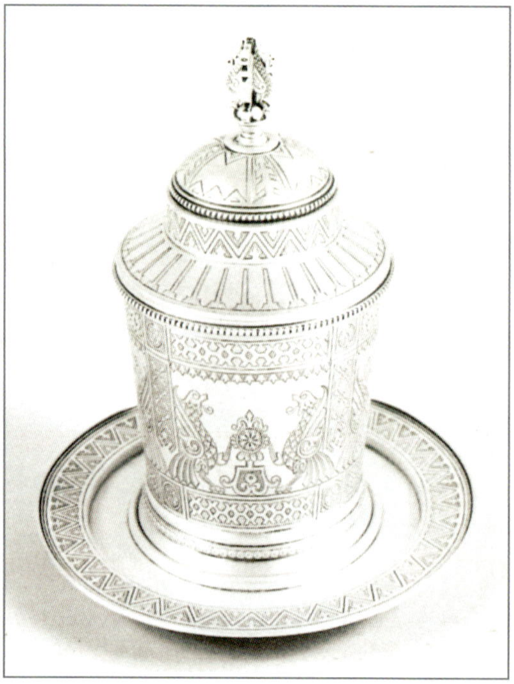

Enameled box with image of the Boyar Wedding sold for $5000 in 1969. *Courtesy of Sotheby's*

The covered silver caviar bowl on the right sold for $1,760. *© 1984 Christie's Images Ltd.*

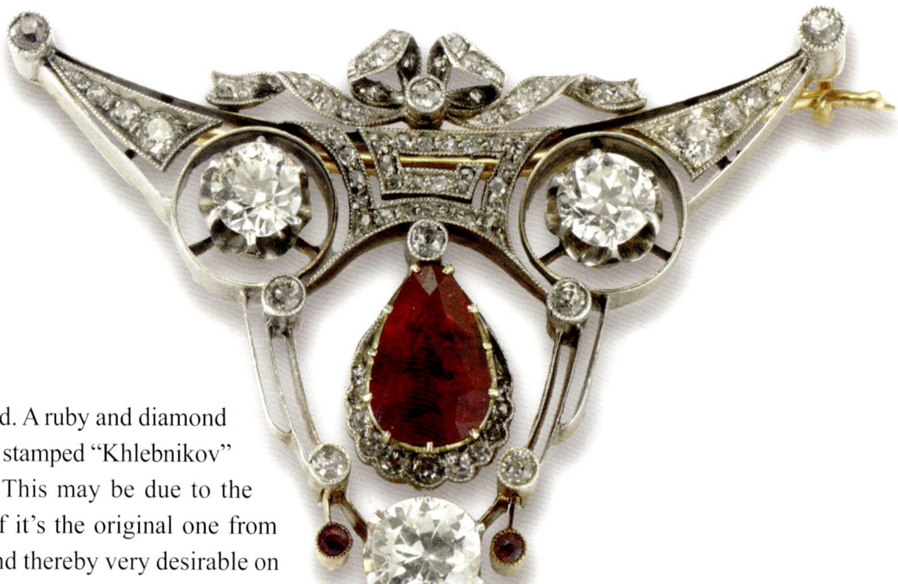

Khlebnikov jewelry has all but vanished. A ruby and diamond brooch in a box that was newly refitted and stamped "Khlebnikov" sold in New York in 2007 for $51,000. This may be due to the quality of the pear-shaped ruby, which, if it's the original one from Khlebnikov's workshop, was untreated, and thereby very desirable on the gem market.[50] However, another gold brooch, this one set with a hexagonal cut amethyst and in the original fitted box, fetched only $3,375 in 2009 and failed to sell when reoffered in 2011. Although rare, the amethyst was a bit pale, and perhaps the buying public did not equate Khlebnikov with jewelry. In St. Petersburg in the 1860s, however, the firm traded more in jewelry than silver, but most examples seem to have disappeared forever.

A ruby and diamond brooch by Khlebnikov. *Courtesy of Sotheby's*

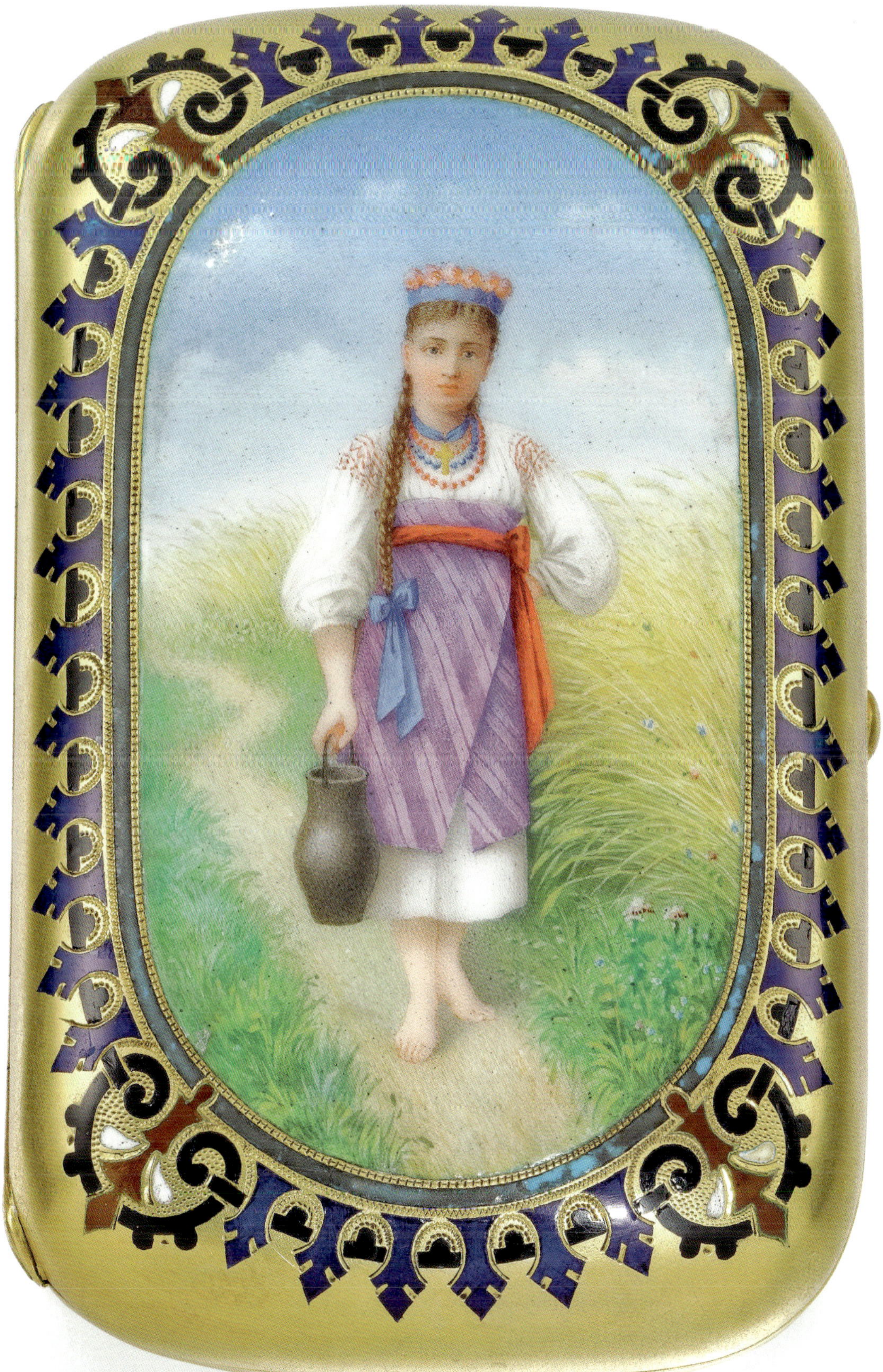

Enamel pictoral cigarette case.
Courtesy of Sotheby's

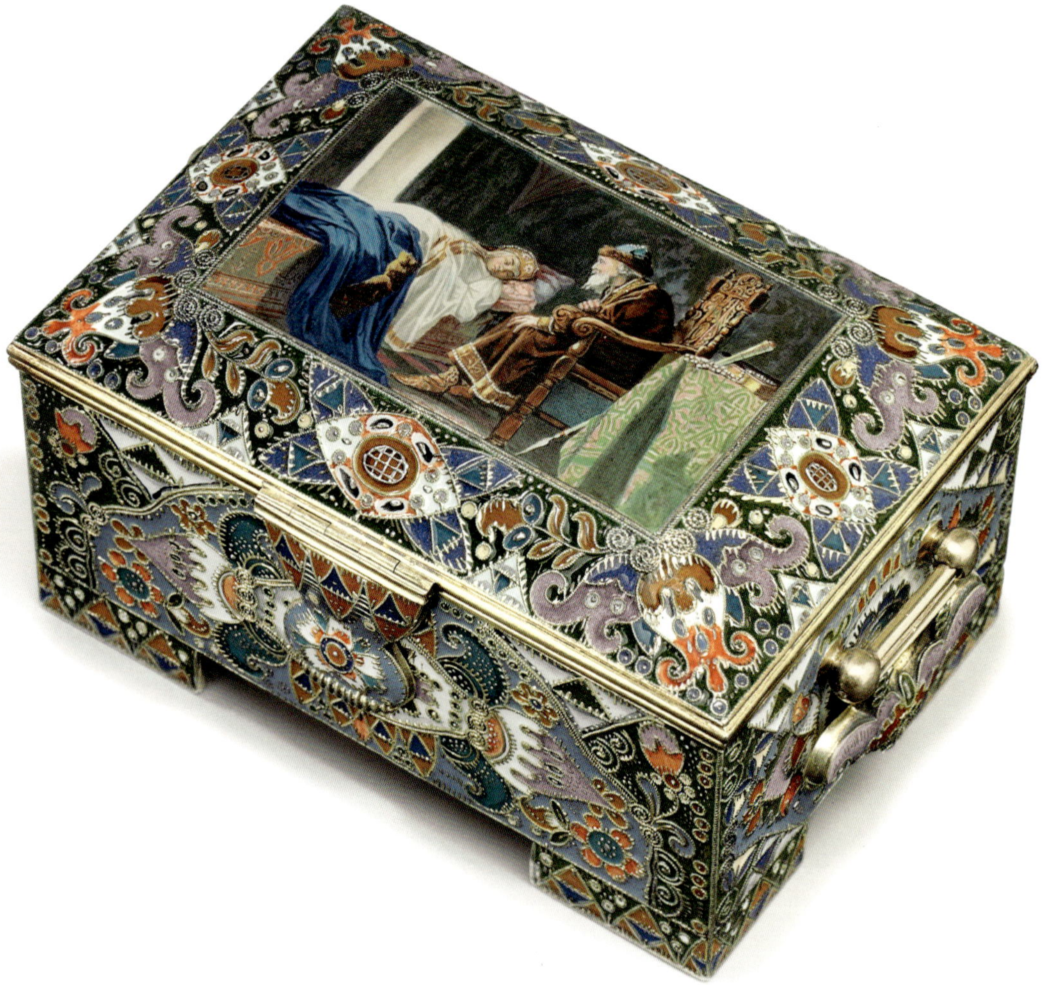

Rückert box depicting Ivan the Terrible admiring Vasilisa Malentieva.
© 2014 Christie's Images Ltd.

Following page:
Rückert kovsh depicting the first Romanov tsar, Michael Fedorovich, in ceremonial attire. *Courtesy of the Walters Art Gallery, Baltimore*

Rückert

Of all the great Moscow enamels, per square inch it is the works created by Fedor Rückert, especially those that were retailed by Fabergé, that command the highest prices.

Rückert items fetch more than comparably sized enamels by the three other greats: Ovchinnikov, Khlebnikov and Kurliukov. For example, a pair of enameled napkin rings by Rückert sold in 2017 for $9,689.

Auction houses love featuring close-up illustrations of Rückert enamels since they are so impeccably detailed. It is curious to note that although they are over 100 years old (Rückert died in 1917), Rückert enamels are seldom seen in poor condition. This is perhaps due to careful preservation or, in some cases, skilled restoration.

Rückert connoisseurs look for telltale signs of the master's production: Russian Revival style in cloisonné and en plein enamel, always of distinctive design and enhanced by creative wirework scrolls and fine detail. Those with pictorial scenes and figures always bring more. Rückert hallmarks matter—not all his works are stamped—but his style is so distinctive that it can be spotted across the room. The hallmarks are ФР (*FR* in Cyrillic), for Fedor Rückert, and if retailed by Fabergé, that firm's name is spelled in full, also in Cyrillic, below an imperial warrant, in a separate punch. This will indicate that the item was made by Rückert and sold by Fabergé in Moscow. Sellers of such items can and do call them "Fabergé," even though Rückert was not strictly a Fabergé workmaster.[51]

Rückert had his own workshop, which was independent of the House of Fabergé. Other retailers also sold his wares, notably the House of Marshak in Kiev, as well as Kurliukov, Khchekleev and Krakov in Moscow. A prime example was the Alexander II commemorative box by Rückert, which sold at Sotheby's in 2011 (see "A Mysterious Monument by Marshak," page 200). Because it was retailed by Marshak and not Fabergé, the price of $287,000 could have been much higher. Today Rückert is regarded as one of the finest enamelers in history.

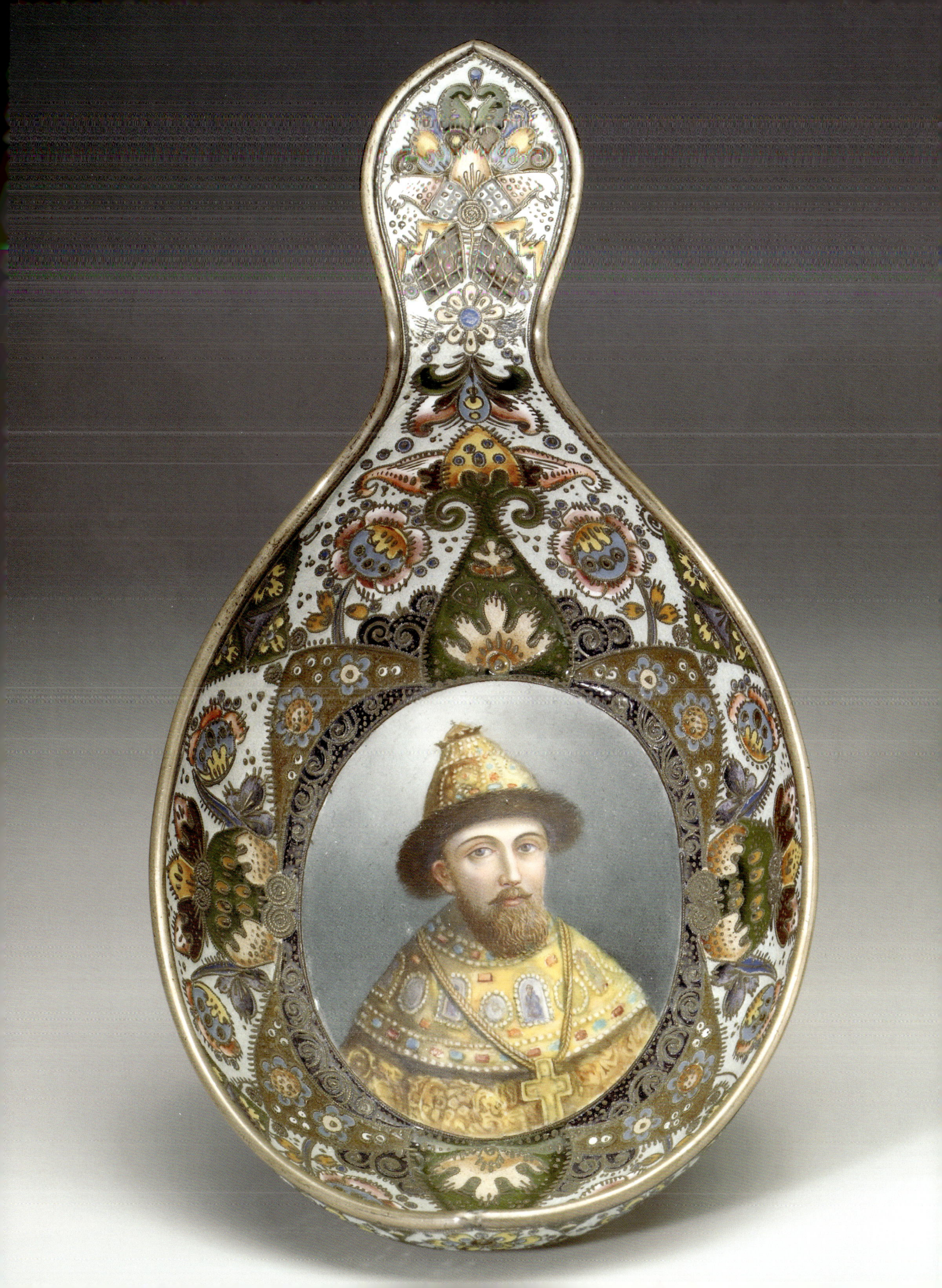

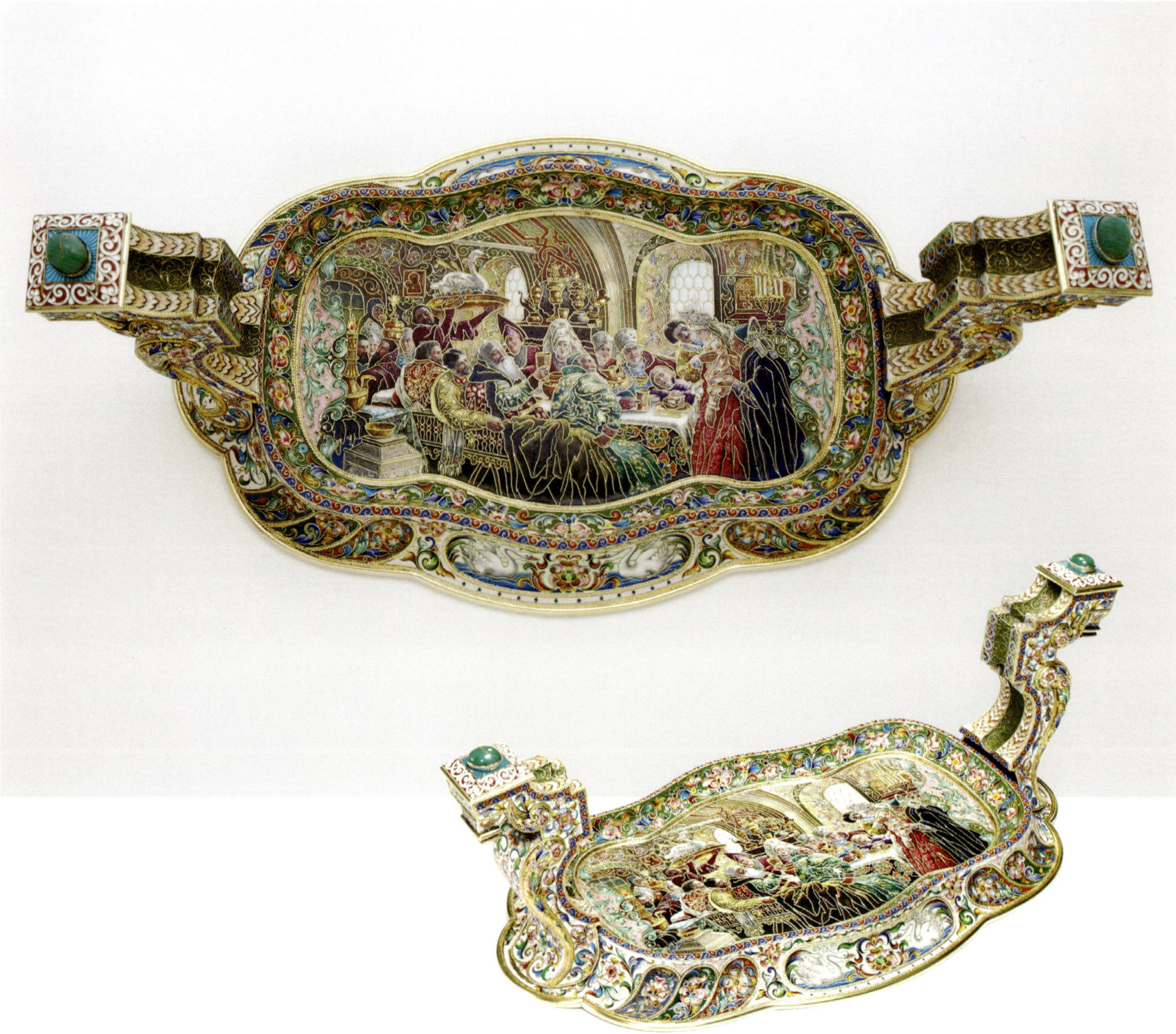

Enameled Boyar Wedding Feast tray by Kurliukov. *Courtesy of Sotheby's*

Following page: This enameled tea caddy by Kurliukov sold for $9,000 in 1971. *Courtesy of Sotheby's*

Kurliukov

Market values for Kurliukov items, although not as well known as Khlebnikov, are almost as high due to the scarcity and high quality of works by this enamel master. In 2006, a two-handled tray featuring the iconic Boyar Wedding Feast sold for $632,000.

Smaller items tend to fall within the same price range as other Moscow enamels. An enameled tea caddy by Kurliukov sold in New York in 1971 for $9,000, one of a pair. Combining Asian and Old Russian design, it depicts a Chinese woman holding a box of tea with a Russian dedication inscription, which was no doubt made as a special order. At the same venue, an enameled dinner plate sold for only $10,450 10 years later, while a bowl with characteristic swans and fowls in 2012 fetched $7,414.

Two similar silver samovars by Kurliukov in the Kokoshnik style, judging from their openwork cover, sold in 1993 for $17,250 and in 2011 for $362,500, a perfect example of sky-rocketing values for typically Russian styles by known Russian silversmiths at the peak of the market.

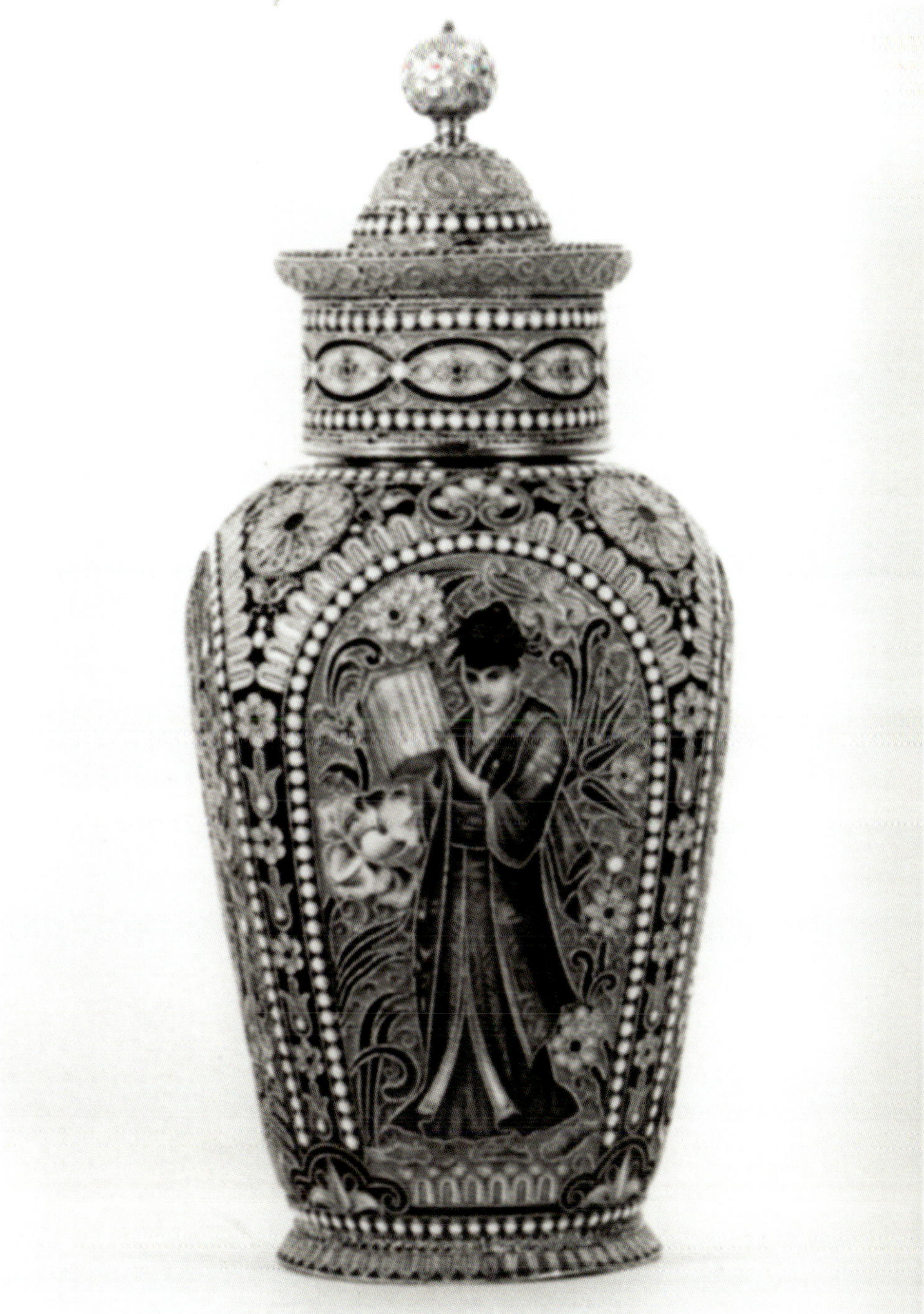

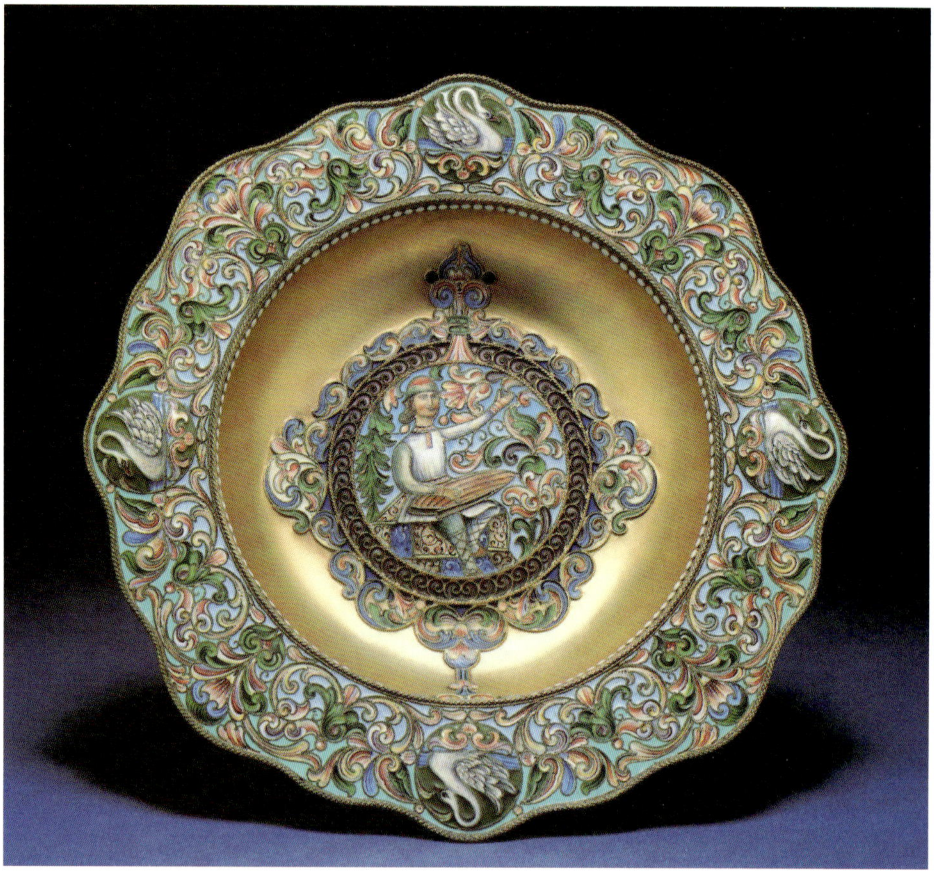

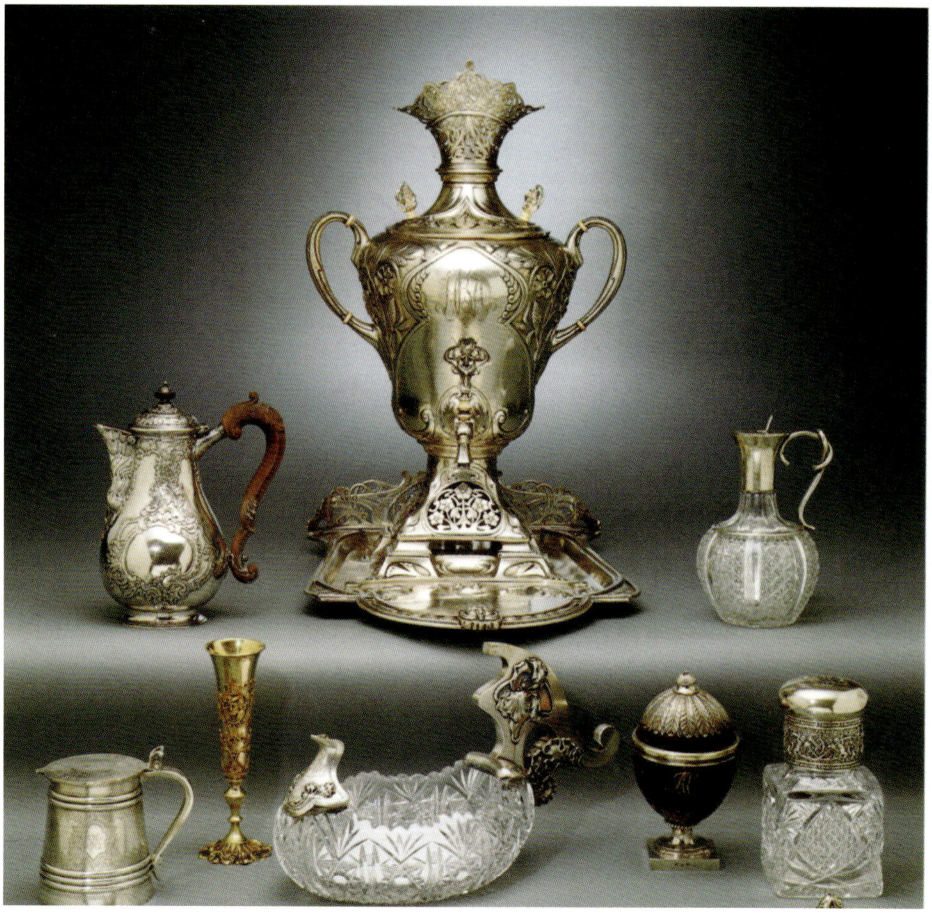

Enameled dinner plate.
Courtesy of Sotheby's

Silver samovar by Kurliukov.
Courtesy of Sotheby's

Following page:
Another Russian silver Kurliukov samovar.
Courtesy of Sotheby's

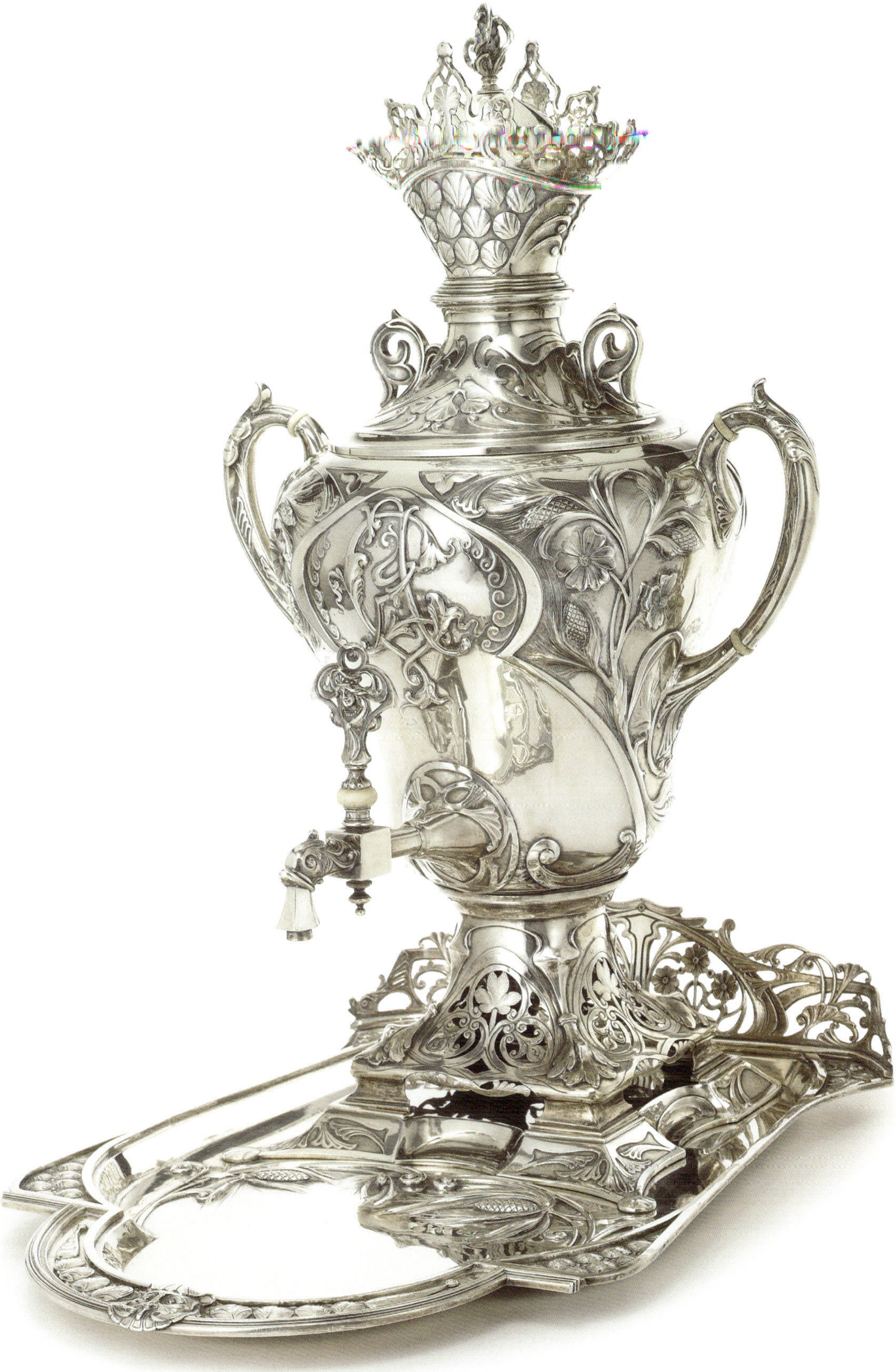

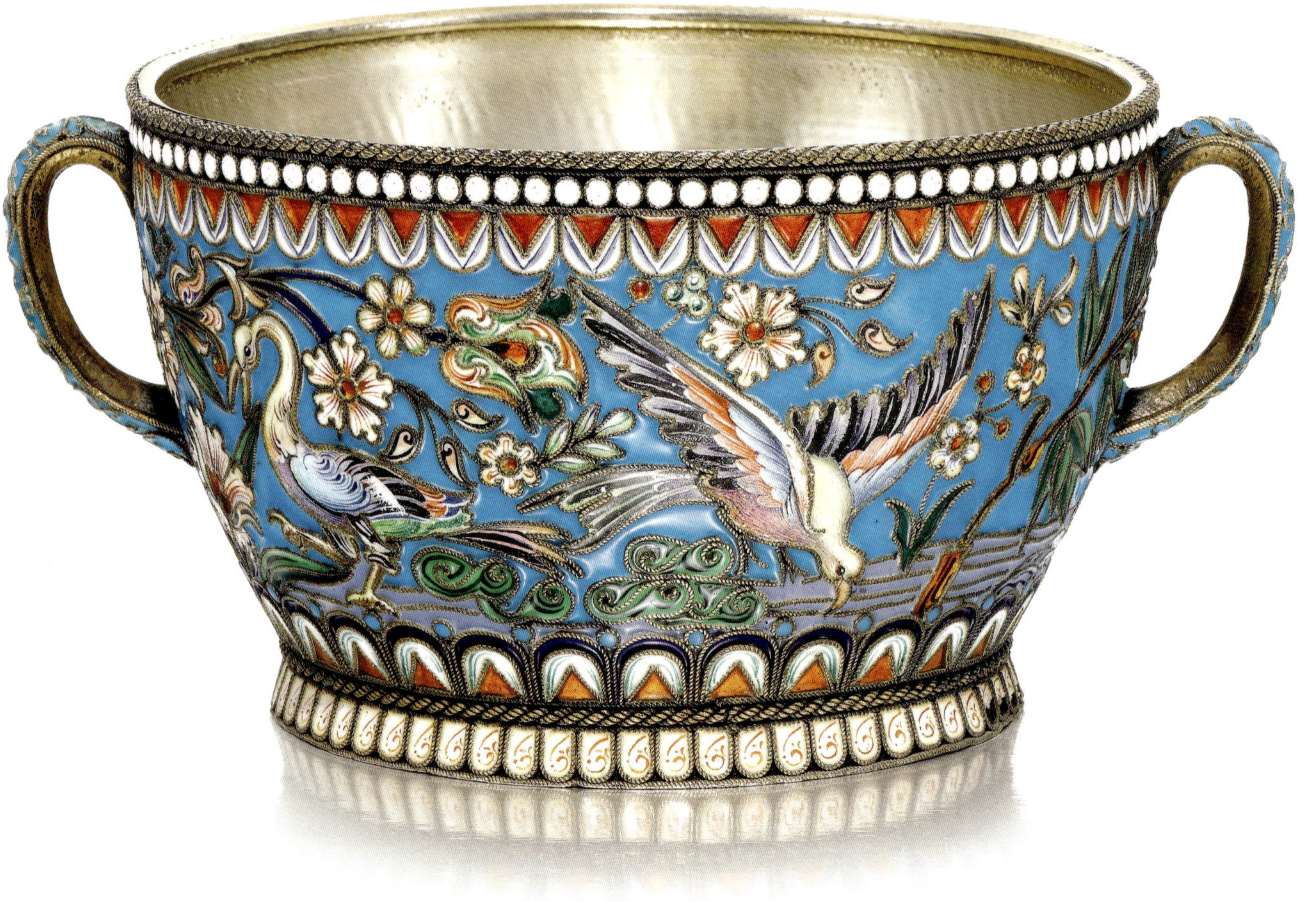

Enameled bowl with vibrant colors characteristic of Kurliukov.
Courtesy of Sotheby's

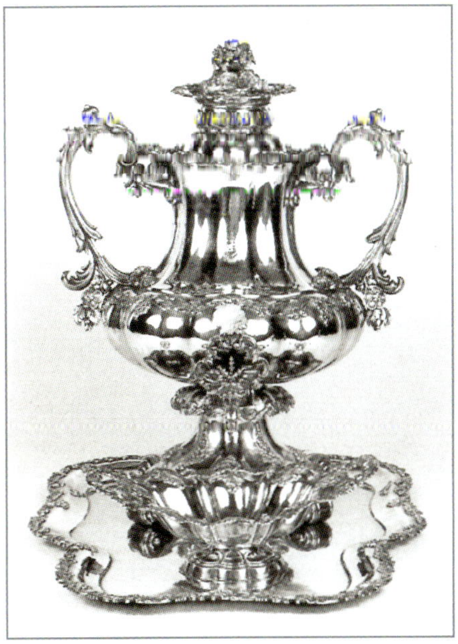

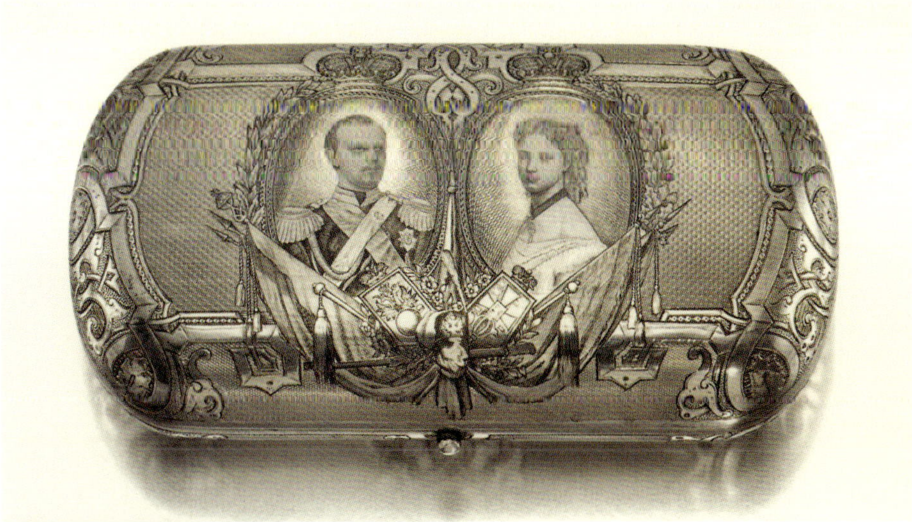

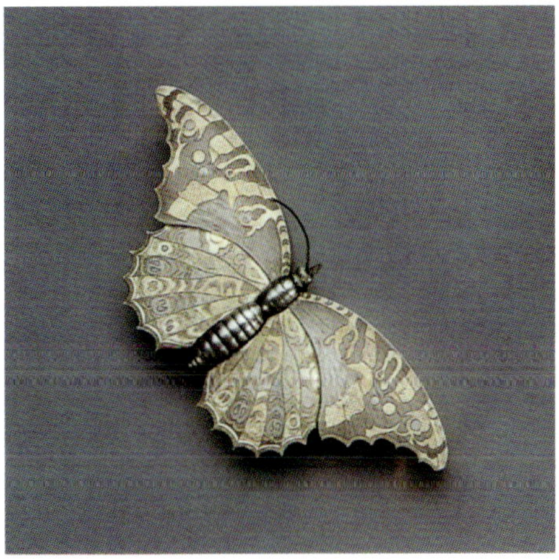

This neo-Rococo silver samovar complete with tray and waste bowl belonging to a Russian princess fetched $26,026 in 1988. Thirty years later the samovar alone sold for $105,567. Gubkin created the portrait presentation box for the marriage of Grand Duke Alexander Aleksandrovich and Grand Duchess Maria Feodorovna in 1867 which sold in London in 2009 for over $80,000 as part of a famous Romanov Grand Ducal sale. A Gubkin Japanese inspired moth shaped box realized $8,446 in 1995. © *1988 Christie's Images Ltd and Sotheby's*

Gubkin

I love Gubkin silver but don't see enough of it. Apart from one or two recent auction records, I found more examples in older catalogues with black-and-white images and from a Soviet-era reference book on Russian silver. One of my favorites is a nielloed box in the form of a moth. It shows excellent work and design. I learned about this wonderful silversmith when I bought a Gubkin tray in 2010, as part of a larger tea and coffee service that had belonged to Prince Sergei Galitzine.

KIEV AND ODESSA MARKET

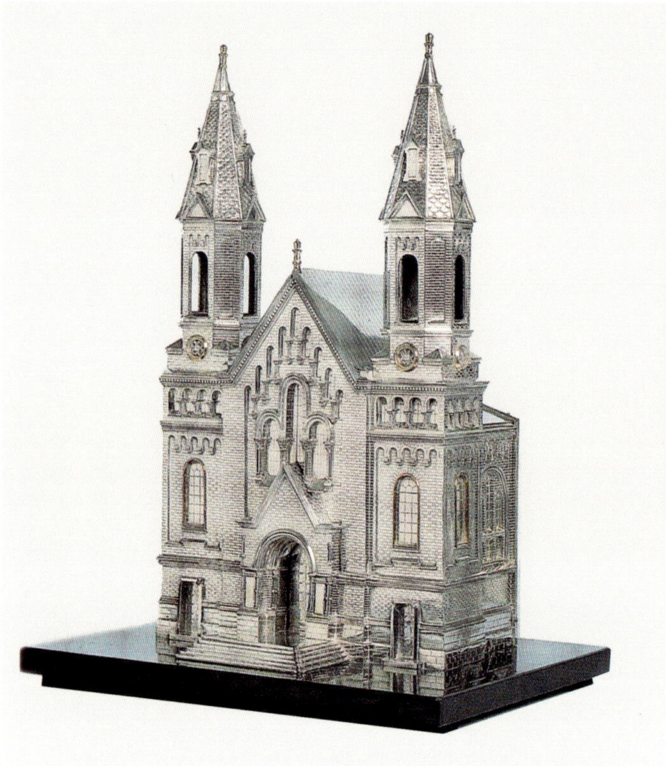

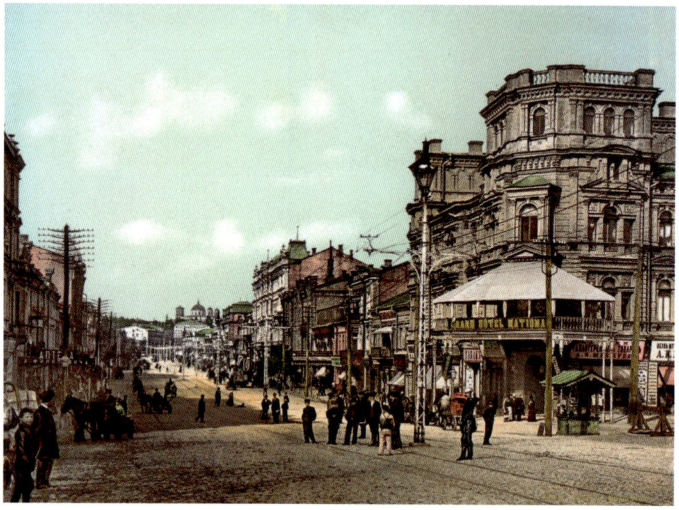

Silver Marshak model of St. Joseph's, a Catholic church in Ukraine. © *1987 Christie's Images Ltd.*

View of the Kreshchatik, ca. 1900, Kiev's main commercial street, where many jewelers had their shops, including Marshak and Fabergé. *Source: Wikimedia Commons*

Marshak

Marshak excelled in freestanding miniature silver models of buildings, boats and automobiles, although few survive. One exception is an intriguing silver rendition of a twin-spired church, which surfaced three times at auction in the West after having passed through the London dealer Wartski. Catalogue descriptions vary and the dates are wrong. However, thanks to Valentin Skurlov, we now know that the church, previously described as Protestant, was a silver replica of St. Joseph's Catholic Church in Nikolaev (near Odessa) and was presented to the local priest by parishioners, most likely around the date of its consecration in 1898.[52] Housing an hour or half-hour repeater clock (descriptions vary) with Roman numerals, it failed to sell in 1980 and 1987 in New York and in Geneva, respectively, but found a buyer in 2003 at Sotheby's New York for a mere $27,000. Intricate in detail, with gold trim and chased and engraved to simulate masonry, this model's quality rivals those made by Fabergé, which can bring 10 times more.[53]

A small, silver, Style Russe enameled patch box by Marshak sold in New York in 1981 for $1,100. In 1994 I found a silver-mounted, cut-glass jardinière in the shape of a Viking ship that brought $6,525, a good price then. In 2005, a Marshak silver kovsh with two smaller kovsh as cups, en suite, which was presented to the First Company of the 44th Kamchata Infantry Regiment in Kiev and applied with the city's coat of arms, brought six times its presale estimate, $103,704. In 2012, a silver samovar realized $50,000, although this may reflect the fact that Russian imperial silver samovars today are very rare and desirable no matter who made them.

Auction records for Marshak's creations are uneven, although items offered by the Kievan goldsmith seem to outnumber those made by Fabergé's Kiev branch.[54] Alas, his jewelry is almost nonexistent. In 2013, a gold ruby-and-diamond bracelet by Finikov retailed by Marshak in original fitted case sold for $12,500. For smaller items, since 2002, I counted only about a dozen by Marshak. A Britsyn white-enameled cigarette case, retailed by Marshak, was offered but failed to sell twice, for reasons unknown to me. Like many Russian goldsmiths, Iosif

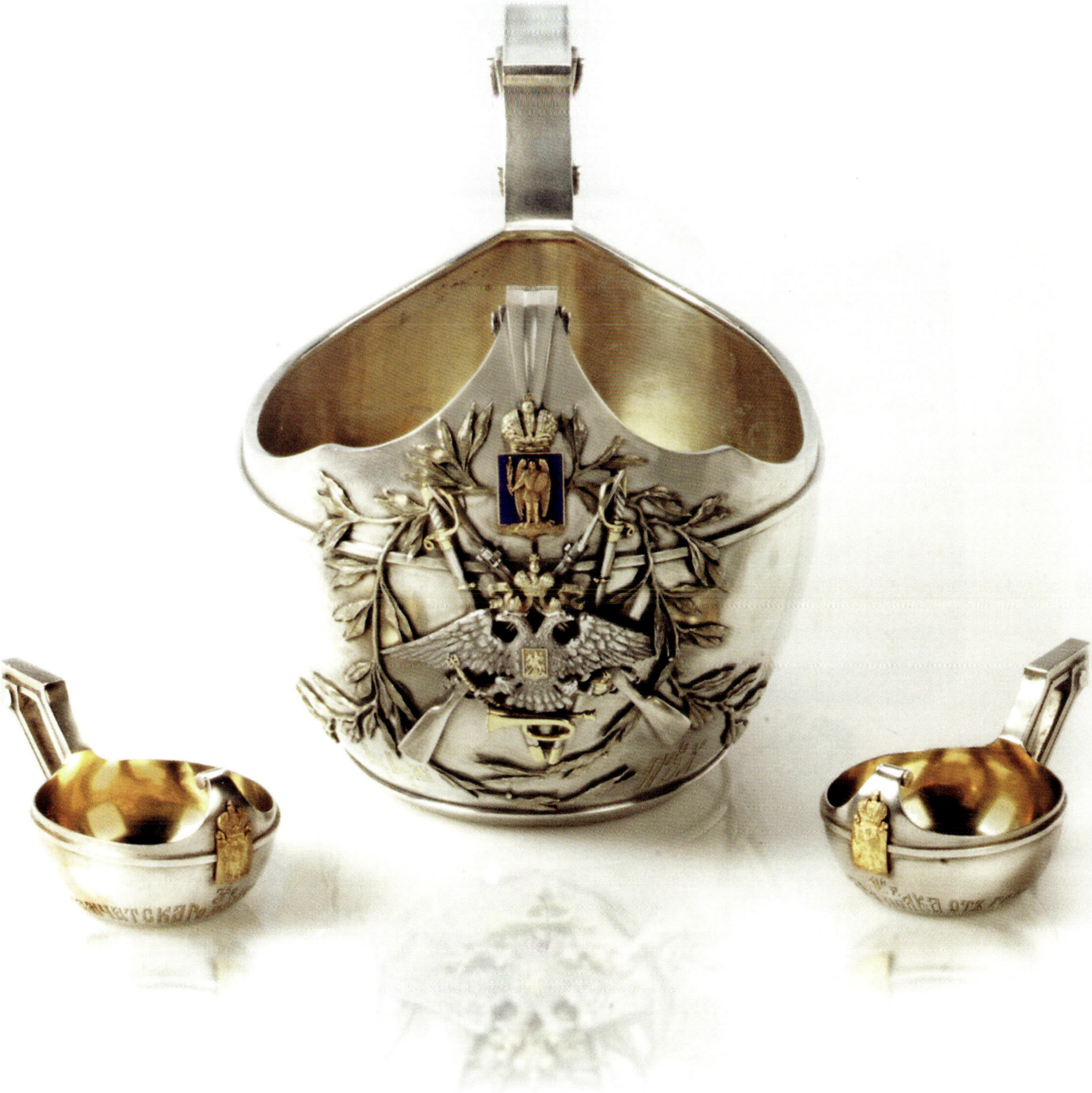

Silver punch set in the form of kovshs.
Courtesy of Sotheby's

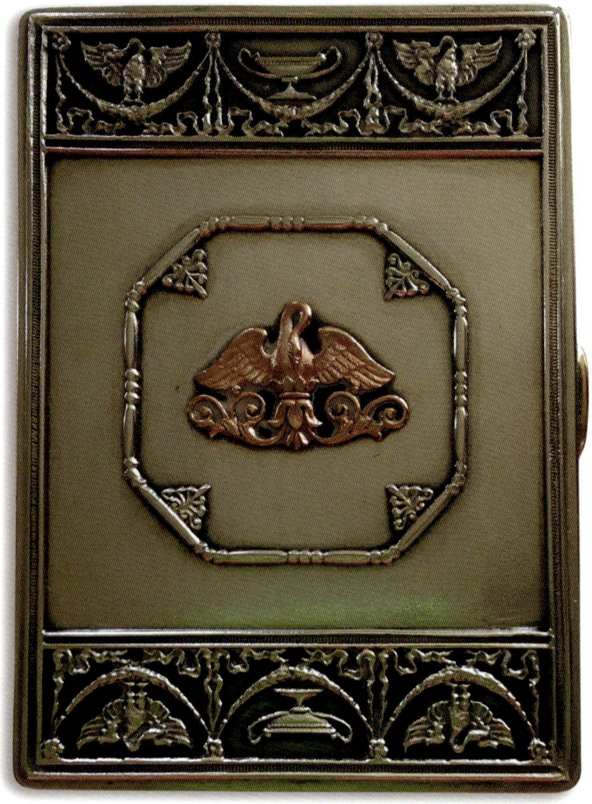

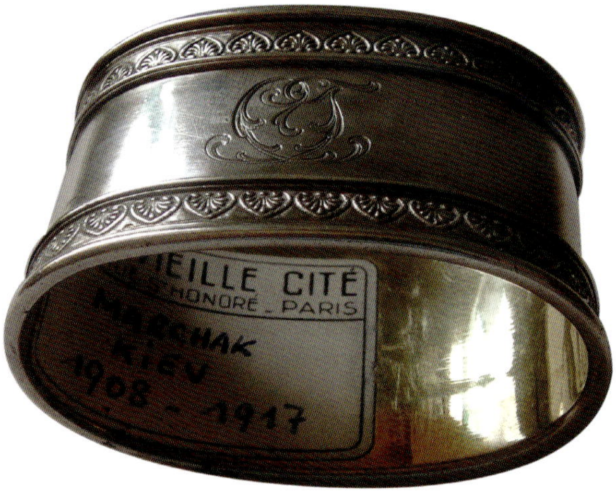

Cigarette case by Marshak.
Private collection

Napkin ring by Marshak.
Private collection

produced many cigarette cases. One in *samorodok*, or textured gold simulating molten metal, sold in 2005 for $8,246. That same case, or a similar one, had fetched only $636 in 2000. Smaller Marshak objects tend to maintain but not exceed their value over the years, such as a silver page turner ($2,150 in 2007), and a vodka cup in the form of a dancing muzhik ($2,250 in 2009).

Is the Kievan Marshak firm now recognized for its excellent works? This remains to be seen. The true test of a firm's market value is if fakes start appearing under its name. A dubious pair of silver putti of poor quality on wooden plinths surfaced in Sweden in 2013 with false Marshak hallmarks for St. Petersburg, instead of Kiev. Forgers are now turning to lesser-known Russian silversmiths, having run out of ideas for faking Fabergé objects. Despite a downturn in the Russian market, prices for important objets d'art by Marshak will no doubt rise as the name begins to mean something to buyers and connoisseurs alike in the West.

Rokhumovskii

Time was not a factor for Israel Rokhumovskii. Some of his projects took years to complete, and few survive. Those that have may be in private collections, since they are not evident on the market.[55] One shining exception is an astonishing miniature gold skeleton complete with an ornate silver sarcophagus, which took him no less than ten years. He took pride in this chef d'oeuvre, signed it accordingly, and wrote, "With the help of minute ball bearings, all body members can move in all directions, and even the lower jaw can be opened and closed. . . . I was entirely satisfied," and, once completed, he decided the skeleton "deserved a beautiful sarcophagus."[56]

When I held it in my hands at a Sotheby's in 2013, its workmanship defied description. Created in solid gold with all moving parts and joints, it measured only 3½ inches long. Inside the showcase, I maneuvered the skeleton in different positions on and off a silver, velvet-lined sarcophagus, which was equally fascinating. When first sold at Christie's Amsterdam in 1998, the skeleton and sarcophagus fetched $311,530. Curiously, 15 years later it brought only $365,000, perhaps due to its macabre theme.

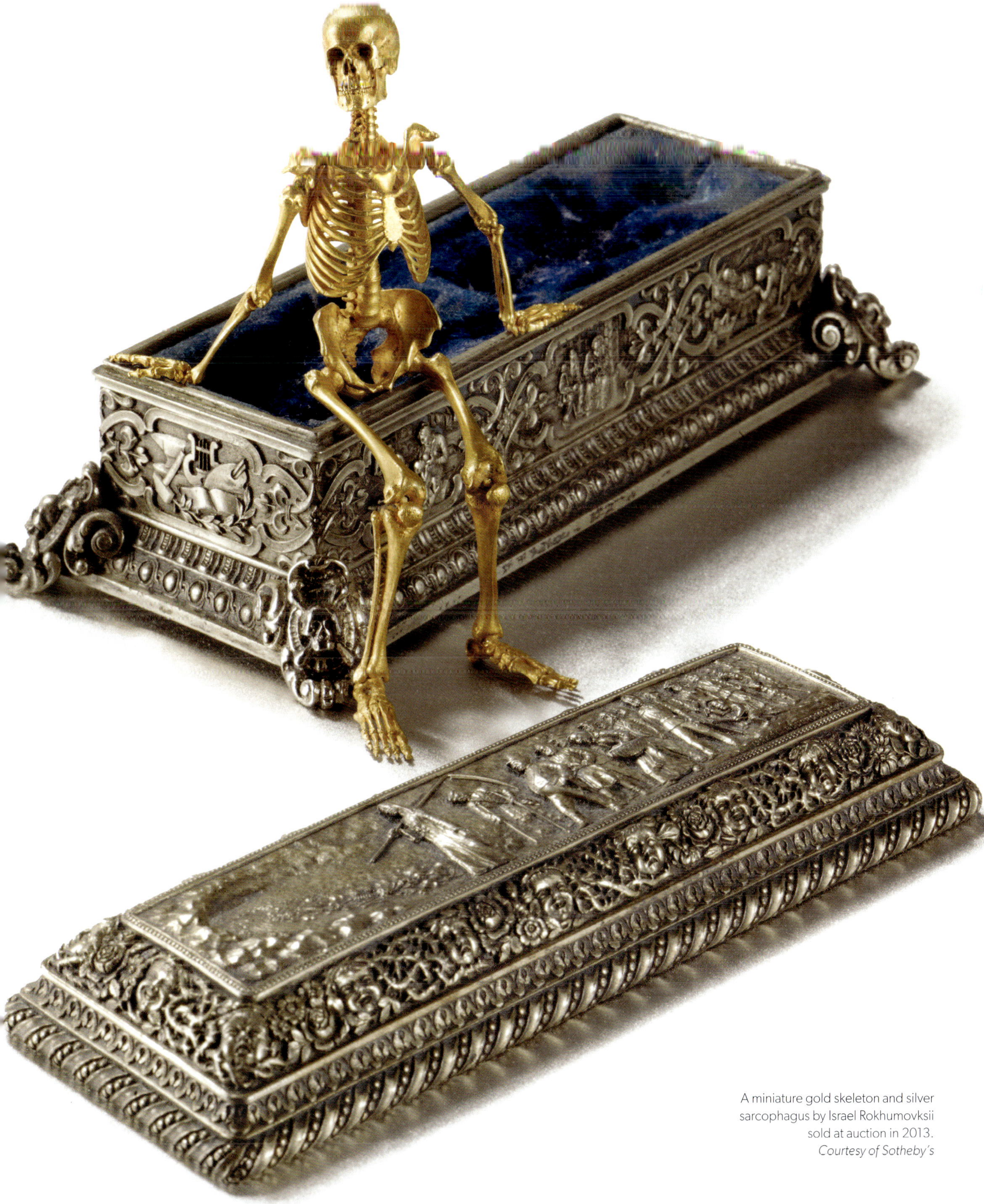

A miniature gold skeleton and silver sarcophagus by Israel Rokhumovksii sold at auction in 2013. *Courtesy of Sotheby's*

Iosif Marshak, Kiev's star jeweler, liked the skeleton. Already in 1893, he displayed one in the Chicago World's Fair. It was said to have been a gift from the ever-generous Rokhumovskii.[57]

Few of Rokhumovskii's creations have surfaced at auction, at least not in America. Christie's New York offered a miniature pendant in the form of the Tiara of Saitapharnes in 1994 in New York, but it failed to sell, proving a difficult market for works by this brilliant creator. Another, a ring, may have been a reproduction. From the image, it looked cast rather than done by hand and brought only $1,875 in a midwestern US auction in 2014, although it had French stamps on it as well. An enameled frame, again probably by the master, sold for around $11,000 in Paris in 2016. Since the Odessan goldsmith lived in Paris for years, more treasures may materialize there, perhaps once again to fool us all (see "Israel Rokhumovskii and the Case of the Counterfeit Crown").

LIFE AS A DEALER

I love my job, most of the time. Like any career, there are highs and lows. It's fascinating and rewarding work, but I will admit that even today, I make mistakes—miss a deal, overpay, or get too excited in my pursuit. The latter part is a bit tricky. Emotions often surface when I'm buying Russian jewels and this never helps me get good prices. When selling, though, it works.

The thrill of discovery is what keeps me going. I love the hands-on aspect and the immediacy of what I do. Dealers, auction specialists and collectors have an advantage over others in this regard. We see volumes of goods and handle the best and the worst, while knowing or striving to know how to sort it all out, usually under pressure. Often from previous errors, we learn to separate real from fake and pristine from doctored, aware that there are always more challenges ahead. For us dealers, it's a question of should we buy, is it a good value, has it had market exposure, do we have a client, what will it sell for, what if we want to keep it and does it have a story?

After leaving Christie's, I did shows and met Cindy and Joe Fanelli, who invited me to sell my jewels in their renowned Madison Avenue store: Fanelli Antique Timepieces. Cindy Fanelli taught me everything I know about retail. Today I sell online and continue to buy mostly from the public.

Early on I purchased every piece of Russian jewelry and silver I could find. Because there was so little of it around, I also began buying French jewels and making frequent trips to Paris, my birthplace. But Russian was an undeniable part of me.

Then it dawned on me: Marie, just be yourself. Why not build on that passion for Russian jewels? So I started to write this book (seven years in the making), giving lectures and, since 2017, leading jewelry-focused, small group tours of St. Petersburg and beyond. Now in the best of both worlds, I can wax lyrical about Russian treasures with you, *in situ*! I've since added Moscow to the St. Petersburg leg in our *Jewels in the Crown Tour*, and two more exciting journeys to Paris and London: www.Mariebetteley.com/tours.

To all aspiring dealers, I would say: seek advice from seasoned dealers, buy what you love, spend time with it and research. You may uncover a provenance or a maker or a story and make a coup!

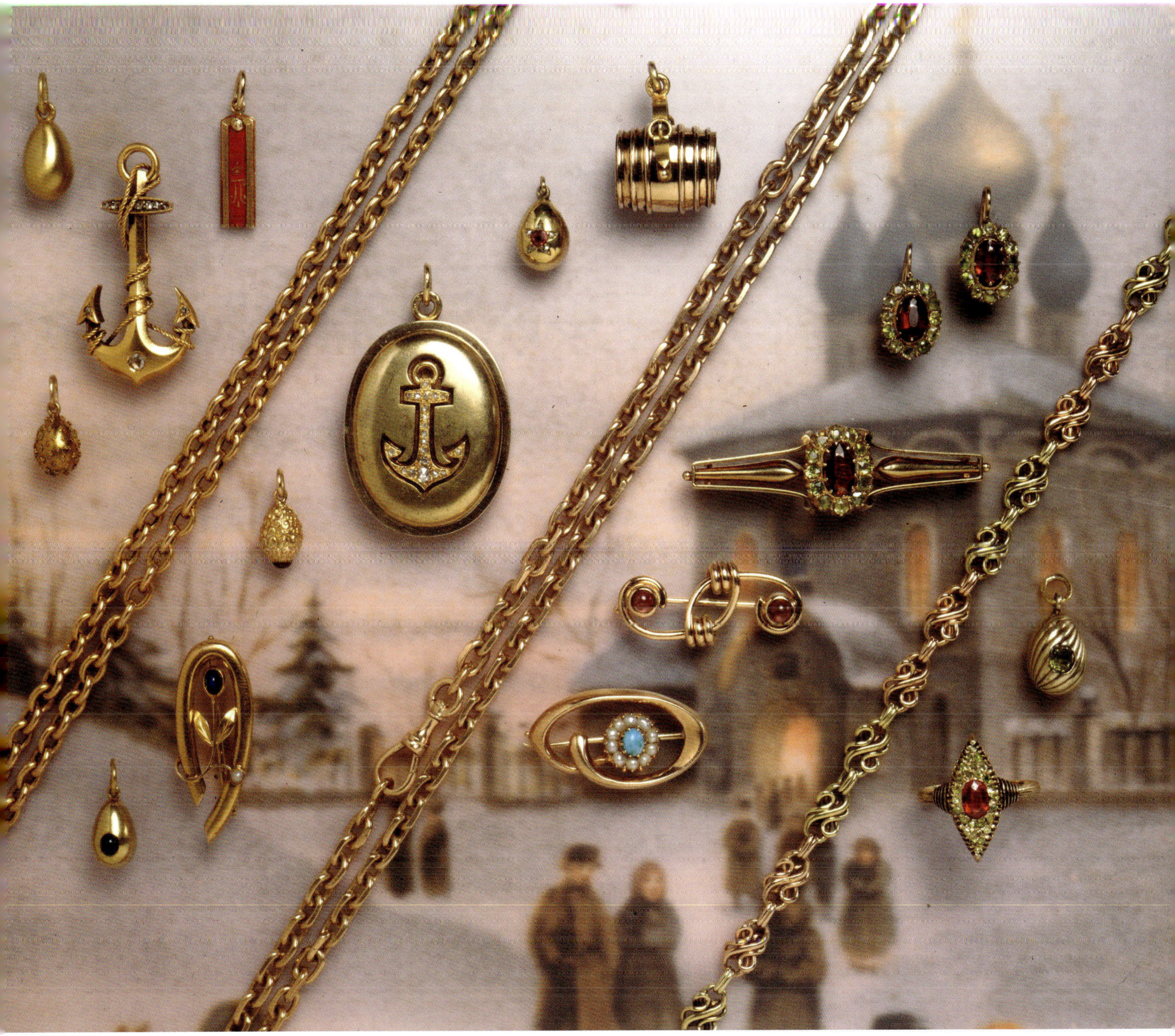

Imperial-era Russian gold jewels on a Romanov postcard from the period. *Marie Betteley, photo by Roger Bester*

NOTES

1. Sotheby's, London, December 1, 2005, lot 347.

2. A midwestern scrap metal dealer came dangerously close to melting down the 1887 Fabergé egg in 2012. Sissi Cao, "How the World's Most Expensive Easter Egg Ended Up in a US Flea Market as Scrap Metal," The Observer, 20 April 2019.

3. Sotheby's, New York, December 14 and 15, 1983, lot 509; and Christie's, London, December 2, 2009, lot 38.

4. Christie's, New York, April 15, 1997, lot 120; and Sotheby's, London, December 1, 2015, lot 401.

5. One exception is with two almost identical pink topaz crosses that were sold within 10 years of each other. One, offered at Christie's in 2001 and attributed to the Odessa goldsmith named N. Chistiakov (sometimes associated with Fabergé and identified as such in the catalogue), sold for $17,625. Its companion, but this one made in St. Petersburg, realized $232,690 only 11 years later. The two are identical except for the central stone, which varies from old-mine-cut diamond to square-cut pink topaz. Is it any wonder that unscrupulous jewelers today continue to refine their fake punches for hallmarking jewels in order to pass them off as by Fabergé?

6. Sotheby's, New York, June 6, 1995, lot 140; and David Killen Gallery, New York, September 27, 2015, lot 196.

7. The best source of information on Fabergé and the market is the *Fabergé Research Newsletter*, https://Fabergéresearch.com.

8. Parke-Bernet Galleries, New York, October 28 and 29, 1960, lots 291 and 292. The Fabergé triptych, in color, was given to Tsar Alexander III for a heroic deed: Christie's, New York, October 27, 1987, lot 93. The Hahn triptych was auctioned 46 years later for $284,800: Sotheby's, New York, April 28, 2006, lot 446.

9. Christie's, New York, May 10, 1989, lot 38.

10. Sotheby's, New York, June 28 and 29, 1979, lot 59; New York, December 8, 1992, lot 184; and London, December 1, 2015, lot 420. In the latter sale, the Hahn box sold for $641,623, while the one by Fabergé (lot 419) in nephrite brought $451,191.

11. Christie's, New York, May 20, 2015, lot 22.

12. Tillander-Godenhielm, "Russian Imperial Awards System," 218. The Bulgarian minister's family claims the box was stolen during the Allied bombing in Europe, and, at the time of writing, was suing the auction house for its return.

13. Christie's, New York, *Property from the Estate of Mrs. Charles W. Engelhard*, March 18, 2005, lot 74; London, December 1–2, 2009, lot 42; and London, June 8, 2010, lot 160.

14. For a jeweled arrow pin and a nephrite paper knife retailed by Tiffany and Hammer Galleries, respectively, see Sotheby's, New York, June 10–11, 1981, lots 349 and 402. The Schaffer Collection of Russian Imperial Treasures sold a small Köchli frame with miniature of Tsar Nicholas in 1935.

15. Parke-Bernet Galleries, New York, May 17, 1967, lot 96; and Sotheby's, New York, June 20–21, 1984, lot 308A.

16. Christie's, Geneva, November 17, 1981, lots 152 and 154, $3,300 and $2,200.

17. Ivanov, *Gold and Silversmiths in Russia*, 2:293–94.

18. Sotheby's, New York, April 12, 2011, lot 230.

19. Christie's, South Kensington, November 21, 2001, lot 77; and London, November 29, 2010, lot 263.

20. Christie's, South Kensington, *Arts & Textiles of the Islamic and Indian Worlds*, April 11, 2014, lot 222.

21. Christie's, New York, April 12, 1988, lot 83; and Sotheby's, London, May 31, 2006, lot 358.

22. Bonham's, London, May 30, 2012, lots 172 and 173, for two commemorative jetons by Arnd, $9,479 and $11,375, and June 5, 2013, lot 90 for a stickpin of the Preobrazhenskii Life Guards Regiment, $6,275.

23. Sotheby's, London, June 12, 2008, lot 590.

24. Christie's, Geneva, May 25 and 26, 1993, lots 433 to 439.

25. Bonham's, London, November 27, 2013, lot 110.

26. South Kensington, *Christie's Interiors—Style & Spirit*, February 17, 2015, lot 94.

27. Sotheby's, London, June 10, 2009, lot 566.

28. Tillander-Godenhielm, *Jewels from Imperial St. Petersburg*, 276, no. 97.

29. Sotheby's, London, November 28, 2006, lot 252, $41,904.

30. Sotheby's, New York, April 21–22, 2010, lot 178.

31. Christie's, New York, *The Van Cliburn Collection*, May 17, 2012, lots 21 and 22.

32. Christie's, London, June 2, 2014, lot 334.

33. Sotheby's, London, May 31, 2006, lot 338.

34. Christie's, New York, April 24, 2006, lot 240.

35. Bonham's, London, November 27, 2013, lot 109. The following lot of six Arnd stirrup cups also sold for an average of $11,000 each.

36. Sotheby's, New York, April 21, 2005, lot 18.

37. Christie's, New York, June 6, 2011, lot 233.

38. Sotheby's, New York, April 16, 2013, lot 96.

39. Rossini, Paris, April 26, 2013, lot 62.

40. Christie's, London, October 5, 1989, lot 32; and Bonham's, London, June 3, 2015, lot 92.

41. Christie's, Geneva, November 16, 1988, lot 39, $6,844.

42. Phillips, London, November 15, 1994, lot 164, $4,230.

43. Sotheby's, New York, February 29 and March 1, 1980, lot 129, $20,000.

44. Sotheby's, Geneva, May 11, 1983, lot 226.

45. Sotheby's, New York, April 16, 2008, lot 521.

46. Sotheby & Co, London, December 4, 1972, lots 79 and 80.

47. Ovchinnikov and Khlebnikov reproductions have appeared in the last 25 years in the form of Japonisme-style beakers and large silver kovshs, some with dedication inscriptions, enameled tankards, and trompe l'oeil baskets. While they lack quality and finesse, and poor enameling is visible even from images, the hallmarks or maker's stamps look convincing even to the experts.

48. Fabergé et al., *Fabergé: A Comprehensive Reference Book*, 111.

49. Sotheby's, New York, December 15, 1987, lot 271.

50. Sotheby's, New York, April 16, 2007, lot 54.

51. In 1912 Rückert presented Carl Fabergé a colorful beaker depicting an en plein enamel of the facade of Fabergé Moscow shop, in commemoration of their 25-year collaboration.

52. Skurlov et al., *K. Faberzhe i Iosif Marshak*, 32–33.

53. Sotheby's, London, June 23 and 24, 1980, lot 676; Christie's, Geneva, May 13, 1987, lot 53; and Sotheby's, London, *A Celebration of the English Country House Sale*, April 30, 2003, lot 23.

54. Skurlov, introduction, in Skurlov et al., *K. Faberzhe i Iosif Marshak*.

55. Pictures and descriptions of these appeared in B. Sapozhnikov, *Israel Rochoumovsky and His Works* (n.p., n.p., 1903), and are included in Ivanov, *Gold and Silversmiths in Russia*, 1.17–48.

56. Sotheby's, New York, *A Treasured Legacy*, April 29, 2013, lot 291; and Christie's, Amsterdam, *Fine Dutch and Foreign Silver, Judaica, Russian Works of Art and "Objects of Vertu,"* November 24, 1998, lot 505. The 1998 catalogue entry quotes from the jeweler's memoirs, translated from Israel Rouchomovsky, *Mein Leben und Meine Arbeit* (Paris: 1928), 214–17

57. Sapfirova, "Antikvarnyi rynok," 29.

GLOSSARY OF JEWELERS AND SILVERSMITHS IN RUSSIA FROM THE 18TH CENTURY TO 1917

This list is a practical guide for collectors, dealers, researchers and anyone else curious to know more about the origin of Russian objects or jewels. It is not comprehensive. While it includes the more prominent jewelers and silversmiths working in Russia from the 18th century to the Bolshevik Revolution of 1917, some are not featured because their works are not seen on the Western market. This may change with new discoveries. Purveyors to the imperial and grand ducal courts and the dates of receiving the warrants after 1855, when they were standardized by the tsar, are listed according to information provided by Valentin Skurlov. An eagle following an entry denotes purveyor to the imperial court of Russia. Gem dealers, designers and most watchmakers, except for those who supplied the major houses, are not included.

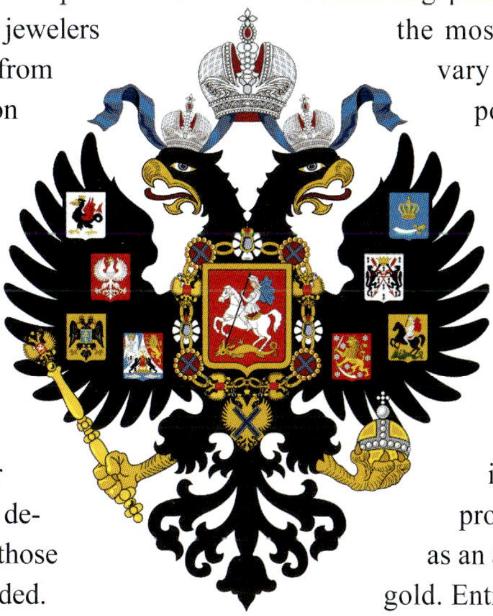

Russian names follow in parentheses for those of foreign birth who became Russian citizens. Sources sometimes list conflicting patronymics and dates. This list is based on the most-credible information available but may vary with other references. The two most important streets in St. Petersburg for jewelers and goldsmiths as well as silversmiths were the Bolshaia Morskaia Street and the Nevskii Prospect, and in Moscow, Kuznetskii Most. Many jewelers, especially in St. Petersburg, had several locations, usually serially, moving when they lost their leases, had a death in the family, or saw greater opportunity in more-central locations. Makers' hallmarks provided are not all inclusive but appear here as an aid to identifying stamped items of silver or gold. Entries in blue appear on the map on page 56.

— *Aarne, Johan Victor (1863–1934)* —

Finnish master craftsmen who worked for Fabergé from 1880 to 1890 and again from 1891 to 1904, after which he sold his workshop to Hjalmar Armfelt, another Finnish goldsmith, for 8,000 rubles. His workshop address was **42 Ekaterinskaia Canal**, where Andre Adler also lived, and **Demidov Lane**.

Hallmark: 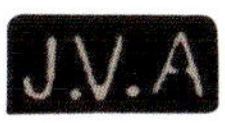

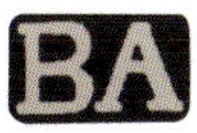

— *Abrosimov, Petr Evstratovich* — *(active 1869–1908)*

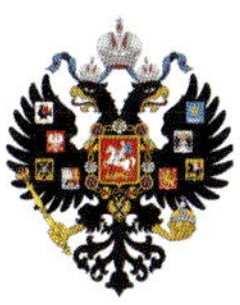

Moscow silversmith, founded his workshop in 1869. In 1887 he had 45 workers; in 1894, 60 workers. Received the title of purveyor to the imperial court on April 21, 1903.

Hallmark: 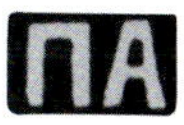

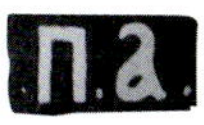

— *Adler, Andre Karlovich (active–1917)* —

Swiss goldsmith who founded Adler & Company in St. Petersburg in 1855 at **42 Ekaterinskii Canal**. Victor Aarne lived and worked in the same building. The firm was co-owned with his brother, Eugene Karlovich Adler, who left in 1904. Adler specialized in gold and silver items, decorations, medals and tokens. Adler bought the Arnd workshop in St. Petersburg from Dimitrii Osipov in 1902.

Hallmark: 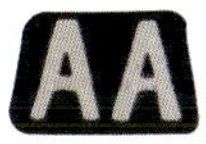

— *Adler, Maria V.* —

Moscow enameler who owned a gold and silverware workshop between 1879 and 1898. She had 74 workers and held a drawing class for training apprentices, with an annual turnover of 75,000 rubles. There is a miniature enameled chair by Adler in the Walters Art Gallery in Baltimore, Maryland.

Hallmark: MA 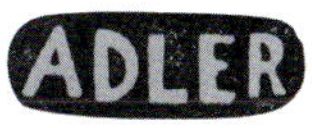

— Ador, Jean Paul (1724–84) —

Swiss-born court jeweler to Empress Catherine the Great. He founded a goldsmith company near Geneva before immigrating to St. Petersburg around 1750. In 1779 the empress commissioned Ador to create a solid-gold coffee service for her eldest grandson, the two-year-old Alexander Pavlovich (later Emperor Alexander I). Ador was especially famous for his imperial snuffboxes and jewels, some of which are preserved in the Hermitage. He occupied **24 Bolshaia Morskaia Street**, at the same location as Carl Fabergé but over 100 years earlier. Ador signed his works in script *Ador a St. Petersbourg* or *IA*, crowned or inside a crown.

Hallmark: 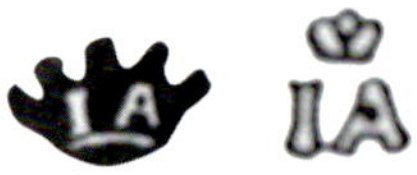

— Afanasev, Fedor Alekseevich — (1870–after 1927)

A native Russian silver and goldsmith, he apprenticed with a Finnish silversmith in St. Petersburg, then worked for Carl Bock and later Carl Fabergé. Afanasev specialized in small jewels and miniature eggs.

Hallmark: 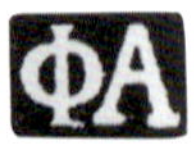

— Agofonov, Vasili Semenovich — (active 1895–1917)

Owned a silver and gold workshop in Moscow from 1895 to 1917. In the 1890s he had 80 workmasters. An Agofonov dragonfly pin set with pearls, rubies and diamonds is in the Moscow Historical Museum.

Hallmark: 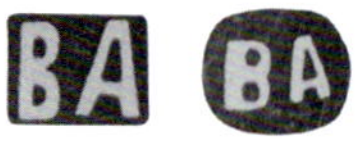

— Albrecht, Carl Julius (Kirill Fedorovich) — (1836–98)

A St. Petersburg silversmith who founded a workshop at 17 **Bolshaia Morskaia Street**. Albrecht was supplier to the imperial court from 1870 to 1880.

Hallmark: KA.

— Andreev, Daniil or Dmitrii (active 1840s) —

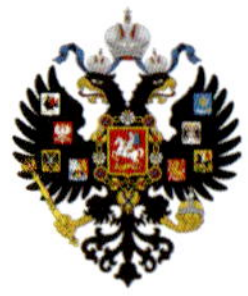

Court silversmith specializing in liturgical objects, tableware, he received a gold medal in the St. Petersburg exhibition in 1841. Received the imperial warrant and grand ducal warrant of Alexander Nikolaevich in 1845.

Hallmark:

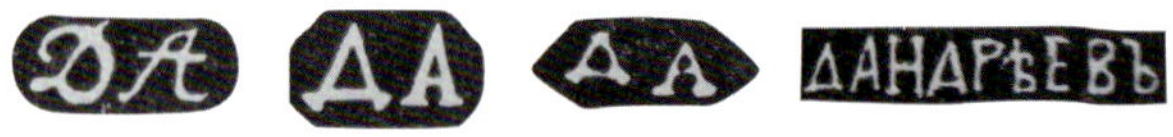

— Armfelt, Carl Gustav Hjalmar (1873–1959) —

Finnish goldsmith from a noble family, trained at Baron Stieglitz School of Art in St. Petersburg and under Anders Nevalainen from 1895 to 1904. Worked for Fabergé mostly in silver and was located at **35 Kazanskaia Street** in 1912.

Hallmark: 

— Arnd(t), Samuel (1812–90) —

Master goldsmith whose firm changed hands several times. It was located at **18 Nevskii Prospect** in St. Petersburg. The Arnd workshop supplied the firms of Nicholls & Plincke (from 1845) and Fabergé from 1902 to 1906. Arnd was married to Sophia Tegelsten, daughter of silversmith Carl Tegelsten, who also worked for Nicholls & Plincke. See "Nicholls & Plincke: Silver Purveyors to the Tsars."

Hallmark: SA

— Barbé, Carl Helfried (1777–?) —

Born near Frankfurt-on-Main, Barbé became a master goldsmith in 1806 and left the foreign guild to join the Russian one upon becoming a Russian citizen in 1811. In 1828, Barbé made a gold snuffbox commemorating the death of Empress Maria Fedorovna, which contained a lock of her hair, now in the Gold Treasury Room in the Hermitage. A goldsmith named Ivan Ustinovich Barbé, possibly a son, is listed at **15 Bolshaia Morskaia Street** in the 1820s.

Hallmark: CB, CHB. 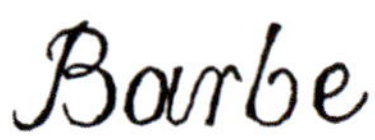

— *Barbé, Johann Christian (1780–1843)* —

Became a master goldsmith in 1804 and worked with his brother, Carl, in St. Petersburg. In 1834, he created a gold military presentation cup in the Russian neoclassical style, which was presented to Count Stepan Apraksin by the Imperial Horse Guards, now in the Hillwood Museum.

Hallmark: J.C. 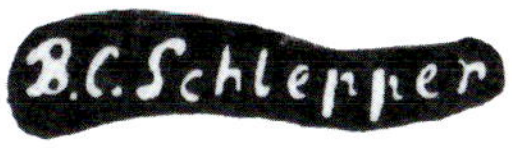

— *Beilin-Leskov Abram Solomonovich (b. 1840)* —

Beilin-Leskov made cigarette cases as well as brooches with diamond crowns and eagles and supplied items to the Moscow branch of Fabergé. Beilin was a merchant of the First Guild, lived at **22 Sadovaia Street**, and owned a workshop beginning in 1882. In 1897 he had 15 workers and in 1901 founded the trading house Beilin and Son with his son David, a graduate of the Riga Polytechnic Institute. From 1901 to 1917, Beilin produced numerous gold chains for Pavel Buhré, the imperial watchmaker on the **23 Nevskii Prospect**.

Hallmark: АБ, АСБDS

— *Blank, Carl Carlovich (active 1882–1917)* —

Finnish born, a diamond workmaster for Carl Hahn for many years, he opened his own business after the death of Hahn's son Dmitrii in 1911. Blank produced diamond decorations and imperial presentation boxes for the imperial court. His workshop was located at **36 Gorokhovaia Street**. He was appointed appraiser to the cabinet and hereditary honorary citizen in 1915. See "Carl August Hahn: The Diamond King."

Hallmark: 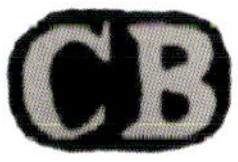

— *Blumentaller, Carl Petrovich* —

In 1902 he had a workshop at **15 Bolshaia Morskaia Street** in St. Petersburg, steps away from the Fabergé shop at 24. He dealt in corals and micromosaics.

Hallmark: КБ, КПБ

— *Bock, Aleksander Carlovich* —

Son of Carl, jeweler who took over his father's business. In 1922, he helped catalogue the crown jewels for the Bolsheviks, along with Agathon Fabergé, Carl's son.

— *Bock, Carl Ivanovich (1851–after 1914)* —

Member and cochair of the Union of St. Petersburg Jewelers. Opened a jewelry workshop in St. Petersburg in 1874 and was appointed purveyor to the imperial court on May 16, 1901. In 1894 his workshop was listed at **9 Bolshaia Morskaia Street**. By 1900 he had added a Moscow shop on the **Kuznetskii Most**. Both were on the same street as Fabergé's shops. See "Carl Bock: Jeweler Entrepreneur."

Hallmark: 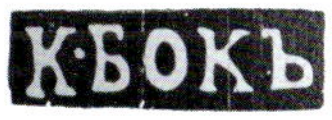 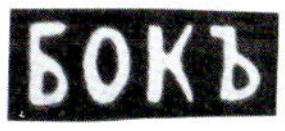

— *Boitsov, Vasili Vasilievich* — *(active 1890–1905)*

Enameler whose workshop was located at **33 Gorokhovaia Street** and who supplied the House of Fabergé.

Hallmark: 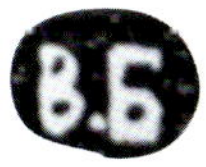

—*House of Bolin* —

Russia's most important jewelry firm. Founded by **Carl Edvard Bolin (1805–64)**, a Swedish-born bookkeeper who married Ernestine, daughter of St. Petersburg court jeweler Andreas Römpler. After the death of his brother-in-law Gottlieb Jahn, a goldsmith, Carl established Bolin & Jahn with Jahn's widow. The firm won a medal at the Great Exhibition of Industry of All Nations in London of 1851 and made imperial snuffboxes and jeweled sets for the imperial family of several consecutive Russian sovereigns. Under Carl Edvard, the House of Bolin flourished and became known for the most important jewels and precious objects of the Russian Empire. Edvard Ludwig Bolin (1842–1926) and Gustav Oscar Friedrich Bolin (1844–1916), sons and successors of Carl Edvard Bolin, continued the business in St. Petersburg. Both received the title of purveyor to the imperial court from Tsar

Nicholas II on April 21, 1902. Henrik Conrad Bolin (1818–88), Carl Edvard's younger brother, founded of the Moscow branch of Shanks & Bolin in 1852. Like the Nicholls & Plincke enterprise, the store was also called Magasin Anglais. Wilhelm James (Vasili Andreevich) Bolin (1861–1934), son of Henrik Conrad, took over his father's business in Moscow until the Russian Revolution. Was awarded title of supplier to the imperial court on December 25, 1912. See "Bolin: The Brightest Star."

Hallmark:

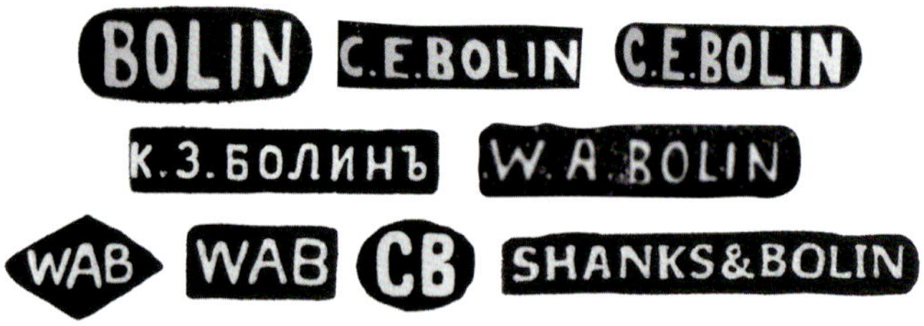

— *Boudde, Jean Francois (Xavier)* —

An 18th-century court jeweler from Hamburg who specialized in gold snuffboxes and objets d'art in the French style, with en plein enameling. He became a master goldsmith in 1769 in St. Petersburg and alderman of the foreigner's guild 10 years later. Several of his works are preserved in the Hermitage, including a gold filigree chalice said to have been presented by Catherine the Great to Prince Potemkin.

Hallmark: 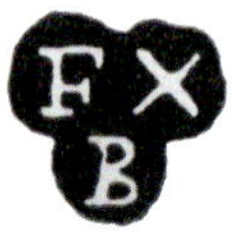

— *Bragin, Andrei Stepanovich* — *(active from 1852)*

Silversmith located on **4 Spasskii Lane** in St. Petersburg; specialized in church plate, tableware, chandeliers and other items. Produced silver for **I. Marshak** of Kiev, among others. Received important commissions such as the Neptune kovsh.

Hallmark: 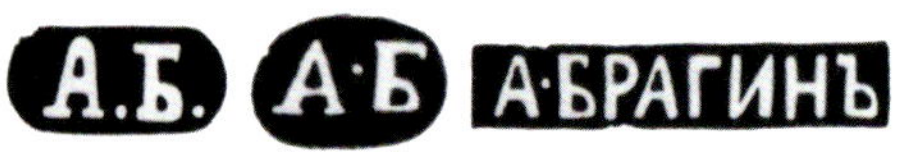

— *Bredenberg, Carl Frederick (Friedrich)* —

Finnish-born silversmith who worked for the imperial court and lived in St. Petersburg from 1798 to 1808.

Hallmark: 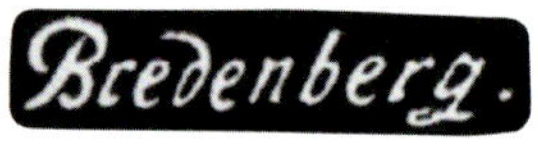

— *Breitfuss, Ludwig (1820–68)* —

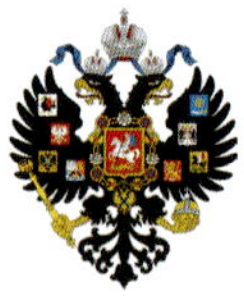

Continued the Breitfuss firm founded by his father, Heinrich Ludwig, in 1812, who was appraiser for the imperial cabinet in 1851 and appointed court jeweler in 1859. German-born Carl Breitfuss helped catalogue the crown jewels along with Bolin and Seftigen in 1868. He became court jeweler in 1867 and obtained hereditary honorary citizenship the same year. His address is listed at **11 Nevskii Prospect**. Other locations mentioned under Breitfuss, Aleksander Carlovich, his son, are **17 Gorokhovaia Street** and **15 or 17 Bolshaia Morskaia Street**.

Hallmark: ЛБ

— *Britsyn, Ivan Savelievich (1870–1952)* —

Becoming master goldsmith in 1903, Britsyn owned a St. Petersburg workshop at **12 Malaia Koniushennaia Street**, near Nevskii Prospect after 1910, producing gold, silver and guilloché enamel wares. Britsyn supplied Marshak of Kiev. Light-blue enamel was his trademark. One of the few jewelers to remain in Petrograd after 1917.

Hallmark: 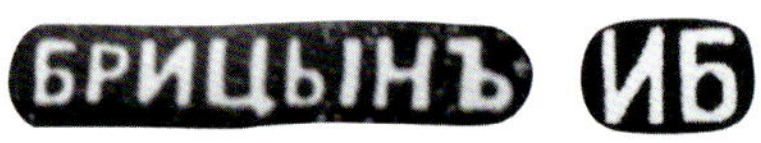

— *Buch, Iver Winfeldt (1776–1811)* —

Born in Norway, of Danish extraction, Buch created liturgical services in the 1790s for Empress Catherine the Great, with gems she had chosen from the imperial treasury, a gold chalice of which is now in the Hillwood Collection. He joined the St. Petersburg Foreign Guild in 1776 and employed six apprentices. Buch worked in the neoclassical style. He supplied four large silver chandeliers to the Winter Palace. He also made a solid-gold tea and coffee service for the wedding of Emperor

Paul I's daughter Grand Duchess Elena Pavlovna (1784–1803) that weighed 239 troy oz. (7,433 grams).

Hallmark: 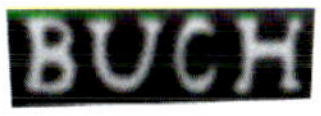

— *Bucknall, Charles Herbert (1864–1938)* —

Traded in gemstones with French partner Georges Sachs and acted as his representative at **8 Maksimilianovskii Lane** when Sachs lived abroad. The firm G. Sachs & C. H. Bucknall is also listed at **5 Lakhtinskaia Street**, along with Fabergé enameler Petrov and Fabergé designer François Birnbaum, and later at **3 Italianskaia Street**. Bucknall also supplied the firm of A. Tillander. He died in England.

Hallmark: ЧБ, ЧГБ

— *Firm of Pavel Buhré* —

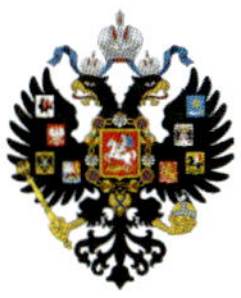

Founded by Swiss watchmaker Paul Eduard Buhré (1810–68), a merchant of the Third Guild in St. Petersburg. He set up shop in a building owned by Count Stroganov, at **23 Nevskii Prospect**. Around 1861, he became merchant of the Second Guild and received the grand ducal warrant of Maria Nikolaevna. His son, Pavel Leopold Karlovich (1842–1892 or 1897?), took the shop over upon his death. An Honorary Citizen, Pavel *fils* received the imperial warrant on January 14 and again on August 28, 1884, from Tsars Alexander II and Alexander III. Also in 1884, on April 14, he received title of purveyor to the grand ducal court of Vladimir Aleksandrovich and became valuer of the imperial cabinet, technician of the imperial Hermitage and consul of the Republic of Venezuela. On July 30, 1891, he received title of purveyor to the grand ducal courts of Vladimir Aleksandrovich for the second time, and of his brother Pavel Aleksandrovich. The Buhré firm enjoyed the patronage of the imperial family for decades. The tsar bought enormous quantities of pocket watches from Buhré as gifts to be distributed to artists and actors, and on state visits within the empire and abroad. After the death of Pavel Leopold (1897?), the firm passed into the hands of Jean Georges Pfund and Pavel Girard, Swiss watchmakers. Pfund and Girard were awarded the title of court purveyors in 1902, 1908 and 1909 and added branches in Moscow and Switzerland. Imported hundreds of thousands of timepieces from Switzerland for an annual revenue of seven million rubles around 1910.

Burchard, Edward (also Burhkardt) —

Active in St. Petersburg since 1889 as a jewelry, watch and clock retailer. One of the founders of the St. Petersburg Jewelry Society in 1911. From 1897 to 1904, Burchard was mentioned under the two addresses of **6 and 34 Nevskii Prospect**, the latter also occupied by the Grachev Brothers. See "Jewelers of St. Petersburg Unite!"

— *Buhler, Christian R. (b. 1855)* —

A citizen of Württemberg, he was supplier to the imperial court in the 1870s. In 1878 he owned a shop at **9 Bolshaia Morskaia Street** in St. Petersburg, where he traded in diamonds and jewels. The firm was later bought by his partner Carl Bock. See "Carl Bock: Jeweler Entrepreneur."

— *F. Butz Firm* —

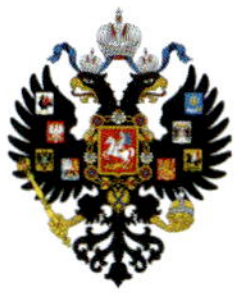

— *Butz, Friedrich Daniel (1820–82?)* —

One of the most prominent jewelry firms in St. Petersburg from the 1850s to the First World War. Founder and master jeweler in St. Petersburg, Friedrich Butz, along with Seftigen and Bolin, was appraiser to the imperial court. In 1849 he had a workshop on **Bolshaia Morskaia Street**. On May 8, 1863, he was awarded title of supplier to the court of Grand Duchess Alexandra Iosifovna (1830–1911), and on November 11, 1870, and October 25, 1870, he was awarded purveyor titles from Grand Dukes Vladimir Aleksandrovich and Alexis Aleksandrovich and Emperor Alexander II, respectively. In 1865, Grand Duke Alexander Aleksandrovich (future Tsar Alexander III) conferred the grand ducal warrant on Butz, which he upgraded to an imperial warrant upon his accession to the throne in 1881. Still listed at **25 Bolshaia Morskaia Street** in 1894. Son Julius Butz (1847–1912), a member of the Union of St. Petersburg Jewelers (See "Jewelers of St. Petersburg Unite!"), took the business over upon his father's death. Fellow student of Carl Fabergé at the Annenschule, a German secondary school, they traveled together in the mid-1860s throughout Europe. In 1896 the company was listed as Julius Butz & Co., jointly owned with Carl Oskarovich Engelman, an arrangement that lasted until 1908, after which time no mention is made of Engelman. Julius also received the title of purveyor to the imperial court.

Hallmark: FB

— *Cheriatov, Egor (Georgii) Kuzmich* — *(active 1900–17)*

Moscow silversmith and jeweler; owner of a factory of 15 workers in 1905; specialized in tableware, cutlery, glass vases, kovshs, vodka cups and enamel wares. He worked for Fedor Lorié, and several of his creations are housed in the Moscow Historical Museum.

Hallmark:

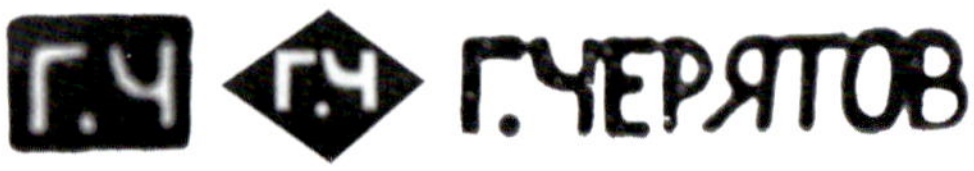

— *Chernokov, Nicholas Andreevich* — *(sometimes Chernakov)*

A Bolin workmaster with a workshop at **40 Liteinyi Prospect**, at the Bolin location, and **55 Moika Embankment**. Chernokov produced items for the Romanov tercentenary. See "Bolin: The Brightest Star."

Hallmark: 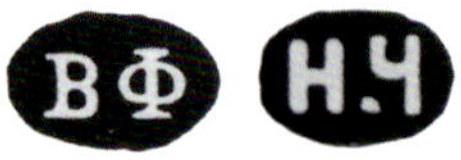

— *Chichelev (Tschitscheleff), Ivan Dmitrovich* — *(1815–88)*

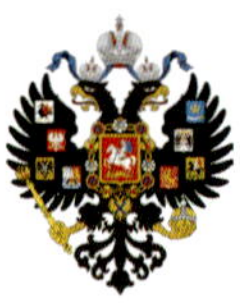

One of the best-known 19th-century jewelers in Moscow in the 1860s. At the Vienna's World's Fair of 1873, he won acclaim for a tiara set with sumptuous gemstones. The jeweler also exhibited in London, Philadelphia, Paris and St. Petersburg. He owned a gold and silver workshop specializing in gold jewelry in the Byzantine style. It is said he received the imperial warrant from the tsar as well as that of the Austro-Hungarian emperor Franz Joseph and King Victor Emmanuel of Italy.

— *Deichmann, Zacharias (1709–76)*—

Court silversmith for Empress Catherine the Great. He was admitted to the Guild of Foreign Masters in 1731 in St. Petersburg and in 1766 made a large silver service for Tsarskoe Selo. Some say he came from Olenets in northern Russia and was trained in Moscow.

Hallmark: 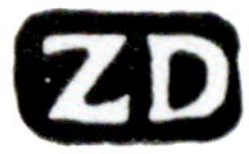

— *Denisov-Uralskii, Aleksei Kuzmich* — *(Kozmich) (active 1880s–1918)*

From Ekaterinburg, son of a stonecutter and specialist who operated a workshop in the Urals. He studied sculpture at the Ekaterinburg guild of sculptors in 1884, and at the St. Petersburg Society for the Encouragement of the Arts. Founder of A. K. Denisov-Uralskii & Co., a shop specializing in jewels, gold, silver and decorative hardstones at **27 Bolshaia Morskaia Street** after 1910. He won several prizes at shows for his creations, including a silver award in the 1887 Ekaterinburg industrial exhibition, and others in 1889 in Paris and 1890 in Kazan. His firm distributing minerals of Russia was located at **42 Moika Embankment**. A member of the Union of St. Petersburg Jewelers. See "Jewelers of St. Petersburg Unite!"

— *Dietwald, Eduard Fernandovich*— *(1868–1910)*

Owner of the firm Eduard. A specialist of medals, orders and diamond-set decorations, Eduard was purveyor for the Chapter of Imperial Orders in 1906 for three years and again in 1909. Located at **10 Nevskii Prospect**. The firm was continued by his widow, Vera Petrovna Dietwald, who joined the Union of St. Petersburg Jewelers. Eduard is mentioned in the January 1913 issue of their periodical, *Russkii iuvelir*.

Hallmark: ЭД, ЭФД, ВД

— *Drevsen, Johann Friedrich* —

St. Petersburg silversmith, member of the foreign guild in 1818. In 1849 he owned a workshop and produced silver for the imperial court.

Hallmark: 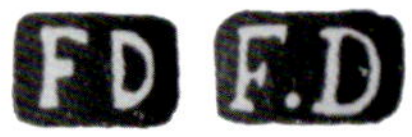

— *Drozhin, Mikhail Ivanovich* —

A St. Petersburg master silversmith in 1906 and merchant of gold and silver objects in 1911; merchant of the Second Guild and Honorable Hereditary Citizen. The store's addresses were **416 Apraksin Court** and **9 Karavannaia Street**. A former master with the Fabergé firm. See "Jewelers of St. Petersburg Unite!"

Hallmark: 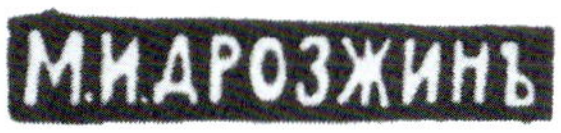

— *Duval, Louis David (1727–88)* —

Son of French Huguenots, born in Geneva. Duval arrived in St. Petersburg in 1753, partnered with Jérémie Pauzié in 1754, and became court jeweler to Catherine the Great and Paul I. He imported jewels, gold boxes and pinchbeck from the London firm of Rundell, Bridge and Rundell and was located at **24 Bolshaia Morskaia Street** (the same address as Carl Fabergé after 1900.) In 1789, he founded the firm Louis David and Son. He made the first smaller diamond coronation crown for Empress Consort Maria Fedorovna for the 1797 coronation of Paul I. His sons, Jacob David (1768–1844) and Jean Francois André (1776–1854), continued the business and made wedding jewels for all five daughters of Tsar Paul I.

— *Eckhardt, Georg Friedrich* — *(active 1730s–60s)*

According to archival documents it was Eckhardt, not Pauzié, who designed the final version of the great diamond crown for the coronation of Catherine II, while Jérémie Pauzié chose and set the gemstones. See "Jérémie Pauzié: A Jewel in the Crown."

— *Eckhardt, Johann (active 1820s–50s)* —

A jeweler from Latvia who in the 1840s founded a workshop in St. Petersburg and collaborated with Gustav Fabergé. He sold his business to Christian Buhler, who subsequently sold it to Carl Bock.

— *Fabergé, Gustav Petrovich (1814–94)* —

Goldsmith trained by court jewelers Andreas Spiegel and Johann Keibel. Moved to St. Petersburg from Reval (now Tallinn) in the 1830s and opened a shop. He added a posh accented *é* to Gallicize his original surname of Faberg in 1842. Father of Carl Fabergé. The workshop was located at **11 Bolshaia Morskaia Street** from 1842 to 1854. See "Fabergé in Perspective."

— *Fabergé, Carl Gustavovich (1846–1920)*

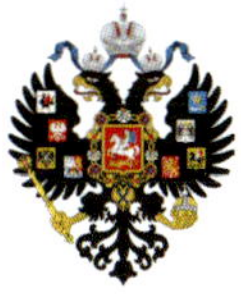

Imperial Russia's most celebrated goldsmith, son of St. Petersburg goldsmith Gustav Petrovich. His world-renowned firm created 50 Easter eggs for Tsars Alexander III and Nicholas II, to be presented to their consorts and Maria Fedorovna, as dowager empress after the death of her husband. Branches in Moscow, Kiev, Odessa and London. On May 1, 1885, he became purveyor to the imperial court of Tsar Alexander III, and on January 29, 1911, court jeweler for Tsar Nicholas II. Often, alongside the firm's hallmark, are the initials of St. Petersburg masters, some of whom, but not all, worked exclusively for the firm. Makers often associated with Fabergé are V. Aarne, F. Afanasev, H. Armfelt, A. Gorianov, A. Hollming, A. Holmström, E. Kollin, A. Nevalainen, G. Niukkanen, M. Perchin, O. Pihl, J. Rappaport, W. Reimer, T. and A. Ringe, V. Solovev, A. Thielemann, H. Wigström and the Väkeväs. See "Fabergé in Perspective."

Hallmark:

LONDON IMPORT: 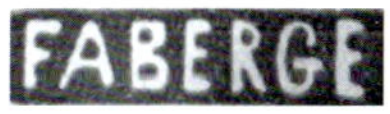

MOSCOW: 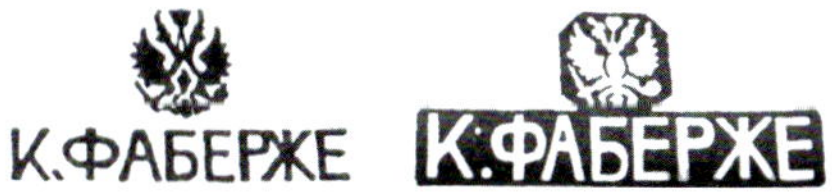

ST. PETERSBURG: 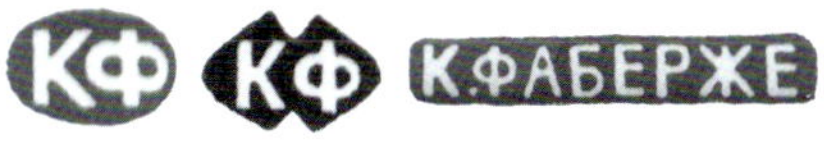

— *Finikov, Vladimir Iakovlevich (until 1916)* —

Bolin's chief jeweler, he owned a workshop from 1880 to 1892 at **55 Moika Embankment**. In 1897, he had 15 workers and made bracelets, brooches, cuff links, rings and cigar cases for 23,000 rubles. Finikov worked for Bolin from 1900 to 1908. In 1883, Mikhail Perchin, Fabergé's head workmaster, married Finikov's daughter. See "Bolin: The Brightest Star."

Hallmark: 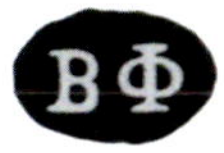

— *Fulda, Fedor* —

Moscow jeweler who received the title of purveyor to the court of Tsar Alexander II on August 28, 1866. M. Fulda & Sons (relation unknown) exhibited a jeweled butterfly, bracelets and other jewels, eliciting praise from the French jury, and was featured in a story in the official catalogue of the Paris Universal Exposition of 1867.

— *Galitzine, Vladimir Pavlovich* —

Owned a factory (workshop) of gold- and silverware in Moscow, which had three different locations between 1900 and 1917, ending at **5 Zvonarskii Street**. Is said to have partnered or collaborated with Moscow silversmiths Egor Cheriatov and Fedor Lorié.

Hallmark: ВГ

— *Gordon, Vladimir Alekseevich* —

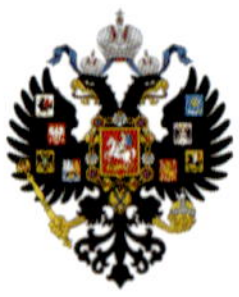

Prominent St. Petersburg silversmith, traded in gold, silver and jewelry in the **Gostinnyi Dvor, 40 Zerkalnaia** line. Said to have worked for both Fabergé and Bolin. On May 12, 1911, he received title of purveyor to the grand ducal and princely courts of Olga Aleksandrovna and Petr Aleksandrovich Oldenburg, respectively.

Hallmark: 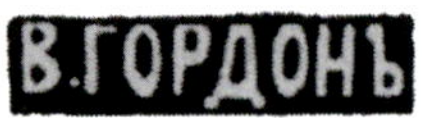

— *Gorianov, Andrei (active 1903–17)* —

Goldsmith worked for Carl Fabergé at **11 Bolshaia Morskaia Street**.

Hallmark: АГ

— *The Grachev Brothers* —

One of the most prominent silver firms in St. Petersburg, the Grachev Brothers were principal suppliers to the courts of Tsars Alexander III and Nicholas II. Silversmith Gavrill Petrovich Grachev (d. 1873) founded the factory in 1866. Upon his death, the business was passed on to his sons. After 1888, the firm participated in the All-Russia and World Art and Industrial Fairs and received prizes in international exhibitions, including the Columbian Exposition in Chicago (1893). In 1892, the company, then situated at **14 Pevcheskii Lane**, was granted the title of supplier to the imperial court. See "The Grachev Brothers: A Dynasty of Silversmiths."

— *Grachev, Mikhail Gavrilovich (b. 1863)* —

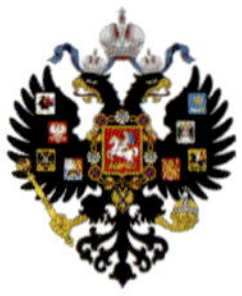

Creative force and eldest of Grachev Brothers Company in St. Petersburg. Appraiser to the imperial court in 1892, he was awarded several medals at international and Pan-Russian shows. He received title of purveyor to the grand ducal courts of Alexis Aleksandrovich (the future tsar) on December 7, 1882, and to Michael Nikolaevich on October 29, 1883. His shop was located at **34 Nevskii Prospect**. The firm became court suppliers in 1901. See "The Grachev Brothers: A Dynasty of Silversmiths."

Hallmark:

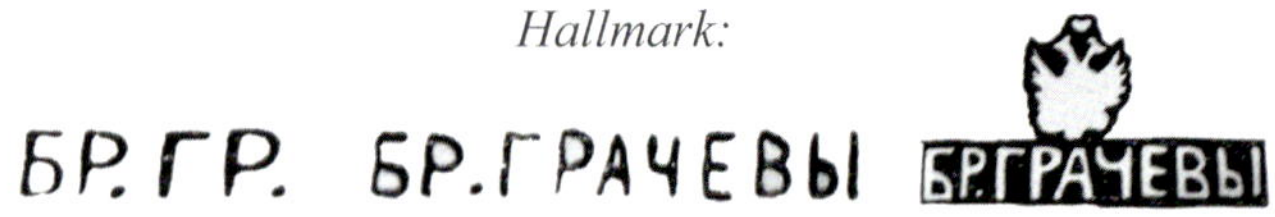

— *Graveraux (Gravero), Benoît — (1695 or 1700–1766)* —

Parisian-born court jeweler to Empress Anna Ioannovna. Trained one of Russia's most famous 18th-century court jewelers, Jérémie Pauzié. See "Jérémie Pauzié: A Jewel in the Crown."

— *Gubkin, Ivan Semyonovich* —

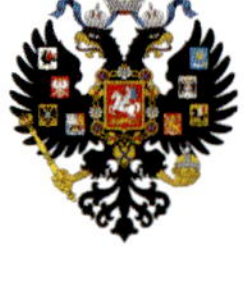

Founder of a silver factory in Moscow in 1841. Both he and his son, Dmitrii, received title of purveyor to the court, in 1855 and on May 5, 1868, respectively, from Tsar Alexander II. See "Ivan Gubkin: Master of the Trompe l'Oeil."

Hallmark:

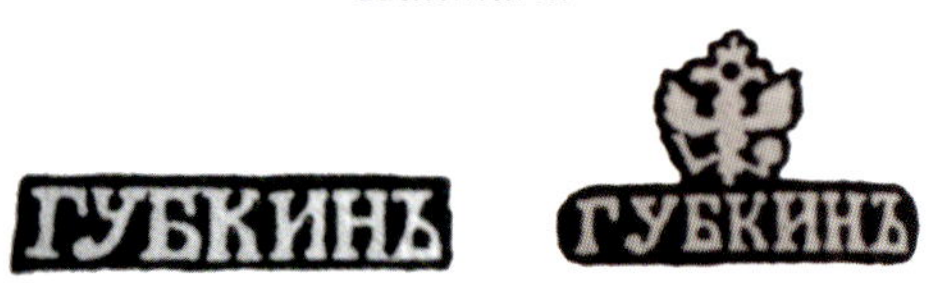

— *Gunst, Johann Aleksandrovich (1830–72)* —

Jeweler who first worked for Sazikov, then Gustav Fabergé. Upon his death his stock went to court jeweler Seftigen.

— *Hahn, Carl August Ferdinand (1836–?)* —

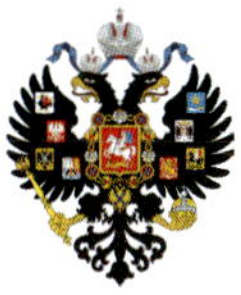

Austrian-born master court jeweler in St. Petersburg, Hahn created diamond decorations, necklaces, maid-of-honor badges, metropolitan crosses and gem-encrusted batons for the imperial court. His workshop was located on **26 Nevskii Prospect**. Hahn's greatest achievement was the diamond coronation crown of Empress Alexandra Fedorovna. On April 18, 1895, Hahn received the title of purveyor to the grand ducal court of Alexander Mikhailovich; on September 27, 1896, purveyor to the imperial court of Tsar Nicholas II; and on December 20 of the same year, the grand ducal warrant of George Aleksandrovich. His son, Dmitrii, received the same title of court purveyor on March 31, 1903, but died in 1911, forcing Hahn père to sell the shop to Alexander Tillander. Hahn's workmasters were Carl Blank and Alexander Treiden. See "Carl August Hahn: The Diamond King."

Hallmark: KG, КГАН, КГ

— *Helenius, Edward Ioannovich* —

Independent St. Petersburg goldsmith who worked for Fabergé in 1910. He owned a gold and silver workshop on **9 Demidov Lane**, the same address as workmaster Erik Kollin.

Hallmark: 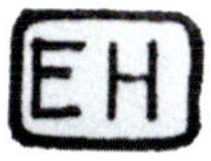

— *Hollming, August (1854–1913)* —

Born in Finland, Hollming was a Fabergé workmaster who qualified as a master jeweler in 1880. His workshop was located at **35 Kazanskaia Street** and moved to the Fabergé building when it opened in 1900 at **24 Bolshaia Morskaia Street**.

Hallmark: 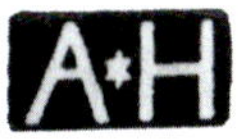

— *Holmström, Albert Augustovich (1876–1925)* —

A Fabergé workmaster, trained musician and master jeweler, Albert was the son of master jeweler August, with a workshop located at **36 Kazanskaia Street**. He took over his father's business after his death in 1903.

Hallmark: 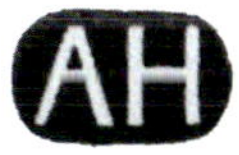

— *Holmström, August Wilhelm (1829–1903)* —

A Fabergé workmaster who, along with Wilhelm Reimer, was one of the early jewelers to work under Gustav Fabergé. Together with children Albert and Alma Pihl, his workshop created the famous Nobel ice jewels and Nobel Egg, a miniature of the imperial diamond regalia, the surprise to the Memory of Azov Egg (a miniature replica of the vessel on which the Tsarevich Nicholas sailed on his world tour), and several imperial eggs, including the third imperial egg of 1887 (rediscovered in 2013), the Diamond Trellis Egg of 1892 and the Mosaic Egg of 1914. His workshop was located at **36 Kazanskaia Street**.

Hallmark: 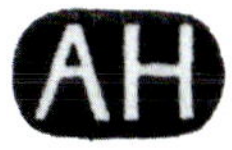

— *Holmström, Hilma Alina (1875–1936)* —

Employed as designer in her father's workshop (August Holmström). A graduate of the Baron Stieglitz School of Art.

— *Ivanov, Aleksander Dementevich* —

St. Petersburg goldsmith located at **32 Nevskii Prospect**. This jeweler is said to have purchased a 10-strand necklace of natural pearls from a convent for a low price, the sale of which subsequently made him a wealthy man. Ivanov also made an expensive imperial presentation box for Tsar Nicholas II, which was presented to the Emir of Bukhara in 1906 (see "Hahn Market").

Hallmark: 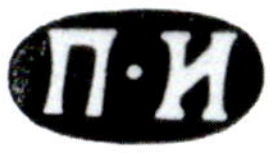

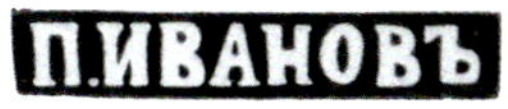

— *Jacobson, Evgenii Eduardovich (1877–1940)* —

A graduate of the Baron Stieglitz School of Art in St. Petersburg, Jacobson was a designer and miniature painter who specialized in the Siamese style and worked for Fabergé. Drew caricatures of Fabergé staff.

— *Jahn (Jan), Gottlieb Ernst (active 1812–36)* —

German goldsmith and forefather of the House of Bolin. Appraiser and jeweler to the imperial court of Tsar Alexander I. Was head of production in 1812 of Römpler's workshop, made partner of Römpler & Jahn, and like Carl Bolin, his future partner, married one of Römpler's daughters. See "Bolin: The Brightest Star."

Hallmark: GJ, GEJ

— *Kämmerer, Wilhelm Heinrich (1786–1854)* —

One of St. Petersburg most famous jewelers, also known as Kammerger, he specialized in diamond creations, orders and decorations from a shop on the **Nevskii Prospect**. His brother, Andrei Kämmerer, was the "court mineralogist" and a tutor of the tsar's children (the mineral kammerite was named in his honor). Appraiser to the imperial cabinet in 1835. Appointed court jeweler to Tsar Nicholas I in 1839, along with Carl Edvard Bolin and Sofia Jahn (widow of Gottlieb Ernest Jahn). Joined forces with Seftigen and won the highest honor: the Council Medal for a diamond-and-emerald bryony wreath and currant necklace at the Great Exhibition in London of 1851. Wilhelm Kämmerer and Johann Keibel were entrusted with the official orders and decorations in 1836. See "The Seftigens: Illustrious Swiss Court Jewelers."

— *House of Keibel* —

—*Keibel, Albert (active 1882–1910)* —

Produced enamel orders and decorations; a son of Julius. His workshop was located at **10 Bolshaia Zelenina Street**.

Hallmark: Keibel

— *Keibel, Johann Wilhelm (1788–1862)* —

Master goldsmith in St. Petersburg, son of court jeweler Otto Keibel. Johann took over his father's workshop and specialized in enamelware, including court decorations, church plate and snuffboxes. Keibel restored the coronation crown of Tsar Nicholas I in 1826, became head of the foreign guild in 1828, and received hereditary honorary citizenship in 1859. He was court purveyor for the Chapter of Imperial and Royal Orders. Wilhelm Kämmerer and Johann Keibel were entrusted with the official orders and decorations in 1836. His diamond creations garnered praise in the 1839 All-Russian Exhibition in St. Petersburg and won first prize along with Valliant in the same exhibition in 1849. He made numerous multirow diamond bracelets for Empress Alexandra Fedorovna and most likely produced the lavish diamond rivière that Tsar Nicholas I gave her in 1843 to mark their 25th wedding anniversary and the birth of their children. Gustav Fabergé (Carl's father) was one of Keibel's apprentices.

Hallmark: K, 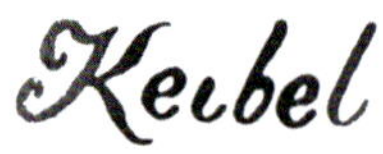

— *Keibel, Julius (1825–82)* —

A master jeweler since 1859, son of Johann Wilhelm, merchant of the First Guild, and Honorary Citizen, a title he inherited from his father. His home-workshop was located at **24 Bolshaia Zelenina Street** in St. Petersburg.

Hallmark: Keibel

— *Keibel, Otto Samuel (1768–1808)* —

Prussian court jeweler in St. Petersburg, one of the best of his time. Some of his work is kept in the Imperial Hermitage Gallery. His son Johann took over the workshop after his death.

Hallmark: 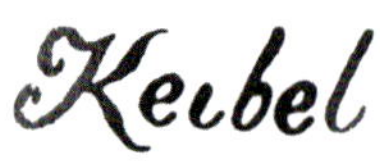

— *Khlebnikov, Ivan Petrovich* —

Master Moscow silversmith and founder of Khlebnikov, I. P. and Sons. Won awards at international and Russian expositions. as well as the grand ducal warrants of Constantine Nikolaevich and Elizabeth Fedorovna (Ella) on February 9, 1909. Khlebnikov could also count Empress Maria Fedorovna, Emperor Franz Joseph I and Tsar Alexander III as patrons. The firm also supplied the courts of the Danish, Dutch and Serbian kings. By 1910 the annual turnover had risen to 700,000 rubles, just behind that of Morozov and Fabergé. See "Ivan Khlebnikov: Enameler to the Tsars."

Hallmark: 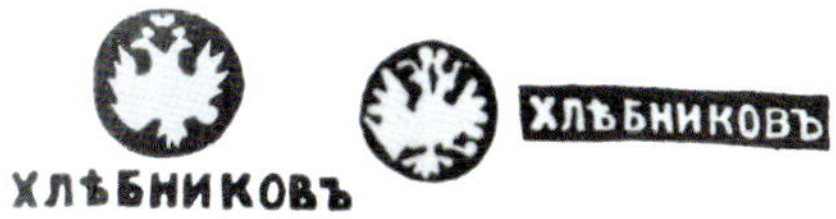

— *Klingert, Gustav Gustavovich* —

Enameler and silversmith, founded his firm in 1867, employed 55 workers, excelled in turquoise enamel with filigree scrolls and the "beehive" design in blue and white. Exhibited at the Chicago World Fair of 1893 under the name "G. Klingert J. Levitt."

Hallmark:

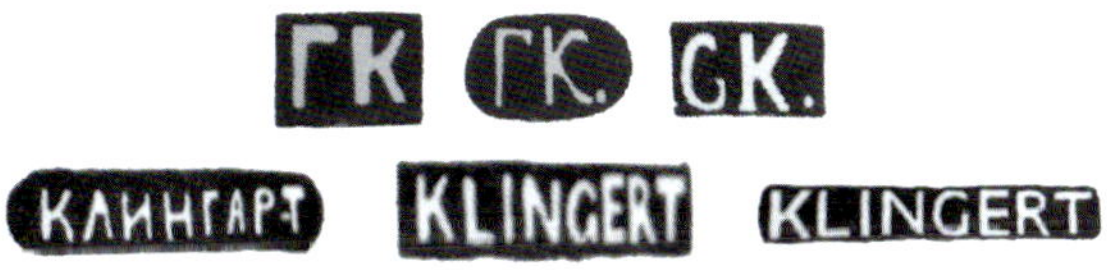

— *Köchli, Friedrich Christian (1837–1906)* — *(Fedor Ivanovich)*

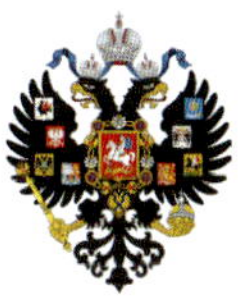

One of St. Petersburg's most prominent imperial jewelers during the reigns of Alexander III and Nicholas II. Köchli became court purveyor of the dowager empress on January 10, 1898, and of Grand Duke Vladimir Aleksandrovich on February 28 the same year, and of his consort, Grand Duchess Maria Pavlovna, on October 20, 1898. Followed by, on July 2, 1899, the individual grand ducal warrants of Serge Aleksandrovich, Paul Aleksandrovich and Maria Aleksandrovich, Duchess of Saxe-Coburg and Gotha. His shop was on **17 Gorokhovaia Street**. See "Friedrich Köchli: The Grand Dukes' Favorite."

Hallmark: 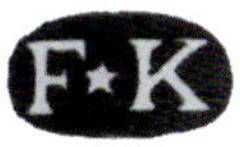

— *Köchli, Theodor Friedrich* — *(Fedor Fedorovich, active 1890s–1911)*

Son of Friedrich and co-owner of FI and FF Köchli. Theodor graduated from the Imperial Academy of Arts in 1890 and joined his father in the business until 1909, when the firm closed. See "Friedrich Köchli: The Grand Dukes' Favorite."

— *Köpping, Johann Friedrich (1718–83)* —

One of the finest 18th-century silver masters in Russia, Swedish-born Köpping was court silversmith to Empresses Elizabeth Petrovna and Catherine II for a period of 32 years. He was the son and apprentice of Claus Jacob, who, as one of the first masters of the foreign guild to settle the new imperial capital, arrived in St. Petersburg in 1718. Like his father, he became master of the foreign guild in 1748. Koepping made the Oranienbaum Service for presentation to the future Peter II by Elizabeth Petrovna.

Hallmark: JFK, J.F.K.

— *Kokhun, Robert Yakovlevich (b. 1807)* —

One of the owners of the building of Nicholls & Plincke, he was also an important silversmith for the firm. See "Nicholls & Plincke: Silver Purveyors to the Tsars."

Hallmark: PK, P.K.

— *Kolb, Friedrich Joseph (active 1806–26)* —

German born, arrived in St. Petersburg in 1793. Descended from a family of goldsmiths. Known as one of the finest gold and silversmiths of the time and received many orders from the imperial cabinet for the court of Tsar Alexander I, for whom he held the warrant from 1820 to 1825.

Hallmark: FK, JF Kolb à St. Petersbourg.

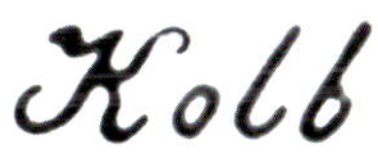

— *Kollin, Erik (1836–1901)* —

A Finnish goldsmith, he worked for August Holmström and then opened his own shop in 1870, about the same time that Carl Fabergé joined the family firm. Kollin produced the copies of ancient jewels, which gave Fabergé its initial triumph. He became head workmaster for Fabergé but was replaced in 1886 by Michael Perchin, his former employee. In 1898, he opened a workshop on **Demidov Lane** in St. Petersburg.

Hallmark: 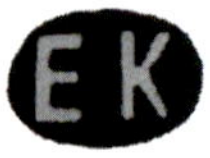

— Kortmann, Eduard Johann (1838–1904) —

Member of the Union of St. Petersburg Jewelers and supplier to the Russian imperial court, Kortmann owned a gold and silver workshop since 1848 (1869 according to another source). Located at **34, Nevskii Prospect, suite 12**, his firm is most renowned for producing enameled jetons, imperial badges and other fine gold objects, as well as for training over 400 medal engravers from 1870 to 1895. Kortmann excelled in guilloché enamel and was a chief rival of but also supplier for Fabergé. The jeweler received the Order of St. Stanislas, Third Class, and the Order of St. Anna, Second Class. See "Jewelers of St. Petersburg Unite!"

Hallmark: ЭК, КОРТМАНЪ

— Kurliukov, Orest Fedorovich —

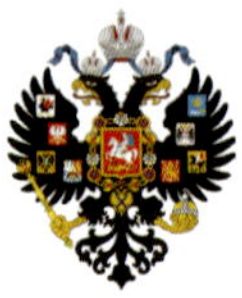

A Moscow merchant of the Second Guild. He worked with his father-in-law, Ivan Khlebnikov until he opened his own firm in 1879. Kurliukov was one of the best-known silver enterprises from 1884 to 1916. The firm collaborated with Fedor Rückert and Carl Fabergé. From 1892 to 1898 Kurliukov was a member of the supervisory board for production of gold and silver of the Moscow Commercial Court. In 1895 he received a medal from the Ministry of Finance. Nikolai Kurliukov continued the work of his father's firm. There were 40 employees in 1901 and 63 in 1907, and the turnover was 100,000 rubles. On July 31, 1903, he received the title of purveyor to the court of Tsar Nicholas II. See "Orest Kurliukov: Maestro of the Magical."

Hallmark: 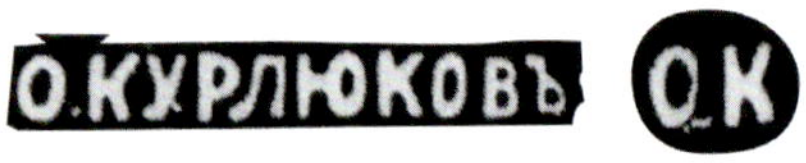

— Kuzmichev, Antip —

Founded a firm specializing in enamels in Moscow in 1856, much of which was exported to America and sold via Tiffany's and various department stores. The company produced plique-à-jour enamel but was better known for its mastery of champlevé.

Hallmark: AK

— Laksin —

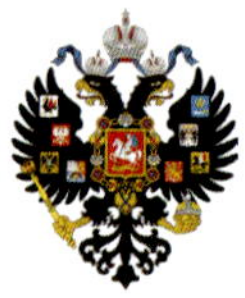

A jeweler from Tiflis who received the title of purveyor to the grand ducal court of Michael Nikolaevich on June 28, 1871.

— Linden, Nikolai Gustavovich — (active 1883 or 1888 to 1915)

Member of the Union of St. Petersburg Jewelers and hereditary honorary citizen, Linden opened a workshop dealing in gold, silver, watches, jetons and church plate in 1883 or 1888, trading under the name of Nikolai Linden & Co. at **83 Nevskii Prospect**. Linden was one of the few Russian jewelers, apart from Fabergé, who produced items for the Buddhist community and Siamese aristocracy. He received the imperial warrant from Tsar Nicholas II on May 29, 1912. See "Jewelers of St. Petersburg Unite!"

— Linke, Konstantin Eduardovich — (1865–after 1917)

Silversmith for Bolin and Lorié and eldest son of Maria Linke. He had his own workshop at **19 Kuznetskii Most** in Prince A. G. Gagarin's house. See "Bolin: The Brightest Star."

Hallmark: 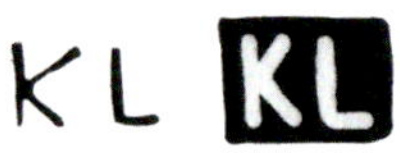

— Linke, Maria Ivanovna (active 1866–94) —

Bolin workmaster along with her husband, Carl. She employed 36 workers and supplied silver to Shanks & Bolin, Lorié and Fabergé before the firm opened its own Moscow shop. Owned a workshop from 1866 to 1894. Matriarch of a silversmith family, including sons Konstantin, Evgraf and Nikolai. See "Bolin: The Brightest Star."

Hallmark: 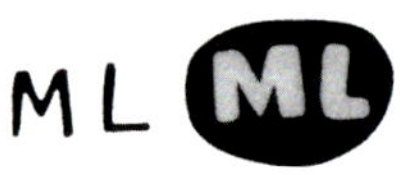

— Liubavin, Aleksander Benediktovich —

Founded his workshop in the 1850s and traded in silver with his mother at **Gostinnyi Dvor at 31 Zerkalnaia Line**. Although based in St. Petersburg, like Grachev he produced cloisonné enamelware. The firm received gold medals at the Nizhni Novgorod and Stockholm exhibitions in the 1890s. His son, Nikolai Aleksandrovich, carried on the business. Tsar Nicholas II conferred the title of purveyor to the court on Aleksander on July 26, 1900, and on his son Nikolai on August 8, 1905. The firm closed in 1917.

Hallmark:

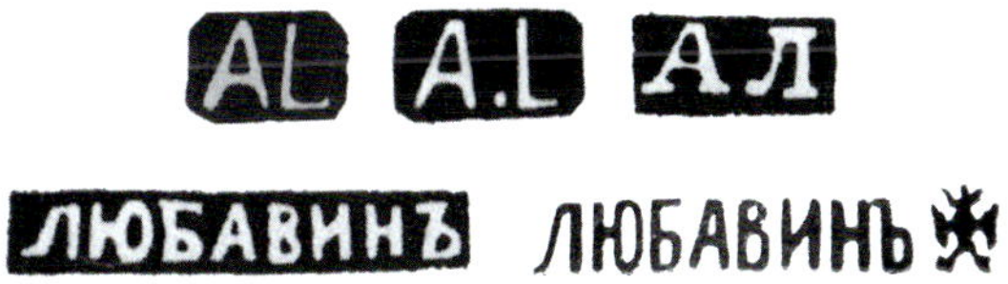

— Lorié, Fedor Anatolevich —

Owner of F. A. Lorié, a Moscow silver and jewelry firm active from 1871 to 1917, located at **4 Kuznetskii Most** in Moscow in the house of the Merchants' Society. Excelled in the art nouveau style, sometimes combined with French glass or en plein enamel.

Hallmark:

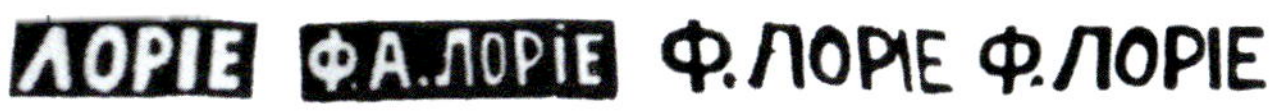

— Margolin, Ilia Berkovich —

Margolin was the imperial cabinet's most important supplier of precious stones and pearls at the turn of the 20th century. From 1887 to 1894, he provided 447,000 rubles worth of stones to the cabinet, and in 1890 alone his cache was worth 93,000 rubles. He provided many gems for snuffboxes and brooches to Fabergé for the 1896 coronation and, along with three other gem dealers, diamonds for the Fabergé imperial eggs.

— Marshak, Iosif Abramovich (1854–1918) —

Marshak opened a workshop in Podil, Ukraine, in 1878 and within a year had moved to the courtyard of 4 Kreshchatik in Kiev, joining dozens of other talented goldsmiths. In 30 years, I. Marshak grew into the most important gold and silver enterprise in Ukraine, producing artistic virtuoso silver centerpieces and jewels that compare in quality to works by Carl Fabergé. Marshak won numerous awards in All-Russian and international exhibitions and created magnificent gifts for the tsar. See "Iosif Marshak. The Cartier of Kiev" and "A Mysterious Monument by Marshak."

Hallmark:

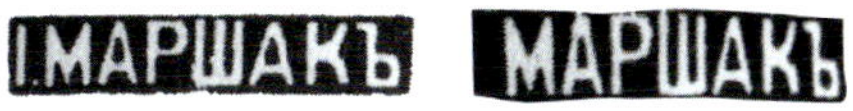

— Melik-Magamed-Bek-Gadzhi Iosif-Belk-Ogli —

Jewelers in Baku during the reign of Tsar Alexander II. On August 31, 1867, appointed purveyor to the court of Grand Duke Michael Nikolaevich, Viceroy of the Caucasus (1862–82).

— Meliksetbegov, Mikirtich —

Silversmith from Tiflis, awarded the imperial warrant by Tsar Alexander II on February 12, 1872.

— Miliukov, Petr Pavlovich — (active 1877–1912)

Miliukov owned a silver enterprise in Moscow from 1877 to 1912. In 1894 he employed 33 workers.

Hallmark:

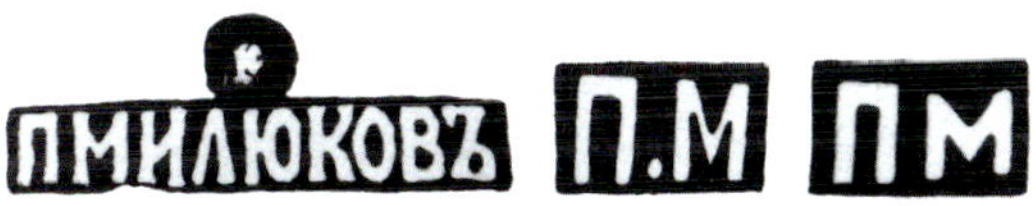

— Morozov, Ivan Ekimovich (1825–85) —

Master goldsmith founded I. E. Morozov in 1849 in **Gostinnyi Dvor** in St. Petersburg, which became the largest enterprise in the capital after Fabergé by 1904. Named supplier to the court in 1884. See "Ivan Morozov: Jeweler and Silversmith to the Tsar."

Hallmark: AH, B.M., JA, A.L.

— Morozov, Sergei Ivanovich —

Brother of Vladimir and silversmith, he owned a workshop on the silver row at **31 or 35 Nevskii Prospect** in St. Petersburg. See "Ivan Morozov: Jeweler and Silversmith to the Tsar."

Hallmark: CM

— Morozov, Vladimir Ivanovich — (active 1892–1908)

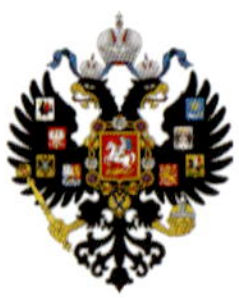

Member of the Union of St. Petersburg Jewelers and, in 1912, elected its chairman. Successor of Ivan Morozov. Continued the business for over 20 more years until his early death. Also sold silverware from the Warsaw firm of Hempel Brothers. The Morozov workshop was considered one of Russia's finest. See "Jewelers of St. Petersburg Unite!" and "Ivan Morozov: Jeweler and Silversmith to the Tsar."

Hallmark: BM

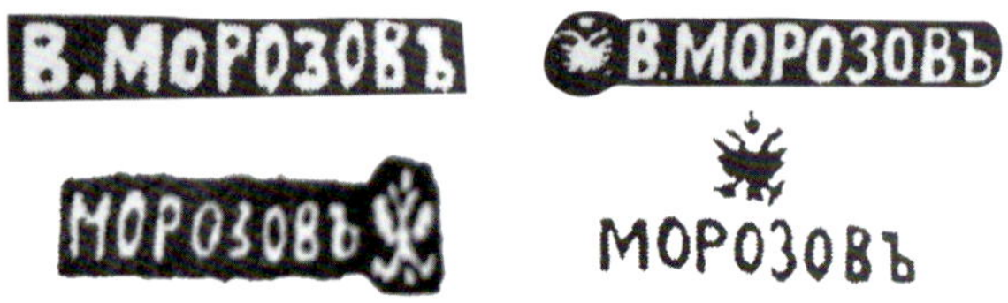

— Morozov, Maria Ivanovna —

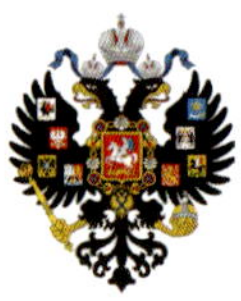

Widow of Sergei Ivanovich, she continued the silver business after his death and received title of purveyor to the imperial court of the tsar in 1912.

Hallmark: MM

— Nemirov-Kolodkin, Nikolai Vasilievich —

Founder of a prominent gold and silver enterprise in Moscow. The firm existed from 1872 to 1917 selling jewelry, silver, church utensils and icons. Nemirov-Kolodkin supplied jewels to the court of Grand Duchess Elizabeth Fedorovna (Ella), sister of Tsarina Alexandra Fedorovna and received the right to use her grand ducal warrant on January 8, 1910, and have fitted cases stamped with her crowned initials. His silver was also sold by Tiffany & Company in America.

Hallmark: H K

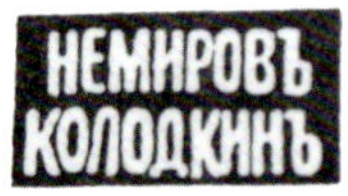

— Nevalainen, Antti (1858–1933) —

Finnish-born St. Petersburg silversmith active in St. Petersburg from 1885 to about 1909. He worked for Fabergé, at first in A. Holmström's workshop, then on his own. Located at **9 Demidov Lane** and **35 Kazanskaia Street**.

Hallmark:

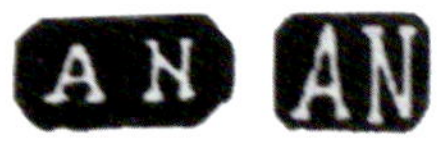

— Nicholls & Plincke (active 1804–1880s) —

Court jewelers for Tsar Nicholas I. Founded by Englishmen Constantin Nicholls and William Plincke, the firm was initially known as the Magasin Anglais. St. Petersburg's most successful jeweler in the first half of the 19th century, and famous for its English-style pieces, silver centerpieces, sumptuous gilded table services and English silver. The store was located at **14 Bolshaia Morskaia**. Employed goldsmith Samuel Arnd and silversmiths Robert Kokhun and Carl Tegelsten. See "Nicholls & Plincke: Silver Purveyors to the Tsars."

Hallmark:

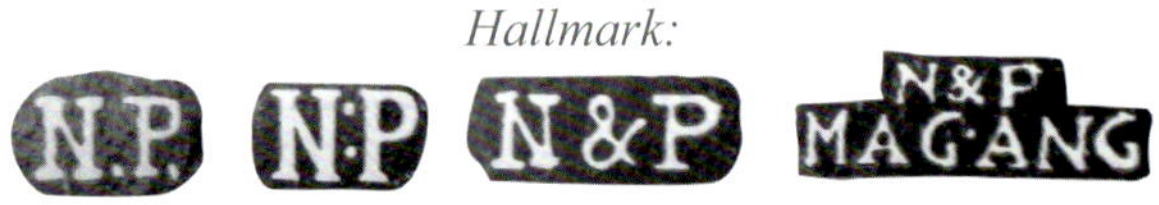

— Nicholls, Constantine (active 1829–52) —

English-born merchant of the First Guild and co-owner with William Plincke of Nicholls & Plincke (before 1854) of the Magasin Anglais. Became a Russian citizen in 1804 and named hereditary honorary citizen. See "Nicholls & Plincke: Silver Purveyors to the Tsars."

— *Nicholls-Ewing, Nicholas (b. 1839)* —

Founded Nicholls-Ewing, a St. Petersburg jewelry firm in the second half of the 19th century. Produced along with Bolin and Fabergé a parure for the wedding of Grand Duchess Xenia Aleksandrovna. He had a shop at **47 Bolshaia Morskaia Street**.

Hallmark: A H

— *Niukkanen, Gabriel (active 1889–1917)* —

Finnish master goldsmith located at **39 Kazanskaia Street** in St. Petersburg. He worked for Fabergé and managed his Odessa shop for a time. Niukkanen made miniature eggs and cigarette cases, some overlaid with a distinctive black enamel spiderweb design on gold.

Hallmark: 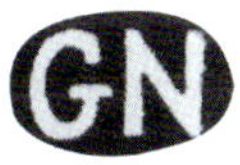

— *Olovianishnikov P. I. & Sons* —

A Russian merchant dynasty of Yaroslav descent, largest manufacturer of bells in the Russian Empire. This prominent enterprise, founded by Ilia Olovianishnikov, began in Yaroslav as a bell foundry in 1776, then flourished in Moscow in 1848 as a major supplier of church utensils, icons and other religious silver. Olovianishnikov P. I. & Sons opened a store in St. Petersburg, was Fabergé's greatest rival in ecclesiastical objects, and in 1909 was appointed suppliers to the imperial court. Designs were influenced by artistic director Sergei Vashkov. Turnover was 200,000 rubles in 1910. Located at **89 Gostinnyi Dvor**. The 1911 International Exhibition in Turin included objects from the firm.

Hallmark: 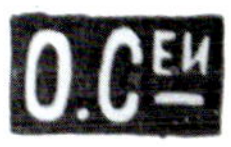

— *Olsonius, Johan Ferdinand (1823–88)* —

Born in Finland, became a master jeweler in Russia in 1852 and merchant of the Second Guild. Olsonius worked for the Grachev Brothers and is known for his silver masterpieces, including a series of engraved cartographic card cases. His shop was at **52 Nevskii Prospect**. See "The Grachev Brothers: A Dynasty of Silversmiths."

Hallmark: J.O

— *Osipov, Dimitrii Ivanovich — (1860–after 1917)*

A member of the Union of St. Petersburg Jewelers, from a family of jewelers with a firm in his own name. His workshop was located at **30 Gorokhovaia Street** in 1884. A merchant of the Second Guild, Osipov produced orders, jetons, badges and name plates and was court purveyor for the Chapter of Imperial Orders. He was a partner of Arnd from 1890 to 1900 and sold his firm to Adler in 1902. Also traded from **42 Ekaterinskaia Canal** in St. Petersburg.

Hallmark: ДО, ДИО

— *Ovchinnikov, Pavel (1830–81)* —

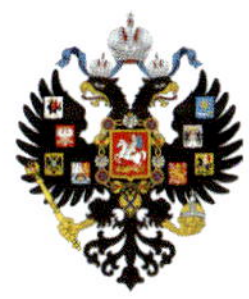

Moscow silversmith and enameler, he opened a workshop in 1853 and by 1881 had built a silver dynasty that was the largest in the Russian Empire. Received title of purveyor to the imperial court from Tsar Alexander III on August 18, 1881, and to the grand ducal court of Michael Nikolaevich on May 21, 1878. His sons (Mikhail, Alexei, Pavel and Nikolai) each received the title of court purveyors on May 17, 1894, and again on March 8, 1896. In St. Petersburg, Ovchinnikov occupied **35 Bolshaia Morskaia Street**. See "Pavel Ovchinnikov: From Serf to Silversmith."

Hallmark: 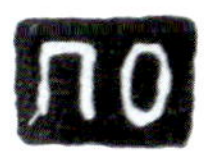

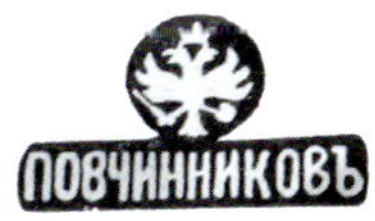

— *Pauzié, Jérémie (1716–79)* —

Legendary court jeweler to Empresses Elizabeth and Catherine the Great. Arrived on foot from Geneva at age 13 and apprenticed to Parisian diamond and gem master Benoît Gravereaux. Pauzié opened his first workshop in 1740 on **Artillereiskaia Street** in the Liteinyi District, just north of Nevskii Prospect. Produced gem-encrusted, chased gold snuffboxes and flower vases, imperial diamond orders and Catherine the Great's famous diamond coronation crown. Several of his creations are preserved in the Gold Treasury Room in the Hermitage. See "Jérémie Pauzié: A Jewel in the Crown."

— *Pendin, (Pontinen) Hiskias (1823–81)* —

Arrived in St. Petersburg from Finland as a boy and was apprentice to a goldsmith by 1840. Pendin worked for Gustav Fabergé and mentored his son Carl, instilling a high standard of quality in his pupil. When Gustav moved to Dresden in 1860, he took over the firm and had full responsibility for Carl's well-being.

— *Perchin, Michael Evlampevich (1860–1903)* —

Fabergé head workmaster of Russian nationality, Perchin was journeyman in the workshop of Erik Kollin, became a master jeweler in 1884 and opened a workshop at **11 Bolshaia Morskaia Street**. Created many Fabergé imperial Easter eggs, including the Serpent Clock Egg of 1895 and the Memory of Azov Egg of 1891, as well as numerous jeweled and enameled presentation boxes for the tsar. Perchin mastered the neo-Renaissance and rococo styles that made Fabergé famous.

Hallmark: 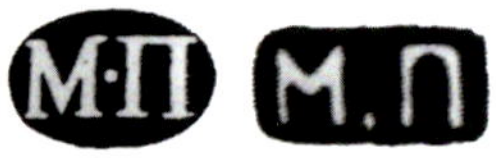

— *Pfisterer, Leopold (active 1760s–90s)* —

Viennese jeweler to Prince Dimitrii Mikhailovich Golytsin (Galizine), Catherine the Great's ambassador to the Habsburg court from 1762 to 1792. When Pauzié returned to Switzerland in 1764, Pfisterer replaced him as the empress's court jeweler. Worked in St. Petersburg for three decades, where he made several diamond crown jewels. See "The Fate of the Russian Crown Jewels."

— *Pihl, Alma Theresia (1888–1976)* —

Jewelry designer, niece and apprentice of Fabergé workmaster Albert Holmström. Designed the snowflake "Frost Flower" diamond jewels for Emanuel Nobel, as well as Fabergé's Winter Egg of 1913 and Mosaic Egg of 1914.

— *Pihl, Knut Oscar (1860–97)* —

Fabergé workmaster and former apprentice of August Holmström. Married August's daughter, Fanny Holmström, in 1887. That year, Carl Fabergé chose Pihl to head the newly opened jewelry workshop in Moscow, a position he held for 10 years until his death at the age of 37. Pihl's daughter, Alma Theresia, continued the Fabergé tradition in the family as designer for August Holmström's son, Albert.

Hallmark: 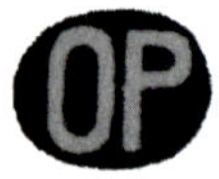

— *Pihl, Oscar, Jr. (1891–1959)* —

Like his sister, Alma Pihl, Oscar Jr. was designer for his uncle Albert Holmström (son of August). After the revolution he returned to Helsinki and worked for Tillander for many years.

— *Plincke, William (active 1829–52)* —

English-born merchant of the First Guild and owner with partner Constantin Nicholls of Nicholls & Plincke (before 1854 the Magasin Anglais). Became a Russian citizen in 1804 and named hereditary honorary citizen. See "Nicholls & Plincke: Silver Purveyors to the Tsars."

— *Postnikov, Andrei Mikhailovich* —

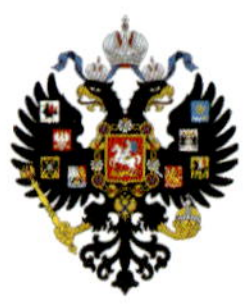

Founded an important factory in Moscow producing gold, silver and enameled items in 1868. Annual turnover was 250,000 rubles by 1870, with various workshops specializing in casting, forging and making simulated gemstones. Established a jewelry school in the 1870s and supplied the British crown and the Russian imperial court, receiving the right to display the imperial warrant on December 6, 1879. In 1883, he became purveyor to three grand ducal courts: Vladimir Aleksandrovich, Alexander Mikhailovich and Michael Nikolaevich. The firm participated in the All-Russian Industrial Exhibition in St. Petersburg in 1898.

Hallmark: АП, А. ПОСТНИКОВЪ

— *Rakhmanov, Nikolai Mikhailovich (b. 1840)* —

St. Petersburg goldsmith who owned a workshop in the former Sazikov factory. Like Fabergé in 1882, he won a gold medal on a St. Stanislaus ribbon. He later collaborated with Fabergé.

Hallmark: HP

— *Rappaport, (Isaac) Julius Abramovich 1851–1917)* —

Apprenticed for Fabergé in the 1880s, became a master and director of the Fabergé silver workshop at **9 Kazacheskaia Street** in St. Petersburg in the early 1900s. The workshop was bought by the Third Artel.

Hallmark: 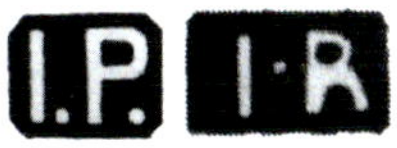

— *Razumnyi, Vladimir* —

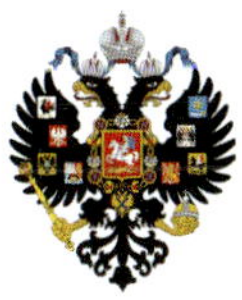

A gold- and silversmith from Sebastopol, and purveyor to the imperial court.

Dates and Hallmark: unknown

— *Reimann, Jan* —

A member of the Union of St. Petersburg Jewelers, Reimann opened a shop in the 1840s at **31 Nevskii Prospect**, selling popular jewels, including brooches in the form of butterflies and beetles, Ural gems, bohemian garnets, gold, silver and watches. His son **Zdenek Ivanovich** ran a shop in the **Gostinnyi Dvor** in the early 20th century.

Hallmark: ЯР

— *Reimer, Wilhelm Carl (1835–1908)* —

Master craftsman and workshop owner from Pernau, Estonia, Reimer also worked for Gustav Fabergé at **11 Bolshaia Morskaia Street** until 1901. His father, Heinrich Reimer, married Gustav Fabergé's sister, Carolina.

Hallmark: 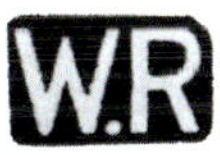

— *Ringe, Anna Carlovna (1840–1912)* —

Widow of Friedrich-Theodor Ringe, Anna took over the shop after his death in 1894 and worked for Fabergé from several independent St. Petersburg workshops, which changed location over the years.

— *Ringe, Friedrich Theodor (1824–94)* —

Became a master goldsmith in St. Petersburg in 1882 and worked for Fabergé as an independent master. His workshop was located at one time at **12 Malaia Morskaia**.

Hallmark: 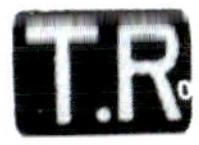

— *Römpler, Christoph Andreas — (Andrei Grigorevich, active 1790–1829)* —

German-born jeweler and diamond merchant in St. Petersburg, forefather of the Bolin dynasty and father-in-law of Carl Edvard Bolin, he was appraiser to the court of Tsar Alexander I. See "Bolin: The Brightest Star."

Hallmark: CR, CAR

— *Rokhumovskii, Israel (1860–1934)* —

Brilliant and reclusive goldsmith from Odessa whose talents reproducing ancient gold artifacts unwittingly fooled the Louvre. See "Israel Rokhumovskii and the Case of the Counterfeit Crown."

— *Rückert, Friedrich Mauritz — (Fedor Ivanovich) (1840–1917)*

One of Russia's greatest enamelers, Rückert moved from Alsace Lorraine to the ancient capital of Moscow at the age of 14 and worked with his five sons as an independent silversmith and supplier to Fabergé, Ovchinnikov and Kurliukov in Moscow and to Marshak in Kiev. Around 1908 his style changed from pastel-colored enamels indistinguishable from those of his Moscow contemporaries to darker hues, more intricate cloisonné work and the inclusion of miniature en plein enameled scenes in the Russian revivalist style, some based on paintings by Victor Vasnetsov and Konstantin Makovksii.

Hallmark: 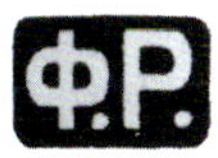

— *Sachs, Georges Abraham (d. 1920)* —

French jeweler, lived abroad from 1896. Proxy to Charles Herbert Bucknall, **8 Maksimilianovskii Lane**, "trade in diamonds and gemstones." In 1911, Bucknall, a British citizen, is listed as residing at **5 Lakhtinskaia Street**. Georges Sachs was a merchant of the First Guild, renowned for his purchase in 1906 of precious gemstones from the imperial cabinet for 1,075,000 rubles, outbidding both Bolin and Fabergé. His Paris office was at 35 rue du Chateaudun. He was known to have dealings with both Fabergé and Bolin before 1906.

Hallmark: GS

— *Saltykov, Ivan Dmitriievich*—

Renowned Moscow silversmith who founded a workshop in 1884 and produced enameled silver for various venues, including Fabergé. By 1897, his firm employed 23 workers and eight apprentices.

Hallmark: ИС, ИДС

— *Sazikov, Ignatii Pavlovich (1793–1868)* —

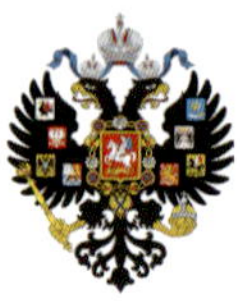

Son and successor of Pavel Fedorovich, became purveyor to the imperial court in 1837 for Tsar Nicholas I and again on November 16, 1857, for Tsar Alexander II. His son, Valentin, continued the business in St. Petersburg at **29 Bolshaia Morskaia Street**. See "Sazikov: The Pioneers."

Hallmark: CAC,

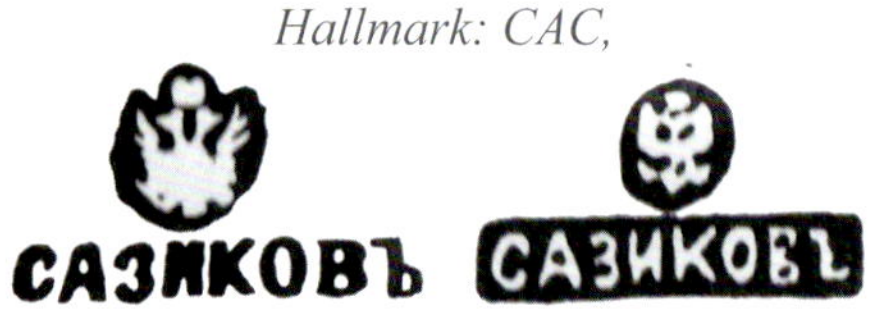

— *Sazikov, Pavel Fedorovich* —

Father of Russia's silversmiths. In 1793 founded one of the empire's finest silver firms. Received a gold medal in the 1849 All-Russian Exhibition in St. Petersburg. See "Sazikov: The Pioneers."

Hallmark: CAC

— *Sbitnev, Grigorii Mikhailovich* — (active 1893–early 20th century)

Owner of a business manufacturing gold, silver and shaded enamelware in Moscow. In 1897, he had 40 workers and a turnover of 100,000 rubles.

Hallmark: Г. С, ГС

— *Schramm, Eduard Wilhelm (b. ca. 1850)* —

Independent German-born master goldsmith who specialized in hammered gold with cabochon sapphires and supplied Bolin and Fabergé. In 1900 his address was **20 Nevskii Prospect**; in 1906, **31 Bolshaia Koniushennaia Street** in St. Petersburg.

Hallmark: 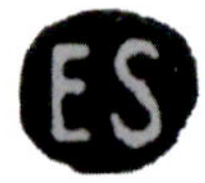

— *Schubert, Carl Reinhold (Ivanovich)* — (active 1844–80)

Goldsmith and jeweler from Germany who founded the Schubert firm in St. Petersburg in 1844. Alexander Tillander worked as journeyman in his shop when it was located on Gorokhovaia Street in the mid-19th century.

— *Schubert, Edward-Wilhelm (1819–1903)* —

Gold master jeweler from 1867 with a shop at **7 Vladimirskii Prospect**. In 1868 he was listed in the Merchant Handbook as 49 years old, guild member, paid dues from second half of 1866, temporarily merchant of the Second Guild. He was awarded a gold medal on Stanislav ribbon as chief jeweler of K. E. Bolin, at the close of 1882 All-Russian Exhibition in Moscow.

— *Schubert, Eduard Karlovich* —

A member of the Union of St. Petersburg Jewelers, Schubert was a master goldsmith whose family firm was founded in 1844, probably by his father, Carl Reinhold Schubert. Schubert had various locations: in 1895 and 1896 at **29/31 Italianskaia Street**, and at the turn of the 20th century at **42**

Moika Embankment, not far from the Yusupov Palace. From 1911 onward, his name appears in the Merchant Handbook, as merchant of the Second Guild. He also traded in diamonds and gold and made jewelry for Empress Maria Fedorovna and her son Grand Duke Paul Aleksandrovich. He took his own life in 1912. See "Jewelers of St. Petersburg Unite!"

Hallmark: ЭШ, ЭКШ

— *Schwan (Schwen), Robert Fedorovich (Friedrikhovich)* —

Goldsmith working exclusively for Bolin, Schwan created exceptional jewels for aristocracy and the imperial court. Awarded a silver medal at the Pan-Russian Exhibition of Industry and the Arts in Moscow in 1882. His son, Robert Robertovich Schwan (in 1915 an engineer at the Putilov Factory), was among founding members of the Russian Gemstone Society (*Russkie Samotsveti*) together with A. K. Denisov-Uralskii, K. F. Verfelemi and others. See "Bolin: The Brightest Star."

Hallmark: 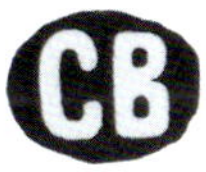

— *Schwan (Schwen), Sophia Ivanovna (active 1898–1917)* —

Gold and silver master at **55 Moika Embankment**. Widow of Robert; continued the business and excelled in invisibly set diamond mounts for Bolin. See "Bolin: The Brightest Star."

Hallmark: 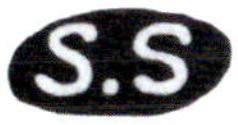

— *Seftigen (Zeftigen, Saefftigen), Adolf Leopold (Leopold Carlovich) (1821–88)* —

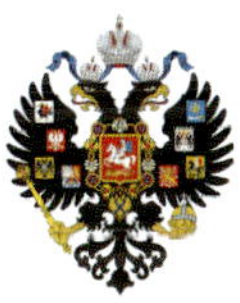

Leopold was famous for making a diamond crown for the coronation of Maria Aleksandrovna and Alexander II in 1855, now in the Diamond Fund in the Moscow Kremlin. At the Crystal Palace Exhibition of 1851 in London, his firm (as Kämmerer and Seftigen) won the Council Medal (the highest prize) for a diamond-and-emerald bryony wreath and currant necklace. Leopold Seftigen was appointed supplier to the imperial court on December 23, 1859; appraiser of the imperial cabinet two years later; and in 1869 jeweler of His Imperial Majesty. Also purveyor to the grand ducal courts of Alexandra Iosifovna, Constantine Konstantinovich and Vladimir Aleksandrovich in 1891 and 1895, respectively. Along with C. E. Bolin, Seftigen was a leading maker of gold and enamel presentation boxes during this period. His son, Julius Otto Seftigen, inherited the business, retaining the title of appraiser of the imperial cabinet and added a workshop at **16 Nevskii Prospect**. *Russkii iuvelir* magazine in 1914 notes that Leopold Seftigen in 1880 was the richest jeweler in St. Petersburg. See "The Seftigens: Illustrious Swiss Court Jewelers."

Hallmark: ЛЗ, ЗЕФТИГЕНЪ

— *Seftigen (Zeftigen, Saefftigen), Carl Emmanuel* —

From Switzerland, Carl arrived in St. Petersburg in the 1830s. He came from a long line of jewelers in his native land. Carl married Elizaveta Eleonora (née Spiegel), who was probably the sister of Andreas Spiegel, a court jeweler who had apprenticed with Seftigen. His sons Leopold and Constantin continued the business. See "The Seftigens: Illustrious Swiss Court Jewelers."

— *Seftigen (Zeftigen, Saefftigen), Constantin Friedrich (Constantin Carlovich) (Active 1840s–1899)* —

Brother of Adolf, also active in the business.

— *Seftigen (Zeftigen, Saeftigen), Julius Otto — (1860–1914)*

Son of Leopold, in 1903 he was located at **52–24 Kazanskaia Street** in St. Petersburg. Continued his father's business until 1895, then he became an appraiser in St. Petersburg Lending Treasury. In 1889, Julius Otto Seftigen, 28 years of age, is listed as keeping shop at **16 Bolshaia Morskaia Street**.

— *Semenov, Vasilii Semenovich* —

A silversmith, he founded his workshop in Moscow in 1852 and participated in important exhibitions in Paris and St. Petersburg (1867 and 1870), among others. He is best known for his fine nielloed designs.

Hallmark: 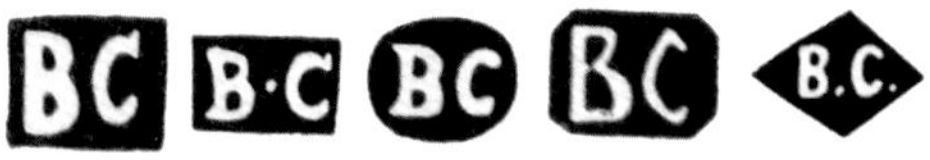

— *Semenova, Maria Vasilevna* —

Maria inherited the workshop of her father, Vasilii Semenov, in 1896. She specialized in shaded enamel kovshs, small bowls, boxes and spoons of floral design, often in pastel colors. The business continued until 1917 in Moscow and was said to have 100 employees at one time. Her wares are highly sought after.

Hallmark: 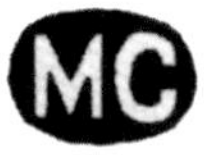

— *Shanks, James Stuart (1826–1911)* —

British-born merchant, joint owner of Shanks & Bolin, Magasin Anglais, with Henrik Bolin, founded in Moscow in 1852. After Bolin's death in 1888, Shanks opened his own firm specializing in silver, accessories and diamond jewels under the name **Shanks & Co.**

Hallmark: 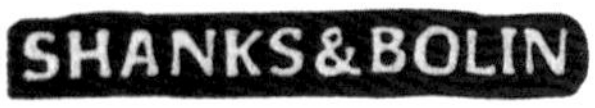

— *Siepel, Carl Adolf (1820–91)* —

St. Petersburg silversmith active between 1846 and 1876. Carl owned a workshop on **4/6 Chubarov Lane**, not far from the Moscow train station, where he had 20 apprentices.

Hallmark: 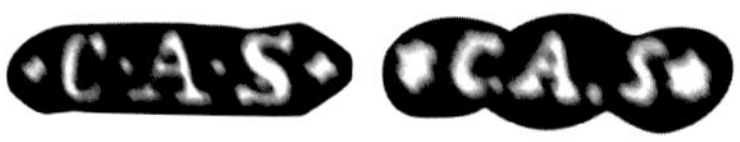

— *Smirnov, Dmitrii Lukich* —

Founder of a silver workshop in Moscow in 1883 specialized in tableware, church utensils and religious icons. In 1912, he had 15 workers and was granted the title of supplier to the imperial court.

Hallmark: Д. С.

— *Sokolov, Aleksander Nikolaevich* — *(active 1858–?)*

St. Petersburg silversmith who established his workshop in 1858, producing silver, gold and bronze items. Recorded a turnover of 75,000 rubles and a staff of 50. Items with his stamp from as late as the 1890s appear on the market. In February 1873, a silversmith named Andrei Nikolaevich Sokolov, possibly a brother, received the imperial warrant from Tsar Alexander II. The quality of Sokolov's creations is high, and, of those that survive at least, whimsical and in the Old Russian taste.

Hallmark: А. СОКОЛОВЪ

— *Spiegel, Andreas Ferdinand (1797–1862)* —

Apprenticed with Carl Emanuel Seftigen. A master goldsmith in St. Petersburg, Spiegel trained Gustav Fabergé (Carl's father). Spiegel made chased gold snuffboxes, some set with miniatures, others with gemstone mosaics and won a prize at the All-Russian Industrial Art Exhibition of 1829.

Hallmark: 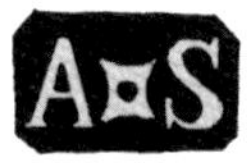

— *Spiegel, Annette (active 1867–?)* —

Widow of Andreas, she took over his workshop and was listed in 1867 as a merchant of the Second Guild with her own hallmark. A gold wedding parure in the form of myrtle branches by Spiegel is illustrated in *Jewels from Imperial St. Petersburg*, while a suite of jewels by Spiegel was illustrated in the All-Russian St. Petersburg Exhibition catalogue of 1870.

Hallmark: А Ш

— *Stang, Ferdinand Gotthard (1780–1821)* —

Exceptional silversmith born in Reval (now Tallinn), who arrived in St. Petersburg in 1806, joining the foreign guild and later becoming a Russian citizen. His widow and son carried on the workshop after his early death.

Hallmark: 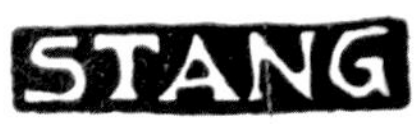

— *Sumin, Avenir Ivanovich* —

Lapidarist and owner of a hardstone workshop begun by his father, Ivan (d. 1894), with shops first located at **46 Nevskii Prospect** and then **60 Nevskii Prospect** after 1911. He sold and restored engraved gemstones for the Russian imperial court.

Hallmark: АС, АИС, СУМИНЪ

— *Tegelsten, Carl Johan (1798–1852)* —

Born in Finland, Tegelsten immigrated to St. Petersburg in 1817 and became a master silversmith in 1833. Owned a silver and bronze factory and made the wedding silver services for several daughters of Tsars Nicholas I and Alexander II. Worked for Nicholls & Plincke. The business continued under his widow, Eva Elisabeth Lönnquist, and son Carl Julius Tegelsten until 1855. See "Nicholls & Plincke: Silver Purveyors to the Tsars."

Hallmark: CT, C.T

— *Thérémin, Pierre Etienne (1764–1802)* —

A Huguenot born in Prussia, Thérémin was apprenticed to his brother, Francois-Claude, in Berlin as engraver and jeweler and settled in St. Petersburg in 1793, joining the foreigners' guild. Became jeweler to the imperial court, specializing in enameled classical themes or *garlanderie*, which was popular in Geneva. Produced four gold boxes in 1801 for Tsar Alexander I for 1,580 rubles. Thérémin married Marianne Jacqueline Renée Duval, daughter of Russian court jeweler Louis Duval, in 1794. Left St. Petersburg in February 1799, although the business continued until 1801.

Hallmark: 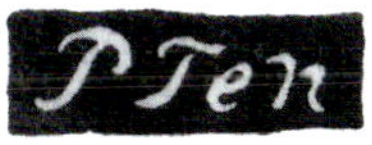

— *Thielemann, Alfred Rudolf (active 1898–1909)* —

Inherited a workshop in St. Petersburg making medals and badges from his father, Carl Rudolf. In 1894 Alfred's shop was listed at **11 Bolshaia Morskaia Street**, where he worked for Fabergé. Other sources list a workshop at **18 Nevskii Prospect**, in the same building previously occupied by Samuel Arnd.

Hallmark: 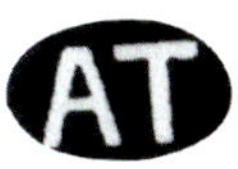

— *Tillander, Alexander Edvard (1837–1918), and Alexander Theodor (1870–1943)* —

Alexander Edvard, Finnish-born jeweler, opened a workshop in St. Petersburg in 1860. Located on the **corner of Bolshaia Morskaia and Gorokhovaia Streets**, the firm was patronized by Dowager Empress Maria Fedorovna, Grand Duchess Olga (the tsar's sister) and many of the Russian grand dukes, including all the family members of Grand Duke Boris Vladimirovich (1877–1943), third son of Grand Duke Vladimir Aleksandrovich. Alexander Theodor bought Hahn's lease in 1911. See "The Tale of Tillander."

Hallmark: 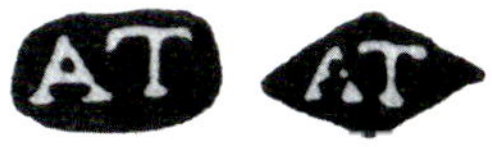

— *Treiden, Aleksander Aldolfovich (1858–?)* —

Member of the Union of St. Petersburg Jewelers. Hahn's head workmaster along with Carl Blank; produced many important imperial presentation pieces. Located at **42 Nevskii Prospect**, Treiden excelled in gold and enameled *objets*, including triptychs and kovsh. See "Carl August Hahn: The Diamond King."

Hallmark: AT, AAT

— *Utkin, Georgi Ivanovich (1870–?)* —

A board member of the Union of St. Petersburg Jewelers in 1912, with a retail shop at **7 Vladimirskaia Street**, advertising "fortuitous [*sluchainye*] brilliants, gold and silver objects." Merchant of the Second Guild and supplier to the court. See "Jewelers of St. Petersburg Unite!"

Hallmark: ГУ, ГИУ

— *Vaillant, Jean-Baptiste (1814–92)* —

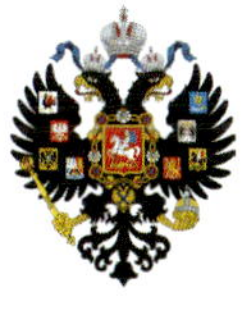

Born in France, the jeweler became famous for his massive silver compositions, including presentation trophies and candelabra, as well as precious stone jewels of refined taste and excellent workmanship. Arrived in St. Petersburg in the 1840s and set up shop on **Italianskaia Street** and in 1867 at **32–34 Nevskii Prospect**. The imperial court commissioned silver from him beginning in 1848, and he received a gold medal for his creations in the All-Russian Exhibition in St. Petersburg in 1849. The imperial cabinet granted the firm Jean Valliant & Gilles de Villefin the imperial warrant on November 11, 1891.

— *Väkevä, Stefan (active 1856–1917), and Aleksander Väkevä (1870–1957)* —

Born in St. Petersburg, Aleksander trained as a silversmith with his father, Stefan, whose workshop supplied Fabergé with silver flatware, tea services and large presentation items. After his father's death in 1910, Aleksander took over the business and produced items in silver, gold, enamel and hardstone.

Hallmark: 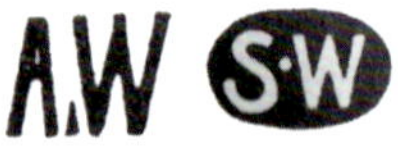

— *Vasilev, Vasilii Vasilevich* —

Vasilev registered for a hallmark in St. Petersburg in 1874 and owned a gold workshop at **40–26 Ekaterinskii Canal**.

Hallmark: BB, BBB

— *Verkhovtsev, Fedor Andreevich (1804–67)* —

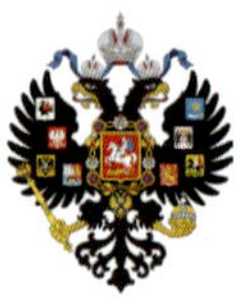

Leading producer of ecclesiastical works in St. Petersburg, including silver and jeweled icon covers, altar crosses and Bible covers. He won a silver medal in the Moscow All-Russian Exhibition of 1831 and founded his workshop producing gold, silver and bronze items. His son, Sergei Fedorovich (1843–93), an Academy of Arts graduate, continued the business as a silver enterprise. Named purveyor to the imperial court on October 10, 1871. In 1881 the turnover was 113,500 rubles.

Hallmark: Ф.В., ФВ, ФВЕРХОВЦЕВЪ

— *Weide, Rudolf Konstantinovich — (active 1874–1915)*

A board member of the Union of St. Petersburg Jewelers, Weide, who was born in Estland (now Estonia), was a goldsmith and silversmith with workshops at **74 Nevskii Prospect** and also, and from 1910 onward, at **53 Gorokhovaia Street**. In 1899, he was elected deputy examiner of trade establishment as the official of assay supervision. His firm was still listed in city merchants guide in 1917.

Hallmark: PB, PKB

— *Wigström, Henrik (1862–1923)* —

One of Fabergé's most famous workmasters, he first had a workshop at **11 Bolshaia Morskaia Street** before moving into **24 Bolshaia Morskaia Street**, the flagship store in 1900. Wigström was responsible for most of the tsar's imperial Easter eggs for 1904–1917. See "Fabergé in Perspective."

Hallmark: 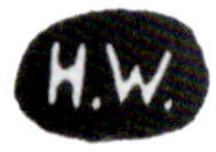

— *Zaionchkovskii, Valery Andreevich — (active 1860–72)*

Workshop manager of Gustav Fabergé from 1860 to 1872, after which Gustav's colleague Henkias Pendin took over, followed by his eldest son, Carl Fabergé (in 1882). A diamond merchant, he was registered at **16 Bolshaia Morskaia Street**, along with the court jeweler Leopold Seftigen, and from 1867 was also listed at **20 Bolshaia Morskaia Street, Apartment 6**.

Hallmark: B3, BA3

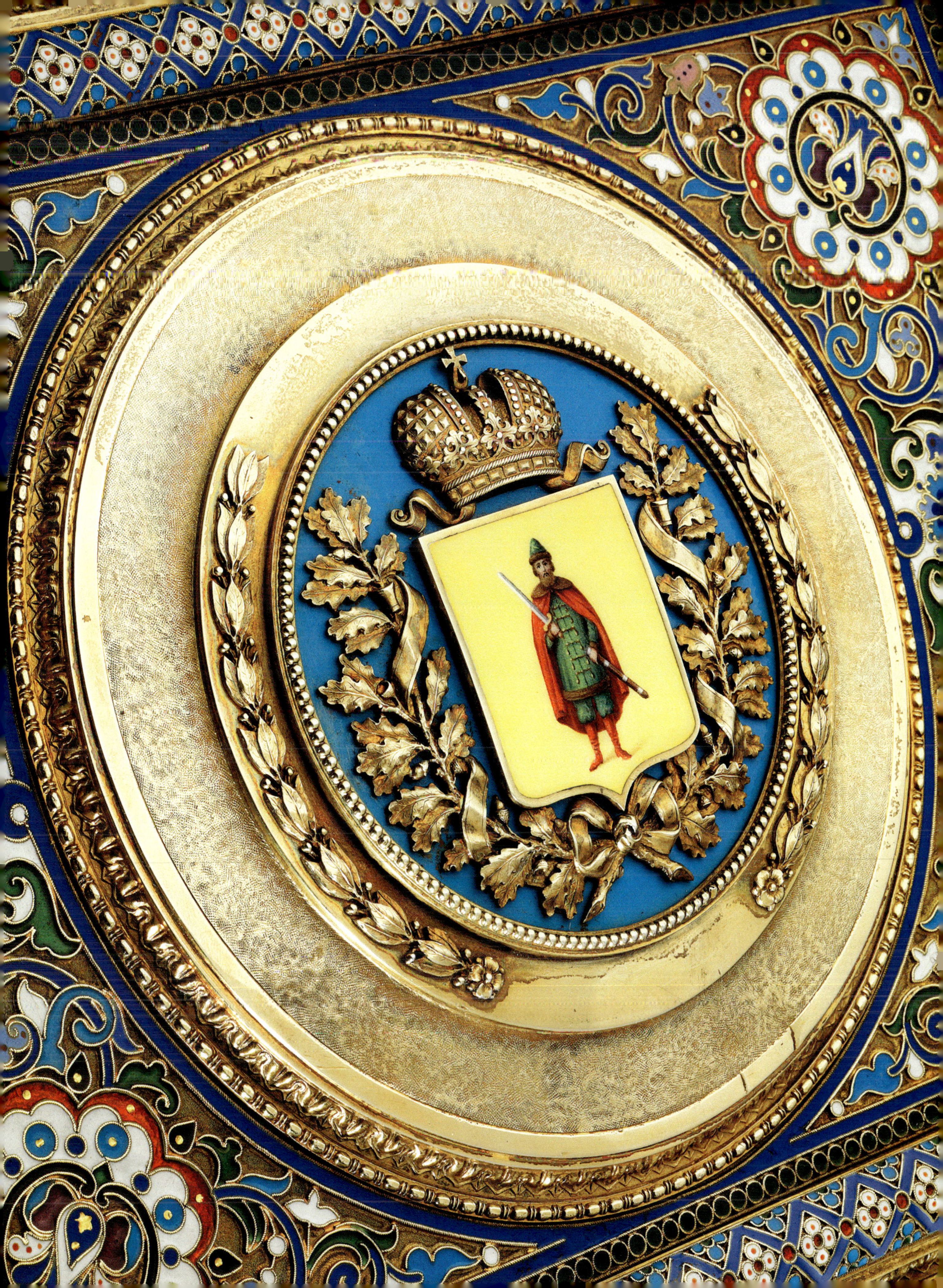

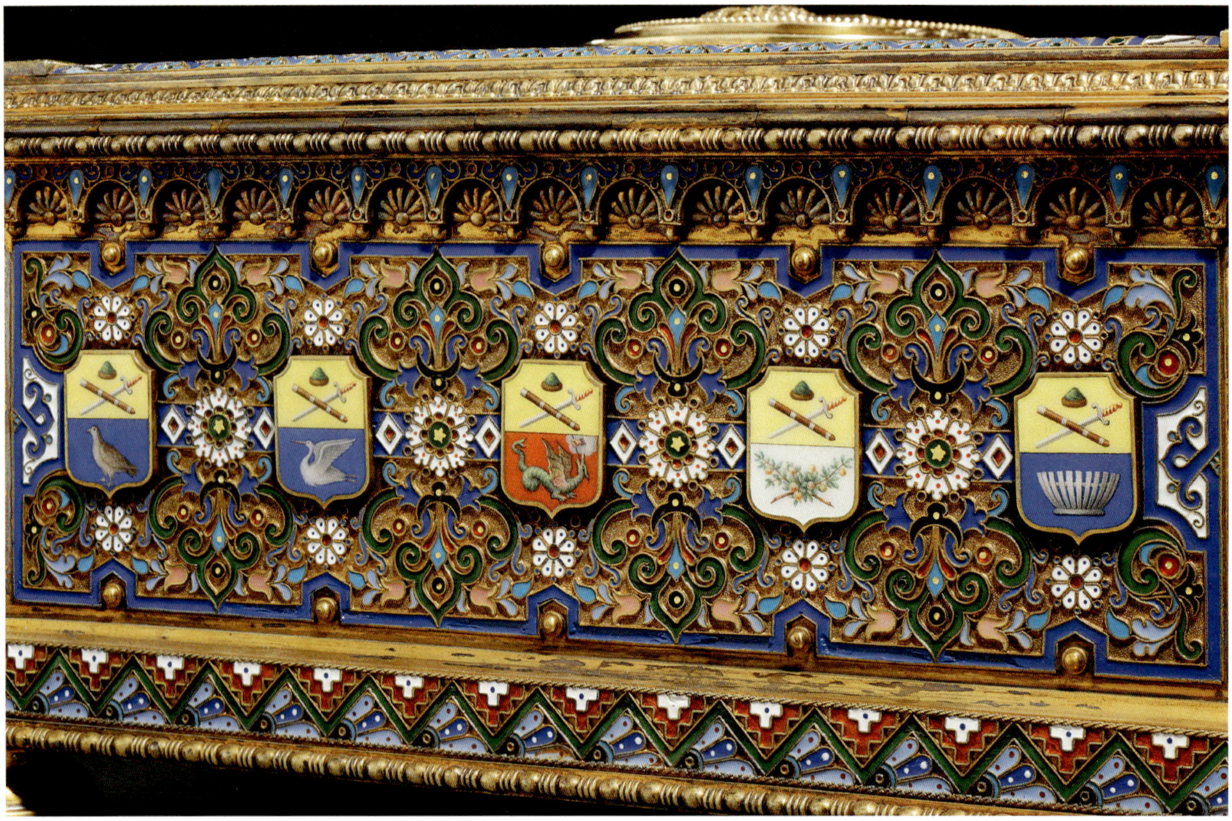

Detail of Ovchinnikov presentation box, dated 1893. © *2008 Christie's Images Ltd.*

SOURCES

Archives

Russian State Historical Archive (RGIA), St. Petersburg

Central State Archive of Film and Photography in St. Petersburg

Public and University Library of Geneva

Auction Catalogues

Bonham's

Christie's

Doyle Auctioneers and Appraisers

Lyon & Turnbull

Nagel Auction

Parke-Bernet Galleries, Inc.

Rossini

Sotheby's

Stair

Stockholm Auktionswerk

Periodicals

Antikvarnoe obozrenie

Apollo

The Connoisseur

Dilletant

Fabergé Research Newsletter

Magazine Antiques

Nashe nasledia

Rodina

Russkii iuvelir

Starye gody

Stolitsa i usadba

Books, Articles and Dissertations

Avdusina, T. D., and N. S. Vladimirskaia. *Kremlin Gold: 1,000 Years of Russian Gems and Jewels*. New York: Harry A. Abrams, 2000.

Beaugrand, M. *Rapport sur les Orfèvres et Bijoutiers de L'Exposition de 1867*. Paris, 1868.

Beglova, Natalia. "Bratia Diuval: Shveitsarskie iuveliry v Rossii; Chast I." *Nasha Gazeta*. http://nashagazeta.ch/news/les-gens-de-chez-nous/bratya-dyuval-shveycarskie-yuveliry-v-rossii-chast-i-brilliantovyy.

———. "Bratia Diuval: Shveitsarskie iuveliry v Rossii; Chast II; Zhenevskoe prikliuchenie Oresta Kiprenskogo." *Nasha Gazeta*. http://nashagazeta.ch/news/les-gens-de-chez-nous/bratya-dyuval-shveycarskie-yuveliry-v-rossii-chast-ii-zhenevskoe.

Betteley, Marie E. "A Bid for the Best Backfires." *Russian Life*, March–April 2017: 46-49.

Birnbaum, Franz. *The History of the House of Fabergé*. Edited by Tatiana Fabergé and Valentin Skurlov. St. Petersburg: Russkie samotsvety, 1992.

Blumay, Carl, and Henry Edwards. *The Dark Side of Power: The Real Armand Hammer*. New York: Pocket Books, 1993.

Bolin, Christian and Pavel Bulatov, eds., *W. A. Bolin in Russia: Court Jeweller Late XIX – Early XX Centuries*. Moscow: Novyi Ermitazh-odin, 2001.

Bond, Edward A., ed. *Russia at the Close of the Sixteenth Century*. London: Hakluyt Society, 1856.

Bonus, Wendy. *The Fabergé Connection: A Memoir of the Bowe Family*. New York: iUniverse, 2010.

Budrina, Liudmilla Alekseevna. "Stilevaia evoliutsiia kamnereznogo i iuvelirnogo iskusstva Rossii vtoroi poloviny 19-nachala 20 veka. V teni imeni Faberzhe: Kamenreznoe i iuvelirnoe tvorchestvo A. K. Denisova-Uralskogo." Candidate's dissertation, Ural State University, 2004.

Catalogue of the Russian Section, World's Columbian Exposition, 1893, Chicago. St. Petersburg: Imperial Russian Commission, Ministry of Finance, 1893.

Catalogue spécial de la section Russe à l'exposition universelle de Vienne en 1873. St. Petersburg: Imprimerie de l'Académie impériale des sciences, 1873.

Cerval, Marguerite de, ed. *Dictionnaire international du bijou*. Paris: Regard, 1998.

Cerwinske, Laura. *Russian Imperial Style*. New York: Prentice Hall, 1990.

Chavchavadze, David. *The Grand Dukes*. New York: Atlantic International, 1990.

Coleman Sparke, Cynthia. *Russian Decorative Arts*. Woodbridge, UK: Antique Collectors' Club, 2014.

Coxe, William. *Travels into Poland, Russia, Sweden, and Denmark*. London: J. Nicholls, 1784.

Cross, Samuel Hazzard, and Olgerd P. Sherbowitz-Wetzor, eds. and trans. *The Russian Primary Chronicle: Laurentian Text*. Cambridge, MA: Mediaeval Academy of America, 1973.

Dostoevskii, F. M. *Polnoe sobranie sochinenii*. Vol. 5. Edited by V. G. Bazarov et al. Leningrad: Nauka, 1972.

Draveny, Mélanie. "Edition critique introduite et commentée du mémoire de Jérémie Pauzié, joaillier à la Cour de Russie de 1730 à 1763." Master's thesis, University of Geneva, 2004.

———. "Jérémie Pauzié, joallier genevois à la cour des tsars." In *Svejcarija-Russie-Lausanne*. [Wabern-Bern, Switzerland]: Benteli, 2006, 53–60.

———. "Genevois et Vaudois, joailliers de la Couronne et de la Cour. In *Suisses en Russie de Pierre le Grand à Alexandre Ier*. Edited by Jean-René Bory, 135–40. Pregny, Switzerland: Institut national de recherches de la Suisse avec l'étranger, 1996.

Durov, V. A. *The Orders of Russia*. Moscow: Voskresene, 1993.

Dzevanovskii, V. M. "Armin Evgenevich von Felkersam (1861–1917): Khranitel' Gallerei dragotsennostei Imperatorskogo Ermitazha." *Antikvarnoe obozrenie* 4 (November 2012): 80–93.

"Exhibit of the Russian Empire." In *Centennial Exposition Described and Illustrated*. Edited by J. S. Ingram, 470–85. Philadelphia: Hubbard Bros., 1876.

Fabergé, Tatiana F., A. S. Gorynia, and Valentin V. Skurlov. *Faberzhe i Peterburgskie iuveliry*. St. Petersburg: Neva, 1997.

Fabergé, Tatiana F., Eric-Alain Kohler, and Valentin Skurlov, eds. *Fabergé: A Comprehensive Reference Book*. Geneva: Slatkine, 2012.

"Fabrika bratev Grachevykh ('Br. Grachevy'), 1866–1918 g.g." https://lermontovgallery.ru/spravochnik-antikvariata/fabrika-bratev-grachevykh/.

"Fabrika I. P. Khlebnikova, 1871–1917 gg." https://lermontovgallery.ru/spravochnik-antikvariata/fabrika-khlebnikova/.

Falk, Fritz, ed. *Gold of the Tsars: 100 Masterpieces of the Goldsmith's Art of the Hermitage, St. Petersburg; The Guild of the Foreign Masters*. Stuttgart: Arnoldsche, 1995.

Fedorov, Oleg. "Drevnerusskii zhenksii iuvelirnyi golovoi ubor XI–XXX veki." www.kulturologia.ru/blogs/220912/17139/.

Fersman, A. E. *Ocherki po istorii kamnia*. Moscow: Izd-vo Akademii nauk SSSR, 1954.

Fersman, Alexander E. *Russia's Treasures of Diamonds and Precious Stones*. Moscow: People's Commissariat of Finances, 1925.

Fölkersam, Baron Armin von. *Alfavitnyi ukazatel k S-Peterburgskikh zolotykh i serebrianykh del masterov, iuvelirov, graverov i proch: 1714–1814*. St. Petersburg: Starye gody, 1907.

———. "Inostrannye mastera zolotogo i serebrianago dela." *Starye gody*, June–September 1911: 95–113.

———. "Iuvelirnye izdeliia vremen Aleksandra I." *Starye gody*, July–September 1908: 529–46.

———. "Nekotorye svedeniia o S.-Peterburskikh zolotykh i serebrianykh masterakh za sto let (1714–1814)." *Starye gody*, January 1907.

Gibbs-Smith, C. H. *The Great Exhibition of 1851*. London: H.M.S.O., 1964.

Gorewa, Olga W., Irina F. Polynina, Nikolai Rachmanov, and Alfons Raimann. *Joyaux du trésor de Russie*. Paris: La Bibliothèque des Arts, 1991.

Great Britain, Commissioners for the Exhibition of 1851. *Official Descriptive and Illustrated Catalogue*. 3 vols., plus supplementary vol. London: Spicer, 1851.

———. *Reports by the Juries on the Subjects in the Thirty Classes into Which the Exhibition Was Divided*. London: Spicer, 1852.

Habsburg, Geza von. *Fabergé: Objects of Vertu and Russians Works of Art*. Geneva, Switzerland: Habsburg, Feldman Editions, 1987.

———. *Fabergé Revealed at the Virginia Museum of Fine Arts*. New York: Skira-Rizzoli, 2011.

———. *Hofjuwelier der Zaren*. Tübingen, Germany: Wasmuth, 1986.

Habsburg, Geza von, and Marina Lopato, eds. *Fabergé: Imperial Jeweler*. Washington, DC: Fabergé Arts Foundation, 1993.

Habsburg, Geza von, Alexandre de Solodkoff, and Robert Bianchi, eds. *Fabergé: Imperial Craftsman and His World.* London: Booth-Clibborn Editions, 2000.

Hakluyt, Richard, ed. *The Principal Navigations, Voyages, Traffiques and Discoveries of the English Nation*. Vol. 3. New York: Kelley, 1969.

Herberstein, Baron Sigismund von. *Description of Moscow and Muscovy, 1557*. New York: Barnes and Noble, 1969.

Hughes, Graham. *Modern Silver throughout the World, 1880–1967*. London: Studio Vista, 1967.

Hughes, Lindsey. "Attitudes towards Foreigners in Early Modern Russia." In *Russia and the Wider World in Historical Perspective: Essays for Paul Dukes*. Edited by Cathryn Brennan and Murray Frame. Basingstoke, UK: Macmillan, 2000, 1–23.

Iljine, Nicholas, and Natalya Semyonova. *Selling Russia's Treasures: The Soviet Trade in Nationalized Art, 1917–1938*. New York: Abbeville, 2014.

"Istoriia fabriki serebrianykh izdelii I. S. Gubkina." https://lermontovgallery.ru/spravochnik-antikvariata/fabrika-serebryanykh-izdeliy-gubkina/

Iudin, Mikhail Olegovich. "Zoloto-serebrianaia firma Ovchinikova: Russkii stil i natsionalnye traditsii v izdeliiakh predpriatiia." Candidate's dissertation, State Institute for Art Studies, 2004.

Ivanov, Alexander Nikolaevich. *Gold and Silversmiths in Russia (1600–1926): A Guide for Art Experts*. 2 vols. Moscow: Russkii natsionalnyi muzei, 2002.

Ivanova, Nadezhda Iurevna. "Iuvelirnoe iskusstvo Moskvi kontsa XIX—nachala XX veka." Candidate's dissertation, Stroganov Academy of Arts and Industry, 2006.

Jaques, Susan. *The Empress of Art: Catherine the Great and the Transformation of Russia.* New York: Pegasus, 2016.

Jones, Mark, Paul T. Craddock, and Nicholas Barker, eds. *Fake? The Art of Deception*. Berkeley: University of California Press, 1990.

Kirichenko, Evgenia. *Russian Design and the Fine Arts, 1750–1917*. Compiled by Mikhail Anikst. New York: Harry N. Abrams, 1991.

Kolpakova, Olga. *Karl Faberzhe i russkie iuveliry*. Moscow: Belyi gorod, 2008.

Korsh, E. "Russkoe serebriannoe delo XVII veka i ego ornamentatsiia." *Starye gody,* July–September 1909, 404–424.

Koshun, Vasilii. "Vysochnye ukrasheniia drevnykh slavian: Khronologiia, tipologiia, simvolika." www.kulturologia.ru/blogs/040713/18513/.

Kostiuk, Olga. "'Chesmenkie' tabakerki i mastera ekaterinskogo vremeni." *Nashe Nasledie* 95 (2010).

Krog, Olle Villumsen, ed. *Ruslands Skatte: Kejserlige gaver*. Copenhagen: Det Kongelige Sølvkammer, 2002.

Kuznetsova, Liliia. "Iskusstvo peterburgskikh iuvelirov vtoroi polovine XVIII stoletii." Candidate's dissertation, Leningrad State University, 1984.

———. *Pamiatniki kul'tury: Novye otkrytiia*. Moscow: Nauka, 1989.

———. *Peterburgskie iuveliry: Dnei Aleksandrovykh prekrasnoe nachalo*. Moscow and St. Petersburg: Tsentrpoligraf, 2012.

———. *Peterburgskie iuveliry XIX-nachala XX v.: O shedevrakh, ikh sozdateliakh*. Moscow: Tsentrpoligraf, 2017.

———. *Peterburgskie iuveliry: Vek vosemnadtsatyi, brilliantovyi*. Moscow: Tsentrpoligraf, 2009.

Lincoln, Bruce W. *Sunlight at Midnight: St. Petersburg and the Rise of Modern Russia*. New York: Basic Books, 2002.

Londonderry, Lady Frances Anne Vane. *Russian Journal of 1836–1837*. Edited by W. A. L. Seaman and J. R. Sewell. London: John Murray, 1973.

Lopato, Marina. *Iuveliry starogo Peterburga*. St. Petersburg: State Hermitage Publishers, 2006.

———. "Les joailliers suisses à Saint-Pétersbourg." In *Suisses à Saint-Pétersbourg: Au tricentenaire de la fondation de Saint-Pétersbourg*. By Madelaine Isabelle Lüthi et al. St. Petersburg: Verlag für typografie, 2003, 222–30.

———. "Serebrianyi serviz 'protiv ordinarnogo vtroe.'" *Nashe Nasledie* 95 (2010).

Lowes, Will, and Christel Ludewig McCanless. *Fabergé Eggs: A Retrospective Encyclopedia*. Lanham, MD: Scarecrow, 2001.

Lure, Lev. *Grad obrechennyi: Putevoditel po Peterburgu pered revoliutsiei*. St. Petersburg: BKhV-Peterburg, 2018.

Martynova, V. I. *Precious Stone in Russian Jewelry Art in XIIth–XVIIIth Centuries*. Moscow: Iskusstvo, 1973.

Medvedeva, Galina, ed. *Russian Jewellery 16th to 20th centuries: From the Collection of the Historical Museum, Moscow*. Moscow: Sovetskii khudozhnik, 1987.

Meylan, Vincent. *Archives Secrètes: Boucheron*. Paris: Ed. SW Télémaque, 2009.

Michael of Greece, Prince. *Jewels of the Tsars*. New York: Vendome, 2006.

Montclos, Brigitte de, ed. *Moscou: Splendeurs des Romanovs*. Monaco: Grimaldi Forum Monaco, 2009.

Mukhin, Vyacheslav, ed. *The Fabulous Epoch of Fabergé*. Moscow: Nord, 1992.

Munn, Geoffrey C. *Tiaras: A History of Splendour*. Woodbridge, UK: Antique Collector's Club, 2001.

Muntian, Tatiana. "Semia iuvelirov Bolin: Peterburg—Moskva—Stockholm." *Nashe Nasledie* 59–60 (2001). http://www.nasledie-rus.ru/podshivka/6025.php.

Muntian, Tatiana, comp. *The World of Fabergé*. Moscow: Red Square, 2000.

Odom, Anne. *Russian Enamels: Kievan Rus to Fabergé*. Baltimore: Walters Art Gallery, 1996.

———. *Russian Silver in America: Surviving the Melting Pot*. Washington, DC: Hillwood Museum, 2011.

Odom, Anne, and Liana Paredes Arend. *A Taste for Splendor: Russian Imperial and European Treasures from the Hillwood Museum*. Alexandria, VA: Art Service International, 1998.

Odom, Anne, and Wendy Salmond, eds. *Treasures into Tractors: The Selling of Russia's Cultural Heritage, 1918–1936*. Washington, DC: Hillwood Museum, 2009.

Polak, Ada. "Iver Winfeld Buch: Imperial Russian Goldsmith." *The Connoisseur*, May 1968.

Postnikova-Loseva, M. M. *Russkoe iuverlirnoe iskusstvo: Ego tsentry i mastera.* Moscow: Nauka, 1974.

"Predpriatie 'P. A. Ovchinnikov,' 1851–1917 g.g." https://lermontovgallery.ru/spravochnik-antikvariata/predpriyatie-ovchinnikova/.

"Pridvornyi fabrikant serebrianykh izdelii Ignatii Pavlovich Sazykov: Istoriia firmy, kleima." https://lermon-tovgallery.ru/spravochnikantikvariata/pridvornyy-fabrikant-serebryanykhizdeliy-ignatiy-pavlovich-sazikov-istoriya-firmy-kleyma/.

Pushkarev, I. I. *Opisanie Sankt-Peterburga i uezdnykh gorodov S.-Peterburskoi gubernii*. Vol. 3. St. Petersburg: Tip. S. Peterburgskogo gubernskago pravlenia, 1841.

Pyliaev, M. I. *Dragotsennye kamni: Ikh svoistva, mestonakhozhdeniia i upotrebleniia*. St. Petersburg: Suvorin, 1896.

Reimers, G. von. *Adresnaia i spravochnaia kniga na rus., nem., i frants. iazykakh*. St. Petersburg, 1809.

Reynolds Brown, Katherine. "Russo-Byzantine Jewelry in the Metropolitan Museum of Art." *Apollo* 111, no. 215 (January 1980): 6–9.

Ribbing, Magdalena, et al. *Smycken & silver för tsarer, drottningar och andra / Jewellery and Silver for Tsars, Queens and Others*. Stockholm: W. A. Bolin, 1996.

Rimmel, Eugène, *Recollections of the Paris Exhibition of 1867*. London: Chapman & Hall, 1868.

Romanov, Grand Duke Alexander Mikhailovich. *Once a Grand Duke*. New York: Farrar & Rhinehart, 1932.

Ruby, Scott. "The Crystal Palace Exhibition and Britain's Encounter with Russia." In *A People Passing Rude: British Responses to Russian Culture*. Edited by Anthony Cross. Cambridge: Open Book, 2012, 89–96.

Rudoe, Judy. "Jewellery at the Great Exhibition." *American Society of Jewelry Historians Newsletter* 20 (May 2003): 13–28.

Saloniemi, Marjo-Riitta, ed. *The Era of Fabergé*. Tampere: Vapriikki, 2006.

Scherer, Barrymore Lawrence. "Glittering Competition: The Rivals of Faberge." *Magazine Antiques*, March 2010. https://www.themagazineantiques.com/article/faberge/.

Schrader, T. A. "Semia finlianskikh iuvelirov Tillander v Sankt-Peterburge (XIX-nachalo XX v.)" in V. N. Baryshnikova and P. A. Kostova, eds., *Sankt-Peterburg i strany severnoi Evropy: Materialy odinnadtsatoi ezhegodnoi mezhdunarodnoi nauchnoi konferentsii*. St. Petersburg: RKhGA, 19-28.

Schroeder-Gudehus, Brigitte, and Anne Rasmussen. *Les Fastes du Progrès: Le Guide des Expositions Universelles, 1851–1992*. Paris: Flammarion, 1992.

Shepelev, L. E. "Imperatorskii dvor: Pridvornye tituly i mundiry." Tituly, mundiry i ordena Rossiiskoi imperii. www.bibliotekar.ru/CentrTitul/30.htm.

Siegel, Jennifer. *For Peace and Money: French and British Finance in the Service of Tsars and Commissars*. Oxford: Oxford University Press, 2014.

Skurlov, Valentin. *Postavchiki imperatorskogo dvora*. St. Petersburg: Antikvarnoe obozrenie, 2008.

Skurlov, Valentin, and I. N. Ivanov. *Kleimenie russkikh zolotykh i serebrianykh izdelii na rubezhe XIX-XX vekov*. St. Petersburg: Liki Rossii, 2001.

Skurlov, Valentin, N. Sapfirova, and Tatiana Fabergé. *K. Faberzhe i Iosif Marshak*. St. Petersburg: Tipografiia "NP-Print," 2015.

Skurlov, Valentin, and Galina Smorodinova. *Faberzhe i russkie pridvornye iuveliry*. Moscow: Terra-Knizhnyi klub, 2001.

Smorodinova, Galina. "Aristokrat iuvelirnogo dela." *Diletant* 41 (2019), 70–71.

———. "Zolotoe i serebrianoe delo Moskvy rubezha XIX i XX vekov: Iz sobraniia Gosudarstvennogo Istoricheskogo Muzeia." www.raruss.ru/russe_moderne/3973_smorodinova_russian_silver.html.

Snowman, Kenneth A., ed. *The Master Jewellers*. London: Thames & Hudson, 1990.

Solntsev, Fedor. *Drevnosti Rossiiskogo Gosudartsva*. 6 vols. St. Petersburg: Tip. Aleksandra Semenova, 1849–65.

Solodkoff, Alexander von. *The Jewel Album of Tsar Nicholas and a Collection of Private Photographs of the Russian Imperial Family*. London: Ermitage, 1997.

———. *Russian Gold and Silverwork, 17th–19th Century*. New York: Rizzoli, 1981.

Solovev, S. M. *Sochineniie v vosemnadtsatykh knigakh*. 18 vols. Moscow: Mysl', 1988–95.

Staël-Holstein, Germaine de. *Mémoires de Madame de Staël (Dix années d'éxil)*. Paris: Charpentier, 1861.

Talbot-Rice, Tamara. *A Concise History of Russian Art*. London: Thames & Hudson, 1963.

Tennant, James. "On Gems and Precious Stones." In *Lectures on the Results of the Great Exhibition of 1851: Delivered before the Society of Arts, Manufactures and Commerce*. London: David Bogue, 1853.

Tillander-Godenhielm, Ulla. *Fabergé: His Masters and Artisans*. London: Unicorn, 2018.

———. *Jewels from Imperial St. Petersburg*. London: Unicorn, 2012.

———. "The Russian Imperial Award System." *Journal of the Finnish Antiquarian Society* 113 (2005).

Toumanoff, Frà Cyrille. *L'Ordre de Malte et l'Empire de Russie*. Rome: Palazzo Malta, 1979.

Troinitskii, S. "Medalnyy tabakerki vrememi Imperatritsy Ekateriny II." *Starye gody*, June 1915, 41–49.

———. "Tabakerki v pamiat semiletnei voiny." *Starye gody*, April–May 1915, 51–57.

Trombly, Margaret Kelly, ed. *Fabergé and the Russian Crafts Tradition: An Empire's Legacy*. London: Thames & Hudson, 2017.

Troyat, Henri. *La vie quotidienne en Russie au temps du dernier tsar*. Paris: Hachette, 1969.

Tutova, T. A. *Sud'ba dvortsovikh tsennostei Rossiiskogo imperatorskogo doma: Zhurnaly raboty Komissii 1922 goda v Moskovskom Kremle*. 2 vols. Moscow: Moskovskii Kreml, 2015.

Whittaker, Cynthia Hyla, ed. *Visualizing Russia: Fedor Solntsev and Crafting a National Past*. Leiden, The Netherlands: Brill, 2010.

Wortman, Richard. *Scenarios of Power: Myth and Ceremony in Russian Monarchy*. 2 vols. Princeton, NJ: Princeton University Press, 1995–2000.

Zabozlaeva, T. B. *Dragotsennosti v russkoi kulture XVIII–XX vekov*. St. Petersburg: Iskusstvo-SPB, 2003.

Zavyalova, Anna. "Russian Fine Arts Section at the World's Columbian Exposition 1893: Notes on Organization and Reception." *MDCCC 1800* 6 (2017): 119–30.

Zhirov, Evgenii. "Iuvelirnaia zabota." *Kommersant*, October 31, 2005.

Zhuravleva, V. L., I. D. Kostina, and T. N. Mutian. *Iskusstvo russkikh iuvelirov: Deviat vekov istorii*. Moscow: Khudozhnik i kniga, 2004.

Zimin, I. V. *Tsarskie dengi: Dokhody i raskhody Doma Romanovykh*. Moscow: Tsentropoligraf, 2011.

Zimin, I. V., and A. Sokolov. *Iuvelirnye sokrovishcha Rossiiskogo imperatorskogo dvora*. Moscow: Izd-vo Tsentrpoligraf, 2013.

Following page:
Gold and cabochon sapphire miniature egg pendant, circa 1900. *Marie Betteley, photo by Rob Wayman*

Page 380:
Gold pearl bracelet by Mikhailov of St. Petersburg, circa 1870. *Marie Betteley, photo by Josh Gaddy*

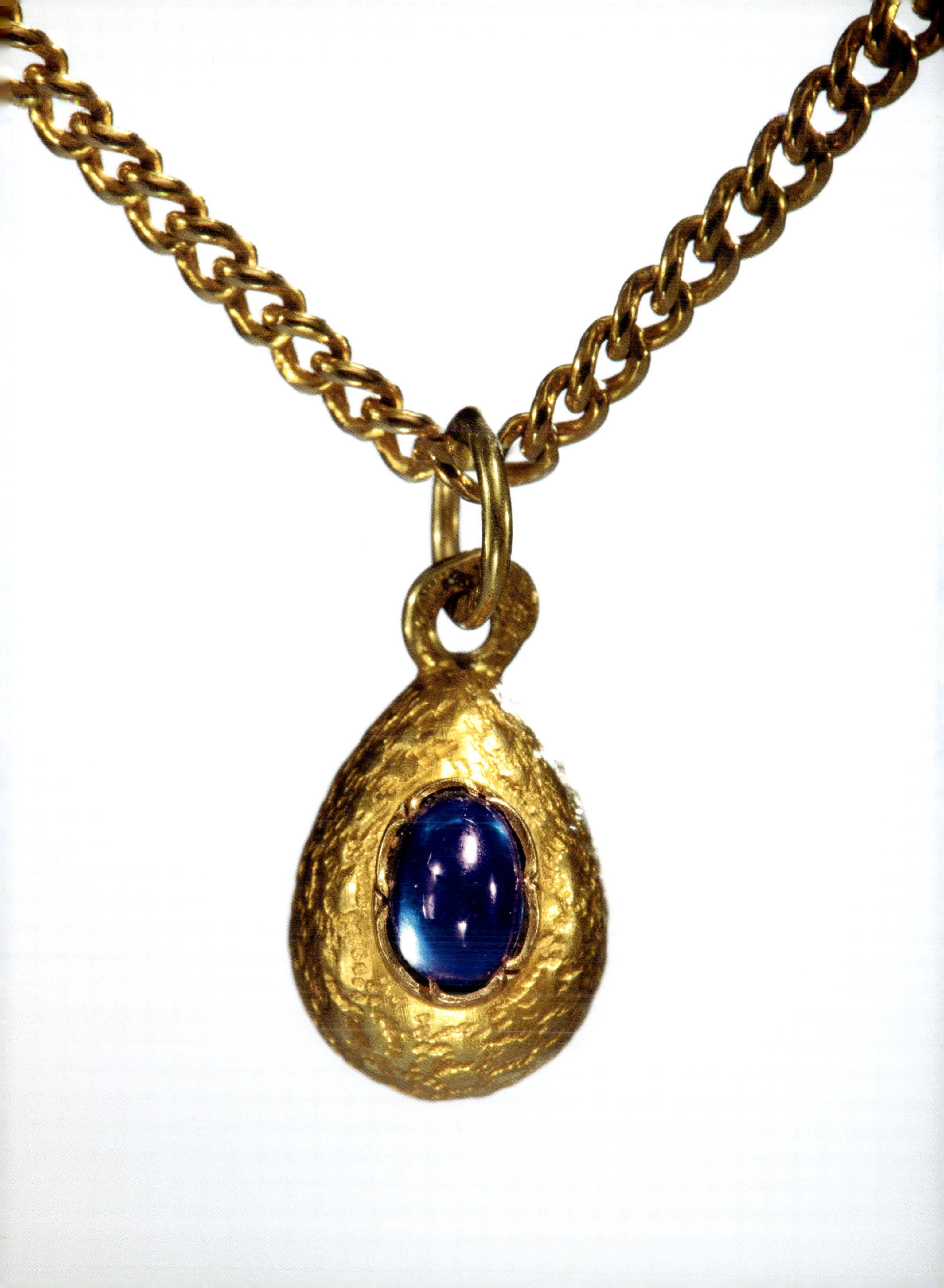

INDEX

F

G

H

I

J

K

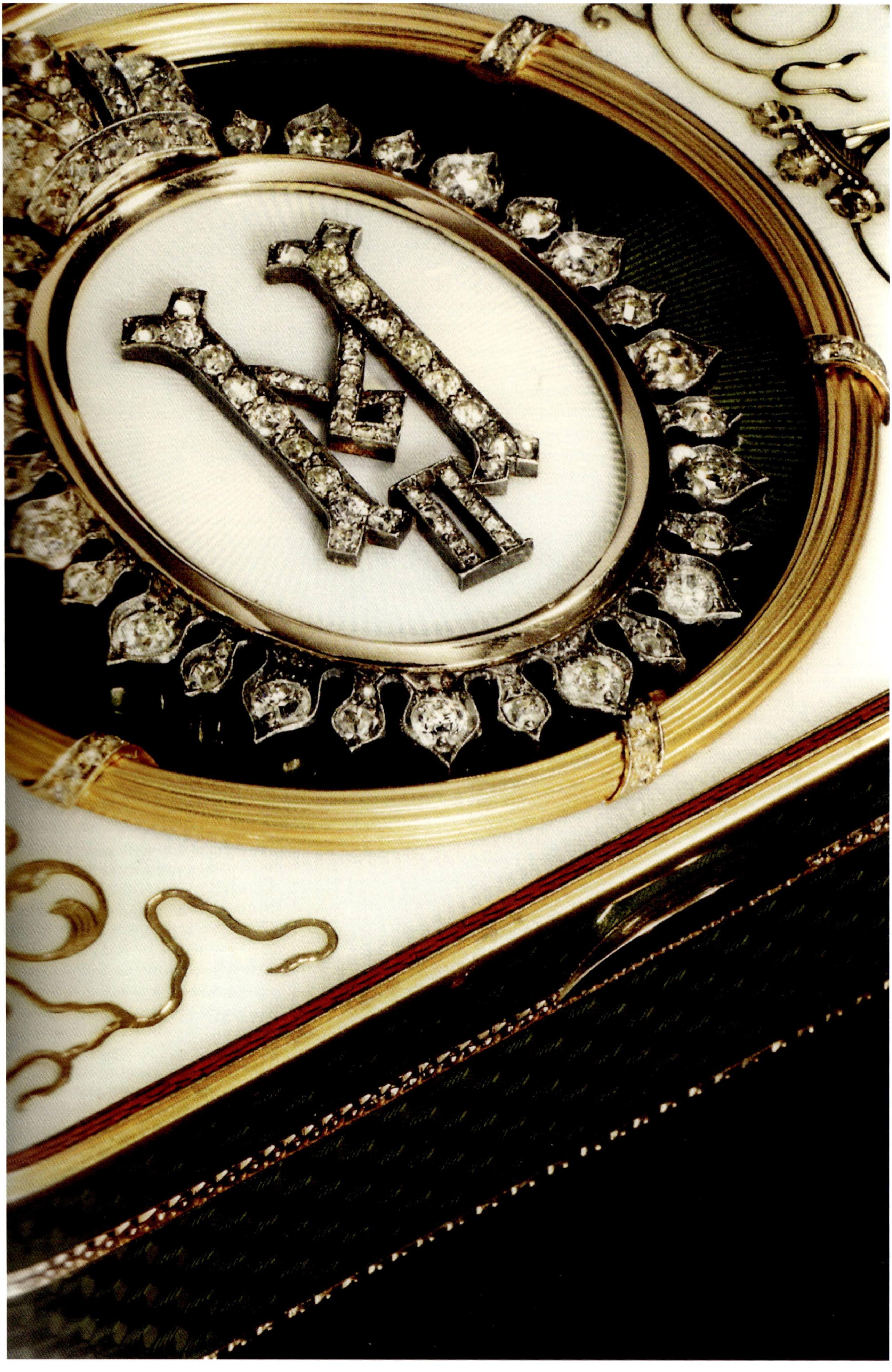